CITE THIS READING MATERIAL AS:

Realty Publications, Inc.

Property Management

Sixth Edition

Cutoff Dates:

Legal editing of this book was
completed October 2019.

Printed in California

Editorial Staff

Legal Editor/Publisher:
Fred Crane

Project Editor:
Connor P. Wallmark

Senior Editor:
Giang Hoang-Burdette

Contributing Editors:
Oscar M. Alvarez
Carrie B. Reyes
Benjamin J. Smith

Graphic Designer:
Mary LaRochelle

Comments or suggestions to:
Realty Publications, Inc., P.O. Box 5707, Riverside, CA 92517
contact@realtypublications.com

Table of Contents

Ownership and Possession

Property Management and Agency

**Rents
and
Deposits**

**Enforcing
Rents;
Forfeiting
Tenancies**

Maintenance and Security

Commercial Lease Provisions

Table of Forms

For a full-size, fillable copy of any form cited in this book plus our entire library of 400+ legal forms, go to *www.realtypublications.com/forms.*

Full Forms

**Partial
Forms**

Chapter

1

Fee vs. leasehold

After reading this chapter, you will be able to:
- identify the different possessory interests held in real estate, and the rights and obligations associated with each;
- distinguish the individual rights which collectively comprise real property;
- identify the different types of leasehold interests held by tenants;
- understand leasehold interests which convey special rights, such as a ground lease, master lease or sublease.

Learning Objectives

estate	**life estate**
fee estate	**master lease**
fixed-term tenancy	**parcel**
ground lease	**profit a prendre**
impairment	**sublease**
leasehold estate	**tenancy-at-sufferance**
legal description	**tenancy-at-will**

Key Terms

Real estate, sometimes legally called *real property* or *realty*, consists of:
- the land;
- the improvements and fixtures attached to the land; and
- all rights incidental or belonging to the property.[1]

A matter of possession

---

1 Calif. Civil Code §658

parcel
A three-dimensional portion of real estate identified by a legal description.

A **parcel** of real estate is located by circumscribing its **legal description** on the "face of the earth." Based on the legal description, a surveyor locates and sets the corners and surface boundaries of the parcel. The legal description is contained in deeds, subdivision maps or government surveys relating to the property.

legal description
The description used to locate and set boundaries for a parcel of real estate.

All permanent structures, crops and timber are part of the parcel of real estate. The parcel of real estate also includes buildings, fences, trees, watercourses and easements within the parcel's boundaries.

A parcel of real estate is three dimensional. In addition to the surface area within the boundaries, a parcel of real estate consists of:

- the soil below the parcel's surface to the core of the earth, including water and minerals; and
- the air space above it to infinity.

For instance, the rental of a boat slip includes the water and the land below it. Both the water and land below the boat slip comprise the real estate, the parcel leased. Thus, landlord/tenant law controls the rental of the slip.

In the case of a statutory condominium unit, the air space enclosed within the walls is the real estate conveyed and held by the fee owner of the unit. The structure, land and air space outside the unit are the property of the **homeowners' association (HOA)**.

Possessory interests in real estate

The ownership interests a person may hold in real estate are called **estates**. Four types of *estates* exist in real estate:

- *fee estates*, also known as *fee simple estates, inheritance estates, perpetual estates*, or simply, *the fee*;
- *life estates*;
- *leasehold estates*, sometimes called *leaseholds*, or *estates for years*; and
- *estates at will*, also known as *tenancies-at-will*.[2]

estate
The ownership interest a person may hold in real estate.

In practice, these estates are separated into three categories: *fee estates, life estates* and *leasehold estates*. Estates at will are considered part of the leasehold estates category. Leasehold estates are controlled by landlord/tenant law.

Fee estates: unbundling the rights

A person who holds a **fee estate** interest in real estate is a fee owner. In a landlord/tenant context, the fee owner is the landlord.

Editor's note — If a sublease exists on a commercial property, the master tenant is the "landlord" of the subtenant.

fee estate
An indefinite, exclusive and absolute legal ownership interest in a parcel of real estate.

A fee owner has the right to possess and control their property indefinitely. A fee owner's possession is exclusive and absolute. Thus, the owner has the

---

2 CC §761

Case in point

Separation of fee interests

> *Consider a fee owner who grants separate fee interests in their property to two individuals. One individual receives the land's surface and air space rights. The other individual receives the subsurface oil and mineral rights.*
>
> *The surface owner claims title to the entire parcel of real estate should be vested — quieted — in their name. The subsurface owner objects, claiming the surface owner's real estate interest is less than the entire fee estate in the property.*
>
> *Here, the surface owner's fee interest in the parcel of real estate is separate from the subsurface ownership and possession of the oil and mineral rights. Also, they are not co- owners of the real estate. Both owners hold an individual fee estate in mutually exclusive and divided portions of the same parcel. [**In re Waltz** (1925) 197 C 263]*

right to deny others permission to cross their boundaries. No one can be on the owner's property without their consent, otherwise they are trespassing. The owner may recover any money losses caused by the trespass.

A fee owner has the exclusive right to use and enjoy the property. As long as local ordinances such as building codes and zoning regulations are obeyed, a fee owner may do as they please with their property. A fee owner may build new buildings, tear down old ones, plant trees and shrubs, grow crops or simply leave the property unattended.

A fee owner may occupy, sell, lease or encumber their parcel of real estate, give it away or pass it on to anyone they choose on their death. The fee estate is the interest in real estate transferred in a real estate sales transaction, unless a lesser interest such as an easement or life estate is noted. However, one cannot transfer an interest greater than they received.

A fee owner is entitled to the land's surface and anything permanently located above or below it.[3]

Separate interests

The ownership interests in one parcel may be separated into several fee interests. One person may own the mineral rights beneath the surface, another may own the surface rights, and yet another may own the rights to the air space. Each solely owned interest is held in fee in the same parcel. [See Case in point, "Separation of fee interests"]

In most cases, one or more individuals own the entire fee and lease the rights to extract underground oil or minerals to others. Thus, a fee owner can convey a leasehold estate in the oil and minerals while retaining their fee interest. The drilling rights separated from the fee ownership are called **profit a prendre**.[4]

profit a prendre
The right to remove minerals from another's real estate.

Profit a prendre is the right to remove profitable materials from property owned and possessed by another. If the profit a prendre is created by a lease agreement, it is a type of easement.[5]

---

3 CC §829
4 **Rousselot** v. **Spanier** (1976) 60 C3d 238
5 **Gerhard** v. **Stephens** (1968) 68 C2d 864

Life estates and the life tenant

life estate
An interest in a parcel of real estate lasting the lifetime of the life tenant.

A **life estate** is an interest in a parcel of real estate lasting the lifetime of an individual, usually the life of the tenant. *Life estates* are granted by a deed entered into by the fee owner, an executor under a will or by a trustee under an inter vivos trust.

Life estates are commonly established by a fee owner who wishes to provide a home or financial security for another person (the life tenant) during that person's lifetime, called the controlling life.

Life estates terminate on the death of the controlling life. Life estates may also be terminated by agreement or by merger of different ownership interests in the property.

For example, the fee owner of a vacation home has an elderly aunt who needs a place to live. The fee owner grants her a life estate in the vacation home for the duration of her lifetime. The aunt may live there for the rest of her life, even if she outlives the fee owner who granted her the life estate.

Although the aunt has the right of exclusive possession of the entire parcel of real estate, the fee owner retains title to the fee estate. Thus, the conveyance of a life estate transfers a right of possession which has been "carved out" of the fee estate. This is comparable to possession under a leasehold estate since it is conveyed for its duration out of a fee estate. Unlike a lease, a life estate does not require rent to be paid.

On the aunt's death, possession of the property reverts to the fee owner, their successors or heirs. The right of possession under the life estate is extinguished on the aunt's death.

The holder of a life estate based on their life has the right of possession until death, as though they were the owner in fee. The holder of a life estate is responsible for taxes, maintenance and a reasonable amount of property assessments.[6]

The life estate improves or impairs the fee

impairment
The act of injuring or diminishing the value of a fee interest.

The holder of a life estate may not *impair* the fee interest.[7]

For instance, the holder of a life estate may not make alterations which decrease the property's value, such as removing or failing to care for valuable plants or demolishing portions of the improvements or land.

Conversely, the owner of the life estate has the right to lease the property to others and collect and retain all rents produced by the property during the term of the life estate.

In addition, a life tenant is entitled to be reimbursed by the fee owner for the fee owner's share of the costs to improve the property.

---

6   CC §840
7   CC §818

Leasehold estates, or *tenancies*, are the result of rights conveyed to a tenant by a fee owner (or by the life estate tenant or master lessee) to possess a parcel of real estate.

Tenancies are created when the landlord and the tenant enter into a rental or lease agreement that conveys a possessory interest in the real estate to the tenant.

The tenant becomes the owner of a leasehold with the right to possess and use the entire property until the lease expires. The ownership and title to the fee interest in the property remains with the landlord throughout the term of the leasehold. The landlord's fee interest is subject to the tenant's right of possession, which is carved out of the fee on entering into the lease agreement.

In exchange for the right to occupy and use the property, the landlord is entitled to rental income from the tenant during the period of the tenancy.

Four types of leasehold estates exist and can be held by tenants. The interests are classified by the length of their term:

- a **fixed-term tenancy**, simply known as a *lease* and legally called an *estate for years*;
- a **periodic tenancy**, usually referred to as a *rental*;
- a **tenancy-at-will**, previously introduced as an *estate at will*; and
- a **tenancy-at-sufferance**, commonly called a *holdover tenancy*.

A *fixed-term tenancy* lasts for a specific length of time as stated in a lease agreement entered into by a landlord and tenant. On expiration of the lease term, the tenant's right of possession automatically terminates unless it is extended or renewed by another agreement, such as an option agreement. [See Figure 1, Form 552 §2]

Periodic tenancies also last for a specific length of time, such as a week, month or year. Under a periodic tenancy, the landlord and tenant agree to automatic successive rental periods of the same length of time, such as in a month-to-month tenancy, until terminated by notice by either the landlord or the tenant.

In a **tenancy-at-will** (also known as an *estate at will*) the tenant has the right to possess a property with the consent of the fee owner. Tenancies-at-will can be terminated at any time by an advance notice from either the landlord or the tenant or as set by agreement. Tenancies-at-will do not have a fixed duration, are usually not in writing and a rent obligation generally does not exist.

A **tenancy-at-sufferance** occurs when a tenant retains possession of the rented premises after the tenancy granted terminates. [See Chapter 3]

Leasehold estates held by tenants

leasehold estate
The right to possess a parcel of land, conveyed by a fee owner (landlord) to a tenant.

Types of leaseholds

fixed-term tenancy
A leasehold interest which lasts for the specific lease period set forth in a lease agreement. A fixed-term tenancy automatically terminates at the end of the lease period. [See **RPI** Form 550 and 552]

tenancy-at-will
A leasehold interest granted to a tenant, with no fixed duration or rent owed. A tenancy-at-will can be terminated at any time by an advance notice from either party.

tenancy-at-sufferance
A leasehold interest held by a tenant who retains possession of the rented premises after the termination of the tenancy. [See **RPI** Form 550 §3.3]

2. TERM OF LEASE:

2.1 The lease granted commences _____, 20_____, and expires _____,20_____.
   a. The month of commencement is the anniversary month.

2.2 The lease terminates on the last day of the term without further notice.

2.3 If Tenant holds over, the monthly rent will be increased to 120% of the monthly rent applicable immediately preceding the termination of this lease agreement, prorated at 1/30th of the monthly rent for each day until the Premises is delivered to Landlord.

2.4 Tenant may surrender this lease only by a written surrender agreement with Landlord. [See **RPI** Form 587]

2.5 ☐ This lease agreement is a sublease of the Premises which is limited in its terms by the terms and conditions of the attached master lease agreement.

Leaseholds conveying special uses

In addition to the typical residential and commercial leases, you will find *special use* leases.

Oil, gas, water and *mineral leases* convey the right to use mineral deposits below the earth's surface.

The purpose of an oil lease is to discover and produce oil or gas. The lease is a tool used by the fee owner of the property to develop and realize the wealth of the land. The tenant provides the money and machinery for exploration, development and operations.

The tenant pays the landlord rent, called a *royalty*. The tenant then keeps any profits from the sale of oil or minerals the tenant extracts from beneath the surface of the parcel.

A **ground lease** on a parcel of real estate is granted to a tenant in exchange for the payment of rent. In a *ground lease*, rent is based on the rental value of the land in the parcel, whether the parcel is vacant or improved. Fee owners of vacant, unimproved land use leases to induce others to acquire an interest in the property and develop it.

ground lease
A leasehold interest in which rent is based on the rental value of the land, whether the parcel is vacant or improved.

Ground leases are common in more densely populated areas. Developers often need financial assistance from fee owners to avoid massive cash outlays to acquire unimproved parcels. Also, fee owners of developable property often refuse to sell, choosing to become landlords for the long-term rental income they will receive.

An original tenant under a ground lease constructs their own improvements. Typically, the tenant encumbers their possessory interest in a ground lease with a trust deed lien to provide security for a construction mortgage.

master lease
A leasehold interest which grants a master tenant the right to sublease a property in exchange for rent paid to the fee owner.

Master leases benefit fee owners who want the financial advantages of renting fully improved property, but do not want the day-to-day obligations and risks of managing the property.

For instance, the fee owner of a shopping center and a prospective owner-operator agree to a master lease.

As the master tenant, the owner-operator will collect rent from the many subtenants, address their needs and maintain the property. The master tenant is responsible for the rent due the fee owner under the master lease, even if the subtenants do not pay their rents to the master tenant.

The *master lease* is sometimes called a *sandwich lease* since the master tenant is "sandwiched" between the fee owner (the landlord on the master lease) and the many subtenants with their possession under subleases.

The master lease is a regular, commercial lease agreement form with the clauses prohibiting subletting removed. A **sublease** is also a regular, commercial lease agreement with an additional clause referencing the attached master lease and declaring the *sublease* subject to the terms of the master lease. [See Figure 1, Form 552 §2.5]

sublease
A leasehold interest subject to the terms of a master lease.

Another type of special-use lease is the *farm lease*, sometimes called a *cropping agreement* or *grazing lease*. Here, the tenant operates the farm and pays the landlord either a flat fee rent, a percentage of the value of the crops or livestock produced on the land.

Editor's note — For simplicity, the remainder of the book will treat the landlord as the fee owner, unless a sublease is specifically referenced. Fee owners will be referred to as "landlords," or, if a distinction is required, simply as "owners."

Chapter 1 Summary

The ownership interests a person may hold in real estate are called estates. Four types of estates exist in real estate:
- fee estates;
- life estates;
- leasehold estates; and
- estates at will.

In practice, estates at will are considered leasehold estates. Leasehold estates are controlled by landlord/tenant law.

Four types of leasehold interests exist and can be held by tenants:
- fixed-term tenancies;
- periodic tenancies;
- tenancies-at-will; and
- tenancies-at-sufferance.

A fixed-term tenancy lasts for a specific length of time as stated in a lease agreement entered into by a landlord and tenant. On expiration of the lease term, the tenant's right of possession automatically terminates unless it is extended or renewed by another agreement.

Periodic tenancies last for a specific length of time. Under a periodic tenancy, the landlord and tenant agree to automatic successive rental periods of the same length of time, such as in a month-to-month tenancy, until terminated by notice by either the landlord or the tenant.

Under a tenancy-at-will, the tenant has the right to possess a property with the consent of the fee owner. Tenancies-at-will can be terminated at any time by an advance notice from either the landlord or the tenant or as set by agreement. Tenancies-at-will do not have a fixed duration.

A tenancy-at-sufferance occurs when a tenant retains possession of the rented premises after the tenancy granted terminates.

In addition, several special use leases exist, including ground leases, master leases and subleases.

**Chapter 1
Key Terms**

Quiz 1 Covering Chapters 1-4 is located on page 633.

Chapter
2

License to use land

After reading this chapter, you will be able to:
- identify the limited rights to use another person's real estate that comprise a license to use land; and
- distinguish a license to use land from the use of property under a leasehold or due to an easement.

Learning Objectives

dominant tenement	**license**
irrevocable license	**servient tenement**

Key Terms

By granting a license, a property owner transfers rights to use the property to another. A license is similar to an easement and a lease since it transfers a right to use a property, yet it is neither. The use granted by a license is a personal right, not a right held due to ownership of another property.

Similar to an easement or a lease, a license is an agreement. However, a license is often oral instead of written. Unlike an easement, a license does not have a perpetual life, nor need it have a specific expiration date like a lease.

As with an easement, a property burdened with a license is referred to as the **servient tenement**. Unlike an easement, a license is a personal right and thus has no **dominant tenement** (another property) which benefits from the license. Accordingly, a license is not appurtenant to any property.

Unlike an easement or a lease, a license is a personal privilege held by an individual, not an appurtenant right belonging to another property for its future owners to receive and use. Since a license is not an appurtenant right

A personal right to use another's property

servient tenement
A property burdened by a license or easement.

dominant tenement
The property benefitting from an easement on a servient tenement.

but is a personal right, called *in gross,* and thus does not benefit another property, the right given by the license cannot be conveyed to another individual as there can be no *successors or assigns* to the interest.

As with an easement, the holder of a license does not usually pay rent for the right to use the burdened property. When consideration for the license exists, it is typically in the form of an expenditure of time and money by the licensee to improve or maintain the use authorized on the burdened property, such as an irrigation ditch, roadway, fence, recreational activity, etc.

No right to exclusive possession of a burdened property (the *servient tenement)* for an authorized use exists. Therefore a license — like an easement and unlike a lease — permits only the nonexclusive use of the property by the licensee. The licensee may not exclude others from the property.

Possessory interests conveyed

Unlike either a rental or lease agreement or an easement deed, which are conveyances of possessory interests in real estate, a license agreement conveys no interest in real estate. The right to use a property granted by a license is a mere personal privilege. It is held by an individual under an agreement with the owner of the burdened property. The license is revocable by the owner of the burdened property at any time, unless revocation is deemed unfair to the licensee.

A license agreement often arises from an informal agreement between a property owner and a neighbor or friend. For example, a property owner may accept of an informal offer by their neighbor to jointly or separately make use of the owner's property for hunting activities. Thus, the neighbor is given a license to use the property. The individual given the license agrees to maintain or improve the property for the agreed-to hunting privileges.

A license to use

A **license** is the nonexclusive right to use a space or area within a parcel of real estate (or its improvements) which is owned by another person. The individual who holds the right to use by agreement does not receive any rights to assign the right or to privacy. A *license* is subject to termination at will by the owner of the burdened property, unless it has become irrevocable.

license
The personal, unassignable right held by an individual to the non-exclusive use of property owned by another.

Consider a property owner who contracts for development work to be done on their property. The owner allows the construction company to store excess excavated dirt on one of the owner's adjacent lots until the construction company can haul it away.

While the dirt remains on the vacant lot, an adventurous dirt biker enters the property and is injured. The injured dirt biker claims the construction company is a licensee who is not in possession of the real estate and thus is liable for their injuries. The construction company claims they have a *recreational use immunity* since they have an interest in the property as a licensee with a right to use it for the agreed-to purpose.

Case in Point

Use as a personal privilege

A broker wants to increase the exposure of their business to the public by billboard advertising.

The broker has a friend and business acquaintance who owns vacant property adjacent to a highway. The property owner is willing to allow the broker to place a billboard on their vacant land.

The broker and property owner enter into an oral understanding allowing the broker to put up a billboard for the broker's use only. It is agreed the broker may enter and exit the property at will to install and maintain the billboard.

A time limitation is not specified for maintaining the billboard on the property, nor is any fee or other compensation established. Critically, the property owner does not relinquish any control over the real estate since they do not give the broker any other right to use the property.

Have the broker and property owner established a landlord/tenant relationship or an easement?

Neither! The broker has only been given a license to use the owner's property.

Unlike a landlord/tenant relationship or an easement, a license to use real estate is a personal privilege, unattached to any property owned by the broker. Thus, the use is non-assignable to others by the broker and, unless agreed to the contrary or is unfair, is revocable by the property owner at any time.

In this example, the holder of any interest in the property is exempt from liability for injuries incurred by others arising out of their **recreational use** of private property. The property interest exempt from liability may be either possessory or nonpossessory.

Since a licensee has a *nonpossessory* interest in the property, they also have recreational use immunity even though the owner remains in possession and control of the land and the licensee has only a nonexclusive personal right to use the property.[1]

Thus, the construction company is not liable for injuries which occur during the dirt biker's recreational use of the property since the construction company holds an interest in the property under their license to use.

License vs. lease

A license is often confused with a lease. A **lease** conveys a possessory interest in real estate which allows the tenant to exclude others from occupying the leased premises. This possessory interest is called a leasehold estate or a lease.[2]

A license-to-use another person's real estate is a personal privilege held by an individual. However, a license is neither personal property nor real property. Also, a license is neither owned by a person nor is it an appurtenance to adjoining real estate. Thus, a license, not being property or capable of ownership, cannot be transferred to the licensee's successors or assigns.[3]

---

1 Calif. Civil Code §846
2 CC §761
3 **Beckett** v. **City of Paris Dry Goods Co.** (1939) 14 C2d 633

License vs. lease, cont'd

Characteristics which distinguish a license from a lease include:

- no writing to formalize the agreement;
- no rental payments;
- no specific location on or within the property where the use will occur;
- no intent to convey a leasehold estate;
- no right to exclude others;
- no termination date; and
- termination at the owner's will, unless the license is irrevocable.

In our previous example, the broker may use their business acquaintance's property to set up their billboard and leave it in place on the property. Also, the broker (or their representative) has the right to go back and forth across the property to maintain or repair the billboard. Thus, the property is a servient tenement subject to the terms of the license held by the broker. However, no *dominant tenement* exists since no other property benefits from the license; only the broker individually benefits as the licensee.

Thus, the owner of the property may demand removal of the broker's billboard from the property at any time, and the broker needs to immediately remove it.

A common thread which runs through both a lease and license is the right to use the property. The glaring distinction between the two is that the license does not include the right to exclude any other person from possession, as does a lease.

Continuing with our example, the broker may not fence off, lock out or quarantine in any way the ground under or around their billboard from the property owner or any other person. The license affords the broker no greater right to be on the property than anyone else the owner might allow to concurrently use the property.

License distinguished from a lease

When an agreement with a property owner gives another person an exclusive right to *possess* the property against all others, including the owner, it is a leasehold estate — not a license.

Conversely, when the agreement confers only the *privilege to use* property which remains under the owner's day-to-day control, it is a license.[4]

For example, an owner of a packing company enters into an agreement to purchase raw materials from a wholesale merchant. The wholesale merchant supplies the packing company with raw materials over a three-year period. In exchange, the packing company pays the agreed-to price for the materials and allows the wholesale merchant the right to use an unlocked storage unit to temporarily stockpile their materials. The packing company also allows the merchant to use desk space in an office at the packing facility to conduct business.

---

4   **Von Goerlitz** v. **Turner** (1944) 65 CA2d 425

The agreement does not designate the exact spaces to be used by the merchant. Also, the packing company concurrently uses the same space used by the merchant.

Two years into the arrangement, the packing company is sold. The new owner demands the wholesale merchant move out immediately. The wholesale merchant claims a lease existed between himself and the previous owner, allowing him to remain on the property until the lease expires.

However, no dollar rental amount had been established. Importantly, the wholesale merchant did not have exclusive possession of the spaces they occupied.

Instead of a lease, the wholesale merchant held a license agreement to use space under which the packing company had a superior possessory right to the premises. Thus, the wholesale merchant's use of unlocked space, concurrently occupied by the original owner, was not a lease.

The mere permission of an owner to let someone use and occupy non-specific space in a structure in a non-exclusive manner when the owner retains possession and total control over the premises constitutes a license.[5]

Even if a written agreement identifies the interest given as a license, the actual language and provisions of the agreement may render it a lease which is improperly titled and referred to as a license.

Terms implying a lease

For example, an optometrist enters into a written agreement with an operator of a box store to establish an optical department on the premises. The written agreement is entitled a license.

The agreement allows the store to determine the space the optometrist will occupy, set the rent at a percentage of the optometrist's total sales and require the optometrist to make nightly deposits of receipts with the store's cashier. Also, the optometrist has the exclusive right to manage and operate their trade within their space. The agreement prohibits the optometrist from assigning their business and the occupancy to another without the store's prior consent.

The agreement is for a term of three years, at which time the optometrist agrees to surrender the premises in good condition.

Two years after commencement of the agreement, the store hands the optometrist a notice of cancellation of their agreement (rather than a three-day notice to perform or quit) for the optometrist's failure to deposit their daily cash receipts with the store cashier.

The optometrist refuses to vacate, claiming they are a tenant of the store under the written agreement. The store contends the agreement was a license, terminable at any time and the optometrist must leave.

---

5   **Caldwell** v. **Gem Packing Co.** (1942) 52 CA2d 80

Case in Point

What steps does a landlord take to serve an unlawful detainer on a holdover tenant?

Consider a corporation which owns 150 units in a resort condominium and sells time-share memberships in the resort. A member may purchase up to four one-week time share interests.

However, a member is not entitled to reserve any particular unit in advance of occupancy. The assignment of units for actual occupancy during the time period selected is left up to the discretion of the corporation's board of directors.

*The **Department of Real Estate (DRE)** issues a restraining order, stopping sales of these time-share memberships because the corporation failed to first obtain a permit and a public report from the DRE to sell fractional interests in real estate.*

Editor's note — This case was decided before the DRE changed its name to the California Bureau of Real Estate (CalBRE) in 2013.

The corporation contends the memberships are mere licenses held by the members to use unidentified space and are not a lease or other conveyance of space to the members which require a permit and public report. The corporation further contends the members do not hold an interest in the real estate since they do not have exclusive right to the possession of any specific unit.

*Here, the occupancy rights held by the members constitute a lease. The units to be occupied are identical, the duration of occupancy is specific and each member has the right to exclusive occupancy of a unit. [**Cal-Am Corporation** v. **Department of Real Estate** (1980) 104 CA3d 453]*

However, the terminology in their agreement and the payment of rent is more in line with a lease than a license, indicating the parties created a landlord/tenant relationship by their arrangements.

Similar to a lease, the provision prohibiting assignment is only applicable to the ownership of an interest in real estate since a license is non-assumable as nothing is actually owned for the licensee to assign. Also, the optometrist was given exclusive possession of a designated space within the store for a fixed period of time which eliminates the owner's right to enter the optometrist's space at any time.

Thus, the arrangement by the content of the written agreement was a lease. The right to exclude others from entry for a stated term, coupled with assignment rights and rent, are characteristics of a landlord/tenant relationship, not a license.[6]

If an occupancy agreement contains words or phrases like "lease," "rental," "demise" or "good tenantable condition," the agreement will be construed to be a lease rather than a license.

Know your tenancy or lose time

A license is usually oral with very few terms agreed to except the permission to use or conduct an activity on a property. All the while, the owner remains in actual possession and retains the right to exclude others, including the licensee. Above all else, a license does not carry with it the right to exclude anyone from the property.

---

6   Beckett, *supra*

However, with every additional condition agreed to between an owner and user, a license begins to **recharacterize** itself more and more into a lease.

For example, a broker has an office with unoccupied desks. The broker wants to operate alone and avoid commitments to manage and supervise associate licensees. However, the broker is willing to share space in the office with other brokers.

The broker offers another broker the use of an office, desk space, a telephone line and secretarial services. The brokers orally agree each will pay their own proportionate share of utilities, secretarial services and rent.

A time period for the use is not specified. The office space selected by the other broker is unlocked and open to the entire office.

In this instance, the original broker may terminate this "rent-a-space" relationship at any time without prior notice or cause since the other broker has been given no more rights than a licensee to use office space.

Conversely, when a broker offers space in their office under a written agreement providing for lockable office space and a specific period for occupancy, the agreement is a lease. With a lease (or a month-to-month rental agreement) in hand, the broker creates a landlord/tenant relationship, not a license.

On some occasions, a license and a lease co-exist and are held by the same person.

A license coupled with a lease

A person who is a tenant with exclusive occupancy to part of the space on the premises of a shopping center also holds a license to use an adjacent portion of the premises as well.

For example, a retail tenant leases space in a shopping center. The tenant has exclusive possession of their store space controlling who may enter. However, the tenant shares use of the sidewalks and parking lots with other shopping center tenants and all the customers of the shopping center.

The tenant has no right to exclusive possession of the sidewalk and parking area, only the space enclosed within their unit. Thus, the tenant holds a license for access and non-exclusive use of the parking area and a lease for the space within the shopping center.

Occasionally an individual makes substantial expenditures to improve or maintain their use of another person's property. When they do so over a long period of time in reliance on their oral agreement with the owner of the property, the license becomes irrevocable. A property owner may not terminate an irrevocable license at will.

An irrevocable license

irrevocable license
The right to enter and use property when the specific activity granted by the license is maintained by the licensee's on-going expenditure of money or equivalent labor, and remains feasible.

An **irrevocable license** grants an individual the right to enter and use property when the specific activity granted by the license remains feasible, maintained by the licensee's on-going expenditure of money or equivalent labor.

Consider the construction of a privacy wall between adjacent lots. The lots are located on a hillside, one above the other. Each lot is flat with a graded slope between them to adjust for the difference in the elevation. Each lot is improved with a residence.

The boundary line between the lots is located at the bottom of the slope. However, for a wall to give the owner of each lot privacy, the wall needs to be located at the top of the slope, entirely on the uphill parcel and several feet from the boundary line.

The owner of the uphill lot agrees to allow the neighbor below to construct a masonry wall with its foundation on the top of the slope. The owner and the neighbor agree on the height of the wall and that the neighbor may use the slope between the wall and the property line.

The uphill lot owner orally agrees to the wall as an encroachment. However, they do not reduce the agreement to a writing and thus no easement is created.

Irrevocable by conduct

Continuing the previous example, the neighbor constructs the masonry wall as agreed at the top of the slope. They also build a gazebo within the slope area between the fence and property line.

The owner of the uphill lot sells the property. The buyer as the new owner has the lot surveyed and demands the neighbor remove the wall and gazebo since they encroach on the buyer's property.

The neighbor claims they have an *irrevocable license* to maintain the encroachments. The neighbor may use the slope since they spent considerable time and money to construct the encroaching wall and gazebo structures in reliance on the prior owner's oral agreement which allowed them to build the wall and use the slope.

The buyer claims they cannot be barred from revoking the license since they had no notice the license existed and the use was not reduced to an enforceable easement.

However, the license became irrevocable due to the neighbor's substantial effort or expenditures made in reliance on the oral agreement with the property owner allowing the use. Further, the buyer — as a successor owner of the property burdened with the use allowed by the oral license agreement — need not have any knowledge of the irrevocable license to be barred from denying the neighbor's continual use to maintain the existing wall and gazebo under the oral agreement.[7]

---

7   **Noronha** v. **Stewart** (1988) 199 CA3d 485

Chapter 2 Summary

Unlike an easement or a lease, a license is a personal privilege held by an individual, not an appurtenant right belonging to another property for its future owners to receive and use. Since a license is a personal right and does not benefit another property, the right given by the license cannot be conveyed to another individual as there can be no successors or assigns to the interest.

A holder of a license does not usually pay rent for the right to use the burdened property. If consideration for the license exists, it is typically in the form of an expenditure of time and money by the licensee to improve or maintain the use authorized on the burdened property.

On some occasions, a license and a lease may sometimes co-exist and be held by the same person. For example, a person who is a tenant with exclusive occupancy to part of the space on the premises of a shopping center also holds a license to use an adjacent portion of the premises as well.

However, with every additional condition agreed to between an owner and user, a license begins to recharacterize itself more and more into a lease. Words or phrases like "lease," "rental," "demise" or "good tenantable condition" are characteristic of a lease rather than a license.

Chapter 2 Key Terms

Quiz 1 Covering Chapters 1-4 is located on page 633.

Notes:

The tenancies in real estate

After reading this chapter, you will be able to:

- differentiate between the four distinct possessory types of tenancies;
- understand the rights held under each type of tenancy;
- determine how a tenancy is established or changed; and
- serve the proper notice required to terminate a tenancy.

Learning Objectives

holdover rent	**reservation agreement**
holdover tenant	**transient occupancy**
lease agreement	**trespasser**
rental agreement	**unlawful detainer**

Key Terms

A landlord and tenant enter into a lease agreement. The lease agreement does not include an option to renew or extend the term of the occupancy on expiration of the lease.

Several months before the lease expires, they begin negotiations to enter into a modified or new lease agreement to extend the term of occupancy. The landlord and tenant do not reach an agreement before the lease expires. On expiration of the lease, the tenant remains in possession of the property.

The landlord and tenant continue lease negotiations. Meanwhile, the landlord accepts monthly rent at the same rate the tenant paid under the expired lease agreement.

Know your tenancy or lose time

Ultimately, they fail to agree on the terms for an extension or a new lease agreement. The landlord serves a notice on the tenant to either stay and pay a substantially higher monthly rent, or vacate and forfeit the right of possession. [See **RPI** Form 571; see Form 569 in Chapter 29]

The tenant does neither. The tenant remains in possession on expiration of the notice, but does not pay the increased rent.

Can the landlord evict the tenant by filing an unlawful detainer (UD) action on expiration of the notice?

Yes! The tenant's right of possession went from an initial *fixed-term tenancy* to a *tenancy-at-sufferance* when the lease expired. When the landlord accepted rent for the continued occupancy, the tenancy-at-sufferance became a *periodic tenancy*. The tenant's failure to pay the higher rent demanded in the notice terminated the tenant's right of possession under the periodic tenancy on expiration of the notice to pay rent or quit.

Different types of tenancies and properties trigger different termination procedures for the landlord, and different rights for the tenant. [See Chapters 25, 41 and 50]

Tenancies as leasehold estates

Recall from Chapter 1 that *leasehold estates*, or *tenancies*, are possessory interests in real estate. Four types of *tenancies* exist:

- *fixed-term tenancies*;
- *periodic tenancies*;
- *tenancies-at-will*; and
- *tenancies-at-sufferance*, also called *holdover tenancies*.

To initially establish a tenancy, a landlord needs to transfer to the tenant the right to occupy the real estate. This right is conveyed either orally, in writing or by the landlord's conduct, called a grant. If the landlord does not transfer the right to occupy, the person who takes possession as the occupant is a **trespasser**.

trespasser
A person who occupies a property without the landlord's transfer of the right to occupy.

Fixed-term tenancies, periodic tenancies and tenancies at will have agreed-to termination dates, or can be terminated by notice.

A *holdover tenancy* occurs when a tenant unlawfully continues in possession of the property after their right to occupy has expired. This unlawful possession of the property without contractual right is called **unlawful detainer (UD)**.

unlawful detainer
The unlawful possession of a property. [See **RPI** Form 575-578]

A landlord needs to file a *UD* action in court to evict a holdover tenant. A tenant's right of possession under the tenancy is terminated either by service of the proper notice or expiration of the lease before he can be evicted. Plainly speaking, the tenant needs to unlawfully detain possession of the property before the tenant can be evicted for unlawful detainer.

> *A landlord and tenant orally agree to a six-month lease, with rent payable monthly. At the end of six months, the landlord and tenant orally agree to another six-month lease.*
>
> *At the end of the second term, the tenant refuses to vacate, claiming the landlord nees to first serve them with a notice to vacate.*
>
> *Here, the tenant is not entitled to any further notice beyond the agreed-to termination date. The oral occupancy agreement was not a periodic tenancy, even though it called for monthly rent payments. Instead, the occupancy agreement created a fixed-term lease with a set expiration date. Thus, the tenant's right of possession terminated on expiration of the orally agreed-to six-month period. The oral lease agreement was enforceable since it was for a term of less than one year. [**Camp** v. **Matich** (1948) 87 CA2d 660]*

Since the type of notice required to terminate a tenancy depends on the period of the tenancy, period of the occupancy and location of the property (e.g., rent control), landlords and property managers needs to understand how each type of tenancy is created.[1]

The fixed-term tenancy

A fixed-term tenancy, also called a lease or estate for years, is the result of an agreement between the landlord and the tenant for a fixed rental period. If the rental period is longer than one year, the lease arrangements need to be in writing and signed by the landlord and tenant to be enforceable. The written document which sets the terms of a fixed-term tenancy is called a **lease agreement.** A *lease agreement* has a commencement date and an expiration date.[2] [See Form 550 in Chapter 50]

lease agreement
The written document which sets the terms of a fixed-term tenancy. [See **RPI** Form 550, 552 and 552-4]

During the term of the lease, the tenancy can only be terminated and the tenant evicted for cause. Even then, service of a three-day notice to cure the breach or vacate the property is required. [See Form 576 in Chapter 26]

Without an exercise of a renewal or extension option, a fixed-term tenancy automatically terminates on the expiration date, no notice required. [3]

If a renewal or extension option exists, the lease is renewed or extended by the tenant's exercise of the option or the landlord's acceptance of rent called for in the option.[4] [See Case in point, "Second lease term is not a periodic tenancy"]

A fixed-term tenancy provides a tenant with several advantages:

- the right to occupy for the fixed term;
- a predetermined rental amount; and
- limitations on termination or modification.

---

1 **Colyear** v. **Tobriner** (1936) 7 C2d 735
2 CC §§761, 1624
3 CCP §1161(1)
4 CC §1945

However, a fixed-term tenancy also has disadvantages for the fixed-term tenant:

- the tenant is liable for the total amount of rent due over the entire term of the lease (less rent paid by any replacement tenant located by the landlord to mitigate his losses) [See Chapter 30]; and

- the tenant may not vacate prior to expiration of the rental period and assign or sublet the premises to a new tenant if prohibited by the lease agreement.

The periodic tenancy

periodic tenancy
A leasehold interest which lasts for automatic successive rental periods of the same length of time, terminating upon notice from either party. [See **RPI** 551 and 552-5]

rental agreement
The written document which sets the terms of a periodic tenancy. [See **RPI** Form 551 and 552-5]

If the landlord finds a fixed-term tenancy too restrictive or inflexible for their requirements, a periodic tenancy may be more suitable.

A **periodic tenancy** automatically continues for equal, successive periods of time, such as a week or a month. The length of each successive period of time is determined by the interval between scheduled rental payments. A *periodic tenancy* is automatically renewed when the landlord accepts rent.

Examples of periodic payment intervals include:

- annual rental payments, indicating a year-to-year tenancy;

- monthly rental payments, indicating a month-to-month tenancy; and

- weekly rental payments, indicating a week-to-week tenancy.

A periodic tenancy is intentionally created by a landlord and tenant entering into a **rental agreement**. A *rental agreement* is the agreement which sets the terms of a periodic tenancy.

However, the tenancy can also arise due to a defective lease agreement. A tenant who enters into possession under an unenforceable lease agreement (e.g., oral, or unsigned) and pays rent in monthly intervals that the landlord accepts is a month-to-month tenant.

A periodic tenancy continues until terminated by a notice to vacate. This makes a periodic tenancy flexible, since it allows the landlord and the tenant to terminate a month-to-month tenancy by giving the appropriate notice to vacate to the other party.[5] [See Forms 569 in Chapter 29 and 572 in Chapter 22]

To terminate a periodic tenancy, the notice period needs to be at least as long as the interval between scheduled rental payments, but need not exceed 30 days. An exception exists: a 60-day notice is required to terminate a residential periodic tenancy if the tenant has occupied the property for more than 12 months.[6] [See Form 569-1 Chapter 29]

On a breach of the rental agreement, a three-day notice to vacate can also be used to terminate a periodic tenancy. [See Form 577 in Chapter 26]

---

5   **Kingston** v. **Colburn** (1956) 139 CA2d 623; CC §1946
6   CC §1946.1

Case in point

Periodic tenancy or tenancy-at-will?

Consider a property manager who rents an apartment to a tenant under a fixed-term lease. At the end of the leasing period, the tenant retains possession and continues to pay rent monthly, which the property manager accepts.

Later, the tenant is served with an appropriate notice to vacate. On the running of the notice period, the tenant refuses to vacate. The tenant claims the notice to vacate served by the landlord merely terminated the tenant's right of possession and made it a tenancy-at-will on expiration of the notice. As a tenant-at-will, they are entitled to an additional three-day notice to vacate before they are unlawfully detaining the property.

*However, an occupancy agreement for an indefinite term with a monthly rent schedule is a month-to-month tenancy. Thus, a tenant is only entitled to one notice to vacate which needs to expire before a UD action may be filed to evict them. [**Palmer** v. **Zeis** (1944) 65 CA2d Supp. 859]*

The tenancy-at-will: consent but no rent

The characteristics of a tenancy-at-will include:

- possession delivered to the tenant with the landlord's knowledge and consent;
- possession for an indefinite and unspecified period; and
- no provision for the payment of rent.

Situations giving rise to a tenancy-at-will include:

- when a tenant is granted the right to indefinitely occupy the property in exchange for services rendered [See Form 591 in Chapter 10];[7]
- when a tenant takes possession of the property under an unenforceable lease agreement (e.g., a written lease not signed by either party with terms orally agreed to) — unless rent is accepted to create a periodic tenancy;[8] or
- when a tenant is given possession of the property while lease negotiations regarding the rent amount are still in progress and rent is not accepted.[9]

For a tenancy-at-will, a written notice to pay rent or quit is required to implement any change in the right to continue to occupy the premises, e.g., change it to a different kind of tenancy or terminate the tenancy. However, the parties can always agree to a shorter or longer notice period to accommodate the change.[10] [See Case in point, "Periodic tenancy or tenancy-at-will?"]

Written notice required before any change in the right to occupancy

Consider, an owner-occupant who agrees to sell their office building. The terms of the purchase agreement allow them to retain the free use and possession of the property until they can occupy an office building they are constructing. Thus, a tenancy-at-will is created.

---

7 **Covina Manor Inc.** v. **Hatch** (1955) 133 CA2d Supp. 790
8 **Psihozios** v. **Humberg** (1947) 80 CA2d 215
9 **Miller** v. **Smith** (1960) 179 CA2d 114
10 CC §§789, 1946

The buyer agrees in the purchase agreement to give the seller a 90-day written notice to pay rent or vacate the property.

The buyer resells the property to a new owner. The new owner serves notice on the tenant-seller to pay rent or vacate in three days' time. The new owner claims they are not subject to the prior owner's unrecorded agreement to give a 90-day notice.

However, the new owner acquired the property subject to unrecorded rights held by the tenant in possession. Thus, the new owner is charged with constructive knowledge of the unrecorded agreement regarding 90-day notices to vacate and took title subject to the terms of the agreement.

Until the tenant-at-will receives the appropriate notice to vacate, they are not unlawfully detaining the property and the owner/landlord cannot proceed with a UD action to recover possession.[11]

However, a tenancy-at-will is automatically terminated if the tenant assigns or sublets their right to occupy the property to another tenant. The new tenant becomes a holdover tenant. Either form of possession is an unlawful detainer and grounds for eviction without notice.[12]

Also, a tenancy-at-will terminates on the death of either the landlord or tenant, unless an agreement to the contrary exists.[13]

The holdover tenancy

When a fixed-term or periodic tenancy terminates by prior agreement or notice, the tenant who remains in possession unlawfully detains the property from the landlord. Likewise, a tenant-at-will who receives the appropriate notice to vacate and who remains in the property also unlawfully detains the property. These scenarios create a tenancy-at-sufferance, commonly referred to as a holdover tenancy. [See Case in point, "What steps does a landlord take to serve an unlawful detainer on a holdover tenant?"]

A holdover tenancy also arises on termination of a resident manager when the resident manager's compensation includes the right to occupy a unit rent-free. When the landlord terminates the employment and the resident manager fails to vacate immediately, the resident manager unlawfully detains the premises as a holdover tenant.[14] [See Form 591 in Chapter 10]

A **holdover tenant** retains possession of the premises without any contractual right to do so. Their tenancy has been terminated. Thus, the landlord is not required to provide a holdover tenant with any additional notice prior to commencing eviction proceedings.[15]

A *holdover tenant* no longer owes rent under the expired lease or terminated rental agreement since they no longer have the right of possession. However,

holdover tenant
A tenant who retains possession of the rented premises after their right of possession has been terminated.

holdover rent
Rent owed by a holdover tenant for the tenant's unlawful detainer of the rented premises. [See **RPI** Form 550 §3.3]

---

11 **First & C. Corporation** v. **Wencke** (1967) 253 CA2d 719
12 **McLeran** v. **Benton** (1887) 73 C 329
13 **Dugand** v. **Magnus** (1930) 107 CA 243
14 **Karz** v. **Mecham** (1981) 120 CA3d Supp. 1
15 CCP §1161

Facts: An apartment landlord filed an unlawful detainer (UD) against a tenant who was unlawfully holding over. The landlord attempted to personally serve the UD on the tenant at the apartment address numerous times but the tenant was out of state. The landlord posted the notice on the property and mailed a copy to the tenant's last known address, which was at the apartment. No other address for the tenant was available. The tenant did not receive or respond to the UD and the landlord took possession of the property.

Claim: The tenant sought to restore their tenancy claiming the landlord's attempts to serve the UD were deficient since all the attempts were executed at the apartment address while the tenant was out of state and no other actions were taken to reach the tenant.

Counter claim: The landlord sought to prevent the tenant from restoring their tenancy, claiming sufficient actions were taken to notify the tenant of the UD since multiple attempts to notify the tenant were executed at the apartment address without response before posting the notice on the premises and no other address for the tenant was available.

Holding: A California Court of Appeals held the tenant may not regain possession since personal service was attempted and the notice was posted at the apartment address and no other address for the tenant was available for personal service or mailing. [*The Board of Trustees of the Leland Stanford Junior University v. Ham* (2013) 216 CA4th 330]

Editor's note – A landlord is not required to expend an indeterminate amount of time and resources to track down an absent tenant in order to serve a UD. If the UD cannot be personally delivered, the landlord may leave a copy with a competent adult at the property or post it on the property, then send¬ the documents by mail to the last known address of the tenant.

Case in point

What steps does a landlord take to serve an unlawful detainer on a holdover tenant?

the rental or lease agreement usually includes a **holdover rent** provision which calls for a penalty rate of daily rent owed for each day the tenant holds over.

If the rental or lease agreement does not contain a *holdover rent* provision, the tenant owes the landlord the reasonable rental value of the property. This is a daily rate owed for each day the tenant holds over. [See Case in point, "Reasonable rental value in a holdover tenancy"; see **RPI** Form 550]

Holdover rent is due after the tenant vacates or is evicted. At that time, the holdover period is known and the amount owed can be determined, and demanded. If it is not paid on demand, it can be collected by obtaining a money judgment.

But a caution to landlords: acceptance of holdover rent prior to a tenant vacating or being evicted has unintended consequences, as discussed in the next section.

Case in point

Reasonable rental value in a holdover tenancy

A tenant with a fixed-term lease holds over after the lease agreement expires. The lease agreement contains no provisions for the amount of rent due during any holdover period.

On the tenant's failure to vacate, the landlord serves the tenant a notice to either pay a rent amount substantially higher than rental market rates, or vacate. The tenant refuses to pay any rent or vacate.

On expiration of the notice, the landlord files a UD action seeking payment of rent at the rate stated in the notice, since the tenant did not vacate.

At the UD hearing, the landlord is awarded the reasonable market rental value for the entire time the tenant held over after the lease expired, not the higher rent demanded in the notice.

*A UD court will only award a reasonable rental value for the time period the tenant held over. [**Shenson** v. **Shenson** (1954) 124 CA2d 747]*

Changing the type of tenancy

A landlord, by using a proper notice, can create a different tenancy relationship from the one they initially conveyed to the tenant. A tenant's possessory interest in real estate can shift from one type of tenancy to another due to:

- a notice;
- expiration of a lease; or
- by conduct.

A classic example involves a change in the type of tenancy which arises when a holdover tenant becomes a month-to-month (periodic) tenant.

A landlord who accepts any rent from a holdover tenant under an expired lease has elected by their conduct to treat the continued occupancy as a periodic tenancy.[16]

Thus, the prerequisite to a UD eviction is the service of a proper notice to vacate on the holdover tenant who paid rent for the continued occupancy, rent the landlord accepted to create a periodic tenancy.[17]

If a landlord accepts rent from a holdover tenant after a fixed-term tenancy expires, the expired lease agreement is renewed on the same terms except for the period of occupancy, which is now periodic.[18]

On expiration of a fixed-term lease, the landlord's continued acceptance of rental payments does not renew the tenancy for another term equal to the term of the original lease. Rather, the tenancy is extended as a periodic tenancy for consecutive periods equal to the interval between rent payments — hence, one month if rent is paid monthly.[19]

A landlord who wants to terminate a periodic tenancy they created by accepting rent after expiration of a lease needs to serve the tenant with the

16 **Peter Kiewit Sons Co.** v. **Richmond Redevelopment Agency** (1986) 178 CA3d 435
17 Colyear, *supra*
18 CC §1945
19 CC §1945

proper notice to vacate and let it expire. On expiration of the notice, the tenant who remains in possession of the premises is unlawfully detaining the premises and the landlord may file a UD action to evict them.

Other rules for terminating a tenancy

A landlord and tenant can establish a shorter or lengthier notice period by agreement. However, the notice period cannot be less than seven days.

Other specialized rules exist for different types of properties and situations. For example, in a rent-controlled tenancy, terminating the right of possession is restricted by local ordinances.

In a tenancy-at-will in a mobile home park, the tenant needs to be given a 60-day written notice.[20]

Industrial and commercial tenants typically require three months minimum notice due to the time spent receiving and responding to a notice since it goes through multiple tiers of corporate management before a decision can be made.[21]

In some instances, an extended 90-day notice is required to terminate residential tenancies in foreclosed properties. [See Chapter 29]

Transient occupants and their removal

Another type of occupancy is to be differentiated from the leasehold interests discussed in this chapter. **Transient occupancy** is the occupancy of a vacation property, hotel, motel, inn, boarding house, lodging house, tourist home or similar sleeping accommodation for a period of 30 days or less. This type of occupant is classified as a *guest*, also called a *transient occupant*.

A transient occupant occupies property known as lodging, accommodation or unit, not space or premises. The property is not called a rental. The term "rental" implies a landlord/tenant relationship exists. Further, landlord/tenant law does not control *transient occupancy*.

The guest's occupancy is labeled a *stay*, not possession. During a guest's stay in the lodging, the owner or manager of the property is entitled to enter the unit at check-out time even though the guest may not yet have departed.

The contract entered into for the lodging is usually called a **reservation agreement**, but never a rental agreement or lease agreement. [See **RPI** Form 593]

Guests pay a daily rate, not a daily or weekly rent. They arrive at a pre-set date and time for check-in, not for commencement of possession. Likewise, guests depart at an hour on a date agreed to as the check-out time. Unlike a tenant, a guest does not vacate the premises; they check out.

transient occupancy
The occupancy of a vacation property, hotel, motel, inn, boarding house, lodging house, tourist home or similar sleeping accommodation for a period of 30 days or less. [See **RPI** Form 593]

reservation agreement
The written document which sets the terms of a transient occupancy. [See **RPI** Form 593]

---

20 CC §798.55(b)
21 CC §1946

When a guest fails to depart at the scheduled check-out hour on the date agreed, no holdover tenancy is created. Thus, an unlawful detainer does not exist as with a tenancy conveyed by a rental or lease agreement. A UD action or court involvement is not required to remove the guest.[22]

However, for the owner or manager to avoid the landlord-tenant UD eviction process, the guest, when checking in, needs to sign a notice stating:

- the unit is needed at check-out time for another guest who has been promised the unit; and
- if the guest has not departed at check-out time, the owner or manager may enter, take possession of the guest's property, re-key the doors and clean up the unit for the next guest.[23] [See **RPI** Form 593]

Property manager's self-help to remove guests

To remove a guest who fails to timely depart the unit and remains in the unit after a demand has been made to leave, the manager can intervene to remove the guest, a solution called *self-help*. If the manager's intervention might cause a breach of the peace, the manager may call the police. The police or the sheriff will assist, without the need for a court order, to remove the guest and prevent a danger to persons or property during the re-keying, removal of possessions and clean up for the arrival of the next guest.[24]

Transient occupancies include all occupancies that are taxed as such by local ordinance or could be taxed as such by the city or by the county.

Taxwise, the guest occupancy is considered a personal privilege, not a tenancy. Time share units when occupied by their owners are not transient occupancies and are not subject to those ordinances and taxes.[25]

Transient units do not include residential hotels since the occupants of residential hotels treat the dwelling they occupy as their *primary residence*. Also, the occupancy of most individuals in residential hotels is for a period of more than 30 days.

Avoidance of month-to-month status

Also, the operator of a residential hotel may not require a resident to change units or to check out and re-register in order to avoid creating a month-to-month tenancy which would place the occupancy under landlord/tenant law. A residential hotel operator violating this rule is liable for a $500 civil penalty and attorney fees.[26]

A broker or any other person who manages "vacation rental" stays for owners of single family homes, units in a common interest development (condominium project), units in an apartment complex or any other residence subject to a local transient occupancy tax, is to maintain accounting records.

---

22 CC §1940(b)
23 CC §1865
24 Calif. Penal Code §602(s)
25 Calif. Revenue and Taxation Code §7280
26 CC §1940.1

Further, the property manager needs to send a monthly accounting statement to each landlord they represent and make the records available for inspection and reproduction by the owner. They need to also comply with the transient occupancy tax regarding collection, payment and record keeping.[27]

---

27 CC §1864

Chapter 3 Summary

A fixed-term tenancy is the result of an agreement between the landlord and the tenant for a fixed rental period. A periodic tenancy automatically continues for equal, successive periods of time, such as a week or a month.

In a tenancy-at-will, possession is delivered to the tenant with the landlord's knowledge and consent for an indefinite and unspecified period, usually without requiring rent. A holdover tenancy is the result of a tenant retaining possession of a rented premises without any contractual right to do so.

A tenant's possessory interest in real estate can shift from one type of tenancy to another based on conduct of the landlord.

The type of notice required to terminate occupancy depends on the period of the tenancy or occupancy and the property type and location.

Chapter 3 Key Terms

Quiz 1 Covering Chapters 1-4 is located on page 633.

Notes:

Chapter
4

Landlord's right to enter

After reading this chapter, you will be able to:

- understand the relationship between a tenant's right to privacy and the landlord's need to access the leased space;
- distinguish the circumstances under which a landlord may enter a leased premises;
- properly serve a 24-hour notice of entry on a tenant in advance of the entry; and
- identify resolutions to possessory conflicts arising from the landlord-tenant relationship.

Learning Objectives

business goodwill

forcible entry

notice of entry

punitive damages

restitution

self-help

Key Terms

Unknown to a residential landlord, a tenant changes the locks on the door to the rented unit. Several months later, the tenant is arrested by law enforcement officers as they step out of their apartment. The tenant is hastily escorted away, leaving lights on and their pet inside, but locking the door.

The landlord becomes aware of the tenant's dilemma. Fearful the gas stove was also left on, the landlord attempts, but is unable to enter with their key.

The landlord calls the police to witness their entry and inspection of the apartment to make sure it is in a safe and secure condition. The landlord then enters the apartment through a window. The police are let in to observe the landlord's conduct.

The police proceed to make a visual inspection of the apartment.

Conflict with occupant's right to privacy

The police find illegal possessions in plain view casually lying around the kitchen and dining area of the apartment.

Did the landlord have the right to enter the apartment? Did the landlord have the right to allow the police to enter the apartment?

Yes to both! The landlord had the right to enter since they reasonably believed the safety of their other tenants and the building may be in jeopardy.

Also, the police were present at the request of the landlord to act as eyewitnesses so the tenant may not claim the landlord removed any of the tenant's possessions. [1]

In contrast, consider the landlord who permits the police to enter and search a tenant's garage without a warrant.

The police have reason to believe the tenant is manufacturing drugs, an illegal use of the premises and of concern to the landlord.

May a landlord collaborate with the police at their request and allow them to enter a tenant's garage?

No! The landlord has no right of possession when the tenant's right of possession has not expired or been terminated. This is true even if the tenant has vacated and only one day remains under a 30-day notice to vacate.

Landlord may not interfere with tenant's possessory right

If the tenant's right of possession has not expired, the landlord has no possessory right. Thus, they are prohibited from entering the property or letting the police enter the property, even if the landlord suspects the tenant of using the premises to commit a crime. The police need to first obtain a search warrant to legally authorize them to come onto the premises occupied by the tenant when the landlord has no right to entry. [2]

However, a landlord does have the right to enter and also to allow police to enter a unit which has been abandoned or vacated by the tenant if the tenancy has been terminated under state law rules of abandonment or surrender. [3] [See Chapter 30 and 31]

Further, "lock-box" entry by the police in collaboration with a multiple-listing service (MLS) member to check out a crime is prohibited without a warrant. The entry violates the purpose of a seller's broker's agency and lock-box authority. The broker may enter only to show the premises to prospective tenants who accompany them (or other authorized agents). [4]

---

1 **People** v. **Plane** (1969) 274 CA2d 1
2 **United States** v. **Warner** (9th Cir. 1988) 843 F2d 401
3 **United States** v. **Sledge** (9th Cir. 1981) 650 F2d 1075
4 **People** v. **Jaquez** (1985) 163 CA3d 918

A landlord's right to enter a residential or commercial unit during the period of the tenant's right to occupy the premises is severely limited. The possessory rights to occupy the property have been conveyed to the tenant and are no longer held by the landlord, until a reversion of possession occurs on termination of the tenancy.

A residential landlord may enter the tenant's actual dwelling space during the term of the rental or lease agreement only in limited circumstances:

- in an emergency;
- to make repairs, alterations, improvements, or supply services that are either necessary or previously approved by the tenant;
- to complete a pre-expiration inspection for deficiencies which would result in a deduction from the security deposit [See Chapter 19];
- to show the unit to prospective buyers, prospective tenants, lenders, repairmen or contractors;
- when the tenant has vacated the premises and their right to occupy has been terminated by surrender or abandonment; or
- under a court order allowing entry.[5]

A property manager's entry into a tenant's unit out of concern for the safety of the property or other tenants constitutes an emergency. The property manager may properly enter the unit without the tenant's knowledge and permission for the limited purpose of dealing with the emergency.[6]

Landlord's right to enter another's space

Consider a commercial lease agreement that prohibits any tenant violations of government laws and regulations. [See **RPI** Form 552 §7.3]

The landlord asks the tenant for permission to conduct tests on the property and investigate whether the leased property contains any contamination from hazardous waste. The tenant refuses to give the landlord permission to conduct the investigation, claiming the landlord does not have a right to determine whether contamination exists until the lease expires.

Here, the landlord, on advance notice to the tenant, has the right to access the property to determine if contamination has or is occurring on the property. Hazardous waste contamination is a violation of law and a breach of the lease provision prohibiting unlawful activities which adversely affect the value of the property.[7]

Entry to conduct a hazardous waste investigation

Before a residential landlord may proceed with any maintenance or services which require entry into a tenant's unit, the tenant needs to be given a written notice of the landlord's intent to enter. Maintenance includes all routine or non-emergency repairs, decorations, alterations, improvements, replacements or services, whether or not agreed to by the tenant.[8] [See Form 567 accompanying this chapter]

Notice of entry for repairs

5 Calif. Civil Code §1954

6 Plane, *supra*

7 **Sachs** v. **Exxon Company, U.S.A.** (1992) 9 CA4th 1491

8 CC §1954

Case in point

Do city inspections violate tenants' rights to privacy?

Facts: A residential landlord owned several rental properties. The city enacted an ordinance requiring annual inspections of all residential rental properties to identify substandard properties. The ordinance required inspectors to obtain consent from landlords and tenants prior to entering units for inspections. However, the ordinance allowed inspectors to enter properties without consent if the inspector had reason to believe a dangerous condition of the property required an immediate inspection for public safety.

Claim: The landlord sought to invalidate the ordinance, claiming the ordinance violated tenants' right to privacy since the inspections allowed searches without a warrant.

Counter claim: The city claimed the ordinance did not violate tenants' right to privacy since landlord and tenant consent was a prerequisite to property inspections, unless an emergency threatened public safety.

Holding: A California court of appeals held the ordinance did not violate tenant privacy since inspectors were required to receive consent before entry, unless an emergency threatened public safety. [*Griffith* v. *City of Santa Cruz* (2012) 207 CA4th 982]

The written notice gives the tenant a reasonable time period to prepare for the entry. A 24-hour notice is considered reasonable, unless extenuating circumstances known to the landlord or their property managers, such as the tenant's vacation or business trip, indicate the tenant needs more time to receive the notice and prepare for the entry.

Service of a 24-hour **notice of entry** in advance of the entry is accomplished by any one of the following methods:

notice of entry
A written document giving a tenant advance notice of a landlord's intent to enter a tenant's unit to perform maintenance, make repairs or inspect. [See **RPI** Form 567]

- handing a written notice to the tenant personally;
- handing the notice to an occupant of the unit who appears of suitable age and discretion to relay the notice to the tenant; or
- posting the notice on, near or under the usual entry door so it will be discovered by the tenant.

Mailed notice of entry

Alternatively, the notice may be mailed, but at least six days is to pass after mailing before the intended entry can be scheduled to occur.[9]

A notice is sufficient to request entry during normal business hours, emergencies excepted. However, to request entry after business hours, the tenant's consent needs to be obtained "at the time of entry."

The *notice of entry* procedures may not be used to harass a tenant in a retaliatory or abusive manner.[10]

A tenant in a community apartment project or a homeowner in a common interest development (CID) is to receive at least 15 days but no more than 30 days written notice when the management or association needs the occupants to vacate the project in order to treat termites. Condominium projects and planned unit developments are examples of CIDs.[11]

---

9 CC §1954
10 CC §1954
11 CC §1364(d)(2)

Form 567

Notice of Intent to Enter Dwelling

NOTICE OF INTENT TO ENTER DWELLING

NOTE: This form is used by a property manager or landlord when maintenance services need to be provided to an occupied unit, to provide the tenant a written notice 24-hour notice of the landlord's intent to enter the leased premises.

DATE: _____, 20_____, at _____, California.
Items left blank or unchecked are not applicable.

FACTS:

1. You are a Tenant under a rental or lease agreement
   1.1 dated _____, at _____, California.
   1.2 entered into by _____, as the Tenant,
       and _____, as the Landlord,
   1.3 regarding real estate referred to as _____
       _____

NOTICE TO TENANT:

2. Landlord will enter the above premises at or around the normal business hour of _____,
   on _____, 20_____ for the following checked purposes:
   2.1 ☐ To make necessary or agreed repairs of _____
       _____
   2.2 ☐ To decorate the unit by _____
       _____
   2.3 ☐ To alter or improve the unit by _____
       _____
   2.4 ☐ To supply necessary or requested services of _____
       _____
   2.5 Other _____
       _____

3. You are not required to be on he premises during this entry. A passkey will be used in the event of your absence.

Date: _____, 20_____
Landlord/Agent: _____ CalBRE: _____

Signature: _____
Address: _____
_____
Phone: _____
Fax: _____
Email: _____

FORM 567   03-11   ©2016 **RPI — Realty Publications, Inc.**, P.O. BOX 5707, RIVERSIDE, CA 92517

Editor's note — When a landlord or property manager needs to temporarily displace a tenant to fumigate or conduct invasive repairs, mutually agreed-to terms need to be set out in writing by the landlord and tenant. [See Chapter 26; see **RPI** *Form 588]*

A residential landlord may enter a tenant's unit after further notice to the tenant when the tenant requests a joint pre-expiration inspection of the premises. The tenant's request is usually in response to the landlord's initial notice mandated to inform the tenant of the tenant's right to a joint inspection. [See Chapter 19]

Entry for pre-expiration inspection

Form 116

Right to Enter and Exhibit Unit to Buyers

RIGHT TO ENTER AND EXHIBIT UNIT TO BUYERS
For Residential and Nonresidential Rentals (Calif. Civil Code §1954)

Prepared by: Agent _____   Phone _____
             Broker _____   Email _____

NOTE: This form is used by the owner of a rental property when listed for sale and before showing rented units to prospective buyers, to advise the tenants the property is "For Sale" and that during the next 120 days the owner or their agent intend to enter their unit on 24 hours' telephonic notice and show it to prospective buyers.

DATE: _____, 20_____, at _____, California.
Items left blank or unchecked are not applicable.

FACTS:

1. You are a Tenant under a rental or lease agreement
    1.1 dated _____, at _____, California,
    1.2 entered into by _____, as the Tenant,
         and _____, as the Landlord,
    1.3 regarding real estate referred as _____
         _____

NOTICE TO TENANT:

2. You are advised the premises you occupy has been placed on the real estate market "For Sale".
3. During the period of 120 days following the date of this notice, Landlord or their authorized Agent for the sale of the property may need to enter your unit during normal business hours for the purpose of showing the premises for review by prospective or actual Buyers.
4. At least 24 hours prior to entry for this purpose, you will be given telephonic or personal notice of our intent to enter.
5. You are not required to be present on the premise during the entry and showing. A passkey will be used should you be absent.
6. On departing the premises, Landlord or their Agent will leave a written note identifying themselves and indicating they have entered and completed their showing of the unit to Buyers. [See **RPI** Form 116-1]

Date: _____, 20_____
Landlord: _____
Listing Agent: _____   CalBRE #: _____

Signature: _____
Address: _____

Phone: _____   Cell: _____
Fax: _____
Email: _____

FORM 116   07-14   ©2016 RPI — Realty Publications, Inc., P.O. BOX 5707, RIVERSIDE, CA 92517

The purpose of the pre-expiration inspection prior to termination of the tenancy is to advise the tenant of any deficiencies in the condition of the premises. The tenant can then correct or eliminate any deficiencies before vacating and avoid deductions from the security deposit.

Before the residential landlord may enter to conduct the agreed-to pre-expiration inspection, the tenant is given a 48-hour written notice stating the date and time for the inspection.[12]

Service of the 48-hour notice of entry is accomplished in the same manner as for the 24-hour notice of advance entry to complete repairs. However, the tenant may waive the 48-hour notice if both the tenant and the landlord sign a written waiver.[13]

---

12 CC §1950.5(f)(1)
13 CC §1950.5(f)(1)

NOTICE TO OCCUPANT OF ENTRY AND COMPLETION OF SHOWING
For Residential and Nonresidential Rentals (Calif. Civil Code §1954(d)(2))

Prepared by: Agent _____ Phone _____
Broker _____ Email _____

NOTE: This form is used by the owner of a rental property listed for sale when with a prospective buyer they have entered and shown the unit based on the 120-day "For Sale" notice previously served on the tenant to advise the tenant the entry occurred and has been completed.

DATE: _____, 20____, at _____, California.
Items left blank or unchecked are not applicable.

FACTS:

1. You are a Tenant under a rental or lease agreement
   1.1 dated _____, at _____, California,
   1.2 entered into by _____, as the Tenant,
   and _____, as the Landlord,
   1.3 regarding real estate referred as _____
   _____

NOTICE TO TENANT:

2. On _____, 20____, you were given notice of Landlord's or their Agent's intent to enter the leased premises you occupy to show the unit to prospective Buyers. [See RPI Form 116]

3. You are advised the showing of your unit has been completed by
   _____, as the Agent, or
   _____, as the Landlord.

Date: _____, 20____
Landlord: _____
Agent: _____ CalBRE #: _____

Signature: _____
Address: _____
_____

Phone: _____ Cell: _____
Fax: _____

FORM 116-1   03-11   ©2016 RPI — Realty Publications, Inc., P.O. BOX 5707, RIVERSIDE, CA 92517

A residential or commercial property occupied by a tenant is called a rental. Real estate brokers who list rentals for sale need to inform the seller of the seller's right to coordinate prospective buyer inspections of the property. These inspections can be completed using one of two notice procedures.[14]

The first notice procedure works exactly the same as the 24-hour written notice of entry for repairs. This notice may also be mailed, as discussed in the prior section.

The second, or alternative notice procedure to the 24-hour written notice is a 120-day "For Sale" notice. The "For Sale" notice may be given to the tenant personally or by regular mail at any time after the seller enters into a listing to sell the property.[15] [See Form 116 accompanying this chapter]

The "For Sale" notice commences a 120-day "for sale" period. During this period, the seller or the seller's agent may enter the unit during normal business hours with a prospective buyer to conduct an inspection of the unit. [See Case in point, "Are weekends normal business hours?"]

Entry during "For Sale" period

14 CC §1954
15 CC §1954(d)(2)

Prior to the time for entry during the "for sale" period, the tenant receipt of the notice is to be given no less than 24 hours advance notice by phone or in person of the actual entry date and time. The actual entry is conditioned on the listing agent leaving a written note in the unit regarding the entry and completion of the inspection. [See Form 116-1 accompanying this chapter]

Here, the giving of the 24-hour notice by phone, during the 120-day period following service of the written "For Sale" notice, is exclusively the right of the seller and their listing agent. The buyer's agent needs to arrange for the listing agent to give the 24-hour advance telephonic notice. The buyer's agent does not have, and may not be given the authority to notify the tenant (unless they are also the listing agent).

On taking a listing to sell property occupied by tenants, the listing agent needs to inform the seller of the two available notice-of-entry procedures.

Once resolved as to which notice procedure the seller is willing to authorize in the listing agreement, the information is shared with buyer's agent.

This information regarding a buyer's access to the listed property is reported in MLS listings under "showing instructions." For example, "Call the listing office (LO) or listing agent (LA) to arrange for 24-hour telephonic (or alternative written) notice of entry."

Once informed of the procedure for entry and inspection, some sellers may restrict inspections of the property to qualified buyers who have entered into a purchase agreement. Thus, sellers might not allow prospective buyers to preview the premises until they have entered into a purchase agreement and been financially qualified as capable buyers.

Entry on surrender, abandonment or forfeiture

A landlord or their manager may enter a unit when:

- the tenant's right of possession has been terminated; and
- the tenant has vacated the unit.

Caution: the tenant vacating the property does not automatically trigger a termination of the tenant's right of possession. The tenant's leasehold right of possession is terminated by:

- the expiration of a lease (or rental agreement, by a proper notice to vacate);
- a properly-established *surrender* [See Chapter 30];
- an *abandonment*, with a notice of abandonment; or
- *a forfeiture*, with a three-day notice containing a *declaration of forfeiture*. [See Chapter 24]

> **Facts:** *A landlord and tenant enter into a residential lease agreement. The landlord later lists the property for sale and intends to hold an open house on the weekend for the purpose of marketing the property to prospective buyers. The tenant refuses to permit the landlord to hold an open house on the weekend.*
>
> **Claim:** *The landlord sues to hold an open house on the weekend, claiming they have the right to show the property during a real estate agent's normal business hours, which include weekends.*
>
> **Counter claim:** *The tenant seeks to prevent the landlord from showing the property on weekends, claiming the tenant is not required to allow weekend access since the weekend is outside normal business hours.*
>
> **Holding:** *A California Court of Appeals held the landlord is allowed to hold open houses during reasonable hours on the weekend since a real estate agent's normal business hours include weekends.* [**Dromy** v. **Lukovsky** (2013) 219 CA4th 278]

Case in point

Are weekends normal business hours?

A landlord has the right to recover possession of the premises due to a forfeiture declared in a three-day notice to quit, or expiration of the rental or lease agreement. However, a landlord may only enforce their right to recover possession from a holdover tenant by the legal eviction process. **Self-help** is absolutely unacceptable.

For example, in an unlawful detainer (UD) action, a landlord obtains a UD judgment against a tenant when the tenant fails to promptly answer the UD lawsuit. Before the eviction is carried out under the court order, the court "sets aside" the judgment. The court-ordered eviction order is now invalid.

Even though the landlord knows the eviction order is invalid, the landlord privately calls on two uniformed county marshals to assist in the eviction. Without knowing the eviction order is invalid, the two marshals demand the tenant vacate the unit.

The tenant leaves the unit immediately and the landlord takes possession. Later, the tenant seeks a money judgment against the landlord claiming the conduct of the landlord was a *forcible entry* and detainer of the premises.

The landlord claims their conduct cannot be considered a *forcible entry* and detainer since the method used to evict the tenant did not lie entirely outside the law. The landlord obtained a court order (although they knew it was invalid) and did not personally evict the tenant (they used law enforcement officers instead).

However, the landlord is liable for forcible entry and detainer. They caused the tenant to be evicted by using a judgment which they knew to be invalid. The landlord's use of uniformed law officials to carry out the entry and removal of the tenant does not excuse the landlord's use of a known invalid eviction order. The landlord is still using *self-help* methods to regain possession of the premises since the eviction was not court-ordered.[16]

Entry by court order

self-help
A landlord's own method of recovering possession from a tenant outside the legal eviction process.

---

16 **Bedi v. McMullan** (1984) 160 CA3d 272

Good faith reliance on erroneous court orders

Now consider a commercial landlord who obtains only a money judgment against their tenant for unpaid rent. The landlord does not obtain an order authorizing the tenant's eviction. However, a court clerk erroneously issues a **writ of possession** authorizing the landlord's recovery of the property, via the sheriff. Consequently, the tenant is evicted by the sheriff.

The tenant now seeks to recover possession. The money judgment did not award the landlord possession of the premises or include an eviction order. The court later recalls the writ as having been erroneously issued, but refuses to order the landlord to surrender possession of the property to the tenant.

The tenant seeks to recover their money losses for the eviction. The tenant claims the landlord is liable for forcible entry and detainer since the landlord had the tenant removed under an invalid writ of possession.

The landlord claims they are not liable for forcible entry or detainer since they relied on court authorization to evict the tenant and recover possession of the premises.

Here, the landlord is not liable for the tenant's money losses. Imposing liability on landlords who, in good faith, rely on erroneous court orders would undermine the public policy favoring orderly judicial process (instead of *self help*).[17]

Tenant's right to privacy on default

Rental and lease agreements occasionally contain an unenforceable provision stating the landlord has the right to enter and retake possession of the premises upon a tenant's breach of the rental or lease agreement. However, the tenant's default does not alone constitute a forfeiture or convey the leasehold and its possessory rights to the landlord.

To terminate the tenant's right of possession after a breach, the landlord serves the tenant with a three-day notice to cure the breach, pay rent or quit. The notice includes a declaration of lease forfeiture if the landlord is to terminate the tenant's right of possession on expiration of the notice.

If the landlord attempts self-help and takes possession without the tenant's consent, the landlord is committing a forcible entry. The landlord thus becomes liable for the tenant's money losses.[18]

A tenant's right of possession arises out of their ownership of a leasehold estate in the property.[19]

The tenant retains the right of possession unless and until it is terminated by proper notice or the expiration of a lease agreement. The only other enforceable transfer of the right of possession is through voluntary conveyance.

17 **Glass** v. **Najafi** (2000) 78 CA4th 45
18 **Lamey** v. **Masciotra** (1969) 273 CA2d 709
19 CC §1953(a)(l)

To recover the property after the tenant's breach, the landlord either serves the tenant with the required notice or the tenant voluntarily conveys the right of possession back to the landlord. Again, the landlord's self-help is not an enforceable transfer of the tenant's right of possession.

In exchange for voluntarily giving up possession, the tenant usually seeks a cancellation of the lease agreement (or some other consideration).

Consider an owner who goes on an extended overseas vacation. The owner rents out their home to a tenant for the duration of their trip. The rental agreement provides for the tenant to vacate on the owner's return.

The owner returns from their trip, but the tenant refuses to relinquish possession of the house. While the tenant is at work, the owner enters the house, removes the tenant's belongings and retakes possession of the property based on a provision in the rental agreement stating they have the right of re-entry.

Can the owner use self-help to dispossess the tenant?

No! So long as the tenant's right of occupancy remains unterminated by notice or agreement, the tenant has the right to exclude others, including the fee owner, from possession. This right is created by all rental or lease agreements since they grant an exclusive right of possession.

An owner, even though entitled to possession by agreement, cannot re-enter the premises without first obtaining a court order.

Forcible entry by a landlord or property manager is an unlawful activity consisting of:

- peaceable entry by open doors, windows or other parts of the premises without permission, prior notice or justification;

- entry by any kind of violence or threat of terror; or

- peaceable entry after which threats, force or menacing conduct is used to dispossess the tenant.[20]

Actions by a landlord, property manager or resident manager construed as an illegal forcible entry include:

- entry resulting from any physical acts of force or violence;

- entry through a window and removal of the tenant's belongings in the occupant's absence;[21]

- entry under the false pretense of making an inspection and then taking possession from the tenant;[22]

- entry by unlocking the door of the unit in the tenant's absence;[23]

No self-help to dispossess a tenant

Forcible entry by management

forcible entry
The unlawful entry of any individual into a rented property without permission, prior notice or justification.

---

20 Calif. Code of Civil Procedure §1159
21 **Bank of California** v. **Taaffe** (1888) 76 C 626
22 **White** v. **Pfieffer** (1913) 165 C 740
23 **Winchester** v. **Becker** (1906) 4 CA 382

- entry accomplished by a locksmith who opens the door during the tenant's absence;[24] and

- entry by breaking locks.[25]

Forcible entry and self-help

Consider an occupant whose rent is paid by their employer under a lease agreement entered into solely by the employer and the landlord. It names the employer as the tenant on the lease.

Later, the occupant's employment is terminated and the employer informs the occupant and the landlord that the employer will no longer pay the rent. Upon a request from the employer, the landlord enters without the occupant's permission, changes the locks and forces the occupant to vacate the premises. No notice is served on the occupant and no UD action is filed.

Is the landlord guilty of forcible entry even though the occupant was no longer employed by the tenant, and was not named as the tenant on the lease?

Yes! While the occupant's employment was terminated and the employer informed the landlord they would no longer pay rent, the occupant was in possession under a lease agreement which had not been terminated. The landlord's attempt to oust the occupant by entering against the occupant's will and changing the locks on the employer's breach of the lease is an example of both forcible entry and self-help.[26]

Tenant's possessions as security

Some lease agreements contain an unenforceable clause purporting to give the landlord the right to take or hold the tenant's personal property as security upon the tenant's default on the lease.

For example, a tenant enters into a lease agreement and occupies the unit. The agreement authorizes the landlord to re-enter the unit on the tenant's default in the payment of rent and take the tenant's personal possessions as security until the rent is paid.

The tenant fails to pay rent and the payment becomes delinquent. To enforce the security provision in the lease, the landlord uses their key to enter the unit in the tenant's absence and remove the tenant's possessions. The landlord then refuses to allow the tenant to re-enter the unit until the rent is paid.

Here, the landlord may not enter and interfere with the tenant's continued access to the premises based on the tenant's default on the lease agreement. The landlord needs to first obtain a court order. It does not matter how peaceably the landlord accomplished the entry, since without a court order they are guilty of forcible entry and detainer.[27]

---

24 **Karp** v. **Margolis** (1958) 159 CA2d 69
25 **Pickens** v. **Johnson** (1951) 107 CA2d 778
26 **Spinks** v. **Equity Residential Briarwood Apartments** (2009) 171 CA4th 1004; CCP §§1159, 1160
27 **Jordan** v. **Talbot** (1961) 55 C2d 597

Forcible entry into premises leased to a tenant occurs whenever anyone enters the tenant's premises without the tenant's present consent.

Consider a hotel operator who as a tenant encumbers their leasehold interest in a hotel with a trust deed to provide security for a mortgage. The trust deed states the lender may appoint a trustee to take possession of the real estate and operate and manage the hotel when the hotel operator defaults on repayment of the mortgage.

The operator defaults on the mortgage. The lender appoints a trustee in compliance with the trust deed provisions. The trustee goes to the hotel to remove the hotel operator from the premises as agreed by the provision in the trust deed.

The trustee, although not entering the premises by force, breaks and replaces locks on the storage cabinets. The trustee raids cash registers and threatens to harm the hotel operator if they refuse to relinquish possession of the hotel.

Is the trustee guilty of forcible entry onto the property even though the trustee was appointed under a trust deed provision agreed to by the operator and used non-violent means to enter the premises?

Yes! The trustee holds the same status as the secured lender. They have no more right of possession than the lender. This is in spite of prior agreements granting authority to the trustee to take possession on default.

The trustee's right of possession, like that of a landlord, may only be lawfully obtained by a UD action against the interest in the property encumbered by the trust deed. After obtaining ownership of the tenant's rights by holding a trustee's sale of the tenant's rights under the leasehold interest securing the mortgage, the trustee or the lender (or other highest bidder) is then required to serve the appropriate notice to vacate. Only upon the expiration of the notice to vacate would they be able to file a UD action and obtain possession.[28]

Forcible entry by others

Even a tenant can be guilty of a forcible entry.

Consider a prospective tenant who enters into a rental agreement without inspecting the premises.

When they inspect just before taking possession, they discover the physical condition of the premises is unacceptable and refuse to take possession. As a result, the landlord does not give the tenant a key or any other means of access to the premises.

The landlord, realizing they will not be able to rent the property until the premises is restored, renovates the property. Upon the landlord's completion of the renovations, the would-be tenant climbs through an open window in the landlord's absence and takes possession of the premises. They claim the rental agreement the landlord and tenant entered into grants them the right of possession of the unit.

Forcible entry by the tenant

---

28 Calidino Hotel Co. of San Bernardino v. Bank of America Nat. Trust & Savings Ass'n (1939) 31 CA2d 295;

Here, the tenant did not have authority from the landlord to occupy the premises. The rental agreement was canceled by the tenant's conduct when they refused to accept delivery of possession and was not given access to the premises. The tenant's occupancy was gained only by their unauthorized and peaceful entry, legally called **forcible entry**.[29]

Landlord as co-tenant with roommates

Consider the owner of a single family residence who rents rooms to individuals, called roommates. Soon, the owner spends less and less time residing on the property. However, the owner continues to maintain their mailing address at the residence.

After a week-long absence, the owner returns and discovers the locks on all the doors have been changed. They break a window and enter the property. The roommates claim the owner is guilty of forcible entry since they broke into the property.

Did the owner's roommates have the exclusive right of possession barring the owner from entering the property without prior notice?

No! The owner was not attempting to regain lost possession. Rather, they were a co-occupant in actual possession of the premises with others at the time of their entry.

The owner and their roommates had joint possession. No one roommate had been given exclusive possession against any other roommate. As a joint possessor with the right to occupy the premises concurrently with others, the owner is not liable for forcible entry.[30]

Losses due to wrongful dispossession

A tenant wrongfully removed from their rented premises by a landlord or property manager is entitled to a return of their possession of the premises for the duration of the lease. This is called **restitution**.[31]

In addition to recovery of possession, a tenant may recover all money losses caused by the landlord's wrongful entry. The tenant may only collect losses incurred while they were dispossessed of the property, but retained a legal right of possession. Thus, they are not entitled to any losses incurred after the expiration or termination of their tenancy under a rental or lease agreement.[32]

restitution
The return of possession of the rented premises to a wrongfully removed tenant.

For example, a commercial tenant is served a 30-day notice to vacate to terminate their month-to-month tenancy.

Then, the tenant defaults on the rental agreement. Prior to the expiration of the notice to vacate and due to the default, the landlord bars the tenant from entering the premises. The tenant is unable to continue operating their business from the property. The tenant does not regain possession of the premises before their right of possession is terminated by expiration of the notice to vacate.

---

29 **McNeil** v. **Higgins** (1948) 86 CA2d 723
30 **Bittman** v. **Courington** (1948) 86 CA2d 213
31 CCP §§1174(a)
32 CCP §1174(b); **Orly** v. **Russell** (1921) 53 CA 660

Is the tenant entitled to recover business income losses due to the landlord's unlawful detainer of the property?

Yes! A tenant whose possession is interfered with can recover their money losses due to:

- lost profits, limited to the net operating income (NOI) they failed to earn during the balance of the unexpired term;[33]

- rental value of the lost use of the premises;[34]

- emotional distress caused by the landlord or property manager's conduct towards the tenant;[35] and

- loss of **business goodwill** (earning power of the business).[36]

business goodwill The earning power of a business.	

If the tenant has built up goodwill with the customers of their business, the remaining days of their period of tenancy are used to advise customers of their expired lease and new location. The landlord who forcibly enters the leased premises during the remaining period of the tenancy is liable for the tenant's money losses due to loss of *business goodwill.*[37]

Punitive damages for malicious acts

A landlord who willfully or maliciously takes possession from the tenant is liable to pay up to three times the tenant's actual money losses to the tenant. These treble damages are inflicted as a judicial punishment to deter bad acts, and are known as **punitive damages**.

For example, a landlord seeking to collect a debt owed by their tenant bars the tenant's employees from the leased premises by changing the locks and refusing the tenant access to records and personal property.

punitive damages
Monies awarded in excess of actual money losses in order to deter unlawful actions.

Here, the landlord is acting with malice and the tenant may recover treble the amount of their actual money losses.[38]

A landlord or property manager using actual force or violence to enter a leased unit is guilty of a misdemeanor crime.[39]

---

33 Orly, *supra*
34 Stillwell Hotel Co., *supra*
35 **Newby** v. **Alto Riviera Apartments** (1976) 60 CA3d 288
36 **Schuler** v. **Bordelon** (1947) 78 CA2d 581
37 Schuler, *supra*
38 **Civic Western Corporation** v. **Zila Industries, Inc.** (1977) 66 CA3d 1
39 Calif. Penal Code §418

Chapter 4 Suumary

A landlord may enter a rented premises:

- in an emergency;
- to make repairs or improvements;
- to complete a pre-expiration inspection;
- to show the unit to prospective buyers, tenants, lenders, repairmen or contractors;
- when the tenant has vacated the premises and their right to occupy has been terminated by surrender or abandonment; or
- under a court order allowing entry.

In most circumstances, prior notice of the entry is to be given to the tenant.

A landlord (or any other person) who enters the property without permission is guilty of unlawful forcible entry.

Chapter 4 Key Terms

Quiz 1 Covering Chapters 1-4 is located on page 633.

Chapter

5

Tenant leasehold improvements

After reading this chapter, you will be able to:
- identify the different types of tenant improvements;
- understand the landlord's rights regarding tenant improvements on the termination of a lease; and
- determine the landlord or tenant's obligation to complete or pay for the construction of tenant improvements.

Learning Objectives

further-improvements provision	**permissive improvement**
mandatory improvement	**real estate fixture**
mechanic's lien	**reversion**
notice of nonresponsibility	**tenant improvements**
	trade fixtures

Key Terms

A retail business owner enters into a commercial lease agreement to occupy commercial space as a tenant. The leased premises do not contain **tenant improvements** since the building is nothing more than a shell.

The tenant agrees to make all the *tenant improvements* needed to occupy the premises and operate a retail business (i.e., interior walls, flooring, ceilings, air conditioning, electrical outlets and lighting, plumbing, sprinklers, telephone and electronic wiring, etc.).

The lease agreement provides for the property to be delivered to the landlord on expiration of the lease "in the condition the tenant received it," less normal wear and tear. No other lease provision addresses whether tenant improvements will remain with the property or the property is to be restored to its original condition when the lease expires.

Ownership rights when a tenant vacates

tenant improvements
Improvements made to a rented property to meet the needs of the occupying tenant. [See **RPI** Form 552 §11]

On expiration of the lease, the tenant strips the premises of all of the tenant improvements and vacates. The building is returned to the landlord in the condition it was found by the tenant: an empty shell, less wear and tear. In order to relet the space, the landlord replaces nearly all the tenant improvements that were removed.

Is the tenant liable for the landlord's costs to replace the tenant improvements removed by the tenant on vacating?

Yes! Improvements made by a tenant that are permanently affixed to real estate become part of the real estate to which they are attached. Improvements remain with the property on expiration of the tenancy, unless the lease agreement explicitly requires the tenant improvements to be removed and the property to be restored to its original condition.[1]

Landlord's right to improvements

However, the landlord's right to improvements added to the property or paid for by the tenant depends upon whether:

- the tenant improvements are permanent (built-in) or temporary (free-standing); and
- the lease agreement requires the tenant to remove improvements and restore the premises.

All improvements attached to the building become part of the real estate, except for *trade fixtures* (discussed later in this chapter).[2]

Examples of improvements that become part of the real estate include:

- built-ins (i.e., central air conditioning and heating, cabinets and stairwells);
- fixtures (i.e., electrical and plumbing);
- walls, doors and dropped ceilings; and
- attached flooring (i.e., carpeting, tile or linoleum).

Leasehold improvement provisions

Commercial lease agreements typically contain a **further-improvements provision** allowing the landlord to either:

- retain tenant improvements and alterations made by the tenant; or
- require restoration of the property to its original condition on expiration of the lease. [See **RPI** Form 552 through 552-5]

Further-improvement provisions usually include clauses stating:

- who will make the improvements (landlord or tenant);
- who will pay for the improvements (landlord or tenant);
- the landlord's consent is required before the tenant makes improvements;

further-improvements provision
A commercial lease provision which allows a landlord to retain tenant improvements or require the restoration of the property to its original condition upon expiration of the lease. [See **RPI** Form 552 §11.3]

---

1 Calif. Civil Code §1013
2 CC §660

- any *mechanic's liens* due to improvements contracted by the tenant will be removed;
- the condition of the premises on expiration of the lease; and
- whether the improvements are to remain or be removed on expiration of the lease. [See **RPI** Form 552 §11]

Failure to make improvements

A landlord under a lease agreement who agrees to make improvements to the rented premises needs to complete the improvements in a timely manner. If the landlord fails to make timely improvements, the tenant may cancel the lease agreement. [See **RPI** Form 552 §3.3]

For example, a landlord agrees to make all the improvements necessary to convert a ranch into a dairy farm for a tenant who operates a dairy.

The landlord is obligated to construct a barn and several sheds that are essential to the operation of the tenant's dairy business.

The tenant moves into the property before the improvements begin. Several months pass and the landlord does not begin construction on the promised improvements. The tenant vacates the property since it is impossible to conduct a dairy business without the dairy barn.

Here, the landlord's failure to make the promised improvements is a breach of the lease agreement.

Since the landlord has breached an essential provision of the lease, the tenant may vacate the property and cancel the lease agreement without obligation to pay further rent.[3]

Improvements promised by the tenant

Conversely, lease agreement provisions can obligate a tenant to construct or install improvements on the rented property, whether improved or unimproved. The time period for commencement and completion needs to be provided for in the lease agreement. If not agreed to, a reasonable period of time is allowed.[4]

However, a tenant may fail to make or complete mandated improvements prior to expiration of the lease. If the improvements are to remain with the property, the tenant is liable to the landlord for the cost the landlord incurs to complete the agreed-to improvements.

For example, a tenant agrees to construct additional buildings on a leased property in lieu of paying rent for one year. When the lease expires, the improvements will remain with the property since the lease agreement does not call for restoration of the premises.

---

3   **Souza** v. **Joseph** (1913) 22 CA 179
4   CC §1657

Case in point

The controlling lease agreement

A landlord agrees to construct the shell of a building for a tenant. The tenant agrees to install all other improvements and fixtures required to occupy and use the property.

Before the building is completed by the landlord, the building code is changed to require the installation of a sprinkler system. The tenant demands the landlord pay the cost of installing the sprinkler system since the tenant cannot occupy the premises without the sprinkler system.

The landlord refuses to pay the additional cost to install the sprinkler system, claiming the lease agreement calls for them to build the structure, not to make it ready for occupancy.

Is the tenant responsible for the costs to install the sprinkler system?

*Yes! The tenant is responsible for making the alterations or improvements required to bring the building into compliance with use ordinances. The tenant had agreed in the lease agreement to make all improvements within the structure needed to take occupancy. [**Wong** v. **diGrazia** (1963) 60 C2d 525]*

---

mandatory improvement
An improvement required to be made under the terms of the lease or rental agreement.

The tenant fails to construct the buildings during the term of the lease. The tenant claims the obligation to build was not a **mandatory improvement**, but *permissive*. According to the tenant, the obligation to build only existed if it was necessary for the operation of the tenant's business.

Here, the improvements were agreed to in exchange for rent. Accordingly, the tenant was required to make the improvements since the landlord bargained for them in the lease agreement. Thus, the landlord is entitled to recover an amount equal to the cost of the improvements the tenant failed to construct.[5]

Additionally, if the tenant agrees to but does not complete the construction of improvements that are to remain with the property on expiration of the lease, the landlord may complete those improvements. The tenant is then financially responsible for the landlord's expenditures to construct the improvements.[6]

Even after the expiration of the lease, a landlord is entitled to recover lost rent and expenses resulting from the tenant's failure to construct the improvements as promised.

Tenant's failure to construct improvements

Consider a landlord who enters into a lease agreement calling for the landlord to construct a building on the leased property. After the foundation is laid, the landlord and tenant orally modify the construction provisions. The tenant agrees to finish construction of the building in exchange for the landlord forgoing their construction profit.

The tenant then breaches the oral modification of the written lease agreement by failing to complete the construction. The breach places the landlord in financial jeopardy as they now needs to complete the building. The landlord terminates the tenant's right to occupancy, evicts the tenant and completes the construction promised by the tenant.

---

5 **Simen** v. **Sam Aftergut Co.** (1915) 26 CA 361
6 **Sprague** v. **Fauver** (1945) 71 CA2d 333

Here, the tenant is not only responsible for the landlord's costs of construction, they are also liable for future rents under the lease agreement. In addition, they are liable for any expenses the landlord incurs to relet the property since the landlord's conduct did not cancel the lease agreement.[7] [See Case in point, "The controlling lease agreement"]

Lease provisions often allow a tenant to make improvements to the leased premises. However, *further-improvement provisions* typically call for the landlord to approve the planned improvements before construction is commenced.

For example, a tenant wishes to add additional space to the premises they leased for use in the operation of their business. The tenant begins construction without obtaining the landlord's prior approval as required by the lease agreement. Further, the addition is located outside the leased premises, an encroachment on other land owned by the landlord.

In the past, the landlord had approved tenant improvements. This time, however, the landlord refuses to give consent and complains about the construction and the encroachment.

The landlord continues to accept rent while the landlord and tenant negotiate the approval of the additional improvements and the modification of the lease agreement to include use of the area subject to the encroachment.

After a few years of negotiations without resolution, the landlord declares a forfeiture of the lease. The forfeiture is based on both the breach of the provision requiring the landlord's prior consent to construction and the encroachment of the unapproved improvements.

The tenant then claims the landlord waived their right to declare a forfeiture of the lease since the landlord continued to accept the rent from the tenant after the breach of the tenant-improvement provision and encroachment.

However, as long as negotiations to resolve the breach continue, a landlord may accept rent from the tenant without waiving their right to consent to additional improvements.[8]

Likewise, consider a tenant with an option to buy the property they rent. The tenant makes improvements with the expectation of ultimately becoming the owner of the property by exercising the option to buy.

Here, the tenant is not entitled to reimbursement for the cost of improvements if the fail to exercise their purchase option. Holding an option to buy is not fee ownership and the improvement becomes part of the real estate. Thus, the improvements will not belong to the tenant unless the tenant exercises their option to buy and becomes the owner of the property.[9]

Landlord's consent to improvements

---

7 **Sanders Construction Company, Inc.** v. **San Joaquin First Federal Savings and Loan Association** (1982) 136 CA3d 387

8 **Thriftimart, Inc.** v. **Me & Tex** (1981) 123 CA3d 751

9 **Whipple** v. **Haberle** (1963) 223 CA2d 477

Permissive improvements by the tenant

Some lease agreement provisions allow a tenant to make necessary improvements without the landlord's further consent. These improvements are not specifically mandated, or required to be completed in exchange for a reduction in rent. Recall that this nonmandatory type of improvement is called a **permissive improvement**.

> **permissive improvement**
> A nonmandatory improvement authorized to be completed by the tenant without further landlord consent.

For example, a landlord and tenant sign a long-term lease agreement. Its further-improvements provision authorizes the tenant to demolish an existing building located on the property and construct a new one in its place without first obtaining the landlord's consent. The rent is based solely on the current value of the premises.

The further-improvements provision does not state a specific time period for demolition or construction.

The tenant makes no effort to tear down the old building or erect a new one. Ultimately, the landlord claims the tenant has breached the lease agreement for failing to demolish the existing building and construct a new one.

Here, the tenant has not breached the lease agreement. The agreement contained no promise by the tenant to build and the rental amount was not based on the construction. The tenant was authorized to build without need for the landlord's approval, but was not obligated to do so. Thus, the improvements on the tenant's part were permissive, not mandatory.[10]

Mandatory improvements

A further-improvements provision that requires a tenant to construct improvements at a rent rate reflecting the value of the land, has different consequences.

If a date is not specified for completion of the improvements, the tenant needs to complete construction within a reasonable period of time since construction of improvements is mandated to occur.

For example, a landlord leases unimproved land to a developer who is obligated to build improvements, contingent on obtaining a construction mortgage. A time period is not set for commencement or completion of the construction. However, a cancellation provision gives the tenant/developer the right to cancel the lease agreement within one year if financing is not found to fund the construction. No provision authorizes the landlord to terminate the lease if the required construction is not completed.

Due to the onset of a recession, the tenant is unable to arrange financing within the one-year period. However, they do not exercise their right to cancel the lease agreement and avoid payment of future rents. Instead, the tenant continues their good faith effort to locate and qualify for construction financing. Ultimately, financing is not located and construction is not commenced.

---

10 **Kusmark** v. **Montgomery Ward and Co.** (1967) 249 CA2d 585

A few years later, as the economy is showing signs of recovery, the landlord terminates the lease. The landlord claims the lease agreement has been breached since the promised construction was not completed.

The tenant claims the landlord cannot terminate the lease as long as the tenant continues their good faith effort to locate financing and remains solvent to qualify for the financing.

Here, the tenant has breached the lease agreement. They failed to construct the intended improvements within a reasonable period of time. The original purpose of the lease was to have buildings erected without specifying a completion date. Following the expiration of the right to cancel, the landlord gave the tenant a reasonable amount of time in which to commence construction before terminating the lease.

When the original purpose for the lease was the construction of a building by the tenant, a landlord cannot be forced to forgo the improvements bargained for.[11]

All tenant improvements are to remain with the leased property on termination of a lease unless the lease agreement permits or mandates their removal by the tenant as a restoration of the premises.

Most lease agreements merely provide for the property to be returned in good condition, minus ordinary wear and tear for the years of the tenant's occupancy. Thus, the tenant is not required to restore the property to its actual condition when they took possession since tenant improvements are part of the real estate.

A provision calling for the tenant's ordinary care of the premises does not also require the tenant to remove their improvements or renovate the premises to eliminate deterioration, obsolescence or normal wear and tear caused by the tenant's permitted use of the property.[12]

Now consider a landlord and tenant who enter into a lease of commercial property. The lease agreement contains a provision requiring the tenant, at the landlord's demand, to restore the premises to the original condition received by the tenant, less normal wear and tear.

The tenant makes all the tenant improvements necessary to operate their business, such as installation of a concrete vault, the removal of partitions and a stairway, and the closing of two entrances into the premises.

On expiration of the lease, the tenant vacates the premises. The landlord exercises their right to require removal of tenant improvements by making a demand on the tenant to restore the premises. The tenant rejects the landlord's demand.

The landlord incurs costs to restore the premises for reletting to a new tenant.

Surrender of improvements

---

11 **City of Stockton** v. **Stockton Plaza Corporation** (1968) 261 CA2d 639

12 **Kanner** v. **Globe Bottling Co.** (1969) 273 CA2d 559

The landlord claims the tenant is liable for the landlord's costs incurred to restore the premises since the tenant's improvements radically altered the premises and made it unrentable to others.

The tenant claims they are not liable for the landlord's costs to restore the premises to its original condition since the alterations became part of the real estate and were beneficial to the property.

Is the tenant liable for the landlord's costs to restore the premises to a rentable condition?

Yes! Here, the landlord exercised their option to call for removal of the improvements under the lease agreement provisions. The lease provisions called for restoration of the premises to its original condition on a demand from the landlord.

On the tenant's failure to restore the premises, the landlord was forced to incur restoration costs to relet the premises. The tenant is liable for the landlord's expenditures to restore and relet the premises to a new tenant.[13]

If a lease does not require the tenant to restore the property to the condition it was in when received, the tenant may only remove their personal improvements, called *trade fixtures*.

Real estate fixtures vs. trade fixtures

Two types of fixtures exist distinguishing improvements installed in a building:

- **real estate fixtures**; and
- **trade fixtures**.

A *real estate fixture* is personal property that is attached to the real estate. It becomes part of the real estate it is attached to and is conveyed with the property.[14]

real estate fixture
Personal property attached to the real estate as an improvement, which becomes part of the conveyable real estate.

For example, if a tenant rents an office and builds bookshelves into the wall rather than merely anchoring them to the wall, the bookshelves become part of the improvements located on the real estate.

trade fixture
Fixtures used to render services or make products for the trade or business of a tenant.

When the lease expires, real estate fixtures become the landlord's property. The landlord takes possession of the real estate fixtures as part of the real estate forfeited or surrendered to the landlord, unless the lease agreement provides for restoration or permits removal by the tenant. The conveyance of real estate fixtures from tenant to landlord on expiration of the lease is called **reversion**.[15]

reversion
The conveyance of real estate fixtures from a tenant to landlord on expiration of a lease.

Conversely, *trade fixtures* do not revert to the landlord on expiration of the lease. A trade fixture is an improvement that is attached to the real estate by the tenant and is unique to the operation of the tenant's business, not the use of the building.

---

13 **Masonic Temple Ass'n. of Sacramento** v. **Stockholders Auxiliary Corporation** (1933) 130 CA 234
14 CC §§660; 1013
15 **City of Beverly Hills** v. **Albright** (1960) 184 CA2d 562

Consider a tenant who leases property to operate a beauty salon. The tenant moves in work-related furnishings (i.e., mirrors, salon chairs, wash stations and dryers), necessary to run the business. The items are attached to the floor, walls, plumbing and electrical leads.

On expiration of the lease, the tenant removes the fixtures that were used to render the services offered by the business. The landlord claims the fixtures are improvements to the property and cannot be removed since they became part of the real estate when installed.

However, furnishings unique to the operation of a business are considered trade fixtures even though the furnishings are attached and built into the structure. Trade fixtures are removable by the tenant.

A tenant may, at the end of or anytime during the lease term, remove any fixture used for trade purposes if the removal can be done without damaging the premises.[16]

Fixtures that have become an integral part of the building's structure due to the way they are attached or the general purpose they serve cannot be removed. Examples of fixtures which cannot be removed include toilets, air conditioners, vent conduits, sprinkler systems and lowered ceilings.[17]

What compensation may be due to a tenant who has improved the property and is wrongfully evicted prior to expiration of a lease?

A tenant who is wrongfully evicted is entitled to the rental value of their improvements for the remainder of their unexpired lease term. Without reimbursement, the landlord receives a windfall profit for their use of the tenant's improvements until they revert to the landlord on expiration of the original lease.

The tenant is not, however, entitled to reimbursement for the market value or cost of the improvements.

Thus, a wrongfully evicted tenant is limited to collecting the reasonable value for the landlord's use of the improvements during the remainder of the term on the original lease.[18]

Reimbursement for tenant improvements on wrongful eviction

Lease agreements often contain a default provision prohibiting the tenant from removing the trade fixtures when the agreement is breached. The tenant (and their unsecured creditors) no longer has a right to the trade fixtures under a default provision.

Consider a tenant who signs a commercial lease agreement to use the premises to operate a frozen packaging plant. The lease agreement states all fixtures, trade or leasehold, belong to the landlord if the lease is terminated due to a breach by the tenant.

Trade fixtures as security

16 **Beebe** v. **Richards** (1953) 115 CA2d 589
17 CC §1019
18 **Asell** v. **Rodrigues** (1973) 32 CA3d 817

The tenant later encumbers the existing trade fixtures by borrowing money against them. The tenant then defaults on their lease payments. While in default on the lease, the tenant surrenders the property to the landlord, including all trade fixtures.

Does the lender on the mortgage secured by the trade fixtures have a right to repossess them?

No! The tenant lost their ownership right to remove the trade fixtures under the terms of the lease agreement that was entered into before they encumbered the trade fixtures. Any right to the fixtures held by the secured lender is similarly lost since the lender is junior in time and thus subordinate to the landlord's interest in the fixtures under the lease agreement.

However, if the trade fixtures installed by the tenant are owned by a third party, or if a third party had a lien on them at the time of their installation, the landlord has no more right to them than the tenant.[19]

Notice of nonresponsibility

Tenants occasionally contract for improvements to be constructed on the premises they have leased. Any **mechanic's lien** by a contractor for nonpayment initially attaches to the tenant's leasehold interest in the property.[20]

However, the mechanic's lien for unpaid labor and materials may also attach to the *fee simple interest* held by the landlord if the landlord or the landlord's property manager:

- acquires knowledge the construction is taking place; and
- fails to post and record a **Notice of Nonresponsibility**. [See Form 597 accompanying this chapter]

A *Notice of Nonresponsibility* is a written notice which needs to be:

- posted in a conspicuous place on the premises within ten days after the landlord or their property manager first has knowledge of the construction; and
- recorded with the county recorder's office within the same ten-day period.[21]

However, the landlord who becomes aware of the construction and fails to post and record the Notice of Nonresponsibility is not personally liable to the contractor. Rather, the contractor can only lien the landlord's interest in the real estate and foreclose on their mechanic's lien to collect for unpaid labor and materials delivered to improve the property under contract with the tenant.[22]

mechanic's lien
A lien entitling a contractor or subcontractor to foreclose on a job site property to recover the amount due and unpaid for labor and materials they provided.

notice of nonresponsibility
A notice used by a landlord to declare that they are not responsible for any claim arising out of the improvement being constructed on their property. [See **RPI** Form 597]

---

19 **Goldie** v. **Bauchet Properties** (1975) 15 C3d 307
20 CC §8442(a)
21 CC §8444
22 **Peterson** v. **Freiermuth** (1911) 17 CA 609

RECORDING REQUESTED BY

AND WHEN RECORDED MAIL TO

Name

Street
Address

City &
State

SPACE ABOVE THIS LINE FOR RECORDER'S USE

NOTICE OF NONRESPONSIBILITY
From Landlord (California Civil Code §3094)

NOTE: This form is used by a property manager or income property owner when a tenant commences construction of improvements on premises leased from the owner, to declare the property owner is not responsible for any claim arising out of the tenant improvements being constructed on the property.

DATE: _____, 20_____, at _____, California.

NOTICE IS HEREBY GIVEN:

1. _____ is the vested and legal owner of real property located in the County of _____, State of California, identified as

   1.1 Common address _____

   1.2 Legal description

2. _____ is:

   2.1 ☐ The Buyer of the property under a purchase agreement, option or land sales contract, or

   2.2 ☐ The Tenant under a lease of the property.

3. Within 10 days before the posting and recording of this notice, the undersigned Owner or Agent of Owner obtained knowledge that a work of improvement has commenced on the site of the property involving ☐ construction, ☐ alteration, or ☐ repair.

4. Owner will not be responsible for any claim arising out of this work of improvement.

5. I declare under penalty of perjury under the laws of the State of California that the foregoing is true and correct.

Date: _____, 20_____   Name: _____

Signature: _____

☐ Owner, or ☐ Agent of Owner

A notary public or other officer completing this certificate verifies only the identity of the individual who signed the document to which this certificate is attached, and not the truthfulness, accuracy, or validity of that document.

STATE OF CALIFORNIA
COUNTY OF _____

On _____ before me, _____

_____ *(Name and title of officer)*

personally appeared _____

who proved to me on the basis of satisfactory evidence to be the person(s) whose name(s) is/are subscribed to the within instrument and acknowledged to me that he/she/they executed the same in his/her/their authorized capacity(ies), and that by his/her/their signature(s) on the instrument the person(s), or the entity upon behalf of which the person(s) acted, executed the instrument.

I certify under PENALTY OF PERJURY under the laws of the State of California that the foregoing paragraph is true and correct.

WITNESS my hand and official seal.

Signature: _____

(This area for official notarial seal)   *(Signature of notary public)*

FORM 597   03-15   ©2016 RPI — Realty Publications, Inc., P.O. BOX 5707, RIVERSIDE, CA 92517

Further, if the lease requires the tenant to make *mandatory improvements*, a mechanic's lien attaches to the landlord's interest even when the landlord has posted and recorded a Notice of Nonresponsibility.

For example, a lease states the tenant is to make certain improvements as a condition of renting the property. Since the improvements are mandatory improvements rather than permissive improvements, the tenant is deemed to be the landlord's agent. The tenant is contracting for the construction of the mandated improvements on behalf of the landlord.

Nonresponsibility on mandatory improvements

Figure 1

Form 436-1

UCC-1 Financing Statement

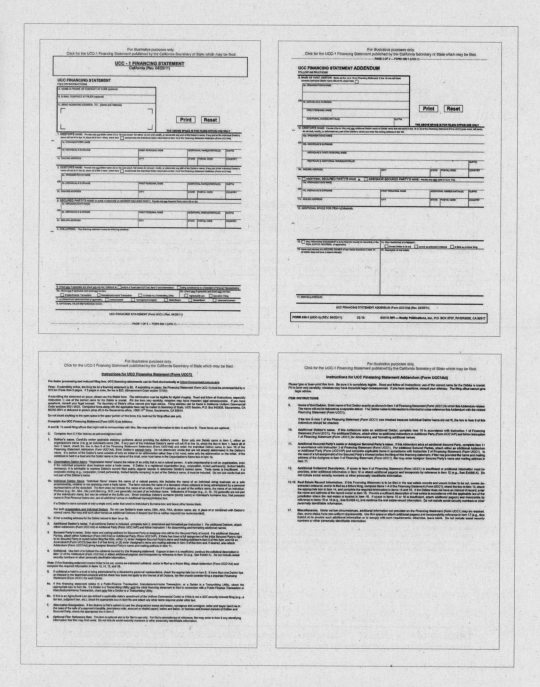

Thus, the mechanic's lien incurred by the tenant will attach to both the tenant's and the landlord's interest in the property, despite any posted and recorded Notice of Nonresponsibility.[23]

Had the lease merely authorized the tenant to make nonmandatory (permissive) improvements, the tenant will not be acting as an agent for the landlord. In that case, the landlord's interest in the property is not subjected to a mechanic's lien if the Notice of Nonresponsibility is timely posted and recorded on discovery of the tenant improvements.[24]

---

23 **Los Banos Gravel Company** v. **Freeman** (1976) 58 CA3d 785
24 **Baker** v. **Hubbard** (1980) 101 CA3d 226

Additionally, a mechanic's lien cannot be recorded against the landlord if the improvements are removed by the contractor recording the lien.

For example, a tenant contracts to have air conditioning installed in the building the tenant rents. The contractor sells the equipment to the tenant under a conditional sales contract. The contractor retains title to the equipment as security until the sales contract debt is paid.

The landlord's consent to the improvements is not obtained by the tenant, but the landlord has knowledge the work has commenced. The landlord does not post a *Notice of Nonresponsibility*.

Later, after the air conditioning units are installed, the tenant vacates the property.

The contractor is not paid and files a mechanic's lien against the landlord's fee interest in the property. Further, the contractor repossesses the air conditioning units and resells them at a loss. The contractor then seeks to recover their losses under the mechanic's lien.

However, by electing to repossess the units, the contractor waived their right to pursue the mechanic's lien to foreclosure.

Whether the air conditioning units are considered a removable fixture due to the financing, or a property improvement permitting the recording of a mechanic's lien, is no longer an issue after their removal. The contractor removed the units and chose to treat the units as personal property. Thus, the contractor lost their lien rights for nonpayment.[25]

Consider the tenant who leases a property containing tanks for holding gasoline. The tenant negotiates a reduced rental payment in exchange for installing fuel pumps free of any liens.

The tenant purchases the pumps on credit and the pumps are installed. The supplier of the pumps does not receive a **Uniform Commercial Code (UCC-1)** financing statement from the tenant. Thus, the supplier does not file a UCC-1 with the Secretary of State, a requisite to perfecting the supplier's lien on the pumps. [See Figure 1, Form 436-1]

Later, the pump supplier claims title to the pumps due to the unpaid installation debt and seeks to repossess them.

However, the landlord owns the pumps as fixtures which became part of the real estate. The landlord gave consideration in the form of reduced rent to acquire the pumps. More importantly, the pump supplier failed to perfect its lien on installation of the pumps.[26]

Removal of fixtures by contractor

Failure to perfect a lien

---

25 **Cornell** v. **Sennes** (1971) 18 CA3d 126

26 **Southland Corp.** v. **Emerald Oil Company** (9th Cir. 1986) 789 F2d 1441

Chapter 5 Summary

Tenant improvements are improvements made to a rented property to meet the needs of the occupying tenant. The landlord's right to tenant improvements depends upon whether the tenant improvements are a real estate fixture or a trade fixture, and whether the further-improvements provision in the lease agreement requires the tenant to remove improvements and restore the premises.

A tenant's or landlord's liability for failing to construct or pay for tenant improvements depends on whether the tenant improvements are mandatory or permissive.

Chapter 5 Key Terms

Quiz 2 Covering Chapters 5-8 is located on page 634.

Chapter
6

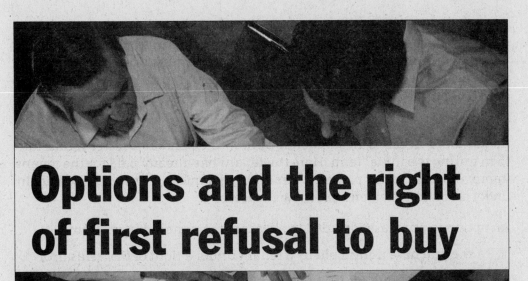

Options and the right of first refusal to buy

After reading this chapter, you will be able to:

- identify the various agreements granting a tenant the right to buy;
- differentiate between an option to renew and an option to extend;
- understand how different lease provisions impact the right to buy; and
- advise tenants how to properly exercise their right of first refusal to buy a leased premises.

call option	**option to extend**
option period	**option to renew**
option to buy	**right of first refusal**

Learning Objectives

Key Terms

Tenants with rights to acquire the premises

Tenants often need to invest substantial dollar amounts in **tenant improvements** to tailor newly leased premises to their needs. Whether contracted for by the tenant or the landlord, the tenant pays for the improvements in:

- a lump sum;
- upfront expenditures; or
- payments amortized over the initial term of the lease, calculated by the landlord and included in the monthly rent.

Installation of racks, cabinets, shelving, trade fixtures, lighting and other interior tenant improvements will also be paid for by the tenant. Further, the business builds up a significant degree of goodwill with customers due to the fixed location over a number of years. Thus, the location and improvements become part of the income generating value of the tenant's business.

All these expenditures will be lost if the landlord refuses to extend the lease, or if their demands for increased rent under an **option to extend** compel the tenant to relocate. A retail tenant with even a small degree of insight into their future operations at the location will attempt to negotiate some sort of option to purchase the property.

option to extend
An agreement granting a tenant the right to extend possession under the original lease agreement on terms set out in the option to extend. [See **RPI** Form 565]

The tenant who has paid rent that includes the amortization of TIs paid by the landlord needs to negotiate an *option to extend* at a lesser rental rate than during the initial term. Here the tenant has already paid for the tenant improvements on the property, a monthly payment that is not paid again under an option to extend or renew the lease.

An option to purchase included in a lease agreement is distinct from:

- the purchase rights held by a tenant under a right of first refusal; or
- the ownership rights held by a buyer under a lease-option sales arrangement. [See **RPI** Form 163]

Option to buy vs. right of first refusal

A landlord grants a tenant an option to purchase by entering into either:

- an irrevocable right to buy the property within a specific time period, called an **option to buy**; or
- a pre-emptive right to buy the property if the landlord later decides to sell the property, called a **right of first refusal**.

option to buy
An agreement granting an irrevocable right to buy property within a specific time period. [See **RPI** Form 161]

right of first refusal
A pre-emptive right to buy a property if the owner decides to sell. [See **RPI** Form 579]

The *option to buy* is typically evidenced by a separate agreement attached to the lease agreement. An option to buy includes terms of purchase, none of which are related to the lease of the property. The option to buy is to always be referenced in the lease agreement and attached as an addendum.

An option to buy contains all terms needed to form an enforceable purchase agreement for the acquisition of the real estate. The tenant holding an option to buy has the discretionary right to buy or not to buy on the sales terms stated in the option. To exercise the option, the tenant does so within an agreed-to time period. No variations are allowed. Thus, the option is a purchase agreement offer irrevocably agreed to by the seller to sell, but the buyer has not agreed to buy. [See Form 161 accompanying this chapter]

To actually buy the property under an option, the tenant exercises their right to buy through acceptance of the irrevocable offer to sell granted by the option. Conversely, the *right of first refusal* is a short agreement with its provisions either included in the body of the lease agreement or by an addendum. Unlike the option to buy, the right of first refusal provisions rarely contain any terms of a sale.

The option agreement

Under an option to buy agreement, the tenant is not obligated to buy the leased property. The tenant is merely given the right to buy if they so choose. This is a type of **call option**. [See **RPI** Form 161]

Facts: *A tenant enters into a commercial lease agreement. The agreement provides for the tenant to renew the lease, though it does not specify how many times the tenant is able to exercise the option to renew, and includes provisions indicative of a short-term lease. The tenant renews the lease at the end of the first term, then attempts to renew again at the end of the second term which the landlord rejects.*

Claim: *The landlord seeks to terminate the lease, claiming they were not obligated to provide another renewal since the original lease did not explicitly offer an unlimited number of renewals, and the lease was consistent with a traditional, short-term lease, rather than a perpetual lease.*

Counter claim: *The tenant claims the original lease allows for an unlimited number of renewals since it does not directly state it allows only one lease renewal.*

Holding: *A California appeals court held the landlord may terminate the lease since unlimited renewals may only be enforced if the lease demonstrates the landlord's intent to offer unlimited renewals, which it did not as the lease included provisions typical of a short-term lease.* **[Ginsberg** v. **Gamson** *(2012) 205 CA4th 873]*

For the option to be enforceable, the purchase price of the property and terms of payment on exercise of the option are included in the option agreement. If the dollar amount is not set as a specific amount in the option agreement, the purchase price may be stated as the fair market value of the property at the time the option is exercised.

The right to buy is exercised by the tenant within a specified time period, called the **option period**. The option period typically runs until the lease expires, including extensions/renewals, or is terminated. [See Form 161 §4]

If the option is not exercised precisely as agreed during the *option period*, the option period expires of its own accord. On expiration, the option no longer exists and the tenant is without an enforceable right to acquire the property.[1]

When options to renew or extend leasing periods are negotiated as part of the leasing arrangements, the expiration of the option to buy is tied by agreement to either:

- the expiration of the initial lease term; or
- the expiration of any renewal, extension or continuation of the tenant's lawful possession.

For example, a tenant rents space under a ten-year lease with an *option to extend* the term of the lease. The tenant also holds an option to buy the leased property. The option references the lease term as the period for exercise of the option to buy.

If the lease is later extended, the option period is automatically extended with the extension of the lease. Here, the option to buy allows the tenant to exercise the option during the lease term which includes any extensions.[2]

call option
An agreement giving a buyer the right to buy property within a specified time or upon an event at a specified price with terms for payment. [See **RPI** Form 161]

option period
The specified time period during which the tenant has the right to buy under an option agreement. [See **RPI** Form 161 §4]

---

1   **Bekins Moving & Storage Co.** v. **Prudential Insurance Company of America** (1985) 176 CA3d 245
2   **In re Marriage of Joaquin** (1987) 193 CA3d 1529

Form 161

Standard Option to Purchase

Page 1 of 2

STANDARD OPTION TO PURCHASE
Irrevocable Right-to-Buy

NOTE: This form is used by a leasing or sales agent when offers to rent or buy a property include a purchase option exercisable without extensions, to prepare an option as an irrevocable offer to sell with a price and terms for payment exercisable during a single period as an attachment to a lease agreement or an offer to grant an option.

DATE: _____, 20_____, at _____, California.
Items left blank or unchecked are not applicable.

1. OPTION MONEY:
Optionor herewith receives from Optionee option money in the amount of $_____, evidenced by:
☐ cash, ☐ check, or ☐ _____, given in consideration for this option to purchase real property.

2. REAL PROPERTY UNDER OPTION:
Address _____
Legal description/Assessor's parcel number _____

3. ADDITIONAL CONSIDERATION:
As further consideration for this option, Optionee is to obtain at their expense and deliver to Optionor prior to expiration % of this option the following checked items regarding the property:
☐ Property survey report by licensed California surveyors   ☐ Off-site improvement plans
☐ Architectural plans and specifications   ☐ Soil engineer's report
☐ On-site engineering plans   ☐ Land use study
☐ Zoning ordinance request   ☐ Application for a conditional use permit
☐ Application for a parcel map or waiver   ☐ _____

4. OPTION PERIOD:
Optionor hereby grants to Optionee the irrevocable option to purchase the Optionor's right, title and interest in the property on the terms stated, for a period commencing with the acceptance of this option and expiring _____, 20_____, or ☐ on termination of Optionee's leasehold interest in the property.

5. EXERCISE OF OPTION:
Optionee may exercise this option during the option period by:
5.1   Signing escrow instructions identical in provisions to those attached as **Exhibit A** and delivering the instructions to escrow [See **RPI** Form 401];
5.2   Depositing cash in escrow of $_____; and
5.3   Delivering an escrow-certified copy of the signed escrow instructions to Optionor within the option period, in person or by both certified and regular mail.

6. ESCROW CONTRACT:
In the event this option is exercised, the transaction will be escrowed with _____.
6.1   Escrow will close within _____ days after exercise.

7. DELIVERY OF TITLE:
On Optionee's exercise of this option, Optionor will timely place all documents and instruments into escrow required of the Optionor as necessary for escrow to close as scheduled.

8. BROKERAGE FEE:
Optionor agrees to pay a brokerage fee of $_____, or _____% of the selling price, IF:
8.1   This option is exercised;
8.2   Within one year after expiration of option period and any extension or renewal, Optionor enters into an agreement to option, sell, lease or exchange with Optionee, or their assigns or successors; or
8.3   Optionor wrongfully prevents the exercise of this option:
8.4   Fee payable to Broker(s) _____.
8.5   Optionor and Optionee acknowledge receipt of the Agency Law Disclosure. [See **RPI** Form 305]

9. SALE TERMS:
Price of $_____ payable as follows:
9.1   ☐ All cash.
9.2   Cash down payment in the amount of $_____.
9.3   ☐ Take title subject to, or ☐ Assume, an existing first trust deed note held by_____,
with an unpaid principal balance of $_____, payable $_____ monthly, including interest not exceeding _____%, ☐ ARM, type _____, plus a monthly tax/insurance impound payment of $_____.
a.   At closing, loan balance differences per beneficiary statement(s) to be adjusted into:
☐ cash, ☐ carryback note, or ☐ sales price. [See **RPI** Form 415]
b.   The impound account to be transferred: ☐ charged, or ☐ without charge, to Optionee.

-- PAGE 1 OF 2 — FORM 161 --

---

option to renew
An agreement granting an irrevocable right to buy property within a specific time period. [See **RPI** Form 565]

Now consider a lease agreement which contains an **option to renew** the lease agreement instead of an option to extend. This is a distinction with a complication. The renewal option requires the preparation and signing of a new lease agreement on identical terms to the original lease agreement. The initial lease agreement, by way of a referenced attachment, provided the tenant with an option to buy which can be exercised prior to the expiration of the lease.

On renewal of the lease agreement, the tenant needs to ensure the option to buy is not left to expire at the end of the initial lease term. The new lease

------------------------------ PAGE 2 OF 2 — FORM 161 ------------------------------

9.4 □ Take title subject to, or □ Assume, an existing second trust deed note held by _____, with an unpaid principal balance of $_____, payable $_____ monthly, including interest not exceeding _____%, □ ARM, type _____, due _____, 20_____.

9.5 A note for the balance of the purchase price in the amount of $_____ to be executed by Optionee in favor of Optionor and secured by a trust deed on the property junior to the above referenced financing, payable $_____ monthly, or more, beginning one month after closing, including interest at _____% per annum from closing, due _____ years after closing.

    a. This note and trust deed to contain provisions to be provided by Optionor for:
      □ due-on-sale, □ prepayment penalty, □ late charges, □_____

    b. □ The attached Financial Disclosure Statement is an addendum to this agreement (mandatory on four-or-less residential units). [See **RPI** Form 300]

    c. □ Optionee to provide a Request for Notice of Default and Notice of Delinquency to senior encumbrancers. [See **RPI** Form 412]

10. GENERAL PROVISIONS:

10.1 □ **See attached addendum for additional provisions.** [See **RPI** Form 250]

10.2 Attached as addenda are the following checked disclosures mandated on four-or-less residential units:
    a. □ Condition of Property Disclosure — Transfer Disclosure Statement (TDS) [See **RPI** Form 304]
    b. □ Natural Hazard Disclosure Statement [See **RPI** Form 314]
    c. □ Disclosure of Sexual Predator Database [See **RPI** Form 319]
    d. □ Hazard Disclosure Booklet, and related Optionor disclosures, containing Environmental Hazards, Lead-based Paint and Earthquake Safety [See **RPI** Forms 313 and 315]
    e. □ Documentation on any Homeowners' Association (HOA) involved. [See **RPI** Form 309]
    f. □ Notice of Supplemental Property Tax Bill [See **RPI** Form 317]

10.3 Possession of the property to be delivered on:
    □ close of escrow, or □ see attached Occupancy Agreement. [See **RPI** Forms 271 and 272]

10.4 Both parties reserve their rights to assign, and agree to cooperate in effecting an Internal Revenue Code §1031 exchange prior to close of escrow, on either party's written notice.

11. EXPIRATION OF OPTION:

This offer to sell will be deemed expired if not accepted by exercise during the option period.

11.1 This option contract will automatically terminate by expiration on _____, 20_____.

OPTIONOR'S BROKER:_____	**OPTIONEE'S BROKER:**_____
Broker's CalBRE #: _____	Broker's CalBRE #: _____
Buyer's Agent: _____	Agent's Name: _____
Agent's CalBRE #: _____	Agent's CalBRE #: _____
Signature: _____	Signature: _____

Is the agent of: □ Optionor exclusively
                □ Both Optionor and Optionee.
	Is the agent of: □ Optionee exclusively.
	                □ Both Optionor and Optionee.

Address: _____	Address: _____
Phone: _____ Cell: _____ Email: _____	Phone: _____ Cell: _____ Email: _____
I hereby grant this option and agree to the terms stated above.	**I hereby accept this option and agree to the terms stated above.**
Date: _____, 20_____	Date: _____, 20_____
Optionor: _____	Optionee: _____
Signature: _____	Signature: _____
Signature: _____ address: _____	Signature: _____ address: _____
Phone: _____ Fax: _____ Email: _____	Phone: _____ Fax: _____ Email: _____

FORM 161   12-14   ©2016 RPI — Realty Publications, Inc., P.O. BOX 5707, RIVERSIDE, CA 92517

agreement is a different contract and needs to also reference the option to buy (as part of the identical terms of the original lease) since a new lease is not an extension of any of the terms of the original lease.[3]

A tenant's right to buy under a right of first refusal agreement can be triggered by any indication of the landlord in a decision to sell the property, including:

- listing or advertising the property for sale;
- offering the property for sale to a buyer;

The right of first refusal to buy

3 In re Marriage of Joaquin, *supra*

- accepting an offer or making a counteroffer involving a sale to a buyer; and

- granting a purchase option.

As shown, the landlord does not need to first agree to sell the leased property by entering into a purchase agreement with another person to trigger the right of first refusal.

Decision to sell triggers option to buy

Consider a buyer who contacts the landlord of leased commercial property to make an offer to purchase the property. The buyer is informed the major tenant holds the right to buy the property under a right of first refusal provision in the lease.

The buyer attempts to circumvent the right of first refusal by negotiating an option to buy the property, exercisable only after the tenant's right of first refusal expires. The landlord grants the buyer an option to buy the property. The granting of the option — an irrevocable offer to sell — now binds the landlord unconditionally to sell the property if the option is exercised.

Here, the landlord's granting of the option to sell the property is a clear indication of their intention to sell, triggering the right of first refusal. The tenant is now allowed to purchase the property on the same terms as contained in the buyer's option.[4]

Editor's note — The right of first refusal is not triggered by conveyance of the property to the landlord's heirs on the landlord's death. The heirs take title subject to the right of first refusal. However, the right of first refusal is triggered by a sale of the property ordered by the probate court or entered into by the heirs. To exercise the right of first refusal, the tenant matches the highest offer submitted in open bidding and approved by the court, or the listing or sale of the property by an executor.[5]

Once notice of the landlord's decision to sell is delivered to the tenant, the right of first refusal is transformed into an option to buy. Control of the transaction then passes to the tenant holding the right of first refusal. The tenant's position under the right of first refusal is converted to that of an optionee on terms set by the landlord, unless the right of first refusal provisions set some or all of the terms.

The landlord may not now retract their decision to sell the property without breaching the right of first refusal provision.

Matching the back-up offer

The landlord subject to a right of first refusal held by a tenant is obligated to notify the tenant of the terms of any sales listing, option to buy, offer to purchase, counteroffer or acceptance of an offer to purchase which triggers the tenant's right to buy under the right of first refusal provision. [See Form 579 accompanying this chapter]

---

4 **Rollins v. Stokes** (1981) 123 CA3d 701
5 **Estate of Patterson** (1980) 108 CA3d 197

Form 579

Right of First
Refusal to Buy

RIGHT OF FIRST REFUSAL TO BUY

Addendum

NOTE: This form is used by a leasing agent or prospective tenant when negotiating a rental or lease agreement, to provide in an addendum the landlord's grant to the tenant of a right of first refusal to purchase the leased premises.

DATE: _____, 20_____, at _____, California.

TO: _____

Items left blank or unchecked are not applicable.

FACTS:

1. This is an addendum to a rental or lease agreement

    1.1 ☐ of same date, or dated _____, 20_____, at _____, California,

    1.2 entered into by _____, as the Tenant, and

    1.3 _____, as the Landlord,

    1.4 regarding the leased premises referred to as _____

    _____.

AGREEMENT:

In addition to the terms of the agreement referenced above, Tenant and Landlord agree to the following.

Right of first refusal to buy:

2. Landlord hereby grants Tenant a right of first refusal to purchase the leased premises, for a term commencing _____, 20_____, and expiring _____, 20_____, or ☐ on termination of Tenant's right of occupancy.

3. If Landlord decides to sell the premises during the term of Tenant's right of first refusal, Landlord will notify Tenant of the terms on which Landlord is willing to sell. [See **RPI** Form 579-2]

    3.1 Tenant has the option, for a period of _____ days after receiving Landlord's written notice sent by certified mail or personal delivery, to agree to purchase the premises on the terms stated in the notice.

    3.2 If Tenant fails to exercise the option within the option period, Landlord has the right to sell the premises to a third party on the same terms stated in Landlord's notice to Tenant.

    3.3 Any sale on different terms reinstates the Tenant's right of first refusal.

4. If Landlord has not closed a sale of the property within six (6) _____ months after Tenant's receipt of Landlord's notice, Tenant's right of first refusal is reinstated.

5. _____
    _____
    _____
    _____
    _____
    _____

Tenant: I agree to the terms stated above.	**Landlord: I agree to the terms stated above.**
☐ See attached Signature Page Addendum. [RPI Form 251]	☐ See attached Signature Page Addendum. [RPI Form 251]
Date: _____, 20_____	Date: _____, 20_____
Tenant: _____	Landlord: _____
By: _____	By: _____
Tenant: _____	Landlord: _____
By: _____	By: _____

FORM 579   03-15   ©2016 RPI — Realty Publications, Inc., P.O. BOX 5707, RIVERSIDE, CA 92517

The tenant who decides to purchase the property agrees to match the sales terms within the time period set in the right of first refusal provision. Failure to do so is a failure to exercise their right of first refusal, resulting in a loss of their right to buy.

Consider a tenant who holds a right of first refusal on the industrial property they lease. A buyer makes an offer to purchase the property. The terms for the payment of the price in the buyer's offer include cash and an assumption of the existing first trust deed on the property.

The property is also encumbered with a nonrecourse second trust deed to be paid off and reconveyed on closing under the terms of the buyer's offer.

The landlord accepts the offer and notifies the tenant, giving the tenant the opportunity to match the buyer's offer under the right of first refusal provision in the lease agreement.

The tenant exercises their right of first refusal by agreeing to purchase the property at the same price. However, the tenant alters the terms for payment of that price as they will assume both the existing first trust deed and nonrecourse second, paying the remainder of the price in cash.

The landlord rejects the tenant's conditions and refuses to sell to the tenant.

Here, the landlord is to comply with the tenant's terms for payment of the price since they are the financial equivalent of the proposed sale. The tenant need merely provide the same net financial result to the landlord as the offer being matched — a cash-out of the landlord's equity in the property.

The tenant's performance under the right of first refusal does not need to be identical in all aspects to the buyer's offer.

Thus, the landlord is to perform and deliver title to the tenant. Here the landlord's net proceeds, economic benefits and liabilities resulting from the terms for performance set by the tenant are the same as those the landlord experiences under the purchase offer which triggered the right of first refusal.[6]

Deficient offer constitutes a waiver

Consider a buyer who offers to purchase property leased to a tenant who holds a right of first refusal. The terms in the buyer's purchase agreement call for a cash down payment and a note executed by the buyer for the balance of the landlord's equity. The note is to be secured by a trust deed on other property with adequate value as security.

The landlord accepts the offer and notifies the tenant, who agrees to match the buyer's offer. However, the value of the property offered by the tenant as security is inadequate, causing the landlord to refuse to accept it.

Here, the tenant's offer is not financially equivalent to the buyer's offer since the value of the security offered by the tenant is inadequate, even if the note is identical. In the tenant's offer, the risk of loss on default has been increased.

The landlord is not obligated to accept the tenant's deficient exercise of their preemptive right to buy. Here, the tenant's deficient offer constitutes a waiver of the tenant's right to buy. The landlord may now sell the property to the buyer — but only on the terms initially agreed to with the buyer or the right of first refusal is reinstated.[7]

Reinstatement of the right of first refusal

A *right of first refusal* provision is automatically reinstated when:

- the landlord agrees to sell the property on terms different from those terms offered to the tenant; or

6   **C. Robert Nattress & Associates** v. **CIDCO** (1986) 184 CA3d 55

7   **McCulloch** v. **M & C Beauty Colleges** (1987) 194 CA3d 1338

Figure 1

Form 163

Lease-Option – Contract for Deed

LEASE-OPTION
Contract for Deed

Prepared by: Agent ________ Phone ________
Broker ________ Email ________

NOTE: This form is used by an agent when a seller holds out property for sale under a lease-option sale arrangement, to structure the change in ownership as a lease-option sale with the seller conveying title on the buyer's full performance of the lease and exercise of the option.

DATE: ________, 20____, at ________, California.
Items left blank or unchecked are not applicable.

FACTS:

1. This lease agreement and option to purchase is entered into by Lessor/Optionor and Lessee/Optionee, regarding property situated in the City of ________, County of ________ California, referred to as ________.
Personal property, ☐ see attached Personal Property Inventory [See RPI Form 256], ________
2. **This agreement is comprised of this three page form and the following checked attachments:**
☐ Credit Application [See RPI Form 302]
☐ Residential Earthquake Hazards Report [See RPI Form 315]
☐ Occupant's Operating Expense Sheet [See RPI Form 562]
☐ Addendum — General Use [See RPI Form 250]
☐ Notice of Your Supplemental Property Tax Bill [See RPI Form 317]
☐ Natural Hazard Disclosure Statement [See RPI Form 314]
☐ Financial Disclosure Statement [See RPI Form 309]
☐ Brokerage Fee Addendum [See RPI Form 273]
☐ Lead-Based Paint Disclosure [See RPI Form 313]
☐ Condition of Property Disclosure [See RPI Form 304]
3. **Term of Lease:**
This lease commences ________, 20____ and continues until ________, 20____.
3.1 The lease terminates on the last day of the term without further notice.
3.2 If Lessee holds over, Lessee to be liable for rent at the daily rate of $________.
4. **Rent:** Lessee to pay, in advance, a base monthly rent of $________ due on the ____ day of each calendar month.
4.1 Rent to be paid by: ☐ personal check made payable to ________, or ☐ ________.
4.2 Rent to be tendered by: ☐ mail, or ☐ personal delivery.
4.3 Lessee to pay a late charge of six percent of all rent amounts due in the event rent is not received within ten days of the due date.
4.4 Lessee to pay $________ for each rent check returned for insufficient funds and thereafter pay rent by cash or cashier's check.
5. **Additional Rent:** In addition to the base monthly rent, Lessee to pay additional monthly rent equal to the increased costs incurred by Lessor after entering into this lease-option, due to:
a. ☐ variable/adjustable interest rate on existing loans secured by the property;
b. ☐ variable/adjustable monthly principal or acceleration of existing loans secured by the property;
c. ☐ property taxes on the property;
d. ☐ fire and extended coverage insurance premiums on the property;
e. ☐ any Homeowners' Association (HOA) assessments;
f. ☐ any special or improvement assessments on the property; and
g. ☐ any other expenditures required of Lessor to protect his interest.
5.1 The additional monthly rent will be the actual monthly cost increase and 1/12th of any annual cost increase
5.2 The additional monthly rent is due on, or beginning with, the monthly rent payment next due following notice to Lessee by Lessor.
6. **Utilities:** Lessee will pay all costs of public utilities to the property, including any required deposits, installation, or service fees.

PAGE 1 OF 3 — FORM 163

PAGE 2 OF 3 — FORM 163

7. **Maintenance of Premises:** Lessee agrees to maintain and perform all necessary repairs to the property during the lease term at his sole expense.
8. **Insurance:** Lessee will maintain at their sole expense, naming Lessor as an additional insured:
8.1 ☐ A standard fire insurance policy with extended coverage, vandalism and malicious mischief endorsements, fully covering the replacement cost of all structures on the property during the entire term of the lease; and
8.2 ☐ Public liability and property damage insurance with a single combined liability limit of at least $300,000 and property damage limits of at least $100,000, insuring against all liability of Lessee arising out of Lessee's use or occupancy of the premises.
9. **Use of the Property:** The property is to be used only as a private residence occupied by Lessee and for no other purpose. Lessee will comply with all laws regarding the use of the property, and will not allow any waste or nuisance to occur on the property.
10. **Assignment and Subletting:** Lessee will not assign this lease, nor sublet or encumber any interest in the property without the prior written consent of Lessor. Any transfer of an interest in the property by Lessee without the prior written consent of Lessor will, at the option of Lessor, terminate this lease and call for payment of all sums due.
11. **Waiver of Damage:** Lessee releases Lessor from liability for loss or damage to Lessee or any property of Lessee caused by water leakage, breaking pipes, theft, vandalism, or any other cause beyond the reasonable control of Lessor
12. **Hold Harmless:** Lessee will indemnify Lessor from liability, damages, and/or expenses arising from the death or injury of any person, including Lessee, or from the damage or destruction of any property, including property owned by Lessee, caused or allegedly caused by some condition of the property, or some act or omission of Lessee or any other person.

OPTION TO PURCHASE:

13. **Option Money:** Optionor acknowledges receipt of option money in the amount of $________, given in consideration for this option to purchase the property leased.
14. **Option Period:** Optionor hereby grants to Optionee the irrevocable option to purchase the Optionor's right, title and interest in the property under the sales terms for a period commencing with the acceptance of this option and expiring on termination of the lease.
15. **Exercise of Option:** Optionee may exercise this option during the option period by:
15.1 Preparing and signing escrow instructions with ________;
15.2 Depositing cash in Escrow of $________; and
15.3 Delivering a certified copy of the signed escrow instructions to Optionor within the option period in person or by certified mail.
16. **Delivery of Title:** Within ____ days after exercise, Optionor and Optionee will place in Escrow all documents and instruments necessary to close.
17. **Sale Terms:** The purchase price is $________, payable:
17.1 ☐ In cash.
17.2 ☐ Down payment in the amount of $________.
17.3 The cash price or down payment to be credited for $________ of option money paid, and for ____%, or $________, of each payment of base monthly rent.
17.4 ☐ Take title subject to, or ☐ Assume, the existing trust deed note with an approximate unpaid balance of $________, currently payable $________ monthly, including principal and interest at ____%, ☐ adjustable, monthly impounds being an additional $________.
17.5 ☐ Take title subject to, or ☐ Assume, a trust deed note with a principal balance of $________, currently payable $________ monthly, including principal and interest at ____%, due ________.
17.6 Loan balance differences to be adjusted in: ☐ cash, ☐ §17.8 Note, or ☐ price.
17.7 ☐ Assume bonds or assessment liens of record in the approximate amount of $________.
17.8 A Note for the balance of the purchase price in the amount of $________, to be executed by Buyer in favor of Seller and secured by a trust deed on the property, payable $________ monthly, or more, commencing one month after closing, including interest at ____%, due ________ years after closing.
a. The Note and Trust Deed will not contain provisions for due-on clauses, prepayment penalties, or late charges.
b. ☐ Optionee to provide a Request for Notice of Default and Notice of Delinquency to senior encumbrancers. [See RPI Form 412]
c. ☐ The Note is an All-Inclusive Trust Deed Note.

PAGE 2 OF 3 — FORM 163

PAGE 3 OF 3 — FORM 163

d. As additional security, Optionee to execute a security agreement and file a UCC-1 financing statement on any personal property included in the price.
18. **General Provisions:**
18.1 Lessee/Optionee and Lessor/Optionor acknowledge receipt of the Agency Law Disclosure. [See RPI Form 305]
18.2 Optionee's transfer of any interest in this option terminates the option.
18.3 Before any party to this agreement files an action on a dispute arising out of this agreement which remains unresolved after 30 days of informal negotiations, the parties agree to enter into non-binding mediation administered by a neutral dispute resolution organization and undertake a good faith effort during mediation to settle the dispute.
18.4 The prevailing party in any action on a dispute will be entitled to attorney fees and costs, unless they file an action without first offering to enter into mediation to resolve the dispute.
19. **Power of Sale:** If this document is characterized as a security device, on default of rental payments or failure to exercise the option, the Lessor/Optionor may call all sums due and elect to proceed with a power of sale by a trustee substituted under Civil Code §2934(a), noticed and held in accordance with Civil Code §§2924 et seq.
20. **Lessor/Optionor Default:** If the Lessor/Optionor defaults on any obligation impairing the Lessee/Optionee's interest under this agreement, Lessee/Optionee may cure the default and demand reimbursement from the Lessor/Optionor of the amount advanced, and if not paid, deduct the amount paid from periodic payments and the purchase price due the Lessor/Optionor.
21. **Expiration of Option:** This option to purchase will be deemed expired if not exercised during the option period, and if not previously terminated, will automatically expire/terminate on ________, 20____.
22. **Brokerage Fee:** Optionor to pay brokerage fees as follows:
22.1 ____% of the option money on receipt; plus
22.2 ____% of each month's base rent on receipt; and
22.3 $________ on exercise of the option.
22.4 Optionee's Broker and Optionor's Broker, respectively, to share the brokerage fee ____:____.
23. ________

Lessee/ Optionee's Broker: ________	Lessor/ Optionor's Broker: ________
By: ________	By: ________
Is the agent of: ☐ Lessee/Optionee exclusively; or ☐ Both Parties.	Is the agent of: ☐ Lessor/Optionor exclusively; or ☐ Both Parties.
I agree to the terms stated above. ☐ See attached Signature Page Addendum. [RPI Form 251]	**I agree to the terms stated above.** ☐ See attached Signature Page Addendum. [RPI Form 251]
Date: ________, 20____	Date: ________, 20____
Lessee/Optionee: ________	Lessor/Optionee: ________
Signature: ________	Signature: ________
Lessee/Optionee: ________	Lessor/Optionee: ________
Signature: ________	Signature: ________
Address: ________	Address: ________
Phone: ________ Cell: ________	Phone: ________ Cell: ________
Email: ________	Email: ________

FORM 163 12-14 ©2015 RPI — Realty Publications, Inc., P.O. BOX 5707, RIVERSIDE, CA 92517

For a full-size, fillable copy of this or any other form in this book that may be legally used in your professional practice, go to realtypublications.com/forms

- the property remains unsold after the running of an agreed-to period of time following the tenant's waiver of the right to buy. [See Form 579 §4]

Consider a landlord who, under a right of first refusal, notifies their tenant of the purchase terms on which they have listed the property for sale. The tenant chooses not to exercise their option to buy at the price and on the terms offered. The landlord later modifies the listing by lowering the sales price or altering the terms for payment of the price.

The price reduction or modification of terms automatically reinstates the tenant's right of first refusal obligating the landlord to re-notify the tenant of new terms for purchase of the property. The tenant only waived their right of first refusal for a sale based on the terms originally given to them by the landlord, not on the different price or set of terms.

When a buyer purchases the property on terms other than those offered to the tenant, the buyer takes title subject to the tenant's preemptive right to buy. This right is reinstated due to the sale on different terms. Thus, the buyer is to resell to the tenant on the same price and terms the buyer paid. The buyer had either actual or constructive notice of the tenant's unrecorded right to acquire the property due to the tenant's possession of the property.

Chapter 6 Summary

A landlord gives a tenant the right to buy rented property by granting either:

- an option to buy, which is an irrevocable right to buy the property within a specific time period; or
- a right of first refusal, which is a pre-emptive right to buy the property if the landlord later decides to sell the property.

The right to buy under an option to buy will be exercised by the tenant within the option period. The option period typically runs until the lease term expires or is terminated.

A tenant's right to buy under a right of first refusal agreement is triggered by any indication of the landlord's decision to sell the property, including:

- listing or advertising the property for sale;
- offering the property for sale to a buyer;
- accepting an offer or making a counteroffer involving a sale to a buyer; and
- granting a purchase option.

To exercise the right of first refusal to buy, the tenant needs to agree to match the sales terms set by the landlord within the time period set in the right of first refusal provision.

Chapter 6 Key Terms

Quiz 2 Covering Chapters 5-8 is located on page 634.

Chapter
7

Property management licensing

Learning Objectives

certified CID manager   **power of attorney**

contingency fee

Key Terms

An individual owns and operates income-producing real estate. As the owner-operator, they locate and qualify tenants, prepare and sign occupancy agreements, deliver possession, contract for property maintenance, collect rent, pay expenses and mortgages, serve any notices and file any *unlawful detainer (UD)* actions to evict tenants.

When is a DRE license required?

Does the owner-operator need a Department of Real Estate (DRE) broker license to perform these activities?[1]

No! The owner of income-producing real estate does not need a real estate broker license to operate as a *principal*. The owner-operator is not acting on behalf of someone else as an agent when managing their own property.[2]

Editor's note — Here, the generic term "agent" refers to anyone who acts on behalf of another. Confusingly, the term "agent" is also used in the real

---

1 The Department of Real Estate (DRE) was referred to as the California Bureau of Real Estate (CalBRE) between July 1st, 2013 through July 1st, 2018.

2 Calif. Business and Professions Code §10131(b)

DCA Guide for Landlords and Tenants

The California Department of Consumer Affairs (DCA) publishes a booklet titled: **California Tenants: A Guide to Residential Tenants' and Landlords' Rights and Responsibilities**. *The purpose of the booklet is to equip tenants with the knowledge to act as savvy consumers during lease negotiations and to protect themselves from ignorant or unethical landlords during tenancy.*

It also includes valuable information for landlords and property managers.

California Tenants solely address residential tenancies and includes practical information on topics including:

- *security deposits;*
- *habitability of rented or leased premises;*
- *disclosure requirements; and*
- *fair housing laws.*

This publication is updated regularly by the DCA and is available from their website.

estate industry to refer to a DRE-licensed sales agent, or salesperson. To simplify, the rest of this chapter will only use the term "agent" to refer to a DRE-licensed individual.

On the other hand, if the owner-operator decides to hire an individual to take over the general management of the apartment complex, the individual employed to act as property manager needs to under most circumstances be licensed by the DRE as a California real estate broker.

Editor's note — A broker has the authority to act as a property manager by virtue of their DRE license alone. There is no special "property management" license or endorsement required under California law. Optional designations are discussed later in this chapter.

Performance of services in exchange for a fee requires a license

An individual or corporation is to hold a broker license if they perform or offer to perform any of the following services on behalf of another in exchange for a fee:

- listing real estate for rent or lease;
- marketing the property to locate prospective tenants;
- listing prospective tenants for the rental or lease of real estate;
- locating property to rent or lease;
- selling, buying or exchanging existing leasehold interests in real estate;
- managing income-producing properties; or
- collecting rents from tenants of real estate.[3]

An individual employed by a broker to perform any of the above services needs to also be licensed by the DRE, either as a broker or sales agent, unless exempt.

---

3   Bus & P C §10131(b)

Administrative and non-discretionary duties performed by an employee of a broker who manages transient housing or apartment complexes are *exempt* from real estate licensing requirements while the employee is under the broker's supervision and control.[4]

Unlicensed vs. licensed activities

Thus, an employee hired to assist the broker in the rental and leasing of residential complexes, other than single family units, may be either:

- **licensed**; or
- **unlicensed**.

Unlicensed employees may perform tenant-related negotiations in apartment and vacation rentals, such as:

- showing rental units and facilities to prospective tenants;
- providing prospective tenants with information about rent rates and rental and lease agreement provisions;
- providing prospective tenants with rental application forms and answering questions regarding their completion;
- accepting tenant screening fees;
- accepting signed lease and rental agreements from tenants; and
- accepting rents and security deposits.[5]

Licensed employees may perform any activities unlicensed employees perform. However, licensed employees are additionally able to perform activities relating to contacts with the landlord, as opposed to the tenant, about the leasing, care of the property and accounting.

License required

Activities which only licensed employees may perform include:

- landlord-related solicitations;
- entering into property management or leasing agent agreements with the landlord;
- listings and rental or lease negotiations;
- care and maintenance of the property;
- marketing of the listed space; and
- accounting.

Also exempt from licensing is an individual who has been given authority to act as an "attorney in fact" under a **power of attorney** to *temporarily manage* a landlord's property.[6] [See **RPI** Form 447]

Power-of-attorney exemption

However, a *power of attorney* may not be used as authority to continuously manage real estate and does not substitute for a broker license.

power of attorney
A temporary authority granted to an individual to perform activities during a period of the owner's incapacity or travel. [See **RPI** Form 447]

---

4   Bus & P C §10131.01(a)
5   Bus & P C §10131.01(a)(1)
6   Bus & P C §10133(a)(2)

Consider a landlord who can no longer handle the responsibilities of managing their property due to illness. The landlord grants a power of attorney to a friend to manage the property. The landlord pays their friend for performing property management tasks, including locating tenants, negotiating leases and collecting rent.

After the landlord's recovery from their illness, they continue to employ their friend to perform these management tasks.

Does the landlord's friend need a real estate broker license to perform property management tasks on a regular, on-going basis in exchange for a fee, even though the landlord has given them a power of attorney?

Yes! The power-of-attorney exemption may only be used in situations where the landlord is compelled by necessity, such as a vacation or illness, to authorize another person to complete a specific or isolated transaction.

A person receiving a fee for the continuous performance of property management tasks requiring a broker license may not rely on the power-of-attorney exemption to avoid licensing requirements.[7]

Apartment resident manager exemption

Apartment building management has special licensing rules distinguishing resident managers from nonresident property managers.

A *resident manager* is employed by either the landlord or the broker who manages the apartment building or complex. The resident manager lives on the premises as a requirement of their employment.

A resident manager and their employees do not need a real estate license to manage the apartment complex.[8]

However, a resident manager of one apartment complex is barred from being the property manager of a separate apartment complex unless they are licensed. In managing two complexes, the resident manager becomes a nonresident property manager of one complex. Thus, they need to be licensed.[9]

Apartment complexes with 16 or more units are required to have a resident manager.[10]

Other licensing exceptions

A person is not required to have a real estate broker license when they are acting:

- as an attorney performing management as part of their legal services[11]; or

- under court appointment, such as a receiver or bankruptcy trustee.[12]

---

7   **Sheetz** v. **Edmonds** (1988) 201 CA3d 1432
8   Bus & P C §10131.01(a)(1)
9   Bus & P C §10131(b)
10 25 Calif. Code of Regulations §42
11 Bus & P C §10133(a)(3)
12 Bus & P C §10133(a)(4)

These exceptions are usually short-term and refer to specific properties.

A person whose business is advertised or held out as including property management for others needs to comply with the licensing laws. Individuals managing property without a license and without qualifying for an exemption will not be able to enforce collection of the fee they were to receive.[13]

If a landlord is a corporation, limited liability company (LLC) or partnership, any officer of the entity may manage the entity's property without a broker license.[14]

However, the unlicensed officer may not receive any contingency fees or extra compensation based on activities that require a license. They are to be salaried or on wages.

For example, a corporation owns a shopping mall managed by an officer of the corporation. The officer's duties include maintaining the premises, locating tenants and collecting rents.

As the manager, the corporate officer is paid an annual salary as a base pay. Whenever a vacancy occurs in the mall, the manager locates a new tenant and negotiates the lease for the corporation. For each new tenant, the manager receives an *incentive fee* over and above their corporate salary. This acts as a bonus for their successful efforts.

Here, the manager needs to be licensed as a broker even though they are an officer and employee of the corporation that owns the property. The manager's earnings include extra compensation based on their performance of real estate management activities requiring a license.

The manager's receipt of an incentive bonus payment for leasing space establishes that the manager is acting as a broker, not merely as a salaried officer of the corporate owner. If the corporation holds a DRE corporate license, then the employed individual only needs to be a licensed salesperson. The exclusion of employees from licensing in residential rental complexes for tenant-related contacts does not apply to commercial leasing.

Similarly, where an LLC owns the property, the manager of the LLC need not be licensed to manage the property — provided fees are not paid based on the quantity of leases negotiated or the LLC's rental income.[15]

If the LLC manager receives a percentage of gross rents as compensation, the compensation is considered a contingent fee unless all the members of the LLC receive the same percentage.

A property manager paid on a **contingency fee** basis, or any other employee or officer whose pay is structured as a *contingency fee*, of an office building,

Contingent fees and bonus awards

No license for LLC manager

contingency fee
An incentive bonus paid upon successfully completing or hitting certain benchmarks, or received as compensation on the occurrence of an event.

13 Bus & P C §10137
14 Bus & P C §10133(a)(1)
15 Bus & P C §10133(a)(1)

shopping center, industrial park, apartment building or other income property will need a broker license if their duties include recruiting tenants, negotiating leases or collecting rents. However, employees of a broker dealing exclusively with prospective tenants for units in apartment complexes or vacation rentals are not required to possess a license.[16]

Bonus, award, commission, incentive or *contingency fee* programs in excess of a base salary require the person receiving them to be licensed by the DRE, whether they are resident managers, assistant resident managers or maintenance personnel. Examples of these programs include:

- a flat dollar fee for each new tenant;
- a monthly flat dollar fee for each new tenant;
- a percentage fee based on increases in rents; and
- a percentage of monthly gross rents if rents collected for the month exceed a percentage of scheduled income.

Certification to manage a CID

A broker license does not automatically confer on the broker the designation of **certified common interest development (CID) manager**. Also, it is not mandatory for a broker to be "certified" to manage a common interest development, but some employers may request it. [See Chapter 8]

The benchmark professional certification is the Certified Community Association Manager. This certification is issued by the California Association of Community Managers. This designation is not an activity involving the DRE. However, the minimum educational criteria for becoming a certified CID manager are set by California law.[17]

certified CID manager
A non-required professional designation certifying an individual has met legislated educational requirements specific to managing common interest developments.

When earning a designation as a certified CID manager, the manager is tested for competence in CID management in the following areas:

- all subjects covered by the Davis-Stirling Common Interest Development Act[18];
- personnel issues related to independent contractor or employment status, laws on harassment, the Unruh Civil Rights Act, The California Fair Employment and Housing Act and the Americans with Disabilities Act;
- risk management, including insurance coverage and residential hazards; and
- federal, state and local laws governing the affairs of CIDs.

Any program claiming to certify CID managers will also instruct and test managers for competency in general management and business skills, such as:

- trust fund handling, budget preparation, and bankruptcy law;
- contract negotiation;

---

16 Bus & P C §10131(b)
17 Bus & P C §§11502. 11503
18 CC § 4000

- supervision of employees and staff;
- management and administration of maintenance, and CC&R's
- owner/resident relations and conflict resolution and avoidance mechanisms;
- architectural standards;
- how to implement association CC&Rs; and
- ethics, professional conduct and standards of practice for CID managers.[19]

It is considered an unfair business practice for a broker to label or advertise themselves as "certified" to manage CIDs if the broker has not completed such a course.[20]

It is a widely held misconception that property managers are required to hold a Certified Property Manager (CPM) membership with the *Institute of Real Estate Management (IREM)* to perform property management activities.

The CPM designation is a non-required unofficial designation bestowed by a private non-regulatory organization. Brokers and agents may earn them by completing private coursework and submitting proof of a certain number of years of property management experience.

Other non-required third-party property management designations include:

- the certified apartment manager (CAM) designation;
- the accredited resident manager (ARM) designation;
- the registered in apartment management (RAM) designation; and
- the certified apartment supervisor (CAPS) designation.

Like the certified CID manager designation, the CPM designation is not required to be employed. Unlike the CID manager designation, the criteria for obtaining these designations are entirely determined by private organizations.

The designations are often costly, and do not guarantee employment in property management. Some employers may favor such designations, while others may not recognize them at all.

A common "licensing" misconception

19 Bus & P C §11502
20 Bus & P C §11504

Chapter 7 Summary

An individual or corporation need to hold a broker license if they perform or offer to or perform any property management services on behalf of another for a fee. An individual employed by the broker to perform activities related to contacts with the landlord also needs to hold a broker or sales agent license.

However, several licensing exemptions exist. A broker who manages apartment complexes and vacation properties may hire unlicensed staff to perform administrative and non-discretionary duties. Resident managers, attorneys, bankruptcy trustees, and (to a limited extent) those who hold power of attorney are not required to be licensed.

Third-party property management designations exist, but are not required for employment.

Chapter 7 Key Terms

Quiz 2 Covering Chapters 5-8 is located on page 634.

Chapter 8

Property management agreement

After reading this chapter, you will be able to:

- understand the function of a property management agreement to grant authority to operate a rental property and specify the performance expectations of the landlord and the manager;
- handle rental payments received from tenants and operating expenses, and provide periodic trust fund accounting to the landlord;
- distinguish the different ways a property manager may structure their fee schedule for their management of a property;
- perform duties specific to a common interest development (CID) upon entering into a property management agreement with the homeowners' association (HOA) controlling the CID; and
- identify and apply the landlord's and property manager's rights and responsibilities under the management agreement.

Learning Objectives

common interest development	property management agreement
managing agent	

Key Terms

A property manager's authority to take possession and control of income-producing real estate and manage its leases, rents, expenses, mortgage payments and accounting in expectation of a fee is established in a **property management agreement.** The *property management agreement* sets out the specific rights, responsibilities and expectations of the property manager and the landlord, including authorized activities, performance standards and expense limitations. [See Figure 1, Form 590]

Authority to operate a rental property

property management agreement
An employment agreement setting the rights, responsibilities and expectations of both the property manager and the landlord. [See **RPI** Form 590]

Landlord responsibilities include providing the property manager with the information and items necessary to manage the property and its tenants, such as:

- lease/rental agreements;
- service and maintenance contracts;
- utilities information;
- keys and security devices;
- security deposits; and
- information on hazard and worker's compensation insurance for the property and employees.

The property management agreement authorizes the property manager to:

- locate tenants;
- enter into rental and lease agreements, including leases for a term of over one year;
- deliver possession of units or space;
- collect rents;
- incur operating expenses; and
- disburse funds to pay expenses, mortgage payments and management fees.[1]

Short-form vs. long-form agreements

Brokers who manage property need to enter into highly detailed property management agreements, not generalized "short-form" property management agreements.

Short-form agreements neither specifically identify nor clarify the performance and expectations of either the property manager or the landlord. Instead, short-form agreements imply industry customs will be followed — whatever those unregulated customs might be or become.

These implied standards, while familiar to the broker, are often misunderstood or unknown to the landlord. Disputes usually result when landlords have high expectations and then receive less than they believe they bargained for when they employed the property manager.

Management obligations detailed in a long-form agreement provide greater protection for a broker from claims they have breached their duties to the landlord. Surprises are eliminated and client expectations are more realistic.

Property managed "as is"

Some landlords want their property maintained at a below-standard level. A broker taking on the management of a property from such a landlord needs to document the maintenance they recommend. This can be accomplished by adding an addendum to the property management agreement or by

---

1   Calif. Civil Code §1624(a)(3)

Figure 1

Form 590

Property Management Agreement

PROPERTY MANAGEMENT AGREEMENT

NOTE: This form is used by a licensed broker or their agent when entering into an employment to act as a property manager for an owner's rental property, to document the employment and set forth the rights, responsibilities and expectations of the property manager and the landlord, including authorized activities, performance standards and expense limitations.

DATE: ______________, 20______, at ____, California.
Items left blank or unchecked are not applicable.

1. RETAINER PERIOD:
1.1 Owner hereby retains and grants Broker the exclusive right to lease, rent, operate and maintain the property as Property Manager, commencing ______________, 20______, and continuing for one year and thereafter until terminated.

2. RECEIPT OF SECURITY DEPOSITS:
2.1 Owner hands $______________ to Broker for deposit into the trust account towards Owner's security deposit obligation to Tenants.

3. RECEIPT OF CASH RESERVE:
3.1 Owner hands $______________ to Broker as a deposit towards Owner's obligation under the agreement.
3.2 Owner to maintain a minimum cash reserve, in addition to any security deposits, in the amount of $______________. On request from Broker, Owner will advance additional funds to maintain this minimum balance.
3.3 The cash reserve may be used to pay costs diligently incurred by Broker or due Broker in fulfilling Broker's obligations.

4. BROKERAGE FEE:
NOTICE: The amount or rate of real estate fees is not fixed by law. They are set by each Broker individually and are negotiable between Owner and Broker.
4.1 Broker compensation to be:
a. ______% of all rents collected and deposited by Broker during the month, except for any first month's rent for which a Broker fee is paid under §4.1 b as follows,
b. ______% of the first month's rent collected and deposited under ☐ rental agreements, and ☐ leases,
c. All sums remaining from credit check fees in excess of credit report expenses, and
d. ☐ Late payment charges and returned check charges paid by a tenant.

5. TRUST ACCOUNT:
5.1 Broker will place Owner's deposit for costs and security deposits into ☐ Broker's trust account, or ☐ separate trust account for Owner, maintained with ______________________ at their ______________________ branch
a. This account will be ☐ non-interest bearing, or ☐ interest bearing.
5.2 All funds received by Broker for the account of Owner will be placed in the trust account.
5.3 Amounts to pay and satisfy the obligations incurred by Broker may be disbursed from the account after payment is due.
5.4 On termination of this agreement, Broker will return to Owner all remaining trust funds belonging to Owner.

6. PERIODIC ACCOUNTING:
6.1 Within ten days after each calendar ☐ month, or ☐ quarter, and on termination of this agreement, Broker will deliver to Owner a Statement of Account for all receipts and expenditures, together with a check to Owner for any funds in excess of minimum reserves under §3.2.
6.2 Amounts to compensate Broker under §4 may be withdrawn from the trust account.
6.3 Each Statement of Account delivered by Broker will include no less than the following information for the period:
a. Amount of security deposits received or refunded.
b. Amount of rent or receipts, itemized by unit.
c. An itemized description of disbursements.
d. End of month balance of the income, expense and security deposit trust accounts.
6.4 ☐ Broker to reserve and disburse from the trust account any property and employee taxes, special assessments, insurance premiums, loan payments and other payments required to be made by the owner.
6.5 Advertising costs incurred to locate new tenants to be paid ☐ by Owner, or ☐ by Broker.

PAGE 1 OF 3 — FORM 590

PAGE 2 OF 3 — FORM 590

7. TITLE CONDITION AND LOANS:
7.1 The property is referred to as ____
7.2 Owner's interest in the property is:
☐ Fee simple, ☐ ______________________________
7.3 Loan payments are to be timely disbursed by Broker to:
a. Lender ______________________________
Address ______________________________
Phone ______________________________
Payment of $______________, due on the ______ day and delinquent on the ______ day of each month.
b. Lender ______________________________
Address ______________________________
Phone ______________________________
Payment of $______________, due on the ______ day and delinquent on the ______ day of each month.

8. BROKER AGREES TO:
8.1 Use diligence in the performance of this employment.
8.2 Continuously maintain a California real estate broker's license.
8.3 Collect all rents, security deposits or other charges and expenses due Owner, and timely refund tenants' security deposits, less allowable deductions and including any interest due tenants.
8.4 Prepare and place advertisements for prospective tenants.
8.5 Show property to prospective tenants, obtain credit reports and confirm creditworthiness of tenants before executing rental or lease agreements.
8.6 Execute, renegotiate or cancel rental or lease agreements with tenants.
No lease to exceed _______ months.
8.7 Serve rent collection and other notices, file unlawful detainer and money damage actions, recover possession of premises or settle with delinquent tenants.
8.8 Inspect the property monthly and each unit when tenants vacate.
8.9 Maintain and periodically confirm the inventory of personal property on premises.
8.10 Evaluate rental and lease agreements periodically for income, expense and provision updates.
8.11 Contract for utilities, services and equipment to operate and maintain the property and safeguard the tenants.
8.12 Contract for any repairs, maintenance or improvements needed to rent or lease the property.
a. Owner to approve all repairs in excess of $______________.
8.13 Obligate Owner to no unauthorized agreement or liability.
8.14 Protect and enhance the goodwill of Owner's rental business and keep confidential and secure any knowledge of Owner's business activities acquired during this employment.
8.15 Hire, supervise and discharge ☐ a resident manager, and ☐ an assistant resident manager.
8.16 Inspect and take any action necessary to comply with federal, state, county or municipal safety and building codes affecting the property.
8.17 Notify Owner of any potential hazards to the tenants or property, and Owner to respond within seven (7) days. Should an emergency situation arise placing the tenants or property in jeopardy, Broker may immediately remedy the situation without further authority from Owner.

9. OWNER AGREES TO:
9.1 Hand Broker all keys and entry codes to the property, and copies of rental and lease agreements with existing tenants.
9.2 Hand Broker (if Broker is to disburse) loan payment coupons/envelopes, property tax bills, insurance premium billings and ______________________.
9.3 Indemnify Broker for the expense of any legal action arising out of Broker's proper performance of this agreement.

PAGE 2 OF 3 — FORM 590

PAGE 3 OF 3 — FORM 590

9.4 Provide public liability, property damage and workers' compensation insurance sufficient in amount to protect Broker and Owner, naming Broker as an additional insured.
9.5 Owner's insurance agent is ______________________________

10. TERMINATION:
10.1 This agreement will continue until terminated by mutual written agreement or until either party, for legally justifiable cause, serves a written Notice of Termination. [See RPI Form 590-2]
10.2 Owner may terminate this agreement at any time during the initial one-year term by paying Broker a fee equal to three times Broker's management fee earned during the month preceding termination.
10.3 On termination, Owner will assume the obligation of any contract entered into by Broker under this agreement.

11. GENERAL PROVISIONS:
11.1 Broker is authorized to place a *For Rent/Lease* sign on the property and publish and disseminate property information.
11.2 Owner authorizes Broker to cooperate with other brokers and divide with them any compensation due.
11.3 The authorized agent-for-service is ☐ Broker, ☐ Owner, ☐ ______________________
11.4 Broker may have or will contract to represent Owners of comparable properties or represent Tenants seeking comparable properties during the retainer period. Thus, a conflict of interest exists to the extent Broker's time is required to fulfill the fiduciary duty owed to others he now does or will represent.
11.5 Before any party to this agreement files an action on a dispute arising out of this agreement which remains unresolved after 30 days of informal negotiations, the parties agree to enter into non-binding mediation administered by a neutral dispute resolution organization and undertake a good faith effort during mediation to settle the dispute.
11.6 The prevailing party in any action on a dispute will be entitled to attorney fees and costs, unless they file an action without first offering to enter into mediation to resolve the dispute.
11.7 If this agreement authorizes Property Manager to execute and negotiate lease terms greater than one year, Landlord acknowledges receipt of the Agency Law Disclosure. [See RPI Form 305]
11.8 ☐ See attached addendum(s) for additional terms. [See RPI Form 250]
11.9 ______________________________

Broker:	**Owner:**
I agree to render services on the terms stated above.	**I agree to employ Broker on the terms stated above.**
☐ See attached Signature Page Addendum. [RPI Form 251]	☐ See attached Signature Page Addendum. [RPI Form 251]
Date: ______________, 20_____	
Broker's Name: ______________	Date: ______________, 20_____
Broker's CalBRE #: ______________	Owner: ______________
Agent: ______________	Signature: ______________
Agent's CalBRE #: ______________	Owner: ______________
Signature: ______________	Signature: ______________
Address: ______________	Address: ______________
Phone: ______________ Cell: ______________	Phone: ______________ Cell: ______________
Email: ______________	Email: ______________

FORM 590 12-14 ©2016 RPI — Realty Publications, Inc., P.O. BOX 5707, RIVERSIDE, CA 92517

For a full-size, fillable copy of this or any other form in this book that may be legally used in your professional practice, go to realtypublications.com/forms

sending estoppel letters to the landlord stating the maintenance situation, the broker's recommendations, and a request for authority to act on the recommendations.

For example, a property manager needs to document a landlord's refusal to maintain landscaping, as overgrown or top-heavy landscaping can result in structural damage, injury to the tenants or a failure of proper security.

Also, a property manager needs to note any advice given, explained and then rejected by the landlord regarding the installation or maintenance of security systems, lighting or other improvements or maintenance needed to eliminate dangerous conditions.

Handling rents and expenses

Property management agreements authorize the property manager to act on behalf of the landlord to handle all income received and incur expenses in the operation of the property.

The property manager's responsibilities regarding the property's income and expenses include:

- collecting rents and other amounts due, such as common area maintenance charges (CAMs) and assessments for property insurance and real estate taxes;
- collecting, accounting for and refunding security deposits;
- paying expenses and mortgage payments from rents received from tenants; and
- complying with any local rent control ordinances.

Trust accounts for the landlord's funds

A property management agreement spells out which maintenance expenses, insurance premiums, utilities, mortgage payments, management fees and property taxes are to be disbursed by the property manager, and which are to be separately paid by the landlord.

The receipt and accounting for cash reserves, security deposits, rent and other sums received from tenants, coin-operated machines and concessions will be handled as trust funds owned by the landlord. Trust funds by their nature need to be deposited into a trust account in the name of the property manager as trustee.

Accounting provisions in the property management agreement:

- authorize the property manager to pay, out of the income and reserve funds held in the trust account, obligations incurred in the management and ownership of the property;
- specify the bank to be used; and
- call for remaining funds held on behalf of the landlord to be disbursed to the landlord periodically and on termination of the property management agreement.

Periodic accounting by the manager

The property management agreement sets the amount of cash reserves the landlord will deposit in the property manager's trust account as a minimum balance for payment of operating expenses and fees.

A landlord is entitled to a statement of accounting:

- at least once a quarter; and

- when the property management agreement is terminated.[2]

The property management agreement sets forth the time periods within which the property manager needs to deliver the statement of accounting to the landlord. While not required on a monthly basis, it is most efficient for a property manager to provide a monthly statement to the landlord since they need to reconcile trust account balances for each client once a month. [See Chapter 9]

The accounting provisions also indicate the property manager will disburse to the landlord, with each accounting, any funds exceeding the minimum balance to be held for reserves. The property manager's authority to withdraw their management fee from the trust account is included.

A property manager who fails to give the landlord a timely and accurate accounting faces loss of their real estate broker license on a complaint from the landlord.[3]

Broker fee enforcement for management services

Property managers cannot enforce collection of their management fees without a *written agreement* with the person agreeing to the payment, typically the landlord.

A prudent property manager will not orally agree with the landlord to the payment of management fees. If the landlord fails to pay fees or interferes with the manager's disbursement of fees, without a signed writing the property manager is unable to enforce their collection.[4]

Thus, the property management agreement sets forth the fees due the property manager.

The property manager needs to also keep all documents connected with any transaction requiring a real estate broker license for three years. These documents include property management and accounting files.[5]

Structuring management fees

Property managers structure management fee schedules in several different ways:

1. *A percentage of the rents collected.*

   The property manager is entitled to charge a set percentage of the rents collected as a fee. Customarily, the fee is typically 5% to 10% of the rents collected and is payable monthly. A percentage fee is a proper method for establishing the amount of fees.

2. *Fixed fee.*

   The property manager and landlord agree in advance to a set dollar amount – a fixed fee – to be charged monthly for management services.

---

2 Calif. Business and Professions Code §10146

3 **Apollo Estates Inc.** v. **Department of Real Estate** (1985) 174 CA3d 625

4 **Phillippe** v. **Shapell Industries Inc.** (1987) 43 C3d 1247

5 Bus & P C §10148

REQUEST FOR HOMEOWNER ASSOCIATION DOCUMENTS
(California Civil Code §1368.2)

NOTE: This form is used by a seller's agent when preparing a listing/marketing package or performing a due diligence investigation on a unit in a common interest development (CID), to obtain homeowners' association (HOA) documents for disclosing the condition of the property and CID to a buyer.

DATE: _____, 20_____, at _____, California.

TO HOMEOWNERS' ASSOCIATION (HOA):
HOA's name _____
Representative's name _____
Address _____
_____
Phone _____ Cell _____
Email _____

FROM SELLER'S AGENT:
Agent's name _____
Broker's name _____
Address _____
_____
Phone _____ Cell _____
Email _____

1. Property address: _____
    _____
    Seller of property: _____
    Seller's mailing address: _____

2. The HOA is kindly requested to provide the Seller's Agent with the HOA documents referenced on page two and three within 10 calendar days of this request.

3. The HOA is authorized by the Seller to supply Seller's Agent the requested copies of the HOA documents.

4. Once complete:
    ☐ mail a physical copy of the requested documents to Seller's Agent's address above;
    ☐ email a copy of the requested documents to Seller's Agent at _____.
       CC Seller at _____; or
    ☐ inform Seller's Agent where the requested documents are available in digital form online.

5. Please send the HOA's billing for the actual costs of copying and delivering the requested documents to Seller's Agent.

I agree to the terms stated above
Date: _____, 20 _____
Seller's Name: _____

Signature: _____
Seller's Name: _____

Signature: _____

Date: _____, 20 _____
Broker's Name: _____
CalBRE#: _____
Agent's Name: _____
CalBRE#: _____

Signature: _____

------- PAGE 1 OF 3 — FORM 135 -------

The amount stays constant whether or not the units are rented. This method, while proper, lacks the motivational incentive to induce the property manager to generate maximum rental income.

3. *Fixed fee per unit.*

Usually applied to large apartment complexes or condominium associations, a set dollar amount is charged for each unit the property manager manages. In addition to the basic fee, property managers often charge a one-time fee each time a unit is re-rented.

4. *A percentage of the first month's rent.*

A front-end fee paid to the property manager is called a **leasing** or **origination fee.** If the landlord agrees, a fee can be charged when any tenant exercises an option to renew or extend, or when the premises is relet to an existing tenant.

Fees are negotiated and set between each individual property manager and landlord.[6]

However, no matter how customary and prevalent it is in the real estate industry to collectively and conscientiously charge a particular percentage fee, fees may not be set by collusion between brokers, or as a result of peer pressure among brokers to maintain equivalent fees. Unfortunately, this conduct still permeates the brokerage industry as a violation of antitrust laws in the form of conscious parallelism.[7]

common interest developments
Condominiums projects, cooperatives or single family residences in a planned unit development. [See **RPI** Form 135]

Management of CIDs

Developments consisting of condominiums, cooperatives or single family residences (SFRs) in a planned unit development (PUD) are projects called **common interest developments (CIDs).** Brokers may be retained by the homeowners' associations (HOAs) of CIDs to manage membership, exercise control over the common areas and structures and account for assessment revenues, expenses and reserves. A broker who acts as a CID manager is called a managing agent.

Before a broker enters into a property management agreement to act as a **managing agent** for a CID, the broker needs to disclose:

managing agent
A broker who manages membership, common areas and accounting for a common interest development.

- the names and addresses of the owners of the their employing brokerage company if it is an entity;

- the relevant licensing of the owners, such as for architectural design, construction, engineering, real estate or accounting, and the effective dates of the licenses;

- the relevant professional designations held by the owners, what organizations issued the designation, the issuance dates and any expiration dates;[8]

- fidelity insurance sufficient to cover the current year's operating and reserve funds of the association;

- the possession of any real estate license and whether or not the license is active; and

- if certified to manage CIDs, the name, address and telephone number of the organization issuing the certification, the date the broker was certified and certification status.[9] [See Chapter 7]

Funds received by the managing agent belong to the HOA. If the HOA does not have a bank account, the managing agent will maintain a separate trust fund account as trustee for the HOA funds. Extensive statutory controls are placed on the handling of the trust fund account held for CIDs.[10]

---

6 Bus & P C §10147.5
7 **People** v. **National Association of Realtors** (1984) 155 CA3d 578
8 CC §5375
9 Bus & P C §11504
10 CC §5380

Upon the sale of any unit in a CID, the managing agent may be required to supply a prospective buyer with documentation of *CID covenants, conditions and restrictions (CC&Rs)* as well as accounting, insurance information and any fees, fines or levies assessed against the seller's interest in the property. Also liens against the seller's interest in the CID unit for any unpaid late fees or accrued interest are disclosed by the managing agent on request prior to the transfer of title.[11] [See Figure 2, Form 135]

---

11 CC § 4525

Chapter 8 Summary

A property management agreement sets out the specific rights, responsibilities and expectations of both the property manager and the landlord. Property management agreements authorize the property manager to handle and account for all income received and expenses incurred in the operation of the property.

Property management agreements also set the fees paid to the property manager, structured as:

- a percentage of the rents collected;
- a fixed fee for the manager's monthly management services;
- a fixed fee per unit; or
- a percentage of the first month's rent.

Brokers retained to manage common interest developments (CIDs) are called managing agents. A managing agent needs to perform duties specific to CIDs upon entering into a property management agreement with the homeowners' association controlling a CID.

Chapter 8 Key Terms

common interest developments .... pg. 85
managing agent .... pg. 85
property management agreement .... pg. 80

Quiz 2 Covering Chapters 5-8 is located on page 634.

A property manager's responsibilities

Chapter

9

After reading this chapter, you will be able to:

- recognize and act on a property manager's responsibilities and obligations owed the landlord;
- generate a reasonable income from a rental property while maintaining its safety, security and habitability;
- conduct property operations in compliance with the prudent investor standard;
- diligently manage trust accounts for funds received while managing a property; and
- implement a property manager's best practices in fulfilling the responsibilities of their employment.

Learning Objectives

commingling	**start-up fee**
property profile	**trust account**
prudent investor standard	**trust funds**

Key Terms

Property management is an economically viable and personally rewarding real estate service permitted for real estate licensees. Serious brokers and agents often turn their attention from an interest in residential sales to the specialized and more disciplined industry of property management.

A broker's primary objective as a property manager operating a rental property is to:

- fill vacancies with suitable tenants;
- collect rent;
- incur and pay expenses; and
- account to the landlord.

An evolving standard of conduct

Thus, a property manager needs to have spent time accumulating experience by actively overseeing and operating like-type rental properties before being entrusted to their management.

Recall that in California, an individual who acts as a property manager on behalf of another for a fee needs to hold a valid Department of Real Estate (DRE) broker license. Any licensed agent or broker associate employed by the broker acts on behalf of their broker, not independent of their broker.[1] [See Chapter 7]

The duty of care a property manager owes a landlord is the same duty of care and protection a broker in real estate sales owes their sellers and buyers. As a property manager, the broker is an agent acting in capacity of a trustee on behalf of the landlord. Agents acting on behalf of the broker perform property management services as authorized by the broker.

A property manager's real estate broker license may be revoked or suspended if the property manager demonstrates negligence or incompetence in performing their management tasks. This includes negligent supervision of their employees, be they licensed or unlicensed employees.[2]

Requisite competence to manage

To be successful in the property management field, a broker initially acquires the minimum knowledge and experience through training sufficient to adequately perform their tasks.

A broker acquires property management expertise through:

- courses required to qualify for and maintain a real estate license;[3]
- on-the-job training as an agent;
- experience as a landlord;
- practical experience in the business management field; and/or
- exposure to related or similar management activities.

Owners measure how capable a broker will be at handling their properties by judging the caliber of the broker's management skills. Most owners look to hire an experienced property manager with well-earned credentials and a responsive staff who will perform to the landlord's expectations.

Other indicators that a property manager will successfully handle rental property include:

- prior experience handling and reporting **trust account** activities;
- a knowledge of current programs used to record and track activity on each property managed by the property manager; and
- a competent staff to perform office and field duties and to quickly respond to both the landlord's and the tenants' needs.

trust account
An account separate and apart and physically segregated from a broker's own funds, in which the broker is required by law to deposit all funds received for clients.

---

1   Calif. Business and Professions Code §§10130, 10131(b)
2   Bus & P C §§10177(g), 10177(h)
3   Bus & P C §§10153.2, 10170.5

A property manager's obligations to a landlord include:

- holding a broker license;
- diligently performing the duties of their employment;
- sufficient oversight of the broker's employees acting on behalf of the landlord;
- handling and accounting for all income and expenses produced by the property;
- contracting for services, repairs and maintenance on the property as authorized;
- monitoring utility services provided by the landlord;
- advertising for prospective tenants;
- showing the property and qualifying tenants;
- negotiating and executing rental and lease agreements;
- responding in a timely manner to the needs of the tenants;
- evaluating rental and lease agreements periodically;
- serving notices on tenants and filing *unlawful detainer (UD)* actions as needed;
- performing regular periodic property inspections; and
- keeping secure any personal property.

In addition to these tasks, the property manager:

- confirms the existence of or obtains general liability and workers' compensation insurance sufficient to protect the landlord, naming the property manager as an additionally insured;
- obligates the landlord to only those agreements authorized by the landlord;
- maintains the property's earning power, called **goodwill**;
- hires and fires resident managers and other on-site employees as needed;
- complies with all applicable codes affecting the property; and
- notifies the landlord of any potentially hazardous conditions or criminal activities affecting the health and safety of individuals on or about the property.

Management obligations owed the landlord

A property manager has a duty to employ a higher standard of conduct regarding the operation of a property than a typical landlord might apply. This standard is called the **prudent investor standard**.

A prudent investor is a person who has the knowledge and expertise to determine the wisest conduct for reasonably managing a property. The *prudent investor standard* is the minimum level of competency expected of a property manager by a landlord, whether or not the landlord is familiar with it.

The prudent investor standard

prudent investor standard
A property management standard reflecting the expectations of a well-informed investor for efficient and effective management of rental income and expenses.

In contrast, the expectations of resident and non-resident landlords may not necessarily be based on obtaining the maximum rental income or incurring only those minimal expenses needed to maintain the long-term income flow of rents from tenants.

Resident owners are more apt to maintain property in a condition which they find personally satisfying, not necessarily in accord with sound economic principles. Often they are not concerned about the effect of the marketplace on their property's value until it is time to sell or refinance.

Likewise, the landlord may not have the *knowledge* or *expertise* to effectively manage the property. Most owners of rental income property pursue unrelated occupations which leave them very little time to concentrate on the management of their properties.

However, property managers are employed to manage property as their primary occupation, one in which they have developed an expertise. A landlord's primary reason for hiring a property manager is to have the property manager maintain the condition of the property at the least cost necessary and keep the rental income stable and as high as the market permits at a reasonable vacancy rate.

Thus, the property manager bases decisions on the need to generate the maximum income from the property and incur only those expenses necessary to maintain the property's good will and preserve the safety, security and habitability of the property.

Property analysis to understand the tasks

To conduct property operations in compliance with the *prudent investor standard*, a property manager considers the following factors:

- the type of the property and its niche in the market;
- the socioeconomic demographics of the area surrounding the property's location;
- the competition currently existing in the local market;
- the current physical condition of the property; and
- the existing liens on the property.

The manager's ability to locate tenants willing and able to pay the rent rate sought by the landlord depends on the competition in the area of the property.

For example, when more tenants seek space than there are units available to rent, the property manager may be able to increase the rent (excluding units covered by rent control ordinances) and still maintain occupancy levels.

Conversely, if the number of rental units or spaces available exceeds the quantity of tenants available to occupy them, a property manager has less pricing power. Special programs to better retain tenants and attract new, long-term ones may be necessary to keep the units at optimum levels of occupancy.

The current physical condition (particularly *curb appeal*) of the property reflects the attitude of the ownership towards tenants. A property manager needs to analyze the repairs, maintenance, landscaping and improvements needed to improve the property's visual appearance and ambiance. Then, they are able to determine the amount of cost involved for any upgrade and the amount of rent increase the upgrades will bring in. The analytical property manager works up a cost-benefits analysis and reviews it with the landlord to consider what will or will not be done.

A prospective tenant's immediate concern when viewing rental property will be the lure of the landscaping, the freshness of exterior finish and the overall care and tidiness of the premises. More importantly, existing tenants stay or leave based on these observances.

Along with the condition of the property, a property manager operating commercial property reviews the status of trust deed liens on the landlord's property. Both the property manager and the tenants are ultimately affected by the burden existing financing places on the landlord's cash flow, and possibly the landlord's ability to retain ownership.

A property manager cannot perform economic miracles for a landlord when payments on the financing encumbering the property are inconsistent with the property's capacity to generate sufficient rents to produce a positive cash flow after mortgage payments. Worse yet, in some cases mortgage payments may consume such a high percentage of rents as to obstruct payment of maintenance or property management fees.

Also, a thoughtful property manager will apprise the landlord when the opportunity arises in the mortgage market to refinance the property with more advantageously structured financing. The property manager may charge an additional fee for soliciting or arranging financing. [See **RPI** Form 104]

The tenant's right to possess the property is usually subject to an existing lender's right to foreclose and terminate the tenancy. A commercial tenant's move-in costs and tenant improvements are at risk of loss if the pre-existing lender forecloses.

It is good practice, and in the property manager's best interest, to run a cursory title check on the property they intend to manage.

A *title check*, commonly called a **property profile**, is supplied online by title companies. A *property profile* will confirm:

- how ownership is vested and who has authority to employ management;
- the liens on the property and their foreclosure status;
- any use restrictions affecting tenants; and
- comparable sales information for the area.

Liens affect commercial tenants

Title profile analysis avoids surprises

property profile
A report from a title company providing information about a property's ownership, encumbrances, use restrictions and comparable sales data.

Any discrepancy between information provided by the landlord and a property profile report is resolved with the landlord prior to taking over management of the property.

Due diligence and the paper trail

A property manager's efforts to locate tenants are documented on a **file activity sheet** maintained for each property. This paper trail is evidence the property manager has diligently pursued activities leading to the renting and maintenance of the property. Keeping a *file activity sheet* reduces the risk of claims that the property manager failed to diligently seek tenants or operate the property.

For example, any advertisements placed by the property manager need to focus on and clearly identify the property to be rented. When the advertisement identifies the property, the landlord is properly billed for the expense of the advertisement. Whenever an advertisement is placed, a purchase order is prepared, whether or not the paperwork is given to the publisher or printer.

As in any business, a purchase order contains the dates the advertisement is to run, the advertising copy, which vendor (newspaper or printer) it was placed with and the property to be charged. This billing referencing the purchase order is a written or computer generated reminder to the property manager of their activity and which landlord to charge. Computer programs for bookkeeping provide for the entry, control and printout of this data.

The goal in property management is to make a diligent effort to locate a tenant and rent the property as quickly as possible.

Failing to set or keep appointments to meet with prospective tenants is inexcusable neglect. Prospective tenants do respond to an advertisement. Thus, the property manager or an office employee needs to be available to show them the property, unless the property has a resident or on-site manager.

When the property manager cannot timely perform or complete the management tasks undertaken, they need to delegate some of this work load to administrative employees or resident managers. This delegation is permitted since the property manager is charged with oversight as the responsible supervisor and employer.

Handling UD actions in small claims

A property manager may file a small claims action on behalf of the landlord to recover amounts due and unpaid under a lease or rental agreement if:

- the landlord has retained the property manager under a property management agreement;
- the agreement was not entered into solely to represent the landlord in small claims court; and
- the claim relates to the rental property managed.[4]

---

4 Calif. Code of Civil Procedure §116.540(h)

A property manager may also file small claims actions to collect money on behalf of a *homeowners' association (HOA)* created to manage a *common interest development (CID).*[5]

However, for the property manager to represent the landlord in a small claims action, the property manager is required to file a declaration in the action stating the property manager:

- is authorized by the landlord to appear on the landlord's behalf under a property management agreement; and
- is not employed solely to represent the landlord in small claims court. [6]

Consider a licensed real estate broker who operates a property management business as a sole proprietorship under their individual DRE broker license. The broker manages an apartment complex for a landlord under a property management agreement.

A party other than the landlord files the UD

The property management agreement gives the broker all care and management responsibilities for the complex, including the authority to:

- enter into leases and rental agreements as the landlord;
- file UD actions; and
- hire an attorney to handle evictions, if necessary.

The broker signs all lease and rental agreements in their own name *as the landlord* under the authority given them in the management contract. The landlord's name does not appear on any lease or rental agreement as authorized by the terms of the property management agreement.

A tenant of the complex fails to pay rent under a rental agreement entered into with the broker. The broker serves a three-day notice to pay rent or quit the premise on the tenant. [See **RPI** Form 575]

The tenant does not pay the delinquent rent within three days and remains on the premises. The broker files a UD action to recover possession by an eviction of the tenant, appearing as the named plaintiff on the UD complaint.

The tenant defends against the eviction by claiming the broker may not maintain a UD action to evict the tenant since the broker is not the owner of the real estate or the owner's attorney.

May the broker file and maintain a UD action against the tenant in their own name?

Yes! The broker may file and persecute the UD action even though they are not the true landlord (owner). The broker entered into the lease agreement and delivered possession as the named lessor on the rental or lease agreement, and is now recovering possession from the tenant in their own name as the lessor.[7]

---

5 CCP §116.540(i)

6 CCP §116.540(j)

7 **Allen** v. **Dailey** (1928) 92 CA 308

As the lessor under the lease, the property manager has the greater right of possession of the premises than the tenant, even though the owner is known by the court to be the true landlord.

Thus, as the lessor named on the lease, the property manager may maintain the UD action against the tenant and recover possession of the premises.

A property manager's frequent and well-documented inspections of property are nearly as important as their accurate accounting of income and expenses through their *trust account*. Inspections determine the:

- physical condition of the property;
- availability of habitable units or commercial space; and
- use of the leased premises by existing tenants.

Property inspections by the manager

When a property manager conducts an inspection of the property, they do so for one of several key situations:

1. *When the property manager and landlord enter into a property management agreement.*

   Any deferred maintenance or defect which might interfere with the renting of the property is to be discussed with the landlord. The property manager resolves the discrepancy by either correcting the problem or noting it is to be left "as is." However, conditions which might endanger the health and safety of tenants and their guests may not be left "as-is."

2. *When the property manager rents to a tenant.*

   A walk-through is conducted with a new tenant prior to giving them occupancy. The property's condition is noted on a condition of premises addendum form and signed by the tenant. [See **RPI** Form 560]

3. *During the term of the lease.*

   While the tenant is in possession, the property is periodically inspected by the property manager to make sure it is being properly maintained. Notes on the date, time and observations are made in the property management file. File notes are used to refresh the property manager's memory of the last inspection, order out maintenance and evidence the property manager's diligence.

4. *Two weeks prior to a residential tenant vacating.*

   Residential property is inspected prior to termination of possession if the tenant requests a joint pre-expiration inspection on receipt of the mandatory notice of right to a wear and tear analysis to be sent by the landlord or the property manager. [See Chapter 19]

5. *When the tenant vacates.*

   The property's condition is compared against its condition documented when first occupied by the tenant. Based on any differences in the property's condition, a reasonable amount may be deducted from the tenant's security deposit for the cost of corrective repairs. Cost deductions are to be documented when accounting for the return of the deposit.

6. *When the broker returns management and possession of the property back to the landlord or over to another management firm.*

   Documenting all property inspections helps avoid disputes with the landlord or tenants regarding the condition of the property when possession or management was transferred to and from the property manager.

The property's condition is noted on a form, such as a condition of property disclosure, and approved by the property manager and the landlord. The property manager keeps a copy in the property's file as part of the paper trail maintained on the property. [See **RPI** Form 304]

Inspections that coincide with key events help establish who is responsible for any deferred maintenance and upkeep or any damage to the property.

On entering into a property management agreement, a broker conducts a comprehensive review of all lease and rental agreement forms used by the landlord, including changes and the use of other forms proposed by the broker.

Periodic review of the leases

Also, the competent property manager prepares a worksheet containing the dates of lease expirations, rent adjustments, tenant sales reports, renewal or extension deadlines, and grace periods for rent payments and late charges. Computer programs have made this tracking easier.

Periodic evaluations by the property manager of existing leases and rental agreements are undertaken to minimize expenses and maximize rental income. Vacant units are evaluated to determine the type of tenant and tenancy desired (periodic versus fixed-term), how rents will be established and which units consistently under-perform.

The amount of rental income receipts is directly related to the property manager's evaluation of the rents charged and implementation of any changes. A re-evaluation of rents includes the consideration of factors which influence the amount to charge for rent. These factors include:

- market changes, such as a decrease or increase in the number of tenants competing for a greater or lesser availability of units;
- the physical condition and appearance of the property; and
- the property's location, such as its proximity to employment, shopping, transportation, schools, financial centers, etc.

A property manager's duty includes keeping abreast of market changes which affect the property's future rental rates. With this information, they are able to make the necessary changes when negotiating leases and rental agreements. The more curious and perceptive the property manager

Awareness of market changes

is about tenant demands and available units/spaces as future trends, the more protection the landlord's investment will likely receive against loss of potential income.

Maintenance and repairs as a responsibility

Obtaining the highest rents available requires constant maintenance and repair of the property. Possibly, this includes the elimination of physical obsolescence brought on by ageing. The property manager is responsible for all the maintenance and repairs on the property while employed by the landlord. This responsibility still exists if the property manager delegates the maintenance of the units to the tenants in lease agreements.

The *responsibility for maintenance* includes:

- determining necessary repairs and replacements;
- contracting for repairs and replacements;
- confirming completion of repairs and replacements;
- paying for completed repairs and replacements; and
- advising the landlord about the status of repairs and replacements in a monthly report.

Different types of property require different degrees of maintenance and upkeep. For instance, a commercial or industrial tenant who occupies the entire property under a net lease agreement will perform all maintenance and upkeep of the property. [See **RPI** Form 552-2 and 552-3]

The broker, as the property manager, then has a greatly reduced role in the care and maintenance of the property under a net lease agreement. The property manager simply oversees the tenant to confirm they are caring for the property and otherwise fully performing the terms of the lease agreement.

Property manager of an HOA

On the other hand, consider an HOA requirement that maintains common areas for the benefit of the homeowners within a CID. The HOA hires a property manager to undertake these duties. A property manager acting on behalf of an HOA exercises a high degree of control over the maintenance and upkeep of the property and the security of the occupants. The management of a CID is nearly comparable to the management of any other multi-tenant structure, such as an apartment building which has not been converted to a CID.

Usually, landlords set a ceiling on the dollar amount of repairs and maintenance the property manager has authority to incur on behalf of the landlord. The property manager does not exceed this dollar ceiling without the landlord's consent even though the landlord receives a benefit from the expenditure.

A property manager discloses to their employing landlord any financial benefit the property manager receives from:

- maintenance or repair work done by the property manager's staff; or
- any other materials purchased or services performed.

When benefiting from repairs, the property manager prepares a repair and maintenance disclosure addendum and attaches it to the property management agreement. This addendum covers information such as:

- the types of repairs and maintenance the manager's staff will perform;
- hourly charges for jobs performed;
- costs of workers' compensation and method for charging the landlord;
- any service or handling charges for purchasing parts, materials or supplies (usually a percentage of the cost);
- whether the staff will perform work when they are available and qualified, in lieu of contracting the work out (i.e., no bids will be taken); and
- to what extent repairs and maintenance will generate net revenue for the management company, constituting additional income to the property manager.

To eliminate the risk of accepting undisclosed earnings, the property manager makes a written disclosure of any ownership interests or fee arrangements they may have with vendors performing work, such as landscapers, plumbers, etc.

Undisclosed earnings received by the property manager for work performed by the property manager or others on the landlord's property are improperly received and can be recovered by the landlord. [See **RPI** Form 119]

Additionally, the landlord may recover any other brokerage fees they have already paid when the property manager improperly or intentionally takes undisclosed earnings while acting as the landlord's agent.[8]

The way a property is operated develops a level of **goodwill** with tenants. Economically, *goodwill* equates to the earning power of the property. A property manager in the ordinary course of managing property will concentrate on increasing the intangible image — goodwill — of the property.

Goodwill is maintained, and hopefully increased, when the property manager:

- cares for the appearance of the property;
- maintains an appropriate tenant mix (without employing prohibited discriminatory selection); and
- gives effective and timely attention to the tenants' concerns.

---

8 Jerry v. Bender (1956) 143 CA2d 198

A prudent property manager makes recommendations to the landlord about maintaining the property to eliminate any accumulated wear and tear, deterioration or obsolescence. Thus, they help enhance the property's "curb appeal."

The manager who fails to promptly complete necessary repairs or correctly maintain the property may be impairing the property's goodwill built up with tenants and the public. Allowing the property or the tenancies to deteriorate will expose the property manager to liability for the decline in revenue.

Reserves and deposits in the trust account

To accommodate the flow of income and expenditures from the properties and monies they manage, the property manager maintains a trust account in their name, as trustee, at a bank or financial institution.[9]

Generally, a property manager receives a cash deposit as a reserve balance from the landlord. The sum of money includes a **start-up fee**, a cash reserve for costs and the tenants' security deposits.

A *start-up fee* is usually a flat, one-time management fee charged by the property manager to become sufficiently familiar with the property and its operations to commence management activities.

The cash reserve is a set amount of cash the landlord agrees to maintain as a minimum balance in the broker's trust account. The cash reserve is used to pay costs incurred when costs and mortgage payments exceed rental income receipts. Security deposit amounts are separate from the client's cash reserves.

The prudent property manager insists that all security deposits previously collected from existing tenants are deposited into the property manager's trust account.

The security deposits need to be accounted for separately from other client funds in the trust account, though this separation of a client's funds is not required. Security deposits belong to the tenant, though the landlord and the property manager have no obligation to handle them differently than funds owned by the landlord.

On a tenant vacating, their deposit is returned, less reasonable deductions. For a residential tenant, an accounting is mailed within 21 days of the tenant's departure. For commercial properties, the security deposit accounting is mailed 30 days after a commercial tenant's departure.[10] [See Chapter 19]

A property manager is required to deposit all funds collected on behalf of a landlord into a trust account within three business days of receipt. These funds are called **trust funds**.

start-up fee
A flat, one-time fee charged by a property manager for the time and effort taken to become sufficiently familiar with the operations of the property to commence management.

trust funds
Items which have or evidence monetary value held by a broker for a client when acting in a real estate transaction.

---

9 Calif. Code of Regulations §2830
10 Calif. Civil Code §1950.5(g)(1); 1950.7(c)(1)

Trust funds collected by a property manager include:

- security deposits;
- rents;
- cash reserves; and
- start-up fees.[11]

Again, trust accounts are maintained in accordance with standard accounting procedures. These standards are best met by using computer software designed for property management.[12]

Also, withdrawals from the trust fund account may not be made by the landlord, only by the property manager.

However, a property manager may give written consent to allow a licensed employee or an unlicensed employee who is bonded to make withdrawals from the trust account.[13]

No matter who the property manager authorizes to make the withdrawal, the property manager alone is responsible for the accurate daily maintenance of the trust account.[14]

The property manager's bookkeeping records for each trust account maintained at a bank or thrift include entries of:

- the amount, date of receipt and source of all trust funds deposited;
- the date the trust funds were deposited in the trust account;
- the date and check number for disbursements of trust funds previously deposited in the trust account; and
- the daily balance of the trust account.[15]

Entries in the general ledger for the overall trust account are kept in chronological order and in a column format. Ledgers may be maintained in a written journal or one generated by a computer software program.[16]

In addition to the general ledger of the entire trust account, the property manager maintains a separate **subaccount ledger** for each landlord they represent. Each *subaccount ledger* accounts for all trust funds deposited into or disbursed from a separate landlord's trust account.

Each separate, individual subaccount ledger identifies the parties to each entry and include:

- the date and amount of trust funds deposited;

**Separate
ledger for
each landlord**

**Separate
subaccount
ledger for
each landlord**

---

11 Bus & P C §10145(a); California Bureau of Real Estate Regulations §2832
12 DRE Reg. §2831
13 DRE Reg. §2834(a)
14 DRE Reg. §2834(c)
15 DRE Reg. §2831(a)
16 DRE Reg. §2831(c)

- the date, check number and amount of each related disbursement from the trust account;

- the date and amount of any interest earned on funds in the trust fund account; and

- the total amount of trust funds remaining after each deposit or disbursement from the trust account.[17]

Like the general ledger for the entire trust account, entries in each client's subaccount record are kept in chronological order, in columns and on a written or computer journal/ledger.[18]

Manager's trust account supervision

If a property manager or their employees delay the proper maintenance of a trust account, the property manager is in violation of their duty to the landlord to maintain the trust account. This violation places the broker's license at risk of loss or suspension.

To avoid mishandling of the trust account, the property manager:

- deposits the funds received, whether in cash, check or other form of payment, within three business days;[19]

- keeps trust fund account records for three years after the transaction;[20]

- keeps a separate ledger or record of deposits and expenditures itemized by each transaction and for each landlord;[21] and

- keeps accurate trust account records for all receipts and disbursements.[22]

Accounting to the landlord

Tied to the property manager's duty to properly maintain their trust account is the duty to account to the landlord.

All landlords are entitled to a statement of accounting no less than at the end of each calendar quarter (i.e., March, June, September and December).

The accounting is to include the following information:

- the name of the property manager;

- the name of the landlord;

- a description of the services rendered;

- the identification of the trust fund account credited;

- the amount of funds collected to date;

- the amount disbursed to date;

- the amount, if any, of fees paid to field agents or leasing agents;

- the overhead costs; and

---

17 DRE Reg. §2831.1
18 DRE Reg. §2831.1(b)
19 DRE Reg. §2832
20 Bus & P C §10148
21 DRE Reg. §2831.1
22 DRE Reg. §2831

- a breakdown of the advertising costs, a copy of the advertisement, the name of the newspaper or publication and the dates the advertisement ran.

Also, the property manager hands the landlord a full accounting when the property management agreement expires or is terminated. Any discrepancy or failure by the property manager to properly account for the trust funds will be resolved against them and in favor of the landlord. Even if the property manager's only breach is sloppy or inaccurate accounting, they are responsible as though misappropriation and commingling occurred.

Although the property manager is required to account to the landlord no less than once each calendar quarter, best practices call for a monthly accounting. They may then rightly collect their fee at the end of each month after they have fully performed and their fee is due. In this way, the property manager avoids the receipt of advance fees. Accounting for the collection of advance fees requires a DRE-approved form.[23]

Again, a property manager on the receipt of monies while acting on behalf of the landlord places them into a *trust account*. As trust funds, these monies need to be diligently managed to avoid claims of mishandling, misappropriation or the **commingling** of the landlord's funds with the property manager's personal funds.

Consider a landlord who hires a broker to act as a property manager. In addition to paying for expenses and costs incurred, the property manager is instructed and authorized to pay the monthly mortgage payments.

The property manager locates a tenant and collects the initial rent and security deposit. After depositing the funds in the property manager's trust account, but prior to disbursing the mortgage payment, the property manager withdraws:

- the leasing fee for locating the tenant; and
- the monthly property manager's fee.

Both fees are due the property manager for work completed under the property management contract.

However, the withdrawal of the property manager's fees leaves insufficient funds in the trust account to make the authorized mortgage payment. The property manager then issues a check on funds held in one of the property manager's personal accounts to make the landlord's mortgage payment. However, this account also has insufficient funds.

Meanwhile, the lender sends the landlord a late payment notice for the mortgage delinquency. The landlord immediately contacts the property manager regarding the delinquent payment. The property manager says they will cover it and does so.

Handling of trust account funds

commingling
The mixing of personal funds with client or third-party funds held in trust.

---

23 Bus & P C §10146

More than three months later, the landlord terminates the property management agreement.

Failure to account for funds

Continuing the previous example, the property manager sends a closing statement on the account containing some erroneous deductions. The closing statement is the only accounting the property manager ever prepared for the landlord.

After discussion with the landlord, the property manager corrects the errors in the closing statement, issues the landlord a check for the remaining balance, closes the account and destroys the landlord's file.

Later, the landlord files a complaint with the DRE regarding the property manager's conduct while under contract.

The DRE investigates and concludes the property manager breached their agency duties. The property manager issued a check for a mortgage payment from an account other than the trust account, an activity that automatically constitutes *commingling* of the property manager's personal funds with trust funds.

Also, the property manager knew they had insufficient funds when they issued the check. This constituted a dishonest act.

In addition, the property manager failed to accurately account for funds taken in or expended on behalf of the landlord. Worse, the property manager neglected their duty to provide an accounting at least every quarter.

Finally, the property manager destroyed the records prior to the expiration of the three-year minimum record keeping requirement. Based on these many violations, the DRE properly revokes the property manager's real estate broker license.[24]

Management conflicts with sales operations

A broker who operates a real estate sales office, in conjunction with a property management operation, has a potential conflict of interest that may need to be disclosed to their clients.

For example, a creditworthy prospective tenant responding to a rental advertisement might be swayed by the broker's sales staff to purchase a residence instead of renting. Sales fees are typically greater than leasing fees for the time spent. Conversely, sales fees are one-shot fees, not continuously recurring fees.

Any active attempt to convert a prospective tenant to a buyer when the prospect has responded to a rental advertisement paid for by a landlord or provided as part of the property management services, suggests improper conduct. The broker's conduct may range from "bait and switch" techniques

---

24 **Apollo Estates Inc.** v. **Department of Real Estate** (1985) 174 CA3d 625

with prospective tenants to diverting the landlord's existing tenants through efforts purportedly expended on the landlord's behalf or interfering with the landlord's best interests.

A property manager takes care to keep their sales and management operations sufficiently separate from one another. When in contact with a creditworthy prospective tenant applying to rent a property they manage, the manager needs to diligently pursue rental or lease agreements with them. The conflict of interest arising when a client seeks the same or different purposes does not bar a broker from conflicting activities so long as the conflict has been timely and properly disclosed. [See **RPI** Form 527]

The landlord comes first. The broker's concern for greater fees comes second.

A property manager employs a higher standard of conduct regarding their operation of a property than a typical landlord might, referred to as a prudent investor standard. The property manager applies this higher standard of conduct when:

- overseeing the maintenance of rental property;
- filling vacancies with suitable tenants;
- collecting rents;
- handling trust funds; and
- accounting to the landlord.

All trust accounts are to be maintained in accordance with standard accounting procedures. A property manager needs to be diligent in the management of their trust accounts to avoid claims of mishandling, misappropriation or commingling of funds. The property manager is also required to provide the landlord they represent with a statement of their separate account.

Chapter 9 Summary

Chapter 9 Key Terms

Quiz 3 Covering Chapters 9-13 is located on page 635.

Notes:

Chapter
10

Resident managers

After reading this chapter, you will be able to:

- use a resident manager agreement to employ a manager to oversee the daily management of a property;
- describe the duties generally performed by a resident manager, such as screening tenants, negotiating leases, collecting rents and serving notices;
- comply with minimum wage requirements for resident managers; and
- properly terminate a resident manager's employment and occupancy.

resident manager   **resident manager agreement**

Learning Objectives

Key Terms

Employees: not independent contractors, not tenants

A broker, retained to manage a residential income property, enters into an employment agreement with a *resident manager* to oversee the daily management of the property. This employment agreement is called a **resident manager agreement**. [See Form 591 accompanying this chapter]

Under the *resident manager agreement*, the resident manager:

- acknowledges employment by the property manager;
- accepts the occupancy and use of an apartment unit rent-free as compensation for the employment; and
- agrees to vacate the property on termination of employment.

The resident manager's job is to show vacant units, run credit checks, negotiate and sign leases, collect rents, supervise repairs and maintenance, serve notices and perform other non-discretionary administrative activities.

Later, the property manager terminates the resident manager's employment.

The property manager demands the resident manager immediately vacate the premises and relinquish possession of the unit.

However, the resident manager claims to be a tenant, entitled to a notice and time to vacate, not just a notice terminating employment and their right of possession of the unit. [See Chapter 29]

Is the resident manager entitled to a notice and time to vacate on termination of employment?

No! A resident manager who continues to occupy a unit after their employment is terminated becomes a holdover tenant. They unlawfully detain the unit and have no right to a notice other than the notice terminating their employment. A resident manager's *occupancy is fixed*, not periodic. It is established in the resident manager agreement that the resident manager's tenancy ends on the date their employment is terminated.[1] [See Form 591 §§4.2 and 4.9]

Also, the resident manager's eviction by an unlawful detainer (UD) action is not protected by rent control ordinances. Further, they may not defend their continued possession by demanding the property manager or landlord show good cause for terminating their employment.[2]

If the resident manager does not relinquish possession on termination of the resident manager's employment, the property manager may immediately file a UD action, without further notice, to have the resident manager evicted.

However, a resident manager agreement may provide for the creation of a tenancy following the termination of a resident manager's employment. When a tenancy is agreed to, the resident manager's right of possession is not terminated on termination of the resident manager employment, but under landlord-tenant rules of notice before eviction.[3]

Resident manager activities

A **resident manager** is an individual employed by the property manager or landlord to live on-site at the managed complex and see to its daily operations. A *resident manager's* duties may include:

- screening tenants and negotiating leases;
- cleaning vacated units;
- supervising landscaping, maintenance and repairs;
- serving notices; or
- attending to tenant inquiries.

resident manager
An individual employed by the property manager or landlord to live onsite at the managed complex property and handle its daily operations. [See **RPI** Form 591]

1   **Karz** v. **Mecham** (1981) 120 CA3d Supp. 1
2   **Tappe** v. **Lieberman** (1983) 145 CA3d Supp. 19
3   Calif. Code of Civil Procedure §1161(1)

Both residential income property and commercial property may have resident managers. However, apartment buildings with 16 or more units are required to have a landlord, resident manager or responsible caretaker living on the premises to manage the property.[4]

Resident managers do not need to be licensed as a real estate broker or agent to negotiate leases or collect rents. However, if a nonresident property manager is not the landlord, the nonresident property manager needs to be licensed by the Department of Real Estate (DRE) as a real estate broker.[5] [See Chapter 7]

A property manager who employs a resident manager is responsible for the following brokerage activities:

- selecting and hiring the resident manager;

- maintaining worker's compensation, liability insurance and any bonding requirements of the landlord or property manager;

- keeping payroll records, including information about withholding and employer contributions;

- supervising the resident manager; and

- terminating the resident manager's employment.

The resident manager's status as an employee is established in an employment agreement called the **resident manager agreement**. [See Form 591]

Family members who live with the resident manager are listed in the *resident manager agreement*. Further, a statement noting these family members are not tenants is to be included. Thus, the family members' right to occupy the property terminates with the resident manager's right to occupy the property (e.g., the termination of the resident manager's employment).

References to the parties in the resident manager agreement need to identify the property manager/landlord as "employer" and the resident manager as "employee." [See Form 591 §4.9]

Depending on the size of the complex, the resident manager may receive occupancy of a unit in the complex as compensation for their services based on:

- a rent reduction given in exchange for the dollar value of the resident manager's services;

- no rent charge, the rental value given in exchange for services; or

- no rent charge, plus an additional monthly salary paid in further exchange for services.

The resident manager agreement states the salary paid to the resident manager is a monthly amount. The fair rental value of the resident manager's unit is deducted from their salary. After the rent deduction, the resident

Hiring a resident manager

resident manager agreement
An employment agreement which establishes the rights and duties of a resident manager and the obligations of the property manager and landlord. [See **RPI** Form 591]

Payment for services, withholding, benefits

---

4 25 Calif. Code of Regulations §42
5 Calif. Business and Professions Code §10131.01

Form 591

Resident
Manager
Agreement

Page 1 of 2

RESIDENT MANAGER AGREEMENT

Prepared by: Agent _____   Phone _____
Broker _____   Email _____

NOTE: This form is used by an owner or property manager when employing a resident manager to oversee the daily management of the owner's rental property, to document the resident manager's non-discretionary administrative duties, hours of work and the manager's occupancy of an apartment unit as part of their compensation.

DATE: _____, 20_____, at _____, California,
Items left blank or unchecked are not applicable.

1. RETAINER PERIOD:

1.1   Employer hereby employs _____, as the Employee,
1.2   as Resident Manager of the rental property commonly referred to as_____
_____,
1.3   located at _____ in _____, California,
1.4   commencing _____, 20_____ and continuing until terminated.

2. EMPLOYEE AGREES TO:

2.1   Collect all rents, security deposits or other charges due Owner and maintain collection records.
2.2   Advertise available rental units.
2.3   Screen and select tenants.
2.4   Show rental units to prospective tenants.
2.5   Negotiate, execute or cancel rental or lease agreements with tenants. No lease is to exceed _____ months.
2.6   Serve three-day notices as needed.
2.7   Clean, repair and maintain the rental real estate, inside and outside, as needed to promote the occupancy of the units.
2.8   Daily inspect the structure, grounds, parking lots, garages, and vacant units of the rental property for cleanliness and repairs.
2.9   Maintain receipt books, key racks and petty cash records in good order.
2.10 Conduct all minor maintenance and repairs not exceeding $500 in cost or $_____   if   Employee holds a contractors license. All materials to be purchased out of petty cash.
2.11 Contact the material and labor suppliers retained by the Employer to conduct all major repairs and maintenance. Employer to approve all repairs in excess of $_____.
2.12 Notify Employer immediately of any potential hazards to the tenants or property. Should an emergency situation arise placing tenants or property in jeopardy, Employee may immediately take action without further authority from Employer.
2.13 Conduct no other business on the premises nor solicit the tenants for any business other than the rental of the property.

3. BANKING:

3.1   Employee will place all rents, security deposits, and other funds received for the benefit of the Owner into an account maintained by Employer with _____
at their _____ branch.
3.2   On depositing funds into the Employer's account, Employee will deliver to Employer a copy of the bank deposit identifying the itemized deposits by the unit from which they were collected.

4. COMPENSATION OF EMPLOYEE AND HOURS WORKED:

4.1   As compensation for services, Employee will be paid a total monthly salary, from all sources, of $_____.
4.2   In part, Employee's salary will be in the form of possession to rental unit _____, which is to be occupied as a condition of employment. The rental credit toward the monthly salary is $_____.   The   utilities including gas, electricity, and trash removal ☐ are, ☐ are not, included with the occupancy.
4.3   The balance of the Employee's salary will be paid ☐ monthly, ☐ semi-monthly, on the _____ of each calendar month.
4.4   Employee will not work more than _____ hours per day and _____ hours per week.
4.5   Employee to have _____ days off weekly being the weekdays of _____.
4.6   Employee agrees to obtain Employer's consent if the hours required to carry out duties exceeds the agreed-to hours.
4.7   Employee will notify Employer within 48 hours of additional hours worked in an emergency situation.

-------------------------------- PAGE 1 OF 2 — FORM 591 --------------------------------

---

manager is paid any balance of their salary. Utilities may also be included as part payment for the resident manager's services or treated separately from the agreed-to salary. [See Form 591 §4]

As an employer, the property manager or landlord is responsible for withholding and forwarding federal and state income taxes. The property manager also makes all required payments for social security, unemployment insurance and disability insurance.[6]

---

6 Calif. Unemployment Insurance Code §13020

```
-------------------------------- PAGE 2 OF 2 — FORM 591 --------------------------------

    4.8   Employee acknowledges they are not a tenant, but an employee for purpose of occupancy of the unit provided
          for their on-site residency.
    4.9   _____
          _____
          _____
          _____
          _____
          _____

 5.  EMPLOYER AGREES TO:
    5.1   Hand Employee all keys and entry codes to the property, and copies of rental and lease agreements with existing
          tenants.
    5.2   Provide public liability, property damage and workers' compensation insurance sufficient in amount to protect the
          Employee and Employer.
    5.3   Hand to Employee $_____ to be accounted for as petty cash to pay costs incurred in performing
          Employee's duties, and to replenish this amount on Employee's request.
    5.4   Withhold all Employee's social security, federal and state income taxes, and disability insurance from cash salary
          paid.
    5.5   Pay all federal and state unemployment insurance, workers' compensation and Employer's social security
          payments.
 6.  GENERAL PROVISIONS:
    6.1   Before any party to this agreement files an action on a dispute arising out of this agreement which remains
          unresolved after 30 days of informal negotiations, the parties agree to enter into non-binding mediation
          administered by a neutral dispute resolution organization and undertake a good faith effort during mediation to
          settle the dispute.

 EMPLOYEE:                                        EMPLOYEE:
 I agree to perform on the terms stated above.    I agree to employ on the terms stated above.
 Date: _____, 20_____                   Date: _____, 20_____
 Employee: _____              Employee: _____
 Address: _____              Address: _____
 _____               _____
 Phone: _____              Phone: _____
 Cell: _____              Cell: _____
 Email: _____              Email: _____



 By: _____               By: _____

 FORM 591      02-16      ©2016 RPI — Realty Publications, Inc., P.O. BOX 5707, RIVERSIDE, CA 92517
```

Form 591

Resident Manager Agreement

Page 2 of 2

The property manager or landlord is required to carry workers' compensation insurance to cover resident manager injuries on the job. Providing workers' compensation coverage is imperative for any persons who employ individuals other than for casual labor.

The degree of control the property manager or landlord retains over a resident manager classifies the resident manager as an employee. A resident manager simply will not qualify as an independent contractor. Thus, the landlord or property manager who hires a resident manager may not avoid tax withholding, employer contributions or workers' compensation premiums.

Consider a property manager who hires a resident manager to run a large apartment complex. As part of their salary, the resident manager receives a unit rent-free plus a fixed monthly salary.

Is the value of the unit occupied by the resident manager considered income for state or federal tax reporting?

Rental value is not taxable income

No! Taxwise, the value of the apartment is not reportable income for the resident manager. The reduction or elimination of rent is not declared as income when the unit occupied by the resident manager is:

- located on the premises managed;
- a convenience for the property manager or landlord; and
- occupied by the resident manager as a condition of employment.[7]

Minimum wage requirements apply

A resident manager's employment is subject to **minimum wage laws** even though the portion of the wages paid by a reduction or elimination of rent is not taxable as personal income.[8]

Minimum wage requirements apply to resident managers. Resident managers carry out the instructions of the property manager or landlord. They do not have the authority to independently make their decisions on their own management policies. They are functionaries who carry out the decisions made at the discretion of the landlord or property manager.[9]

Even though the rent-free compensation is not taxed as income, the rent credit is included and considered when determining the resident manager's pay for minimum wage requirements. The rent credit is used as all or part of the wages received per hour of work performed by a resident manager, limited by caps on the rent credit.

Two "caps" limit minimum wage calculations to control the amount of the rent credit. The caps limit the rent credit to two thirds of the fair rental value of the unit and to an amount no greater than $621.28 per month in 2019 (and $677.75 in 2020). For a couple employed as resident managers, the rent credited toward hourly pay may not exceed $919.02 per month in 2019 (and $1,002.56 in 2020).[10]

Married resident managers

For example, a broker employs an individual as a resident manager of a 20-unit apartment complex in 2019. Later, the resident manager marries and their spouse moves into the resident manager's unit. The spouse is not employed to manage the residential property.

The following month, the broker subtracts $919.02 from the resident manager's salary (for the free rent allocation) to calculate the manager's hourly pay. The broker claims they are now able to deduct the maximum amount for couples since two people inhabit the resident manager's unit.

The resident manager claims the maximum amount used to calculate their hourly pay is the individual maximum of $621.28 since the spouse was not also employed by the broker.

---

7   26 CFR §1.119-1(b)
8   Calif. Labor Code §1182.8
9   8 CCR §11050(1)(B)(1)
10 8 CCR §11050(10)(C); Labor C §1182.13

May the broker use the maximum allowable rent credit for a couple employed as resident managers when the broker employs only one of them?

No! The broker may only calculate the minimum hourly rate based on a total monthly rental credit of $621.28. Only one of the two people residing in the rental unit is employed as a resident manager, the resident manager agreement not modified to also employ the spouse.[11]

To keep wages per hour from dropping below the minimum dollar amount capped by the government, the property manager requires the resident manager to:

- prepare time cards;
- limit the number of hours per week the resident manager may work so wages per hour do not drop below the minimum dollar amount; and
- make provisions for the payment of any overtime permitted.

By requiring and reviewing these weekly work reports, the property manager may confirm the hours worked by the resident manager and that pay is in line with minimum wage requirements.

These reports will shield the property manager from a resident manager's claim that they worked excessive hours in relation to their salary and the maximum rent credit allowed. [See Form 591 §4]

Thus, all work requiring additional hours, except emergency work, is to be approved by the property manager as a matter of management policy.

For example, consider a resident manager who is provided with a unit and a **base salary**. The resident manager is required to remain on the premises at all times. However, they are only authorized to perform required work for a limited number of hours per day. The number of hours is set by the resident manager agreement. [See Form 591 §4.4]

The resident manager claims to be entitled to overtime pay for the hours they are required to remain on the premises even though they are not working.

However, the resident manager is only entitled to receive compensation for the time they actually performed work agreed to in the resident manager agreement. No compensation is due for the time they were required to *remain on call*, but were not working.[12] [13]

A resident manager is an employee of the property manager or the landlord who hires them. As an employer, the property manager or landlord is liable to others injured due to the resident manager's negligence.[14]

Compliance with minimum wage requirements

Mismanaged, negligent resident managers

---

11 8 CCR §11050(10)(C)

12 **Brewer** v. **Patel** (1993) 20 CA4th 1017

13 **Isner** v. **Falkenberg** (March 18, 2008) 160 CA4th 1393

14 Calif. Civil Code §2338

A resident manager has managed a large complex for many years as an agent for the property manager. The resident manager is over 62 years of age.

The property manager hires a new, younger resident manager and relegates the old resident manager to a lesser position. The property manager constantly suggests to the older resident manager that they retire. Further, the property manager demotes the older resident manager to even lesser positions while dramatically reducing their compensation.

Has the property manager discriminated against the older resident manager?

Yes! The property manager's basis for demoting the older resident manager was age, criteria placing the older resident manager in a protected class.

*As a result, the property manager is responsible for monetary losses suffered by the employee for emotional distress and attorney fees. [**Stephens** v. **Coldwell Banker Commercial Group, Inc.** (1988) 199 CA3d 1394]*

To avoid liability for negligent violations of law or personal injuries to others, the conduct of resident managers needs to be closely supervised by the property manager or landlord. Business liability insurance is a necessity for the landlord and the property manager. This insurance covers the landlord and the property manager for the liability exposure created by their own conduct or by the resident manager's actions.

Termination of the resident manager

A resident manager agreement creates an at-will employment between the resident manager and the employing property manager or landlord. Thus, the resident manager's employment may be terminated at any time and without prior notice.

While a landlord or property manager does not need to have a good reason to terminate a resident manager, they may not have an improper reason for terminating the resident manager. A property manager or landlord may not terminate the resident manager or otherwise harass them based on:

- disability;
- race;
- creed;
- color;
- gender; or
- age.

An improper termination exposes the employing property manager or landlord to liability.[15] [See Case in point, "An improper termination"]

---

15 **Stephens** v. **Coldwell Banker Commercial Group, Inc.** (1988) 199 CA3d 1394

Recall from the opening scenario that the resident manager agreement controls the resident manager's right to occupy their unit as an employee. No separate lease or rental agreement is entered into or required (unless the property manager or landlord specifically intend to create a tenancy).

The resident manager agreement also controls when that right to occupy the unit is terminated. If a resident manager agreement requires the resident manager to surrender their unit upon termination of employment, the resident manager is not entitled to any notice to quit. The termination of employment is sufficient to terminate the resident manager's occupancy.

If the terminated resident manager remains in possession of the property after their employment is terminated, they are unlawfully detaining the property and may be evicted.

Editor's note — Under rent control ordinances, a holdover tenant needs to receive a notice to vacate to terminate the tenancy. However, courts in rent-controlled areas have exempted employee-tenants from rent control protection by classifying them, for purposes of rent control only, as licensees rather than tenants. They are not considered licensees for any other purposes.[16]

To avoid creating a tenancy that continues on termination of the resident manager's employment, the resident manager agreement will state:

- possession is incidental to employment;
- possession automatically ends concurrent with termination of employment; and
- failure to perform managerial duties constitutes a breach of the resident manager agreement and is grounds for immediate termination and eviction.

However, a caution: a property manager or landlord's conduct can change the resident manager's right of occupancy.

Consider the landlord of an apartment complex who hires a resident manager to run the complex. In exchange for their services, the resident manager receives a monthly salary and an apartment, rent-free.

Under the resident manager agreement, the resident manager is to vacate the apartment unit on termination of their employment. Thus, the right of possession is extinguished when employment is terminated.

The landlord terminates the resident manager's employment. The landlord then decides to serve the resident manager with notice to:

- immediately vacate and relinquish possession of the unit; or
- stay and pay monthly rent.

Terminating a resident manager's occupancy

Conduct changes manager's occupancy rights

---

16 **Chan** v. **Antepenko** (1988) 203 CA3d Supp. 21

Case in point

How does a landlord calculate the rental payments of a former resident manager who remains as a tenant?

Facts: A residential tenant of an apartment complex is employed as a resident manager. For managerial services, payment of the monthly rent is waived and applied as a credit toward wages due the resident manager. During the manager's employment, rental rates for all tenants in the complex are increased to the maximum amount permitted by rent control annually. [See Chapter 57]

Several years later, the landlord terminates the resident manager and the manager continues in occupancy of the unit as a tenant. Later, the landlord serves the former manager with a notice of a rent increase, adjusting the rental rate upward to include all of the past annual adjustments permitted by rent control during the period of employment as the resident manager. The former manager refuses to pay the adjusted rental rate.

Claim: The former manager claims the landlord may not calculate the new rental rate based on all annual adjustments which occurred during the employment period since the increased rental rate violates the Rent Stabilization Ordinance (RSO) which does not permit retroactive or cumulative annual adjustments.

Counter claim: The landlord claims entitlement to a rental rate based on all previous adjustments is permitted by rent control since under local RSO a landlord may adjust the rent due from a resident manager who on termination remains as a tenant by calculating for all annual adjustments allowed during their employment.

*Holding: The California Supreme Court held the landlord was entitled to base the rental rate increase on all past annual adjustments permitted by rent control since the RSO allows a landlord to adjust a former resident manager's rental rate to include any annual adjustments implemented during the manager's employment when they remain as a tenant. [**1300 N. Curson Investors, LLC** v. **Drumea** (2014) 225 C4th 325]*

The resident manager remains in possession of the apartment, but fails to also pay the monthly rent called for in the notice to quit. Without further notice, the landlord begins UD proceedings to regain possession of the apartment from the terminated resident manager.

The resident manager claims that due to the notice they are now a tenant and the landlord needs to serve them with a notice to quit before the landlord may evict the resident manager in a UD action.

The landlord claims the resident manager is a holdover tenant unlawfully detaining the premises since the termination of their employment.

Is the resident manager entitled to a notice to vacate?

Yes! By serving the resident manager with a notice to quit which included an offer to remain in possession, the property manager converted the resident manager's occupancy as an employee to a month-to-month tenancy.

Here, the resident manager's continued occupancy of the apartment constituted acceptance of the new tenancy offered by the landlord. The failure to pay rent is merely a breach of the new tenancy agreement noted in the notice to stay and pay.

Thus, the landlord's UD action may not be filed until proper notice to vacate is given to terminate the resident manager's new tenancy.[17]

---

17 *Karz. supra;* CC §1946

Chapter 10 Summary

A resident manager is an individual employed by a property manager to live on-site at the managed property and see to its daily operations. A property manager and a resident manager have an employer/employee relationship. A resident manager's duties include:

- screening tenants and negotiating leases;
- cleaning vacated units;
- supervising landscaping, maintenance and repairs;
- serving notices; or
- attending to tenant inquiries.

The resident manager may receive rent-free occupancy of a unit in the complex as compensation for their services. Taxwise, the value of the apartment is not reportable income for the resident manager. In contrast, a resident manager's employment is subject to minimum wage laws.

The property manager is liable to others injured due to the resident manager's negligence. The resident manager's employment may be terminated at any time and without prior notice. A resident manager agreement may require the resident manager to surrender their unit upon termination of employment.

Chapter 10 Key Terms

Quiz 3 Covering Chapters 9-13 is located on page 635.

Notes:

Chapter

11

Identification of property manager or owner

After reading this chapter, you will be able to:
- authorize brokers under an agent-for-service clause in management agreements to act on behalf of an owner to accept service of legal documents and notices from tenants;
- appoint an agent-for-service; and
- determine the disclosures to be given to residential tenants identifying the owner, the property manager and the owner's agent-for-service.

Learning Objectives

agent-for-service clause   **agent-for-service process**

Key Terms

An owner of a residential income property employs a broker to manage the property. The broker will operate the property acting as the landlord under the *property management agreement*, which includes all contact with the tenants on behalf of the owner. [See Chapter 8]

One of the owner's objectives is to become as anonymous as possible and avoid giving tenants any personal information or otherwise interacting with them.

The owner is advised they can avoid being identified to the tenants by appointing another individual to act as their agent-for-service of process, such as the broker or the owner's attorney. The **agent-for-service of process**, acting on behalf of the owner, will accept service of legal documents and notices initiated by tenants.[1]

Notice to tenant of agent-for-service

agent-for-service process
An individual who acts on behalf of the owner, accepting service of legal documents and notices initiated by tenants.

---
1 Calif. Civil Code §1962(a)(1)(B)

Here, when the owner appoints an *agent-for-service of process*, the owner's name and address need not be disclosed to any tenant, even if the tenant demands the information so they can sue the owner. Serving the agent-for-service with the lawsuit is the same as serving the owner.[2]

Editor's note — The identity of an owner is easily located by a search of the county records. If title to the property is vested in the name of a limited liability company (LLC), corporation, or other entity, a review of other records with the Secretary of State will identify and locate the manager of the entity.

Appointing the agent-for-service

An owner is the object of the service of notices and legal documents by a tenant. However, a residential income property owner may appoint any individual, including their property manager or attorney, to be their *agent-for-service*. Importantly, this appointment allows the owner to avoid personal service on themselves.

The property manager may be appointed as the owner's agent-for-service by including an **agent-for-service clause** in the *property management agreement* employing the broker. [See **RPI** Form 590]

agent-for-service clause
A section in the property management agreement which appoints the owner's agent-for-service. [See **RPI** Form 590 §11.3]

As the owner's agent-for-service, the broker accepts personal service of legal documents on behalf of the owner, such as notices and lawsuits initiated by tenants. However, both the broker and the owner need to first consider whether it is prudent for the broker to act as the owner's agent-for-service.

The broker's additional responsibility of accepting service of tenant complaints on the owner's behalf conflicts with the broker's main responsibility as a property manager. An owner might prefer to appoint an attorney as their agent-for-service to avoid the broker's potential conflict of interest.

Who is identified to the tenant?

The names and addresses of the following individuals will be disclosed to all residential tenants:

- the owner or other individual appointed by the owner as their agent-for-service;
- any property manager; and
- any resident manager.[3]

The addresses provided for the property manager, resident manager and agent-for-service are street addresses where legal notices can be personally served. A post office box will not suffice.[4]

The individual responsible for making the disclosures is:

- the owner; or
- the individual authorized to enter into rental and lease agreements on behalf of the owner, such as the property manager or resident manager.[5]

---

2 CC §1962(a)(1)(B)
3 CC §1962(a)
4 CC §1962(a)(1)
5 CC §1962(a)

The names and addresses of the owner's property manager, the resident manager and agent-for-service are disclosed in:

- the rental and lease agreements entered into with each tenant; or

- a notice posted on the property.[6]

When the disclosure notice is posted, the notice will be posted in two conspicuous places on the property.[7]

If the rental property contains elevators, the written notice will be posted in:

- every elevator in the building; and

- one other conspicuous place on the property.[8]

If the residential rental or lease agreement is oral, a written statement containing the names and addresses of the property manager, resident manager and agent- for-service will be provided to all tenants.[9]

Delivery of the notice

The owner, property manager or resident manager responsible for entering into rental and lease agreements is to notify all tenants of the name and address for service on the owner of a notice or complaint initiated by the tenant. This information is handed to the tenants within 15 calendar days after any change in:

- the manager of the property;

- the owner of the property, unless the new owner appoints an agent-for-service; or

- the owner's agent-for-service.[10] [See Form 554 accompanying this chapter]

Change in ownership and management

To disclose a *change in ownership or management*, the property manager or resident manager responsible for leasing is to:

- prepare the notice of change of ownership or property management as an addendum to each existing rental or lease agreement and hand it to each tenant to sign and return [See Form 554]; or

- post on the property the names and addresses of the property manager, resident manager and owner's agent-for-service.

The notice also includes information regarding how and when rent will be paid. A successor owner or property manager may not serve a tenant with a notice to pay rent or quit, or file an unlawful detainer action based on rent unpaid and due during the period in which the successor owner or property manager failed to provide rent payment information.[11]

However, the owner or property manager's failure to timely provide rent payment information does not excuse a tenant of their obligation to pay rent.

---

6   CC §1962(a); CC §1962.5(a)
7   CC §1962.5(a)(2)
8   CC §1962.5(a)(1)
9   CC §1962(b)
10 CC §1962(c)
11 CC§1962(c)

Form 554

Change of
Owner or
Property
Manager

Page 1 of 2

CHANGE OF OWNER OR PROPERTY MANAGER
Addendum To Rental Or Lease Agreement (California Civil Code §1962(c))

Prepared by: Agent _____   Phone _____
Broker _____   Email _____

NOTE: This form is used by a property manager or landlord when a change of ownership or property manager has occurred on a residential rental property, to notify each tenant of the change and confirm the status of their rent and other monetary obligations.

DATE: _____, 20_____, at _____, California.
To Tenant: _____
Items left blank or unchecked are not applicable.
FACTS:
1. This is an addendum to the ☐ lease, ☐ rental agreement,
    dated _____, 20_____, at _____, California,
    1.1 entered into by _____, as the Landlord,
    1.2 and _____, as the Tenant(s),
    1.3 recorded on _____, as Instrument No. _____,
         in the records of _____ County, California,
    1.4 regarding real estate referred to as _____
         _____

AGREEMENT:

2. This notice is to advise you of a change in ownership or management of the premises you occupy as indicated below:
    2.1 ☐ The ownership of the real estate you lease or rent has been transferred.
    2.2 The new property management broker is _____
         Address _____
         Phone _____
    2.3 The new resident manager is _____
         Address _____
         Phone _____
3. Beginning _____, 20_____, your monthly rent due is to be paid by ☐ check, ☐ credit card, ☐ cash, or
    ☐ cashier's check, made payable to _____
    3.1 Rent may be tendered by ☐ personal check, or ☐ _____,
         to

         _____
         (Name)

         _____
         (Address)

         _____
         (Phone)

         a. Personal delivery of rent will be accepted during the hours of _____ a.m to _____ p.m.
             on the following days _____
    3.2 Rent may also be paid by deposit into account number _____
         at _____
         (Financial Institution)

         _____
         (Address)

    3.3 If rent is to be paid by credit card, the credit card number is _____/_____/_____/_____,
         exp. date _____, 20_____ issued by _____,
         which Landlord will charge each month for the rent due.

-------------------------------------- PAGE 1 OF 2 — FORM 554 --------------------------------------

A residential property manager (or resident manager) in charge of leasing who fails to provide the name and address of the owner or their agent-for-service:

- automatically becomes the owner's agent-for-service of process and agent for receipt of all tenant notices and demands;[12] and

- is treated as the owner, not the owner's agent, and liable for performing all obligations described under rental and lease agreements with tenants.[13]

_____

12 CC §1962(d)(1)
13 CC §1962(d)(2)

-- PAGE 2 OF 2 — FORM 554 ---

3.4   Your current monthly rent is $_____.

3.5   Your rent has been paid up to and including _____, 20_____.

4.   Your security deposit of $_____.

   4.1   ☐ has been transferred to the new owner.

   4.2   ☐ has been transferred to the new property manager.

5.   No breach of your lease or rental agreement by Landlord or Tenant currently exists, except

_____

_____

_____

_____

_____

_____

6.   Any notices or demands on Owner by Tenant, including service of process, may be served on

Name _____

Address _____

Phone _____

7.   All terms and conditions of your lease and rental agreement remain effect.

I agree to the terms stated above.

Date: _____, 20_____

Landlord: _____

Agent: _____

Agent's CalBRE #: _____

Signature: _____

Address: _____

Phone: _____ Cell: _____

Fax: _____

Email: _____

I agree to the terms stated above.

Date: _____, 20_____

Tenant: _____

Signature: _____

Tenant: _____

Signature: _____

Address: _____

Phone: _____ Cell: _____

Fax: _____

Email: _____

FORM 554   06-14   ©2016 RPI — **Realty Publications, Inc.**, P.O. BOX 5707, RIVERSIDE, CA 92517

When the person signing the lease or rental agreement for the owner fails to make the disclosures, the tenant may have no indication the person signing is not the owner. However, this does not relieve the owner of liability to tenants. It merely extends liability to the property manager or resident manager who failed to give the required agency notice identifying themselves as agent for the owner.[14]

---

14 CC§1962(e)

Chapter 11 Summary

An agent-for-service of process may act on behalf of the owner, accepting service of legal documents and notices initiated by tenants. The agent-for-service provision in a property management agreement identifies the individual acting in this capacity.

The owner, property manager and resident manager on any change in ownership or management disclose their addresses to all residential tenants and how and when rent is to be paid in notices handed to the tenants.

Failure to disclose imposes liability for tenant claims on the property manager and the resident manager.

Chapter 11 Key Terms

Quiz 3 Covering Chapters 9-13 is located on page 635.

Chapter 12

Exclusive authorization to lease

After reading this chapter, you will be able to:

- understand the broker's right to compensation for services when employed by a commercial owner under an exclusive authorization to lease;
- use a fee schedule to establish the broker's right to a fee for future extensions, renewals and other continuing leasehold and purchase arrangements which might be later entered into by the tenant and the owner;
- distinguish the various provisions in an authorization to lease which protect the leasing agent's fee; and
- identify situations in which the leasing agent/broker has earned a fee.

Learning Objectives

Key Terms

contingency fee clause

early termination clause

exclusive authorization to lease

exclusive right-to-collect clause

full listing offer to lease

leasing agent

open listing

safety clause

Leasing agent's bargain for fees

Consider commercial property that is offered for lease by the owner. A broker makes an appointment with the owner to discuss the possibility of becoming their **leasing agent**.

During the discussion, the broker explains they can best help lease the property when operating under an **exclusive authorization to lease**, also called a *listing* or *employment agreement*.

> **leasing agent**
> A broker who markets the availability of space to rent and locates and negotiates the terms of a lease with suitable tenants.

Under the listing, the broker, on the owner's behalf, will be able to:

- market the space and locate prospective tenants [See Figure 1, Form 110 §1];
- publish the terms under which a tenant can lease and occupy the space [See Figure 1, Form 110 §8];
- share fees with brokers representing the tenants [See Figure 1, Form 110 §4.2];
- conduct negotiations with tenants or their brokers [See Figure 1, Form 110 §4.3] ; and
- accept deposits with offers to lease the space.

A broker who acts solely as a leasing agent does not manage or operate the property for the owner. The duties of a leasing agent are limited to locating prospective tenants and negotiating a lease agreement for their occupancy of the space.

Right to compensation for services

An *exclusive authorization to lease* entered into by the owner assures the leasing agent they will be paid a fee for their efforts *if anyone procures* a tenant for the identified space during the listing period, either on:

- the leasing terms sought in the listing; or
- any other terms accepted by the owner.

However, an owner may be reluctant to give up the ability to lease the property independently. Further, an owner may want to avoid employing a leasing agent and paying a brokerage fee if the owner locates the tenant.

On the other hand, an owner has a better chance of finding a tenant on acceptable terms if they employ a leasing agent that is known in the community of local leasing agents. An effective leasing agent takes the owner's "rough edges" out of negotiations and is constantly involved in leasing discussions with others in the trade.

Written authorization to lease

Consider an owner who prefers to orally agree to employ a broker to find tenants for the owner's property. The owner confirms they will work exclusively with the leasing agent to market the space and locate a user. The owner does not, however, believe it is necessary to commit all these arrangements to a written agreement.

exclusive authorization to lease
A written agreement between a broker and client employing the broker to render services in exchange for a fee on the leasing the property to a tenant located by anyone. Also known as a listing. [See **RPI** Form 110]

The broker explains an **exclusive authorization to lease** must be written and signed by the owner for the broker to be entitled to collect a fee. No signed writing, no services.

Is the broker correct?

Yes! A written agreement signed by the client is the only way a broker can protect their right to compensation for services. More importantly, a written

Figure 1

Form 110

Exclusive Authorization to Lease Property

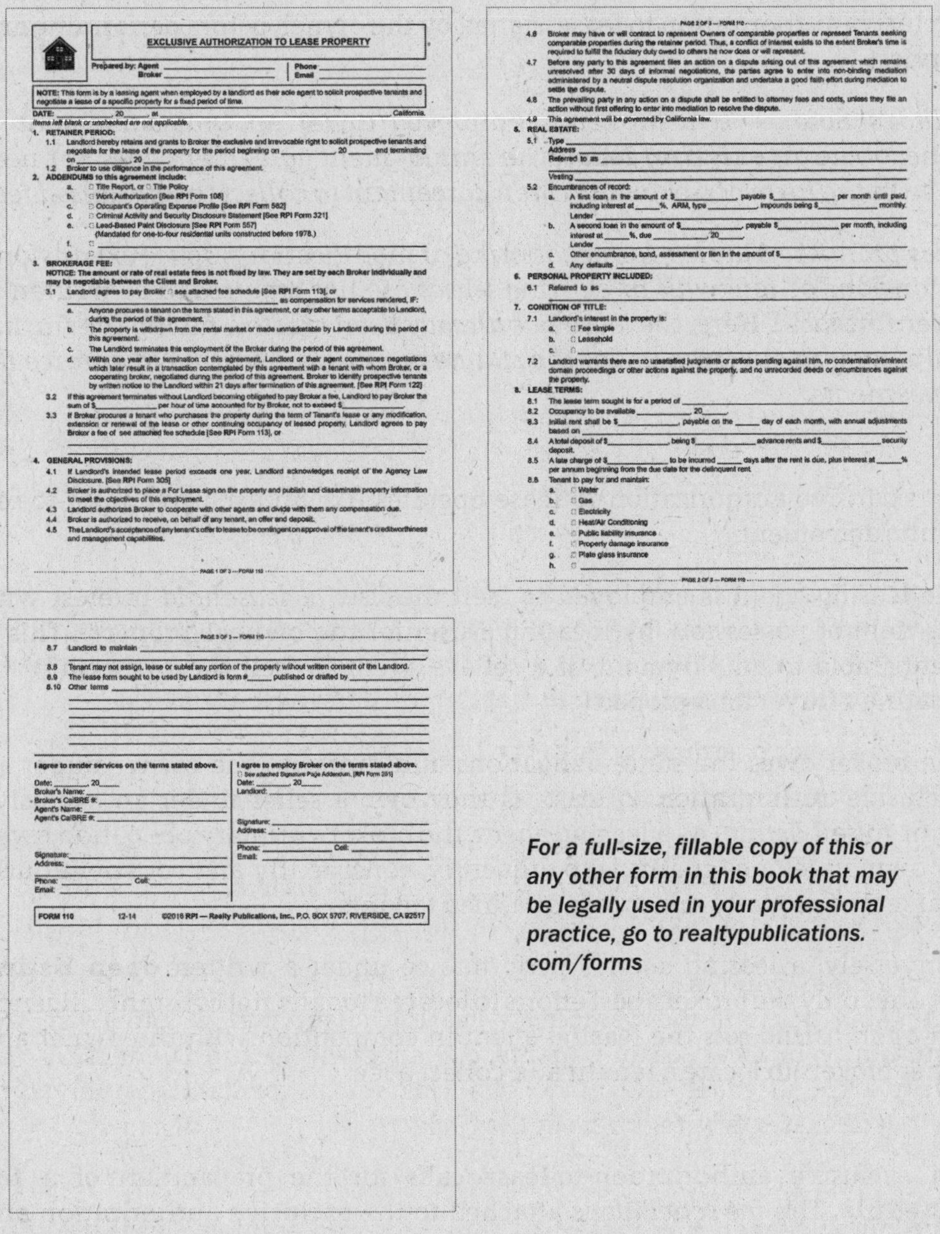

EXCLUSIVE AUTHORIZATION TO LEASE PROPERTY

Prepared by: Agent ____________ Phone ____________
Broker ____________ Email ____________

NOTE: This form is by a leasing agent when employed by a landlord as their sole agent to solicit prospective tenants and negotiate a lease of a specific property for a fixed period of time.

DATE: __________, 20____, at ______________________________, California.
Items left blank or unchecked are not applicable.

1. **RETAINER PERIOD:**
   1.1 Landlord hereby retains and grants to Broker the exclusive and irrevocable right to solicit prospective tenants and negotiate for the lease of the property for the period beginning on __________, 20____ and terminating on __________, 20____.
   1.2 Broker to use diligence in the performance of this agreement.
2. **ADDENDUMS to this agreement include:**
   a. ☐ Title Report, or ☐ Title Policy
   b. ☐ Work Authorization [See RPI Form 108]
   c. ☐ Occupant's Operating Expense Profile [See RPI Form 562]
   d. ☐ Criminal Activity and Security Disclosure Statement [See RPI Form 321]
   e. ☐ Lead-Based Paint Disclosure [See RPI Form 557] (Mandated for one-to-four residential units constructed before 1978.)
   f. ☐ ____________
   g. ☐ ____________
3. **BROKERAGE FEE:**
   NOTICE: The amount or rate of real estate fees is not fixed by law. They are set by each Broker individually and may be negotiable between the Client and Broker.
   3.1 Landlord agrees to pay Broker ☐ see attached fee schedule [See RPI Form 113], or ____________ as compensation for services rendered, IF:
      a. Anyone procures a tenant on the terms stated in this agreement, or any other terms acceptable to Landlord, during the period of this agreement.
      b. The property is withdrawn from the rental market or made unmarketable by Landlord during the period of this agreement.
      c. The Landlord terminates this employment of the Broker during the period of this agreement.
      d. Within one year after termination of this agreement, Landlord or their agent commences negotiations which later result in a transaction contemplated by this agreement with a tenant with whom Broker, or a cooperating broker, negotiated during the period of this agreement. Broker to identify prospective tenants by written notice to the Landlord within 21 days after termination of this agreement. [See RPI Form 122]
   3.2 If this agreement terminates without Landlord becoming obligated to pay Broker a fee, Landlord to pay Broker the sum of $__________ per hour of time accounted for by Broker, not to exceed $__________.
   3.3 If Broker procures a tenant who purchases the property during the term of Tenant's lease or any modification, extension or renewal of the lease or other continuing occupancy of leased property, Landlord agrees to pay Broker a fee of see attached fee schedule [See RPI Form 113], or ____________.
4. **GENERAL PROVISIONS:**
   4.1 If Landlord's intended lease period exceeds one year, Landlord acknowledges receipt of the Agency Law Disclosure. [See RPI Form 305]
   4.2 Broker is authorized to place a For Lease sign on the property and publish and disseminate property information to meet the objectives of this employment.
   4.3 Landlord authorizes Broker to cooperate with other agents and divide with them any compensation due.
   4.4 Broker is authorized to receive, on behalf of any tenant, an offer and deposit.
   4.5 The Landlord's acceptance of any tenant's offer to lease to be contingent on approval of the tenant's creditworthiness and management capabilities.

PAGE 1 OF 3 — FORM 110

PAGE 2 OF 3 — FORM 110

   4.6 Broker may have or will contract to represent Owners of comparable properties or represent Tenants seeking comparable properties during the retainer period. Thus, a conflict of interest exists to the extent Broker's time is required to fulfill the fiduciary duty owed to others he now does or will represent.
   4.7 Before any party to this agreement files an action on a dispute arising out of this agreement which remains unresolved after 30 days of informal negotiations, the parties agree to enter into non-binding mediation administered by a neutral dispute resolution organization and undertake a good faith effort during mediation to settle the dispute.
   4.8 The prevailing party in any action on a dispute shall be entitled to attorney fees and costs, unless they file an action without first offering to enter into mediation to resolve the dispute.
   4.9 This agreement will be governed by California law.
5. **REAL ESTATE:**
   5.1 Type ____________
   Address ____________
   Referred to as ____________
   Vesting ____________
   5.2 Encumbrances of record:
      a. A first loan in the amount of $__________, payable $__________ per month until paid, including interest at ____%, ARM, type __________, impounds being $__________ monthly.
      Lender ____________
      b. A second loan in the amount of $__________, payable $__________ per month, including interest at ____%, due __________, 20____.
      Lender ____________
      c. Other encumbrance, bond, assessment or lien in the amount of $__________.
      d. Any defaults ____________
6. **PERSONAL PROPERTY INCLUDED:**
   6.1 Referred to as ____________
7. **CONDITION OF TITLE:**
   7.1 Landlord's interest in the property is:
      a. ☐ Fee simple
      b. ☐ Leasehold
      c. ☐ ____________
   7.2 Landlord warrants there are no unsatisfied judgments or actions pending against him, no condemnation/eminent domain proceedings or other actions against the property, and no unrecorded deeds or encumbrances against the property.
8. **LEASE TERMS:**
   8.1 The lease term sought is for a period of ____________
   8.2 Occupancy to be available __________, 20____.
   8.3 Initial rent shall be $__________, payable on the ____ day of each month, with annual adjustments based on ____________.
   8.4 A total deposit of $__________, being $__________ advance rents and $__________ security deposit.
   8.5 A late charge of $__________ to be incurred ____ days after the rent is due, plus interest at ____% per annum beginning from the due date for the delinquent rent.
   8.6 Tenant to pay for and maintain:
      a. ☐ Water
      b. ☐ Gas
      c. ☐ Electricity
      d. ☐ Heat/Air Conditioning
      e. ☐ Public liability insurance
      f. ☐ Property damage insurance
      g. ☐ Plate glass insurance
      h. ☐ ____________

PAGE 2 OF 3 — FORM 110

PAGE 3 OF 3 — FORM 110

   8.7 Landlord to maintain ____________
   8.8 Tenant may not assign, lease or sublet any portion of the property without written consent of the Landlord.
   8.9 The lease form sought to be used by Landlord is form #____ published or drafted by __________.
   8.10 Other terms ____________

I agree to render services on the terms stated above.
Date: ________, 20____
Broker's Name: ____________
Broker's CalBRE #: ____________
Agent's Name: ____________
Agent's CalBRE #: ____________
Signature: ____________
Address: ____________
Phone: ________ Cell: ________
Email: ____________

I agree to employ Broker on the terms stated above.
☐ See attached Signature Page Addendum. [RPI Form 251]
Date: ________, 20____
Landlord: ____________
Signature: ____________
Address: ____________
Phone: ________ Cell: ________
Email: ____________

FORM 110 12-14 ©2016 RPI — Realty Publications, Inc., P.O. BOX 5707, RIVERSIDE, CA 92517

For a full-size, fillable copy of this or any other form in this book that may be legally used in your professional practice, go to realtypublications.com/forms

agreement memorializes the leasing agent's obligation to conscientiously and continuously work to meet the client's objectives, whether representing a tenant or an owner.

An oral fee agreement between a broker and their client is unenforceable by the broker and leaves the broker without evidence of the agency created. This is true even when the broker documents the existence of an oral agreement by referencing the fee and terms of payment in written correspondence sent to and acted on by the client. Without the client's signature promising to pay, the broker cannot enforce collection of the orally promised fee.[1]

1 **Phillippe** v. **Shapell Industries, Inc.** (1987) 43 C3d 1247

Thus, a broker protects their right to collect a fee by entering into a form exclusive authorization to lease, signed by the owner, before performing any services.

*Editor's note — If a broker is employed under an oral agreement to renegotiate an **existing lease**, the employment agreement does not need to be in the form of a signed written agreement to collect the promised fee.*

Fees promised a broker for negotiating of modifications, space expansions, extensions or renewals of existing leases are not required to be written to be enforceable. Here, the lease has already been created, taking the further employment out from under the statute requiring a writing to enforce fee agreements.[2]

Exclusive authorization to locate a user

An exclusive authorization to lease operates like an exclusive right-to-sell listing agreement.

The leasing agent is employed to "sell the use," a *leasehold* interest with the right of possession, by locating a user for the owner's property. This is comparable to employment of a seller's agent to "sell the ownership" by locating a buyer for a property.

open listing
An employment entered into by a broker to render real estate services on a best-efforts basis under which a fee is due to the broker if they achieve the client's objective of the employment before the client or another broker separately first meet the objective, such as the sale or locating of a property.

The broker owes the same obligations and duties to the owner under an exclusive authorization to lease as they owe a seller under an exclusive *right-to-sell listing*. As a leasing agent, the broker's primary obligation owed an owner seeking tenants is to diligently, consistently and conscientiously market the property and locate qualified tenants.

Conversely, a leasing agent's performance under a written **open listing** requires only the broker's best efforts to locate a tenant, not constant diligence. An *open listing* sets the leasing agent in competition with the owner and other brokers to locate a tenant and collect a fee.

Fee schedule establishes broker's right to a fee

An exclusive authorization-to-lease calls for the preparation of a **fee schedule**. The *fee schedule* is attached to the exclusive authorization and references leasing situations which trigger the broker's right to be paid a fee when earned. The fee schedule includes fees for future extensions, renewals and other continuing leasehold and purchase arrangements which might be entered into in the future by the tenant and the owner. [See **RPI** Form 113; see Chapter 41]

The amounts established in the fee schedule are earned and due to the broker when:

- an *exclusive right-to-collect clause* assures payment of the agreed-to fee if anyone procures a tenant on the terms in the listing, or on any other terms accepted by the owner [See Figure 1, Form 110 §3.1a];

---

2   **Shell** v. **Darneille** (1984) 162 CA3d 957

- an *early termination clause* assures payment of the fee if the owner withdraw the property from the rental market during the listing period [See Figure 1, Form 110 §3.1b];

- a **termination-of-agency clause** assures payment of the fee if the owner cancels the employment without cause before it expires under the listing, whether or not the owner intends to continue to market the property for sale [See Figure 1, Form 110 §3.1c]; and

- a *safety clause* assures payment of the fee if, within one year after termination of the exclusive authorization to lease, the owner enters into negotiations resulting in a leasing or sale of the property to a prospective tenant the broker negotiated with during the listing period. [See Figure 1, Form 110 §3.1d]

termination-of-agency clause
A provision which assures payment of the broker's fee if the owner cancels the employment without cause before the listing expires. [See **RPI** Form 102 §3.1(c), 103 §4.1(b), 110 §3.1c]

Now consider a broker who is employed by an owner under an exclusive authorization to lease.

The authorization states the owner will pay the broker a fee if the broker, or anyone else, produces a tenant ready, willing and able to lease the property on the same terms specified in the exclusive authorization to lease. [See Figure 1, Form 110 §3.1a]

The broker produces a creditworthy tenant who is financially capable of leasing the premises on the terms set forth in the exclusive authorization to lease. [See Figure 1, Form 110 §8]

The broker prepares and submits the tenant's offer to lease on terms substantially identical to the leasing terms in the authorization, called a **full listing offer to lease**. [See **RPI** Form 556]

The owner then demands higher rental rates and refuses to accept the offer.

The broker claims to be entitled to a fee since they produced a tenant who was ready, willing and able to lease the property on the terms stated in the exclusive authorization to lease.

The owner claims the broker is not entitled to a fee since the property was never leased.

Here, the broker has earned their fee. The exclusive authorization to lease included a written fee agreement obligating the owner to pay the broker a fee once the broker located a tenant ready, willing and able to lease the property on the terms set forth in the exclusive authorization to lease.[3]

Ready, willing and able tenant condition

full listing offer to lease
A buyer's or tenant's offer to buy or lease on terms substantially identical to the employment terms in the owner's listing agreement with the broker. [See **RPI** Form 556]

---

3 **Twogood** v. **Monnette** (1923) 191 C 103

An exclusive right-to-collect clause

Now consider a broker whose exclusive authorization to lease contains a fee provision that states they are entitled to a fee if the owner rents the space during the listing period. This clause is called the **exclusive right-to-collect clause**. It is the exclusive right-to-collect clause which makes a listing exclusive. The clause states "a fee is due if anyone procures a tenant." [See Figure 1, Form 110 §3.1a]

The broker, as part of their efforts to locate a tenant, places a "For Lease" sign on the premises. The sign is seen by a prospective tenant.

The prospective tenant contacts the owner of the premises directly.

Before the exclusive authorization to lease period expires, the prospective tenant and owner enter into a lease agreement. The terms of the lease agreement are different from those specified in the broker's exclusive authorization to lease.

Even though the owner's broker had no contact with the prospective tenant (other than the sign exposure) and the terms are different from the listing, the broker has earned a fee. A tenant's offer to lease was accepted by the owner during the exclusive authorization period.[4]

Early termination by owner triggers fee

A typical exclusive authorization to lease contains boilerplate wording in the fee provision stating the owner will pay the broker the agreed-to fee if the property is:

- withdrawn from the rental market;
- transferred or conveyed;
- leased without the broker's consent; or
- otherwise made unrentable by the owner. [See Figure 1, Form 110 §3.1b]

Collectively, this boilerplate provision is known as the **early termination clause**. An early termination clause protects the broker from loss of time and money spent in a diligent effort to locate a tenant when the owner's conduct effectively removes the property from the rental market before the listing expires. When the owner interferes with the broker's objective — to produce a ready, willing and able tenant on the terms stated — a fee has been earned and is immediately due.

Consider a broker and owner who enter into an exclusive authorization to lease that expires in six months. The agreement contains a fee provision with an early-termination clause.

The broker diligently attempts to locate a tenant for the owner's property.

During the listing period, the owner notifies the broker the property is no longer for lease. The broker is instructed to stop marketing the property. In compliance with the owner's instructions, the broker takes the property off the market.

---

4 **Carlsen** v. **Zane** (1968) 261 CA2d 399

The broker then makes a demand on the owner for a *full listing fee*. The broker claims the early termination clause provides for payment of the broker's fee by the owner when the owner withdraws the property from the rental market before the listing period expires.

The owner claims the broker cannot collect a fee under the early termination clause since it is an unenforceable penalty provision.

Is the broker entitled to a fee on the client's termination of the broker's employment?

Yes! The broker is entitled to a fee. The early termination clause is not a penalty provision since the owner has an alternative. It simply gives the owner the option to cancel the exclusive authorization agreement in exchange for paying the broker a fee instead of allowing the listing to expire without interference with the broker's marketing efforts. The owner exercises the right to cancel by conduct which interferes with the broker's ability to lease the property, such as taking the property off the market. Thus, the owner is required to pay the fee on exercise of their option to cancel the listing agreement.[5]

Editor's note — See **RPI** *Form 121 for an agreement to cancel an exclusive authorization to lease during the listing period.*

A **safety clause** protects a leasing agent's fee when their efforts produce results during the year after the listing expires. This one-year period is known as the *safety clause period*. [See Figure 1, Form 110 §3.1d]

Under the safety clause, the owner owes the leasing agent the scheduled fee if:

- during the *safety clause period,* the owner enters into negotiations with a tenant located by the leasing agent during the listing period; and

- the negotiations result in a lease agreement.

The safety clause includes a provision which calls for the leasing agent as a condition precedent to collecting a fee to provide the owner with a list of the prospective tenants located by the leasing agent during the listing period. [See **RPI** Form 122]

Consider a broker and an owner who enter into an exclusive authorization to lease. The exclusive authorization to lease contains a fee provision with a safety clause.

On expiration of the listing period, the broker supplies the owner with the names of prospective tenants they have contacted and who received information regarding the property. Thus, each of these prospective tenants is "registered" with the owner.

Safety clause covers prospects who lease

safety clause
A provision in an exclusive listing agreement earning the broker a fee during an agreed safety period after expiration of the employment for marketing efforts with identified buyers, tenants or property, if the client sells the listed property to an identified buyer or purchases or leases an identified property during the safety period. [See **RPI** Form 102 §3.1(d), 103 §4.1(c) and 110 §3.1(d)]

---

5 **Blank** v. **Borden** (1974) 11 C3d 963

After the listing expires, the owner employs a second broker without discussing the terms of the prior listing.

Within the safety period of the first broker's listing, the second broker leases the premises to a tenant registered by the first broker. The lease is arranged without the first broker's participation in negotiations or the fee paid on the transaction.

Here, the owner owes the first broker the entire amount of the agreed-to fee even though the property was leased while listed exclusively with another broker.

The exclusive authorization to lease entered into by the owner and the first broker promised the first broker a fee if, within one year after expiration of the listing, the owner enters into negotiations which result in a lease with a prospective tenant registered with the owner by the first broker.[6]

As a "safety net" for brokerage services rendered, the clause discourages the owner from attempting to avoid payment of a leasing agent's fee by:

- waiting until the exclusive authorization agreement expires and then directly or indirectly approaching a prospective tenant located and solicited by the leasing agent; or

- making special fee arrangements with a second leasing agent which re-ignite negotiations with a prospective tenant located and exposed to the property by the first leasing agent broker.

Contingency fees due on owner's breach

contingency fee clause
A provision in an offer-to-lease which states the broker's fee is payable on the transfer of possession to the tenant. [See **RPI** Form 556 §15]

An offer-to-lease form is used by prospective tenants to begin negotiations with the owner to lease a property. Along with a prospective tenant's desired lease terms, offer-to-lease forms typically contain a provision stating the broker's fee is payable on the transfer of possession to the tenant. This provision is called a **contingency fee clause**. [See **RPI** Form 556]

Consider an owner who accepts an offer to lease submitted by a broker on behalf of a prospective tenant. The signed offer to lease contains a fee provision which states the broker's fee is payable by the owner on change of possession. [See **RPI** Form 556]

Later, the owner wrongfully refuses to enter into a lease agreement and convey the leasehold interest as agreed in the offer to lease. The broker makes a demand on the owner for payment of a fee.

The owner claims the broker is not entitled to receive a fee since the leasehold was never conveyed to the prospective tenant.

Is the broker entitled to their fee?

Yes! The owner cannot avoid paying the fee the broker has already earned by claiming a lease was never signed. Here, the owner's breach of the agreement to lease prevented the transfer of occupancy to the tenant. The owner failed

---

6 **Leonard** v. **Fallas** (1959) 51 C2d 649

to deliver the lease agreement and possession as agreed in the offer to lease. Thus, the failure to enter into the lease triggers payment of the fee previously earned when the owner accepted the tenant's offer to lease.

The contingency fee clause included in the offer to lease merely designates the time for payment of a fee the broker previously earned on locating a tenant or the acceptance of the tenant's offer. The contingency fee clause in the offer does not defeat the broker's right to compensation simply because the owner later wrongfully refused to enter into the lease.[7]

The contingency fee clause in an offer to lease shifts the time for payment of the fee from the time the fee is earned under an exclusive authorization agreement to the time a lease is entered into in the offer to lease.

Also, unless the leasing agent approves, the owner cannot include and enforce a fee provision in the offer to lease that is unacceptable to the broker or contrary to the terms of the fee schedule in the exclusive authorization to lease.[8]

Exclusive authorizations to lease have fee schedules attached which contain formulas for calculating the brokerage fee earned based on the length of the lease negotiated with the tenant. Further, they usually state the broker will receive an additional fee for any extension, renewal or modification of the tenant's occupancy under the original lease. [See Chapter 41]

Additional fees on extension of lease

For example, a broker operating under the authority of a written exclusive authorization to lease procures a tenant who signs a ten-year lease. The broker is paid the fee called for in the listing agreement fee schedule.

The fee schedule also provides for a percentage fee to be paid if the owner and tenant enter into an agreement for the tenant's continued occupancy of the premises on expiration of the original lease.

On expiration of the original lease, the owner and tenant negotiate a new lease for the tenant's continuing occupancy and use of the premises. A brokerage fee is not paid for the tenant's continued occupancy.

The broker makes a demand for an additional fee under the original listing agreement. The broker claims the new lease, which the broker did not negotiate, earned the broker a fee.

The owner claims they do not owe the broker a fee since the new lease is a separate agreement, not an extension, renewal or modification of the original lease.

However, the broker is due an additional fee from the owner as agreed in the original listing since the new lease constitutes an extension of the original possession.

---

7 **Steve Schmidt & Co.** v. **Berry** (1986) 183 CA3d 1299
8 **Seck** v. **Foulks** (1972) 25 CA3d 556

Here, the tenant located by the broker continued in possession and use of the premises on expiration of the original lease. The listing agreement stated the broker was to be paid a fee on this event. The form of documentation used to permit the continued occupancy of the premises is of no importance.[9]

---

9   **John B. Kilroy Company** v. **Douglas Furniture of California, Inc.** (1993) 21 CA4th 26

Chapter 12 Summary

An exclusive authorization to lease entered into by the owner assures the leasing agent will be paid a fee for their efforts if anyone procures a tenant for the identified space during the listing period, either on:

- the leasing terms sought in the listing; or
- any other terms accepted by the owner.

An exclusive authorization-to-lease calls for the preparation of a fee schedule. The fee schedule is attached to the exclusive authorization and references leasing situations which trigger the broker's right to be paid a fee when earned. The fee schedule includes fees for future extensions, renewals and other continuing leasehold and purchase arrangements which might later be entered into by the tenant and the owner.

Numerous provisions exist in the exclusive authorization to lease which protect a leasing agent's right to a fee, including the:

- exclusive right-to-collect clause;
- early termination clause;
- safety clause; and
- contingency fee clause.

Chapter 12 Key Terms

Quiz 3 Covering Chapters 9-13 is located on page 635.

Chapter
13

Exclusive authorization to locate space

After reading this chapter, you will be able to:
- use an exclusive authorization to locate space to assure payment of a fee for assisting prospective tenants;
- determine a tenant's needs and expectations for leasing a property using a tenant lease worksheet; and
- understand the benefits for prospective tenants and brokers employed under an exclusive listing agreement.

Learning Objectives

agency duty	**exclusive authorization to**
consultation fee	**locate space**
dual agency	**general duty**

Key Terms

A landlord of a commercial property holds an open house attended by leasing agents. The purpose of the open house is to induce the leasing agents to locate tenants for the landlord's vacant space.

A leasing agent and the commercial tenant

Leasing agents attending the open house are handed the landlord's brochure on available space and lease terms. The information includes an unsigned schedule of broker's fees the landlord will pay if a broker procures a tenant who leases space in the property. The informational handout also includes a tenant registration form for brokers to fill out when showing the space to prospective tenants.

One of the brokers who received a brochure inspects the property with their client, a prospective tenant.

Case in point

To know
the tenant's
expectations

Tenant needs and expectations

To effectively negotiate a commercial lease arrangement on behalf of a tenant, a leasing agent needs to possess a high level of knowledge and expertise regarding the alternative terms of a lease agreement. Further, to select qualifying space and negotiate the best terms for a tenant, the agent first identifies the tenant's needs and expectations for leasing a property.

When gathering leasing information from a tenant, the agent needs a checklist of pertinent items to consider. This objective is best met by using a tenant lease worksheet. [See **RPI** *Form 555]*

In the process, the leasing agent needs to uncover the tenant's precise reasons for moving to be better equipped to find a suitable new location and premises, or possibly negotiate a renewal or extension of the tenant's existing lease.

Know the tenant's business projections

When a prospective tenant is starting a new business, the leasing agent initially needs information on the tenant's business projections, which may be overly optimistic. The tenant may want space that is simply too large or in too expensive a location. The tenant may have to settle for incubator space in a less desirable location which accepts "start-up" business tenants.

Conversely, a tenant may underestimate the potential future growth of their business. The premises they favor may be too small to accommodate their short-term growth, hindering attempts to expand. The tenant will be forced to relocate again prematurely. To ensure room for future growth, the leasing agent considers:

- *options to lease space;*
- *the right of first refusal on additional space; or*
- *a lease cancellation or buyout provision to vacate the premises.*

Completed tenant regstration form

The broker completes the tenant registration form identifying the broker and prospective tenant. The registration form itself does not reference the fee schedule or any amount payable to the broker as a fee.

The registration form is handed to the landlord, or the landlord's employee, who signs it and returns a copy to the broker.

Later, the broker prepares an offer to lease, which is signed by the tenant and submitted to the landlord. The offer to lease form contains a provision calling for the landlord to pay a broker's fee. [See **RPI** Form 556]

The offer to lease is not accepted or rejected by the landlord. The landlord does not make a counteroffer. However, without contacting the broker, the landlord and the tenant engage directly in lease negotiations. Later, they enter into a lease which does not provide for a fee to be paid to the broker.

In the lease, the landlord agrees to be responsible for payment of any broker's fee due as a result of the lease.

Also, over projection of the potential income of a tenant's business under a percentage-rent lease agreement will reduce the landlord's projected rental income. Unless the leasing agent considers the space needs and gross income of the tenant, the leasing agent's long-term service to either the landlord or tenant is limited. Thus, the leasing agent needs to consider a system to help them match up the right landlord with the right tenant.

Using a tenant lease worksheet

The tenant lease worksheet covers three key areas the leasing agent is to consider:

- *the tenant's lease agreement obligations for their existing space;*
- *the tenant's present and future needs for leased space; and*
- *the tenant's financial condition and creditworthiness for ability and capacity to make rent payments. [See RPI Form 555]*
- *Regarding the tenant's space requirements, the leasing agent considers:*
- *current square footage needs;*
- *future square footage needs;*
- *phone, utilities, computer and information technology (IT) needs;*
- *heating and air conditioning requirements;*
- *parking, docking, turn-around and shipping requirements;*
- *access to freeways, airports and other public transportation;*
- *access to civic, financial, legal, governmental or other "downtown" facilities;*
- *response time for police and fire departments;*
- *access to housing areas; and*
- *any needs peculiar to the tenant.*

Some tenants focus on specific geographic locations among businesses or in population centers. Others may need the lowest rent possible, regardless of location.

On discovering the tenant's occupancy, the broker seeks payment of their fee from their client the tenant, not the landlord. The broker claims the tenant interfered with or breached the broker's fee provision in the offer to lease (which was signed by the tenant) by failing to provide for payment of the fee the broker earned when the tenant leased the property.

The tenant claims they are not liable for payment of the broker's fee since the offer to lease called for the landlord to pay the broker's fee.

Can the broker recover their fee from the tenant?

Yes! The offer to lease signed by the tenant contains a fee provision which states the broker will receive compensation for their efforts if the tenant leases the premises. It is not important that the tenant's offer called for the landlord to pay the fee.

exclusive authorization to locate space
An employment agreement by a broker and a prospective tenant which authorizes the broker to act as the tenant's leasing agent to locate suitable space and negotiate a lease agreement. [See **RPI** Form 111]

Thus, the broker is able to enforce collection of a fee from the tenant. The tenant signed an offer to lease the property, which contained a provision calling for the broker to be paid a fee. The tenant breached that fee provision by failing to provide for payment of that broker's fee. In doing so, the tenant incurred liability for the fee.[1]

Conversely, a broker locating space for a client puts their fee orally promised by the landlord at risk if the prospective tenant does not sign an agreement — such as an **exclusive authorization to locate space** or *offer to lease* — containing provisions for the payment of a broker's fee if the tenant leases property. An oral agreement to pay a broker's fee is unenforceable against the person making the oral promise.[2]

Various written fee agreements

A leasing agent has the opportunity to enter into a written fee agreement signed by either the tenant or the landlord on at least four occasions during lease negotiations:

- when the leasing agent solicits a commercial landlord for authorization to represent the landlord to locate users and negotiate acceptable leasing arrangements; [See Form 110 in Chapter 12]

- when the leasing agent solicits (or is solicited by) a commercial tenant for authorization to represent the tenant to locate suitable space and negotiate leasing arrangements acceptable to the tenant; [See Form 111 accompanying this chapter]

- when the leasing agent prepares a tenant's offer to lease by including a broker's fee provision within the body of the offer signed by the tenant; and

- when the leasing agent prepares the lease agreement by including provisions for fees.

Employment agreements with a user

A broker needs to enter into an employment agreement with a tenant before extensively analyzing the tenant's needs for space the broker intends to locate. The employment agreement is entered into and signed prior to locating space or exposing the tenant to available space not listed with the broker. [See Form 111]

This employment agreement, called an *exclusive authorization to locate space*, assures the broker a fee will be received if the tenant ultimately leases space of the type and in the area noted in the authorization. Through the exclusive authorization, the tenant commits to work with the broker to accomplish the objective of the employment — to rent space. The leasing agent's commitment to the tenant under the employment is a promise to use diligence and care in locating suitable space on terms acceptable to the tenant.

---

1   **Rader Company** v. **Stone** (1986) 178 CA3d 10
2   **Phillippe** v. **Shapell Industries, Inc.** (1987) 43 C3d 1247

Form 111

Exclusive
Authorization to
Locate Space

EXCLUSIVE AUTHORIZATION TO LOCATE SPACE

Prepared by: Agent _____ Phone _____
Broker _____ Email _____

NOTE: This form is by a leasing agent when employed by a tenant as their sole agent to locate property and negotiate terms and conditions for its rental or lease for a fixed period of time.

DATE: _____, 20_____, at _____, California.
Items left blank or unchecked are not applicable.

1. RETAINER PERIOD:
   1.1   Tenant hereby retains and grants to Broker the exclusive right to locate space of the type described below and to negotiate terms and conditions for its rental acceptable to Tenant, for a retainer period beginning on _____, 20_____, and terminating on _____, 20_____.

2. BROKER'S OBLIGATIONS:
   2.1   Broker to use diligence in the performance of this employment.
   2.2   If Tenant's intended lease period exceeds one year, Tenant acknowledges receipt of the Agency Law Disclosure. [See **RPI** Form 305]

3. GENERAL PROVISIONS:
   3.1   Tenant authorizes Broker to cooperate with other agents and divide with them any compensation due.
   3.2   Broker may have or will contract to represent Owners of comparable properties or represent Tenants seeking comparable properties during the retainer period. Thus, a conflict of interest exists to the extent Broker's time is required to fulfill the fiduciary duty owed to others he now does or will represent.
   3.3   Before any party to this agreement files an action on a dispute arising out of this agreement which remains unresolved after 30 days of informal negotiations, the parties agree to enter into non-binding mediation administered by a neutral dispute resolution organization and undertake a good faith effort during mediation to settle the dispute.
   3.4   The prevailing party in any action on a dispute shall be entitled to attorney fees and costs, unless they file an action without first offering to enter into mediation to resolve the dispute.
   3.5   This agreement will be governed by California law.

4. BROKERAGE FEE:
NOTICE: The amount or rate of real estate fees is not fixed by law. They are set by each Broker individually and may be negotiable between the Tenant and Broker.
   4.1   Tenant agrees to pay Broker ☐ see attached fee schedule [See **RPI** Form 113], or ☐ _____ _____ of the rental price of the space located, IF:
      a.   Tenant, or any person acting on Tenant's behalf, leases space located during the retainer period;
      b.   Tenant terminates this employment of Broker during the retainer period; or
      c.   within one year after termination of this agreement, Tenant or their agent commences negotiations which later result in a transaction contemplated by this agreement with a landlord with whom Broker, directly or indirectly, negotiated during the period of this agreement. Broker to identify prospective properties by written notice to Tenant within 21 days after termination of this agreement. [See **RPI** Form 123]
   4.2   If this agreement terminates without Tenant becoming obligated to pay Broker a fee, Tenant to pay Broker the sum of $_____ per hour of time accounted for by Broker, not to exceed $_____.
   4.3   If Landlord of space leased to Tenant agrees to pay a fee acceptable to the Broker, Tenant's obligation to pay a brokerage fee will be satisfied. _____

TYPE OF SPACE SOUGHT:
GENERAL DESCRIPTION _____
LOCATION _____ SIZE _____
RENTAL AMOUNT/TERM _____

I agree to render services on the terms stated above.	I agree to employ Broker on the terms stated above.
Date: _____, 20_____	☐ See attached Signature Page Addendum. [RPI Form 251]
Broker's Name: _____	Date: _____, 20_____
Broker's CalBRE #: _____	Tenant: _____
Agent's Name: _____	
Agent's CalBRE #: _____	Signature: _____
	Tenant: _____
Signature: _____	Signature: _____
Address: _____	Address: _____
Phone: _____ Cell: _____	Phone: _____ Cell: _____
Email: _____	Email: _____

FORM 111   12-14   ©2016 RPI — **Realty Publications, Inc.**, P.O. BOX 5707, RIVERSIDE, CA 92517

The exclusive authorization to locate space form is similar in structure and purpose to a exclusive authorization to lease entered into by a landlord and includes:

- the term of the retainer period;

- the formula for calculating the broker's compensation and who will pay the fee [See Form 113 in Chapter 41];

- a description of the type and location of space or property sought by the tenant; and

- identification of the broker as the agent and the tenant as the client.

The description of the property in the exclusive authorization to locate space specifies the space requirements, location, rental range, terms and other property conditions sought by the tenant.

Exclusive authorization ensures collection of a fee

Based on the fee provisions in an exclusive authorization to locate space, the broker earns a fee when the tenant enters into a lease agreement for space similar to the space sought under the exclusive authorization. The fee is collectible no matter who locates acceptable space or negotiates the lease agreement, established by the exclusive clause in the employment agreement. [See Form 111 §4.1a]

Also, fee provisions containing a safety clause allow the broker to collect a fee if property located by the broker and disclosed to the tenant during the retainer period is later leased by the tenant in negotiations commenced during the one-year period after the exclusive authorization expires. [See Form 111 §4.1c]

If the tenant decides not to lease space during the exclusive authorization period, the fee provision is structured so the broker can include payment of a **consultation fee**. A *consultation fee* is charged on an hourly basis for the time spent locating rental property. [See Form 111 §4.2]

consultation fee
A fee the broker charges for the time spent locating rental property if the tenant decides not to lease space during the exclusive authorization period. [See **RPI** Form 111 §4.2]

Benefits of exclusive authorization

An exclusive authorization to locate space is mutually beneficial to a prospective tenant and a broker. The employment commits the commercial tenant and broker to work together to accomplish a single objective — the leasing of space.

Understandably, an unrepresented tenant is at the mercy of the leasing agent employed by the landlord. An agent employed by a landlord owes the employing landlord an **agency duty** to use diligence in seeking the most qualified tenant and negotiating terms for a lease most favorable to the landlord.

agency duty
The fiduciary duty a broker owes a client to use diligence in attaining the client's real estate goals. [See **RPI** Form 305-1 and 550-2]

Conversely, the landlord's broker only owes a **general duty** to a non-client tenant. The general duty requires the leasing agent to disclose to the tenant all material facts about the property which might adversely affect its rental value.

The exclusive authorization to locate space is an employment agreement. It imposes on the broker an agency duty owed to the tenant, even though the fee will most likely be paid by the landlord.

general duty
The duty a licensee owes to non-client individuals to act honestly and in good faith with upfront disclosures of known conditions which adversely affect a property's value. [See **RPI** Form 305-1 and 550-2]

The prospective tenant who exclusively authorizes a competent broker to locate space saves time and money. The licensed advisor conducts the search and handles negotiations to lease property on the prospective tenant's behalf.

However, a tenant working directly with a landlord's broker will initially (and properly) only be first shown space the broker has been employed by a landlord to lease.

In a rising market, when available space is scarce, landlords have superior negotiating power. Thus, it is in the tenant's best interest to employ a different broker from the landlord's broker as their exclusive representative.

Curiously, when a rising market allows landlords to control negotiations in real estate transactions and when prospective tenants most need representation, brokers tend to avoid entering into employment agreements with prospective tenants. It seems to be easier, during periods of rapidly rising prices and rents, to list property and lay back, waiting for the tenant to contact the landlord's broker, instead of the reverse activity of an agent locating property on behalf of a prospective tenant.

However, in a falling market, the opposite happens. Tenants have more negotiating power than landlords due to the increasing availability of space and properties. The result is that brokers have more trouble obtaining written employment agreements from prospective tenants than during periods of reduced availability of space.

Also, when the market position of landlords weakens, landlords eventually become more flexible in lease negotiations. During such markets, landlords are more apt to employ brokers to locate tenants and fill vacant space, particularly builders and developers.

Consider a commercial landlord who orally promises a broker to pay a fee if the broker locates a prospective tenant. A prospective tenant is located by the broker. The tenant is orally advised by the broker that the landlord has agreed to and will pay the broker's fee. No retainer agreements (listings) are entered into by the broker.

After seeing the property and before signing an offer to lease (with fee provisions), the tenant contacts the landlord directly to negotiate a lease. Ultimately, the tenant and landlord enter into a lease agreement. The documentation does not contain provisions for a broker's fee.

Here, the broker cannot enforce collection of their fee from the landlord since the landlord's promise to pay was oral.

However, the tenant has a different liability exposure. While the tenant did not promise to pay a fee, the broker makes a demand on the tenant for payment of an amount equal to the broker's fee promised by the landlord. The broker claims the tenant is liable since the tenant knew about the landlord's oral promise to pay the broker's fee, and interfered with that promise.

The tenant claims the broker is not entitled to recover the fee from them since a written fee agreement did not exist to evidence the fee agreement with the landlord.

Is the tenant liable for payment of the broker's fee?

Yes! The tenant is liable for the broker's fee the landlord promised to pay since the tenant:

Who controls the negotiations?

Pay if you interfere with a broker's economic advantage

- was aware the landlord had promised to pay the broker a fee if the tenant leased the property; and

- excluded the broker from lease negotiations with the intent of avoiding payment of the fee.[3]

When a tenant induces a landlord to deny the broker's fee agreed to by the landlord, the tenant becomes liable for the fee. It does not matter whether the employment agreement between the broker and the landlord is oral or written.

The broker may not pursue the person who orally agreed to pay the fee. However, they may pursue a person who interferes with another person's oral agreement to pay.[4]

Understanding dual agency

Now consider a broker engaged to locate space on behalf of a prospective tenant. The broker fails to ask for and is not employed under an exclusive authorization to locate space. The broker extends the search to space other than the space they have listed for lease.

The broker locates space acceptable to the tenant. The landlord has not listed the space for lease with any broker.

To assure payment of a fee, the broker enters into a so called "one-time" or *"one-party" listing agreement* with the landlord.

The broker does not advise the landlord about the broker's working relationship with the prospective tenant, which was an agency established by the broker's prior efforts to locate suitable space on behalf of the tenant.

On receiving the "one-party" listing for the property, the broker presents the landlord with the tenant's signed offer to lease or **letter of intent (LOI)**. The landlord rejects the offer by making a counteroffer. Again, no disclosure or confirmation of the agency relationship with the tenant is made to the landlord.

Negotiations conducted by the broker between the tenant and the landlord ultimately result in an agreement to lease. The agreement also contains a provision stating the broker's fee will be paid by the landlord.

Before the tenant takes possession and the broker is paid their fee, the landlord discovers the broker was also acting as an agent on behalf of the tenant. This **dual agency** relationship was not disclosed to the landlord when they were induced to employ the broker under the listing. The landlord delivers possession to the tenant, but refuses to pay the broker's fee.

The broker makes a demand on the landlord for payment of the fee. The broker claims they acted as the exclusive agent of the tenant at all times. The

dual agency
The agency relationship that results when a broker represents both the buyer and the seller in a real estate transaction. [See **RPI** Form 117]

---

3 **Buckaloo** v. **Johnson** (1975) 14 C3d 815
4 **Della Penna** v. **Toyota Motor Sales, U.S.A., Inc.** (1995) 11 C4th 376

broker further claims they undertook no agency duty to act on behalf of the landlord in entering into the "one-party" listing to document collection of a fee from the landlord.

The landlord claims the broker is not entitled to a fee since the broker failed to disclose they were representing both parties as a dual agent prior to entering into the employment agreement.

Can the broker enforce collection of the fee?

No! The broker is not entitled to a fee. They were an undisclosed dual agent in the transaction.

The broker became the tenant's agent when they undertook the task of locating and submitting all available suitable space to the tenant, particularly space not listed with the broker.

The broker also became employed as the landlord's agent upon entering into the listing agreement with the landlord. The result was a conflicting employment. Upon entering into the employment with the landlord, the broker had a duty to disclose the resulting dual agency to both the landlord and tenant.[5]

Continuing the previous example, to avoid losing the right to collect a fee on the transaction, the proper practice for the broker is to negotiate with the tenant, not the landlord, to enter into a written employment agreement.

Need for a written employment agreement

Also, an agency relationship with the landlord is unnecessary when the broker prepares and submits the tenant's offer to lease to the landlord. The landlord may agree to pay the fee in an offer to lease or the lease agreement without ever becoming the employer of the broker as their agent. Thus, the issue of a dual agency does not arise.

---

5 **L. Byron Culver & Associates** v. **Jaoudi Industrial & Trading Corporation** (1991) 1 CA4th 300

Chapter 13
Summary

In a rising market when available space is scarce, landlords have superior negotiating power. Thus, it is in the tenant's best interest to employ a different broker from the landlord's broker as their exclusive representative. In a falling market, tenants have more negotiating power than landlords due to the increasing availability of space and properties. The result is that brokers have more trouble obtaining written employment agreements from prospective tenants than during periods of short supply of space.

An exclusive authorization to locate space entered into by a prospective tenant assures the broker a fee if the tenant ultimately leases space of the type and in the area noted in the authorization. An exclusive authorization to locate space is mutually beneficial to a prospective tenant and a broker since it commits a commercial tenant and broker to work together to accomplish a single objective — the leasing of space.

A leasing agent is to investigate and confirm why the tenant wants to move if they are to understand the tenant's needs. When gathering information from a tenant, a diligent agent prepares a tenant lease worksheet to assess the tenant's space requirements and the financial strength of the tenant's business. By uncovering the precise reasons for moving, the agent is best able to find a suitably located space, or negotiate a renewal or extension of the tenant's existing lease.

Chapter 13
Key Terms

Quiz 3 Covering Chapters 9-13 is located on page 635.

Chapter
14

Cost of operating in leased space

After reading this chapter, you will be able to:
- use the property expense profile to disclose to prospective tenants the costs they will likely incur to use and maintain a property;
- understand the duties owed a tenant by the landlord's leasing agent to disclose facts about the property that adversely affect the tenant's use of the property;
- distinguish the additional duties owed a tenant by their agent to advise on the consequences of the property operating facts disclosed by the landlord's agent; and
- apply property operating data to assist prospective tenants in the selection of suitable space.

Learning Objectives

common area maintenance charge	**nonrecurring deposits or charges**
comparative cost analysis	**operating costs**
further-approval contingency	**property expense profile**
letter of intent	**property operating data**
	recurring operating expenses

Key Terms

Property operating data is readily available as property management services are computerized. As a result, prospective tenants making decisions about leasing property have greater awareness and higher expectations when seeking a broker's advice.

Yet, brokers have not delivered more information in response to tenant demand. Rather, tenants continue to suffer adverse results when renting for failure to receive property information known and undisclosed by the brokers and agents involved. [See Form 562 accompanying this chapter]

Disclosures by leasing agents

This failure has prompted the legislature to take action, expanding a broker's duty to disclose known and knowable facts which might adversely affect a property's value. Brokers are charged with knowing readily available facts affecting the rental pricing and utility of the property they are marketing.[1]

Furthermore, when representing a prospective tenant, a broker and their agents need to take reasonable steps to care for and protect the client's interest.[2]

Peer pressure among leasing agents to remain silent about conditions, such as local governmental use requirements for occupancy certificates, often keeps prospective tenants unaware of property-related issues that will adversely affect their use of the property.

A broker representing tenants bears a greater burden to investigate and advise their client about property conditions than does the landlord's broker. Knowing the tenant's needs and capacities is also essential to properly managing the broker-tenant agency relationship as well as the broker's selection of suitable space.

Upon locating a qualifying property, the tenant's broker needs to base their property disclosures on their own investigations, not conjecture before executing leases. Earlier property representations credited to another source and not known or believed to be false by the broker are acceptable to get negotiations underway. Eventually, when commitments are to be made by the tenant, the property information from others needs to be *confirmed* or *corrected*.[3]

Tenant's cost of occupancy and ongoing operations

As couriers of information and the "gatekeepers" for almost all real estate transactions, brokers are retained by consumers (prospective tenants and buyers) to inform them of relevant conditions surrounding a property. Brokers and their agents are the presumed experts, licensed and trained in the issues that affect pricing and users of property. Relevant information includes the costs of occupying and ongoing operations within a space, collectively called **operating expenses**.

operating expenses
The total annual cost incurred to maintain and operate a property for one year. [See **RPI** Form 352 §3.21]

As for a landlord and their leasing agent, their role in marketing space is limited to:

- disclosing *facts* about the property that adversely affect the value and use of the property; and
- avoiding *misleading disclosures*.

The duty the landlord's broker owes tenants does not require them to advise tenants about any adverse consequences the disclosed facts might have on the tenant. Advice on the consequences of the facts disclosed is the duty owed to the tenant by the tenant's broker.

---

1   **Jue** v. **Smiser** (1994) 23 CA4th 312; Calif. Civil Code §2079
2   **Easton** v. **Strassburger** (1984) 152 CA3d 90
3   **Field** v. **Century 21 Klowden-Forness Realty** (1998) 63 CA4th 18

The tenant needs to seek out this advice from an agent so they can make an informed decision when selecting among all available properties.

It is the role and burden of the tenant's leasing agent to fully ascertain the consequences of a property's essential facts, or see to it the tenant investigates, and make relevant recommendations to assist the tenant to meet their goals.

The factual information and assistance which a landlord's broker can offer prospective tenants falls into one of three general categories for analysis:

1. *The property's physical aspects*, including square footage, shipping facilities, utilities, HVAC units, tenant improvements, sprinkler system, condition of the structure, soil, geologic hazards, toxic or noise pollution, parking, etc.;

2. *The conditions of occupancy affecting the use and enjoyment of the property*, i.e., facts available on request from title companies (CC&Rs, trust deeds and vesting), planning departments (uses permitted), redevelopment agencies, business tax rates, police and fire department response times, security, natural hazards and conditions of the neighborhood surrounding the location; and

3. *The cost of operating the leased premises when put to the expected use.*

A property's *operating costs* include business taxes local agencies charge a tenant for locating and conducting business in their jurisdiction. Taxes weigh on the selection of available space, as does access to highways and the client's market. Business taxes vary greatly from city to city, as do police response time and criminal activity.

A property's *operating expenses* are part of its signature, distinguishing it from other available properties. Data on a property's operating costs are gathered and set forth on the *property expense profile* which is handed to prospective tenants. These profiles are used by leasing agents to induce tenants to rent their landlord-client's space rather than other comparable space. [See Form 562]

Property-related expenditures incurred by a tenant of a specific property during the leasing period are classified as:

- **recurring operating expenses**;
- **nonrecurring deposits or charges** [See Chapter 19]; or
- rent and payments on mortgages secured by the tenant's leasehold.

Tenants, their leasing agents, and property managers compare the costs a tenant will incur to occupy and operate in a particular space against the costs to operate in other available space, a type of **comparative cost analysis**. Tenant improvements are a type of acquisition cost that the tenant has to contend with (paid for up front or over the initial term of the lease), whether constructed by the landlord or the tenant.

Tenant's expected costs as part of a marketing package

Operating costs disclosed to tenants

recurring operating expenses
The regular and continuing costs of using and maintaining a property.

nonrecurring deposits or charges
One-time costs for which the tenant is responsible. [See **RPI** Form 550 §2]

Form 562

Tenant's Property Expense Profile

TENANT'S PROPERTY EXPENSE PROFILE

Prepared by: Agent _____ Phone _____
Broker _____ Email _____

NOTE: This form is used by an owner and their leasing agent when preparing a marketing package for the lease of a residential property and disclosing the property's operating costs, to prepare a worksheet to be handed to prospective tenants for their review of the monthly property operating costs and deposits they will likely incur on taking possession of the property.

DATE: _____, 20_____, at _____, California.
PROSPECTIVE TENANT _____
1. **PROPERTY TYPE** _____
    1.1   Location _____
    1.2   Expense figures are estimates reflecting:
          a.   ☐ current expenses of occupancy.
          b.   ☐ forecast of anticipated expenses of occupancy.

2. **MONTHLY OPERATING EXPENSES:**
    2.1   Electricity .... $_____
    2.2   Gas .... $_____
    2.3   Water .... $_____
    2.4   TV (cable/satellite) .... $_____
    2.5   Phone .... $_____
    2.6   Internet .... $_____
    2.7   Trash .... $_____
    2.8   Sewage .... $_____
    2.9   General obligation bonds .... $_____
    2.10 Lawn/Gardening .... $_____
    2.11 Maid/Housekeeping .... $_____
    2.12 Pool/Spa .... $_____
    2.13 Homeowners' Association (HOA) .... $_____
    2.14 Maintenance and repair .... $_____
    2.15 Property management services .... $_____
    2.16 Insurance _____ .... $_____
    2.17 Taxes _____ .... $_____
    2.18 Other _____ .... $_____
    2.19 **Total Operating Expenses** .... $_____
    2.20 Monthly Lease Payment .... $_____
    2.21 **Total Monthly Expenses** .... $_____

3. **DEPOSITS:**
    3.1   Rental security deposit .... $_____
    3.2   Electricity deposit .... $_____
    3.3   Water deposit .... $_____
    3.4   Sewage and rubbish deposit .... $_____
    3.5   Gas service deposit .... $_____
    3.6   Phone service deposit .... $_____
    3.7   Other _____ .... $_____
    3.8   **Total Deposits** .... $_____

-------------------- PAGE 1 OF 2 — FORM 562 --------------------

---

comparative cost analysis
A comparison of the costs a tenant will incur to occupy and operate in a particular space against the costs to operate in other available space. [See **RPI** Form 562]

The tenant's *comparative cost analysis* is even more relevant to negotiations during periods of economic slowdown. Overbuilding or a decline in the number of commercial tenants increases vacancy levels. When this occurs, the economic function of the marketplace will dictate a reduced rent rate until demand for space fills up the present supply of available space and rental rates rise.

When tenants search for space without the pressure of high occupancy levels and the attendant scarcity of space, they are more likely to compare properties. They are also more likely to select a property based on operating costs or the cost of **tenant improvements (TIs)**, rather than rent alone.

Figure 1

Form 185

Letter of Intent

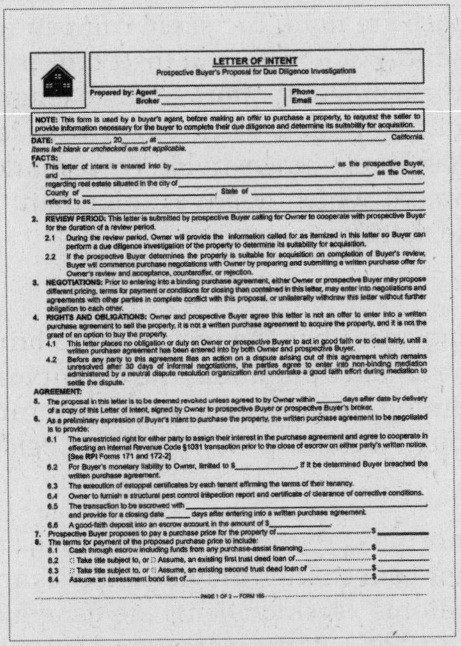

LETTER OF INTENT

Prospective Buyer's Proposal for Due Diligence Investigations

Prepared by: Agent ______________ Phone ______________
Broker ______________ Email ______________

NOTE: This form is used by a buyer's agent, before making an offer to purchase a property, to request the seller to provide information necessary for the buyer to complete their due diligence and determine its suitability for acquisition.

DATE: ____________, 20_____, at ______________________________, California.

Items left blank or unchecked are not applicable.

FACTS:

1. This letter of intent is entered into by ______________________, as the prospective Buyer, and ______________________, as the Owner, regarding real estate situated in the city of ______________, County of ______________, State of ______________, referred to as ______________________.

2. **REVIEW PERIOD:** This letter is submitted by prospective Buyer calling for Owner to cooperate with prospective Buyer for the duration of a review period.
   - 2.1 During the review period, Owner will provide the information called for as itemized in this letter so Buyer can perform a due diligence investigation of the property to determine its suitability for acquisition.
   - 2.2 If the prospective Buyer determines the property is suitable for acquisition on completion of Buyer's review, Buyer will commence purchase negotiations with Owner by preparing and submitting a written purchase offer for Owner's review and acceptance, counteroffer, or rejection.

3. **NEGOTIATIONS:** Prior to entering into a binding purchase agreement, either Owner or prospective Buyer may propose different pricing, terms for payment or conditions for closing than contained in this letter, may enter into negotiations and agreements with other parties in complete conflict with this proposal, or unilaterally withdraw this letter without further obligation to each other.

4. **RIGHTS AND OBLIGATIONS:** Owner and prospective Buyer agree this letter is not an offer to enter into a written purchase agreement to sell the property, it is not a written purchase agreement to acquire the property, and it is not the grant of an option to buy the property.
   - 4.1 This letter places no obligation or duty on Owner or prospective Buyer to act in good faith or to deal fairly, until a written purchase agreement has been entered into by both Owner and prospective Buyer.
   - 4.2 Before any party to this agreement files an action on a dispute arising out of this agreement which remains unresolved after 30 days of informal negotiations, the parties agree to enter into non-binding mediation administered by a neutral dispute resolution organization and undertake a good faith effort during mediation to settle the dispute.

AGREEMENT:

5. The proposal in this letter is to be deemed revoked unless agreed to by Owner within ______ days after date by delivery of a copy of this Letter of Intent, signed by Owner to prospective Buyer or prospective Buyer's broker.

6. As a preliminary expression of Buyer's intent to purchase the property, the written purchase agreement to be negotiated is to provide:
   - 6.1 The unrestricted right for either party to assign their interest in the purchase agreement and agree to cooperate in effecting an Internal Revenue Code §1031 transaction prior to the close of escrow on either party's written notice. [See RPI Forms 171 and 172-2]
   - 6.2 For Buyer's monetary liability to Owner, limited to $____________, if it be determined Buyer breached the written purchase agreement.
   - 6.3 The execution of estoppel certificates by each tenant affirming the terms of their tenancy.
   - 6.4 Owner to furnish a structural pest control inspection report and certificate of clearance of corrective conditions.
   - 6.5 The transaction to be escrowed with ______________________, and provide for a closing date ______ days after entering into a written purchase agreement.
   - 6.6 A good-faith deposit into an escrow account in the amount of $____________.

7. Prospective Buyer proposes to pay a purchase price for the property of .... $ ________

8. The terms for payment of the proposed purchase price to include:
   - 8.1 Cash through escrow including funds from any purchase-assist financing .... $ ________
   - 8.2 ☐ Take title subject to, or ☐ Assume, an existing first trust deed loan of .... $ ________
   - 8.3 ☐ Take title subject to, or ☐ Assume, an existing second trust deed loan of .... $ ________
   - 8.4 Assume an assessment bond lien of .... $ ________

PAGE 1 OF 3 — FORM 185

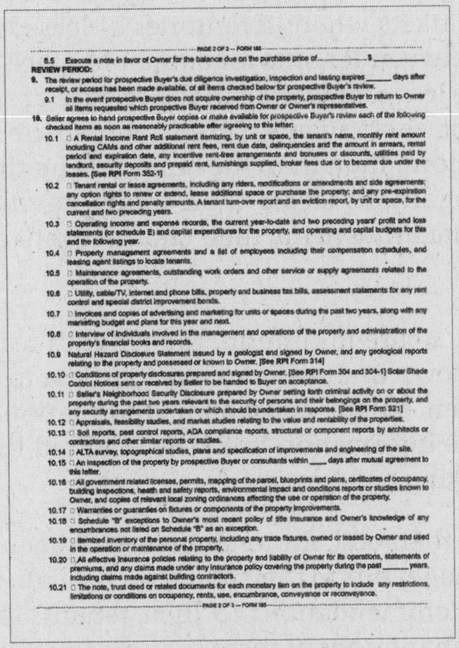

PAGE 2 OF 3 — FORM 185

- 8.5 Execute a note in favor of Owner for the balance due on the purchase price of .... $ ________

REVIEW PERIOD:

9. The review period for prospective Buyer's due diligence investigation, inspection and testing expires ______ days after receipt, or access has been made available, of all items checked below for prospective Buyer's review.
   - 9.1 In the event prospective Buyer does not acquire ownership of the property, prospective Buyer to return to Owner all items requested which prospective Buyer received from Owner or Owner's representatives.

10. Seller agrees to hand prospective Buyer copies or make available for prospective Buyer's review each of the following checked items as soon as reasonably practicable after agreeing to this letter:
   - 10.1 ☐ A Rental Income Rent Roll statement itemizing, by unit or space, the tenant's name, monthly rent amount including CAMs and other additional rent fees, rent due date, delinquencies and the amount in arrears, rental period and expiration date, any incentive rent-free arrangements and bonuses or discounts, utilities paid by landlord, security deposits and prepaid rent, furnishings supplied, broker fees due or to become due under the leases. [See RPI Form 352-1]
   - 10.2 ☐ Tenant rental or lease agreements, including any riders, modifications or amendments and side agreements; any option rights to renew or extend, lease additional space or purchase the property; and any pre-expiration cancellation rights and penalty amounts. A tenant turn-over report and an eviction report, by unit or space, for the current and two preceding years.
   - 10.3 ☐ Operating income and expense records, the current year-to-date and two preceding years' profit and loss statements (or schedule E) and capital expenditures for the property, and operating and capital budgets for this and the following year.
   - 10.4 ☐ Property management agreements and a list of employees including their compensation schedules, and leasing agent listings to locate tenants.
   - 10.5 ☐ Maintenance agreements, outstanding work orders and other service or supply agreements related to the operation of the property.
   - 10.6 ☐ Utility, cable/TV, internet and phone bills, property and business tax bills, assessment statements for any rent control and special district improvement bonds.
   - 10.7 ☐ Invoices and copies of advertising and marketing for units or spaces during the past two years, along with any marketing budget and plans for this year and next.
   - 10.8 ☐ Interview of individuals involved in the management and operations of the property and administration of the property's financial books and records.
   - 10.9 Natural Hazard Disclosure Statement issued by a geologist and signed by Owner, and any geological reports relating to the property and possessed or known to Owner. [See RPI Form 314]
   - 10.10 ☐ Conditions of property disclosures prepared and signed by Owner. [See RPI Form 304 and 304-1] Solar Shade Control Notices sent or received by Seller to be handed to Buyer on acceptance.
   - 10.11 ☐ Seller's Neighborhood Security Disclosure prepared by Owner setting forth criminal activity on or about the property during the past two years relevant to the security of persons and their belongings on the property, and any security arrangements undertaken or which should be undertaken in response. [See RPI Form 321]
   - 10.12 ☐ Appraisals, feasibility studies, and market studies relating to the value and rentability of the properties.
   - 10.13 ☐ Soil reports, pest control reports, ADA compliance reports, structural or component reports by architects or contractors and other similar reports or studies.
   - 10.14 ☐ ALTA survey, topographical studies, plans and specification of improvements and engineering of the site.
   - 10.15 ☐ An inspection of the property by prospective Buyer or consultants within _____ days after mutual agreement to this letter.
   - 10.16 ☐ All government related licenses, permits, mapping of the parcel, blueprints and plans, certificates of occupancy, building inspections, health and safety reports, environmental impact and conditions reports or studies known to Owner, and copies of relevant local zoning ordinances affecting the use or operation of the property.
   - 10.17 ☐ Warranties or guaranties on fixtures or components of the property improvements.
   - 10.18 ☐ Schedule "B" exceptions to Owner's most recent policy of title insurance and Owner's knowledge of any encumbrances not listed on Schedule "B" as an exception.
   - 10.19 ☐ Itemized inventory of the personal property, including any trade fixtures, owned or leased by Owner and used in the operation or maintenance of the property.
   - 10.20 ☐ All effective insurance policies relating to the property and liability of Owner for its operations, statements of premiums, and any claims made under any insurance policy covering the property during the past ______ years, including claims made against building contractors.
   - 10.21 ☐ The note, trust deed or related documents for each monetary lien on the property to include any restrictions, limitations or conditions on occupancy, rents, use, encumbrance, conveyance or reconveyance.

PAGE 2 OF 3 — FORM 185

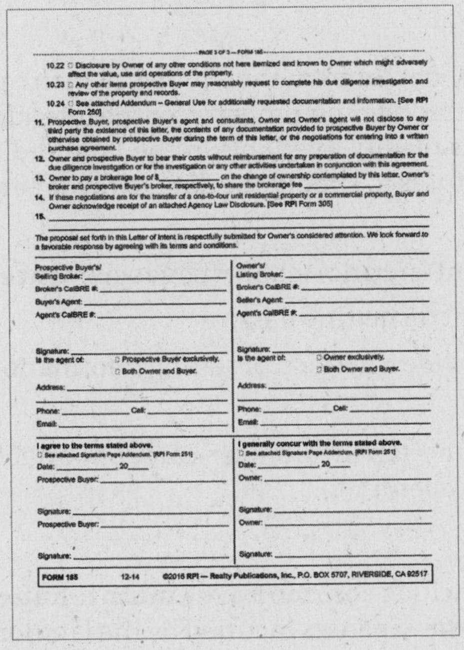

PAGE 3 OF 3 — FORM 185

   - 10.22 ☐ Disclosure by Owner of any other conditions not here itemized and known to Owner which might adversely affect the value, use and operations of the property.
   - 10.23 ☐ Any other items prospective Buyer may reasonably request to complete his due diligence investigation and review of the property and records.
   - 10.24 ☐ See attached Addendum – General Use for additionally requested documentation and information. [See RPI Form 250]

11. Prospective Buyer, prospective Buyer's agent and consultants, Owner and Owner's agent will not disclose to any third party the existence of this letter, the contents of any documentation provided to prospective Buyer by Owner or otherwise obtained by prospective Buyer during the term of this letter, or the negotiations for entering into a written purchase agreement.

12. Owner and prospective Buyer to bear their costs without reimbursement for any preparation of documentation for the due diligence investigation or for the investigation or any other activities undertaken in conjunction with this agreement.

13. Owner to pay a brokerage fee of $____________ on the change of ownership contemplated by this letter. Owner's broker and prospective Buyer's broker, respectively, to share the brokerage fee ________:________.

14. If these negotiations are for the transfer of a one-to-four unit residential property or a commercial property, Buyer and Owner acknowledge receipt of an attached Agency Law Disclosure. [See RPI Form 305]

15. ____

The proposal set forth in this Letter of Intent is respectfully submitted for Owner's considered attention. We look forward to a favorable response by agreeing with its terms and conditions.

Prospective Buyer's/ Selling Broker: ______	Owner's/ Listing Broker: ______
Broker's CalBRE #: ______	Broker's CalBRE #: ______
Buyer's Agent: ______	Seller's Agent: ______
Agent's CalBRE #: ______	Agent's CalBRE #: ______
Signature: ______	Signature: ______
Is the agent of: ☐ Prospective Buyer exclusively. ☐ Both Owner and Buyer.	Is the agent of: ☐ Owner exclusively. ☐ Both Owner and Buyer.
Address: ______	Address: ______
Phone: ______ Cell: ______	Phone: ______ Cell: ______
Email: ______	Email: ______
I agree to the terms stated above. ☐ See attached Signature Page Addendum. [RPI Form 251]	**I generally concur with the terms stated above.** ☐ See attached Signature Page Addendum. [RPI Form 251]
Date: ______, 20____	Date: ______, 20____
Prospective Buyer: ______	Owner: ______
Signature: ______	Signature: ______
Prospective Buyer: ______	Owner: ______
Signature: ______	Signature: ______

FORM 185 12-14 ©2015 RPI — Realty Publications, Inc., P.O. BOX 5707, RIVERSIDE, CA 92517

For a full-size, fillable copy of this or any other form in this book that may be legally used in your professional practice, go to realtypublications.com/forms

Landlords leasing their properties for below-market rents need to be queried for information and history on the operating costs the tenant will incur in addition to the rent. Below-market rent raises suspicions of property *obsolescence* due to aging and loss of function, or excessive operating costs such as utility charges, local taxes, security needs, use requirements, neighborhood issues, crime, etc.

Without knowledge of property operating costs, the prospective tenant is left to speculate about the costs (other than rent) of leasing the property. For the tenant, this is a financially unsound starting place for negotiating a lease.

Nondisclosure of operating costs is more likely to occur during tight rental markets when inventories of leased space are tight. Increased competition between tenants for available space induces landlords and their brokers to be less cooperative in the release of adverse property information to tenants and their agents. This asymmetric condition provides the tenant with less information than the landlord and the landlord's broker holds. These market conditions create a predatory environment which deprives the tenant of data influencing their choice to rent and ability to negotiate.

The duty of a tenant's agent to investigate and advise

At a bare minimum, the tenant's leasing agent has the obligation to bring known and readily available data to the tenant's attention. The tenant may then obtain additional information during negotiations or by requiring the information from the landlord through a contingency provision before taking occupancy.

At their best, the tenant's leasing agent not only advises, but also investigates and reports to their client on the data they collect. They provide analysis and recommendations to their tenant. Landlords' leasing agents are generally unhappy about these inquiries, preferring reduced transparency and instant uninformed action.

property operating data
The actual costs of operating a property for its intended use.

The landlord either knows, or can easily obtain from their property manager or current tenant, the actual costs of operating their property for the intended use. Thus, **property operating data** is readily available to the landlord. If the landlord or the landlord's broker refuses to supply the data to the tenant, the tenant's broker can:

- investigate the expenses the current and prior tenants have experienced;
- make any offer to lease contingent on getting data; or

letter of intent
A non-binding proposal signed and submitted to a property owner to start negotiations.

- use a **letter of intent (LOI)** to provide a method of getting information. [See Figure 1, Form 185]

Armed with knowledge of the costs, the tenant's broker can comfortably disclose the operating expenses to their client.

CAMs incurred by the landlord, paid by the tenant

Leases on commercial properties often include **common area maintenance charges (CAMs)**. *CAMs* are intended to be expenses incurred by the landlord and paid by the tenant as rent additional to the base rent, adjustments and percentages. However, the use of CAMs set as a percentage of the base rent are used to effectively increase rental income (and make the property's published rental rate appear advantageous) without ever incurring or accounting to the tenant for amounts spent.

The prospective tenant and their agent need to insist on the seller providing an operating cost sheet itemizing the monthly CAMs the tenant will incur for their share of the common area maintenance.

Information about CAMs paid by the prior occupant of the space might affect the tenant's negotiations and rental commitment. Thus, such information is a material fact essential to the tenant's decision-making process. It's all part of the rent payments to the landlord structured essentially as net leasing arrangements for multi-tenant properties, not single user property. [See **RPI** Form 552-3]

During a tight leasing market with reduced availability of space, landlords sometimes deceptively increase their net income by adding fixed amounts as CAMs instead of directly raising rents. Thus, they fractionalize the rent to distract the prospective tenant with what initially appears to be a competitive rent, until the extent of the CAMs are brought up well into negotiations.

The landlord's broker has a duty to disclose the actual costs which have been incurred by tenants in the space. If hard numbers are not available, a landlord's broker may provide estimates. However, estimates are required to be reasonably accurate, not the product of guesswork. Further, the landlord's broker needs to state they are estimates when they are not data actually experienced.

Also, the landlord's broker needs to identify the source of the data provided to the tenant and rate its reliability as known to the broker. If the data or source of the data is questioned, the offer to lease (or counter offer) needs to include a **further-approval contingency**. [See Figure 1, Form 185 §9]

The *further-approval contingency* provision allows the tenant time to investigate and confirm the property information disclosed by the landlord. If the information cannot be confirmed, or is contrary to the information disclosed, the tenant their agent may cancel or renegotiate the offer to lease.[4]

Best practices when disclosing operating costs include:

- the preparation of a **property expense profile** for each available unit, prepared by the landlord or property manager and signed by the landlord [See Form 562]; and
- a comparison by the tenant and the tenant's broker of the economic cost of rent, and other operating expenses for one space versus operating costs and rent incurred in other qualifying spaces.

With documentation and a comparative analysis of rent and operating costs complete, the tenant and the tenant's broker can intelligently negotiate the best lease arrangements available for the tenant in the local market.

Occasionally, a landlord may want to be "tight-lipped" about the operating data due to various different arrangements with numerous tenants. In this case, the landlord may insist on (or be offered by the tenant) a confidentiality agreement before releasing any data to the prospective tenant.

Tenants who forego representation by an agent lose the benefit of a comparative analysis. They also incur risk since they will miss out on the experience and advice of a licensee retained to represent their best interests.

common area maintenance charge
Property operating expenses incurred by a commercial landlord and paid by the tenant as rent in additonal to the base rent, adjustments and percentages. [See **RPI** Form 552 §6]

Accurate estimates by leasing agents

further-approval contingency
A provision in an offer to rent property which allows the tenant time to investigate and confirm the property information disclosed by the landlord.

property expense profile
An itemized analysis of the costs a tenant or landlord will incur to operate and maintain a particular property. [See **RPI** Form 562]

---

4 **Ford** v. **Cournale** (1973) 36 CA3d 172

Chapter 14 Summary

A property's operating costs are part of its signature, distinguishing it from other available properties. Data on a property's operating costs are gathered and set forth on the property expense profile which is handed to prospective tenants. These profiles are used by leasing agents to induce tenants to rent their landlord-client's space rather than other comparable space.

The duty the landlord's broker owes tenants does not require them to advise tenants about any consequences the disclosed facts might have on the tenant. Advice on the consequences of the facts disclosed is the duty owed to the tenant by the tenant's broker. Thus, it is the role and burden of the tenant's leasing agent to fully ascertain a property's essential facts and make relevant recommendations to assist the tenant to meet their goals.

Without knowledge of property operating costs, the prospective tenant is left to speculate about the costs (other than rent) of leasing the property. For the tenant, this is a financially unsound starting place for negotiating a lease. The tenant's comparative cost analysis is even more relevant to negotiations during periods of economic slowdown.

Chapter 14 Key Terms

Quiz 4 Covering Chapters 14-18 is located on page 636.

Tenant profiles

After reading this chapter, you will be able to:

- ascertain a tenant's needs when leasing property; and
- manage tenant requirements during leasing negotiations.

exclusive authorization to locate space   **tenant lease worksheet**

Learning Objectives

Key Terms

A broker negotiating a commercial lease on behalf of a client needs to possess a high level of knowledge and expertise regarding different aspects of leasing, including:

- the economic attributes and financial results of lease agreements;
- the legal consequences of lease agreement provisions and title conditions affecting the tenant's right to possession; and
- the tax implications of the lease transaction.

Get the negotiations rolling

A broker's technical expertise enables them to ascertain their client's needs and requirements, whether their client is a landlord or a tenant. Once the broker understands their client's objectives, the broker can locate either a suitable tenant (a **user**) or property (the **space** or **premises**). Then, what remains is to enter into lease negotiations.

Most commercial tenants are completely consumed by the constant demands of their business. They usually do not have sufficient time to devote to making decisions in real estate leasing transactions. Further, annual operating costs of leasing property represent a small fraction of the business's gross income, somewhere between 2% and 4%. High traffic shopping center space is the exception.

On the other hand, most landlords are primarily concerned with efforts to get vacant space rented. Consequently, landlords and tenants rely on brokers as their leasing agents to put the lease package together, which consists of property data disclosures and lease documents.

The final lease agreement negotiated by a leasing agent will be the result of:

- the relative bargaining strength of the landlord and tenant under current market conditions;
- the time the landlord and tenant are willing to devote and the urgency given to negotiating the leasing details;
- the expertise exercised and attention given to property and leasing details by their respective leasing agents; and
- local market conditions affecting user demand for the property and rent amounts.

The tenant's letter of intent

The broker usually gets the negotiations started with an **offer to rent** or **letter of intent (LOI)**. Once negotiations are underway, a broker's advice to their client helps shape the final terms. The tenant's broker drafts the initial offer or LOI. The lease agreement needs to be prepared by the tenant's agent if they are to maintain their advantage of making the first offer. Landlords with larger leasing operations often prepare their own documents "in house," or retain legal counsel to do so.

A leasing agent best determines the tenant's intentions for leasing property by preparing:

- a tenant lease worksheet to assess the tenant's space requirements and, with financial statements, the financial condition of the tenant's business [See Form 555 accompanying this chapter]; and
- an offer to lease and attached lease agreement to commit the tenant so an acceptance by the landlord will bring about an enforceable contract set by the terms of a lease agreement or a viable counteroffer. [See **RPI** Form 556]

A LOI will probably precede the tenant's actual offer in a casual effort to "feel out" the landlord. But this may backfire on the leasing agent if the landlord simply responds with a lease agreement as their proposal, stripping the tenant's leasing agent of control over lease agreement content.

List the tenant

With or without a written retainer agreement with a tenant, the leasing agent who undertakes the task of locating space for the tenant assumes agency obligations to act on behalf of, and in the best interest of, the tenant.

However, without a written agreement, the leasing agent has no assurance their fee, if earned, will be paid.[1]

---

1 **Phillippe v. Shapell Industries, Inc.** (1987) 43 C3d 1247

Thus, the prudent leasing agent only undertakes the duty to represent a tenant when the tenant signs an **exclusive authorization to locate space**. [See **RPI** Form 111]

Under a tenant's *exclusive authorization to locate space*, the broker is formally retained as the tenant's representative. Thus, the broker will be paid a leasing fee, either by the landlord or the tenant, if the tenant enters into a lease for the type of property described in the tenant's exclusive authorization agreement. [See **RPI** Form 111]

A leasing agent acting on behalf of a tenant needs to investigate and confirm why the tenant wants to move if the leasing agent is to better understand their user's needs.

For example, the tenant's existing space may have become too large or too small for their current or future needs. Alternatively, the tenant may be arguing with their current landlord over:

- the rent, common area maintenance charges (CAMs) or assessments when renewing a lease;
- the tenant's current space requirements that conflict with space provided for under an option to renew or extend; or
- a lease assignment or sublease of a portion of the leased space.

By uncovering the precise reasons for moving, the tenant's agent is better able to find a suitable new location and premises, or negotiate a renewal or extension of the tenant's current lease.

Tenant conferences

exclusive authorization to locate space
An employment agreement by a broker and a prospective tenant which authorizes the broker to act as the tenant's leasing agent to locate suitable space and negotiate a lease agreement. [See **RPI** Form 111]

The tenant's future needs

When a prospective tenant is starting a new business, the leasing agent needs to get information on the tenant's business projections at the outset. A tenant's new business projections may be overly optimistic. They may want space that is simply too large or in too expensive a location. The tenant may have to settle for incubator space in a less desirable location which accepts "start-up" business tenants. Rent might be paid by the landlord accepting a fractional participation in the ownership of the tenant's business.

Conversely, a tenant may underestimate the potential future growth of their business. The premises they favor may be too small to absorb their growth, frustrating later attempts to expand. The tenant will be forced to relocate again prematurely. In this case, the tenant may require options or the right of first refusal on additional space, or a lease cancellation or buyout provision so they may vacate the premises without liability for future rents under their lease agreement.

Also, over projection of the potential income of a tenant's business when entering into a percentage-rent lease will reduce the landlord's projected rental income. Unless the leasing agent considers the space needs and gross income of a user, the leasing agent's long-term service to either the landlord or tenant is limited. Thus, the leasing agent needs to develop a system to match the right landlord with the right tenant.

TENANT LEASE WORKSHEET

Prepared by: Agent _____ Phone _____
Broker _____ Email _____

NOTE: This form is used by a leasing agent when representing a prospective commercial tenant in need of space, to determine the tenant's motivations, business needs and financial status, and the type of property and lease terms sought by the tenant.

DATE: _____, 20_____, at _____, California.

1. **GENERAL INFORMATION:**
   Tenant's name _____
   Business address _____
   Phone _____ Fax _____
   Email _____
   Type of business _____

2. **Information on space presently occupied by Tenant:**

   2.1 Type of building: ☐ Multi-tenant ☐ Free-standing
   2.2 Location: ☐ Good ☐ Adequate ☐ Poor
   2.3 Suitability to business: ☐ Good ☐ Adequate ☐ Poor
   2.4 Square feet _____ determined by _____
   2.5 Tenant utility costs:
       a. ☐ Lighting/electrical. . . . . $_____
       b. ☐ Gas. . . . . $_____
       c. ☐ Water. . . . . $_____
       d. ☐ _____ . . . . $_____
       TOTAL . . . . $_____

   2.6 Tenant operating costs:
       a. ☐ Common area maintenance (CAM). . . . . $_____
       b. ☐ Casualty insurance. . . . . $_____
       c. ☐ Use fees. . . . . $_____
       d. ☐ Real property taxes. . . . . $_____
       e. ☐ Maintenance. . . . . $_____
       f. ☐ Assessments. . . . . $_____
       g. ☐ Property management. . . . . $_____
       h. ☐ Janitorial services. . . . . $_____
       i. ☐ Parking. . . . . $_____
       j. ☐ Fire insurance. . . . . $_____
       k. ☐ _____ . . . . $_____
       l. ☐ _____ . . . . $_____
       TOTAL . . . . $_____

   2.7 Rooms/offices (number of):
       ☐ Offices . . . . _____
       ☐ Reception area. . . . . _____
       ☐ Storage rooms . . . . _____
       ☐ Kitchen. _____
       ☐ Conference rooms . . . . _____
       ☐ Lab/R&D rooms . . . . _____
       ☐ Restrooms. . . . . _____
       ☐ Dressing rooms . . . . _____
       ☐ Computer room . . . . _____
       ☐ Hallways . . . . _____
       ☐ Lunchroom . . . . _____
       ☐ _____ . . . . . _____
       ☐ _____ . . . . . _____
       ☐ _____ . . . . . _____

   2.8 Tenant improvements and trade fixtures _____
   _____

Using a tenant lease worksheet

Consider a tenant who runs an insurance agency that has more employees and files than the premises it now occupies will accommodate. The tenant has three agents and a support staff of eight people, including secretaries, an office manager and a full-time computer technician and webmaster.

The tenant expects the economy to allow the business to continue to grow. Thus, they need a larger space to meet their present and expanding needs.

3. information on space sought by tenant:

3.1 Type of building: ☐ Multi-tenant ☐ Free-standing ☐ Rural

3.2 Location preference: ☐ Downtown ☐ Suburbs

City _____ County _____

3.3 Access needed:

☐ Residential	☐ Legal/civic centers	☐ Shopping centers
☐ Agricultural	☐ Hotels	☐ Restaurants
☐ Industrial	☐ Libraries	☐ Redevelopment areas
☐ Mountain areas	☐ Universities/Colleges	☐ Government-state
☐ Freeways	☐ Financial services	☐ Government-federal
☐ Public transit	☐ Warehouses	☐ Publishing houses
☐ Parking	☐ Office centers	☐ Manufacturing centers
☐ Airports	☐ Convention centers	☐ Disposal facilities
☐ Coastal	☐ Sports facilities	☐ Trains
☐ Shipyards	☐ Near competition	☐ _____
☐ Trucking	☐ Medical/hospital	

3.4 Space needs:

a. Square feet _____

b. Rooms/offices:

☐ Offices	_____	☐ Storage rooms	_____
☐ Conference rooms	_____	☐ Restrooms	_____
☐ Computer rooms	_____	☐ Lunch rooms	_____
☐ Reception area	_____	☐ Kitchen	_____
☐ Lab/R&D rooms	_____	☐ Dressing rooms	_____
☐ Hallways	_____	☐ _____	_____

3.5 Physical plant needs:

☐ Signs	_____	☐ Ceilings	_____
☐ Stairwells	_____	☐ Walls	_____
☐ Finishing	_____	☐ Floors	_____
☐ Partitions	_____	☐ Painting	_____
☐ Carpeting	_____	☐ Ramps/parking	_____

3.6 Utility needs:

☐ Lighting/electrical	_____	☐ Computer	_____
☐ Water	_____	☐ Gas	_____

4. Tenant business goals:

4.1 Short term (3-5 years)

_____
_____
_____
_____

4.2 Long term (5-10 years)

_____
_____
_____
_____

5. Lease terms on space now occupied by Tenant:

5.1 Type: ☐ Office ☐ Shopping center ☐ Retail
☐ Industrial ☐ Light business

5.2 Term _____ Expiration date _____ / _____ / _____

5.3 Base rent $_____ payable _____

5.4 Current rent $_____ payable _____

5.5 Rent based on: ☐ Per sq. ft. ☐ Percent gross sales

The tenant contacts a leasing agent to locate space with tenant improvements suitable for their staff to occupy. The leasing agent explains they are the leasing agent for a number of landlords in the area and will be able to find suitable space for the tenant. The tenant is advised that, if needed, planners are available to design the use of the space and specify the tenant improvements for occupancy.

The leasing agent prepares a **tenant lease worksheet**. [See Form 555 accompanying this chapter]

Form 555

Tenant Lease Worksheet

Page 2 of 3

tenant lease worksheet
A document the leasing agent uses to analyze the tenant's current financial condition and needs for leased space. [See **RPI** Form 555]

---------------------------------- PAGE 3 OF 3 — FORM 555 ----------------------------------

5.6 Rental adjustments based on: ☐ CPI ☐ Reappraisal
    ☐ Graduated ☐ Fixed ☐ _____

5.7 Security deposit . . . . $_____

5.8 Prepaid rent . . . . $_____

5.9 Option to renew/extend: ☐ Yes ☐ No

5.10 Opiton to buy: ☐ Yes ☐ No

5.11 Option to lease additional space: ☐ Yes ☐ No

5.12 Lease assignment: ☑ Freely ☐ Landlord consent

5.13 Other _____

5.14 Landlord's name _____

    Business address _____

    Phone _____ Fax _____

    Agent's name _____

    Phone _____ Fax _____

6. Lease terms sought:

6.1 Desired monthly base rent $_____

6.2 Rent based on: ☐ Per sq. ft. ☐ Percent gross sales

6.3 Rental adjustments based on: ☐ CPI ☐ Reappraisal
    ☐ Graduated ☐ Fixed ☐ _____

6.4 Landlord responsibility for utilities:
    ☐ Lighting/electrical ☐ Gas
    ☐ Water ☐ _____

6.5 Landlord responsibility for operating costs:
    ☐ Maintenance ☐ Insurance
    ☐ Property mgmt. ☐ Parking
    ☐ Use fees ☐ Janitorial
    ☐ Taxes ☐ _____

6.6 Common area maintenance (CAM) provision cap:
    ☐ _____ Per sq. ft. ☐ _____% Per year

6.7 Security deposit . . . . $_____

6.8 Prepaid rents . . . . $_____

6.9 Option to renew: ☐ Yes ☐ No [See **RPI** Form 565]

6.10 Option to buy: ☐ Yes ☐ No [See **RPI** Form 161]

6.11 Option to lease additional space: ☐ Yes ☐ No [See **RPI** Form 579-1]

6.12 Lease assignment: ☐ Freely ☐ Landlord consent [See **RPI** Form 595]

6.13 Other _____

_____

_____

_____

_____

_____

_____

The *worksheet* covers three key areas the leasing agent needs to consider and analyze:

- the tenant's current lease agreement obligations and conditions of their existing space;
- the tenant's current and likely future needs for leased space; and
- the tenant's financial condition and creditworthiness.

Regarding the tenant's existing space, the leasing agent will determine:

- the type of building;
- the square footage;
- the monthly operating and utility costs; and
- the tenant improvements and trade fixtures.

A necessary review of the tenant's current lease includes:

- the expiration date;
- monthly rent and periodic adjustments and assessments;
- the obligation to continue to occupy the premises;
- the obligation to restore the premises or remove tenant improvements;
- options to extend or renew the lease or buy the premises;
- the tenant's ability to assign or sublease; and
- the amount of the security deposit.

These facts will help the leasing agent determine the tenant's rights and obligations under their present lease for timing the tenant's relocation. When representing the tenant, the leasing agent needs to point out and explain, to the best of their ability, their knowledge of the beneficial or detrimental effect any lease provisions have on the tenant.

When representing an owner, the leasing agent will advise them which terms the tenant is unhappy with and which lease provisions are "throw away" clauses. Such clauses are designed for negotiations and are of little or no concern to the owner.

Next, the leasing agent ascertains the tenant's needs and goals for the new space.

Regarding the space requirements, the leasing agent will need to uncover the tenant's:

- current square footage needs;
- future square footage needs;
- phone, utilities and computer facility needs;
- heating and air conditioning requirements;
- parking, docking, turn-around and shipping requirements;
- access to freeways, airports and other public transportation;
- access to civic, financial, legal, governmental or other "downtown" facilities;
- response time for police and fire departments;
- access to housing areas, shopping and restaurants; and
- any needs peculiar to the tenant.

Some tenants may focus on specific geographic locations in the business market or population centers. Others may need the lowest rent possible, regardless of location within the geographic area they wish to conduct business.

On completing a tenant lease worksheet, the leasing agent discovers the tenant wants to:

- stay in the same community because of their many strong business and social ties to the area;
- keep their rent fixed or have predictable (fixed) annual adjustments over the next three to five years; and
- move closer to the freeway for quick access to customers in outlying areas.

Tenant needs

The tenant currently needs 4,000 square feet to accommodate:

- four private offices;
- a computer room;
- a reception area;
- a conference room;
- a storage room;
- restrooms;
- a lunch room; and
- areas for sales staff and secretaries.

Financially, the business is profitable, but the tenant wants to keep rent at no more than 4% of gross income. Additionally, the tenant is concerned future inflation will mount. Thus, they do not want their rent adjustments tied to the Consumer Price Index (CPI). If they have to be, then a ceiling needs to be set on any annual rise in the CPI beyond 3%.

Also, the leasing agent might suggest negotiating for an option to lease additional space if adjacent space becomes available and necessary for expansion (and an additional fee for the leasing agent if exercised).

Finally, the leasing agent and the tenant need to discuss the rental terms available in the leasing market. Several provisions in leases have a financial impact, favorable or not, on the landlord and the tenant. Financial aspects of a lease agreement include:

- base monthly rent;
- periodic rental adjustments (CPI or percentage);
- payment of real estate taxes and insurance premiums;
- tenant improvements;
- responsibility for general maintenance (CAMs);
- structural, roofing and HVAC maintenance;
- government ordered retrofitting;
- lease assignability and subletting authority;
- options to renew or extend, or to buy; and
- personal guarantees or letters of credit.

Chapter 15 Summary

The prudent leasing agent only undertakes the duty to represent a tenant when the tenant signs an exclusive authorization to locate space.

The leasing agent's goal to locate space for the tenant involves several steps. First the leasing agent prepares a tenant lease worksheet. The worksheet covers three key areas the leasing agent needs to consider and analyze:

- the tenant's current lease conditions and existing space;
- the tenant's current and future needs for leased space; and
- the tenant's financial condition and creditworthiness.

These facts will help the leasing agent determine the tenant's rights and obligations under their present lease agreement.

Next, the leasing agent ascertains the tenant's needs and objectives to be met in the new space. Finally, the leasing agent and the tenant need to discuss the rental terms available in the leasing market.

Chapter 15 Key Terms

Quiz 4 Covering Chapters 14-18 is located on page 636.

Notes:

Chapter
16

Offers to lease

After reading this chapter, you will be able to:

- appreciate the legal significance of written negotiations; and
- distinguish between submitting an offer to lease and a proposal to lease.

letter of intent   **offer to lease**

Learning Objectives

Key Terms

Negotiating the commercial lease

Once a leasing agent locates suitable premises for a prospective tenant, the agent brings the landlord and tenant together through negotiations to develop the terms of a lease acceptable to all.

The role the broker plays in negotiations and their duties as a leasing agent depends on whom they represent in the transaction: the landlord, the tenant or both. How aggressive a role a broker may play on behalf of their client depends on the bargaining power held by the landlord or tenant during the current phase of the cyclical market conditions.

When representing the tenant, the broker needs to initially determine their need for space and the rental amount the tenant is willing and able to pay for the space. The broker uses a tenant lease worksheet, when first interviewing the tenant to gather and review this information. [See **RPI** Form 555; see Chapter 15]

When representing the landlord, the broker needs to know the rental terms and leasing conditions the landlord desires for the space, and perform a due diligence review of the space for rent. Usually, this data is set out in the exclusive authorization to lease property. [See **RPI** Forms 110 and 590]

The offer to lease

Whether a broker represents the tenant or the landlord, the broker initiates negotiations most efficiently by preparing an offer to lease form for the tenant to review and consider for signing. [See Form 556 accompanying this chapter]

The tenant enters into the offer to lease space for the same reasons a buyer signs and submits an offer to purchase real estate.

For example, under an offer to lease, the landlord agrees to convey a right to possession to the tenant for a set period of time under the lease.

Likewise, a buyer of a real estate interest under a purchase agreement acquires either an existing leasehold (held by and being sold by an existing tenant) or fee title (from the owner). This interest is conveyed to the buyer by an assignment or deed.

Thus, like a sales transaction, the arrangement of a lease transaction has two phases:

- the *offer and acceptance* (agreement to lease); and
- the *drafting and signing of the lease* and delivery of funds and possession (the conveyance of the leasehold interest on closing).

In the leasing situation, the broker, the landlord or the landlord's attorney prepares and handles all the closing instruments, such as the lease agreement and transfer of funds.

Leasing is usually accomplished without the benefit of a formal escrow. If documents are to be recorded, such as occurs in a long-term leasing transaction, a title officer and title insurance company become involved with a title search and issuance of a leasehold title insurance policy.

Contents of the offer

To be effective, an **offer to lease** needs to set forth all crucial elements negotiated to bring the landlord and tenant together in final leasing arrangements. [See Form 556]

offer to lease
A document which sets forth all crucial elements typically negotiated to bring the landlord and tenant together in final leasing arrangements. [See **RPI** Form 556]

An *offer to lease*, like an offer to purchase, contains four sections:

- identification of the parties and premises;
- rental payment schedules and period of occupancy;
- property maintenance and terms of possession (use); and
- signatures of the parties.

A floor plan or common description of the premises is usually attached by a reference to it in the identification section.

The tenant is asked to include a good faith deposit as is a fee simple buyer under a purchase agreement. The check for the deposit needs to be made payable to a broker involved, not the landlord.

Upon receipt of the good faith deposit, the broker needs to hold the deposit in a trust account as trust funds. If lease negotiations are unsuccessful, the

---

OFFER TO LEASE

Prepared by: Agent _____ Phone _____
Broker _____ Email _____

NOTE: This form is used by a leasing agent or prospective tenant when negotiating a rental or lease agreement for commercial space, to make an offer on terms sufficiently complete to form a binding agreement on acceptance by the landlord.

DATE: _____, 20_____, at _____, California.
Items left blank or unchecked are not applicable.
Received from _____, the sum of $_____,
evidenced by ☐ check, or _____ ☐, payable to _____,
to be held undeposited until acceptance of this offer as a deposit toward the leasing of the premises referred to as
_____.

The following checked addendums are part of this offer to lease:
☐ Plat map of the premises   ☐ Tenant's financial statements [See **RPI** Form 209-2 and 209-3]
☐ Lease agreement [See **RPI** Form 550]   ☐ Option to Renew/Extend [See **RPI** Form 565]
☐ Standard Option to Purchase [See **RPI** Form 161]   ☐ Right of First Refusal to Buy [See **RPI** Form 579]
☐ Credit Application [See **RPI** Form 302]   ☐ _____

TERMS:
1. The commencement date of the lease to be _____, 20_____, and continue ☐ until the expiration date of _____, 20_____, or ☐ as a month-to-month tenancy.
2. The monthly rent to be payable in advance as follows:
   2.1   ☐ Monthly rent to be fixed at $_____ until expiration of the lease.
   2.2   ☐ Monthly rent to be adjusted from a monthly base rent for the first year of $_____.
         On each anniversary date of the lease, the monthly base rent is to be adjusted upward only based on the annual increase in the Consumer Price Index for All Urban Consumers (CPI-U) for:
         ☐ Los Angeles-Anaheim-Riverside   ☐ San Diego   ☐ _____
         ☐ San Francisco-San Jose-Oakland   ☐ National
         a.   The upward adjustment for any one year is capped at a _____% annual increase.
   2.3   ☐ Monthly rent to be graduated on each anniversary under the following schedule:
         a.   Base year monthly rent of $_____, and on each anniversary month, an upward adjustment in the monthly rent of _____% over the prior year's monthly rent; or _____
         _____.
         b.   Base Year $_____   Second Year $_____   Third Year $_____
              Fourth Year $_____   Fifth Year $_____   Sixth Year $_____
   2.4   ☐ Rent to be the greater of _____% of monthly gross sales/receipts or the total of other rents, taxes, insurance and common area maintenance (CAMs) checked in this offer.
   2.5   ☐ Monthly base rent to be adjusted upward to current market rental value every _____ years.
   2.6   Holdover rent to be $_____ daily.
3. The utility expenses for the space leased to be paid as follows:
   Tenant to pay _____
   Landlord to pay _____
4. ☐ Common Area Maintenance (CAMs) costs for maintaining and operating of the common areas are to be paid by Tenant based on their proportionate share of the total space leased on the premises, or _____%. The CAMs charge will be assessed ☐ monthly, or ☐ quarterly, and is payable within 10 days. The CAM charge will not exceed ☐ _____% of the rent, ☐ _____ cents per square foot monthly, or _____.
5. Real estate taxes and assessments on the real estate will be paid by ☐ Landlord, or ☐ Tenant.
   5.1   Any taxes and assessments paid by Tenant to be capped at a _____% annual increase.
6. A security deposit of $_____ to secure the performance under Tenant's lease to be paid on signing of the lease.
7. ☐ Tenant to have the option to renew or extend the lease as set forth in the attached option to renew/extend. [See **RPI** Form 565]
8. Tenant may assign, sublet or encumber the leasehold interest subject to Landlord's consent.
9. Tenant's intended use of the premises includes _____
   _____

broker returns the good faith deposit to the prospective tenant. If the landlord and tenant enter into a lease agreement, the broker disperses the funds to satisfy the security deposit or rent amount due under the lease agreement. In this case, the broker will deliver the amount of the good faith deposit to either the landlord or the property manager, whomever is designated in the lease agreement.

The section of the offer setting forth the rental payment schedule is a checklist of various rental arrangements which may be selected by the tenant to pay rent, including:

- the duration/term of the initial leasing period;
- the monthly base rent for the first year;

------------------------------------- PAGE 2 OF 2 — FORM 556 -------------------------------------

10. Landlord to make improvements prior to the time Tenant is to take possession as follows _____
     _____.

11. Tenant to make improvements as follows _____

12. Landlord to deliver to Tenant any building plans, blueprints or property documents in Landlord's possession upon
     Tenant's request for additional improvements to be made by Tenant or any government demands made on Tenant
     for their use of the Premises.

13. Tenant may exercise the right to lease additional space from Landlord as follows (note the premises, rent, terms, and
     period) [See **RPI** Form 579-1] _____
     _____.

14. Tenant to maintain insurance on the premises to cover any casualty loss in the amount of $_____.

15. Landlord and Tenant to sign a lease to be prepared by ☐ Tenant, or ☐ Landlord, on a form entitled
     _____ published by _____.

16. Parties to pay Broker(s) a fee of ☐ see attached fee schedule [See **RPI** Form 113], or _____, as follows:
     Landlord to pay the brokerage fee on transfer of possession. The party wrongfully preventing a transfer of possession
     to pay the brokerage fee. Landlord's Broker and Tenant's Broker, respectively, to share the brokerage
     fee _____ :_____.

17. This offer will be deemed revoked unless accepted in writing and personally delivered to Tenant or Tenant's Broker
     on or before _____, 20_____.

18. Before any party to this agreement files an action on a dispute arising out of this agreement which remains unresolved
     after 30 days of informal negotiations, the parties agree to enter into non-binding mediation administered by a neutral
     dispute resolution organization and undertake a good faith effort during mediation to settle the dispute.

19. If Tenant's intended lease period exceeds one year, Tenant acknowledges receipt of the Agency Law Disclosure. [See
     RPI Form 305]

20. _____

Landlord's Broker: _____	Tenant's Broker: _____
Broker's CalBRE Identification #: _____	Broker's CalBRE Identification #: _____
Agent's Name: _____	Agent's Name: _____
Agent's CalBRE Identification # _____	Agent's CalBRE Identification #: _____
Signature: _____	Signature: _____
Is the agent of: ☐ Landlord exclusively.	Is the agent of: ☐ Tenant exclusively.
☐ Both Landlord and Tenant.	☐ Both Landlord and Tenant.
Address: _____	Address: _____
Phone: _____ Cell: _____	Phone: _____ Cell: _____
Fax: _____	Fax: _____
Email: _____	Email: _____
I agree to the terms stated above.	**I agree to the terms stated above.**
☐ See Signature Page Addendum. [RPI Form 251]	☐ See Signature Page Addendum. [RPI Form 251]
Date: _____, 20_____	Date: _____, 20_____
Landlord: _____	Tenant: _____
Agent: _____	
Agent's CalBRE #: _____	
	Signature: _____
	Tenant: _____
Signature: _____	Signature: _____

FORM 556	12-14	©2016 RPI — **Realty Publications, Inc.,** P.O. BOX 5707, RIVERSIDE, CA 92517	

- any rental adjustments during the leasing period for inflation and appreciation;
- responsibility for payment of utilities;
- responsibility for insurance policies, premium payment and payment of property taxes;
- the amount of the security deposit; and
- options to renew or extend the leasing period, or to buy the property.

It is good brokerage practice to reference and attach a copy of the proposed lease agreement form to the offer. It includes boilerplate provisions covering:

- the responsibility for property operating and maintenance expenses;

- the right to assign, sublet or encumber the lease;
- subordination/trust deed lender rights;
- default remedies; and
- eminent domain.

In the offer's miscellaneous leasing provisions, the tenant and landlord further agree to other terms peculiar to leasing, including:

- the tenant's proposed use;
- the lease agreement form to be used;
- responsibility for tenant improvements;
- any alterations by the tenant;
- brokerage fees; and
- the time and manner for accepting the offer to lease.

Some landlords, in response to a letter of intent or offer to lease, initially present prospective tenants with fully prepared but unsigned lease agreements. This landlord negotiating stance works to the landlord's advantage since the issue of whose lease document to be used is ended. The parties then orally negotiate the final terms.

To better clarify negotiations, the broker writes up the offer to lease (and counteroffers). Then, within the offer-counteroffer context, acceptable terms based on signed offers and counteroffers are developed. Expectations are properly reached and negotiations are memorialized in writing to avoid later conjecture.

The final section of the offer to lease is the signature section, where the landlord and tenant sign and agree to the terms stated in the offer.

Miscellaneous provisions

By signing an offer to lease prepared by a broker, a prospective tenant initiates the negotiations in earnest on a property suitable for the tenant's use. The landlord's acceptance concludes the search for space.

The key difference between an offer and a proposal to lease, called a **letter of intent (LOI)**, is the offer on acceptance forms a binding contract. The LOI is a mere proposal and solicitation of the landlord's intentions, binding on no one.

Solicitations, such as an LOI sent to the landlord or their leasing agent by the tenant's agent, require the landlord, if they respond, to clarify their previously announced terms and conditions. A phone call between agents is more efficient than an LOI since no offer exists for the landlord to accept or counter. If the landlord responds, they need to make an offer in writing. This forces the leasing agents to submit the landlord's offer to lease to the tenant for an acceptance, counteroffer or rejection.

Offers to lease vs. proposals

letter of intent
A non-binding proposal signed and submitted to a property owner to start negotiations to rent or buy a property. [See **RPI** Form 185]

Form 180

Counteroffer

COUNTEROFFER

Prepared by: Agent _____ Phone _____
Broker _____ Email _____

NOTE: This form is used by an agent when an offer or counteroffer for the purchase or lease of property is received and rejected by the client, to prepare a counteroffer on modified terms.

DATE: _____, 20_____, at _____, California.
Items left blank or unchecked are not applicable.

FACTS:

1. This is a counteroffer to an offer entitled:
   ☐ Purchase agreement
   ☐ Exchange agreement
   ☐ Counteroffer
   ☐ _____
   1.1 dated _____, 20_____, at _____, California,
   1.2 entered into by _____, as the _____,
   1.3 regarding real estate referred to as _____
   _____.

AGREEMENT:

2. The undersigned includes all the terms and conditions of the above referenced offer in this Counteroffer, **subject to the** following modifications:
   _____
   _____
   _____
   _____
   _____

   2.1 ☐ See attached Addendum. [RPI Form 250]

3. This Counteroffer will be deemed revoked unless accepted in writing and delivered to the undersigned or their broker prior to the time of _____ on _____, 20_____.

Buyer's Broker: _____	Buyer's Broker: _____
By: _____	By: _____
CalBRE#: _____	CalBRE#: _____

I agree to purchase this property as stated above.	**I agree to sell this property as stated above.**
☐ See attached Signature Page Addendum. [RPI Form 251]	☐ See attached Signature Page Addendum. [RPI Form 251]
Date: _____, 20_____	Date: _____, 20_____
Buyer's Name: _____	Seller's Name: _____
Signature: _____	Signature: _____
Buyer's Name: _____	Seller's Name: _____
Signature: _____	Signature: _____
Address: _____	Address: _____
Phone: _____ Cell: _____	Phone: _____ Cell: _____
Email: _____	Email: _____

FORM 180 03-11 ©2016 RPI — Realty Publications, Inc., P.O. BOX 5707, RIVERSIDE, CA 92517

A proposal merely evidences a tenant's or landlord's intent to think about and provide leasing information. The tenant and the landlord are not yet ready to make a binding commitment, otherwise an offer is submitted by one or the other.

Counteroffers focus on negotiations

To form a binding agreement to lease, an offer or counteroffer needs to accepted in its entirety and without qualification or alteration.[1]

When a landlord or tenant conditions their acceptance of an offer to lease by changing or adding specific terms, acceptance does not occur and a binding agreement to lease is not formed.[2]

---

1 Calif. Civil Code §1582
2 CC §1585

Consider a landlord who is currently negotiating with the CEO of a company to enter into a lease agreement. A competing landlord (or their broker) actively solicits the company's officers and board members to lease space from them instead.

Ultimately, the company enters into a lease agreement with the competing landlord.

The landlord who lost out seeks to recover lost rent from the competing landlord, claiming the competing landlord intentionally interfered with their prospective economic advantage which existed with the CEO of the company. The landlord claims the competing landlord induced the officers and board members to consider and accept the competing landlord's proposal while they were completing negotiations with the company's CEO.

However, a competing landlord and their brokers have a privilege of competition. This right allows them to solicit a tenant who they know is negotiating with another landlord. The competing landlord does not engage in unlawful interference with another landlord's prospective tenant when the prospective tenant has not yet finalized negotiations and entered into an enforceable agreement to rent space from the other landlord.

*A landlord who has not yet entered into a binding offer to lease or lease agreement does not hold an economic advantage (in the form of a binding contract) with which a competing landlord may not interfere. [**San Francisco Design Center Associates** v. **Portman Companies** (1995) 41 CA4th 29]*

The added conditions or changes establish a rejection of the offer and create a counteroffer. To avoid altering a signed document (the offer or lease), a counteroffer form referencing the signed document is prepared, signed and submitted. The other party then accepts, rejects or further counters the prior offer.

Thus, if the offer to lease is not acceptable to the landlord or tenant, they may counter by using a counteroffer form to state their acceptable terms. [See **RPI** Form 180 accompanying this chapter]

As written negotiations continue, an acceptable set of terms develops by the use of counteroffer forms. Written counteroffers keep the landlord and tenant focused on the remaining unnegotiated details. LOIs do also if the agents fully note all aspects previously agreed on by the tenant and the landlord. Further, a deposit and credit application delivered with the offer demonstrate to the landlord the tenant's serious intent to rent the property.

After acceptance of the offer or counteroffer to lease, only the following remain to close the lease transaction:

- preparation of the lease agreement (and other closing documents);
- transfer of possession; and
- payment of the security deposits and initial rent.

Chapter 16 Summary

Like a sales transaction, the arrangement of a lease transaction has two phases:

- the offer and acceptance (agreement to lease); and
- the drafting and signing of the lease agreement and delivery of funds and possession (the conveyance of the leasehold interest on closing).

The key difference between an offer and a proposal to lease, called a letter of intent (LOI), is the offer on acceptance forms a binding contract. The LOI is a mere proposal and solicitation of the landlord's intentions, binding on no one.

If the offer to lease is not acceptable to the landlord or tenant, they may counter by using a counteroffer form to state their acceptable terms.

Once an offer or counteroffer is accepted in its entirety, and without qualification or alteration, a binding lease agreement is formed.

Chapter 16 Key Terms

Quiz 4 Covering Chapters 14-18 is located on page 636.

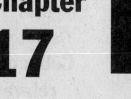

Residential tenant credit checks

Chapter

17

After reading this chapter, you will be able to:
- identify issues to be addressed by a tenant background check; and
- intelligently analyze a prospective tenant's creditworthiness for the payment of rent.

applicant screening fee   **credit reporting agency**

Learning Objectives

Key Terms

Protection for landlords and brokers

A landlord or property manager bases their analysis of a prospective tenant's ability to perform under a lease agreement on:

- a completed **credit application** from the tenant [See Form 302 accompanying this chapter];

- a **credit clearance** through a credit reporting agency as authorized on the credit application; and

- an **unlawful detainer (UD)** clearance through a consumer reporting agency.

Besides relying on financial ratios and formulas to analyze the suitability of an individual as a tenant, on receipt of a rental application a prudent residential landlord or property manager will:

- call prior landlord(s) to confirm the amount of the prospective tenant's prior rent, payment history and personal conduct as an occupant on the premises;

- call the current employer to confirm the employment data on the application;

- confirm other sources of income, expenses and amount of indebtedness disclosed in the credit application; and

- determine whether the prospective tenant is able to make the payments or a guarantee is necessary.

Collecting relevant information

Accurate credit and background information is needed on each prospective tenant to properly analyze the risk of lost rent and enforced collection.

Owners and property managers of income-producing property need information to make informed decisions whether to accept or reject prospective tenants. This information includes:

- prior evictions;
- late rent payments;
- bounced checks; or
- other breaches of lease agreements.

A conclusion on creditworthiness is drawn from the tenant's credit history and financial statements.

In the course of their brokerage business, a property manager makes decisions and advises landlords on the ability (income) and willingness (payment history) of tenants to pay rent and care for the premises.

credit reporting agency
A private agency which collects and reports information regarding an individual's credit history.

Property managers advising landlords on tenants' creditworthiness need to subscribe to the services available from a **credit reporting agency (CRA)**. Apartment owners' associations obtain credit information for their membership from the same private tenant screening services directly available to landlords.

Editor's note — One such service is the Tenant Screening Center, Inc. at 140 Wikiup Drive, Santa Rosa, CA 95403 (1-800-523-2381, info@tsci.com).

Acquiring credit data

A credit report does not guarantee the prospective tenant will perform under the rental or lease agreement. Neither does it establish the prospect's ability to pay rent in the future.

However, the report does reveal the prospect's previous performance in paying their debts (e.g. money owed on finance contracts, utility services or professional services, etc.). It also reveals whether they have incurred late penalty charges on consumer credit accounts or been subjected to judgments or tax liens. Thus, the report gives an indication as to whether the tenant will pay rent and pay it on time.

Property managers seeking credit information need to identify themselves to the *CRA*, state their purpose for seeking the information and certify to the CRA that the information will be used for no other purpose than stated.[1]

---

1 Calif. Civil Code §1785.14(a)

Form 302

Credit Application

Page 1 of 2

CREDIT APPLICATION
Individual

Prepared by: Agent _____ Phone _____
Broker _____ Email _____

NOTE: This form is used by a loan broker or carryback seller and their agent when arranging a mortgage loan or carryback note on a sale and needing a determination of the borrower's/buyer's creditworthiness, to authorize a credit reporting agency to complete a consumer report on the borrower/buyer.

DATE: _____, 20_____, at _____, California.
THIS CREDIT APPLICATION is for the amount of $_____.
Property address: _____
Received from Applicant(s) $_____, ☐ cash, or ☐ check, for a consumer credit report which is a non-refundable cost and not a deposit.
Applicant(s):
Applicant One _____
   (Last Name)   (First Name)   (Middle Name)   (Sr., Jr., etc.)
   Social Sec. # _____ Drivers Lic. # _____ State_____
Applicant Two _____
   (Last Name)   (First Name)   (Middle Name)   (Sr., Jr., etc.)
   Social Sec. # _____ Drivers Lic. # _____ State_____
Additional Occupant(s): Name _____
                           Name _____
Rental History: Have you ever been party to an eviction? ☐ Yes ☐ No   Filed bankruptcy? ☐ Yes ☐ No
Present Address _____
   City _____ Zip _____
   Length of Residency _____ Monthly Rent $_____
   Landlord/Agent _____
   Address _____
   City _____ Zip _____ Phone _____
   Reason for Moving _____ Moving Date _____/_____/_____
Previous Address _____
   City _____ Zip _____
   Length of Residency _____ Monthly Rent $_____
   Landlord/Agent _____
   Address _____
   City _____ Zip _____ Phone _____
Employment:
Applicant One
   Employer _____
   Address _____
   City _____ Zip _____ Phone _____
   Length of Employment _____ Position _____ Wages_____
   Pay Period _____ Union _____
   Previous Employer _____
   Address _____
   City _____ Zip _____ Phone _____
Applicant Two
   Employer _____
   Address _____
   City _____ Zip _____ Phone _____
   Length of Employment _____ Position _____ Wages_____
   Pay Period _____ Union _____
   Previous Employer _____
   Address _____
   City _____ Zip _____ Phone _____
Additional Income Amount $_____ Source _____
Recipient _____

-------------------------- PAGE 1 OF 2 — FORM 302 --------------------------

Even if a broker is approved by a CRA, the agency will not provide a broker with credit information on just anyone. A broker seeking information on a prospective tenant will be refused service unless the tenant signs a release form for the information. [See Form 302]

The requirement for a tenant to first authorize the release of credit information is often waived if the broker is a member of an agency's credit association. Membership is open only to applicants who allow the agency to make a full investigation of their own creditworthiness and professional integrity. Abuse of the credit reporting service leads to termination of membership.

Form 302

Credit Application

Page 2 of 2

PAGE 2 OF 2 — FORM 302

General Credit Information:
Automobile One: Make _____
    Year _____ Model _____ Lic. #/State _____
    Lender _____
Automobile Two: Make _____
    Year _____ Model _____ Lic. #/State _____
    Lender _____
Bank/branch _____
    Check Acc. # _____ Savings Acc. # _____
Bank/branch _____
    Check Acc. # _____ Savings Acc. # _____
Credit References:
    1. _____
    Address _____
    Account # _____ Balance due $ _____ Phone _____
    2. _____
    Address _____
    Account # _____ Balance due $ _____ Phone _____
Personal Reference _____
    Address _____ Phone _____
Personal Reference _____
    Address _____ Phone _____
Nearest Relative (name/relationship) _____
    Address _____ Phone _____

I/We declare all information given in this application is true and correct. I/We authorize your credit reporting agency to obtain and verify a complete consumer report and supply the information obtained to you. This information is not privileged.
Date: _____, 20_____
Name: _____

Signature: _____
    (Applicant 1)
Name: _____

Signature: _____
    (Applicant 2)

I acknowledge receipt of this credit application and accompanying payment.
Seller or Lender: _____

Signature: _____
Phone: _____

FORM 302   03-11   ©2016 RPI — Realty Publications, Inc., P.O. BOX 5707, RIVERSIDE, CA 92517

Credit report contents

Consumer credit reports are limited to specific factual information on a prospective tenant's creditworthiness standing or capacity. Consumer credit reports are used to establish eligibility for:

- credit to be used for personal, family or household purposes;
- employment purposes; and
- the rental of a dwelling unit.[2]

A telecredit check reviews the tenant's check writing history. The broker will be informed if the tenant has written checks on insufficient funds in the past.

2 CC §1785.3(c)

The credit report includes references to the payment status of existing liens, mortgage and finance contracts, charge accounts, delinquencies, rental histories and payments, skips, damages and monies owed landlords and other creditors.

Information not available on a credit report includes:

- bankruptcies pre-dating the report by more than ten years;
- judgments pre-dating the report by the longer of seven years;
- unlawful detainer (UD) actions in which the landlord did not receive a final judgment by default, summary judgment or trial;
- paid tax liens and accounts on collection pre-dating the credit report by more than seven years; and
- criminal activity or other adverse information pre-dating the report by more than seven years.[3]

A prudent property manager uses a service which provides records on unlawful detainer (UD) actions in which the landlord prevailed by receiving a final judgment.

UD reporting services

Some specialty credit services constantly obtain UD information from the municipal courts and landlords who subscribe to their service. These CRAs sell landlords information gathered from public records regarding UD evictions, and from landlords on particular tenants with whom they have adverse relationships. The broker then obtains more detailed information on these tenants by contacting the landlord giving the adverse activity to the CRA.

In the early 1990s, CRAs were singled out and prohibited from disclosing the UD information needed by landlords to analyze their risks. The prohibition was based on the claim the state had an interest in maintaining the availability of rental housing to all individuals, despite their adverse credit history. However, without the information, landlords were unable to analyze the risk they undertake by renting to a particular prospect.

The statute prohibiting credit agencies from reporting UD actions was found to be a violation of landlords' First Amendment rights. Thus, credit agencies now collect and report UD evictions.[4]

However, a tenant may request the agency clarify the disposition of the UD action if the initial report, while technically true, is misleading or incomplete.[5]

Investigative consumer reports provide information on a tenant's character, reputation, personal characteristics and mode of living.

Investigative reports go further

This information is obtained through personal interviews with neighbors, friends and associations of the tenant.

3   CC §1785.13(a)
4   **U.D. Registry, Inc.** v. **State** (1995) 34 CA4th 107
5   **Cisneros** v. **The U.D. Registry, Inc.** (1995) 39 CA4th 548

Investigative consumer reports may be used for:

- insurance or employment purposes; and
- the rental of a dwelling unit.[6]

Investigative consumer reports are commonly used by landlords when hiring a property manager or resident manager, or entering into a percentage lease with a tenant. Before obtaining an investigative consumer report, a landlord needs to notify and receive written permission from the prospective employee or tenant to retrieve and use the investigative consumer report for employment or leasing purposes.[7]

Prior rental history inquiries

Additional information on the tenant's creditworthiness and character is readily available to property managers who contact the tenant's previous landlord. Critical questions to be asked of the prior landlord include:

- Did the tenant cause any damage to the rental property?
- Was the rent paid on time every month? Were partial payments made?
- Were any late charges incurred, and if so, were they demanded and did the tenant pay the late charges?
- Was the tenant ever served a three-day notice?
- Did the tenant leave on friendly terms?
- Did the tenant care for and maintain the premises?
- Did the tenant abide by restrictions in the lease (i.e., pets, guests, building policy, etc.)?
- Did the tenant interfere with or endanger other tenants?

If, after investigating a prospective tenant's background, it seems likely the tenant will damage, deteriorate, or otherwise diminish the value of the property for other tenants, a prudent landlord or property manager may not be willing to lease to the prospect or consent to their assumption of an existing lease.

Evaluating credit information

Once a property manager has obtained the necessary credit information on the tenant, the data needs to be evaluated.

Information provided on forms filled out by the tenant, brokers and landlords may not be used to discriminate against any tenant based on their race, color, religion, sex, sexual orientation, marital status, national origin, ancestry, familial status or disability.[8]

However, each tenant needs to be treated individually when applying income-to-debt or income-to-rent ratios as guidelines to determine a tenant's creditworthiness. A tenant who does not meet an income ratio is not necessarily a credit risk if they have a strong balance sheet (assets and net worth).

---

6   CC §1786.12(d)

7 · CC §1786.12

8   Calif. Government Code §12955

However, a landlord or property manager may analyze a prospective tenant's capability to pay rent by applying a ratio or formula (such as a "three-to-one" income-to-rent ratio) as the only basis for determining the tenant's creditworthiness.[9]

Income-to-debt ratios and percentage income-to-rent standards assume all prospective tenants who do not meet the ratio or percentage are unable to pay. Exclusively using these ratios to qualify prospective tenants sacrifices a thoughtful review of a prospective tenant's ability to pay rent and maintain the premises.

A more thorough review based on the tenant's financial statements and occupancy history will often yield tenants of better financial capacity than a quick, mechanical test of the tenant's financial ability.

Denied due to bad credit

When a tenant is refused occupancy or subjected to increased rent or security deposit due to their credit report, the tenant needs to be:

- told so by the landlord or property manager when relying on the credit report to reject the tenant; and
- given the name of the service that issued the credit report.[10]

Any consumer who is denied credit, i.e., refused as a tenant for lack of creditworthiness, needs to be informed they are entitled to a written statement from the landlord or property manager of the reasons for the denial.[11]

Nonrefundable fees for credit reports

A residential landlord may charge a prospective tenant a nonrefundable credit screening fee to cover the costs of obtaining information about the prospective tenant.[12]

The information requested by the landlord permitting the charge of a credit screening fee includes personal references, investigative reports and credit reports.

The amount of the **applicant screening fee** may not exceed $30 plus annual adjustments based on increases in the Consumer Price Index (CPI), or the lesser amount of:

- out-of-pocket costs for gathering the information; and
- costs of the landlord's time in obtaining the information.[13]

> **applicant screening fee**
> A nonrefundable fee charged to the tenant to reimburse the landlord for the cost to obtain the tenant's credit report.

The landlord needs to provide the prospective tenant with an itemized receipt of the out-of-pocket expenses and time spent to obtain and process the tenant's credit information.[14]

---

9 **Harris v. Capital Growth Investors XIV** (1991) 52 C3d 1142
10 CC §1787.2
11 CC §1787.2(b)(2)(i)
12 CC §1950.6(a)
13 CC §1950.6(b)
14 CC §1950.6(d)

If a personal reference check is not performed or a consumer credit report is not ordered, the landlord needs to refund any amount of the screening fee not used to cover screening costs.[15]

Further, on request from the prospective tenant, the landlord needs to provide the prospective tenant with a copy of the consumer report.[16]

An applicant screening fee may not be charged when a rental unit is presently unavailable or will not be available within a reasonable period of time.[17]

Editor's note — A reasonable time is probably the time period required to notice the termination of a tenancy, such as under a notice to vacate.

---

15 CC §1950.6(e)
16 CC §1950.6(f)
17 CC §1950.6(c)

Chapter 17 Summary

A landlord or property manager bases their analysis of a prospective tenant's ability to perform under a lease agreement on:

- a completed credit application from the tenant;
- a credit clearance through a credit reporting agency as authorized on the credit application; and
- an unlawful detainer (UD) clearance through a consumer reporting agency.

A conclusion on creditworthiness is drawn from the tenant's credit history and financial statements.

A residential landlord may charge a prospective tenant a nonrefundable credit screening fee to cover the costs of obtaining information about the prospective tenant.

Chapter 17 Key Terms

Quiz 4 Covering Chapters 14-18 is located on page 636.

Commercial tenant screening

After reading this chapter, you will be able to:
- identify aspects of a commercial tenant's background needing further investigation prior to entering into a lease agreement; and
- proceed with a credit screening investigation.

balance sheet
profit and loss statement

Learning Objectives

Key Terms

Qualified to stay and pay

An owner's leasing agent, when reviewing an application to rent from a prospective commercial tenant, has a duty to the owner to review the tenant's qualifications. A commercial lender reviews a person's qualifications to borrow money in the same way.

Like lending money, leasing real estate is an extension of credit. Rent paid for the use of property is comparable to interest paid for the use of money. Both financial arrangements have the same economic function since each generates a rate of return — one called **rent**, the other called **interest**.

Further, the owner conveys to the tenant the right to use the property, comparable to a lender advancing money for use by a borrower. Both are on loan. Finally, property let to a tenant is to be returned to the owner, just as money lent to a borrower is returned to the lender without a decrease in value.

Thus, the leasing agent and landlord analyze the prospective tenant's creditworthiness and whether they're qualified to take possession of the property, pay for its use in a timely manner and return it undiminished as agreed.

Credit report partial information

A credit report provides only partial information on a commercial tenant's creditworthiness. Credit reports do not evaluate the tenant's managerial ability to successfully operate their trade or business and care for the premises. Also, they do not consider the tenant's assets (net worth) or the profitability of the business. However, investigative reports carry this type of information.

A tenant, on inquiry from a leasing agent, will provide financial statements on their company. The tenant's business income, expenses and net operating income (NOI) are disclosed in the tenant's **profit and loss statement**, a type of financial statement. The tenant's **balance sheet** is a separate financial statement which sets forth the tenant's net worth (assets) and liabilities (debts). [See Form 209-2 accompanying this chapter; see **RPI** Form 209-3]

profit and loss statement
A type of financial statement which discloses the tenant's business income, expenses and net operating income. [See **RPI** Form 209-2]

Occasionally, start-up companies do not have computer-generated financial statements. In this event, financial statement forms are available from institutional lenders and forms publishers for tenants.

The information contained in financial statements supplied voluntarily by the tenant needs to be confirmed by the owner or their leasing agent. Most credit agencies will perform this activity for a fee. The credit application usually supplies the name and address of banks and creditors of the tenant.

balance sheet
An itemized, dollar-value presentation for setting an individual's net worth by subtracting debt obligations (liabilities) from asset values. [See **RPI** Form 209-3]

Leasing agents may also check out the property currently occupied by commercial tenants to see if the tenant failed to maintain the property. A diminished property value on the tenant's return of possession is what an owner wants to avoid. Investigating the tenant's behavior before entering into a leasing agreement will help establish with more certainty what risk the tenant's conduct poses for the owner.

For managers of commercial property, the added dimension of the tenant's business operations and conduct needs to be considered. The tenant's business acumen and style of marketing from the premises will have an effect on occupants of adjacent space.

Also, leasing agents need to give the same review to a substitute tenant seeking to assume an existing lease and to a prospective tenant negotiating a new lease. When a lease agreement contains an alienation provision stating the owner's consent "will not be unreasonably withheld," the owner needs to hold the substitute tenant to the same standards used to qualify new tenants.

Using different qualifying standards is an unreasonable interference with the commercial tenant's right to sell their business and transfer the leasehold to the substitute tenant for the remainder of the term.

Purpose of background checks

A commercial manager, leasing agent or owner conducts a background check on a new tenant to determine their:

- credit history;
- financial status;
- business track record and proposed business plans;

- compatibility with other tenants and class of clientele;
- ability to manage their business; and
- ability to maintain the property's value.

Credit and financial history

Before a prospective tenant's credit and financial history can be analyzed by the owner, the prospective tenant needs to complete a **credit application**, also called an application to rent. On receiving the tenant's credit application, the owner and their leasing agent may begin the process of verifying the tenant's payment history based on the information supplied by the tenant and reports ordered from credit agencies. [See **RPI** Form 302; see Chapter 17]

Any possible adverse information, such as foreclosures, bankruptcies, tax liens, evictions, violations of use ordinances or records of arrests, needs to be given weight when analyzing the tenant's acceptability.

Editor's note — Litigious and troublesome tenants are to be shunned since they come with baggage and attitudes adverse to problem-free landlord-tenant relationships.

Business track record

Extensive financial data on the prospective tenant's business is readily available to the owner upon request. Financial information on the tenant's business operations is usually provided through financial statements, including:

- *profit and loss*, income and operating statements for the current and preceding year; and
- a *balance sheet* for the last day of the month preceding the application to rent.

Attention needs to be focused on the tenant's:

- prior work experience;
- business or professional licenses;
- familiarity with their proposed use of the property;
- degree of responsibility;
- managerial skills;
- vocational or educational experience;
- business acumen and survivability;
- name recognition and length of time in the community; and
- civic and community involvement.

The prospective commercial tenant's income statement and balance sheet statement need to be examined for:

- income, expenses and net operating income (NOI) ratios;
- ability to maintain or increase sales;
- budget and income projections;

Form 209-2

Profit and Loss Statement

PROFIT AND LOSS STATEMENT
Borrower's Financial Statement (FNMA 1020)

| Prepared by: Agent _____ | Phone _____ |
| Broker _____ | Email _____ |

NOTE: This form is used by a loan broker when processing a mortgage application to be prepared by the borrower for the loan broker, to determine the borrower's sources and amounts of income, personal expenses and net income and set the borrower's debt-to-income (DTI) ratios.

	Servicer Loan Number:
Property Address:	
Is your home listed for sale? ☐ Yes ☐ No	
Agent's Name:	Agent's Phone Number:
Borrower's Name:	Social Security Number:
Mailing Address (P.O Box, Street, Apt):	
Mailing Address (City, State, Zip):	
Total number of persons living at this address:	Number of dependents at this address:
Home phone:	Work phone
Co-Borrower Name:	Social Security Number:
Mailing Address (#, Street, Apt):	
Mailing Address (City, State, Zip):	
Total number of persons living at this address:	Number of dependents at this address:
Home phone:	Work phone
Have you contacted credit counseling services? ☐ Yes ☐ No	
Number of cars you own:	

Monthly Income (wages): $ _____ / mo.

Additional Income (not wages): $ _____ / mo. * Source: _____

* Notice: Alimony, child support or separate maintenance income need not be revealed if the Borrower or Co-Borrower does not choose to have it considered for approval of:

Asset Type:	Estimated value	Liability Type:	Monthly payment	Balance Due
Other Real Estate:	$	Dependent Care:	$	$
Checking Accounts:	$	Rent:	$	$
Savings/Money Market:	$	Other Mortgage(s):	$	$
IRA/Keogh Accounts:	$	Personal Loans(s):	$	$
401(k)/ESOP Accounts:	$	Medical Expense:	$	$
Stocks, Bonds, CDs:	$	HOA Fees/Dues:	$	$
Other Investments:	$	Other:	$	$
Reason for delinquency:				

I (we) agree that the financial information provided is an accurate statement of my (our) financial status. I (we) understand and acknowledge that any action taken by the lender of my (our) mortgage loan on my (our) behalf will be made in strict reliance on the financial information provided: My (Our) signature(s) below grants the holder of my (our) mortgage the authority to confirm the information I (we) have disclosed in this financial statement, to verify that it is accurate by ordering a credit report, and to contact my real estate agent and/or credit counseling service representative (if applicable).

Submitted this _____ Day of _____ 20_____

By: _____
    Signature of Borrower   *Date*

By: _____
    Signature of Borrower   *Date*

* Note: Before mailing. make sure you have signed and dated the form and attached a copy of your most recent pay stub. if you are self-employed. attach a copy of your most recent Federal Tax return.

FORM 209-2   03-11   ©2016 RPI — Realty Publications, Inc., P.O. BOX 5707, RIVERSIDE, CA 92517

- net cash flow;

- age of accounts payable;

- amortization periods and due dates of debts;

- cash reserves;

- ownership and control; and

- product performance and service satisfaction.

Also, most commercial tenants are structured as business entities, not operated as individual proprietorships. With an entity as the tenant, the landlord or leasing agent needs to pull records from the Secretary of State for California to determine if the company is in good standing with the state. It is also needed to determine who is registered with the state as the CEO/President/managing member permitted to enter into contracts, such as a lease agreement, binding the entity to the agreement.

The tenant's future plans for the space and their business objective for the relocation are legitimate concerns of an owner. Some entrepreneurial owners accept stock or other share ownership in the tenant's company in lieu of rent for the leased space, particularly with business start-ups.

Future plans and business goals

Regardless of the form in which rent will be paid, the owner needs to consider questions about the nature and substance of the tenant's operations, including:

- Is the tenant consolidating or expanding their operations?
- Do their income and expense projections, including the rent amounts, make sense?
- Does the business require the infusion of capital to relocate to new space?
- Does the tenant need to increase or reduce their debt or annual debt service?
- For tenants who are a corporation or limited liability company (LLC), is a stockholder or a member willing to personally guarantee the lease agreement or provide security?
- Will the activities of the tenant pose any zoning, ordinance or insurance coverage problems?
- Will the tenant's operations and the type of clientele it attracts enhance or impair the future value of the real estate?

Chapter 18 Summary

The leasing agent and landlord analyze the creditworthiness of prospective tenants. They investigate the tenant to determine whether the prospective tenant is qualified to take possession of the property, pay for its use in a timely manner and return it undiminished as agreed.

A commercial manager, leasing agent or owner conducts a background check on a new tenant to determine their:

- credit history;
- financial status;
- business track record and proposed business plans;
- compatibility with other tenants and class of clientele;
- ability to manage their business; and
- ability to maintain the property's value.

Extensive financial data on the prospective tenant's business is readily available to the owner upon request. Financial information on the tenant's business operations is usually provided through financial statements.

Chapter 18 Key Terms

balance sheet .... pg. 178
profit and loss statement .... pg. 178

Quiz 4 Covering Chapters 14-18 is located on page 636.

Chapter 19

Security deposits and pre-expiration inspections

After reading this chapter, you will be able to:

- understand the use of a security deposit as a source of recovery for money losses incurred by the landlord due to a tenant default on obligations agreed to in a rental or lease agreement;
- notify a residential tenant of their right to request a joint pre-expiration inspection of their unit prior to vacating;
- apply the differing residential and commercial security deposit refund requirements; and
- provide an itemized statement of deductions to account for recoverable expenses and any interest accrued the landlord is to pay on the security deposit.

Learning Objectives

Key Terms

final inspection	**rent**
itemized statement of deduction	**security deposit**
	statement of deficiencies
joint pre-expiration inspection	

Both commercial and residential landlords prudently require a tenant to pay the first month's rent and make a security deposit as a requisite to entering into a rental or lease agreement. [See **RPI** Form 550, 551 and 552]

The **security deposit** provides a source of recovery for money losses incurred due to a default on obligations agreed to in the rental or lease agreement. Tenant monetary obligations include:

- paying rent;

Cover for a tenant's nonperformance

security deposit
A source of funds to pay tenant obligations owed the landlord on the tenant's default in the rental or lease agreement.[See **RPI** Form 550 §2.1 and 552 §1.2]

- reimbursing the landlord for expenses incurred due to the tenant's conduct;

- maintaining the premises during occupancy; and

- returning the premises in the same level of cleanliness as existed at the time possession was initially taken, less ordinary wear and tear.

The amount of *security deposit* the residential landlord may demand and receive is controlled. Further, the amount of any security deposit is greatly influenced by the current condition of the local residential and commercial market. If competition is tight, a landlord may be forced to lower the security deposit amount required to attract tenants.

Aggressively competitive landlords are less likely to require a security deposit. However, this exposes them to an increased risk of loss if the tenant defaults, a foreseeable event.

Rent is paid in advance

Any monies handed to a residential landlord by a tenant on entering into a rental or lease agreement are characterized as one of the following:

- *rent*;

- a *security deposit*;

- a *waterbed administrative fee*; or

- a *tenant screening fee* for processing an application.[1]

rent
Compensation received by a landlord in exchange for the tenant's use, possession and enjoyment of the property.

Rent is compensation, usually paid periodically, received by a landlord in exchange for the tenant's use, possession and enjoyment of the property.[2]

Editor's note — Rent by agreement also includes amounts due from a tenant in payment of late charges on delinquent rent, and bounced check charges.[3]

Residential security deposits: not rents, not fees

Residential tenants, unlike commercial tenants, lack sufficient bargaining power when negotiating a rental or lease agreement. To prevent residential tenants from abuse, California public policy and laws limit the amount of security deposits a residential landlord may demand and collect from a tenant.

Residential security deposits are limited to:

- two months' rent for unfurnished units; and

- three months' rent for furnished units.[4]

A residential landlord may also collect one month's advance rent. This amount is not included in the security deposit limit.

1 Calif. Civil Code §§1940.5(g); 1950.5(b); 1950.6(b)

2 **Telegraph Ave. Corporation** v. **Raentsch** (1928) 205 C 93

3 **Canal-Randolph Anaheim, Inc.** v. **Wilkoski** (1978) 78 CA3d 477

4 CC §1950.5(c)

For residential rental properties, all monies paid to the landlord in addition to the first month's rent are considered part of the security deposit, except screening fees and waterbed administrative fees. [See Case in point, "To defer the first month's rent"]

Landlords often try to "mask" refundable security deposit funds by giving them names such as "nonrefundable deposit", "cleaning charge" or "last month's rent." However, any advance of funds in excess of the first month's rent, screening fees and waterbed administrative fees, no matter how characterized by the residential landlord, are classified as security deposits, subject to the above limits. [5]

A residential landlord has limited authority to also demand and collect a pet deposit as part of the maximum security deposit allowed if the tenant is permitted to keep one or more pets in the unit. However, the total advance funds, including the pet deposit, may still not exceed the above limits.[6]

Any funds received and recharacterized as a security deposit are refundable when the tenant vacates, less permissible deductions.

The amount of a residential security deposit demanded of prospective tenants needs to be uniform based on either the amount of the rent charged or the tenant's creditworthiness.

If the security deposit is based on a tenant's creditworthiness, the landlord needs to establish clear and precise standards for the different levels of creditworthiness (such as credit scoring) they use in the selection of tenants. Further, the security deposit amount set for each level of creditworthiness is to be applied to every prospective tenant who falls within each level. [7]

Further, a landlord cannot require higher security deposits for tenants with children than for tenants without children as this is a prohibited discriminatory act. Any increase in a security deposit for larger versus smaller families is also a prohibited discriminatory practice.[8] [See Chapter 54]

Uniform application of security deposits

An additional security deposit may be demanded and collected when a tenant maintains a waterbed in an unfurnished rental unit. [See **RPI** Form 564]

This waterbed deposit cannot exceed an amount equal to one-half month's rent. This waterbed deposit is in addition to the first month's rent and the maximum permissible security deposit.

The additional waterbed deposit

The landlord may also charge a reasonable fee to cover administrative costs of processing the waterbed arrangements.[9]

Commercial security deposits

5 CC §§1940.5; 1950.5(b), (c); 1950.6
6 CC §1950.5(c)
7 24 Code of Federal Regulations §100.60(b)(4)
8 Calif. Government Code §12955(a); 24 CFR §100.65
9 CC §1940.5(g)

Consider a residential landlord who locates a creditworthy tenant. In addition to the advance payment of the first month's rent, the landlord requires a security deposit equal to one month's rent.

The tenant asks the landlord if they can pay half the security deposit in advance and the other half with the second month's rent. The tenant is unable to pay the security deposit in full until they receive their security deposit refund from their current landlord.

The landlord wants this applicant as a tenant and is willing to extend the credit.

To be cautious, the landlord structures receipt of the tenant's funds as payment of the entire security deposit and half of the first month's rent. The tenant will pay the remaining half of the first month's rent with payment of the second month's rent.

Thus, if the tenant fails to pay the second month's rent and the remainder of the first month's rent when due, the landlord may serve the tenant with a three-day notice to pay rent or quit. Then, if the tenant vacates, the landlord may deduct all rents accrued and due from the security deposit. The reason: an unpaid portion of the security deposit cannot be collected by enforcement while unpaid rent can be collected by deduction from the security deposit.

Conversely, consider a landlord who allows a tenant to allocate their initial payment on the lease to one full month's rent paid in advance, with payment of the balance due on the security deposit spread over two or more months.

Here, if the tenant fails to pay the promised installments of the security deposit, the default is not considered a material breach of the rental or lease agreement. A material breach is necessary before an unlawful detainer (UD) action based on service of a three-day notice to perform can proceed to an eviction. A security deposit is not rent, although it is an amount "owed" to the landlord.

The landlord is protected by classifying the initial advance payment as fully prepaying the security deposit. The security deposit then covers any default in the promise to pay deferred rent.

A tenant's breach must be material and relate to the economics of the rental agreement or lease, such as a failure to pay rent, before the landlord can justify service of a three-day notice. However, while they are considered "rent", a failure to pay late charges, returned check charges and deferred security deposit is considered a minor breach. Thus, failure to pay these amounts does not justify the serving of a three-day notice to quit.

*Failure to deliver rent and other amounts regularly paid to the landlord, such as CAMs on commercial leases, is a material breach supporting forfeiture of the tenant's leasehold and right of possession of the property. [**Baypoint Mortgage** v. **Crest Premium Real Estate Investments Retirement Trust** (1985) 168 CA3d 818*

A commercial landlord has the discretion to set security deposit amounts under a rental or lease agreement. Amounts set for commercial deposits are generally based on the tenant's type of operations, the accompanying risks of damage they pose to the leased property and creditworthiness.

For instance, a small services firm may pay an amount equal to one month's rent as a security deposit, to cover a default in rent. On the other hand, a photography studio which uses chemicals in its rendering of services may be asked to pay an amount equal to two or more month's rent.

Editor's note — A photography studio tenant, laundry facility or other users of chemicals must be required to provide insurance coverage for losses due to toxic conditions created on the property.

Like all other terms in a commercial lease agreement, the amount of the security deposit is negotiable between the commercial landlord and the tenant prior to entering into the lease.

When the availability of unfurnished residential units is tight, residential landlords often require all prospective tenants to advance the maximum permissible amount of rent and security deposit. Landlords charge maximum amounts upfront in hopes of preventing less solvent tenants from renting their units.

For residential rentals, the first and last month's rent are legally recharacterized as the first month's rent and a security deposit equal to one month's rent.[10]

Commercial landlords typically require an advance payment of both the first and last month's rent on a lease. They do so without considering that an advance payment of the last month's rent is economically equivalent to a security deposit, as is mandated by residential rental rules.

Now consider a residential tenant who pays the first month's rent and a security deposit equal to one month's rent.

When the last month's rent becomes due, the tenant does not pay it. The tenant knows the defaulted payment of rent will be deducted from his security deposit. This is a permissible use of the security deposit by the landlord. The landlord does not attempt to have the tenant evicted since the tenant will vacate before an eviction under an unlawful detainer (UD) action is processed.

On expiration of the lease, the tenant vacates the unit. Due to excess wear and tear on the unit inflicted by the tenant, repairs and replacements are required before the unit can be re-rented.

However, after deducting the unpaid last month's rent from the security deposit, no money remains to reimburse the landlord for the cost of the repairs.

The recovery of the repair costs is initiated by a demand on the tenant for payment. If unpaid, a small claims court action may be used to enforce collection.

If the landlord requires advance payment on the first and last month's rent but no security deposit, a similar demand is made on the tenant for payment of repair costs.

The problematic last month's rent

---

10 CC §1950.5(c)

Form 567-1

Notice of Right to Request a Joint Pre-Expiration Inspection

Page 1 of 2

**NOTICE OF RIGHT TO REQUEST
A JOINT PRE-EXPIRATION INSPECTION**

NOTE: This form is used by a property manager or landlord when a residential tenant will be vacating their unit, to notify the tenant of their right to request a joint pre-expiration inspection of the premises they occupy and receive a statement of deficiencies itemizing the repairs and cleaning necessary to be remedied or eliminated by the tenant to avoid a deduction of their costs from the security deposit.

DATE: _____, 20_____, at _____, California.
To Tenant: _____
Items left blank or unchecked are not applicable.
FACTS:
1. You are a Tenant under a rental or lease agreement
　1.1　dated _____, at _____, California,
　1.2　entered into by _____, as the Tenant,
　1.3　and _____, as the Landlord,
　1.4　regarding real estate referred to as _____,
　1.5　which tenancy expires _____, 20_____.
NOTICE:
2. You are hereby advised of your right to request and be present at a pre-expiration inspection of the premises you occupy, and at the time of the inspection, be given Landlord's itemized statement of deficiencies specifying repairs and cleaning which will be the basis for deduction from your security deposit. [See **RPI** Form 567-3]
　2.1　The purpose for the inspection and the statement of deficiencies is to give you the opportunity to remedy or eliminate the itemized deficiencies before vacating to avoid a deduction of their cost from your security deposit.
　2.2　The inspection, if requested by you, may be scheduled no earlier than two weeks before the expiration of your tenancy, and is separate from Landlord's final inspection and accounting for your security deposit within 21 days after you vacate.
　2.3　If you do not request a pre-expiration inspection, no inspection will be made prior to the final inspection after you vacate.
3. You may request an inspection at any time after you are given this notice by preparing the form attached to this notice and giving it to Landlord or their agent.
　3.1　On Landlord's receipt of your request, Landlord will attempt to set a mutually agreeable date and time for the inspection.
　3.2　On Landlord's receipt of your request, you will be given a written 48-hour notice of entry advising you of the date and time scheduled by Landlord for the inspection.
4. On completion of the scheduled inspection, whether or not you are present, Landlord or their agent will hand you or leave on the premises a copy of an itemized statement of deficiencies specifying repairs and cleaning which will be the basis for deductions from your security deposit, unless you remedy or eliminate them prior to your vacating on or before your tenancy expires.
　4.1　Once you have requested an inspection you may withdraw the request at any time prior to the inspection.
5. **Notice:** State law permits former Tenants to reclaim abandoned personal property left at the former address of the Tenant, subject to certain conditions. You may or may not be able to reclaim property without incurring additional costs, depending on the cost of storing the property and the length of time before it is reclaimed. In general, these costs will be lower the sooner you contact your former Landlord after being notified that property belonging to you was left behind after you moved out.

Date: _____, 20_____
Landlord/Agent: _____ CalBRE #: _____

Signature: _____
Address: _____

Phone: _____ Cell: _____
Fax: _____
Email: _____

-------------------- PAGE 1 OF 2 — FORM 567-1 --------------------

Landlord treatment of security deposits

Security deposits are held by the landlord as **impounds**. The funds belong to the tenant who advanced them and are to be accounted for by the landlord.[11]

However, while the security deposit belongs to the tenant, a landlord may commingle the funds with other monies in a general business account. No trust relationship is established when a landlord holds a tenant's security deposit.[12]

Without a trust relationship, the landlord's receipt of a security deposit does not obligate them to pay interest on the security deposit for the period held.

---

11 CC §§1950.5(d); 1950.7(b)
12 **Korens** v. **R.W. Zukin Corporation** (1989) 212 CA3d 1054

**NOTICE OF RIGHT TO REQUEST
A JOINT PRE-EXPIRATION INSPECTION**

DATE: _____, 20_____, at _____, California.
To Landlord:

1. I, the Tenant, hereby request an inspection at the earliest possible date and time during the two-week period prior to the expiration or termination of my tenancy.

2. The dates I prefer for an inspection during normal business hours include _____
    _____

3. I understand you will give me a 48-hour notice prior to the inspection.
    Address of the premises _____
    Tenant's name _____

Signature _____
Daytime telephone number _____
Email _____

FORM 567-1   01-13   ©2016 RPI — Realty Publications, Inc., P.O. BOX 5707, RIVERSIDE, CA 92517

Form 567-1

Notice of Right to Request a Joint Pre-Expiration Inspection

Page 2 of 2

However, some local rent control ordinances require residential landlords to pay interest at or below bank savings account rates to tenants on their security deposits.

Joint pre-expiration inspections and the deposit

A residential landlord is to notify a tenant in writing of the tenant's right to request a **joint pre-expiration inspection** of their unit prior to the tenant vacating the unit.

Editor's note — The notice of right to request a joint pre-expiration inspection must also contain a statement notifying residential tenants of their right to reclaim abandoned personal property. [See Chapter 32; see Form 567-1 §5 accompanying this chapter]

However, unless the tenant requests an inspection after receiving the notice, the landlord and their agents are not required to conduct an inspection or prepare and give the tenant a statement of deficiencies before the tenancy expires and the tenant vacates.

The notice requirement does not apply to tenants who unlawfully remain in possession after the expiration of a three-day notice to pay/perform or quit.

The purpose for the *joint pre-expiration inspection*, also called an *initial inspection*, is to require residential landlords to advise tenants of the repairs or conditions the tenant needs to perform or maintain to avoid deductions from the security deposit.

When a residential tenant requests the pre-expiration inspection in response to the notice, the *joint pre-expiration inspection* is to be completed no earlier than two weeks before the expiration date of:

joint pre-expiration inspection
An inspection conducted by a residential landlord or the property manager to advise a tenant of the repairs the tenant needs to perform to avoid deductions from their security deposit. [See **RPI** Form 567-1]

Form 567-3

Statement of
Deficiencies
on Joint Pre-
Expiration
Inspection

Page 1 of 2

**STATEMENT OF DEFICIENCIES
ON JOINT PRE-EXPIRATION INSPECTION**

NOTE: This form is used by a property manager or landlord when conducting a joint pre-expiration inspection of a leased premises, to provide the tenant an itemization of the repairs and cleaning necessary to be remedied or eliminated by the tenant to avoid a deduction of their costs from the security deposit.

DATE: _____, 20_____, at _____, California.
To Tenant: _____
Items left blank or unchecked are not applicable.

FACTS:

1. On this date, a pre-expiration inspection was conducted by Landlord on the premises and appurtenances which are the subject of a rental or lease agreement

    1.1   dated _____, at _____, California,

    1.2   entered into by _____, as the Tenant(s),
           and _____, as the Landlord,

    1.3   regarding real estate referred to as _____
           _____

    1.4   ☐ Tenant was present and given a copy of this statement prepared and signed by Landlord or their agent.

    1.5   ☐ Tenant was not present and a copy of this statement prepared and signed by Landlord or their agent was left inside the premises.

2. The tenancy under the rental or lease agreement expires on _____, 20_____, by which date you are to vacate the premises.

3. **NOTICE TO TENANT:**

    3.1   You have until the date for expiration of your tenancy to remedy or eliminate the repairs and cleaning specified in this Statement of Deficiencies to avoid the deduction from your security deposit of the cost to repair and clean the identified deficiencies.

    3.2   Unobservable conditions or conditions which occur after the pre-expiration inspection requiring repair and cleaning will be deducted from your security deposit after the final inspection by Landlord or their agent.

STATEMENT OF DEFICIENCIES:

4. The following itemized list of identified deficiencies in repairs and cleaning will be the basis for deductions from your security deposit, unless remedied or eliminated by you prior to vacating and later confirmed by Landlord or their agent during a final inspection after you vacate.

    4.1   Damage to the premises and appurtenances caused by Tenant or their guests, other than ordinary wear and tear, which needs to be repaired are listed as follows: _____
           _____
           _____
           _____
           _____
           _____
           _____
           _____

    4.2   Cleaning which needs to be performed to bring the premises up to the level of cleanliness which existed on commencement of the tenancy is listed as follows: _____
           _____
           _____
           _____
           _____
           _____
           _____
           _____
           _____

-------------------------------- PAGE 1 OF 2 — FORM 567-3 --------------------------------

---

- the lease term; or

- a 30-day notice to vacate initiated by either the landlord or the tenant.[13] [See Form 567-1]

Ideally, the notice advising the tenant of their right to a joint pre-expiration inspection is given to the tenant at least 30 days prior to the end of the lease term. In the case of a rental agreement, the notice is provided immediately upon receiving or serving a 30-day notice to vacate.

---

13 CC §1950.5(f)(1)

Form 567-3

Statement of Deficiencies on Joint Pre-Expiration Inspection

Page 2 of 2

------------------------------ PAGE 2 OF 2 — FORM 567-3 ------------------------------

5. The following recitals are excerpts from Civil Code §1950.5 regarding security deposits:

5.1 1950.5(b) As used in this section, "security" means any payment, fee, deposit or charge, including, but not limited to, any payment, fee, deposit, or charge, except as provided in Section 1950.6, that is imposed at the beginning of the tenancy to be used to reimburse the landlord for costs associated with processing a new tenant or that is imposed as an advance payment of rent, used or to be used for any purpose, including, but not limited to, any of the following:

(1) The compensation of a landlord for a tenant's default in the payment of rent.

(2) The repair of damages of the premises, exclusive of ordinary wear and tear, caused by the tenant or by a guest or licensee of the tenant.

(3) The cleaning of the premises upon termination of the tenancy necessary to return the unit to the same level of cleanliness it was in at the inception of the tenancy. The amendments to this paragraph enacted by the act adding this sentence shall apply only to tenancies for which the tenant's right to occupy begins after January 1, 2003.

(4) To remedy future defaults by the tenant in any obligation under the rental agreement to restore, replace, or return personal property or appurtenances, exclusive of ordinary wear and tear, if the security deposit is authorized to be applied thereto by the rental agreement.

5.2 1950.5(d) Any security shall be held by the landlord for the tenant who is party to the lease or agreement. The claim of a tenant to the security shall be prior to the claim of any creditor of the landlord.

Date: _____, 20_____
Landlord/Agent: _____ CalBRE#: _____

Signature: _____
Address: _____

Phone: _____ Cell: _____
Email: _____

FORM 567-3   03-11   ©2016 RPI — Realty Publications, Inc., P.O. BOX 5707, RIVERSIDE, CA 92517

A period of 30 days allows the tenant time to request and prepare for the inspection. After the inspection, the tenant has time to remedy any repairs or uncleanliness the landlord observes during the inspection. Thus, the tenant is provided time to avoid a security deposit deduction.

When the landlord receives the tenant's oral or written request for a pre-expiration inspection, the landlord serves a written 48-hour *notice of entry* on the tenant stating:

- the purpose of entry as the pre-expiration inspection; and
- the date and time of the entry.

If the landlord and tenant cannot agree to the date and time of the inspection, the landlord may set the time. However, if a mutually acceptable time for the inspection is within 48 hours, a written waiver of the notice of entry is to be signed by both the landlord and tenant.

When the waiver is signed, the landlord may proceed with the inspection.[14] [See **RPI** Form 567-2]

Notice of entry and statement of deficiencies

---

14 CC §1950.5(f)(1)

Form 585

Security Deposit Disposition on Vacating Residential Premises

---

**SECURITY DEPOSIT DISPOSITION
ON VACATING RESIDENTIAL PREMISES**

NOTE: This form is used by a residential property manager or landlord when a tenant has vacated a premises and the landlord holds the tenant's security deposit, to provide the tenant with an itemized statement within 21 days of vacating of the security deposit's disposition and documentation of charges deducted.

DATE: _____, 20_____, at _____, California.
TO TENANT:
Items left blank or unchecked are not applicable.
FACTS:
1.   This is notice to Tenant of any Landlord deductions from the security deposit under the following agreement:
    ☐ Residential lease agreement   ☐ Occupancy agreement
    ☐ Reseidential rental agreement   ☐
    1.1   dated _____, 20_____, at _____, California,
    1.2   entered into by _____, as the Landlord,
    1.3   and _____, as the Tenant,
    1.4   regarding residential premises referred to as _____
DISPOSITION OF DEPOSIT:
2.   Under the above referenced agreement, Tenant handed Landlord a security
    deposit in the amount of . . . . $_____
3.   The following deductions have been made by Landlord from the security deposit:

		Cost
3.1	Repair of damages	
	a. _____	$_____
	b. _____	$_____
3.2	Necessary cleaning of the premises	Cost
	a. _____	$_____
	b. _____	$_____
3.3	Delinquent or holdover rent	Amount
	a. From _____ To _____	$_____
3.4	Replacement/repair of lost or damaged furnishings	Cost
	a. _____	$_____

    3.5   **TOTAL** deductions from security deposit (line 2 less line 3.4) . . . . (-)$_____
4.   **BALANCE DUE TENANT:**
    4.1   Balance of security deposit remaining after deductions (line 2 less line 3.4) . . . .$_____
    4.2   Interest on the security deposit from _____ to _____
        at _____ % per annum . . . .(+)$_____
    4.3   Balance due Tenant is refunded in the amount of (line 4.1 plus line 4.2) . . . . $_____
        by Landlord / Agent's check #_____
5.   **AMOUNT DUE LANDLORD:**
    5.1   The amount due Landlord after deductions (line 2 less line 3.5) . . . . $_____
    5.2   Less interest on the security deposit from _____ to _____
        at _____ % per annum . . . . (-)$_____
    5.3   Tenant to hand or mail Landlord/Agent the balance due of (line 5.1 less line 5.2) . . . .$_____

This statement is true and correct.
Date: _____, 20_____
Landlord/Agent: _____   CalBRE #:_____

Signature: _____
Address: _____

Phone: _____   Cell: _____
Email: _____

FORM 585   01-13   ©2016 RPI — Realty Publications, Inc., P.O. BOX 5707, RIVERSIDE, CA 92517

Following service on the tenant of the 48-hour notice, the landlord may inspect the property whether or not the tenant is present, unless the tenant has previously withdrawn their request for the inspection.

On completion of the joint pre-expiration inspection, the landlord gives the tenant an itemized **statement of deficiencies.** In it, the landlord specifies any repairs or cleaning which need to be completed by the tenant to avoid deductions from the security deposit.

Also, the itemized *statement of deficiencies* is to contain the contents of subdivisions (b) and (d) of Calif. Civil Code §1950.5. [See Form 567-3 accompanying this chapter]

The landlord's pre-expiration inspection statement is prepared at the time of the inspection and delivered to the tenant by either:

- handing the statement directly to the tenant if they are present at the inspection; or

- leaving the statement inside the premises at the time of the inspection if the tenant is not present.[15]

If the tenant chooses to withdraw their request for an inspection after submitting it, the landlord needs to send a memo to the tenant confirming the tenant's decision to withdraw. [See **RPI** Form 525]

Editor's note — The completion of a pre-expiration inspection statement by the landlord does not bar the landlord from deducting other costs from the security deposit for:

- *any damages noted in the joint pre-expiration inspection statement which are not cured;*

- *any damages which occurred between the pre-expiration inspection and termination of the tenancy; or*

- *any damages not identified during the pre-expiration inspection due to the tenant's possessions being in the way.*[16]

> **statement of deficiencies**
> A document a residential landlord presents to a vacating tenant specifying any repairs or cleaning to be completed by the tenant to avoid deductions from the security deposit. [See **RPI** Form 567-3]

Within a window period of 21 days after a residential tenant vacates, the residential landlord is to:

- complete a **final inspection** of the premises;

- refund the security deposit, less reasonable deductions; and

- provide the tenant with an *itemized statement of deductions* taken from the security deposit.[17] [See Form 585 accompanying this chapter]

Also, the residential landlord is to attach copies of receipts, invoices and/or bills to the itemized statement showing charges incurred by the landlord that were deducted from the security deposit.[18]

If repairs by the landlord are not completed and the costs are unknown within 21 days after the tenant vacates, the landlord may deduct a good faith estimated amount of the cost of repairs from the tenant's security deposit.

This estimate is stated on the itemized security deposit refund statement. This statement is to disclose the name, address and telephone number of any person or entity providing repair work, materials or supplies for the incomplete repairs.[19]

Residential deposit refund requirements

> **final inspection**
> An inspection of the premises conducted by the landlord within 21 days after a residential tenant vacates the property. [See **RPI** Form 585]

---

15 CC §1950.5(f)(2)
16 CC §1950.5(f)
17 CC §1950.5(g)
18 CC §1950.5(g)(2)
19 CC §1950.5(g)(3)

Then, within 14 days after completion of repairs or final receipt of bills, invoices or receipts for the repairs and materials, the landlord is to deliver to the tenant a final itemized security deposit refund statement with attached receipts and invoices.[20]

No receipt or invoice copies

It is not necessary for the landlord to provide copies of receipts, bills or invoices for repair work or cleaning to the tenant if:

- the total deduction from the security deposit to cover the costs of repairs and cleaning is equal to or less than $125; or
- the tenant signs a waiver of their right to receive bills when or after notice to terminate their tenancy is given.[21]

If the residential landlord is not required to provide copies of receipts to the tenant, the tenant may still request copies of receipts for repair work or cleaning within 14 days after receipt of the itemized security deposit refund statement. The landlord is then to provide copies of the documents within 14 days after receipt of the tenant's request.[22]

Editor's note — Residential security deposits may be refunded to the tenant electronically by mutual agreement between the landlord and the tenant. The itemized statement of deductions from the security deposit, with copies of receipts, may be delivered via email.[23]

Reasonable deductions from the deposit

Reasonable deductions from a residential tenant's security deposit include:

- any unpaid rent, including late charges and bounced check charges incurred and requested on a proper demand;
- recoverable costs incurred by the landlord for the repair of damages caused by the tenant;
- cleaning costs to return the premises to the level of cleanliness as existed when initially leased to the tenant, less wear and tear; and
- costs to replace or restore furnishings provided by the landlord if agreed to in the lease.[24]

The landlord may not deduct from a tenant's security deposit the costs they incur to repair defects in the premises which existed prior to the tenant's occupancy. To best avoid claims of pre-existing defects, a joint inspection of the unit and written documentation of any defects is completed before possession is given to the tenant. [See Form 560 in Chapter 36] [25]

As previously discussed, when a residential tenant vacates, the landlord provides the tenant with a security deposit refund accounting. If local rent

---

20 CC §1950(g)(3)
21 CC §1950.5(g)(4)
22 CC §1950.5(g)(5)
23 CC §1950.5
24 CC §§1950.5(b); 1950.7(c)
25 CC §1950.5(e)

control ordinances (or state law) require the landlord to pay interest on security deposits, the landlord uses the **itemized statement of deductions** to account for interest accrued on the security deposit. [See Form 585 §4.3]

A residential landlord who, in bad faith, fails to comply with security deposit refund requirements is subject to statutory penalties of up to twice the amount of the security deposit. Additionally, the landlord is liable to the tenant for actual money losses the tenant incurs for the wrongful retention of security deposits.[26]

As an aside, on the landlord's sale of a residential or commercial property, the landlord is to deliver an itemized statement to tenants stating:

- the amount of the tenant's security deposit;
- any deductions made from the security deposit; and
- the name, address and telephone number of the buyer.

The notice, important for the seller, shifts liability to the buyer of the property for the future return of the security deposit to the tenant.[27] [See **RPI** Form 586]

> **itemized statement of deductions**
> A document accounting for the tenant's security deposit, delivered by the landlord to a residential tenant after the tenant vacates. [See **RPI** Form 585 §4.3]

Commercial deposit refund rules

A commercial lease does not need to set forth:

- the circumstance under which a tenant's security deposit will be refunded; or
- a time period within which a landlord will refund a tenant's security deposit. [See **RPI** Form 552 through 552-4]

However, a commercial landlord is to refund the security deposit within 30 days after the transfer of possession of the property from the tenant to the landlord if:

- a refund period is not agreed to; and
- the commercial landlord takes no deductions from the security deposit.

Permissible deductions from the security deposit include unpaid rent, cost of cleaning or repairs.

Occasionally, the security deposit exceeds two months' rent and the only deduction from the deposit is for delinquent rent. Here, the commercial landlord is to return any remaining amount in excess of one month's rent within two weeks after the transfer of possession of the property to the landlord. The remaining amount of the security deposit is to be returned to the tenant or accounted for within 30 days after the transfer of possession.[28]

Unless otherwise stated in the rental or lease agreement, the commercial landlord is prohibited from deducting additional costs from the security deposit for "key money" or to cover attorney's fees incurred in preparing, altering or renewing the lease or rental agreement.[29]

---

26 CC §1950.5(l)
27 CC §§1950.5(h); 1950.7(d)
28 CC §1950.7(c)
29 CC §1950.8(b)

Unlike the residential landlord, the commercial landlord is not required to provide tenants with an itemized statement of deductions when the security deposit is refunded. However, a prudent commercial landlord provides tenants with an itemized statement when they vacate, unless a full refund is made.

An accounting avoids the inevitable demand for documentation which arises when a tenant does not receive a full refund of their security deposit. A commercial landlord who, in bad faith, fails to comply with the refund requirements is liable to the tenant for up to $200 in penalties.[30]

---

30 CC §1950.7(f)

Chapter 19 Summary

The security deposit provides a source of recovery for money losses incurred due to a tenant's default on obligations agreed to in the rental or lease agreement.

The amount of security deposit the residential landlord may demand and receive is controlled by codes. On a commercial landlord's entry into a rental and lease agreement, security deposit amounts may vary at the landlord's discretion.

A residential landlord is to notify a tenant in writing of the tenant's right to request a joint pre-expiration inspection of their unit prior to the tenant vacating the unit. The joint pre-expiration rules require residential landlords to advise tenants of the repairs or conditions the tenant needs to perform or maintain to avoid deductions from the security deposit.

Chapter 19 Key Terms

Quiz 5 Covering Chapters 19-21 is located on page 637.

Residential turnover cost recovery

After reading this chapter, you will be able to:
- analyze the landlord's recovery of residential tenant turnover costs;
- classify funds received from a tenant by a residential landlord as either rent, security deposits, waterbed administrative fees or tenant screening fees;
- avoid liquidated damages and stay-or-pay provisions as unenforceable; and
- mitigate expenses that reduce the landlord's net operating income (NOI) due to tenant turnover.

liquidated damages provision   **"stay-or-pay" clause**

net operating income

Learning Objectives

Key Terms

Following a *cost-reduction review* of management operations, the landlord of an apartment complex is determined to offset the recent increase in the cost of tenant turnover by shifting the costs to tenants.

Each **tenant turnover** requires expenditures to:
- refurbish the unit to eliminate the cumulative effect of normal wear and tear brought about by the tenant's use of the unit;
- advertise the unit's availability to locate a tenant; and
- pay leasing fees to the property manager.

An increasing number of the landlord's tenants are staying for shorter periods of time. On vacating, the units are re-renting quickly. Thus, lost rent due to turnover is kept to a minimum. However, the landlord cannot raise rents to cover the increasing annual costs without losing tenants to competing units.

Rent is set to include all operating expenses

(an unenforceable provision)

*If the tenancy is terminated during the **six-month period** following commencement of this agreement, tenant shall forfeit tenant's security deposit.*

net operating income
The net revenue generated by an income producing property as the return on capital, calculated as the sum of a property's gross operating income less the property's operating expenses. [See **RPI** Form 352 §4]

At issue is the landlord's **net operating income (NOI).** It is being reduced by the increased frequency of refurbishing and reletting costs. [See Figure 3, Form 352]

Worse, any reduction in the NOI due to the increasing turnover costs becomes an equivalent dollar reduction in the landlord's spendable income remaining after payment on mortgage financing.

From an accounting point of view, the *NOI* is calculated by subtracting operating costs from rental income generated by the property.

Also, the landlord is concerned about the economic impact of the decreased NOI on the property's value. The NOI is the basis for establishing the property's market value and maximum mortgage amount.

To maintain or increase the property's NOI and net spendable income (and the property's value), the landlord chooses to add a **"stay-or-pay" clause** addendum to the month-to-month rental agreements.

"stay-or-pay" clause
An unenforceable provision calling for the residential tenant to forego a return of their security deposit if they move before a set date.

The *stay-or-pay clause* states the residential tenant foregoes a return of their security deposit if they move within six months after taking occupancy.

The landlord believes the stay-or-pay clause will dissuade month-to-month tenants from moving for at least six months.

If a tenant is not persuaded and vacates the premises within the first six months, the stay-or-pay clause provides for the landlord to recover "prematurely incurred" turnover costs by retaining the tenant's security deposit.

Can the residential landlord enforce a stay-or-pay clause in rental agreements?

No! The stay-or-pay clause is an unenforceable penalty. It is an illegal forfeiture of the tenant's security deposit. [See Figure 1]

*Editor's note — **RPI** rental and lease agreements do not include a stay-or-pay provision. [See **RPI** Form 550 and 551]*

Refund of the tenant's security deposit

The security deposit is to be fully refunded, regardless of how long the unit remains vacant, if:

- the tenant has not breached the rental or lease agreement; and

- on expiration of proper notice, the tenant has fully paid all rents accrued and returns the unit in the condition it was received, less ordinary wear and tear.

The security deposit may not be used to cover either:

- rent lost due to the vacancy following expiration of a notice to vacate; or
- operating costs incurred to eliminate normal wear and tear and refurbish the unit for the next tenant.[1]

Thus, the landlord cannot use a stay-or-pay clause in tandem with a security deposit to provide more revenue to cover operating costs. Revenue for operating expenses comes *exclusively from rents*, a cost-plus pricing imperative, and not from a one-time lump sum advance payment of any sort.

In review, funds received from a tenant by a residential landlord fall into one of only four classifications of receipts:

- *rent*;
- *security deposits*;
- a *waterbed administrative fee* [See Chapter 19]; or
- a *tenant screening fee* for processing an application.[2]

The amount of the tenant screening fee is capped and may not exceed $50.94 for 2019.

Editor's note — The maximum tenant screening fee can be found on the California Department of Consumer Affairs website, http://www.dca.ca.gov.

Further, the tenant screening fee is limited to:

- the out-of-pocket cost for gathering the information; and
- the cost of the landlord's or property manager's time spent obtaining the information and processing an application to rent.[3]

It is common practice for landlords and property managers to request a tenant to provide them with a copy of the tenant's credit report. A tenant can obtain their credit report online from landlord-tenant screening services for far less than the maximum screening fee, or even free from the major credit reporting agencies.

In the opening scenario, the landlord is shown to fund the care and maintenance of a property from rents rather than an up-front lump sum amount paid by each tenant in addition to rent and a security deposit.

Now consider a residential landlord who requires new tenants to prepay the first month's rent and a refundable security deposit in an amount equal to one month's rent before entering into a rental or lease agreement.

Classifying tenant funds the landlord receives

Is it extra rent or a screening fee?

---

1 Calif. Civil Code §1950.5(e)

2 CC §§1940.5(g); 1950.5(b); 1950.6(b)

3 CC §1950.6(b)

Figure 2

A liquidated
damages
minimum
tenancy
provision

(an unenforceable provision)

Should the tenant choose to terminate this tenancy during the six-month period beginning on commencement of this tenancy, the tenant shall pay as liquidated damages, and not as a penalty or forfeiture, an amount equal to one month's rent in consideration for exercising the right to vacate prematurely.

The landlord also charges an additional one-time, nonrefundable, new-tenant fee, key fee, membership fee, tenant application expense fee or other named garbage fee.

The stated purpose of the nonrefundable fee is to cover administrative expenses and services related to processing the tenant's application to rent the unit, a sort of "key payment."

On vacating the unit, the tenant makes a demand on the landlord to return the one-time extra charge. The tenant claims it is a security deposit since the one-time, lump-sum charge covers expenses which are properly paid from rents. This makes the application fee a *masked security deposit*.

Can the tenant recover the one-time extra charge imposed by the landlord?

Yes, but not as a security deposit! The one-time charge for administrative costs incurred by the landlord to process the tenant's rental application is not a security deposit. A security deposit is imposed and collected to cover the landlord's losses due to future tenant defaults on a rental or lease agreement.[45]

However, this "nonrefundable upfront fee" is an administrative fee controlled by the tenant screening fee statute.

Any overage paid by the tenant above the set limit is refundable as an excess screening fee charge which is neither rent nor a security deposit.

Unenforceable liquidated damages

Consider a residential landlord who includes a **liquidated damages provision** in month-to-month rental agreements in an effort to offset tenant turnover costs. This provisions calls for a penalty payment equal to one month's rent to be taken from the security deposit if the tenant returns possession before six months of occupancy.

In addition to the first month's rent, the landlord properly collects a security deposit from the tenant in an amount equal to one month's rent to cover any future breach of the rental agreement by the tenant.

Before six months passes, the tenant hands the landlord a 30-day notice to vacate, then vacates the unit.

4   **Krause** v. **Trinity Management Service, Inc.** (2000) 23 C4th 11
5   CC §§1950.5; 1950.6

Within 21 days after vacating, the landlord sends the tenant an itemized accounting for the security deposit. One of the itemized deductions is one month's rent as the liquidated damages owed the landlord due to the early termination of the month-to-month rental agreement.

The tenant makes a demand on the landlord to refund the amount withheld from the security deposit for early termination of the rental agreement. The tenant claims a **liquidated damages provision** in a rental or lease agreement is unenforceable as it calls for payment of a forfeiture.

Is the liquidated damages provision in a rental or lease agreement enforceable?

No! A *liquidated damages provision* is unenforceable in rental and lease agreements, as it is in most other real estate transactions. Collectible damages are limited to out-of-pocket money losses.[6] [See Figure 2]

Editor's note — A liquidated damages provision creates wrongful expectations of windfall profits and are nearly always forfeitures and unenforceable. **RPI** *forms do not include liquidated damages provisions.*

> **liquidated damages provision**
> A rental agreement provision which acts as a penalty payment for returning possession before a set date.

Limited circumstances for enforcement

A liquidated damages provision may only be enforced in limited circumstances when accounting conditions make it extremely difficult or impracticable to determine the amount of actual money losses incurred by the landlord. This is never the case with real estate rentals as both the costs and time involved managing the costs are known.[7]

The amount of recoverable losses a residential landlord incurs when a tenant vacates a unit, such as the lost rent and the maintenance costs of labor and materials to cover excess wear and tear, is readily ascertainable.

Further, liquidated damages do not represent a recovery of actual money losses incurred by the landlord. The purpose of the landlord's liquidated damages provisions is not to recover money lost due to unpaid rent or excessive wear and tear, but to increase NOI and spendable income by a windfall.

Even if the landlord does not deduct the liquidated damages amount from the security deposit, they will not be able to recover the liquidated damages from the tenant in a civil action on the rental or lease agreement.

Covering tenant turnover costs

Recovery of a landlord's turnover costs comes from the rents paid by tenants. Refurbishing costs are an expense of operations deducted from rental income.

The costs of refurbishing a unit to eliminate normal wear and tear so it can be re-rented in a "fresh" condition are known, or readily available on inquiry, in advance. Thus, they are not properly the subject of liquidated damages provisions.

---

6 CC §1671(d)
7 CC §1671(d)

Financially, the amount of the refurbishing costs is best viewed as amortized over the length of each tenant's period of probable occupancy. The costs will then be properly recovered as a component factored into the periodic rent charged to a tenant.

However, the local rental marketplace determines rent ceilings, not landlords. The market limits the amount a landlord can charge for rent and successfully compete for tenants.

Thus, a landlord's most logical cost recovery approach is to negotiate with prospective tenants to stretch out their terms of occupancy to an optimal minimum number of months. The longer the average occupancy, the less frequent the tenant turnovers, and the greater the net spendable income.

To lease for a fixed term reduces costs

While the market limits the rent a landlord can charge, different rent rates exist for month-to-month rental agreements and fixed-term lease agreements.

The landlord's best method for recovering turnover costs is to rent to creditworthy tenants on a *lease agreement* with a one-year term or longer. Here again, the local rental market sets the maximum rent amount for this term. Economic conditions may even make six- or nine-month fixed-term leases feasible objectives.

A fixed-term occupancy allows the landlord to amortize the anticipated cost of refurbishing the unit over the term negotiated. Tenants under a lease agreement tend to remain in possession until the lease term expires. Thus, fixed-term arrangements reduce the frequency of move-outs and provide a schedule for turnover maintenance — the same objective sought by exploiting a forfeiture penalty period.

As a result, a landlord usually charges less rent on a lease agreement than under a month-to-month rental agreement. This lower rent is a reflection of lower overall refurbishing expenses, reduced annual vacancy rates, less management time and effort, and less risk of lost rents. Additionally, the lower rent may result in longer periods of occupancy and stave off the inevitable turnover.

As compensation, a landlord is able to charge higher rents for *month-to-month tenancies*. This higher rent reflects the cost-push of higher and more frequent turnover expenses per unit than occur under a lease.

Tiered rents for time in occupancy

A rental or lease agreement can be structured with tiered rents for future periods of continued occupancy. **Tiered rents** provide for a slightly higher rent for initial months included in the first-tier period — such as the first six months of the periodic tenancy — with lower rent amounts set for the following months if the tenant remains in possession.

If the month-to-month tenant continues in occupancy after the first-tier period, the rental agreement calls for a lower rent during a second-tier

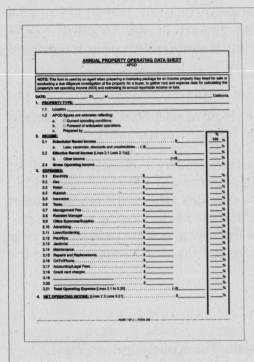

Figure 3

Form 352

Annual Property Operating Data Sheet (APOD)

For a full-size, fillable copy of this or any other form in this book that may be legally used in your professional practice, go to realtypublications.com/forms

period or for the remainder of the occupancy. This encourages tenants to stay longer since their rent will be lower. Both rental rates are consistent with the marketplace.

As a result, the landlord's turnover costs are better amortized, "reserved" from the higher periodic rent charged during the period of the first tier.

However, tiered rents will only avoid the security deposit limitations if:

- the security deposit is a customary amount for the credit risk posed by the tenant;

- the higher monthly rent is consistently charged over a long enough period, say six months, to avoid recharacterization as a disguised or delayed receipt of a security deposit, tenant screening fee or forfeiture; and

- the tenancy is month-to-month.

The same economics and amortization logic applies to the cost of **tenant improvements** made by a commercial landlord (or a tenant).

For example, tenant improvements are recovered by a commercial landlord over the initial years of a lease as part of the rent amount. Rent for an extension (the second tier) is reduced to an amount which reflects the elimination of the improvement charges. This reduction is used to induce the tenant to stay for a greater period of time. The tenant improvements are paid for and now all the landlord needs to collect is rent for the value of the premises, less the paid-for tenant improvements.

Chapter 20 Summary

Each tenant turnover reduces the landlord's net operating income (NOI) due to the increased frequency of refurbishing expenses and lost rents on vacancies. Recovery of a landlord's turnover costs comes from the rents paid by tenants. Refurbishing costs are an expense of operations deducted from rental income.

The security deposit may not be used to cover either:

- rent lost due to the vacancy on expiration after notice to vacate; or
- operating costs incurred to eliminate normal wear and tear and refurbish the unit for the next tenant.

Financially, the amount of the refurbishing costs is best viewed as amortized over the length of each tenant's period of probable occupancy. The costs are then properly recovered as a component factored into the periodic rent charged a tenant.

Liquidated damages and stay-or-pay provisions are unenforceable.

However, the local rental marketplace limits the amount a landlord can charge for rent and successfully compete for tenants. Thus, a landlord's best recovery approach is to negotiate with prospective tenants to stretch out their terms of occupancy to an optimal minimum number of months.

Chapter 20 Key Terms

Quiz 5 Covering Chapters 19-21 is located on page 637.

Accepting partial rent

After reading this chapter, you'll be able to:
- apply in practice the landlord's right to receive partial rent under a partial payment agreement with a tenant;
- distinguish the rights of residential tenants from commercial tenants when paying partial rent; and
- determine when a landlord has the right to file an unlawful detainer (UD) action after receipt of partial rent.

nonwaiver of rights provision   **reservation of rights clause**

partial payment agreement

Learning Objectives

Key Terms

Residential and commercial landlord rights

A commercial tenant experiences cash flow difficulties due to a business downturn. As a result, the tenant becomes delinquent in the payment of rent.

Discussions between the landlord and tenant follow. To enforce collection of the rent, the landlord eventually serves the tenant with a three-day notice to pay rent or quit the premises. [See Form 575 in Chapter 25]

Prior to the filing of an unlawful detainer (UD) action, the tenant offers to make a partial payment of the delinquent rent, if the landlord will accept it. Further, the commercial tenant offers to pay the balance of the delinquent rent by a specific date if the landlord agrees not to file a UD action called a **partial payment agreement**. [See Form 558 accompanying this chapter]

The *partial payment agreement* states:
- the amount received as partial rent;
- the amount of deferred rent remaining unpaid;
- a promise to pay the deferred rent;

> **partial payment agreement**
> An agreement for receipt of partial rent, specifying the amount of deferred rent remaining unpaid and the date for its payment. [See **RPI** Form 558 and 559]

- the date the payment is due; and
- the consequences of nonpayment.

If the deferred rent is not paid as scheduled, the commercial landlord may file a UD action to evict the tenant without serving another three-day notice. [See Form 558 §7]

Here, the partial payment agreement only temporarily delays the commercial landlord's eviction process which commenced with the previous service of a three-day notice on the tenant.

The tenant fails to pay the deferred balance of the delinquent rent on the date scheduled for payment. Without further notice to the tenant, the landlord files a UD action.

The commercial tenant seeks to prevent the landlord from proceeding with the UD action. The tenant claims the landlord's acceptance of the partial rent payment invalidated the prior three-day notice since the notice now states an amount of rent which is no longer due.

Can the commercial landlord accept a payment of partial rent after serving a three-day notice and later file a UD action against the tenant without serving another three-day notice for the amount remaining due and now delinquent?

Yes! A commercial landlord can accept a partial payment of rent after serving a three-day notice and before eviction. Without further notice to the tenant, the commercial landlord can proceed with a UD action and evict the tenant.[1]

Landlord's reservation of rights clause

Continuing our previous example, on accepting a partial payment of delinquent rent, a commercial landlord does not need to agree to a new due date for the remaining rent. They also do not need to enter into any agreement regarding acceptance of the partial payment. However, the commercial tenant needs to be on notice that acceptance of late rent does not waive the landlord's right to enforce any remaining breach of the lease. This notice is called a **reservation of rights clause**.

The *reservation of rights clause* is found in the *nonwaiver of rights provision* in commercial lease agreements as well as in *acceptance of partial rent agreements*. [See **RPI** Form 552 §20]

However, the commercial landlord who memorializes their acceptance of the partial rent payment and the due date for payment of the remaining balance eliminates conflicting claims the tenant may make in a UD action.

The impact of serving a three-day notice, then later accepting partial rent from a commercial tenant is vastly different from the protection a residential tenant is provided in partial rent situations.

reservation of rights clause
A clause in the nonwaiver of rights provision in commercial rental and lease agreements stating acceptance of late rent does not waive the landlord's right to enforce remedies for any remaining breach of the lease agreement by the tenant. [See **RPI** Form 552 §20 and 558 §7]

---

1 Calif. Code of Civil Procedure §1161.1(b)

PARTIAL PAYMENT AGREEMENT
Commercial

NOTE: This form is used by a commercial landlord or their agent when accepting partial payment of delinquent rent and temporarily deferring any eviction activity, to document the terms for payment of the remainder of the delinquent rent and preserve the right to continue any eviction process underway if the tenant defaults.

DATE: _____, 20_____, at _____, California.
Items left blank or unchecked are not applicable.

FACTS:

1. This partial payment agreement pertains to the collection of past due rent under a commercial rental or lease agreement
   1.1 dated _____, at _____, California,
   1.2 entered into by _____, as the Tenant,
   1.3 and _____, as the Landlord,
   1.4 regarding the premises referred to as _____.

AGREEMENT:

2. Tenant has not paid delinquent rent for the period(s) of _____.
3. Landlord hereby accepts partial payment on delinquent rent in the amount of .... $_____
4. The balance of the delinquent rent owed is .... $_____
   4.1 Plus late charges for delinquency(ies) of .... $_____
   4.2 Plus deferred rent processing charges of .... $_____
   4.3 **TOTAL deferred rent** due, including additional charges, is the sum of .... $_____
5. Tenant to pay the total deferred rent on or before _____, 20_____.
   5.1 Rent to be paid by ☐ cash, ☐ check, or ☐ cashier's check, made payable to Landlord.
   5.2 Rent may be tendered by ☐ mail, or ☐ personal delivery, to:
   _____ (Name)
   _____ (Address)
   _____ (Phone)
   a. Personal delivery of rent will be accepted during the hours of _____ to _____ on the following days: _____.
   5.3 Rent may also be paid by deposit into account number _____ at:
   _____ (Financial Institution)
   _____ (Address)
   5.4 No grace period for payment of the deferred rent is granted to Tenant.
   5.5 Delinquent payment of the deferred rent incurs a late charge of $_____.
6. If deferred rent is paid when due, any outstanding three-day notice to pay rent or quit is no longer valid.
7. If the deferred rent is not paid when due, Landlord reserves the right to:
   (Check one box only)
   7.1 ☐ Serve Tenant with a three-day notice to pay the remaining balance of the rent due or quit the premises.
   (Check if a three-day notice has not been served)
   7.2 ☐ Commence, without further notice, an unlawful detainer action to evict Tenant from the premises.
   (Check if a three-day notice has been served)
   7.3 ☐ Continue with the unlawful detainer action on file to evict Tenant from the premises.
   (Check if unlawful detainer action has been filed)
8. No provision of the rental or lease agreement is affected in this agreement.
9. _____

I agree to the terms stated above.
☐ See attached Signature Page addendum. [RPI Form 251]
Date: _____, 20_____
Landlord: _____
Agent: _____ CalBRE #:_____

Signature: _____
Phone: _____ Cell: _____
Email: _____

I agree to the terms stated above.
☐ See attached Signature Page addendum. [RPI Form 251]
Date: _____, 20_____
Tenant: _____

Signature: _____
Tenant: _____

Signature: _____
Phone: _____ Cell: _____
Email: _____

FORM 558 03-11 ©2016 RPI — Realty Publications, Inc., P.O. BOX 5707, RIVERSIDE, CA 92517

A residential landlord who accepts any amount of rent from a tenant after serving a three-day notice waives their right to use that notice as the basis for a UD action. After receiving partial rent, a residential landlord needs to serve the tenant with another three-day notice for the amount now remaining unpaid.[2]

---

2 **EDC Associates, Ltd.** v. **Gutierrez** (1984) 153 CA3d 167

Residential vs. commercial landlords

Acceptance of a partial payment toward delinquent rent is within the discretion of the landlord. A landlord might agree to accept partial payments when:

- the partial payment is at least equal to the rent accrued at the time the tenant offers the payment;
- the tenant is creditworthy;
- the tenant has an adequate payment history; and
- the tenant is one the landlord wants to retain.

Both residential and commercial landlords may accept a partial payment of delinquent rent. Then, unless they have agreed to the contrary, immediately serve the tenant with a three-day notice demanding payment of the balance due or quit. Of course, a landlord may agree in a partial payment agreement not to serve a three-day notice after receipt of the partial payment of rent on the condition the balance is received on or before a specified date. [See Form 558 and 559 accompanying this chapter]

Residential rent paid after notice

If a residential landlord files a UD action and, prior to eviction, accepts a partial payment of rent, the acceptance of rent nullifies the UD action and the landlord may not proceed to eviction. The reason the UD action cannot proceed lies in the difference between:

- the amount of rent demanded in the notice to pay supporting the UD action; and
- the amount actually remaining unpaid at the time of the UD hearing.

In residential UD actions, the amounts in the three-day notice and the amount owed by the tenant are required to be the same. Once the residential landlord accepts a partial payment of delinquent rent, the three-day notice served on the tenant no longer states the correct amount the tenant is to pay to avoid losing the right of possession. This rule does not apply to commercial tenancies.

Also, any three-day notice served on a residential tenant which overstates the amount of delinquent rent due at the time of trial on the UD action is invalid. The UD action in a residential eviction based on an overstated amount in the three-day notice fails.[3]

Commercial nonwaiver requirements

Consider a commercial landlord who serves their tenant with a three-day notice to pay rent or quit. Later, the landlord accepts a partial payment of rent under an agreement with the tenant containing a **nonwaiver of rights provision**. This provision states the acceptance of rent does not waive the landlord's right to enforce a breach of the lease. If the nonwaiver notice is not given, the commercial landlord needs to serve the tenant with another three-day notice for payment of the sums remaining due and unpaid.

---

3 **Jayasinghe** v. **Lee** (1993) 13 CA4th Supp. 33

An alternative scenario exists since a nonwaiver of rights provision also exists in the commercial lease agreement entered into by the tenant. As a result, the tenant has received a nonwaiver of rights notice before the landlord's acceptance of partial rent. Here, the landlord may take the money and file or continue with an already filed UD action to recover possession of the premises.[4] [See **RPI** Form 552 §20]

For example, a commercial tenant defaults on a rent payment called for in their lease agreement which contains a nonwaiver of rights provision. The tenant is served with a three-day notice to pay or quit. The tenant fails to pay the rent before it expires, causing the tenancy to be terminated. The three-day notice to pay does not contain a provision for nonwaiver of rights on acceptance of partial rent.

The landlord then accepts a partial payment of rent without entering into any agreements, except to acknowledge receipt of the amount paid as rent. The commercial landlord files a UD action for the amount remaining due and unpaid.

The tenant claims the landlord cannot proceed with a UD hearing since neither the three-day notice nor the landlord's receipt of the partial rent payment include a nonwaiver of rights provision.

Here, the commercial landlord may proceed with the UD action after receipt of partial rent. The nonwaiver provision in the lease agreement puts the tenant on notice, allowing the landlord to accept rent without waiving enforcement rights. One such right is the right to proceed with a UD action.[5]

A nonwaiver of rights provision in a three-day notice or partial payment agreement provides the landlord with the same right to proceed with the UD action as though the provision existed in the lease agreement.

On accepting a partial payment of rent after a UD action has been filed, the commercial landlord amends the UD complaint to reflect the partial payment received and the amount remaining due and unpaid by the tenant.[6]

Without a *written* partial payment agreement, tenants might claim the landlord who accepted partial rent:

- treated acceptance of partial rent as satisfaction of all the rent due;
- waived their right to continue eviction proceedings; or
- permanently modified the lease agreement, establishing a semi-monthly rent payment schedule.

When a residential or commercial landlord accepts a partial payment of rent, the evidence provided by a signed partial payment agreement overcomes tenant claims that the landlord waived UD enforcement rights by accepting rent.

nonwaiver of rights provision
A commercial rental or lease agreement provision containing the landlord's reservation of rights. [See **RPI** Form 552 §20]

No waiver of rights

Get it in writing

---

4 CCP §1161.1(c)
5 **Woodman Partners** v. **Sofa U Love** (2001) 94 CA4th 766
6 CCP §1161.1(c)

PARTIAL PAYMENT AGREEMENT
Residential

NOTE: This form is used by a residential landlord or their agent when accepting partial payment of delinquent rent and temporarily deferring any eviction activity, to document the terms for payment of the remainder of the delinquent rent and preserve the right to continue any eviction process underway if the tenant defaults.

DATE: _____, 20_____, at _____, California.
Items left blank or unchecked are not applicable.
FACTS:

1. This partial payment agreement pertains to the collection of past due rent under a residential rental or lease agreement
    1.1 dated _____, at _____, California,
    1.2 entered into by _____, as the Tenant,
    1.3 and _____, as the Landlord,
    1.4 regarding the premises referred to as _____
    _____.

AGREEMENT:

2. Tenant has not paid the full rent due for the month(s) of _____
3. Landlord hereby accepts partial payment on the past due rent in the amount of . . . . $_____
4. The balance of the unpaid rent owed by Tenant is . . . . $_____
    4.1 Plus late charges for delinquency of. . . . . $_____
    4.2 Plus deferred rent processing charge of . . . . $_____
    4.3 **TOTAL deferred rent** due, including additional charge, is the sum of . . . . $_____
5. Tenant to pay the total deferred rent on or before _____, 20_____.
    5.1 Rent to be paid by ☐ personal check, or ☐ _____.
    5.2 Rent may be tendered by ☐ mail, or ☐ personal delivery, to:
    _____ (Name)
    _____ (Address)
    _____ (Phone)
       a. Personal delivery of rent will be accepted during the hours of _____
          to _____ on the following days: _____.
    5.3 Rent may also be paid by deposit into account number _____at:
    _____ (Financial Institution)
    _____ (Address)
    _____ (Phone)
    5.4 No grace period for payment of the deferred rent is granted to Tenant.
    5.5 Delinquent payment of the deferred rent incurs a late charge of $_____
6. If the deferred rent is not paid when due, a three-day notice to pay rent or quit may be served at any time. [See **RPI** Form 575 and 575-1]
7. No provision of the rental or lease agreement is affected by this agreement.
8. _____

I agree to the terms stated above.
Date: _____, 20_____
Landlord: _____
Agent: _____

Signature: _____
Address: _____

Phone: _____ Cell: _____
Fax: _____

I agree to the terms stated above.
Date: _____, 20_____
Tenant: _____

Signature:
Tenant: _____

Signature:
Address: _____

Phone: _____ Cell: _____

FORM 559   03-11   ©2016 **RPI** — Realty Publications, Inc., P.O. BOX 5707, RIVERSIDE, CA 92517

Residential partial payment agreement

The *partial payment agreement* entered into by a tenant and a landlord accepting partial rent memorializes:

- the landlord's receipt of partial rent;
- the amount owed on the deferred portion of the delinquent rent;
- the tenant's promise to pay the remaining rent owed on or before a specific date; and
- notification of the landlord's right to serve a three-day notice on failure to pay the remaining balance. [See Form 559]

Consider a prudent residential tenant who informs the landlord they will be unable to pay the full monthly rent before the payment becomes delinquent. The tenant offers to pay part of the rent prior to delinquency and the remainder ten days later.

Since the tenant is creditworthy, has not been seriously delinquent in the past and the landlord wishes to retain the tenant, the residential landlord agrees to accept the partial payment.

However, to avoid disputes regarding the amount of rent remaining due and when it is to be paid, the residential landlord prepares and the landlord and tenant sign a partial payment agreement formalizing their understanding.

Now consider a residential landlord who serves a three-day notice and then accepts a partial payment of rent before completing the eviction process started by the notice. By accepting a partial payment, the residential landlord understands the three-day notice had been rendered invalid and no longer supports a UD action and eviction.

Thus, when the residential landlord accepts payment of partial rent it is on the condition the tenant enters into a partial payment agreement stating the date the balance owed is due. The partial payment agreement prevents disputes with the tenant about when the balance is due or a three-day notice may be served if the balance is not paid.

Prevention of disputes

Chapter 21 Summary

Acceptance of a partial payment toward delinquent rent is within the discretion of the landlord. Both residential and commercial landlords may accept a partial payment of delinquent rent. Different rules apply for commercial and residential partial rent payments.

A commercial landlord may accept a partial payment of rent after serving a three-day notice and before eviction. Without further notice to the tenant, the commercial landlord may proceed with a UD action and evict the tenant.

However, a residential landlord who accepts any amount of rent from a tenant after serving a three-day notice waives their right to use the notice as the basis for a UD action. After receiving partial rent, a residential landlord needs to serve the tenant with another three-day notice for the amount now remaining unpaid.

Chapter 21 Key Terms

Quiz 5 Covering Chapters 19-21 is located on page 637.

Chapter
22

Changing terms on a month-to-month tenancy

After reading this chapter, you will be able to:
- apply the rules to be adhered to when changing the terms of a month-to-month tenancy;
- determine whether a 30- or 60-day notice is to be used by a residential landlord based on the percentage change in rent; and
- implement the proper procedure for serving the tenant with a notice of change in rental terms.

Learning Objectives

| notice of change in rental terms | notice of intent to vacate |
| pro rata rent |

Key Terms

A landlord and tenant enter into a **month-to-month tenancy** under a rental agreement which grants an option to purchase the property. The option expires on termination of the tenancy. [See **RPI** Form 551]

Later, the landlord serves the tenant with a *30-day notice of a change in rental terms*. The notice states the option to purchase expires in 30 days, unless exercised by the tenant. [See Form 570 accompanying this chapter]

After the 30-day notice expires, the tenant, who is still in possession, attempts to exercise the option. In response, the landlord refuses to sell the property under the option. The landlord claims the tenant's right to exercise the purchase option expired due to the change of rental terms in the 30-day notice.

Landlord's notice to tenant

The tenant claims the option to purchase is binding until the tenancy is terminated, and the month-to-month rental agreement and occupancy have not been terminated.

Can the tenant enforce the option to purchase?

No! The option expired, unexercised. The option to purchase was part of the terms of the rental agreement. Thus, on expiration of the 30-day notice terminating the option, the option to purchase was eliminated.

Like any other provision contained or referenced in a month-to-month rental agreement, the option to purchase is part of the tenant's rights and obligations comprising the month-to-month tenancy. Thus, the option was subject to change on 30 days' written notice from the landlord.[1]

Notice of change in rental terms

All conditions in a residential or commercial month-to-month rental agreement or expired lease agreement may be changed on written notice by the landlord. This notice is commonly referred to as a **notice of change in rental terms**.

The most common notice of change in rental terms requires a 30-day notice period. However, a 60-day notice period is required for residential rent increases greater than 10%. The 60-day notice is reviewed in a later subhead.[2]

Editor's note — Conditions in a rental or lease agreement are also commonly referred to as provisions, clauses, terms, conditions, addenda, covenants, etc.

For example, a residential or commercial landlord under a month-to-month rental agreement can increase the rent or shift repair and maintenance obligations to the tenant by serving a 30-day *notice of change in rental terms*. It is also used to change any other terms in a residential month-to-month tenancy. For commercial property, the form is used regardless of the amount of the rent increase or to change any other terms. [See Form 570]

In addition to referencing the rental or expired lease agreement to be modified, the *30-day notice of change in rental terms* provides for:

- change in the rent amount;
- change in the *common area maintenance (CAM)* charge;
- change in utility payment responsibility;
- additional security deposit;
- allocation of new or additional non-smoking areas; and
- a space for additional changes in the terms to the rental or expired lease agreement. [See Form 570]

notice of change in rental terms
Written notice served on the tenant noting changes in the terms or conditions of a month-to-month rental agreement. [See **RPI** Form 570 and 574]

---

1 **Wilcox** v. **Anderson** (1978) 84 CA3d 593
2 Calif. Civil Code §827

Form 570

30-Day Notice of Change in Rental Terms

30-DAY NOTICE OF CHANGE IN RENTAL TERMS

NOTE: This form is used by a seller or seller's agent when a real estate transaction does not close as a result of a buyer's breach and the seller has incurred unrecoverable money losses, to make a demand on and provide the buyer with an itemization of the seller's out-of-pocket losses.

Date: _____, 20____, at _____, California.
To Tenant: _____
Items left blank or unchecked are not applicable.

FACTS:

1. You are a Tenant under a rental agreement or expired lease agreement
    1.1 dated _____, at _____, California,
    1.2 entered into by _____, as the Tenant,
    1.3 and _____, as the Landlord,
    1.4 regarding real estate referred to as _____
    _____

NOTICE:

Thirty (30) days after service of this notice on you, the terms of your tenancy on the real estate are hereby changed as indicated below:

2. Rent will be $_____ payable ☐ monthly, or ☐ _____,
    in advance, and due on the _____ day of the month.
    2.1 Rent to be paid by ☐ personal check, or ☐ _____.
    2.2 Rent may be tendered by ☐ mail, or ☐ personal delivery,
        to _____ (Name)
        _____ (Address)
        _____ (Phone, Fax, Email)
        a. Personal delivery of rent will be accepted during the hours of _____ to _____ on the following days:
        _____
    2.3 Rent may also be paid by deposit into account number _____,
        at _____ (Financial Institution)
        _____ (Address)
3. The common area maintenance charge will be $_____ per month, payable with each payment of rent.
4. Utilities now paid by Landlord to be paid by Tenant as checked:
    ☐ Gas ☐ Electricity ☐ Sewage and Rubbish ☐ Water ☐ Cable TV
5. ☐ Tenant to maintain and properly care for the lawns, gardens, trees, shrubs and watering system.
6. An additional security deposit of $_____ is payable with the next rent payment.
7. _____
    _____

8. **This notice affects no other terms of your tenancy.**

Date: _____, 20_____
Landlord/Agent: _____ CalBRE#:_____

Signature: _____
Address: _____
Phone: _____ Cell: _____
Fax: _____
Email: _____

FORM 570   03-11   ©2016 RPI — Realty Publications, Inc., P.O. BOX 5707, RIVERSIDE, CA 92517

To be enforceable, a notice of change in rental terms is served in the same manner as a three-day notice to pay rent or quit. However, only the landlord may unilaterally change the terms in a rental agreement.[3]

A month-to-month tenant has no ability to alter the terms of the rental agreement, other than to terminate the tenancy and vacate.[4]

In rent control communities, a landlord or property manager needs to comply with rent control ordinances that affect their ability to alter provisions in leases and rental agreements, which is reviewed in a later subhead.

---

3 CC §827
4 CC §1946

Form 572

30-Day Notice to Vacate: From Tenant

30-DAY NOTICE TO VACATE
From Tenant

NOTE: This form is used by a tenant when the tenant occupies the property under a month-to-month rental agreement or occupancy with rent paid under an expired lease agreement, and is vacating the premises, to notify the property manager or landlord the tenant will vacate the premises within 30 days.

Date: _____, 20_____, at _____, California.
To Landlord: _____
Items left blank or unchecked are not applicable.

FACTS:

1. I am a Tenant under a rental agreement or expired lease agreement
    1.1   dated _____, at _____, California,
    1.2   entered into by _____, as the Tenant,
          and _____, as the Landlord,
    1.3   regarding real estate referred to as _____
          _____

NOTICE:

2. Within thirty (30) days after service of this notice, I will vacate and deliver possession of the premises to Landlord or _____.

3. This notice is intended as a 30-day Notice to terminate my month-to-month tenancy.

4. I understand:
    4.1   I will owe pro rated daily rent for any days in the 30-day period I have not prepaid rent.
    4.2   I have previously given Landlord a security deposit of $_____.
          a.   I acknowledge, if I am a residential tenant, that I have the right to request and be present for an inspection of the premises to be conducted within two weeks of expiration of this notice to vacate for the purposes of Landlord providing me with an itemized statement of deductible charges for repairs and cleaning to allow me the opportunity to remedy these deficiencies and avoid a deduction from my security deposit. [Calif. Civil Code §1950.5(f)(1)]
          b.   Within 21 days after I vacate, Landlord will furnish me a written statement and explanation of any deductions from the deposit, and a refund of the remaining amount. [Calif. Civil Code §1950.5(g)(1)]
    4.3   Landlord may deduct only those amounts necessary to:
          a.   reimburse for Tenant defaults in rental payments;
          b.   repair damages to the premises caused by Tenant (ordinary wear and tear excluded);
          c.   clean the premises, if necessary;
          d.   reimburse for loss, damage or excessive wear and tear on furnishings provided to Tenant.
    4.4   Landlord may show the premises to prospective tenants during normal business hours by first giving you written notice at least 24 hours in advance of entry. The notice will be given to you in person, by leaving a copy with an occupant of suitable age and discretion, or by leaving the notice on or under your entry door.

5. The reason for termination is _____.

6. I have served this notice on Landlord or Manager ☐ personally, or ☐ by certified or registered mail.

This statement is true and correct.	For Landlord/Agent's use:
Date: _____, 20_____	Date Received: _____.
Tenant: _____	
Signature: _____	
Forwarding Address:_____	
_____	
Phone: _____ Cell: _____	
Fax: _____	
Email: _____	

FORM 572   03-11   ©2016 RPI — **Realty Publications, Inc.,** P.O. BOX 5707, RIVERSIDE, CA 92517

Calculating rent due after an increase

A landlord or property manager may serve the tenant in possession under a periodic rental agreement with a notice of change in rental terms on any day during the rental period.

Once a notice of change in rental terms is served on a tenant, the new terms stated in the notice immediately become part of the tenant's rental agreement or expired lease agreement, both being month-to-month tenancies.[5]

---

5 CC §827

However, the new rental terms stated in the notice do not take effect until expiration of the 30-day or 60-day period after service of the notice on the tenant.

For example, a property manager prepares a 30-day notice of change in rental terms to increase the rent on a month-to-month tenant. The due date for the payment of rent is the first day of each month.

The tenant is properly served with the 30-day notice on the 10th of June. The tenant intends to remain in possession at the new rent rate.

Since June 11th is the first day of the 30-day notice period, the rent does not begin to accrue at the increased rate until July 11th — the day after the 30-day notice expires. However, rent for all of July is payable in advance on the first day of the month, including the number of days affected by the rent increase.

To calculate the advance rent due and payable on the first day of July, the rent is prorated as follows:

- the old daily rate of rent for the first ten days of the month; and
- the new daily rate of rent for the remaining 20 days in the month of July.

Pro rata rent due on the first is determined based on the number of days in the calendar month, unless the rental agreement contains a provision prorating rent on a 30-day basis.

If a residential landlord decides to increase rent on a tenant under a month-to-month rental agreement, the length of the notice period depends on the amount of the rent increase. Two notices exist:

- the 30-day notice of change in rental terms [See Form 570]; and
- the 60-day notice of change in rental terms. [See **RPI** Form 574]

To determine whether a 30-day or 60-day notice is required, the landlord compares the increased rent sought with the lowest rent amount paid by the tenant during the last 12 months.[6]

When the increase in monthly rent is equal to or less than 10% of the lowest amount of monthly rent paid during the previous 12 months, the landlord may serve the tenant with a 30-day notice of change in rental terms.

However, when the increase in rent is more than 10%, the landlord needs to serve the tenant with a 60-day notice of change in rental terms.[7]

For instance, consider a residential landlord charging a month-to-month tenant a rent of $1,000 per month. The tenant's rent has not been increased during the last 12 months. The landlord now seeks to increase the monthly

Notice periods

---

6   Calif. Civil Code §827

7   CC §827

rent by $100. Since the total rent increase is not more than 10%, the landlord may serve the tenant with a 30-day notice to change the terms of the rental or expired lease agreement.

Now consider a different landlord and tenant situation. Within the past 12 months, the landlord increased the tenant's monthly rent $50 from $950 to $1,000. The landlord currently seeks to increase the monthly rent by an additional $100. The anticipated $100 increase (totaling $1,100) is compared to the lowest amount of rent paid in any month during the past 12 months to determine the percentage increase — the $950. Here, the increase in rent is 15.8%. Since the increase in rent is greater than 10%, the landlord needs to serve the tenant with a 60-day notice of a change in rental terms.

Tenant responses to a change

On being served with a notice of a change in rental terms, the month-to-month tenant has three options:

- remain in possession and comply with the new rental terms;

- serve the landlord with a 30-day **notice of intent to vacate** and continue paying rent through the end of the 30-day period to vacate[8] [See Form 572 accompanying this chapter]; or

- remain in possession, refuse to comply with the rental terms and raise available defenses, such as retaliatory eviction, in the resulting **unlawful detainer (UD)** action. [See Chapter 26]

notice of intent to vacate
A tenant's notice to the landlord signifying their intent to vacate the leased property. [See **RPI** Form 571 and 572]

pro rata rent
Rental payment amount due for the portion of the rental period remaining after a change in the rent amount due. [See **RPI** Form 552 §4.1]

Consider the tenant who receives the landlord's notice changing rental terms to increase the rent. The tenant does not wish to continue in possession at the increased rent amount. Accordingly, the tenant serves the landlord with a 30-day notice of intent to vacate. [See Form 572]

The tenant owes **pro rata rent** at the new rate for the days after the rent increase becomes effective through the date the tenant's notice to vacate expires. The *pro rata rent* is payable in advance on the due date for the next scheduled payment of rent, usually the first.[9]

Rent control restrictions

In communities with low density and rent control, limitations on rent increases exist for older units.

Most rent control ordinances allow a landlord or property manager to increase the rent to:

- obtain a fair return on their investment;

- recover the cost of capital improvements to the property; and

- pass through the cost of servicing the debt on the property.

Thus, without further authority from the rent control board, a landlord whose property is subject to rent control may increase rent in one of three ways:

- increase rent by the maximum percentage set by local ordinance;

---

8   CC §1946
9   CC §14

- increase rent by the maximum percentage of the **consumer price index (CPI)** as set by local ordinance; or

- increase rent by the maximum amount previously set by the local rent control board.

Landlords of newly constructed units or individual units (single family residences/condos) may establish their own rent rates, when they are subject to rent control ordinances established prior to 1995.

Chapter 22 Summary

All conditions in a residential or commercial month-to-month rental agreement may be changed on written notice by the landlord, but not by the tenant. To be enforceable, the notice is served on the tenant in the same manner as a three-day notice to pay rent or quit.

A landlord or property manager may serve a notice of change in rental terms on any day during the rental period. The new rental terms stated in the notice do not take effect until expiration of the notice. The notice period for most changes is 30 days. For residential rent increases greater than 10%, a 60-day notice period is required.

Chapter 22 Key Terms

notice of change in rental terms.. pg. 214

notice of intent to vacate... pg. 218

pro rata rent.. pg. 218

Quiz 6 Covering Chapters 22-24 is located on page 638.

Notes:

Lease guarantees and small claims actions

After reading this chapter, you will be able to:
- distinguish a lease guarantee agreement from a lease agreement;
- understand its separate risk reduction function when used in conjunction with a lease agreement; and
- implement enforcement of a guarantee if a tenant defaults on a lease agreement.

accommodation party   **lease guarantee**

Learning Objectives

Key Terms

Recovery amount limited

> **lease guarantee**
> An agreement committing a person other than the tenant to pay all monies due the landlord under the lease agreement. [See **RPI** Form 553-1]

Consider three young prospective tenants who seek to rent their first apartment as roommates. The prospective tenants lack any rental history or independent source of income.

A landlord agrees to lease to the tenants on the condition a creditworthy parent of one of the tenants signs a **lease guarantee** agreement. A *lease guarantee* is then entered into by the parents of one of the tenants. Under the lease guarantee, the parents are responsible for all monies due the landlord on the lease agreement to be entered into by the tenants if the tenants fail to pay. [See Form 553-1 §4.1 accompanying this chapter]

The tenants enter into a one-year lease. However, before the lease expires, the tenants stop paying rent.

The landlord serves the tenants with a three-day notice to pay rent or quit.

The landlord sends a copy of the notice to the guarantor as required to enforce the guarantee agreement, contractually called a *condition precedent* to exercising the guarantee. [See Form 553-1]

GUARANTEE AGREEMENT
For Rental or Lease

Prepared by: Agent _____   Phone _____
Broker _____   Email _____

NOTE: This form is used by a leasing agent, property manager or landlord when entering into a rental or lease agreement with a prospective tenant in reliance on a guarantee, to document a third-party's guarantee for the payment of rent or other monetary obligation arising out of a default in a rental or lease agreement.

DATE: _____, 20_____, at _____, California.

Items left blank or unchecked are not applicable.

FACTS:

1. This Gurantee Agreement, called Guarantee, is entered into by
   1.1 _____, as the Guarantor,
   1.2 and _____, as the Landlord,
   1.3 as an addendum to a Lease Agreement dated _____, 20_____,
       between _____, as the Tenant,
       and _____, as the Landlord,
   1.4 regarding real estate referred to as _____
       _____
   1.5 The Lease Agreement is entered into by Landlord in reliance on this Guarantee and the financial statements provided by Guarantor. [See **RPI** Form 550 and 551]

2. **LANDLORD AGREES:**
   2.1 To notify Guarantor of any notices served on Tenant for proceedings to enforce the Lease.
   2.2 To apply to the Lease Agreement obligations, in any reasonable manner and in its sole discretion, any payments or recoveries from Tenant or from Guarantor.
   2.3 Any refund to Tenant by Landlord of any payment received by Landlord on the guaranteed Lease Agreement will remain fully guaranteed.
   2.4 Any recovery by Landlord from any other Guarantor or an. Insurer will first be credited to the portion of the indebtedness of Tenant to Landlord which exceeds the maximum liability under this Guarantee.

3. **GENERAL PROVISIONS:**
   3.1 Any communication or notice under this Guarantee is to be in writing and is effective only if delivered by personal service or mailed by registered or certified mail, postage-prepaid and return receipt requested.
   3.2 This Guarantee is binding on Guarantor, their successors and assigns, and inures to the benefit of Landlord and its successors and assigns.
   3.3 No provision of this Guarantee or right of Landlord can be waived, nor can Guarantor be released from their obligations, except in writing signed by Landlord.
   3.4 If Guarantor is a corporation, partnership or Limited Liability Company (LLC), each individual executing this Guarantee on behalf of Guarantor represents and warrants they are duly authorized to execute this Guarantee on its behalf.
   3.5 Before any party to this agreement files an action on a dispute arising out of this agreement which remains unresolved after 30 days of informal negotiations, the parties agree to enter into non-binding mediation administered by a neutral dispute resolution organization and undertake a good faith effort during mediation to settle the dispute.
   3.6 The prevailing party in any action on a dispute will be entitled to attorney fees and costs, unless they file an action without first offering to enter into mediation to resolve the dispute.
   3.7 This Guarantee will be governed by California law.

4. **GUARANTOR AGREES:**
   4.1 To guarantee to Landlord the payment of rent or any other monetary obligation arising under the Lease Agreement.
   4.2 To continue liability under this Guarantee, notwithstanding:
       a. Any modification of the Lease Agreement;
       b. Any waiver or failure to enforce the Lease Agreement;

--- PAGE 1 OF 2 — FORM 553-1 ---

The rent remains unpaid and the landlord files an unlawful detainer (UD) action. As a result, the tenants are evicted.

When the landlord regains possession, they discover the tenants and their guests have extensively damaged the property. The landlord incurs $4,500 in losses due to the cost of preparing the unit for leasing and rents lost before re-letting the unit.

Since the recovery sought under the lease agreement is less than $5,000 and possession is no longer an issue, the landlord files a small claims court action against the tenants who signed the lease agreement, also naming the parents who signed the guarantee.

----------------------------------- PAGE 2 OF 2 — FORM 553-1 ---

   c.   Any release or modification of any security for the Lease Agreement, including other guarantees for performance of the Lease Agreement;

   d.   Any unenforceability of part or all of the provisions of the Lease Agreement.

4.3   To file all claims against Tenant in bankruptcy or other proceeding on any indebtedness of Tenant to Guarantor, and to assign to Landlord all Guarantor's rights on any such indebtedness. If Guarantor fails to file any claim, Landlord is authorized to do so in the name of Guarantor or as Guarantor's attorney-in-fact.

4.4   To subordinate any of Guarantor's claims against Tenant to the Lease Agreement obligations of Tenant to Landlord.

4.5   ☐ The Guarantee is secured by a trust deed. [See RPI Form 451]

5. GUARANTOR WAIVES:

5.1   All right of subrogation to Landlord's rights against Tenant.

5.2   All notices to Guarantor or other persons of the creation, modification, renewal or accrual of any obligations under the Lease Agreement or any other related matter, except under §2.1 of this Guarantee Agreement.

5.3   Any failure to timely enforce the Lease Agreement.

5.4   Any statute of limitations.

5.5   Any duty of Landlord to disclose to Guarantor any facts known or discovered about Tenant which materially increase Guarantor's risks of liability.

5.6   Any circumstances which constitute a legal or equitable discharge of Guarantor.

5.7   The right to require Landlord to first proceed against Tenant and enforce Tenant's obligations under the Lease Agreement or to pursue any remedy or to enforce any right before proceeding on this Guarantee.

5.8   Any Tenant defenses to Landlord's exercise of any of its rights under the Lease Agreement.

6. Other: _____
_____
_____
_____
_____
_____
_____
_____
_____
_____

I agree to the terms stated above.	**I agree to the terms stated above.**
	☐ See attached Signature Page Addendum. [RPI Form 251]
Date: _____, 20_____	Date: _____, 20_____
Landlord's Signature: _____	Guarantor's Signature: _____
Landlord's Signature: _____ Address: _____	Guarantor's Signature: _____ Address: _____
Phone: _____ Cell: _____ Fax: _____ Email: _____	Phone: _____ Cell: _____ Fax: _____ Email: _____

FORM 553-1 06-14	©2015 RPI — Realty Publications, Inc., P.O. BOX 5707, RIVERSIDE, CA 92517

However, at trial, the small claims judge advises the landlord that any award against the parents who guaranteed the lease is limited to $2,500. The landlord is then asked if they want:

- a $2,500 judgment against the guarantors, which would bar any further recovery from the guarantors; or

- a dismissal of the case against the guarantors, which would allow the landlord to file a superior court action against the guarantors to recover on the guarantee.

Is the small claims court judge correct in limiting the landlord's recovery from the parents under the guarantee agreement?

Figure 1

Appearing on
the owner's
behalf

A licensed real estate broker retained solely to manage an owner's rentals, not to represent the owner in a small claims court action, may appear on the owner's behalf in all small claims court actions related to the rental property the broker manages. [CCP §116.540(g)]

However, if the owner seeks to collect amounts which exceed the small claims court's limitations, the action needs to be filed in a municipal court. In a municipal court action, the broker may not represent the owner.

Only the individual owner or an attorney licensed in California may represent the owner in a municipal court action. Also, entities need to be represented by an attorney in these courts.

Yes! The small claims court only has jurisdiction over a person who is liable as a guarantor for the obligations of another if the amount awarded is $2,500 or less.[1]

Thus, if the landlord wants a judgment against the guarantors for the full amount of their losses, the landlord needs to dismiss the small claims action against the parents and seek recovery on the separate guarantee agreement in a superior court action.

When the landlord knows the small claims court limitations from the beginning, they may consider seeking recovery against the guarantor and the tenants in a superior court action by either representing themselves, called *in pro per,* or being represented by an attorney licensed in California. Under some property management situations, the broker managing the property can handle the court action to recover possession and money losses. [See Chapter 9; see Figure 1]

Partners and officers as guarantors

Now consider a corporate tenant who enters into an agreement to lease an office building to be occupied by an incorporated business operation. The president of the corporation signs the lease agreement on behalf of the corporation, acting in an agency capacity as authorized by the board of directors. Thus, the corporation is liable for performance of the lease agreement.

The corporate vice president, in a separate agreement, agrees to personally guarantee as an individual the corporation's promised performance under its lease agreement with the landlord. The guarantee agreement signed by the vice president identifies the guarantor as an individual, not the vice president of the corporation. The guarantee agreement does not contain a description of the guarantor's relationship to the corporation as a corporate officer.

Further, the separate guarantee agreement describes the obligation of the guarantor as a personal obligation. The vice president also supplies the landlord with a financial statement itemizing their personal assets.

---

1   Calif. Code of Civil Procedure §116.220(c)

The vice president signs the guarantee agreement and places the words "Vice President" next to their signature.

The corporation breaches the lease agreement and files for bankruptcy. The landlord then seeks to enforce the guarantee agreement against the vice president, as an individual, to collect their money losses under the separate lease agreement entered into by the corporation.

The vice president claims the guarantee agreement cannot be enforced against them personally since, by identifying themselves as the vice president of the corporation on the guarantee agreement, they were executing the guarantee on behalf of the corporation which entered into the lease agreement, not themselves.

In this example, the guarantee agreement contains words which bind the vice president personally. The fact the words "Vice President" were entered along with their signature does not change the character of the person identified in the guarantee agreement.

Personally binding

The words "Vice President" were merely a description of the individual as a corporate officer. The guarantee agreement did not indicate they were acting as an agent of the corporation, rather than on their own behalf, when they signed it.

The nature of the guarantee agreement identifying the individual and the inclusion of their personal financial statement indicated the vice president was binding themselves personally as an individual.[2]

If the vice president signed the guarantee agreement on behalf of the corporation (as the guarantor of its obligation to pay on the lease agreement), the guarantee agreement is redundant and surplusage. The corporation is already bound by the terms of the lease agreement.

Now consider a landlord who insists on a creditworthy **co-signer** on a lease agreement before they will lease property to a couple who lack sufficient credit and net worth. They intend for a third party to hold the landlord harmless if the actual tenant defaults.

Co-signers on the lease

A co-signer signs the lease agreement but may or may not be identified in the lease agreement as an additional lessee to whom the leasehold is conveyed. The co-signer does not sign a separate guarantee agreement.

However, the co-signer here is not listed as a tenant who will occupy the unit. The co-signer does not occupy the unit or receive any benefit from the landlord or by use of the property for signing the lease agreement.

---

2 **Sebastian International, Inc. v. Peck** (1987) 195 CA3d 803

The tenants default and vacate the property. The landlord now seeks to recover more than $2,500 in damages and unpaid rent from the co-signer. The landlord files a small claims court action against the co-signer to collect lost rent and the cost to repair excess wear and tear to the unit.

The co-signer claims the landlord's recovery is limited to $2,500 since the co-signer was not intended to be a tenant, did not take possession of the property and received no benefit from the leasing transaction.

Here, the co-signer signed the lease agreement merely to assure payment of the rent owed by the tenants. Thus, the co-signer claims they are liable for the actions of the tenants as a guarantor.

Small claims

While case law does not exist regarding the co-signer's guarantor defense, state law does limit a small claims recovery to $2,500 from a defendant who is required to respond to claims by paying for losses based on the default, actions or omissions of another person.

Negotiations conducted prior to the lease agreement establish the separate legal nature of the co-signer's involvement in the leasing transaction as that of a guarantor. Negotiations demonstrate the purpose of the co-signer's involvement was to ensure the landlord received rent payments due under the lease agreement — not to enforce any benefits on behalf of the landlord.

The co-signer argument is similar to the co-signer of a note who receives no benefit from the mortgage proceeds and merely co-signs the note.

Involvement of an accommodation party

As a corollary to the co-signing of a note, the co-signer on a lease agreement claims their activity of co-signing the lease agreement creates a contract obligation similar to an **accommodation party** under California's Commercial Code, and thus, assures payment of a debt (rent) owed by another person (the occupying tenant).

Under the Commercial Code, an *accommodation party* is an individual who:

- signs a note to include liability for a debt evidenced by the note; and
- receives no direct benefit from the debt.[3]

> **accommodation party**
> An individual who signs a note to include liability for a debt evidence by the note and receives no direct benefit from debt.

The co-signer claims the lease agreement needs to be viewed as a note since it is evidence of a debt (rent) owed for letting the premises, a debt economically equivalent to interest owed on principal lent (and evidenced by a note). Also, due to the fact the co-signer was not to take possession under the lease agreement, the co-signer is not primarily liable for payment of the rent and needs to be considered the equivalent of an accommodation party.[4]

An accommodation party's liability is secondary and similar to a guarantor's. Thus, the co-signer argues the landlord's recovery in a small claims court action is limited to $2,500.

3   Calif. Commercial Code §3419(a)
4   Com C §3419

In spite of the reference in the lease agreement to the co-signer as a (non-occupying) tenant, the intent and sole purpose behind the co-signer's execution of the lease was to assure payment of the rent owed by others — the occupying tenants. Thus, the co-signer entered into a guarantee agreement on signing the lease agreement.

Further, the guarantor under a guarantee agreement waives their rights to notices and consent to material changes in the lease agreement. This allows the landlord to terminate the tenancy and pursue collection from the tenant before ever making a demand on the guarantor. [See Form 553-1 §5]

Under a lease guarantee agreement, the guarantors are separately responsible from the tenant for all monies due the landlord on the lease agreement entered into by the tenants.

The purpose of the guarantor's separate involvement from the tenant is to provide an additional source for the landlord to recover monies due under the lease agreement with the tenant.

A co-signer functions similar to a guarantor. The co-signer signs the lease agreement rather than a separate guarantee agreement. A co-signer may or may not be identified in the lease agreement as an additional lessee to whom the leasehold is conveyed.

The co-signer assures payment of rent owed by another person (the occupying tenant), but receives no direct benefit from the debt.

Chapter 23 Summary

Chapter 23 Key Terms

Quiz 6 Covering Chapters 22-24 is located on page 638.

Notes:

Forfeiture of the lease

Learning Objectives

After reading this chapter, you will be able to:

- distinguish a tenant's real property right to occupy real estate versus the landlord's independent contractual right to collect future rents;
- understand how a tenant's right of possession can be terminated under a declaration of forfeiture provision in a three-day notice;
- appreciate how future rent is collected in a separate money action after a tenant's possessory rights have been terminated; and
- instruct a landlord on loss mitigation measures to be implemented to recover future rents when a tenant vacates or is evicted.

Key Terms

declaration of forfeiture provision

default remedies provision

forfeiture of possession

holdover rent provision

loss mitigation

money action

present value

reinstatement period

Lease agreement obligations survive

A tenant's right to occupy real estate is a possessory estate in real property. It is conveyed by the landlord to the tenant by operation of the granting clause in a rental or lease agreement.

Once conveyed, the right of possession is owned by the tenant separate from the rental or lease agreement. The rental or lease agreements contain provisions creating contractual rights and obligations between the landlord and tenant. However, while the tenant holds the right granted to use and

default remedies provision
A lease agreement provision authorizing the landlord on termination of the tenant's lease due to the tenant's default to collect rents for the remaining unexpired lease term. [See **RPI** Form 550 §3.1 and 552 §2.1]

occupy the rented property as a separate real property right from contract rights, the provisions of the rental or lease agreement control the terms and duration of the use and occupancy of the tenant's possessory rights.

One contractual provision in rental or lease agreements is the **default remedies provision**. The *default remedies provision* creates the right for the landlord to collect rents for the full term of the lease. The landlord's contractual right to collect future rents is independent of the tenant's right of possession, continuing after possession is terminated based on the tenant's material breach of the lease agreement. [See **RPI** Form 552]

Forfeiture-of-lease clause is about possession

declaration of forfeiture provision
A lease or rental agreement provision declaring a tenant's failure to cure a breach of the agreement constitutes a forfeiture of the tenant's right of possession. [See **RPI** Form 575 §5]

Consider a tenant who fails to pay rent which becomes delinquent. The landlord serves the tenant with a three-day *notice to pay rent or quit*.

The notice contains a **declaration of forfeiture provision** stating the tenant's right of possession — the real estate leasehold interest owned by the tenant — is forfeited on expiration of the three-day notice unless the tenant first pays the agreed rent. The *declaration of forfeiture provision* is also known as a *forfeiture-of-lease clause*.

Here, the "lease" subject to forfeiture is the property right of possession owned by the tenant, not the lease agreement entered into by the landlord and tenant (which is subject to cancellation, but never a forfeiture since an agreement is not property as is the right of possession). Confusingly, the lease agreement document, the paperwork itself, is often also loosely referred to as the "lease", such as "this is the lease we signed."

If the tenant fails to pay rent before the expiration of the notice, their possessory interest in the real estate is forfeited, as called for in the declaration or forfeiture provision in the notice. On forfeiture, the tenant voluntarily vacates. Alternatively, if the tenant remains in possession without the landlord's consent, the tenant can be evicted through an unlawful detainer (UD) action. [See Form 575 §3 in Chapter 25]

However, the landlord does not file a UD action to regain possession of the property, even though the tenant's continued possession is now unlawful and the landlord accepts no further rent.

holdover rent provision
A rental or lease agreement provision which sets the rent rate during a tenant holdover period. [See **RPI** Form 550 §3.3 and 552 §2.3]

*Editor's note — The landlord may benefit by choosing not to evict the tenant when no other tenant is immediately available to occupy the space. If the lease agreement contains a **holdover rent provision** setting holdover rent rates, the landlord can pursue the tenant for holdover rents in a money action. Holdover rents usually greatly exceed the current rent rate for the space which is all the courts will award in UD actions. Further, occupancy is often required by insurance carriers to remain qualified for hazard coverage. [See Sidebar, "A holdover tenancy"]*

The tenant later voluntarily vacates the property prior to expiration of the lease.

Sidebar

A holdover tenancy

A holdover tenancy occurs when a tenant remains in possession of a property without a valid right of possession. The right of possession expires:

- *at the end of the term granted by the lease agreement;*
- *on expiration of a notice to vacate served by either the landlord of the tenant under a rental agreement; or*
- *on expiration of a notice to quit served on a defaulting tenant if the notice contains a declaration of forfeiture provision.*

When the tenant no longer has the right of possession, the landlord may immediately file an unlawful detainer (UD) action without serving any additional notice. [Calif. Civil Code §1946; Calif. Code of Civil Procedure §1161(1); see Chapter 29]

When a tenant materially breaches a rental or lease agreement, the breach alone does not terminate the tenant's right of possession. A breaching tenant still has a right to possess the property until the landlord acts to terminate the possessory right in the property held and owned by the tenant.

Once the tenant no longer has the right of possession on termination of their tenancy in the real estate, they become a holdover tenant subject to the landlord's UD action.

The landlord then files a separate civil action against the tenant to collect rent for:

- the period prior to termination of the right of possession by forfeiture as declared in the three-day notice;
- the holdover period after the **forfeiture of possession** and prior to vacating; and
- the remaining period under the lease agreement after the tenant vacated until expiration of the lease.

The tenant claims the landlord cannot collect rent called for in the lease agreement for any period after expiration of the three-day notice since:

- the election to forfeit the lease contained in the three-day notice to pay or quit did not just terminate the tenant's real property right to occupy, but cancelled the contractual lease agreement; and
- the landlord's failure to evict the tenant on cancellation of the lease agreement converted the tenant's continued occupancy into a periodic tenancy for which reasonable rent is due, not the holdover rent set in the lease agreement.

forfeiture of possession
The termination of the tenant's right of possession triggered by a declaration of forfeiture in a notice to quit. [See **RPI** Form 575 §5]

Can the landlord collect all rent unpaid as agreed during the tenant's occupancy as well as future rent due for the remaining term of the lease even though the lease was forfeited in the three-day notice?

Yes! But before proceeding, an extremely important distinction needs to be made between:

- the tenant's real property right of possession, called a *lease*, or a leasehold interest as an estate in real property [See Chapter 1]; and

- the lease agreement, which grants the landlord a contract right to collect rents, also commonly referred to as a lease.[1]

A three-day notice to pay or quit that includes a declaration of forfeiture provision terminates the tenant's real property right of possession. It does not also cancel the contract which is the lease agreement. The lease agreement remains intact on forfeiture of possession.[2] [See Chapter 24]

Also, a landlord need not first evict the holdover tenant in a UD action before filing a separate money action to recover rents called for in the lease agreement. Remember, the right of possession and the contractual rights and obligations agreed to in the lease agreement are enforced separately, independent of one another.

Once the tenant's right of possession has expired or been terminated, the landlord can demand and recover holdover rents and unearned future rents remaining under the lease agreement.[3]

First terminate the lease on default

"Termination of the lease" by forfeiture refers exclusively to the termination of the tenant's right of possession in the real estate. Again, the lease agreement remains enforceable to collect unpaid past rents and future rents; it was not cancelled and is unaffected by the termination by forfeiture of the tenant's property rights, with or without the tenant being evicted.

With the tenant's right of possession terminated by the declaration of forfeiture provision in the three-day notice, the landlord may at any time file a UD action and recover possession.[4]

In a UD action, the court initially determines whether the termination of the right of possession under the three-day notice was proper. If proper and the tenant did not cure the breach before the forfeiture became effective, the landlord is awarded possession and the tenant evicted. [See Sidebar, "Abandonment: a passive alternative"]

Rent awarded in a UD action

Rent earned and unpaid up to the time of the UD trial may be awarded in the UD action along with an eviction order. The UD money award for rent due applies only to periods before the UD trial, including:

- the period before termination of the lease for delinquent rent at the rate set by the lease agreement; and

- during the holdover period after termination of the tenant's right of possession up to the UD trial for rent of a reasonable amount as determined by the court.

Editor's note — Typically, UD courts will only award the landlord reasonable rent for rent due in a holdover period. If a lease agreement contains a holdover rent provision, the landlord may consider limiting their recovery

---

1 **Walt** v. **Superior Court** (1992) 8 CA4th 1667
2 **Danner** v. **Jarrett** (1983) 144 CA3d 164
3 Walt, *supra*
4 Calif. Code of Civil Procedure §§1161.1; 1174(c)

in the UD action to a simple recovery of possession. Then, the landlord may file a separate money action to recover the holdover rents due, at the holdover rent rate set in the lease agreement.

A UD award does not include future, unearned rent. Future rents are collected through a separate *money action* on the lease agreement filed after the tenant has been evicted and mitigation of losses undertaken by the landlord.

To review: a landlord who needs to evict a tenant by a UD action may recover possession based on either:

- a termination of the tenant's right of possession under a declaration of forfeiture provision in a three-day notice; or
- leaving the declaration of forfeiture provision out of the three-day notice and allowing the court to terminate the lease on expiration of a five-day *reinstatement period* following a UD award.[5]

With a declaration of forfeiture provision in the three-day notice, the tenant who fails to cure the breach has no continuing right to occupy the real estate after the notice expires.[6]

But what if the three-day notice did not include a declaration of forfeiture provision, deliberately deleted or not? Without including the declaration of forfeiture provision in a notice to quit, the right of possession — the lease — is not terminated until five days has passed after the UD judgment is entered. During this period, called the **reinstatement period**, the tenant may reinstate their yet unforfeited right of possession if they meet the terms set by the UD judgment. If the terms are not met within the reinstatement period of five days, the lease is then forfeited and the tenant evicted.[7]

A landlord might deliberately remove the declaration of forfeiture provision from a three-day notice to give a good tenant extra time to bring overdue rent current. A landlord who deletes the declaration of forfeiture provision effectively gives their tenant the three-day notice period, the length of the UD court process and the five-day reinstatement period to bring the rent current.

If the tenant is able to bring the rent current, the landlord benefits by keeping an otherwise suitable tenant and avoiding a vacancy and turnover costs.

A tenant has no ability to unilaterally restore their right of possession after their leasehold estate in the property has been terminated by forfeiture. Only a court order, or a mutual agreement with the landlord, can restore the tenant's right of possession once terminated.

The relief from forfeiture is sought primarily by commercial tenants who have long-term leases and are prepared to cure any defaults.

Three-day notice without a forfeiture

reinstatement period
The period of time during which the tenant may reinstate their right of possession if they meet the terms set by the unlawful detainer judgment.

Relief from forfeiture of possession

---

5 CCP §1174(a),(c)
6 CCP §1174(a)
7 CC §1174(c)

A tenant who wishes to remain in possession after their right of possession has been forfeited and they have been evicted by UD action may petition the court to restore their right of possession, if:

- the underlying lease had an original term of more than one year;
- the landlord has not retaken possession of the property;
- the tenant has not been removed by the sheriff; and
- the tenant petitions the UD court for relief.[8]

Whether the court will grant the tenant a relief from forfeiture and a reinstatement of the lease is based on the degree of hardship the tenant suffers if evicted. However, if the court does grant the tenant relief from forfeiture, it will be conditioned on:

- the payment of all amounts, including rents, due the landlord; and
- full performance of all rental or lease agreement conditions, whether oral or written.

Also, when the right of possession has already been terminated by a declaration of forfeiture provision in the three-day notice does not concern the court when hearing the tenant's petition for relief from forfeiture.[9]

If an attorney appears on behalf of the tenant seeking relief from forfeiture, a copy of the application for relief and petition for the hearing is to be served on the landlord or property manager filing the UD action at least five days prior to the hearing.[10]

Also, at the UD trial, the landlord needs to be prepared to defend the forfeiture they have declared. This will entail explaining why relief from the forfeiture is unfair to the landlord. The landlord is also required to detail the amounts owed and lease/rental conditions to be cured. The court in a UD action may initiate an inquiry on its own into whether the tenant is entitled to relief from forfeiture.

Also, the tenant may orally request the court at the UD trial to be relieved of the forfeiture and allowed (on conditions) to remain in possession.

The obligation to pay future rent

On termination of the tenant's possessory right to the property — the leasehold— under a declaration of forfeiture provision in any three-day notice or at trial, the landlord is entitled to:

- file a UD action to physically remove the defaulting tenant from actual possession, called **eviction**;
- enforce collection of rent earned and unpaid through entry of the UD judgment; and
- file a separate **money action** to recover future rents and any prior unpaid rent earned but not included in the UD judgment.

money action
Litigation which seeks to recover future rents and any previously unpaid rent earned but not included in an unlawful detainer judgment.

---

8 CCP §1179
9 CCP §1179
10 CCP §1179

*Instead of or in addition to beginning the eviction process by serving a three-day notice with a declaration of forfeiture, a landlord may choose to sever the possession through the abandonment process. [CC §1951.3; see **RPI** Form 581]*

To begin recovering possession through abandonment, a landlord serves a notice of abandonment on the tenant. This notice is served if:

- *rent on the leased property has been due and unpaid for at least 14 days from the due date;*
- *the landlord has a reasonable belief that the tenant has abandoned the property. [Calif. Civil Code §1951.3(b)]*

A notice of abandonment declares the tenant's right of possession (but not the rental or lease agreement) will be terminated due to abandonment on expiration of the notice. A tenant may contest the abandonment within:

- *15 days of the tenant receiving personal service of the notice of abandonment; or*
- *18 days after the notice is placed in the mail by the landlord. [CC §1951.3.(b)]*

If the tenant does not contest the notice of abandonment within the statutory time limit, the landlord has terminated the tenant's right of possession. Remember: the rental or lease agreement remains intact and survives the tenant's loss of possession. Thus, the landlord retains the contract right to collect future rents due under the uncancelled rental or lease agreement.

Serving a notice of abandonment by itself can have significant negative impacts for a landlord. Firstly, it takes 18 days to terminate a tenant's right of possession, as opposed to three days under the three-day notice.

Secondly, the notice of abandonment only addresses a failure to pay rent. It is not triggered by, nor does it address any material breach by the tenant. A three-day notice to quit is triggered by a material breach of the rental or lease agreement.

Thirdly, the landlord's service of an abandonment notice is an inherently passive process. The landlord serves the notice, and effectively waits for the tenant to contest the landlord's notice. The tenant need not take any action to first cure any breach. Contrast this with the three-day notice and the eviction process, in which the tenant is required to cure the breach, or the right of possession is terminated.

Editor's note — Of course, double recovery of rent is not allowed. If the landlord, in their UD action, is awarded (or denied) rents accrued prior to the UD award, the landlord cannot again seek to recover those amounts in the separate money action for rents.

In a *money action* to collect future rents separate from any UD action or other remedies permitted by the lease agreement, the landlord is entitled to recover:

- all unpaid rent earned under the lease agreement up until the tenant's right of possession is terminated;[11]
- reasonable per diem rent from the termination of the right of possession, until entry of the judgment for rent;[12]

---

11 CC §1951.2(a)(1)
12 CC §1951.2(a)(2)

- all unearned rent called for in the lease agreement for the remaining unexpired term of the lease, subject to:
  - loss mitigation;
  - default remedies in the lease agreement;
  - the prior reletting of the premises; and
  - the discounted present worth of the future rent[13];
- costs incurred by the landlord as a result of the tenant's breach[14]; and
- attorney fees incurred if the lease agreement contains an attorney fees provision.[15]

If the lease agreement included a default remedies provision, the separate money action to recover future rents can be filed immediately after the tenant's right of possession terminated. Recall from the opening scenario that a default remedies provision reserves the landlord's right to collect future rent due after the tenant's right of possession has been terminated. [See Figure 1]

If the lease agreement does not contain a default remedies clause, the landlord's right to recover future rents is still allowed by statute as laid out above. This type of recovery of rents is called a **statutory recovery**. However, in a *statutory recovery* the landlord is required to first mitigate their losses by reletting the premises. Only after reletting the premises may the landlord file a money action to recover *future rents* due from the evicted tenant.[16]

Loss mitigation offsets future rents

With or without a default remedies provision in the lease agreement, the landlord who seeks to recover future rents is to make a reasonable, good-faith effort to reduce their loss of rent after the tenant vacates or is evicted. This is known as **loss mitigation**, a requisite to recovery of future rents.

If the landlord does not act to reduce loss of future rental income, a tenant has the right to offset any future rent due by the amount of rent the landlord could have reasonably collected by reletting the space.[17]

Consider a tenant who fails to pay rent as scheduled in the lease agreement.

Ultimately, a UD judgment is entered in the landlord's favor. The tenant is evicted by the sheriff under a writ of possession issued by the court.

The landlord repossesses the property. Then, the landlord takes steps to relet the property. During the effort to relet, the evicted tenant offers to lease the property at the old rent rate. The landlord refuses the evicted tenant's offer, opting to relet the property to a more creditworthy tenant at a lower rent rate.

loss mitigation
The good-faith effort a landlord who seeks to recover future rents makes to reduce their loss of rent after a tenant vacates or is evicted.

13 CC §1951.2(a)(3)
14 CC §1951.2(a)(4)
15 CC §1717
16 CC §1951.2(c)
17 CC §1951.2(c)

The landlord then seeks to recover their money losses from the evicted tenant. The losses equal the difference between:

- the amount of rent agreed to and unpaid through the expiration of the lease term in the lease agreement; and
- the amount of rent the new tenant has agreed to pay.

The evicted tenant claims the landlord is barred from collecting any unpaid future rent since the landlord could have recovered the full amount of rental payments if the landlord had accepted the evicted tenant's offer to lease.

Is the evicted tenant liable for the deficiency created by the difference between all rent remaining unpaid on the lease and the amount of rent the new tenant has agreed to pay?

Yes! The evicted tenant owes the deficiency between the rent owed under the tenant's lease agreement and the lower rent to be paid by the new tenant. Here, the landlord actively sought a new tenant and was unable to get the full amount of the rent the evicted tenant had agreed to pay through the expiration of their lease.[18]

The landlord's effort to mitigate the loss of rents by reletting the property was in good faith and reasonable. The reasonableness of the landlord's conduct undertaken to relet the space is determined based on the actions actually taken by the landlord. Reasonableness is not determined by evaluating available alternative courses of action the landlord could have taken to mitigate damages (such as re-renting to the evicted tenant).

A landlord needs to pursue a course of action that is likely to reduce the amount of future rent the evicted tenant owes after the tenancy is terminated. Otherwise, the tenant is permitted to offset future rents by showing the landlord's efforts to relet the property were unreasonable efforts to mitigate the loss of rent.

Discounted future rent and interest on delinquent rent

The landlord who is entitled to recover future rent under an unexpired lease agreement will only be awarded the *present value* of the unearned future rents.

To determine the **present value** of unearned rent at the time of the court's money award, the future rents will be discounted (to their present value) at the annual rate of 1% over the Federal Reserve Bank of San Francisco (the Fed)'s discount rate. The Fed's discount rate used for calculating the present worth of future rent on an award in 2014 would be 1% over the discount rate of 0.75%.[19]

From the time the tenant defaults on the payment of rent to the time the unpaid rent is awarded, the landlord is entitled to recover interest on unpaid amounts of back rent.

present value
Unearned rent that is discounted at the time of the court's money award at the annual rate of 1% over the Federal Reserve Bank of San Francisco's discount rate.

---

18 **Zanker Development Co.** v. **Cogito Systems, Inc.** (1989) 215 CA3d 1377
19 CC §1951.2(b)

The interest accrued prior to judgment is calculated at the rate agreed to in the lease agreement. If the interest rate is not stated in the lease agreement, the interest will accrue at 10% per annum from the date of default to entry of the money judgment. After judgment is awarded for back rent or discounted future rent, interest accrues at 10% on the money judgment until paid.[20]

Costs to relet

A landlord is entitled to recover all reasonable costs incurred to relet the property once a tenant has prematurely vacated, or been evicted.[21]

Costs incurred to relet the property include:

- costs to clean up the property;
- brokerage and legal fees to find a new tenant;
- permit fees to construct necessary improvements or renovations; and
- any other money losses incurred as a result of the tenant's breach, such as a decline in the property's market value.[22]

---

20 CC §§1951.2(b), 3289
21 CC §1951.2(a)(4)
22 **Sanders Construction Company, Inc. v. San Joaquin First Federal Savings and Loan Association** (1982) 136 CA3d 387

Chapter 24 Summary

A tenant's right to occupy real estate is a possessory estate in real property. It is conveyed by the landlord to the tenant by operation of the granting clause in a rental or lease agreement.

Once conveyed, the right of possession is owned by the tenant separate from the rental or lease agreement. The rental or lease agreements contain provisions creating contractual rights and obligations between the landlord and tenant. However, while the tenant holds the right to use and occupy a rented property as a separate real property right, the provisions of the rental or lease agreement control the terms and duration of the use and occupancy.

A landlord who needs to evict a tenant by an unlawful detainer (UD) action may recover possession based on either:

- a termination of the tenant's right of possession under a declaration of forfeiture provision in a three-day notice; or
- leaving the declaration of forfeiture provision out of the three-day notice and allowing the court to terminate the lease on expiration of the five-day reinstatement period following a UD award.

Rent earned and unpaid up to the time of the UD trial may be awarded in the UD action along with an eviction order. A UD award does not include future, unearned rent, which is collected through a separate money action on the lease agreement.

The landlord who seeks to recover future rents is to make a reasonable, good-faith effort to reduce their loss of rent after the tenant vacates or is evicted, known as loss mitigation. The landlord who is entitled to recover future rent under an unexpired lease agreement will only be awarded the present value of the unearned future rents. To determine the present value of unearned rent, the future rents will be discounted to their present value at the annual rate of 1% over the Federal Reserve Bank of San Francisco (the Fed)'s discount rate.

Chapter 24 Key Terms

Quiz 6 Covering Chapters 22-24 is located on page 638.

Notes:

Chapter
25

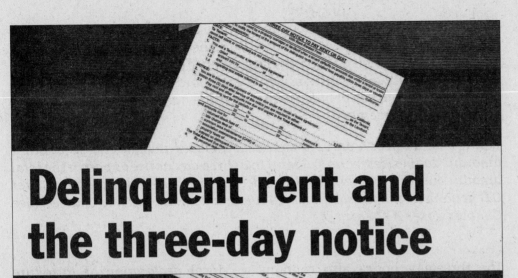

Delinquent rent and the three-day notice

After reading this chapter, you will be able to:
- determine when rent becomes delinquent and a three-day notice to pay rent or quit may be served on a tenant;
- contrast a material breach with a minor breach which alone does not justify service of a three-day notice;
- determine when a notice to quit with no alternative performance is served on a tenant committing an incurable breach; and
- understand the timing, servicing requirements and consequences of a notice to pay rent or quit served on a tenant.

Learning Objectives

delinquency	**late charge provision**
due date	**material breach**
grace period	**minor breach**
incurable breach	**notice to pay rent or quit**

Key Terms

A tenant fails to pay rent on or after the due date and expiration of the grace period set in the rental or lease agreement. The rent is now delinquent. The property manager serves the tenant with a three-day **notice to pay rent or quit**. [See Form 575 accompanying this chapter]

The *three-day notice* states the exact amount of:
- delinquent rent unpaid; and
- other delinquent amounts owed to the landlord and unpaid.

Pay or forfeit your right of possession

> **notice to pay rent or quit**
> A notice served on a tenant by the landlord which states the amount of delinquent rent and any other delinquent amounts owed the landlord. [See **RPI** Form 575 and 575-1]

Editor's note — Some trial judges declare late charges and rent-related fees are not rent in residential agreements. Thus, the delinquency of a late charge payment or rent-related fee properly demanded and unpaid is not properly included as an amount due a residential landlord to be collected by use of a three-day notice to pay or quit. Further, they are not a material breach of the rental or lease agreement

*Before a landlord or a property manager includes any late charge (or other amounts due besides technical rent) in a three-day notice as part of the total amount due, the wise landlord will determine if the judge presiding over UD actions in the jurisdiction will allow a demand for late charges. [See Chapter 28; see **RPI** Form 575-1]*

Declaration of forfeiture provision

The three-day notice also contains a critical *declaration of forfeiture provision*. The forfeiture provision states the tenant's failure to pay the delinquent rent before the notice expires causes the right of possession of the property to revert to the landlord by forfeiture.

After the three-day notice expires, the tenant remains in possession. Later, the tenant tenders payment of the delinquent rent to the landlord. The landlord refuses to accept the payment. The tenant refuses to voluntarily vacate.

The landlord files an unlawful detainer (UD) action to evict the tenant and regain possession of the premises. The landlord claims the tenant's right of possession was terminated on expiration of the three-day notice due to the *declaration of forfeiture provision* it contained. Thus, the tenant cannot now reinstate their terminated right of possession by paying the delinquent rent.

Can the landlord evict the tenant even though the tenant tendered the delinquent rent in full after expiration of the three-day notice?

Yes! The tenant's right of possession was terminated on expiration of the three-day notice since the notice contained a *declaration of forfeiture provision*. Thus, the tenant's continued occupancy became unlawful on expiration of the three-day notice.[1]

On expiration, the landlord is no longer obligated to accept delinquent rent payments or allow the occupancy to be reinstated. Even though the right to possession has been terminated by forfeiture, the rental or lease agreement has not been cancelled (remember, contract rights cannot be forfeited). The rental or lease agreement remains enforceable to collect future rents as scheduled.[2] [See Form 575 §5.1]

Default, notice and cure or vacate

A **tenant defaults** on their rental or lease agreement by failing to:

- pay rent and any other amounts due and called for in the rental or lease agreement; or

---

[1] Calif. Code of Civil Procedure § 1174(a)

[2] CCP §§ 1161(2); 1174(a)

Form 575

Three-Day
Notice to Pay
Rent or Quit
— With Rent-
Related Fees

THREE-DAY NOTICE TO PAY RENT OR QUIT
With Rent-Related Fees

NOTE: This form is used by a property manager or landlord when a tenant defaults on amounts due under a rental or lease agreement, to notify the tenant of the amount of the delinquent rents and related fees payable within three days or vacate and deliver possession.

DATE: _____, 20 _____, at _____, California.
To Tenant: _____
Items left blank or unchecked are not applicable.
FACTS:
1. You are a Tenant under a rental or lease agreement
   1.1 dated _____, at _____, California,
   1.2 entered into by _____, as the Tenant,
   1.3 and _____, as the Landlord,
   1.4 regarding real estate referred to as _____
   _____.

NOTICE:
2. You are in breach of the payment of amounts due under the rental or lease agreement.
3. Within three (3) days after service of this notice you are required to either:
   3.1 Pay rent and other amounts now due and unpaid in the **Total Amount** of . . . . $_____
   representing rent for the periods of
   _____, 20_____ to _____, 20_____ . . . . . . Amount $_____
   _____, 20_____ to _____, 20_____ . . . . . . Amount $_____
   _____, 20_____ to _____, 20_____ . . . . . . Amount $_____
   and amounts due for
   ☐ returned check fees of . . . . $_____
   ☐ late charge fees of . . . . $_____
   ☐ common area maintenance (CAM) of . . . . $_____
   ☐ association assessments of . . . . $_____
   ☐ property taxes of . . . . $_____
   ☐ interest on delinquent rent of . . . . $_____
   The **Total Amount** due may be paid in one of the following manners:
   a. By personal delivery to _____ (Name)
   _____ (Address)
   _____ (Phone)
   Payment of the Total Amount due will be accepted at the above address during
   the hours of _____ to _____ on the following days: _____.
   b. By deposit into account number _____
   at _____ (Financial Institution)
   _____ (Address)
   c. By the electronic funds transfer previsouly established between Landlord and Tenant.
   d. _____
   OR
   3.2 Deliver possession of the premises to Landlord or _____
4. If you fail to pay the Total Amount due or to deliver possession of the premises within three (3) days, legal proceedings will be initiated against you to regain possession of the premises and to recover the amounts owed, treble damages, costs and attorney fees.
5. The Landlord hereby elects to declare a forfeiture of your Right to Possession if you fail to pay the Total Amount demanded above.
   5.1 Landlord reserves the right to pursue collection of any future loss of rent allowed by Civil Code §1951.2.
6. State law permits former Tenants to reclaim abandoned personal property left at the former address of the Tenant, subject to certain conditions. You may or may not be able to reclaim property without incurring additional costs, depending on the cost of storing the property and the length of time before it is reclaimed. In general, these costs will be lower the sooner you contact your former Landlord after being notified that property belonging to you was left behind after you moved out.

Date: _____, 20 _____
Landlord/Agent: _____ CalBRE# _____

Signature: _____
Address: _____
Phone: _____ Cell: _____

FORM 575   01-13   ©2016 RPI — Realty Publications, Inc., P.O. BOX 5707, RIVERSIDE, CA 92517

• perform nonmonetary obligations called for in the rental or lease agreement.

On a tenant's default, the landlord may make a demand on the tenant to cure the default or vacate the premises.

However, only a **material breach** allows the landlord to forfeit the tenant's right of possession. [See Case in point, "When is a failure to perform an eviction-worthy breach?"'

Failure to pay rent or perform other significant obligations called for in the rental or lease agreement is a *material breach*. Conversely, the tenant's

material breach
Failure to pay rent or perform other significant obligations called for in the rental or lease agreement. [See **RPI** Form 577]

A landlord notifies a tenant of a change in the terms of their month-to-month rental agreement requiring the tenant to obtain personal property insurance. The notice of change of terms states failure to comply constitutes grounds for the tenant's forfeiture of the right of possession of their unit. The tenant does not obtain personal property insurance. The landlord serves the tenant with a three-day notice to perform or quit. After expiration of the three-day period, the landlord files an unlawful detainer (UD) action to evict the tenant.

The landlord seeks to remove the tenant and take possession of the unit, claiming the tenant's failure to comply with the new terms of the rental agreement is a material breach allowing the landlord to terminate the tenant's right of possession by use of the declaration of forfeiture provision in the three-day notice.

The tenant seeks to retain possession of the unit, claiming their failure to obtain personal property insurance is not a material breach of their rental agreement warranting termination by forfeiture of their right to possession since personal property insurance is not significant for the landlord as it primarily benefits the tenant.

*The California Superior Court held the landlord cannot terminate the rental agreement and remove the tenant for failure of the tenant to obtain the personal property insurance demanded by the landlord since the requirement primarily benefited the tenant and thus failure to provide it is not a material breach justifying termination of the rental agreement. [**Nivo 1 LLC v. Antunez** (2013) 271 C4th 1]*

minor breach
Failure to pay late charges, interest penalties, bad check charges or security deposits.

incurable breach
Nonmonetary defaults in leases or mortgages that cannot be cured or undone. [See RPI Form 577]

failure to pay late charges, interest penalties, bad check charges or security deposits are **minor breaches**, which alone do not justify a three-day notice to cure or quit. [3]

Some nonmonetary defaults by a tenant cannot be cured. These are known as **incurable breaches**. Incurable breaches include:

- *waste* to the premises;
- *alienation* of the leasehold; or
- significant criminal activity which has occurred on the property.

The landlord's remedy for an incurable breach is to serve notice on the tenant to quit the premises within three days after service. The tenant has no alternative but to vacate. Here, a declaration of forfeiture provision accompanying the three-day notice is unnecessary and ineffective since the failure cannot be cured and the tenancy cannot be reinstated. [4]

Three days between notice and UD

After a landlord serves a tenant with a three-day notice to pay rent or quit, containing a declaration of forfeiture provision, the tenant is required to cure the breach in *three calendar days* to avoid loss of their right to possession and eventual eviction. (The first day in the three-day period is the day after service of the notice.) [5]

The tenant cures the default, retaining the right of possession by paying the amount stated before the three-day notice expires. [6]

3 **Keating** v. **Preston** (1940) 42 CA2d 110
4 CCP §1161(4)
5 Calif. Civil Code §10
6 CCP §1161.5

The tenant may tender payment of the delinquent rent in the same manner the tenant made past rental payments — by personal or business check, money order, cashier's check, credit card, cash or electronic transfer.[7]

Rent paid by check and timely received by the landlord becomes delinquent when the check is returned due to insufficient funds and replacement funds are not received within the established grace period. With rent now delinquent, the landlord may serve a three-day notice to pay or quit.

Editor's note — Under a month-to-month rental agreement, the landlord may modify the tenant's method of payment by serving the tenant with a written 30-day notice of a change in rental terms.[8] [See Chapter 22]

To cure a **delinquency**, the tenant's delinquent rent payment needs to be received by the landlord. For instance, when a check for delinquent rent is returned because of insufficient funds, the delinquent rent demanded in a three-day notice has not been paid. Unless the tenant actually pays the delinquent rent and it is received by the landlord prior to expiration of the notice, the tenant's right of possession will be terminated under the declaration of forfeiture provision. At that point, the landlord may file a UD action if the tenant remains in possession.

delinquency
A tenant or borrower's failure to pay the agreed amounts on or before the due date or expiration of any grace period.

Editor's note — A landlord can require payment of rent in cash if a tenant's check is returned for insufficient funds. However, this cash-only requirement may not extend longer than three months. After that period, the landlord is required to again accept alternate forms of payment.[9] [See **RPI** *Form 552 §3.10]*

One-year delinquent rent limitation for UD

A three-day notice may only demand rents which became due during the one year prior to the date of service. If a three-day notice demands delinquent rents which have been due for more than one year, the notice is defective and will not terminate the right of possession or support a UD action. More rent has been demanded than will be awarded by a court in a UD action. Thus, any UD action based on a notice demanding rent for delinquencies more than a year old will fail.[10]

The landlord may recover rents and other amounts more than one year delinquent by pursuing collection in a money action separate from the UD action. A landlord is allowed four years to bring a civil action to recover due and unpaid amounts.[11]

Before serving a three-day notice

Before serving a tenant with a three-day notice to pay rent or quit, the landlord or property manager needs to consider the following questions:

- Is the rent delinquent?

---

7 **Strom** v. **Union Oil Co.** (1948) 88 CA2d 78

8 CC §827

9 CC §1947.3

10 **Bevill** v. **Zoura** (1994) 27 CA4th 694

11 CCP §337

- What amounts are due and unpaid?
- When can delinquent rent be estimated in the three-day notice?
- What is a reasonable estimate of unknown but delinquent rent?
- When does the three-day notice expire?
- When does the tenant's right of possession terminate?
- Is the rental or lease agreement cancelled? and
- How are subtenants evicted?

When is the rent delinquent?

Rent needs to be delinquent before a three-day notice to pay or quit may be served.

Rent becomes delinquent:

- the business day following the **due date**, unless a grace period is established in the rental or lease agreement; or
- the business day following the last calendar day of the *grace period* established in the rental or lease agreement.

> **due date**
> The date provided in the rental or lease agreement on which rental payments are due. [See **RPI** Form 550 §4.1 and 552 §4.1]

A **grace period** is the time period following the due date during which rent may be paid without incurring a late charge. While rent is past due and unpaid, it is not delinquent until the grace period expires.

When a grace period exists and the day scheduled for payment of rent falls on a legal holiday, the payment is not delinquent if it is tendered on the next business day. For purposes of paying rent, legal holidays include:

> **grace period**
> The time period following the due date for a payment during which payment received by a lender or landlord is not delinquent and a late charge is not due. [See **RPI** Form 550 §4.3 and 552 §4.7]

- Saturdays;
- Sundays; and
- state or federal holidays.[12]

For instance, the last day of a grace period falls on a Saturday. Payment is not delinquent if it is received on or before the following Monday (Tuesday if Monday is a holiday).[13]

Similarly, when the final day of the three-day notice falls on a holiday such as a Saturday, Sunday or other legal holiday, the three-day notice expires on the next business day.[14]

Unlike the service of documents in a civil action, service of a three-day notice by mail following a failed attempt at personal service does not extend the three-day notice period an additional five days.[15]

To initiate the process for collecting delinquent rent from a tenant in possession the landlord serves the tenant with a three-day notice to pay rent or quit. The notice may be served on any day after the grace period expires without prior receipt of the rent.

---

12 CCP §§10; 12a
13 CCP §13; Calif. Government Code §6706
14 **Lamanna** v. **Vognar** (1993) 17 CA4th Supp. 4; CCP §12a
15 **Losornio** v. **Motta** (1998) 67 CA4th 110

Consider a landlord and tenant who enter into a rental agreement which sets the due date for rent on the first day of each month. The rental agreement also contains a **late charge provision** imposing an additional charge if rent payments are not received on or before the 10th of the month. A grace period is not mentioned in the rental agreement.

Each month, the tenant pays rent after the date for incurring a late charge. The landlord accepts the tenant's late rental payments every month, but makes no written demand for payment of the late charges.

Finally, on receipt of yet another late payment, the landlord informs the tenant all future rent payments need to be received by the landlord prior to the date for incurring a late charge.

The next month, the late charge period stated in the rental agreement runs and rent has not been received. On the day the late charge is incurred, the 11th, the landlord serves the tenant with a three-day notice to pay rent or quit that includes a declaration of forfeiture provision. The tenant does not pay rent before the three-day notice expires. The landlord files a UD action.

As in the prior months, the tenant tenders the rent payment to the landlord after the late charge period has expired. However, unlike in prior months, the landlord refuses to accept the payment, claiming the tenant is now unlawfully occupying the premises.

Has the landlord established an unlawful detainer on expiration of the three-day notice?

No! The three-day notice is premature and useless. The tenant's rent had not yet become delinquent. Rent is not delinquent until the grace period — including extensions authorized by the landlord's conduct in accepting late payments — has run without receipt of rent.

When the rental agreement called for a late charge after a day other than the due date, a grace period was established, even though it was not explicitly identified as a "grace period." Further, the landlord extends the grace period by consistently accepting rent payments after the grace period without demanding the late charge, a notice required to enforce collection of a late payment fee.[16]

Thus, the tenant's tender of rent was timely. It occurred after the written grace period but on or before the extended date set by the landlord's conduct.

To reinstate and enforce the written grace period, a landlord first gives the tenant a 30-day notice to reinstate the terms for payment stated in the rental or lease agreement.

The 30-day notice states that all future rent payments becoming due following the expiration of the 30-day notice need to be received within the

Conduct extends the grace period

late charge provision
A provision in the lease agreement which imposes an additional administrative charge if rent payments are not received before the date the charge is incurred. [See **RPI** Form 550 §4.3 and 552 §4.7]

---

16 **Baypoint Mortgage** v. **Crest Premium Real Estate Investments Retirement Trust** (1985) 168 CA3d 818

grace period. If future payments (due after the 30 day period) are not timely received, the landlord will demand the agreed-to late charge and serve a three-day notice on the tenant.

Accurate residential rent demands

To be valid, the three-day notice to pay rent or quit served on a residential tenant needs to state the exact amount of money due and unpaid. Conversely, a *commercial landlord* may estimate the amount of money due and unpaid, when the exact amount cannot be accurately ascertained.

A residential tenant need not pay more than the amount due and unpaid to retain possessory rights under a rental or lease agreement.

However, if the amount stated in a three-day notice served on a residential tenant exceeds the amounts actually due and unpaid at the time of the UD trial, the notice is invalid.[17]

For both residential and commercial tenants, if the amount stated in the three-day notice is less than the actual amount due and unpaid, the tenant may pay the amount stated and avoid eviction. To collect any amounts omitted in a three-day notice, the landlord serves another three-day notice to pay the balance or quit.

Estimated commercial rent

A three-day notice served on a *commercial tenant* may include an estimate of the amounts due if:

- the notice states the amount due is an estimate; and
- the amount estimated is reasonable.[18]

Failure to indicate that an estimated amount due is an estimate renders the three-day notice invalid.

Further, if the landlord knows the exact amount due and states a different amount due as an "estimate" in the three-day notice, the notice is defective and the landlord will be unable to terminate the tenant's right of possession.

An estimate of rent owed in a three-day notice is considered reasonable if:

- the actual amount owed is truly in question; and
- the delinquent amount demanded is neither 20% more or less than the amount determined due at the UD hearing.[19]

An estimate itemizing rent amounts not yet due, such as unbilled common area maintenance expenses (CAMs), is not considered reasonable. Amounts due in the future are not yet due or delinquent, and may not be included in an estimate of delinquent amounts due and unpaid.[20]

---

17 **Jayasinghe** v. **Lee** (1993) 13 CA4th Supp. 33
18 CCP §1161.1(a)
19 CCP §1161.1(e)
20 **WDT- Winchester** v. **Nilsson** (1994) 27 CA4th 516

Case in point

Is a tenant liable for unpaid rent when the lease requires rent to be paid by mail and the landlord does not receive payment?

Facts: A landlord and tenant enter into a residential lease which requires the tenant to pay rent by mail. The tenant timely mails a money order for the correct amount to the address specified in the lease, but the landlord does not receive it. The landlord issues a three-day notice to pay rent or quit and the tenant holds over.

Claim: The landlord seeks possession of the property and money losses, claiming the tenant violated the lease since the landlord did not receive their monthly rental payment.

Counter claim: The tenant seeks to retain possession of the property, claiming they did not violate the lease since they sent their payment by mail as the lease indicates.

Holding: A California court of appeals holds the tenant did not violate the lease agreement since mailing the money order fulfilled the tenant's obligations under the lease and the landlord bears the risk of non-delivery. [*Sleep EZ v. Mateo* (April 4, 2017) _CA4th_]

Now consider a commercial tenant who takes possession of property on entering into a *percentage lease agreement*. [See **RPI** Form 552-4]

The rent provisions in the lease agreement state:

- the rent is payable annually on the anniversary of the lease;
- the tenant is to provide the landlord with the amount of the tenant's gross sales proceeds; and
- rent is an amount equal to 20% of the gross sales proceeds.

The tenant fails to furnish the landlord with the amount of the gross sales proceeds or make the annual rental payment. The landlord serves the tenant with a three-day notice to pay rent or quit. The notice states:

- the amount of rent which is due and unpaid in an amount equal to 20% of the tenant's gross sales proceeds; and
- only the tenant knows the amount of the sales proceeds.

The tenant does not pay the rent before the three-day notice expires. The landlord files a UD action. The tenant claims the three-day notice is invalid since the notice did not state the dollar amount of rent due.

Can the landlord evict the tenant even though the three-day notice did not state the dollar amount of the delinquent rent?

Yes! A commercial tenant cannot prevent the landlord from receiving rent or recovering possession by failing to provide the landlord with the means needed to determine the rental amount.

The purpose of a three-day notice is to give a tenant the opportunity to avoid forfeiture of the leasehold estate by paying the delinquent rent.[21]

Estimating unknown amounts

---

21 **Valov** v. **Tank** (1985) 168 CA3d 867

Rent estimates by commercial tenants

On receiving a three-day notice stating the rental amount due is an estimate, the commercial tenant may respond by tendering the amount of rent the tenant estimates is due.[22]

If the amount the tenant estimates and tenders is equal or greater than the rent due, the tenant will retain the right of possession in a UD action. Likewise, when the amount estimated and tendered by the tenant is less than the amount actually due and was a reasonable estimate, the tenant retains possession by paying the additional amount and other sums awarded the landlord within five days after entry of the UD judgment.[23]

Subtenant evictions by the owner

For an owner to regain possession when the master tenant defaults and a subtenant occupies the premises, the three-day notice served on the master tenant needs to also name the subtenant as a tenant in default. Similarly, the notice is also served on the subtenant.

Serving a subtenant with a copy of the three-day notice that only names the master tenant will result in the subtenant retaining the right of possession.[24]

Evict the master tenant but keep the subtenant

Conversely, an owner who wishes to evict a defaulting master tenant but retain the subtenant may do so. The owner is not required to serve the subtenant with a three-day notice when only the master tenant is being evicted.[25]

For example, an owner consents to a sublease agreement entered into by the master tenant and a subtenant which contains an *attornment clause*. If the master tenant defaults and fails to cure under a three-day notice to pay or quit containing a declaration of forfeiture provision, the master tenant forfeits their right of possession. Here, the owner may enforce the sublease by exercising the owner's rights under the attornment clause in the sublease. [See Chapter 59]

Under the sublease's attornment provision, the subtenant agrees to recognize the owner as landlord if the owner:

- elects to forfeit the master tenant's leasehold; and
- recognizes the subtenant as the owner's tenant.

However, a subtenant who takes possession of the premises after the master tenant has been served with a three-day notice will be evicted on the owner's successful completion of a UD action.[26]

---

22 CCP §1161.1(a)

23 CCP §1161.1(a)

24 **Briggs** v. **Electronic Memories & Magnetic Corporation** (1975) 53 CA3d 900

25 **Chinese Hospital Foundation Fund** v. **Patterson** (1969) 1 CA3d 627

26 CCP §1164

A tenant defaults on their rental or lease agreement by failing to:

- pay rent and any other amounts due and called for in the rental or lease agreement; or
- perform nonmonetary obligations called for in the rental or lease agreement.

Rent needs to be delinquent before a three-day notice to pay or quit may be served. Rent becomes delinquent:

- the business day following the due date, unless a grace period is established in the rental or lease agreement; or
- the business day following the last calendar day of the grace period established in the rental or lease agreement.

Only a material breach allows the landlord to forfeit the tenant's right of possession, such as the failure to pay rent or perform other significant obligations. Conversely, minor breaches alone do not justify a three-day notice to cure or quit.

After a landlord serves a tenant with a three-day notice to pay rent or quit, containing a declaration of forfeiture provision, the tenant is required to cure the breach in three calendar days to avoid forfeiture of the right of possession and eventual eviction.

For an owner to regain possession when the master tenant defaults and a subtenant occupies the premises, the three-day notice needs to also name and be served on the subtenant.

Chapter 25 Summary

Chapter 25 Key Terms

Quiz 7 Covering Chapters 25-28 is located on page 639.

Notes:

Three-day notices to quit for nonmonetary breaches

After reading this chapter, you will be able to:

- differentiate between a curable breach a tenant can resolve and an incurable breach a tenant cannot correct;

- use a three-day notice to pay or quit when a tenant fails to timely pay a money obligation;

- serve a three-day notice to perform or quit when the lease provision breached is not for rent or other money obligation but can be corrected by the tenant; and

- prepare a three-day notice to quit without an alternative when the tenant's breach is incurable or statutory.

Learning Objectives

assignment	notice to quit
curable breach	nuisance
monetary breach	reasonable person test
nonmonetary breach	retaliatory eviction
nonwaiver provision	statutory breach
notice to perform or quit	waste

Key Terms

On a routine inspection of an apartment complex, the property manager observes a pet in one of the units. All the rental and lease agreements with tenants in the complex prohibit housing of a pet on the premises.

As a courtesy, the tenant is asked, both orally and by a personal note, to remove the pet. However, the tenant retains the pet.

Curable and incurable nonmonetary breaches

To enforce the provision prohibiting pets in the tenant's rental or lease agreement, the property manager prepares a three-day *notice to perform or quit*. The notice is served on the tenant. The notice gives the tenant an ultimatum — either remove the pet (the performance required) or vacate the unit within three days (the alternative performance). [See Form 576 accompanying this chapter]

The tenant fails to remove the pet from the premises and remains in the unit after the three-day notice expires.

Can the landlord file an unlawful detainer (UD) action to evict the tenant for failure to either remove the pet or vacate under the three-day notice?

Yes! On expiration of the *three-day notice to perform or quit*, the tenant may be evicted if one of the conditions has not been met. Here, the tenant breached the provision in their rental or lease agreement prohibiting the keeping of a pet on the premises. This type of breach, which can be remedied by the tenant's action, is known as a **curable breach**.[1]

curable breach
A breach of the lease agreement which can be remedied by action from the tenant.

However, if the tenant breaches a provision in their rental or lease agreement that the tenant is unable to perform within three days, the landlord or property manager may serve a *three-day notice to quit* the premises, permitting no alternative action. A breach which cannot be remedied by the tenant during the notice period is classified as an **incurable breach**.[2]

Types of three-day notices for various breaches

The three-day notice served on a tenant needs to be the correct type before an unlawful detainer, or *holdover*, of a premises can be established and the tenant evicted.

Depending on the nature and extent of the tenant's breach, one of the following types of three-day notices may be served:

- a three-day *notice to pay rent or quit* [See Form 575 in Chapter 25];
- a three-day *notice to perform or quit* [See Form 576]; or
- a three-day *notice to quit*. [See Form 577 accompanying this chapter]

When a tenant's breach is the failure to pay rent or other money obligation before it becomes delinquent, the tenant is served with a three-day *notice to pay rent or quit*. This type of breach is known as a **monetary breach** which is curable by paying money.

monetary breach
A tenant's failure to pay rent or other money obligation due.

When the provision breached is not for rent or other money obligation, called a **nonmonetary breach**, and the breach can still be quickly corrected by the tenant, such as the pet situation in the opening scenario, the tenant is served with a three-day *notice to perform or quit*. [See Form 576]

nonmonetary breach
A tenant's breach of any obligation other than an obligation to pay money.

---

1 Calif. Code of Civil Procedure §1161(3)
2 CCP §1161(3)

Form 576

Three-Day Notice to Perform or Quit

THREE-DAY NOTICE TO PERFORM OR QUIT

NOTE: This form is used by a property manager or landlord when a tenant fails to perform a nonmonetary activity called for in a rental or lease agreement which can be performed or rectified within three days, to notify the tenant they are to perform the activity within three days or vacate and deliver up posession

DATE: _____, 20_____, at _____, California.
To Tenant: _____
Items left blank or unchecked are not applicable.

FACTS:

1. You are a Tenant under a rental or expired lease agreement
   1.1 dated _____, at _____, California,
   1.2 entered into by _____, as the Tenant,
   1.3 and _____, as the Landlord,
   1.4 regarding real estate referred to as _____
   _____

NOTICE:

2. You are in breach of the terms of your rental or lease agreement as follows: _____
   _____
   _____

3. Within three (3) days after service of this notice, you are required to either:
   3.1 Perform or rectify the breach by _____
   _____
   _____

OR

   3.2 Deliver possession of the premises to Landlord or _____
   _____

4. If you fail to cure the breach or to deliver possession within three (3) days, legal proceedings may be initiated to regain possession of the premises and to recover the rent owed, treble damages, costs and attorney fees.

5. Landlord hereby elects to declare a forfeiture of your lease if you fail to cure the breach noted above.
   5.1 Landlord reserves the right to pursue collection of any future rental losses allowed by Calif. Civil Code §1951.2.

6. Notice: State law permits former Tenants to reclaim abandoned personal property left at the former address of the Tenant, subject to certain conditions. You may or may not be able to reclaim property without incurring additional costs, depending on the cost of storing the property and the length of time before it is reclaimed. In general, these costs will be lower the sooner you contact your former Landlord after being notified that property belonging to you was left behind after you moved out.

Date: _____, 20_____
Landlord/Agent: _____ CalBRE #:_____

Signature: _____
Address: _____

Phone: _____ Cell: _____
Fax: _____
Email: _____

FORM 576   01-13   ©2016 **RPI — Realty Publications, Inc.**, P.O. BOX 5707, RIVERSIDE, CA 92517

When a tenant is in default for a failure to pay rent as well as a curable nonmonetary breach, a three-day notice to perform or quit is used. The demand to pay rent is listed as an additional (monetary) breach to be cured under the notice to perform or quit.

A three-day *notice to quit* without an alternative requires the tenant to vacate. The notice to quit is served on a tenant when the tenant's breach is:

- a breach impossible to cure in three days;[3] or
- a *statutory breach.*[4]

---

3 **Matthew** v. **Digges** (1920) 45 CA 561
4 CCP §1161(4)

Notice to perform or quit

notice to perform or quit
A notice requiring a tenant to perform an action to remedy a curable nonmonetary breach of the lease agreement. [See **RPI** Form 576]

The **three-day notice to perform or quit** requires the tenant to either:

- perform under the breached lease provision; or
- vacate the premises.[5]

The tenant's breach of a provision in a rental or lease agreement needs to be a significant breach, called a *material breach*, to justify serving a three-day notice. A minor or trivial breach by the tenant will not support a three-day notice.[6]

For a tenant to avoid a forfeiture of their right of possession, they are first given an opportunity to reinstate the rental or lease agreement. The landlord is required to give the tenant an opportunity to remedy the breach if the breach can be cured in three days.

The three-day notice to perform or quit specifies the provision breached and the action to be taken to cure the breach. When the tenant cures the breach before the three-day notice expires, the breach of the rental or lease agreement is eliminated and possession continues as though no breach occurred.

When a tenant fails to cure the breach by performance or by vacating within three days after service of the notice to perform or quit and the notice contains a declaration of forfeiture provision, the landlord may initiate a UD action and have the tenant removed even if the tenant later performs. The declaration of forfeiture in the three-day notice bars the tenant from reinstating their right to possession after the three-day notice expires and they have failed to first perform.[7]

Curable nonmonetary breaches

A tenant operates a retail business on leased premises. The lease agreement requires the tenant to periodically hand the landlord an inventory of their sales merchandise. Also, the landlord is permitted to examine the tenant's business records.

The landlord makes a request for an inventory and access to the records. The tenant does not provide the inventories or permit the landlord to examine their business records.

The landlord serves the tenant with a three-day notice to quit the premises. No alternative performance is given to allow the tenant to rectify the failures and stay. The tenant does not vacate the premises.

The landlord files a UD action, seeking to evict the tenant since the tenant materially breached a lease obligation.

The tenant claims they cannot be evicted since the three-day notice did not give the tenant the alternative to perform by delivering inventory lists and records to avoid a forfeiture of possession.

---

5 CCP§1161(3)

6 **Baypoint Mortgage** v. **Crest Premium Real Estate Investments Retirement Trust** (1985) 168 CA3d 818

7 CCP §1161(3)

Form 577

Three-Day
Notice to Quit

THREE-DAY NOTICE TO QUIT
Residential and Commercial

NOTE: This form is used by a property manager or landlord when a tenant under a rental or lease agreement has committed an incurable breach or failed to perform obligations which cannot be performed or rectified within three days, to notify the tenant they are to vacate and deliver possession within three days.

DATE: _____, 20_____, at _____, California.
To Tenant: _____
Items left blank or unchecked are not applicable.
FACTS:

1. You are a Tenant under a rental or expired lease agreement
   1.1 dated _____, at _____, California,
   1.2 entered into by _____, as the Tenant;
   1.3 and _____, as the Landlord,
   1.4 regarding real estate referred to as _____
   _____

NOTICE:

2. You are in breach of the terms of your rental or lease agreement as follows: _____
   _____
   _____
   _____
   _____
   _____
   _____
   _____

3. Within three (3) days after service of this notice, you are required to vacate and deliver possession of the premises to Landlord or _____.

4. If you fail to vacate and deliver possession of the premises within three (3) days, legal proceedings may be initiated to regain possession of the premises and to recover the rent owed, treble damages, costs, and attorney fees.

5. Landlord hereby elects to declare a forfeiture of your lease.
   5.1 Landlord reserves the right to pursue collection of any future rental losses allowed by Calif. Civil Code §1951.2.

6. **Notice:** State law permits former Tenants to reclaim abandoned personal property left at the former address of the Tenant, subject to certain conditions. You may or may not be able to reclaim property without incurring additional costs, depending on the cost of storing the property and the length of time before it is reclaimed. In general, these costs will be lower the sooner you contact your former Landlord after being notified that property belonging to you was left behind after you moved out.

Date: _____, 20_____
Landlord/Agent: _____ CalBRE #:_____

Signature: _____
Address: _____
_____
Phone: _____ Cell: _____
Fax: _____
Email: _____

FORM 577   01-13   ©2016 RPI — **Realty Publications, Inc.**, P.O. BOX 5707, RIVERSIDE, CA 92517

Can the landlord maintain a UD action against the tenant based on the three-day notice to quit?

No! The three-day notice served on the tenant needs to be in the alternative — perform or quit. Here, the tenant is able to hand over an inventory to the landlord and give the landlord access to the business records, all within three days.[8]

When the tenant is capable of taking steps within three days which cure a breach of a lease provision, the landlord needs to allow the tenant to cure the breach, monetary or nonmonetary.[9]

---

8 **Hinman v. Wagnon** (1959) 172 CA2d 24
9 CCP §1161(3)

Notice to quit; no alternatives

Recall from the opening scenario the use of a three-day **notice to quit** when the tenant's material breach is:

- an *incurable breach*; or
- a *statutory breach*.

Incurable breaches and statutory breaches automatically forfeit the tenant's right of possession. Incurable breaches either cannot be remedied within the notice period, or are incurable by statute.[10]

Statutory breaches, being incurable, include:

- an unauthorized subletting or assignment of the premises;
- *nuisance*; or
- *unlawful use* of the premises.[11]

notice to quit
A notice to vacate served on a tenant for an incurable breach of a rental or lease agreement or due to a statutory breach of the tenancy. [See **RPI** Form 577]

statutory breach
A breach of the lease agreement which automatically forfeits the tenant's right of possession.

The three-day notice to quit does not need to indicate the provision breached or the activity of the tenant constituting the breach. Nor does it need to include a lease forfeiture declaration by the landlord. The tenant's right of possession was automatically forfeited by the tenant's incurable or statutory breach. Since these breaches cannot be cured by the tenant, the right of possession may only be reinstated if the landlord chooses to waive the forfeiture.

However, while a forfeiture of the lease has already occurred, a UD court requires service of a three-day notice before a landlord may recover possession.

Quit! The breach cannot be undone

Consider a tenant who leases agricultural property. The lease agreement states the tenant's use of the property is limited to grazing sheep. However, the tenant plants crops on the property in breach of the lease agreement use provision.

Based on the tenant's unauthorized use of the premises, the landlord initiates the eviction process by serving a three-day notice to quit on the tenant.

The tenant's use of the property to raise crops, instead of the single agreed-to use as a pasture, is an incurable nonmonetary breach of the lease agreement. The tenant cannot reverse the act or the effects of raising the crops on the soil since the activity has already occurred.[12]

In another example, consider a tenant in possession of agricultural property improved with an orchard. The lease obligates the tenant to poison squirrels on the property to control the agricultural pest.

The tenant does not poison the squirrels as required by the lease agreement and the premises becomes infested with squirrels.

The landlord serves the tenant with a three-day notice to quit the premises based on the tenant's failure to eradicate the squirrels with poison.

---

10 CCP §1161(3)
11 CCP §1161(4)
12 **Harris v. Bissell** (1921) 54 CA 307

The tenant does not vacate the premises. The landlord files a UD action to evict the tenant. The tenant claims they cannot be evicted since the proper notice to serve for the failure to poison the squirrels is a three-day notice to perform or quit, allowing the tenant to cure their breach.

However, the three-day notice to quit is the proper notice. The elimination of squirrels by poisoning cannot be performed before the three-day notice to quit expired.[13]

A tenant may be evicted for maintaining a nuisance *or unlawful use* of the premises, even if these activities are not prohibited by the lease agreement.[14]

A **nuisance** includes anything which:

- is injurious to health, such as contamination of the property's soil;
- is offensive to the senses, such as excessive noise levels or obnoxious fumes; or
- obstructs the use and enjoyment of surrounding property.[15]

For example, a tenant in a multi-unit property maintains a nuisance on the premises in the form of excessive late-night noise. The noise interferes with another tenant's use or enjoyment of their premises. As a result, the landlord may serve a three-day notice to quit on the interfering tenant.

Also, a tenant who illegally sells, grows or manufactures controlled substances on the premises has, by their actions, triggered an automatic forfeiture of the leasehold. The tenant may be served with a notice to quit for maintaining a nuisance. If they do not vacate, they may be evicted by a UD action.[16]

A tenant's *unlawful use* of the premises under the statute includes violations of local laws or ordinances if the prohibited use affects the property, such as noncompliance with zoning ordinances restricting the use of the premises. Again, the leasehold is forfeited automatically due to the statutory violation. The three-day notice is required as a requisite to maintaining a UD action when the tenant remains in possession.[17]

However, before the use is unlawful and justifies service of a notice to quit, the use needs to:

- threaten the physical safety of the property;
- stigmatize the premises; or
- impair the landlord's continued receipt of rent.

For example, a tenant's lease agreement contains a provision stating the tenant will not use the premises for any unlawful purpose or to violate any laws, a provision that restates the statute.

Breach of statutory prohibitions is a forfeiture

nuisance
An action which is injurious to health, offensive to the senses, or obstructs the use and enjoyment of surrounding property. [See **RPI** Form 550 §6.7 and 552 §7.3]

Nuisance or unlawful use

13 Matthews, *supra*
14 CCP §1161(4)
15 Calif. Civil Code §3479
16 CCP §1161(4)
17 **Haig** v. **Hogan** (1947) 82 CA2d 876

The tenant's business, which is authorized to operate on the premises, is penalized for conducting the pricing of its services and goods in violation of federal anti-trust laws. The landlord seeks to evict the tenant for unlawful use of the premises in violation of the lease.

Here, the landlord may not evict the tenant. The tenant's violation of anti-trust laws is the unlawful conduct of their lawful business, not an unlawful use of the premises by the tenant.[18]

When a tenant's activity is considered a nuisance or an unlawful use, a three-day notice to quit may be served on the tenant even if the tenant is able to cure the breach by terminating or eliminating the activity within three days. The mere occurrence of the unlawful and endangering activity automatically forfeits the lease, leaving nothing for the tenant to do except vacate or be evicted based on the three-day notice to quit.

Forfeiture on assigning or subletting

Consider a lease provision prohibiting the tenant from entering into a *sublease* or an *assignment* of the lease without first obtaining the landlord's written consent, called a *restraint-on-transfer provision*. Unknown to the landlord or the property manager, the tenant subleases the premises. The property manager discovers the premises is occupied by a subtenant.

The property manager names and serves both the tenant and subtenant with a three-day notice to quit. The subtenant does not vacate the premises. The landlord files a UD action to regain possession from both the tenant and the subtenant.

The tenant claims their leasehold interest cannot be terminated by the three-day notice to quit since the landlord cannot unreasonably withhold their consent to a sublease of the premises.

Can the landlord serve a three-day notice to quit and evict a tenant who subleased the premises without their consent?

Yes! The landlord may proceed to evict the subtenant based on a three-day notice to quit. The tenant's breach was the failure to request the landlord's consent prior to subletting the premises, an event that cannot be cured. Further, as a statutory breach of the lease agreement, the tenant immediately forfeits their right of possession. The landlord need not declare the forfeiture.

The tenant cannot avoid the forfeiture of their right of possession due to the breach by claiming the landlord was unreasonably withholding consent. Here, the landlord was not given the opportunity to grant or withhold their consent.[19]

Assignment or subleasing prohibited

When provisions in a lease agreement prohibit **assignment** or **subleasing** without the landlord's consent, and the tenant does so without obtaining

---

18 **Deutsch** v. **Phillips Petroleum Co.** (1976) 56 CA3d 586
19 **Thrifty Oil Co.** v. **Batarse** (1985) 174 CA3d 770

consent, a three-day notice to quit may be served on the tenant to recover possession. By statute, the act is an incurable activity that terminates the lease, leaving no alternative to vacating.[20]

However, the landlord need not consider the lease terminated when the tenant assigns the lease or sublets the premises without the landlord's consent. The landlord can waive the statutory forfeiture of possession.

Thus, a three-day notice to perform or quit may be served on the tenant. The tenant may then retain their possession by requiring the subtenant to move from the premises within three days.[21]

Waste to the leased premises by a tenant is a breach that cannot be cured. *Waste* terminates the tenant's right of possession. The tenant needs to vacate if the landlord serves a three-day notice to quit. [See Sidebar, "Covering your bases with alternatives"]

However, waste is grounds for eviction only when the value of the leased premises is substantially or permanently impaired due to the tenant's conduct.

Waste occurs when a tenant:

- intentionally damages or destroys the leased premises; or
- neglects the premises and impairs its value by failing to care for and maintain it as agreed.

Consider a tenant in an office building. The tenant's lease agreement obligates the tenant to follow all building rules. The building rules prohibit tenants from adjusting the temperature controls. The tenant's employees adjust the temperature controls, resulting in damage to the thermostat.

The landlord serves the tenant with a three-day notice to quit the premises. The tenant does not vacate. The landlord then files a UD action. The landlord claims the tenant committed waste to the premises since adjusting of the temperature controls damaged the building's thermostat.

The tenant cannot, however, be evicted for waste. The damage to the thermostat was minor and reparable within three days. Also, the landlord was unable to demonstrate the tenant's conduct substantially diminished the property's market value. [22]

Now consider a landlord who discovers a tenant's pets have damaged the wooden floors, doors and plastered walls of the tenant's apartment unit. Unsanitary conditions also exist in the unit.

A three-day notice to quit is served based on the tenant's waste to the unit.

Again, the landlord is unable to evict the tenant for waste. The tenant's failure to maintain the unit has not significantly nor permanently lowered

assignment
A tenant's sublease of a portion of the leased premises.

Waste forfeits the lease

waste
The intentional destruction or neglect of property which diminishes its value. [See **RPI** Form 550 §6.8 and 552 §7.4]

---

20 CCP §1161(4)

21 CCP §1161(3)

22 **Rowe** v. **Wells Fargo Realty, Inc.** (1985) 166 CA3d 310

the market value of the unit. The damage created by the tenant's pets can be repaired and the unit quickly returned to a marketable condition. The three-day notice to quit was inappropriate.[23]

Waiver of breach by conduct

Consider a tenant of commercial property who wants to add further improvements to the leased premises. The lease agreement requires the landlord's written consent before the tenant may make improvements to the premises.

The tenant submits a request to the landlord for approval of additional improvements they want to make. The landlord does not respond to the tenant's request.

Without the landlord's consent, the tenant begins construction on the improvements. The landlord is aware of the construction. Further, the landlord knows the construction extends beyond the area of the leased premises and encroaches onto other property owned by the landlord.

The landlord demands the tenant remove the improvements they have constructed. As a result, the landlord and tenant commence lease negotiations to expand the leased premises to include the property on which the improvements now encroach.

During negotiations, the landlord accepts all rent payments made by the tenant. Ultimately, the landlord and tenant are unable to reach an agreement. The unauthorized construction remains unresolved. The landlord then serves a three-day notice to quit followed by a UD action to evict the tenant.

The tenant claims the landlord's acceptance of rent payments waived the landlord's right to terminate the tenant's possession on the tenant's breach.

Can the landlord evict the tenant?

Yes! The landlord did not waive their right to terminate the tenant's possession by accepting rent addressed in the lease agreement. The landlord *continuously objected* and never acquiesced to the construction of the improvements.

While the landlord accepted rent payments, the landlord demonstrated to the tenant that they did not intend for the tenant to construct the improvements and continue to occupy the premises under the terms of the existing lease agreement.[24]

The nonwaiver provision

Many lease agreements contain an enforceable provision that states a landlord's waiver of a tenant's breach of the lease is not a waiver of similar or subsequent breaches by the tenant. This provision is called a **nonwaiver provision**. [See **RPI** Form 552 §20.1]

---

23 **Freeze** v. **Brinson** (1991) 3 CA4th Supp. 1
24 **Thriftimart, Inc.** v. **Me & Tex** (1981) 123 CA3d 751

Covering your bases with alternatives

A tenant's failure to comply with building rules or to maintain the premises in a clean and sanitary manner are breaches of a lease agreement. Generally these types of breaches can be remedied within three days.

The landlord who serves a three-day notice to perform or quit provides the tenant with an opportunity to comply with building rules, or clean the premises and stay. If the tenant's breach remains uncured after three days, and the tenant remain in possession, the landlord may file an unlawful detainer (UD) action to evict the tenant.

Consider again the tenant who may not be evicted for waste since their failure to follow building rules did not permanently lower the market value of the premises.

A tenant whose breach results from the failure to follow building rules may stop the activity constituting a violation on receiving a three-day notice perform or quit. If the tenant performs on the notice by complying with building rules within the three-day period, the tenant cannot be evicted.

However, the tenant might later resume the breaching activity. The tenant's repeat conduct may then constitute a nuisance, perhaps obstructing other tenants' ability to enjoy the use of the building.

The tenant will likely contest a three-day notice to quit for nuisance. The landlord will then be forced to show how the tenant's conduct constitutes a continuing nuisance. Also, a three-day notice to quit results in a forfeiture of the tenant's right of possession, as no alternative exists — a harsh result courts do not favor.

Thus, if the tenant's breach is non-statutory and can be cured within three days, a three-day notice to perform or quit is the proper notice to serve.

When a landlord is uncertain about whether or not a breach can be cured within three days, a three-day notice to perform or quit will either:

- *cause the tenant to cure the breach within three days; or*
- *support the landlord's UD action to evict the tenant.*

nonwaiver provision
A provision in the lease agreement that states a landlord's waiver of a tenant's breach is not a waiver of similar or future breach. [See **RPI** Form 550 §7.4 and 552 §20.1]

When a nonwaiver provision is in the lease agreement, the landlord's acceptance of rent does not constitute a waiver of their right to evict the tenant for a separate or later breach of the lease.[25]

Landlord's conduct condones breach

Consider a tenant who operates a concession stand on leased property. The lease agreement prohibits camping on the premises and contains a nonwaiver provision.

The tenant is unable to stop campers from using the premises. The tenant installs a sign stating camping is not allowed and erects fences to keep overnight campers off the premises. On a demand from the landlord, the tenant takes down the sign and fences.

On removal of the fence, the tenant advises the landlord of their inability to prevent campers from using the premises without maintaining the sign. The landlord does not respond, but continues to accept rent.

---

25 **Karbelnig** v. **Brothwell** (1966) 244 CA2d 333

After an extended time, the landlord serves a three-day notice to quit for breach of the lease agreement provision prohibiting camping on the premises. The landlord files a UD action to evict the tenant.

Can the landlord evict the tenant?

No! The landlord's conduct misled the tenant into believing the breaching conduct was no longer a concern of the landlord. The landlord was prevented from processing an eviction based on tenant activity authorized by the landlord. This holds even if the lease agreement contains a nonwaiver provision.[26]

Once the tenant's actions breaching a lease agreement provision have been condoned by the landlord, the landlord has waived the nonwaiver provision. They need to take reasonable steps if they intend to reinstate and enforce the nonwaiver provision.

A reasonable step to reinstate enforceability is the use of a written 30-day notice to the tenant, stating the landlord's intent to enforce the nonwaiver provision in the lease agreement on expiration of the 30-day notice if 30 days is sufficient time to cure the breach. [See Form 570 in Chapter 17]

If the tenant continues to breach after expiration of the period for reinstating the provision, the landlord may serve a three-day notice to perform or quit.

Service of notice

Statutory requirements need to be strictly followed when preparing and serving a three-day notice.

If the three-day notice is incorrectly or inaccurately prepared, or improperly served on the tenant, the notice is invalid. To evict the tenant, a new three-day notice needs to be correctly and accurately prepared, and properly served on the tenant.[27]

Further, a **proof of service** form is filled out and signed by the person who serves the three-day notice. Without a proof of service, a UD action cannot be maintained. [See Form 580 accompanying this chapter]

Concurrent service of two notices

A landlord may concurrently serve both a three-day notice to pay (perform) or quit and a 30-day notice to vacate or change terms. However, the notices need to be served separately. If attached or otherwise combined, other than their being served at the same time, they may be reasonably confused as one. The confusion might defeat any UD action based on the three-day notice.

Also, each notice is accompanied by its own separate *proof of service* to clarify their independent existence. [See Form 580]

---

26 **Salton Community Services District** v. **Southard** (1967) 256 CA2d 526
27 **Lamey** v. **Masciotra** (1969) 273 CA2d 709

PROOF OF SERVICE
For Service of Notice to Real Estate Tenants

NOTE: This form is used by a property manager or landlord when serving a tenant a notice to pay, perform, vacate or quit or a notice of change in rental terms, to document the date and time the notice was served and the manner of service for use in any eviction proceeding.

1. I am over 18 years of age.

2. On _____, 20_____, at _____, California, I served the following checked items:

    ☐ Three-Day Notice to Pay Rent or Quit [See **RPI** Forms 575 and 575-1]

    ☐ Three-Day Notice to Perform or Quit [See **RPI** Form 576]

    ☐ Three-Day Notice to Quit [See **RPI** Forms 577 and 578]

    ☐ 30-Day Notice to Vacate [See **RPI** Forms 569, 571 and 573]

    ☐ 60-Day Notice to Vacate [See **RPI** Form 569-1]

    ☐ 30-Day Notice of Change in Rental Terms [See **RPI** Form 570]

    ☐ 60-Day Notice of Change in Rental Terms [See **RPI** Form 574]

    ☐ _____

3. Regarding tenancy of property referred to as _____
    _____

4. On Tenant(s) (name) _____
    _____

5. Manner of service (check the appropriate box):

    5.1 ☐ By personally delivering a copy to each named Tenant;

        a.   ☐ at Tenant's residence;

        b.   ☐ at Tenant's place of business.

    5.2 ☐ By delivering a copy to a person of suitable age and discretion;

        a.   ☐ at the Tenant's residence; or

        b.   ☐ at Tenant's place of business, as the named Tenant was absent from each location;

    and

    mailing by first-class postage prepaid a copy to each named Tenant at his residence.

    5.3 ☐ By posting a copy for each named Tenant in a conspicuous place on the property described in the notice as no person of suitable age or discretion was found at the Tenant's residence or place of business;

    and

    mailing by first-class postage prepaid a copy to each named Tenant at the address of the leased property.

    I declare under penalty or perjury that foregoing is true and correct.

    Date: _____, 20_____

    Name: _____

    Signature: _____

FORM 580   01-13   ©2016 RPI — **Realty Publications, Inc.**, P.O. BOX 5707, RIVERSIDE, CA 92517

For example, a tenant on a month-to-month tenancy breaches their obligation to maintain the premises. The landlord concurrently serves the tenant with both a three-day notice to perform or quit and a 30-day notice to vacate.

Each notice stands alone, unattached to the other, and is separately, but concurrently, handed to the tenant. Each service is returned by the server accompanied by a separate proof of service. The tenant fails to maintain the premises under the three-day notice to perform and remains in possession. The landlord files a UD action based on the service of the three-day notice and its proof of service.

At the UD hearing, the tenant claims they were unaware of their need to vacate within three days since they were also served with a 30-day notice giving the tenant 30 days to vacate.

reasonable person test
A judicial test used to determine reasonable behavior between two parties.

The court examines the content of the separate notices. The court's analysis is based on the **reasonable person test** which sets guidelines for reasonable behavior between the two parties to an action. The court finds that a reasonable person might be confused by the separate requirements contained in the concurrently served notices.

Therefore, the tenant is granted a relief from forfeiture of possession under the three-day notice to perform or quit. The tenant is allowed to stay, on the condition they immediately perform the maintenance addressed in the three-day notice.[28]

Regardless of any confusion the tenant had, in response to the judgment the tenant will either:

- immediately perform the maintenance called for in the notice and retain the right of possession; or
- take no action, and be evicted from the property for failure to perform the maintenance called for in the notice.

Application of the reasonable person test

Now consider a tenant under a month-to-month tenancy who is served with a three-day notice and a separate 30-day notice at the same time. Each notice has its own proof of service statement.

The three-day notice to pay or quit requires the tenant to pay amounts due and delinquent, within three days after service of the notice, or vacate and deliver possession to the landlord.

The 30-day notice to vacate states the tenant is required to vacate and deliver possession of the premises to the landlord within 30 days after service of the notice. [See Chapter 29]

The 30-day notice does not request that the tenant pay any delinquent rent which is due, only the amount which will become due within 30 days on the first of the next calendar month. The tenant pays the rent before the three-day period expires.

Later, at the end of the 30-day period, the tenant refuses to leave. The landlord initiates a UD action on the 30-day notice to vacate. At the UD hearing, the tenant claims they believed that by paying the delinquent rent under the three-day notice, the 30-day notice was no longer applicable.

Again, the court will apply the *reasonable person test* to determine if the notices served might result in the tenant's confusion.

Courts also enforce the legislative scheme to make sure the landlord follows all statutory requirements regarding content and service of the notice. If the landlord is in compliance, the court awards the landlord relief available under the legislative scheme.

---

28 CCP §1179

Here, the contents of the notices show they are mutually exclusive of one another. Further, the three-day notice does not indicate that payment of the delinquency mentioned in the three-day period nullifies the order to vacate in the 30-day notice.

Also, while served concurrently, the landlord did serve the notices separately. Both notices followed their respective legislative schemes:

- one for collecting delinquent rent; and
- the other for terminating the month-to-month tenancy.

Finally, the tenant's supposed confusion is not about the time for performance or vacating while one of the notice periods remained unexpired. Rather, the tenant assumed one notice overrode the provisions of the other, an assumption unfounded and unreasonable, given the explicit content of the notices. Thus, the tenant's purported confusion is not a legal excuse for failing to vacate.

Retaliatory eviction

A tenant under a month-to-month rental agreement continually fails to timely pay rent and becomes delinquent on the current month's rent. In response to the repeated delinquencies, the tenant's landlord concurrently serves the tenant with a three-day notice to pay or quit and a 30-day notice to vacate.

The tenant claims the 30-day notice was served to terminate their tenancy in retaliation for being late with the rent, called a **retaliatory eviction**.

A *retaliatory eviction* occurs when a residential landlord attempts to evict a tenant for:

- exercising their right to file a complaint with an appropriate agency regarding the habitability of the premises;
- orally complaining to the landlord about the *habitability* of the premises;
- filing documents to initiate a judicial or arbitration proceeding regarding the habitability of the premises;
- organizing or participating in a tenant association or an association for tenant's rights; or
- lawfully exercising any rights, such as the refusal to authorize credit reports or personal investigation after taking possession of the premises.[29]

Here, the tenancy was not terminated in retaliation for complaints about the habitability of the premises or for a legal right exercised by the tenant. Instead, the tenant was being evicted for their continued delinquent payment of rents — a breach by the tenant of the month-to-month rental agreement.

> **retaliatory eviction**
> The wrongful eviction attempted by a landlord against a tenant for lawfully exercising any of their rights.

---

29 CC §1942.5

Recall that a notice to vacate need not include a reason for the termination of occupancy. It is therefore up to the tenant to determine whether the landlord's conduct may justify the claim of a retaliatory eviction. [See Chapter 29]

A landlord convicted of a retaliatory eviction is liable for punitive damages up to $2,000 for each act of retaliation.[30]

---

30 CC §1942.5

Chapter 26 Summary

The three-day notice served on a tenant must be the correct type before the tenant's unlawful detainer of a premises can be established and the tenant evicted.

Depending on the nature and extent of the tenant's breach, one of the following types of three-day notices may be served:

- a three-day notice to pay rent or quit;
- a three-day notice to perform or quit; or
- a three-day notice to quit.

A breach which can be remedied by action from the tenant during the notice period is known as a curable breach. A breach which cannot be remedied by action from the tenant is known as an incurable breach.

When a tenant's breach is the failure to pay rent or other money obligation which is due, the tenant is served with a three-day notice to pay rent or quit. This type of breach is known as a monetary breach which is curable by paying money.

When the lease provision breached is not for rent or other money obligation, called a nonmonetary breach, and the breach can still be quickly corrected by the tenant, the tenant is served with a three-day notice to perform or quit.

A three-day notice to quit is used when the tenant's material breach is:

- an incurable breach; or
- a statutory breach.

Chapter 26 Key Terms

Quiz 7 Covering Chapters 25-28 is located on page 639.

Notes:

Proof of service

After reading this chapter, you will be able to:
- identify the type of three-day notice required to be used for various tenant breaches of rental and lease agreements; and
- carry out the proper service of a three-day notice on a tenant.

notice to pay rent or quit   **substituted service**

Learning Objectives

Key Terms

Diligence not required to locate the tenant

Rent owed by a residential tenant under a rental or lease agreement has become delinquent. In a final effort to collect the delinquent rent, the landlord (or property manager or unlawful detainer (UD) service) prepares a **three-day notice to pay rent or quit** to be served on the tenant.

The individual serving the notice, called a process server, is handed the notice and attempts to personally serve the tenant at the tenant's residence. The tenant is not present at the residence and the tenant's place of employment or business is unknown to the landlord.

However, a 16-year-old who responds to the process server at the premises is handed the *three-day notice*. The process server observes that the 16-year-old is of suitable age and discretion to accept service of the notice and pass it along to the tenant. Thus, the process server does not post the notice on the property.

A copy of the three-day notice is also mailed on the same day to the tenant at the residence address since a business address is unknown.

The three-day notice expires without the tenant paying the delinquent rent or vacating. A UD action is filed to evict the tenant.

> **notice to pay rent or quit**
> A notice served on a tenant by the landlord which states the amount of delinquent rent and any other delinquent amounts owed the landlord under a rental or lease agreement. [See **RPI** Form 575 and 575-1]

At the UD hearing, the tenant claims they may not be evicted and the three-day notice was improperly served since a person of suitable age and discretion to accept service needs to be at least 18 years old.

Is handing a copy of a three-day notice to an apparently intelligent 16-year-old on the premises and mailing a copy to the tenant sufficient service to terminate the occupancy and establish the tenant's unlawful detainer of the property on its expiration?

Yes! The tenant's unlawful detainer is established without personal service of the notice on the tenant. After an attempt at personal service, **substituted service** is authorized. Proper *substituted service* of a three-day notice includes delivery of a copy to an intelligent and mature 16-year-old on the leased premises. Thus, having been served, the tenant may be evicted.[1]

substituted service
In place of personally serving the tenant, the notice is personally delivered to a person of suitable age at the tenant's residence or place of business and is mailed to the leased premises, or posted on and mailed to the premises.

If the tenant is not available for personal service at their residence, or their place of business if known to the landlord, the three-day notice may be:

- handed to any person who is of suitable age and discretion at either location; and
- copied and mailed to the tenant at their residence.[2]

The rules for serving a three-day notice do not specify a person of suitable age and discretion needs to be at least 18 years old.

A young person who appears to be of suitable age and discretion, such as a family member or an employee, may be handed the notice as part of the substituted service on the tenant.

Editor's note — A person of suitable age and discretion to accept substituted service of a three-day notice will, on questioning, be able to understand their responsibility to hand the notice to the tenant. If the responsibility is not understood, then the process server will post the notice at the property and mail a copy to the tenant.

Serving a three-day notice

To establish the UD of a property by a tenant or subtenant, a requisite to a UD action, statutory requirements are to be strictly followed when serving a three-day notice.[3]

Both residential and commercial properties are subject to the same three-day notice and service rules.

On the breach of a rental or lease agreement and depending on the type of activity or inaction comprising the breach, one of the following statutory three-day notices is served on the tenant:

- a Three-Day Notice to Pay Rent or Quit [See **RPI** Form 575];
- a Three-Day Notice to Perform or Quit [See **RPI** Form 576]; or
- a Three-Day Notice to Quit.[4] [See **RPI** Form 577]

1 **Lehr** v. **Crosby** (1981) 123 CA3d Supp. 1
2 Calif. Code of Civil Procedure §1162(a)(2), §1162(b)(2)
3 **Lamey** v. **Masciotra** (1969) 273 CA2d 709
4 CCP §1161

The three-day notice may be served on the tenant by:

- personal service;
- leaving a copy with a person of suitable age and discretion at the premises and mailing a copy to the premises if the tenant is not personally served at their residence or place of business, called substituted service; or
- posting the notice on the leased premises and mailing a copy to the premises if the tenant is not available for personal service at their place of business or residence address if known, or a person is not be found to be served at the tenant's residence or place of business.[5]

The first attempt at serving a three-day notice is by personal delivery of a copy to the tenant, called **personal service**.[6]

Personal delivery may be made wherever the tenant is located. *Personal service* will be attempted at both the tenant's residence and place of business, if known. These two attempts to personally serve the notice are a prerequisite to an attempt at substituted service.

Second, the attempt to personally serve the tenant will fail when they are absent from both their residence and place of business (if known). In this event, a copy of the three-day notice may then be:

- handed to a person of suitable age and discretion at either the tenant's residence or place of business; and
- mailed to the tenant at their residence, called substituted service.[7]

Third, both the tenant's residence and place of business may be unknown or the tenant cannot be found for personal service at either the residence or business addresses, or a person of suitable age and discretion cannot be found for substituted service at either place. In this event, the three-day notice may be:

- posted on the leased premises; and
- mailed to the tenant at the address of the leased premises, loosely deemed service by "nail and mail."[8]

Usually, a landlord's resident manager or property manager is responsible for preparing and serving a three-day notice as part of their employment by the landlord. [See **RPI** Forms 590 and 591]

The attorney or UD service handling the anticipated eviction often prepares and causes the notice to be served.

The individual who serves the three-day notice will complete a form confirming they served the notice and the method of service completed. This form is called a proof of service. [See Form 580 accompanying this chapter]

Service by elimination of methods

Documenting service of the three-day notice

---

5   CCP §1162
6   CCP §1162(a)(1), §1162(b)(1)
7   CCP §1162(a)(2), §1162(b)(2)
8   CCP §1162(a)(3), §1162(b)(3)

If a UD action is filed to evict a tenant, a completed proof of service will be produced at trial, evidencing service of the three-day notice.

If the three-day notice is personally served on the tenant, the individual serving the notice will verify in the proof of service that they made the personal service at the address served. [See Form 580 §5.1]

When the server completes a substituted service, they verify in the proof of service:

- their attempts to personally serve the tenant at both addresses were unsuccessful;
- the notice was handed to a person of suitable age and discretion at the tenant's residence or business address; and
- the three-day notice was mailed to the tenant at their residence. [See Form 580 §5.2]

If the notice is served by posting on the premises, the server verifies:

- no person of suitable age or discretion was available at the tenant's residence and business addresses, or the addresses are unknown; and
- the three-day notice was mailed to the tenant at the address of the leased premises. [See Form 580 §5.3]

Full compliance on each attempt

When serving a three-day notice, the landlord first attempts to personally serve the tenant before resorting to substituted service.[9]

Personal service occurs when the three-day notice is handed to the tenant, whether or not the notice is:

- accepted by the tenant; or
- dropped at the tenant's feet after the tenant refuses to accept the notice.

Failure to attempt substitute service at both the tenant's residence and place of business, if known, before posting the property results in defective service. The landlord will be unable to maintain a UD action against the tenant if the tenant successfully challenges the service of the three-day notice.

Merely showing, and not handing, a copy of the three-day notice to a person on the premises and mailing a copy to the address is not proper service.[10]

When leaving a copy with a suitable person or posting a three-day notice on the leased premises, service is completed only if the notice is also mailed to the tenant.[11]

The notice may be mailed by first-class, registered or certified mail.

---

9 **Nourafchan** v. **Miner** (1985) 169 CA3d 746
10 **Kwok** v. **Bergren** (1982) 130 CA3d 596
11 **Jordan** v. **Talbot** (1961) 55 C2d 597

A lender acquired title to a residential property occupied by a tenant at a trustee's sale. The lender posted a 90-day notice to quit on the property and mailed a copy to the tenant's address of record without first attempting personal service of the notice. After 90 days elapsed, the tenant did not vacate. The lender filed an unlawful detainer (UD) action to remove the tenant.

The lender sought possession of the property, claiming the tenant's occupancy was unlawful since the 90-day period had expired.

The tenant claimed they were not required to vacate the premises since the lender did not properly serve the notice to quit as they posted it on the property and mailed it before attempting to serve the tenant personally.

*Here, the tenant was not required to vacate the premises since the lender did not serve the notice to quit properly. State law permits the lender to post and mail a notice to quit only after they have first attempted to serve the tenant personally. [**Bank of New York Mellon** v. **Preciado** (2013) 224 CA4th Supp. 1]*

*In order to properly serve a notice to quit, the lender was required to show that personal service was attempted on a person of suitable age or discretion at either tenant's residence or business address before posting and mailing the notice, called substituted service. This personal service procedure requirement applies to all notices served by landlords and any successors-in-interest. [See **RPI** Form 573]*

Case in point

Improper Service of a Notice to Quit

However, the mailing of a three-day notice is not itself a proper substituted service. The notice needs to first be either handed to an individual of suitable age and discretion or, if such an individual is not available, posted on the premises.[12]

Personal service needs to first be attempted before resorting to substituted service. However, reasonable diligence by the landlord or property manager to locate the tenant so they may be personally served is not required.

For example, consider a property manager of an apartment building who prepares a three-day notice for service on a tenant. The property manager is unaware of any business address for the tenant. No business address is listed on the application to rent or on any other documents received by the landlord or property manager.

The property manager attempts to serve the three-day notice on the tenant at the unit they rented.

The property manager receives no response after ringing the doorbell and knocking on the door of the premises. Thus, no personal or substituted service can be made. The property manager posts the three-day notice to the door and mails another copy addressed to the tenant at the unit they rented by first-class mail.

The tenant does not pay the delinquent rent or vacate before the three-day notice expires. A UD action is filed and served on the tenant.

No diligence required to locate the tenant

---

12 **Liebovich** v. **Shahrokhkhany** (1997) 56 CA4th 511

Form 580

Proof of Service

PROOF OF SERVICE
For Service of Notice to Real Estate Tenants

NOTE: This form is used by a property manager or landlord when serving a tenant a notice to pay, perform, vacate or quit or a notice of change in rental terms, to document the date and time the notice was served and the manner of service for use in any eviction proceeding.

1. I am over 18 years of age.

2. On _____, 20_____, at _____, California, I served the following checked items:

   ☐ Three-Day Notice to Pay Rent or Quit [See **RPI** Forms 575 and 575-1]
   ☐ Three-Day Notice to Perform or Quit [See **RPI** Form 576]
   ☐ Three-Day Notice to Quit [See **RPI** Forms 577 and 578]
   ☐ 30-Day Notice to Vacate [See **RPI** Forms 569, 571 and 573]
   ☐ 60-Day Notice to Vacate [See **RPI** Form 569-1]
   ☐ 30-Day Notice of Change in Rental Terms [See **RPI** Form 570]
   ☐ 60-Day Notice of Change in Rental Terms [See **RPI** Form 574]
   ☐ _____

3. Regarding tenancy of property referred to as _____
   _____

4. On Tenant(s) (name) _____
   _____

5. Manner of service (check the appropriate box):

   5.1 ☐ By personally delivering a copy to each named Tenant;
       a.   ☐ at Tenant's residence;
       b.   ☐ at Tenant's place of business.

   5.2 ☐ By delivering a copy to a person of suitable age and discretion;
       a.   ☐ at the Tenant's residence; or
       b.   ☐ at Tenant's place of business, as the named Tenant was absent from each location;
       and
       mailing by first-class postage prepaid a copy to each named Tenant at his residence.

   5.3 ☐ By posting a copy for each named Tenant in a conspicuous place on the property described in the notice as no person of suitable age or discretion was found at the Tenant's residence or place of business;
       and
       mailing by first-class postage prepaid a copy to each named Tenant at the address of the leased property.

	I declare under penalty or perjury that foregoing is true and correct.
	Date: _____, 20_____
	Name: _____
	Signature: _____

   FORM 580   01-13   ©2016 RPI — Realty Publications, Inc., P.O. BOX 5707, RIVERSIDE, CA 92517

The tenant claims improper service of the three-day notice since the property manager made no effort to locate the tenant's business address and there attempt personal service before posting it to the property and mailing them a copy.

However, the property manager is not required to use diligence, much less investigate the location of the tenant, when attempting personal service of a three-day notice. A review of the property management files and personal knowledge will suffice.

In the previous example, the property manager's use of the post-and-mail alternative for service was proper. When the landlord or property manager is unaware of any address for the tenant other than the leased premises:

- no attempt to ascertain the tenant's other address is necessary; and
- service by posting the premises and mailing to the leased premises is sufficient when no suitable person for substituted service is found at the premises.[13]

Consider an individual who leases space in a retail center to operate their business.

The tenant fails to pay their rent, and the property manager prepares a three-day notice for service on the tenant. The property manager does not know the tenant's residential address.

The property manager attempts to personally serve the tenant with the three-day notice at the leased premises, but the tenant is absent from the business.

The property manager hands the three-day notice to an employee of the tenant and mails a copy to the tenant at the premises.

Is the method of service used by the property manager proper?

Yes! Reasonable diligence to locate the tenant is not required when attempting personal service. Here the property manager need not make a second effort, such as returning to the premises or looking in a directory or voting records, to discover the tenant's residential address.[14]

Even if the attempted service is defective, the tenant's admitted receipt of the three-day notice establishes personal service. Thus, the defective service is no longer an issue.[15]

For example, a property manager sends a three-day notice by certified mail. It is the property manager's only attempt to notify the tenant. No personal service is attempted, or substituted and no notice is posted on the premises.

However, the tenant personally signs the postal receipt accepting the certified mail. The tenant's acknowledgement of receipt confirms they have been personally served (by the post office) with the three-day notice on the date they acknowledged receipt.

The mailing of the notice by the property manager did not constitute service of the three-day notice on the tenant — even though certified mail was used. However, the tenant's signing of the postal receipt is proof the tenant was handed the three-day notice by a post office employee — which is personal service.

---

13 **Hozz** v. **Lewis** (1989) 215 CA3d 314
14 Nourafchan, *supra*
15 **Valov** v. **Tank** (1985) 168 CA3d 867

The tenant who fails to pay the delinquent rent within the three-day period following acknowledgment of their receipt of the three-day notice by mail is unlawfully detaining the premises and may be evicted.

Editor's note — If any person other than the tenant signs acknowledging the receipt of the mail, personal service is not accomplished.[16]

An evasive tenant might not pick up certified mail addressed to them when their rental payment is delinquent.

If personal service cannot be accomplished, the three-day notice period begins to run the day the notice is either served by substituted service and mailed, or posted and mailed. The day following service is day one of three. When a Saturday, Sunday or holiday is the third day, the three-day period then continues through the first following business day.

---

16 Liebovich, *supra*

Chapter 27 Summary

On the breach of a rental or lease agreement and depending on the type of activity or inaction comprising the breach, one of three statutory three-day notices is served on the tenant:

- a Three-Day Notice to Pay Rent or Quit;
- a Three-Day Notice to Perform or Quit; or
- a Three-Day Notice to Quit.

The three-day notice may be served on the tenant by:

- personal service;
- leaving a copy with a person of suitable age and discretion at the premises and mailing a copy to the premises if the tenant is not personally served at their residence or place of business, called substituted service; or
- posting the notice on the leased premises and mailing a copy to the premises if the tenant is not available for personal service at their place of business or residence address if known, or a person is not found to be served at the tenant's residence or place of business.

Chapter 27 Key Terms

Quiz 7 Covering Chapters 25-28 is located on page 639.

Chapter
28

Other amounts due under three-day notices

Learning Objectives

late charge notice

late payment clause

public policy

Key Terms

Know what the judge will allow

A clause in a rental or lease agreement between a landlord and tenant calls for the accrual of interest on delinquent rent from the due date of the payment. This is a type of **late payment clause**.

The tenant fails to pay rent before it becomes delinquent. The landlord then prepares a three-day notice to pay or quit and serves the notice on the tenant. [See Form 575-1 accompanying this chapter and Form 575 in Chapter 20]

The three-day notice itemizes the amounts of delinquent rent and daily interest accrued that are due and unpaid on the date the notice is prepared. The tenant fails to pay or quit during the three-day period. The landlord files an *unlawful detainer (UD)* action to evict the tenant.

At the UD hearing, the tenant claims the landlord cannot terminate the tenant's right to possession of the premises under the three-day notice. The notice demands payment of an amount greater than the rent due under the lease agreement.

> **late payment clause**
> A provision in a rental or lease agreement establishing the landlord's right to demand and receive a late charge when a rent payment becomes delinquent. [See **RPI** Form 550 §4.3 and 552 §4.7]

May a three-day notice include money amounts due under a rental or lease agreement in addition to the rent?

Yes! A three-day notice to pay or quit is not limited to the scheduled amount of periodic rent which is delinquent. While the notice to pay may not be served until rent is delinquent, the notice may include all sums of money which are properly due and unpaid under the rental or lease agreement at the time the notice is served, including the delinquent rent.[1]

That said, late charges raise issues of the need for a demand for their payment, their nature as a cost recovery remedy, their reasonableness and whether they are punitive in amount.

Amounts in addition to scheduled rents

Examples of amounts of money due periodically under a rental or lease agreement, in addition to scheduled rent, include:

- *common area maintenance charges (CAMs);*
- association charges;
- pro rata insurance premiums, property taxes and assessments;
- late payment and bad check charges;
- expenses incurred by the landlord to cure *waste* or failure to maintain the property; and
- other amounts of money properly due as compensation or reimbursement of expenses arising out of the occupancy.

A three-day notice to pay or quit form provides for the itemization of rent and other amounts due which are unpaid and delinquent. [See Form 575 in Chapter 25]

Lump sum late charges

Under a commercial lease agreement entered into by a tenant, rent is typically due and payable on the first day of each month, called the *due date*. The lease agreement contains a late charge provision stating the tenant agrees to pay a specified charge if the rent is not received by the landlord within five days of the due date, called a **grace period**. [See Chapter 25; see **RPI** Form 552 §4.7]

The rent payment is *delinquent the day after the grace period runs, the* seventh day of the month. The delinquency triggers the landlord's right to **demand payment** of the agreed-to late charge, or do nothing and waive it.

The lease agreement also requires the tenant to pay a specific sum for each rent check returned for insufficient funds. [See **RPI** Form 552 §4.9]

One month, the landlord receives the rent after the grace period expires. The landlord as required accepts the rent since the tenant's right of possession has not been terminated by a declaration of forfeiture provision in a three-day notice or expiration of the lease. The landlord then notifies the tenant

---

1 **Canal-Randolph Anaheim, Inc.** v. **Wilkoski** (1978) 78 CA3d 477

in writing of their demand for payment of a late charge, payable with the following month's rent as called for in the lease agreement. [See Form 569 in Chapter 29]

The following month the landlord receives the regularly scheduled rent within the grace period. However, the tenant does not tender the late charge the landlord demanded due to the delinquency of the prior month's rent payment.

The landlord's options to enforce collection of the late charge payment, viable or not, include:

- returning the rent check to the tenant as insufficient payment for the total amount due;

- serving the tenant with a three-day notice to pay or quit;

- deducting the additional charge from the security deposit on written notice to the tenant; or

- filing an action against the tenant in small claims court to collect the late charge.

Returning the rent check to the tenant will result in one of the following scenarios:

- the tenant will submit another check which includes rent and payment of the late charge (which payment will be delinquent and arguably incur another late charge); or

- the tenant will retain the rent check as having been properly tendered and paid, and do nothing more until they send a check for the following month's rent.

A tenant who fails to pay rent or otherwise materially breaches the lease agreement may be served with the appropriate three-day notice. The three-day notice based on a material breach properly includes late charges and any other monetary amounts past due.[2]

If the tenant fails to cure the material breach within three days following service of the notice and remains in possession, the landlord may file a UD action to regain possession.[3]

Landlord's options for collection

A landlord will not succeed in a UD action when the landlord's refusal to accept the tenant's timely tender of a rent check is based solely on the tenant's refusal to pay late charges. Failure to pay the agreed late charge after notice is a **minor breach**.[4]

Refusal to pay late charges is a minor breach

---

2 Canal-Randolph Anaheim, Inc., *supra*
3 Calif. Code of Civil Procedure §1161
4 Canal-Randolph Anaheim, Inc., *supra*

A late charge is properly sought when pursuing delinquent rent. But alone, a late charge (or bounced check charge) is a *minor breach and will not independently support a UD action.*[5]

Thus, the landlord has two viable options for the collection of unpaid late charges from the tenant:

- accept the rent check and deduct the amount of the unpaid late charge from the security deposit, then or later, and advise the tenant of the deduction; or
- accept the rent check and file a money action for the unpaid late charge amounts.

The financially practical action is for the landlord to accept the rent and deduct the demanded late charge from the tenant's security deposit.

Late charges to recover costs

To be enforceable, late charges need to be reasonably related to:

- the actual costs of collecting the delinquent rent (the time, effort and money spent); and
- the delay in its receipt (loss of use, such as interest).

A lump sum late charge is a liquidated damages provision when the amount of the late charge is significantly greater than the actual out-of-pocket losses. As liquidated damages, the charge is a penalty and unenforceable.[6]

Editor's note — Some may argue any lump sum late charge on residential property is void as a liquidated damage since out-of-pocket money losses due to a late payment are readily ascertainable, especially in real estate transactions.

A liquidated damages provision in any agreement is void unless:

- the loss covered is impracticable or nearly impossible to calculate (rarely the case in real estate transactions); or
- the amount of the charge is a reasonable estimate of the landlord's out-of-pocket expenses for the collection effort.[7]

When setting the amount of a late charge, a landlord considers charging an amount equivalent to the late charge allowed on delinquent residential mortgage payments as a public policy set by the state legislature. The late charge formula amount for a delinquent mortgage payment is a good indicator of what is reasonable as a late charge on a delinquent rent payment.

The late charge amount allowed for a delinquent payment on a mortgage secured by residential property is controlled by statute. This is not the case for late charges on rent, which is determined by case law.

---

5   **Baypoint Mortgage** v. **Crest Premium Real Estate Investments Retirement Trust** *(1985) 168 CA 3d 818*
6   **Garrett** v. **Coast and Southern Federal Savings and Loan Association** (1973) 9 C3d 731
7   Calif. Civil Code §1671(d)

Form 575-1

Three-Day
Notice to Pay
Rent or Quit

THREE-DAY NOTICE TO PAY RENT OR QUIT
Without Rent-Related Fees

NOTE: This form is used by a property manager or landlord when a tenant defaults on rent payments under a rental or lease agreement, to notify the tenant of the amount of delinquent rent payable within three days or vacate and deliver possession.

DATE: _____, 20_____, at _____, California.
To Tenant: _____
Items left blank or unchecked are not applicable.
FACTS:
1. You are a Tenant under a rental or lease agreement
   1.1 dated _____ at _____, California,
   1.2 entered into by _____, as the Tenant,
   1.3 and _____, as the Landlord,
   1.4 regarding real estate referred to as _____
   _____

NOTICE:
2. You are in breach of the payment of amounts due under the rental or lease agreement.
3. Within three (3) days after service of this notice you are required to either
   3.1 Pay rent and other amounts now due and unpaid in the **Total Amount** of . . . .$_____
   representing rent for the periods of
   _____, 20_____ to _____, 20_____ . . . . . . Amount $_____
   _____, 20_____ to _____, 20_____ . . . . . . Amount $_____
   _____, 20_____ to _____, 20_____ . . . . . . Amount $_____
   and amounts due for
   ☐ common area maintenance (CAM) of . . . . $_____
   ☐ association assessments of . . . . $_____
   ☐ property taxes of . . . . $_____
   The **Total Amount** due may be paid in one of the following manners:
   a. By personal delivery to _____ (Name)
   _____ (Address)
   Payment of the Total Amount due will be accepted at the above address during
   the hours of _____ to _____ on the following days: _____.
   b. By deposit into account number _____
   at _____ (Financial Institution)
   _____ (Address)
   c. By the electronic funds transfer previsouly established between Landlord and Tenant.
   d. _____
   OR
   3.2 Deliver possession of the premises to Landlord or _____.
4. If you fail to pay the Total Amount due, or to deliver possession of the premises within three (3) days, legal proceedings will be initiated against you to regain possession of the premises and to recover the amounts owed, treble damages, costs and attorney fees.
5. The Landlord hereby elects to declare a forfeiture of your Right to Possession if you fail to pay the Total Amount demanded above.
   5.1 Landlord reserves the right to pursue collection of any future loss of rent allowed by Civil Code §1951.2.
6. State law permits former Tenants to reclaim abandoned personal property left at the former address of the Tenant, subject to certain conditions. You may or may not be able to reclaim property without incurring additional costs, depending on the cost of storing the property and the length of time before it is reclaimed. In general, these costs will be lower the sooner you contact your former Landlord after being notified that property belonging to you was left behind after you moved out.

Date: _____, 20_____
Landlord/Agent: _____ CalBRE# _____

Signature: _____
Address: _____
Phone: _____ Cell: _____

FORM 575-1   01-13   ©2016 RPI — Realty Publications, Inc., P.O. BOX 5707, RIVERSIDE, CA 92517

For example, the lump sum late charge allowed on a mortgage encumbering an owner-occupied, single family residence (SFR) cannot exceed 6% of the delinquent payment (principal and interest only).[8]

Rent is the economic equivalent of interest as they accrue and are paid as consideration for the use of property or money. For purposes of late charges, delinquent rent payments need to be treated no differently than delinquent mortgage payments.

---

8 CC §2954.4(a)

Late charges as liquidated damages

A late charge provision calling for interest to accrue at a predetermined annual percentage rate on delinquent rent is not a *liquidated damages provision*. Thus, late charges are enforceable unless the rate of interest is unconscionable.[9]

However, some landlords wrongfully view late charges as a means for *coercing tenants* to pay rent on time. Thus, landlords set the late charge at a punitive amount which is far greater than the out-of-pocket losses they incurred in time, effort and money. An excessive amount constitutes a penalty assessment and is unenforceable.

A late charge provision calling for a lump sum dollar amount is classified as a *liquidated damages provision*. The charge is a one-time, predetermined fixed amount. It is intended by its nature to reimburse the landlord for the delay in receipt of the rent money and the costs and effort spent to collect the delinquent amount.[10]

Thus, a lump sum late charge provision in a commercial lease agreement is valid unless the tenant can show the amount of the late charge is an unreasonable reimbursement for the delay in receipt of the rent and costs of collection efforts.[11]

A late charge is unenforceable if the charge is so great in comparison to actual losses that it imposes a penalty on the tenant for their late rent payment to the extent the late charge becomes a windfall profit for the landlord.[12]

In a lease agreement for single-user property encumbered by a mortgage, an appropriate late charge for the tenant is equal to the amount of the late charge imposed on the landlord from their mortgage lender. The landlord is simply "passing through" the loss incurred by late receipt of the tenant's rent payment.

However, in a residential lease agreement, a late charge provision setting a fixed amount is void unless the losses suffered by the landlord due to late payment are impracticable to calculate.[13]

Editor's note — Determining money losses suffered due to late payments in any real estate transaction, especially in a residential lease, is not impracticable. A landlord may calculate this by accounting for known costs incurred due to collection efforts and lost use of the funds until received.

Imposing the late charge

A late charge is not automatically due and payable by the tenant when the landlord fails to receive the rent payment within the grace period.

On the failure of a landlord to receive a rent payment prior to its delinquency, the landlord needs to make a written demand on the tenant for payment of the late charge if they intend to enforce collection of the late charge. The demand includes the amount due and the date for its payment.

9 Canal-Randolph Anaheim, Inc., *supra*
10 CC §1951.5
11 CC §1671(b)
12 Garrett, *supra*
13 CC §1671(d)

Thus, a written billing demanding payment of the late charge with the next month's rent is delivered to the tenant to ensure the late charge agreed to is imposed. This is called a **late charge notice**. [See **RPI** Form 568]

The *late charge notice* advises the tenant the landlord is entitled to enforce collection of the unpaid late charge by:

- deducting the unpaid late charge amount from the tenant's security deposit; or
- filing a small claims or municipal court action for unpaid late charge amounts.

late charge notice A landlord's written notice demanding payment of a late charge on a delinquent rent payment. [See **RPI** Form 586]

Too late to collect

Recall that a landlord has only one year from the date of the delinquency to serve a three-day notice to collect delinquent rent due and unpaid.[14]

As an alternative to seeking a recovery of money in a UD action with its one-year limitation, the landlord may file a separate money action within four years of the breach to collect unpaid late charges, returned check handling charges and any other amounts due under the rental or lease agreement.[15]

Ultimately, the landlord may deduct properly demanded late charges from the tenant's security deposit as payment of unpaid amounts due the landlord under the rental or lease agreement.[16]

The UD court problem

The *Canal-Randolph Anaheim, Inc.* case clarified a landlord's right to include any money sums due and unpaid under the lease as an amount due in the three-day notice.

Also, existing statutes do not forbid (or limit) the collection of a late charge in a rental or lease agreement. However, cases do limit the charge to an amount reasonably calculated to cover the losses inflicted by late payment.[17]

Despite the holding of *Canal-Randolph Anaheim, Inc.*, some trial judges in UD actions declare late charges are not *rent* for purposes of enforcing residential rental and lease agreements. Thus, the delinquency of a late charge payment previously demanded is not properly included in their courtrooms as an amount due the landlord to be collected by use of a three-day notice to pay or quit.[18]

These judges hold a late charge or bad check charge cannot be included in the three-day notice as part of the amount due. If included, the demand bars an eviction before those judges.

---

14 CCP §1161(2)
15 CCP §337
16 CC §§1950.5(b)(1); 1950.7(c)
17 Garrett, *supra*
18 CCP §1161(2)

Varying approaches

Before a landlord or a property manager includes any late charge (or other amounts due besides amounts stated in rental or lease agreements as base rent) in a three-day notice as part of the total amount due, the wise landlord will determine if the judge presiding over UD actions in the jurisdiction will allow the inclusion of late charges in the three-day notice and UD action.

Judges in UD actions on residential rental or lease agreements vary in their approach to late charges:

- some allow masked late charges built into the scheduled monthly rent and cloaked as a forgiveness of 6% to 10% of the stated rent if paid on or before the due date or within a grace period;

- some allow a late charge of up to 6% of the delinquent rent as a reasonable charge;

- some disallow fixed-sum late charges as an unenforceable penalty for being delinquent;

- some disallow late charges as a forfeiture of money (since the amount exceeds the costs of collection); and

- some just disallow late charges altogether as an exercise of their discretion.

Information on the treatment given by the local UD trial judge can be obtained from an attorney or other landlords who have experience appearing before the judge.

If the judge will not allow the late charge as part of the amount due from the tenant, the landlord needs to leave it out of the three-day notice. Instead, the landlord's best practice is to either deduct the late charge they have demanded from the security deposit or pursue collection in a separate action for money. Both of these remedies avoid the issue of whether late charges or bounced check charges are proper in the three-day notice for residential tenants.

The landlord needs to inquire into the local judge's behavior to eliminate the risk of getting an erroneous judicial determination that late charges or other monetary amounts due were improperly included in the three-day notice. Such a judgment will result in a denial of the eviction, requiring a new three-day notice and UD process without the late charge or an appeal.

Public policy legislation to set acceptable limits

An obvious solution to the inconsistent rules applied to late charges is **public policy** legislation defining the nature of late charges and acceptable limits on time and amounts for recovery of the cost of collecting delinquent rent. This would provide guidance for all involved in the UD process.

Late charges for rent are best treated like late charges on mortgages. Both serve the same economic function — recovery of costs incurred due to the delayed receipt of funds and resulting collection efforts. The number of homeowners with mortgage payments is almost equal to the number of renters with rental payments in California. Both mortgage payments and rental payments are part of the cost of occupancy and entitled to equivalent legislative controls over residential mortgage lenders and residential landlords.

public policy
A system of laws maintained by local, state or federal government for the conduct of its people.

A rent payment becomes delinquent the day after the grace period runs. The delinquency triggers the landlord's right to demand payment of an agreed-to late charge. But alone, a late charge (or bounced check charge) is a minor breach and will not independently support an unlawful detainer (UD) action.

To be enforceable, late charges need to be reasonably related to:

- the actual costs of collecting the delinquent rent (the time and effort involved); and

- the delay in its receipt (loss of use, such as interest).

The landlord on failure to timely receive a rent payment makes a written demand on the tenant for payment of the late charge and includes the date when the charge is payable. If the amount of the late charge is significantly greater than the landlord's actual out-of-pocket losses, the late charge is unenforceable as a penalty.

Some trial judges hold late charges are not properly included as an amount due residential landlords to be collected by use of a three-day notice to pay or quit. If included, the demand bars an eviction before those judges.

Before a landlord or a property manager includes any late charge (or other amounts due besides technical rent) in a three-day notice as part of the total amount due, the landlord needs to determine if the judge presiding over UD actions in their jurisdiction allows for collection of late charges in a UD action.

Chapter 28 Summary

Chapter 28 Key Terms

Quiz 7 Covering Chapters 25-28 is located on page 639.

Notes:

Notices to vacate

After reading this chapter, you will be able to:

- determine the correct use of a notice to vacate by landlords and tenants to terminate periodic month-to-month tenancies;
- differentiate the circumstances for the use of a 30- or 60-day notice to vacate from those for the use of a three-day notices to quit on a breach;
- apply the requirement of a Section 8 landlord for good cause when using a 30-day notice to vacate to terminate a tenancy; and
- manage service for an owner-by-foreclosure of a 90-day notice to vacate on holdover residential tenants.

Learning Objectives

bona fide lease agreement

cancellation provision

notice to vacate

owner-by-foreclosure

Section 8 housing

Key Terms

A landlord enters into a lease agreement granting the tenant the right to use and occupy a single family residential property. The lease agreement obligates the tenant to maintain the property's landscaping as a condition of the right of possession granted.

The landlord receives complaints from surrounding property owners regarding the tenant's behavior. A high number of visitors arrive at the property late at night producing excessive noise. On more than one occasion, the police have responded to calls from neighbors regarding the noise. Also, the city ordinance compliance department has given notice for the removal of disabled vehicles from the property.

Termination of periodic tenancies

On a *drive-by inspection*, the landlord discovers the landscaping and lawn have deteriorated since the tenant has not kept them watered.

The landlord decides to require the tenant to vacate the property although the tenant consistently pays the rent on time and several months remain on the lease. The tenant's interference with their neighbors' use and enjoyment of their property is a nuisance and the failure to maintain the leased premises is *waste*. Both a nuisance and waste are events automatically terminating the tenant's right of possession.

notice to vacate
A written document used by a tenant or a landlord to terminate a periodic tenancy. [See **RPI** Form 569 and 569-1]

The landlord prepares and serves the tenant with a 30-day **notice to vacate** to avoid stating their reasons for terminating the tenancy.[1] [See Form 569 accompanying this chapter]

The tenant remains in occupancy of the premises after the 30-day notice expires and tenders the next rent payment on time. The landlord refuses to accept the rent payment and files an unlawful detainer (UD) action to evict the tenant.

Can the landlord, subject to an unexpired lease that the tenant has breached, evict the tenant from the premises with a 30-day notice to vacate?

No! When the tenant occupies the property under an unexpired lease, a notice to vacate does not terminate the tenant's right to possession as required to maintain a UD action. Here, the landlord needed to use a three-day notice to quit. The tenancy was already terminated by statute due to the separate issues of nuisance and waste. Thus, the three-day notice to quit is merely required to evict in a UD action.

A residential or commercial notice to vacate is only effective when used by a landlord or tenant to terminate a periodic tenancy, such as a month-to-month tenancy or one created by a continuing occupancy after a lease expires.

Notice to quit versus notice to vacate

Remember that a *notice to quit* is used when the tenant has materially breached a rental or lease agreement and the landlord uses the breach to terminate the lease by a declaration of forfeiture or a statutory forfeiture forcing the tenant to vacate or be evicted in a UD action. A *notice to vacate* is used to terminate a rental agreement and interfere with the automatic renewal of the periodic tenancy when a breach of the rental agreement has not occurred or is not an issue. Exceptions to terminating residential tenancies exist in rent control, Section 8 and occupancies subject to foreclosure sales.

cancellation provision
A lease agreement provision permitting the tenant to terminate their occupancy and rent obligation by paying a set sum of money.

A **cancellation provision** is occasionally included in a residential or commercial lease agreement by negotiations to allow the tenant to terminate their occupancy and vacate prematurely on notice to the landlord accompanied by payment of a set sum of money.

---

1 Calif. Civil Code §1946

30-DAY NOTICE TO VACATE
For Use by Residential Landlord

NOTE: This form is used by a residential property manager or landlord when the landlord is terminating a month-to-month rental agreement and the tenant has occupied the property for less than one year, to terminate the tenancy and require the tenant to vacate.

Date: _____, 20_____, at _____, California.
To Tenant: _____
Items left blank or unchecked are not applicable.
FACTS:
1. You are a residential Tenant under a rental agreement or expired lease agreement
   1.1 dated _____ at _____, California,
   1.2 entered into by _____, as the Tenant,
   1.3 and _____, as the Landlord,
   1.4 regarding real estate referred to as _____
   _____

NOTICE:
2. This notice is intended as at least a thirty (30) day notice prior to termination of your month-to-month tenancy.
3. On or before _____, 20_____, a date at least thirty (30) days after service of this notice, you will vacate and deliver possession of the premises to Landlord, or _____
   _____
4. Rent due prior to the date to vacate includes pro rated rent of $_____, payable on or before _____, 20_____.
5. Landlord acknowledges the prior receipt of $_____ as your security deposit.
   5.1 **Notice:** You have the right to request and be present for an inspection of the premises to be conducted within two weeks of expiration of this notice to vacate for the purposes of providing you with an itemized statement of deductible charges for repairs and cleaning and allowing you the opportunity to remedy these deficiencies and avoid a deduction from your security deposit. [Calif. Civil Code §1950.5(f)(1)]
   5.2 Within 21 days after you vacate, Landlord will furnish you with a written statement and explanation of any deductions from the deposit and a refund of the remaining amount. [Calif. Civil Code §1950.5(g)(1)]
   5.3 Landlord may deduct only those amounts necessary to:
      a. Reimburse for Tenant defaults in rental payments;
      b. Repair damages to the premises caused by Tenant (ordinary wear and tear excluded);
      c. Clean the premises, if necessary; and
      d. Reimburse for Tenant loss, damage or excessive wear and tear on furnishings provided to Tenant.
6. Landlord may show the leased premises to prospective tenants during normal business hours by first giving you written notice at least 24 hours in advance of the entry. The notice will be given to you in person, by leaving a copy with an occupant of suitable age and discretion, or by leaving the notice on or under your entry door.
7. **Notice:** State law permits former Tenants to reclaim abandoned personal property left at the former address of the Tenant, subject to certain conditions. You may or may not be able to reclaim property without incurring additional costs, depending on the cost of storing the property and the length of time before it is reclaimed. In general, these costs will be lower the sooner you contact your former Landlord after being notified that property belonging to you was left behind after you moved out.
8. If you fail to vacate and deliver possession of the premises by the date set for you to vacate, legal proceedings may be initiated to regain possession of the premises and to recover rent owed, treble damages, costs and attorney fees.
9. The reason for termination _____.
   (Required by rent control ordinance or Section 8 housing)

Date: _____, 20_____
Landlord/Agent: _____ CalBRE#:_____
Signature: _____
Address: _____
Phone: _____ Cell: _____
Fax: _____
Email: _____

FORM 569 01-13 ©2016 RPI — Realty Publications, Inc., P.O. BOX 5707, RIVERSIDE, CA 92517

Unlike the extension of a lease which needs to be agreed to, the 30-day rental period under a month-to-month rental agreement (or for any other period, whether residential or commercial) is automatically extended for the same period and on the same terms. [See Forms 569 and 572]

To interfere with the automatic extension of a periodic tenancy and by the same act **terminate** the right to occupancy, either the tenant or the landlord hand the other a notice to vacate. However, to terminate the tenancy of a residential tenant who has resided on the property for one year or more, residential landlords are required to give the tenant a 60-day notice to vacate, not the 30-day notice to vacate commonly used.[2] [See Form 569-1]

Periodic tenancies extended/terminated

2 CC §1946.1

Form 569-1

60-Day Notice to Vacate

60-DAY NOTICE TO VACATE
For Use by Residential Landlord

NOTE: This form is used by a residential property manager or landlord when the landlord is terminating a month-to-month rental agreement or the occupancy of a tenant paying rent under an expired lease, and the tenant has resided in the property for one year or more, to terminate the tenancy and require the tenant to vacate.

Date: _____, 20_____, at _____, California.

To Tenant: _____

Items left blank or unchecked are not applicable.

FACTS:

1. You are a residential Tenant under a rental agreement or expired lease agreement
   1.1   dated _____, at _____, California,
   1.2   entered into by _____, as the Tenant,
   1.3   and _____, as the Landlord,
   1.4   regarding real estate referred to as _____
   _____

NOTICE:

2. This notice is intended as at least a sixty (60) day notice prior to termination of your month-to-month tenancy.

3. On or before _____, 20_____, a date at least sixty (60) days after service of this notice, you will vacate and deliver possession of the premises to Landlord or _____.

4. Rents due and payable by you prior to the date to vacate include:
   a.   Monthly rent of $_____, due _____, 20_____; and
   b.   Prorated rent of $_____ through the date to vacate, due _____, 20_____.

5. Landlord acknowledges the prior receipt of $_____ as your security deposit.
   5.1   Within 21 days after you vacate, Landlord will furnish you with a written statement and explanation of any deductions from the deposit and a refund of the remaining amount. [Calif. Civil Code §1950.5(g)(1)]
   5.2   Landlord may deduct only those amounts necessary to:
   a.   Reimburse for Tenant defaults in rental payments;
   b.   Repair damages to the premises caused by Tenant (ordinary wear and tear excluded);
   c.   Clean the premises, if necessary; and
   d.   Reimburse for Tenant loss, damage or excessive wear and tear on furnishings provided to Tenant.

6. Landlord may show the leased premises to prospective tenants during normal business hours by first giving you written notice at least 24 hours in advance of the entry. The notice will be given to you in person, by leaving a copy with an occupant of suitable age and discretion, or by leaving the notice on or under your entry door.

7. Please contact the undersigned to arrange a time to review the condition of the premises before you vacate.

8. If you fail to vacate and deliver possession of the premises by the date set for you to vacate, legal proceedings may be initiated to regain possession of the premises and to recover rent owed, treble damages, costs and attorney fees.

9. **Notice:** State law permits former Tenants to reclaim abandoned personal property left at the former address of the Tenant, subject to certain conditions. You may or may not be able to reclaim property without incurring additional costs, depending on the cost of storing the property and the length of time before it is reclaimed. In general, these costs will be lower the sooner you contact your former Landlord after being notified that property belonging to you was left behind after you moved out.

10. The reason for termination is _____.
   (Required by rent control ordinance or Section 8 housing)

Date: _____, 20_____

Landlord/Agent: _____   CalBRE#:_____

Signature: _____

Address: _____
_____

Phone: _____   Cell: _____
Fax: _____
Email: _____

FORM 569-1   03-11   ©2016 RPI — Realty Publications, Inc., P.O. BOX 5707, RIVERSIDE, CA 92517

A 30-day notice to vacate on a month-to-month tenancy, whether given by the tenant or the landlord, establishes a tenant's unlawful detainer (UD) of the property when it expires and the tenant remains in possession.[3]

If the notice to vacate expires and the tenant has not vacated, the landlord may file a UD action to evict the month-to-month tenant without further notice.[4]

---

3   **Palmer v. Zeis** (1944) 65 CA2d Supp. 859
4   Code of Civil Procedure §1161(5)

Consider a tenant who enters into a one-year lease of a unit in a residential building. On expiration of the lease, the tenant remains in possession, becoming a holdover tenant unlawfully detaining the premises. However, the tenant continues to pay rent monthly which the landlord accepts.

Later, the residential landlord serves the tenant with a 60-day notice to vacate the property. The notice period expires but the tenant remains in possession. The landlord files a UD action to evict the tenant.

The tenant claims they cannot be evicted based on a 60-day notice to vacate. They hold possession of the unit under a lease agreement. The tenant asserts the lease which had expired was automatically extended for the same period as the term of the original lease when the landlord accepted rent after the lease expired.

Here, the 60-day notice to vacate is effective to terminate possession and the tenant can be evicted when they holdover on expiration of the notice. The landlord's acceptance of monthly rent after the lease expired establishes a month-to-month tenancy on the same conditions for use and occupancy stated in the lease agreement. The tenant under a lease agreement who does not hold an option to extend the lease and continues in possession and pay rent which is accepted by the landlord transforms the lease into a rental agreement on the same terms, except as a periodic tenancy for the rent payment period.[5]

A landlord, residential or commercial, terminates a month-to-month tenancy by preparing and serving the tenant with a 30-day notice to vacate, unless exceptions to this rule control the tenancy. However, when a tenant materially breaches a rental or lease agreement, the landlord uses the appropriate three-day notice to quit to terminate the tenancy. [See **RPI** Form 571; see Form 579 in Chapter 6]

A notice to vacate form (as distinguished from a notice to quit) used by a landlord contains:

- the name of the tenant;
- the address of the premises;
- a reference to the rental agreement or expired lease;
- a statement that the unit needs to be vacant within the applicable number of days (30 or 60) after service of the notice;
- the dollar amount of pro rata rent to be paid when rent is next due;
- a statement regarding the security deposit and its disposition;
- a statement informing the tenant of their right to request a joint pre-expiration inspection of the premises so they may act to avoid deductions from their security deposit; and
- a statement notifying residential tenants of their right to reclaim abandoned personal property. [See Chapter 32]

Lease transformed into a periodic tenancy

Landlord's intent for a tenant to vacate

5 CC §1945

Notices to vacate do not include declarations of forfeiture since a breach is not involved allowing for three days to require the tenant to vacate. When the notice expires, the tenancy automatically terminates since the tenant no longer holds an estate in the property. The content of the landlord's notice to vacate eliminates any confusion over the amount of rent to be paid for the remaining term of the tenancy. [See **RPI** Form 571 §4]

Tenant's intent to vacate

A tenant, residential or commercial, who intends to vacate and avoid further liability under a month-to-month rental agreement serves the landlord with a 30-day advance notice the tenant is vacating. The notice may be in the form of a letter personally delivered to the landlord or their agent, or sent by certified or registered mail.[6]

The tenant and landlord are best served by the landlord handing the tenant a blank 30-day notice to vacate form when entering into a rental agreement, but not when entering into a lease agreement. The tenant will then have the correct paperwork to complete and deliver documentation to the landlord or property manager. Use of a form lends certainty to the tenant's understanding of a critical event. [See Form 572]

Tenant acknowledgement

A 30-day notice used by a tenant to advise the landlord they intend to vacate acknowledges:

- the tenancy is terminated on expiration of 30 days after service of the notice on the landlord or the manager;

- the tenant intends to pay pro rata rent;

- the amount of the security deposit;

- the tenant's right to request a joint pre-expiration inspection and receive an itemized statement of maintenance and cleaning deficiencies for any potential deductions from the security deposit;

- a security deposit statement and refund based on any deductions for cleaning and repairs on a final review of the premises by the landlord or property manager; and

- the landlord's right to show the premises to a prospective tenant on 24 hour notice.

If a tenant serves the landlord or property manager with a 30-day notice to vacate, but fails to vacate the residence after expiration of the notice, they become a holdover tenant unlawfully in possession. The tenancy has been terminated by the tenant's notice and with it the right to occupancy. The landlord may immediately file a UD action to evict the tenant. No further notice to quit is required since the tenancy has already been terminated.

---

6 CC §1946

A notice to vacate may be served at any time during the month.

However, a commercial landlord and tenant may agree in a rental agreement that the 30-day notice to vacate may not be served during the last seven days of the month. In contrast, service of a notice to vacate can occur at any time in a residential periodic tenancy.[7]

To be effective in commercial tenancies, the notice to vacate from a tenant or landlord needs to be served:

- in the same manner as a three-day notice (in person, by substitution or ultimately post and mail); or

- by certified or registered mail, methods of service not available for three-day notices to quit.[8]

The date of service is the date the notice, attempted in the following priorities, is:

- personally served;

- handed to a person of suitable age and discretion at either the residence of the tenant or the tenant's place of business; or

- posted in a conspicuous place on the leased premises and mailed by certified or registered mail.

The minimum period within which the tenant is to vacate begins to run the day after the date of service, which is day one of the 30- or 60-day period.[9]

If the day for expiration of the notice is a Saturday, Sunday or a federal holiday, the tenant is not required to vacate until the next business day.[10]

Most properly completed notice to vacate forms give a specific date by which the tenant needs to vacate, on or before at least 30 days after service of the notice. The day is not left to chance when filling out the notice and, as a practical matter, not set as a weekend day or holiday.

When a residential rental property is located in a **rent control community**, the landlord has less discretion to terminate tenancies and evict tenants with a notice to vacate.

Typically, the termination of a tenancy and evictions are allowed in *rent control communities* when:

- the tenant fails to pay rent or otherwise materially breaches the lease agreement;

- the tenant creates a nuisance;

- the tenant refuses to renew a lease;

- the tenant uses the residence for an illegal purpose; or

Service of the notice to vacate

Rent control limitations on eviction

---

7   CC §1946
8   CC §1946
9   CC §10
10 CCP §12a

> • the landlord or a relative will occupy the unit.

A landlord and their property manager of a property subject to residential rent control need to be aware of local restrictions placed on landlords for the eviction of tenants.

Good reason to evict exception

Generally, a landlord is not required to state their reasons for terminating the occupancy in a notice to vacate, or even have **good cause** for evicting a month-to-month tenant.[11]

Exceptions exist. If a tenant's unit is subject to rent control, the landlord needs to state a *good cause* for terminating the tenancy.

Section 8 housing
A government housing program for low income households which provides qualifying tenants with rent subsidies and minimum habitability standards.

Likewise, when a tenant's rent is subsidized by the Department of Housing and Urban Development's (HUD) **Section 8 housing** program, the landlord will state their good cause in the 30-day notice to vacate as the reason for the termination. Good cause includes:

- the tenant's **material noncompliance** with the rental agreement;
- the tenant's material failure to carry out their obligations under any state or local landlord and tenant act;
- criminal activity conducted by the tenant on the premises that threatens the health, safety, or right to peaceful enjoyment of the premises by other tenants; or
- other good cause.[12]

Material noncompliance

Material noncompliance includes:

- one or more substantial violations of the lease agreement;
- repeated minor violations of the lease agreement, such as violations which disrupt the livability of the project or interfere with the management of the project;
- failure to timely supply required income and eligibility information to the landlord or knowingly providing incomplete or inaccurate information; and
- failure to pay rent or any other financial obligation due under the lease agreement beyond any grace period.

The tenant is given notice of the landlord's good cause so they can prepare any defense they may have to avoid eviction.[13]

Recall that a material breach of a rental agreement is handled by a three-day notice to quit, not a notice to vacate which is used when no tenant breach exists. However, to terminate a tenancy for *Section 8 housing*, a landlord provides the tenant with a separate notice identifying the inappropriate conduct of the tenant which is the basis for "good cause" to terminate the occupancy.[14]

---

11 CC §1946
12 24 Code of Federal Regulations §247.3(b)
13 **Mitchell v. Poole** (1988) 203 CA3d Supp. 1
14 24 CFR §247.3(b)

Whether or not a landlord provides good cause for terminating a tenancy, a landlord may not evict a tenant for a wrong reason. The landlord terminating a tenancy for the wrong reason may find they are not only unable to evict the tenant, but defending against the tenant's claim the eviction is:

- retaliation for the tenant making official complaints about the property or against the landlord;

- based on discriminatory reasons, such as the tenant's ethnicity or marital status; or

- improper because of the landlord's failure to maintain the property in a habitable condition.

The owner of a residential income property is in default on a mortgage secured by a trust deed encumbering the property. While the owner is in negotiations with the lender to modify the mortgage's payment schedule and cure the default, they enter into a two-year lease agreement with a tenant, who takes possession of the property.

Shortly after the residential tenant takes possession, negotiations with the lender break down. The lender records a *notice of default (NOD)*, commencing a trustee's foreclosure on the property. The property is sold at a trustee's sale. The high bidder takes title to the property as the new **owner-by-foreclosure**.

*Editor's note — A notice of sale is to be posted with the notice of trustee's sale on a residential property in foreclosure. The **notice of sale** notifies any occupant of the premises, including tenants, of the potential effect of a trustee's sale on the tenants' right of possession and underlying rental or lease agreement. This notice needs to be mailed to all occupants in possession of the property in foreclosure.[15] [See **RPI** Form 474-1]*

The *owner-by-foreclosure* is a speculator who intends to fix up the property and resell it for a profit. The owner-by-foreclosure has read state law controlling the rights of tenants in possession at the time of the trustee's sale and knows the tenant's leasehold interest in the property has been eliminated by the foreclosure sale. They believe they can terminate the tenancy (at sufferance) rights held by the tenant by serving the tenant with a 60-day notice to vacate due to the foreclosure sale. [See Form 569-1]

The real estate agent hired by the owner-by-foreclosure to handle the resale marketing of the property advises the owner-by-foreclosure to serve the tenant with a 90-day notice to vacate under federal rules since:

- the owner-by-foreclosure acquired the residential property through a trustee's sale;

- the owner-by-foreclosure's resale of the property will be to a buyer who will occupy the property as their primary residence; and

- the sale needs to be set to close on or after the 90-day notice expires.

Residential foreclosure and continuing possession

owner-by-foreclosure
The winning bidder at a trustee's sale who takes title to the property sold by a trustee's deed.

---

15 CC §2924.8

The owner-by-foreclosure ignores their agent's advice and serves the tenant with the 60-day notice to vacate as required by state law for evictions of residential tenants in possession one year or more.[16]

60 days pass following the service of the notice on the tenant, but the tenant remains in possession. Can the owner-by-foreclosure file a UD action and obtain a court order to evict the tenant?

No! An owner-by-foreclosure of a residential property is required to serve a bona fide tenant occupying the property at the time of the foreclosure sale with at least 90 days' notice before the tenant's right of possession is terminated. [See **RPI** Form 573 and 573-1]

The requisite 90-day notice to vacate

An owner-by-foreclosure acquiring tenant-occupied residential property at a trustee's sale for investment purposes terminates the tenant's right to continued occupancy by serving the tenant with a 90-day notice to vacate. This rule expires December 31, 2019, unless extended by legislation.[17] [See **RPI** Form 573 and 573-1]

However, an owner-by-foreclosure may not use a 90-day notice to vacate to avoid:

bona fide lease agreement
A lease agreement with a fair market rent held by a residential tenant when ownership of the property is transferred by a foreclosure sale. [See **RPI** Form 550]

- a **bona fide lease agreement** held by the existing tenant, entered into prior to the foreclosing lender recording the NOD, granting the tenant the right of possession for a period running beyond the 90-day notice period;
- an existing Section 8 or state housing assistance payment contract which subsidizes the tenant's rent; or
- local or state rent control ordinances or codes that provide the residential tenant with a greater time period for occupancy or other tenant benefits such as relocation money.[18]

A *bona fide lease agreement* is one entered into by a tenant and the prior owner in which:

- the tenancy granted was negotiated as an arm's length lease agreement, meaning the tenant is not a parent, spouse or child of the prior owner; and
- the lease agreement calls for payment of a fair market rent at the time entered into.

---

16 Calif. Code of Civil Procedure 1161b(a)
17 CCP §§1161a,1161b
18 CCP §1161b

A tenant enters into a lease agreement and takes possession of a residential unit created by the conversion of a garage. The owner defaults on a mortgage encumbering the property. The lender forecloses and takes title to the property by a trustee's deed. The lender, as the new owner-by-foreclosure managing the property as REO inventory, serves a 90-day notice to vacate by posting the notice on the door of the main house. A notice to vacate is not served on the tenant in the converted garage by personal or substitute service. Prior to the expiration of the lease held by the tenant of the converted garage, the tenant is denied access to the property by a new occupant of the main house.

The tenant seeks to recover their money losses from the REO lender, claiming the lender failed to prevent the interference of the tenant's right to occupy the converted garage for the remainder of the lease term since the lease agreement was entered into prior to the foreclosure sale and remains enforceable after foreclosure for lack of a notice to vacate under the Protecting Tenants Against Foreclosure Act (PTFA).

The lender claims they have no liability exposure for interference of the tenant's possession of the property since the lender fulfilled its PTFA obligations by posting a 90-day notice to vacate on the main building of the property containing the converted garage.

*A California court of appeals held the lender, as the owner-by-foreclosure, was liable for the existing residential tenant's money losses due to the lender's failure to protect the tenant from third party interference with the tenant's use of the property since the lease agreement entered into by the tenant prior to the foreclosure sale remained enforceable. [**Nativi** v. **Deutsche Bank National Trust Company** (2014) 223 CA4th 261]*

*On acquiring a property at a foreclosure sale, the successful high bidder, whether the mortgage lender or a third-party, serves existing tenants with a **90-day notice to quit due to foreclosure** if they intend to force the tenants to vacate. [See **RPI** Form 573]*

*In addition to the 90-day notice to vacate requirements, the owner-by-foreclosure also steps into the position of the **landlord** under the rental or lease agreements entered into by the prior owner. With the original landlord out of the picture, it is the owner-by-foreclosure who needs to manage and maintain the rental property for the occupancy of the preexisting tenants.*

Existing leases and the buyer-occupant exception

Consider an owner-by-foreclosure who is an investor that plans to resell a single family residential property they acquired. A residential tenant is in possession of the property having taken possession before the trustee's sale by entering into a lease agreement. The tenant's lease agreement expires within three months after the trustee's sale.

The owner-by-foreclosure serves the tenant with the required 90-day notice to vacate to terminate their right of possession. If the tenant does not vacate upon expiration of the 90-day notice, the owner-by-foreclosure may evict the tenant in a UD action.[19]

Now consider the same scenario, except the tenant has another six-month term remaining on their lease following the day of the trustee's sale. Here, the tenant may remain in possession of the property until the lease term expires or is terminated due to a tenant default.

---

19 CCP §1161b

However, if this owner-by-foreclosure resells the property to a buyer who will occupy the property as their primary residence, the tenant's lease may be terminated by the service and expiration of a 90-day notice to vacate.[20]

Additionally, if the lease agreement is the subject of the Section 8 voucher program and was entered into prior to the trustee's sale, the tenant may enforce the lease agreement and require the owner-by-foreclosure to honor the Section 8 voucher program until the lease expires.[21]

Bona fide residential tenants and the 90-day notice

Consider an owner-by-foreclosure who acquires a property subject to a residential lease agreement at a fair rent entered into with the prior owner before title is transferred at the trustee's sale. The lease expires 45 days after the date of the trustee's sale.

On expiration of the lease agreement, the owner-by-foreclosure demands the tenant vacate since the lease has expired. The tenant refuses, claiming the owner-by-foreclosure needs to serve the tenant with a 90-day notice to vacate to terminate their right of possession.

May the owner-by-foreclosure file a UD action and succeed in evicting the tenant since the tenant's lease expired after the trustee's sale?

No! All bona fide residential tenants at the time of the foreclosure sale are entitled to remain in possession of their dwelling unit until the expirations of a 90-day notice served on them by the owner, unless a longer period of possession is provided for under:

- an existing lease;
- a Section 8 voucher program entered into prior to the trustee's sale; or
- local rent control ordinances or state law.[22]

The 90-day period applies whether their tenancy was:

- a month-to-month rental agreement;
- an expired lease agreement;
- a tenancy at will; or
- a lease agreement.[23]

A notice to vacate due to domestic violence

A residential tenant who has been, or whose family member has been, the victim of sexual assault, stalking, domestic violence or elder abuse may terminate their tenancy by delivering to their landlord a written 30-day notice to vacate with an attached copy of one of the following documents relating to the sexual assault, stalking, or domestic violence:

- a temporary restraining order;
- an emergency protective order; or

---

20 CCP §1161b
21 CCP §1161b
22 Pub Law 111-22 §702(a)(2)(B); Pub L 111-22 §703 (2)
23 Pub L 111-22 §702 (a)(1)(2)(B)

- a police report.[24]

The notice to vacate needs to be delivered to the landlord within 180 days of the date the corroborating document was issued. Rent is owed for the 30-day period after delivery of the written notice to vacate. On expiration of the 30-day period, the tenant cannot be penalized for ceasing to pay rent.

If the tenant quits the premises within 30 days after delivering the notice to vacate and the premises is rented to another party who takes possession within the 30 day period, the rent due for that period is prorated.

No tenants other than the victim and any family members living in the household are relieved of their obligations under the rental or lease agreement.

---

24 CC §1946.7

A residential or commercial 30-day notice to vacate is used by a landlord or tenant to terminate a periodic tenancy, such as a month-to-month tenancy or a continuing occupancy after a lease expires.

However, a 60-day notice to vacate is used if the property is residential and the tenant has occupied the premises for one year or more.

If the tenant materially breaches the rental agreement, a landlord may use a three-day notice to quit to terminate the tenancy.

A tenant, residential or commercial, who intends to vacate and avoid further liability under a month-to-month rental agreement needs to give 30 days' advance notice to the landlord.

Generally, a landlord is not required to state their reasons in a notice to vacate, or even have good cause for evicting a month-to-month tenant. However, if the tenant's rent is subsidized by the Department of Housing and Urban Development's (HUD) Section 8 housing program, the landlord needs to set forth good cause as the reason for the termination in the 30-day notice to vacate.

An owner-by-foreclosure of a residential property is required to serve a bona fide tenant occupying the property at the time of the foreclosure sale with at least 90 days' notice before the tenant's right of possession is terminated.

**Chapter 29
Summary**

Chapter 29 Key Terms

Quiz 7 Covering Chapters 25-28 is located on page 641.

Chapter 30

Surrender cancels the lease agreement

After reading this chapter, you will be able to:

- identify a surrender as a cancellation of the lease agreement by the landlord when the tenant returns possession of the leased premises;
- use a written surrender to mutually terminate a lease agreement and release the tenant and landlord from any further obligations; and
- distinguish a landlord's inability to collect future rent on a surrender from the landlord's right to collect future rent when a tenant breaches and the landlord forfeits the tenant's right to possession.

Learning Objectives

early-termination fee   surrender

Key Terms

Before a commercial lease expires, consider a tenant who closes out their business operations and vacates the premises, paying no further rent. The landlord serves the tenant with a three-day *notice to pay rent or quit*. [See Form 575 in Chapter 25]

Lost ability to recover future rents

The notice includes a clause declaring a forfeiture of the lease if the tenant fails to pay rent within three days following service of the notice.

The tenant responds to the notice by letter, stating they elect not to pay future rent and accept the landlord's offer to terminate the lease. The key to the premises is returned to the landlord with the letter.

The landlord responds by letter stating:

- neither the landlord nor the tenant owe each other any further obligations under the lease; and

- the tenant is to pay all rent due up to the date the tenant returned the key to the landlord.

The landlord then attempts to relet the premises, but without success.

Later, the landlord makes a demand on the tenant for payment of rents called for in the lease agreement for the entire remaining term of the lease. The landlord claims the forfeiture of the lease in the three-day notice terminated the tenant's right of possession but did not cancel the lease agreement.

The tenant claims the landlord is not entitled to any future rents called for in the lease agreement since the landlord agreed that neither the tenant nor the landlord owed any further obligation under the lease agreement.

May the landlord recover future rents from the tenant based on the lease agreement, notices and letters?

No! The lease agreement was cancelled by the communications agreeing to terminate all obligations under the lease agreement in exchange for possession. Therefore, the lease agreement was no longer enforceable.[1]

Surrender

Continuing our previous example, the tenant's letter "electing to pay no future rent" coupled with the return of the key to the landlord initiated a **surrender.** It signified an implied offer to cancel the lease agreement.

surrender
A mutual cancellation of a lease agreement by the landlord and the tenant, written or by their conduct, when the tenant vacates the leased premises. [See **RPI** Form 587]

The landlord's affirmative response to the tenant's letter foregoing future rents released the tenant from further liability on the lease agreement. The landlord's conduct constituted acceptance of the tenant's offer to cancel the lease agreement obligations.

Editor's note — The declaration of forfeiture did reserve the landlord's right to collect future rents under the lease agreement from the tenant. However, the landlord later effectively cancelled the lease agreement by their conduct in agreeing to the tenant's offer to pay no future rent on return of the keys.[2]

A lease agreement breached and space vacated

Consider a tenant who breaches a commercial lease agreement before the lease expires and vacates the premises without the landlord's service of a *three-day notice to quit* on the tenant. The landlord may respond by taking possession in one of four ways:

- terminate the tenant's *right of possession* and cancel the lease agreement by a *surrender*, then take possession and relet the premises to others or occupy the premises as the owner [See Form 587 accompanying this chapter];
- terminate the tenant's right of possession using a three-day notice containing a *declaration of forfeiture* (or a notice of abandonment),

1 **Desert Plaza Partnership** v. **Waddell** (1986) 180 CA3d 805
2 Calif. Civil Code §1951.2

take possession and relet the premises to mitigate losses before making a demand for payment of future rents [See Chapter 24; see **RPI** Form 575 and 581];

- take possession of the premises and relet it on the tenant's behalf, then collect any monthly losses from the tenant; or

- enforce any *tenant-mitigation provision* in the lease agreement, leaving possession with the tenant to relet the premises to mitigate the tenant's losses. [See Chapter 48]

Only ownership of a real estate interest, such as a leasehold interest, and personal property may be forfeited. However, a contract, such as a lease agreement, is not property. A contract is evidence of rights and obligations. Thus, it may be cancelled, but it cannot be the subject of a forfeiture.

A surrender occurs when:

- a tenant breaches a lease or rental agreement and vacates or intends to vacate the premises; and

- the landlord agrees to accept a return of possession from the tenant in exchange for cancelling the lease agreement.

The cancellation of the lease agreement in a surrender situation occurs by either:

- mutual consent of the landlord and the tenant;[3] or

- operation of law, implied due to the conduct of the landlord.

Editor's note — Avoiding an unintentional surrender is one of the many reasons why a landlord needs to understand the difference between terminating a right of possession (the forfeiture of possession aspect) and the separate act of terminating a lease agreement (the cancellation of the right to future rents). [See Chapter 24]

For a landlord to avoid adverse legal consequences when a tenant prematurely vacates, lease agreements contain a *remedies provision* stating a surrender occurs only if the tenant enters into a written cancellation and waiver agreement. [See **RPI** Form 552 §2.4]

The **Termination of Lease and Surrender Agreement** by RPI provides the writing used to mutually terminate a lease agreement and release the tenant and landlord from any further obligations and liability under the lease agreement. [See Form 587]

Termination of Lease and Surrender Agreement

Lease termination and surrender agreement provisions include:

- the termination date on which the tenant is to quit and surrender possession of the premises to the landlord [See Form 587 §2];

- a release between the landlord and tenant from all claims and obligations, known or unknown, arising out of the lease agreement and possession [See Form 587 §2.1];

---

3   CC §1933(2)

Form 587

Termination
of Lease and
Surrender
Agreement

TERMINATION OF LEASE AND SURRENDER AGREEMENT

NOTE: This form is used by a property manager or landlord when the tenant returns possession of the leased premises and no further obligations remain between the tenant and the landlord, to mutually terminate a lease agreement and release the tenant and landlord from any further obligation and liability under the lease agreement.

DATE: _____, 20_____, at _____, California,
Items left blank or unchecked are not applicable.

FACTS:

1. This mutual lease termination and surrender agreement ("Termination Agreement") pertains to the following Lease Agreement
   1.1 dated _____, 20_____, at _____, California,
   1.2 entered into by _____, as the Tenant,
   1.3 and _____, as the Landlord,
   1.4 regarding real estate referred to as _____
   _____

AGREEMENT:

2. Landlord and Tenant agree the above referenced Lease Agreement is cancelled and terminates on _____, 20_____ ("Termination Date"). Tenant is to quit and surrender possession of the premises to Landlord on the Termination Date in consideration for cancellation of the Lease Agreement.

   2.1 Landlord and Tenant release each other from all claims and obligations, known or unknown, arising out of the Lease Agreement and possession.

   2.2 Tenant to pay Landlord on or before Termination Date the sum of $_____ as further consideration for Landlord's entering into this Termination Agreement.

   2.3 Cancellation of the Lease Agreement is subject to performance of the following conditions (clearance of encumbrances on the tenant's leasehold, fixture, tenant improvements, and title conditions, etc.):
   _____
   _____

   a. ☐ See attached general use addendum. [See **RPI** Form 250]

   2.4 Regarding any subtenant, this Agreement is contingent upon the execution of:
   a. ☐ an amendment to Tenant's sublease agreement with Subtenant on terms and conditions acceptable to Landlord; and
   b. ☐ a release of liability and waiver agreement in favor of Tenant regarding the sublease agreement with Subtenant on terms and conditions acceptable to Tenant.

3. Landlord and Tenant waive any rights provided by Section 1542 of the California Civil Code, which provides: "A general release does not extend to claims which the creditor does not know or suspect to exist in his or her favor at the time of executing the release, which if known by him or her must have materially affected his or her settlement with the debtor."

I agree to the terms stated above.	I agree to the terms stated above.
☐ See Signature Page Addendum. [RPI Form 251]	☐ See Signature Page Addendum. [RPI Form 251]
Date: _____, 20_____	Date: _____, 20_____
Landlord: _____	Tenant: _____
Agent: _____	
Signature: _____	Signature: _____
Address: _____	address: _____
Phone: _____ Cell: _____	Phone: _____ Cell: _____
Fax: _____	Fax: _____
Email: _____	Email: _____

| FORM 587 | 09-13 | ©2016 RPI — Realty Publications, Inc., P.O. BOX 5707, RIVERSIDE, CA 92517 |

- any monetary consideration remaining to be paid by the tenant to the landlord [See Form 587 §2.2];

- a description of any conditions to be performed prior to cancellation, which may include any payment the landlord will make to the tenant, such as a return of deposit, prepaid rent or settlement money on a dispute [See Form 587 §2.3]; and

- conditions pertaining to a subtenant, if any, that needs to be arranged and agreed to. [See Form 587 §2.4]

Consider a tenant who makes a written offer to surrender the leased premises to the landlord.

The landlord believes a new tenant, who will pay more rent for the space than the current tenant, can be quickly located.

Still, the landlord demands an **early-termination fee** equal to three months' rent to cancel the lease agreement. The tenant pays the fee and delivers possession, and the acceptance by the landlord cancels the lease. A surrender has occurred. [See Form 587 §2.2]

Editor's note — Mid-term leases sometimes contain an early-termination provision for a surrender. The provision allows the tenant to cancel the lease agreement on payment of a fee. This termination fee usually is in the amount of two to six months' unearned rent. This is a type of prepayment bonus or liability limitation provision seen in mortgages and purchase agreements.

Under an early termination provision, a surrender functions like a deed-in-lieu of foreclosure that conveys the real estate to the lender (possession returned to the landlord) in exchange for the lender's cancellation of the note obligations (cancellation of the lease agreement).

Now consider a tenant on a lease with a ten-year term. A few years after entering into the lease agreement, the tenant vacates the premises. The tenant removes all of their personal property and returns the key to the landlord. The tenant has no intention of returning and has breached the lease agreement by failing to pay rent.

Since a surrender cancels the landlord's right to future rents due under the lease agreement, the landlord refuses to treat the tenant's return of possession as a surrender.

To avoid a surrender, the landlord promptly informs the tenant they intend to enforce collection of future rent due by the terms of the lease agreement.

Without prior notice to the tenant, the landlord retakes possession, refurbishes the vacated space and leases it to a replacement tenant. The new lease agreement with the replacement tenant is for a lower rent rate than the prior tenant paid under the breached lease. The landlord notifies the prior tenant they have leased the premises to mitigate their loss of rent.

The landlord makes a demand on the prior tenant for the payment of rent. The rent demanded is the difference between:

- the total amount of rents remaining unpaid over the remaining unexpired term of the prior tenant's lease; and
- the amount of rent to be paid during the same period under the new lease by the replacement tenant.

Can the landlord recover the lost rent from the prior tenant who vacated the premises and returned possession to the landlord?

Surrender by mutual consent

early-termination fee
A fee paid to the landlord by the tenant to cancel the lease agreement in exchange for returning possession. [See **RPI** Form 587 §2.2]

Surrender by operation of law

Case in point

Surrender on failure to declare a forfeiture

A tenant breaches their lease agreement. Before the landlord may serve the tenant with a three-day notice containing a declaration of forfeiture provision, the tenant voluntarily vacates the property. Without serving a three-day notice to quit (or a notice of abandonment) and terminating the tenant's right to possession, the landlord takes possession and relets the premises.

Here, the landlord's actions are inconsistent with the tenant's outstanding right of possession. By acting in a manner inconsistent with the tenant's right of possession (which had not been terminated before the landlord retook possession) the underlying lease agreement no longer is enforceable. The landlord's conduct established a surrender.

*Thus, the landlord's right to recover future rents under the lease agreement is eliminated by conduct adverse to their own best interest when they failed to honor the tenant's continued right of possession. The lease agreement now is no longer enforceable. Any losses due to vacancy simply become part of the market risks any landlord assumes as the owner of vacant rental property on expiration of a lease. [**Desert Plaza Partnership v. Waddell** (1986) 180 CA3d 805]*

No! Before entering the space to prepare for reletting the premises, the landlord failed to:

- *terminate the tenancy* by serving a three-day notice with a declaration of forfeiture (or a notice of abandonment); or
- *notify the tenant* they were taking possession of the premises as an agent acting on the tenant's behalf.

The conduct of the landlord at the time they unilaterally took possession to relet the premises violated the tenant's unforfeited and continuing right of possession. Although the landlord did not intend to accept a surrender, they did so by taking possession without first forfeiting the tenant's leasehold (or advising the tenant of the landlord's intent to act on the tenant's behalf to relet the premises).

Here, a surrender by operation of law occurred. The landlord took possession while the tenant still retained their possessory interest in the property as granted by the lease agreement.

Thus, the landlord's interference with the tenant's remaining right of possession constitutes an acceptance by the landlord of an implied offer to surrender initiated by the tenant's vacating the premises.

The result is the tenancy is terminated and the lease agreement cancelled by surrender. This result is avoided when the landlord first serves notice terminating the tenant's right of possession with a declaration of forfeiture provision.[4] [See Case in point, "Surrender on failure to declare a forfeiture"]

---

4 **Dorcich** v. **Time Oil Co.** (1951) 103 CA2d 677

A landlord may not want to terminate the tenancy on evicting the tenant. The landlord might rather retake possession, acting as the tenant's agent to relet the property on the tenant's (rather than the landlord's) behalf.

Here, the landlord omits the declaration of forfeiture from the three-day notice since the landlord intends to leave the tenant's right of possession intact.

Although no longer physically occupying the property, the tenant still owns the leasehold interest in the property and the lease agreement rent remains enforceable as it has not been cancelled. However, the use and occupancy of the premises is now managed by the landlord on the tenant's behalf.

The landlord who intends to take possession and relet the premises as the tenant's agent notifies the tenant about their agency actions twice:

- once before taking possession of the premises; and
- again when the premises is relet.

Even though a tenant fails to pay rent, removes all of their personal property, vacates the leased premises and has no intention of returning, the tenant cannot unilaterally terminate their right to continued possession of the premises, much less escape the obligations to pay future rents called for in the lease agreement.

Until the tenant's right of possession is terminated by a three-day notice containing a declaration of forfeiture provision (or abandonment) served on the tenant by the landlord, no person other than the tenant has the right to occupy the premises.

However, the landlord who does not forfeit the tenant's right of possession may establish themselves as the *agent of the tenant* who has vacated. This is done in an effort to preserve the landlord's reversionary interest from waste.

Consider a tenant who has breached their lease agreement and vacated the premises. The landlord notifies the tenant that the landlord will enter the premises, take possession and relet the premises as the tenant's agent.

The landlord relets the premises for less rent, but for a period extending beyond the expiration of the tenant's lease. The landlord notifies the tenant they have relet the premises on the tenant's behalf.

The landlord then makes a demand on the tenant for the loss in rent resulting from the reletting of the premises at a reduced rent. The tenant refuses to pay since the terms of the lease granted to the new tenant by the landlord exceeded the term of the tenant's remaining right of possession under the breached lease agreement.

Here, the tenant's right of possession which remains unterminated runs only until the expiration of the period fixed by the lease agreement. Had the vacating tenant sought to sublet the premises, the term of the sublease may not extend beyond the expiration date of the tenant's lease.

Repossession on the tenant's behalf

Inconsistent behavior while reletting on tenant's behalf

Thus, the landlord who acts to relet the premises as the tenant's agent for a longer term than the unexpired term remaining on the lease:

- is not renting the premises on behalf of the tenant; and

- has worked a surrender due to conduct inconsistent with the vacating tenant's unexpired and unterminated right of possession.[5]

Maintenance to prevent waste

Now consider a landlord who, on notice to a vacating tenant, takes possession on behalf of the tenant. The landlord maintains and cares for the vacated premises while attempting to relet the premises.

The tenant claims the landlord's care and maintenance of the property constitutes a surrender since the landlord exercised independent control over the premises by their maintenance activity.

However, the landlord has not surrendered the property merely by maintaining it to prevent waste. Acting as the agent of the vacated tenant, the landlord undertakes an obligation to make a good faith effort to lease the premises, called **loss mitigation**. This duty requires the landlord to keep the premises properly maintained. Care and maintenance of the property is activity consistent with the landlord's agency duty owed the tenant when acting on the tenant's behalf.[6]

To avoid adverse legal consequences when a tenant prematurely vacates, lease agreements contain a remedies provision stating a surrender can occur only if the tenant enters into a written cancellation and waiver agreement. [See **RPI** Form 552 §2.4]

However, the landlord's conduct regarding possession in response to a tenant's breach of the lease agreement and vacating of the premises can result in a cancellation of the lease by surrender.

A landlord's conduct supersedes the lease agreement provisions requiring a written agreement to cancel the lease. Landlord/tenant law controls the results of conduct, barring application of contract law principles that ignore the landlord's inconsistent conduct.

---

5 **Welcome** v. **Hess** (1891) 90 C 507
6 **B.K.K. Company** v. **Schultz** (1970) 7 CA3d 786

A surrender occurs when:

- a tenant breaches a lease or rental agreement and vacates or intends to vacate the premises; and

- the landlord agrees to accept a return of possession from the tenant in exchange for cancelling the lease agreement.

The cancellation of the lease agreement in a surrender situation occurs by either:

- mutual consent of the landlord and the tenant; or

- operation of law, implied due to the conduct of the landlord.

When a tenant breaches the lease agreement and vacates the premises without the landlord's service of a three-day notice to quit on the tenant, the landlord may respond to possession in one of four ways:

- terminate the tenant's right of possession and cancel the lease agreement by a surrender, then relet the premises to others or occupy the premises as the owner;

- terminate the tenant's right of possession using a three-day notice containing a declaration of forfeiture (or a notice of abandonment), take possession and relet the premises to mitigate losses before making a demand for payment of future rents;

- take possession of the premises and relet it on the tenant's behalf, then collect any monthly losses from the tenant; or

- enforce any tenant-mitigation provision in the lease agreement, leaving the tenant in possession to relet the premises to mitigate the tenant's losses.

Chapter 30 Summary

Chapter 30 Key Terms

Quiz 8 Covering Chapters 29-32 is located on page 641.

Notes:

Chapter
31

Notice of belief of abandonment

After reading this chapter, you will be able to:
- analyze whether the tenant's conduct constitutes an abandonment of the premises;
- determine whether an abandonment is the best method for terminating the tenancy; and
- initiate the procedure necessary to terminate the tenant's right to possession.

Learning Objectives

abandonment	**surrender**
notice of right to reclaim personal property	**tenant-mitigatin provision**

Key Terms

A tenant who is delinquent in rent payments due under their lease agreement has vacated the premises. The tenant has not been served a notice to quit. Here, the landlord may respond in one of several ways to terminate the tenancy and retake possession.

An alternative forfeiture

The landlord may treat the tenant's right to possession as terminated and the lease agreement as canceled. This is known as a **surrender**.

Alternatively, the landlord may treat the tenant's right to possession as terminated by serving a three-day notice to pay or quit which contains a declaration of forfeiture of the right of possession, or serving an **abandonment** notice. After serving either of these notices, the landlord may enforce the tenant's financial obligations for rent and other amounts due under the lease agreement.

surrender
A mutual cancellation of a lease agreement by the landlord and the tenant, written or by their conduct, when the tenant vacates the leased premises. [See **RPI** Form 587]

abandonment
A unilateral termination of a tenancy by forfeiture, delivered by the landlord based on notices from the landlord. [See **RPI** Form 581]

The landlord may also take possession without terminating the tenant's leasehold interest by serving notice on the tenant stating the landlord is acting as the tenant's agent to relet the property.

Another option remaining for the landlord is to treat the lease as continuing if the lease agreement contains a statutory tenant-mitigation provision. Under this provision and treatment, the landlord may recover rent as it becomes due without repossessing or reletting the property.[1]

Statutory abandonment notice

The *abandonment* rules, like *surrender* rules, apply to both residential and commercial property. The commonality between surrender and abandonment is the tenant's breach of the lease and vacating of the premises.

They differ, however, on the methods for terminating the tenant's right to possession and handling the landlord's rights under the lease agreement regarding the collection of future rent. A surrender is a mutual termination agreed to by tenant and landlord, while an abandonment is a unilateral termination by forfeiture based on notices from the landlord.

Further, abandonment is to be distinguished from a three-day notice containing a forfeiture declaration. Both methods retain the landlord's rights to enforce collection of future rents under the lease agreement while terminating the tenant's right to retake possession. However, their differences are in the time that needs to pass after serving the notices until the landlord may retake possession.

An abandonment may be noticed and carried out when a tenant:

- voluntarily vacates the leased premises with no intention to reoccupy; and
- fails to pay rent with no intention to further perform their obligations on the lease agreement.

However, a tenant does not terminate their lease agreement, nullifying its enforcement, by breaching the lease and vacating the premises. The landlord may terminate the tenant's leasehold right to possession in response to the breach and vacating of the property, permitting the landlord to retake possession.

For the landlord to proceed with the abandonment process, they are to first confirm the tenant's intent to abandon the property and terminate their right to possession. The tenant's intent is confirmed by the landlord serving a statutory abandonment notice on the tenant. [See Form 581 accompanying this chapter]

Notice of Belief of Abandonment

A **Notice of Belief of Abandonment** may be served on a tenant only if:

- the tenant has vacated the premises;

---

1 Calif. Civil Code §1951.4

- the tenant's rent payment is due and unpaid for a period of at least 14 days prior to service of the Notice of Belief of Abandonment; and

- the landlord reasonably believes the tenant has abandoned the premises.[2]

If the tenant's rent due on the first of the month has become delinquent, no portion has been paid and the tenant no longer occupies the property, the landlord may serve the notice on the 15th day of the month. Note that a three-day notice to pay or quit will have already terminated the tenancy and allowed the landlord to enter and take possession of the space.

The notice of abandonment may be served on the tenant by either:

- personal service; or

- first-class mail sent to the tenant's last known address and any other addresses known to the landlord where the tenant might reasonably receive the notice.[3]

If the abandonment notice is personally served on the tenant, the tenant has 15 days after the date of service to respond before the notice expires. If the abandonment notice is served by mail, the notice expires 18 days after the date the notice is deposited in the mail.[4]

When personal service cannot be made, the service requirements for the *Notice of Belief of Abandonment* are different from service requirements for three-day notices. [See Chapter 27]

Once served, the notice of abandonment expires in 15 days unless in the interim the tenant:

- tenders all or partial payment of rent; or

- rejects the abandonment in writing.

On expiration of the notice, the tenant's right to possession is terminated if no rejection or rents are received by the landlord.

Having terminated the tenancy by expiration of the abandonment notice, the landlord may:

- *enter the premises* to remove any personal property left behind by the tenant and relet the premises as the landlord;[5] and

- *collect past and future rents* from the tenant as provided in the lease agreement, less any rents received on reletting.[6]

After the tenant has been served with a notice of abandonment, the tenant may reoccupy the premises. Reoccupying will not stop the abandonment procedure or avoid termination of the tenant's right to possession on

Service of abandonment notice

Tenant's response ends abandonment

2 CC §1951.3(b)
3 CC §1951.3(c)
4 CC §1951.3(d)
5 CC §1954
6 CC §1951.2(a)

expiration of the notice. Once served, further steps beyond merely reoccupying the property need to be taken by the tenant to nullify the abandonment procedure.[7]

After an abandonment notice has been served, the tenant can only disavow an abandonment and avoid the termination of their right to possession by doing one of the following:

- showing the landlord cannot have justifiably believed the tenant had abandoned the premises when the notice was served;

- proving rent was not due prior to 14 days before service of the notice or, if due, was not yet delinquent at the time the notice was served;

- proving some or all of delinquent rent was received by the landlord during the 14-day period preceding the service of the notice;

- paying some or all of the past due rent prior to expiration of the notice; or

- handing a written notice to the landlord before the abandonment notice expires stating the tenant has no intention to abandon the premises and including an address for service on the tenant by certified mail of an unlawful detainer (UD) action.[8]

Thus, when a portion or all of the delinquent rent is tendered, or a statement of no intent to abandon is delivered to the landlord by the tenant prior to the expiration of the abandonment notice, a UD action based on abandonment will fail.

If the tenant reoccupies the premises after the notice is served — before or after its expiration and without paying rent or delivering a statement of no intent to abandon — the tenant may be evicted by a UD action on expiration of the abandonment notice.

Concurrent service with three-day notice

Both a three-day notice to pay or quit (with forfeiture declaration) and a notice of abandonment may be served concurrently under separate proof of service statements. [See Chapter 26]

Since both notices terminate the leasehold on their expiration, a tenant who reoccupies or, on a commercial property tenders only a partial payment of rent that the landlord accepts, may be dealt with quickly by filing a UD action on expiration of the three-day notice.

However, under a UD action based on a three-day notice, the landlord needs to prove their case for eviction.

Conversely, at a UD trial based on a notice of abandonment where the tenant has reoccupied, the tenant needs to prove they may remain on the premises by showing:

- no delinquency existed when the notice was served;

---

7 CC §1951.3(e)
8 CC §1951.3(e)

- a portion or all of the rent was paid within four weeks prior to the expiration of the notice; or
- they delivered the landlord a written statement of their intent to occupy.

Tenants who vacate the leased premises occasionally leave significant personal property behind. When a landlord is confronted with a unit or space vacated by the tenant, but loaded with abandoned personal property, the notice of abandonment may be an efficient way to terminate the tenant's right to possession. Thus, the landlord may take possession on termination of the tenancy without concern for claims by the tenant.

Before serving a notice of abandonment, a residential landlord may temporarily enter the vacated premises to establish their reasonable belief the tenant abandoned the premises.[9]

Even if the tenant has left personal items behind, a landlord's observations while inside the unit or space may lead them to reasonably believe the premises is abandoned.[10]

If the landlord exercises their right to temporarily enter the unit when a tenant appears to have abandoned it, the landlord may inventory the personal property so it can be itemized in the abandonment notice.[11]

Abandoned personal property poses a problem regarding its removal (by the landlord) and recovery (by the tenant). When personal property is left behind by a tenant who has vacated, the landlord is responsible for notifying the tenant of their **right to reclaim** the personal property.[12]

Notice of the tenant's *right to reclaim* personal property may be included in the notice of abandonment.[13] [See Form 581]

When combined in one form, the notice of right to reclaim personal property and the abandonment notice expire simultaneously.

The combined abandonment and right to reclaim property notices are appropriate when the landlord chooses to leave the tenant's personal property on the premises until abandonment of the real estate and the personal property is established by expiration of the notices.

Thus, the landlord avoids moving the tenant's belongings twice by serving the abandonment notice, rather than by preparing both a three-day notice to pay and a later notice to reclaim personal property.

Abandoned personal property

Removal and recovery

notice of right to reclaim personal property
A landlord's notice mailed to a former tenant informing the tenant of their right to reclaim or abandon personal property remaining on the premises. [See **RPI** Form 583 and 584]

---

9 CC §1954(a)
10 CC §1951.3(e)(2)
11 CC §1983
12 CC §1983
13 CC §1991

On termination of the tenancy by expiration of the notice of abandonment, the landlord is entitled to possession of the premises. The landlord may then enter the unit to take possession, refurbish it and relet it to a new tenant without concern for the tenant's terminated possessory rights.[14]

The landlord needs to first terminate the tenant's right to possession by a three-day notice, 30-day notice to vacate or abandonment notice. If the tenant's right to possession is not first terminated, the landlord has interfered with the leasehold estate held by the tenant to occupy the space or unit.

Thus, the landlord who does not first act to terminate the unexpired tenancy before removing personal items or reletting the premises may find themselves on the wrong end of a viable forcible detainer action.[15]

Tenant-mitigation provision

If the tenant's lease agreement, residential or commercial, contains a statutory **tenant-mitigation provision**, the landlord may:

- treat the tenant's leasehold rights to possession as continuing without the landlord taking possession; and

- enforce their landlord rights to recover rent from the tenant as it becomes due under the lease agreement.[16]

tenant-mitigation provision
A provision in a commercial lease agreement allowing the landlord to leave the tenant's leasehold and the lease agreement intact on the tenant's breach, and then recover rent from the tenant for the life of the lease without the landlord first taking steps to mitigate losses. [See **RPI** Form 552 §21.1]

When a residential or commercial tenant breaches their lease agreement and vacates the leased premises, the tenant-mitigation remedy may be enforced when:

- the tenant-mitigation remedy is included as a provision in the lease agreement; and

- the assignment and subletting (alienation) provision in the lease agreement does not prohibit the tenant's subletting or assignment of the leasehold interest.[17] [See Form 596 accompanying this chapter]

The landlord may treat the leasehold and lease agreement as continuing and recover rents as they become due if the lease agreement contains a provision worded substantially as follows:

> *"The lessor has the remedy described in California Civil Code Section 1951.4 (lessor may continue lease in effect after lessee's breach and abandonment and recover rent as it becomes due, if lessee has right to sublet or assign, subject only to reasonable limitations)."*[18]

Shift of responsibility

A landlord's use of the tenant-mitigation remedy shifts the responsibility for mitigating their losses under the lease agreement to the tenant when the tenant vacates the premises and breaches the lease agreement. Instead of the landlord being required to mitigate their loss of rents by reletting the space as a requisite for qualifying to collect future rents, the tenant is to take necessary steps to mitigate their liability to the landlord.

---

14 CC §1954
15 Calif. Code of Civil Procedure §1160
16 CC §1951.4
17 CC §1951.4(b)
18 CC §1951.4(a)

Form 581

Notice of
Belief of
Abandonment

NOTICE OF BELIEF OF ABANDONMENT
Residential or Commercial Property

NOTE: This form is used by a commercial property manager or landlord when rent has been due and unpaid for 14 consecutive days or more and the landlord believes the tenant has vacated the leased premises and left personal property, to commence the landlord-initiated personal property disposition process and advise the tenant of their right to reclaim or abandon it.

DATE: _____, 20_____, at _____, California,
To Tenant: _____
Items left blank or unchecked are not applicable.
FACTS:
1.   You are a Tenant under the rental or lease agreement
   1.1   dated _____, 20_____, at _____, California,
   1.2   entered into by _____, as the Tenant,
   1.3   and _____, as the Landlord,
   1.4   regarding real estate referred to as _____
   _____

YOU ARE HEREBY INFORMED:
Rent on the leased real estate has been due and unpaid for 14 consecutive days or more, **AND** Landlord believes you have abandoned the property. Personal property remains on the premises as described in Section 6.
NOTICE:
2.   This notice expires unless you respond by _____, 20_____, which date is at least 15 days after this notice was personally served, or 18 days after this notice was sent by first class mail, postage prepaid, or emailed.
3.   On expiration of this notice, the real estate will be considered abandoned, your right to possession terminated, and all remaining personal property will be disposed of under Section 8 below.
   3.1   Landlord reserves the right to collect future rent losses allowed by California Civil Code §1951.2.
4.   **YOU MAY AVOID THIS NOTICE,** if before it expires and at the address below, Landlord receives your written notice stating:
   4.1   Your intent not to abandon the real estate, **AND**
   4.2   An address where you may be served by certified mail in any action for unlawful detainer of the real property.
5.   **YOU MAY AVOID DISPOSAL OF PERSONAL PROPERTY** by doing the following before expiration of this notice:
   5.1   Pay the reasonable cost of removal and storage of all the personal property [See **RPI** Form 582-1]; **AND**
   5.2   Take possession of the personal property.
6.   You may minimize the cost of storage if you claim your personal property by:
   _____
7.   You may claim the personal property at _____
   _____
8.   The personal property to be claimed or disposed of is valued as:
   8.1   ☐ Worth more than $700. If you fail to reclaim the property, it will be sold at a public sale after published notice of the sale. You have the right to bid on the property at this sale. After the property is sold and the cost of storage, advertising and sale are deducted, the remaining money will be handed to the county. You may claim the remaining money within one year after the county receives the money.
   8.2   ☐ Worth less than $700. This property is believed to be worth less than $700. Therefore, it may be kept, sold or destroyed without further notice if you fail to reclaim it prior to expiration of this notice. [Calif. CC §1988]
9.   You are required by agreement to pay past due rent. Failure to pay can lead to court proceedings against you.

Date: _____, 20_____
Landlord/Agent: _____

Signature: _____
Address: _____

Phone: _____   Fax: _____

FORM 581   01-13   ©2016 RPI — Realty Publications, Inc., P.O. BOX 5707, RIVERSIDE, CA 92517

When the landlord chooses to enforce the tenant-mitigation remedy, the landlord may engage in the following activities without working a termination of the tenant's right to possession or a surrender of the lease agreement:

- maintenance to preserve the premises from waste;

- appointment of a receiver (by a court) to protect the tenant's interest; or

- the reasonable withholding of consent to an assignment or subletting.[19]

The landlord who includes the *tenant-mitigation provision* in their lease agreement usually is an absentee owner who enters into a long-term, net lease agreement with a creditworthy, well-established user.

---

19 CC §1951.4(c)

RECORDING REQUESTED BY

AND WHEN RECORDED MAIL TO

Name

Street
Address

City &
State

SPACE ABOVE THIS LINE FOR RECORDER'S USE

ASSIGNMENT OF LEASE
By Tenant/Lessee

NOTE: This form is used by an escrow officer or tenant when the buyer of a tenant's leasehold interest in a property takes possession and assumes the tenant's rights and obligations under a rental or lease agreement, to transfer ownership of the tenant's leasehold interest to the buyer.

DATE: _____, 20____, at _____, California.
Items left blank or unchecked are not applicable.

1. This assignment transfers the Lessee's interest in the lease dated _____, 20_____.
   1.1 entered into by _____, as the Lessor, and
   1.2 _____, as the Lessee.
   1.3 recorded on _____, _____, as Instrument No. _____
       in the records of _____ County, California,
   1.4 regarding real estate referred to as _____
       _____.

AGREEMENT:

2. Lessee hereby assigns all of Lessee's interest in the above described lease to
   _____, as the Assignee.

3. Assignee hereby assumes and agrees to timely perform all Lessee's obligations under the lease.
   3.1 This assumption by Assignee is made for the benefit of Landlord under the lease.
   3.2 If Assignee or its successors default in performance of this assumption and Lessee not be released from Lessee liability on the lease, the amount of the default will be a lien in favor of Lessee on the Lessee's interest and Lessee may elect to foreclose on the interest assigned to Assignee under California Civil Code §§2924 et seq.
   3.3 The Assignee will indemnify Lessee against any claim, liability, loss, costs, attorney fees, and other damages incurred by Lessee under the lease.
   3.4 If an action is instituted to enforce this assumption the prevailing party to receive their attorney fees.

I agree to the terms stated above.	**I agree to the terms stated above.**
☐ See attached Signature Page Addendum. [RPI Form 251]	☐ See attached Signature Page Addendum. [RPI Form 251]
Date: _____, 20_____	Date: _____, 20_____
Lessee: _____	Assignee: _____

A notary public or other officer completing this certificate verifies only the identity of the individual who signed the document to which this certificate is attached, and not the truthfulness, accuracy, or validity of that document.

STATE OF CALIFORNIA
COUNTY OF _____
On _____ before me, _____
personally appeared _____ *(Name and title of officer)*
who proved to me on the basis of satisfactory evidence to be the person(s) whose name(s) is/are subscribed to the within instrument and acknowledged to me that he/she/they executed the same in his/her/their authorized capacity(ies), and that by his/her/their signature(s) on the instrument the person(s), or the entity upon behalf of which the person(s) acted, executed the instrument.

(This area for official notarial seal)

I certify under PENALTY OF PERJURY under the laws of the State of California that the foregoing paragraph is true and correct.

WITNESS my hand and official seal.

Signature: _____
(Signature of notary public)

FORM 596   03-15   ©2016 RPI — Realty Publications, Inc., P.O. BOX 5707, RIVERSIDE, CA

The landlord entering into a long-term net lease intends to receive rent payments without expending time and energy managing the property. The tenant usually agrees to pay all costs of ownership of the property.

Assignment or subletting restrictions

Now consider a commercial lease agreement containing the statutory tenant-mitigation provision.

The lease agreement also contains a subletting or assignment provision calling for the landlord's consent, which will not be unreasonably withheld. The assignment provision also calls for the payment of money as a condition for the landlord's consent.[20] [See Form 596]

---

20 CC § 1995.250

A separate lease cancellation provision in the lease agreement further permits the landlord to cancel the lease agreement on their receipt of a request from the tenant to consent to an assignment under the assignment provision.[21]

The tenant stops paying rent and vacates the property.

The landlord elects the remedy available to them under the statutory tenant-mitigation provision in the lease agreement.

The tenant, being responsible for reletting the premises, locates a replacement tenant. The tenant notifies the landlord of their intent to assign the lease and requests the landlord's consent.

On receiving the request for consent to assign, the landlord sends the tenant a notice canceling the lease agreement as permitted by the lease cancellation provision in the lease agreement.

The tenant claims the landlord may not terminate the lease since the landlord's ability to refuse consent is subject to a standard of reasonableness due to the tenant-mitigation provision.

However, the landlord's cancellation of the lease under the lease cancellation provision is neither reasonable nor unreasonable. The lease cancellation provision relieves the tenant who has vacated the premises and breached the lease of any further responsibility under the tenant-mitigation provision in the lease.

Cancellation of the lease agreement terminates the tenant's right to possession and with it their ability to assign their leasehold interest. This creates a "catch-22" for the opportunistic tenant with a leasehold interest of more rental value than the rent obligations due under the lease agreement.[22]

Assignment or subletting restrictions, cont'd

21 CC § 1995.320

22 **Carma Developers, Inc.** v. **Marathon Development California, Inc.** (1992) 2 C4th 342

Chapter 31 Summary

Abandonment rules, like surrender rules, apply to both residential and commercial property. The commonality between surrender and abandonment is the tenant's breach of the lease and vacating of the premises.

They differ, however, on the methods for terminating the tenant's right to possession and handling the landlord's rights under the lease agreement regarding the collection of future rent. A surrender is a mutual termination agreed to by tenant and landlord, while an abandonment is a unilateral termination by forfeiture based on notices from the landlord.

Further, abandonment is to be distinguished from a three-day notice containing a forfeiture declaration. Both methods retain the landlord's rights to enforce collection of future rents under the lease agreement while terminating the tenant's right to retake possession. However, their differences are in the time that needs to pass after serving the notices until the landlord may retake possession.

Chapter 31 Key Terms

Quiz 8 Covering Chapters 29-32 is located on page 641.

Personal property recovered by tenant

After reading this chapter, you will be able to:

- take the proper procedural steps to notify a tenant who left personal property on the premises when they vacated;
- properly handle personal property remaining on the premise after a tenant vacates; and
- understand the requirement to sell abandoned personal property at public sale when the items are valued at $700 or more.

Learning Objectives

landlord-initiated disposition procedure	**notice to landlord to surrender personal property**
notice of right to reclaim personal property	**reasonable belief**
	tenant-initiated recovery procedure

Key Terms

A tenant vacates a rental property, residential or commercial, leaving behind personal belongings.

The tenant vacated because their right of possession had been terminated by expiration of a three-day notice to quit with a provision declaring a forfeiture of the leasehold. The space is immediately re-rented by the property manager and needs to be made ready for the new tenant.

The property manager removes the tenant's belongings from the leased space and stores them in a place of safekeeping. The value of the personal property is determined by the property manager to be less than $700.

Reclaim it on notice or lose it

notice of right to reclaim personal property
A landlord's notice mailed to a former tenant informing the tenant of their right to reclaim or abandon personal property remaining on the premises. [See **RPI** Form 583 and 584]

The property manager immediately mails (or emails) the tenant a notice, called a **notice of right to reclaim personal property**, which:

- describes each item or lot of personal property left on the premises; and
- advises the tenant that the personal property will be discarded if not reclaimed by the tenant within 18 days of mailing the notice.[1] [See Form 584 accompanying this chapter]

Editor's note — Residential landlords serving a tenant with a notice to vacate, or a notice of the tenant's right to request a joint pre-expiration inspection of the property, will include a statement notifying the tenant of their right to reclaim abandoned personal property.

The notice to reclaim property expires without a response from the tenant. The property manager disposes of the tenant's belongings.

Later, the tenant sends the property manager a letter requesting the property manager arrange for them to pick up their personal property. The property manager ignores the tenant's late response and does nothing. The tenant then demands payment for the value of the items left behind.

Here, the landlord is not liable for the value of the personal property left in the unit and unclaimed by the tenant. The property manager followed the statutory procedure for notice and disposal of property estimated to be worth less than $700.[2]

The statutory notice procedure:

- provides the tenant with time in which to reclaim their personal property; and
- protects the landlord from liability on disposition of the personal property if the tenant fails to respond prior to expiration of the notice to reclaim.

Removal of personal property

Before removing a tenant's personal property from a vacant unit, a property manager needs to be legally entitled to enter and take possession of the unit. [See Chapter 4]

The property manager can enter, take possession and dispose of a tenant's personal property when the tenant's right of possession has expired or been terminated by forfeiture. [See Chapter 33]

Returning personal property

Two separate statutory procedures exist for the return of personal property left on the premises by a tenant. One is initiated by the landlord or property manager, the other by the tenant.

Residential and commercial landlords and their property managers may initiate (and control) the process of returning or disposing of the tenant's personal property. The *notice of right to reclaim personal property* prepared

1 Calif. Civil Code §1983
2 CC §§1982, 1984

Form 584

Notice of Right to Reclaim Personal Property

NOTICE OF RIGHT TO RECLAIM PERSONAL PROPERTY
To Residential Tenant After Termination of Tenancy

NOTE: This form is used by a residential property manager or landlord when a tenant has vacated the premises and left personal property behind, to advise the tenant the personal property will be discarded if not reclaimed by the tenant by paying the cost of removal and storage.

DATE: _____, 20_____, at _____, California,
TO FORMER TENANT:
Name: _____
Address: _____

Items left blank or unchecked are not applicable.
FACTS:
1. You were a Tenant under a rental or lease agreement
    1.1 dated _____, at _____, California,
    1.2 entered into by _____, as the Tenant,
    1.3 and _____, as the Landlord,
    1.4 regarding real estate referred to as _____
         _____

NOTICE:
2. When you vacated the premises referenced above on _____, 20_____, the following personal property
    remained _____
    _____
    _____

3. You may claim the personal property at _____
    _____

4. **YOU MAY AVOID DISPOSAL OF PERSONAL PROPERTY** by doing the following before expiration of this notice:
    4.1 Pay the reasonable cost of removal and storage of all the personal property [See RPI Form 582-1]; **AND**
    4.2 Take possession of the personal property.
5. This notice expires unless you respond by _____, 20_____, which date is at least 15 days after this notice
    was personally served, or 18 days after this notice was sent by first class mail, postage prepaid, or emailed.
6. You may minimize the cost of storage if you claim your personal proprty by:
    _____
    (Date not less than two days after Tenant vacated premises)
7. **The personal property to be claimed or disposed of is valued as:**
    7.1 ☐ Worth more than $700. If you fail to reclaim the property, it will be sold at a public sale after published notice
         of the sale. You have the right to bid on the property at this sale. After the property is sold and the cost of
         storage, advertising and sale are deducted, the remaining money will be handed to the county. You may claim
         the remaining money within one year after the county receives the money.
    7.2 ☐ Worth less than $700. This property is believed to be worth less than $700. Therefore, it may be kept, sold or
         destroyed without further notice if you fail to reclaim it prior to expiration of this notice.

This statement is true correct.
Date: _____, 20_____
Landlord/Agent: _____ CalBRE #:_____

Signature: _____
Address: _____

Phone: _____ Cell: _____
Fax: _____
Email: _____

FORM 584	01-13	©2016 RPI — Realty Publications, Inc., P.O. BOX 5707, RIVERSIDE, CA 92517

---

by the property manager needs to be personally served or mailed to the tenant who vacated and left the personal property. The notice advises the tenant of their right to reclaim or abandon the personal property. This process is called the **landlord-initiated disposition procedure**. [See **RPI** Form 581 and Form 584]

landlord-initiated disposition procedure
The process of a landlord mailing a notice of the right to reclaim personal property to a tenant who vacated and left personal property on the premises. [See **RPI** Form 581 and 584]

notice to landlord to surrender personal property
A written request submitted by a former tenant to a landlord for the return of personal property left in the vacated unit. [See **RPI** Form 582]

tenant-initiated recovery procedure
The recovery process initiated by a tenant to retrieve personal property from a landlord within 18 days after vacating rental property. [See **RPI** Form 582]

The other procedure allows a residential tenant acting within 18 days of vacating the premises to initiate a return of personal property they left behind. By handing or mailing to the landlord or property manager a **notice to landlord to surrender personal property,** the tenant may reclaim personal items left behind. This is called the **tenant-initiated recovery procedure**.[3] [See Form 582 accompanying this chapter]

The property manager is not required to use the landlord-initiated disposition procedure when the tenant leaves personal property behind.[4]

However, a property manager who sells or disposes of a tenant's personal property by other than these two procedures can be challenged for their handling of the belongings.

For example, a tenant claims their personal property was left behind inadvertently, not abandoned. The property manager is not entitled to sell or dispose of the tenant's personal property unless the property manager first establishes the tenant's actual intent is not to reclaim the property, but to abandon it.

The preferred method for establishing the tenant's intent to abandon the property left behind is the landlord-initiated disposition procedure. The tenant is notified of their right to reclaim the property they left behind and their need to respond to avoid its disposal. [See **RPI** Form 581 and Form 584]

Residential tenant-initiated recovery

Only a residential tenant may deliver to the landlord or the landlord's agent a written request for the return of personal property left in the vacated unit, called a *notice to landlord to surrender personal property*. [See Form 582]

The residential tenant's request for the landlord's release of belongings the tenant left behind needs to:

- be written;
- be mailed or handed to the landlord or property manager within 18 days after they vacate the unit;
- include the tenant's current mailing address;
- contain an identifiable description of the personal property left behind;
- be received by the landlord or property manager while they are in control or possession of the personal property; and
- be received by the landlord or property manager before they have mailed a *notice of right to reclaim personal property*, commencing the landlord-initiated disposition procedure.[5]

Within five days of receiving the tenant's notice to surrender personal property, the property manager mails, emails or hands the tenant a written

---

3 CC §1965
4 CC §1981
5 CC §1965(a)

Form 582

Notice to
Landlord to
Surrender
Personal
Property

NOTICE TO LANDLORD TO SURRENDER PERSONAL PROPERTY
For Use by Residential Tenants Only

NOTE: This form is used by a tenant when they have left personal property on the premises and the landlord has not begun the disposition process, to initiate a return of personal property they left behind within 18 days of vacating the premises and reclaim it within 72 hours after payment of removal and storage fees.

DATE: _____, 20_____, at _____, California,
To Landlord: _____
Items left blank or unchecked are not applicable.
FACTS:
1. I am a former Tenant under a residential rental or lease agreement
    1.1   dated _____, at _____, California,
    1.2   entered into by _____, as the Tenant,
    1.3   and _____, as the Landlord,
    1.4   regarding real estate referred to as _____
        _____.

NOTICE:
2. Within eighteen (18) days prior to mailing or handing this notice to Landlord, I vacated and delivered possession of the premises to Landlord; or
3. This notice is a request for Landlord to surrender to me personal property not owned by Landlord and described below which was left on the vacated premises.
4. I understand:
    4.1   This notice must be mailed within eighteen (18) days after I vacated the premises.
    4.2   Landlord or the Landlord's Manager must have control or possession of the personal property at the time the Landlord actually receives this notice.
    4.3   I will pay all reasonable costs actually incurred by Landlord for the removal and storage of the personal property as a condition for the release and return of the personal property.
    4.4   Landlord will provide a written itemized demand for payment of reasonable removal and storage fees within five (5) days of actual receipt of this notice unless the property is first returned. The demand for payment of removal and storage fees will be mailed to the address given below or handed to me personally.
    4.5   I will claim and remove the personal property at a reasonable time mutually agreed upon by Landlord and myself to occur within 72 hours after my payment of reasonable removal and storage fees demanded by Landlord.
5. Description of personal property to be reclaimed _____
    _____
    _____
    _____
    _____

This statement is true correct.
Date: _____, 20_____
Tenant: _____

Signature: _____
Current mailing address: _____

Phone: _____ Cell: _____
Fax: _____
Email: _____
For Landlord/Manager's use:
Date Received: _____

By: _____

FORM 582   01-13   ©2016 RPI — Realty Publications, Inc., P.O. BOX 5707, RIVERSIDE, CA 92517

---

demand for reasonable removal and storage costs. This written demand itemizes the costs for removal and storage to be paid before the tenant can remove the property.[6] [See **RPI** Form 582-1]

The tenant or other owner of the personal property is not required to pay any storage costs if:

- their personal property remained on the rented premises; and
- they reclaim their personal property within two days of vacating the premises.

Once the tenant has received notice, it is then the tenant's responsibility to contact the property manager and arrange a mutually agreeable date, time

---

6 CC §1965(a)(3)

and location for the tenant to claim and remove their personal property. However, the tenant or the tenant's agent needs to remove the personal belongings within 72 hours after the tenant pays storage charges demanded by the property manager.[7]

After a tenant mails the property manager a request to surrender personal property, the property manager might receive another request for the same items from the tenant's roommate, a secured creditor or other person with an interest in the property.

The first request received by the property manager controls the return of the property left behind.[8]

The landlord is not obligated to the roommate or anyone else who makes a later request for the same personal belongings.

Which process controls

The tenant-initiated process for residential rentals does not apply if the property manager first mails, emails or personally delivers the notice to the tenant before the landlord or the property manager receives the tenant's notice to surrender personal property.[9]

But what if the property manager's notice to reclaim property and the tenant's request to surrender the property pass in the mail?

The landlord-initiated process begins the moment the property manager deposits the notice of the tenant's right to reclaim property in the mail (first-class, postage prepaid). The tenant-initiated process does not begin until the property manager personally receives the tenant's request. [10]

The property manager who neglects to mail the notice before actually receiving a tenant's request is required to respond to the tenant's request. Under abandonment rules, the landlord no longer controls disposition.

Conversely, if the property manager can show they deposited either the *notice of abandonment* (which covers both the rented real property and the tenant's personal property) or the notice to reclaim personal property in the mail before they actually received the tenant's notice to surrender, the tenant abides by the landlord-initiated disposition procedure. [See Chapter 24]

Residential landlord violations

Consider a residential tenant who has vacated and timely hands the property manager a notice to surrender personal items they left behind.

The property manager makes a demand on the tenant to pay removal and storage costs. The tenant promptly pays the removal and storage costs.

---

7 CC §1965(a)(4)
8 CC §1965(d)
9 CC §1965(c)
10 CC §1983

NOTICE OF RIGHT TO RECLAIM PERSONAL PROPERTY
To Others with an Interest in Property Left by Residential Tenant

NOTE: This form is used by a residential property manager or landlord when a tenant has vacated the premises and left personal property behind, to advise others the landlord believes have any ownership interest in the personal property that it will be discarded if not reclaimed by paying the cost of removal and storage.

DATE: _____, 20____, at _____, California.

TO: (Name) _____
(Address) _____

Items left blank or unchecked are not applicable.

NOTICE:

1. This notice to claim personal property you may have an interest in expires on _____, 20____, which date is at least 15 days after this notice was personally served on you, or 18 days after this notice was sent by first class mail, postage prepaid, to your last known address.

2. When our former Tenant named _____,
vacated premises known as _____
_____
on _____, 20____, the following personal property remained _____
_____
_____
_____

3. If you have an interest in any of this personal property, you may claim it at _____
_____

4. You need to pay the cost of storage on or before taking possession of the personal property you claim. [See **RPI** Form 582-1]

5. You may minimize the cost of storage if you claim your personal property by: _____
_____
(Date not less than two days after Tenant vacated premises)

6. Unless you take possession of the personal property you have an interest in prior to the expiration of this notice, the personal property not claimed will be sold at a public sale by competitive bidding. [Calif. CC §1988

This statement is true and correct.
Date: _____, 20____
Landlord/Agent: _____ CalBRE #:_____

Signature: _____
Address: _____

Phone: _____ Cell: _____
Fax: _____
Email: _____

FORM 584-1   01-13   ©2016 **RPI — Realty Publications, Inc.**, P.O. BOX 5707, RIVERSIDE, CA 92517

If the property manager fails to hand over the items within 72 hours after the tenant (or tenant's agent) pays storage and removal fees, the landlord is liable for:

- damages for the value of the personal items;
- $250 for each violation; and
- attorney fees.[11]

This tenant-initiated procedure is entirely avoided when the property manager merely sends by first-class mail either the notice of abandonment (both real estate and personal property) or a notice to reclaim personal property before they receive the tenant's notice to surrender the property. The notice to reclaim personal property may also be emailed to the tenant. [See **RPI** Form 581 and Form 584]

11 CC §1965(e)

Landlord-initiated abandonment

On mailing or personally delivering the notice of abandonment to the tenant, a residential or commercial property manager commences the landlord-initiated disposition process. [See **RPI** Form 581]

As an alternative to the abandonment procedure, the property manager may deliver a notice to reclaim personal property to the tenant by either:

- personal service;
- email; or
- first-class mail to the tenant's last known address with a duplicate notice mailed to the address of the vacated premises.[12]

Notice is best given promptly on termination of the tenancy, but may be given at any time after the tenant vacates the premises.[13]

As a matter of practice, the tenancy is terminated before entering the premises to determine whether the tenant left personal property, unless the abandonment procedure is used.

Abandonment notices

A property manager may combine the abandoned personal property notice (the right to reclaim personal property notice) with the notice of abandonment of the premises. [See **RPI** Form 581]

The property manager combines the two notices when they believe the tenant has abandoned both the personal property and the premises. The property manager may choose to terminate the tenant's right of possession by establishing an abandonment of the premises instead of using a three-day notice and declaration of forfeiture.[14] [See Chapter 24]

Both abandonment notices from the property manager to the tenant include:

- a description of each item;
- notice that reasonable storage costs will be charged;
- the location where the property may be reclaimed;
- the date by which the tenant is to reclaim their property;
- notice the property will be kept, sold or destroyed if the value is estimated at less than $700; and
- notice the property will be sold by public sale if it is worth $700 or more and is not reclaimed.[15]

If the notice is personally served on the tenant, the notice may expire no less than 15 days after service. If the notice is mailed, the notice may expire no less than 18 days after posting in the mail.[16]

---

12 CC §1983(c)
13 CC §1983
14 CC §1991
15 CC §§1983(b), §1984(b)
16 CC §1983(b)

When personal property worth less than $700 is not reclaimed by a tenant before the notice expires, the property manager may keep, sell or destroy the property without further notice to the tenant.[17]

Under the landlord-initiated procedure, the property manager also notifies any other persons they reasonably believe may have any ownership interest in the personal property left on the premises.[18] [See Form 584-1 accompanying this chapter]

The **reasonable belief** of ownership of the abandoned personal property imposed on a property manager means the actual knowledge a prudent person would have without making an investigation, unless such an investigation is of probable value and reasonable cost.[19]

The property manager is not required to investigate public records unless it is likely they will find information pertinent to locating the owner of the personal property.

Also, if a property manager notices a name or phone number inscribed on the personal items, such as a furniture rental company, they need to further investigate. The landlord will not be protected from liability for failure to do so.

The notice to reclaim personal property needs to list every significant item or "lot of items" left behind.

Although the landlord or their property manager may choose to describe only a portion of the personal property left behind, they are protected from liability only for those items they identify.

A property manager may identify an item simply as a "bundle," a "lot" or a "box" of items. Alternatively, the property manager may look inside the bundle or boxes to determine the contents and their worth. The total value of the items will determine the method the property manager employs to dispose of them.

Additionally, if records remain on the premises after the tenant has vacated or abandoned the property, the tenant alone is presumed to be the owner of the records.

Records include any materials or equipment which record or preserve information such as:

- written or spoken words;
- graphics;
- printed materials; or

Notice to third-party owners

reasonable belief
The actual knowledge a landlord has of the ownership of personal property without investigating.

Identification of personal property

---

17 CC §1984
18 CC §1983(a)
19 CC §1980(d)

- electromagnetically transmitted items.[20]

The landlord, property manager or resident manager needs to consider having a witness present or video record their inventory of the items to confirm their estimated worth. The witness or video will provide evidence the property manager behaved properly if the tenant claims the landlord or their property manager confiscated or damaged items.

The property manager may use *reasonable belief* to estimate the value of the items.

Storage and release of property

Like with the tenant-initiated procedure for reclaiming items, the property manager may charge the tenant for the cost of removal and storage of the property. The property manager may store the personal property in the unit, or remove it to another place of safekeeping, for which they may charge a fee.

Recall, though, that the tenant or owner of the personal property is not required to pay storage costs if the property is kept on the premises, and the tenant recovers it within two days of vacating the premises.

While the property manager needs to exercise care in storing the property, the landlord may be held liable only for damages caused by the property manager's intentional or negligent treatment of the items when removing and storing them.[21]

The property manager releases the personal property to the tenant, or the person who first notifies the property manager of their right to reclaim it, within 72 hours of payment of the storage costs.

The tenant or owner reclaiming the personal items is responsible for storage costs. Any owner other than the tenant is responsible only for the storage costs of property they claim. The property manager may not, however, charge more than one party for storage of any one item.[22]

Sale of the abandoned property

If the total worth of the abandoned personal items is $700 or more, they are sold at public sale by the property manager.[23]

If the abandoned personal property notice states the property is subject to public sale, the property manager will surrender the personal property to the tenant at any time prior to the sale, even after the date specified for expiration in the notice of abandonment.[24]

However, the tenant or the owner of the personal property is required to pay advertising and sale costs in addition to storage costs.[25]

---

20 CC §§ 1980, 1983, 1993 and 1993.03
21 CC §1986
22 CC §1990
23 CC §1988(a)
24 CC §1987
25 CC§ 1987

Chapter 32: Personal property recovered by tenant

Form 582-1

Costs Payable
to Reclaim
Personal
Property

COSTS PAYABLE TO RECLAIM PERSONAL PROPERTY

NOTE: This form is used by a property manager or landlord when a tenant has vacated a premises, left behind personal property and initiated a return of personal property they left behind, to itemize the cost of removal and storage fees payable by the tenant as a requisite to the release of the personal property.

DATE: _____, 20_____, at _____, California.
To Former Tenant:
Name: _____
Address: _____
_____

Items left blank or unchecked are not applicable.
FACTS:
1. You were a Tenant under a rental or lease agreement
    1.1   dated _____, at _____, California,
    1.2   entered into by _____, as the Tenant,
    1.3   and _____, as the Landlord,
    1.4   regarding personal property left on the premises located at _____
    _____

NOTICE:
2. This demand for costs is in response to your request to Landlord to surrender personal property dated _____, 20_____.
3. You or your agent on payment of the cost sought by this demand may claim and remove the personal property at time of payment or within 72 hours after payment.
    3.1   The time to claim and recover the personal property within the 72 hour period needs to be arranged by you and mutually agreed upon by you and Landlord.
4. The reasonable costs incurred by Landlord or the value of labor expended on the removal and storage of the personal property left on the premises by the former Tenant are itemized as follows:
    4.1   Labor to box or disassemble furnishings . . . .$_____
    4.2   Removal and transport to storage . . . .$_____
    4.3   Storage space rental charge . . . .$_____
    4.4   photocopies . . . .$_____
    4.5   Long-distance phone calls . . . .$_____
    4.6   Other . . . .$_____
    4.7   Other . . . .$_____
    4.8   Total costs incurred by Landlord . . . .$_____
5. Demand is hearby made on you for the total costs itemized and totaled at §4.8 to be paid as a requisite to the release of the personal property you may claim.
_____

This statement is true and correct.
Date: _____, 20_____
Landlord/Agent: _____ CalBRE: _____

Signature: _____
Address: _____
_____
Phone: _____ Cell: _____
Fax: _____
Email: _____

FORM 582-1   01-13   ©2016 RPI — Realty Publications, Inc., P.O. BOX 5707, RIVERSIDE, CA 92517

The property manager advertises the public sale prior to its scheduled date in a local county newspaper of general circulation.[26]

The notice of sale appears twice — once each week for two consecutive weeks. The last advertisement may not be later than five calendar days before the date of the public sale. The notice of sale specifies the date, time and location of the sale. Also, the notice of sale needs to sufficiently describe the personal property to allow the owner to identify the property as theirs.

---

26 CC §1988(b)

The timetable before the sale becomes the combination of the 15- or 18-day period for the notice of abandonment and the 14 days of advertising. The highest bidder (including the tenant or landlord) may buy the property.

Any proceeds, minus the costs of sale, advertising and storage, are given to the county treasurer within 30 days of the sale. Once the remaining proceeds have been given over to the county treasurer, the tenant or owner of the personal property has one year to claim the proceeds.[27]

---

27 CC §1988

Chapter 32 Summary

Two separate statutory procedures exist for the return of personal property left on the premises by a tenant. One is initiated by the landlord, the other by the tenant. If initiated by the landlord, the tenant is notified of their right to reclaim the personal property left behind and their need to respond to avoid its disposal.

Only a residential tenant may deliver to the landlord or the property manager a written request for the return of personal property left in the vacated unit.

When personal property worth less than $700 is not reclaimed by a tenant before the notice expires, the landlord or the property manager may keep, sell or destroy the property without further notice to the tenant. If the total worth of the abandoned personal items is $700 or more, the personal property needs to be sold at a public sale by the landlord or the property manager.

Chapter 32 Key Terms

Quiz 8 Covering Chapters 29-32 is located on page 641.

Constructive eviction cancels the lease

Chapter 33

Learning Objectives

After reading this chapter, you will be able to:
- identify the circumstances which constitute a constructive eviction;
- understand the tenant's options when a landlord breaches the implied warranty of habitability; and
- distinguish the concepts of constructive eviction and implied warranty of habitability.

Key Terms

anti-competition clause

constructive eviction

covenant of quiet enjoyment

remedies provision

Interference forces the tenant to vacate

A commercial tenant occupies a building in which they operate their restaurant business. The tenant's lease agreement obligates the landlord to make all necessary repairs to the exterior walls and roof during the term of the lease.

During the tenancy, the roof begins to leak. The tenant notifies the landlord about the leaks and the need for repairs. The landlord makes several personal attempts to repair the roof. However, the roof is never properly repaired and the leaks persist each year during the rainy season. The leaking water damages the interior walls. During rain storms, water runs along beams and down walls. Puddles form on the floors creating hazardous conditions for employees and patrons.

Fed up, the tenant vacates the premises.

The tenant then makes a demand on the landlord to recover their security deposit and business losses. The tenant's losses include lost income from business operations, loss of goodwill, relocation expenses, employee medical expenses and water damage to furnishings and equipment.

Also, the tenant claims the lease agreement has been cancelled due to the landlord's interference with the tenant's occupancy. The landlord failed to meet their contractual obligation to repair the roof resulting in uninhabitable conditions. This caused the tenant to vacate the leased premises, called a **constructive eviction**.

> **constructive eviction**
> A termination of the tenant's right of possession and cancellation of the lease agreement on vacating due to the landlord's failure to maintain the premises as stated in the lease. [See **RPI** Form 552 §6]

The landlord claims their failure to repair the roof was not conduct so intrusive as to result in a *constructive eviction*. According to the landlord, the tenant is only entitled to money for their losses, not a cancellation of the lease agreement and obligation to pay future rent.

Here, the landlord's failure to meet their obligation to repair the roof under the terms of the lease agreement was conduct that terminated the tenant's right of possession and canceled the lease agreement. The leaking roof significantly interfered with the tenant's ability to use the premises to operate a restaurant as permitted by the lease agreement.

Collectively, the landlord's failure to maintain the property and the tenant vacating the premises in response constitute a *constructive eviction*. The tenant recovers the security deposit and any money losses caused by the landlord's interference with possession.[1]

Editor's note — The constructive eviction could easily have been avoided in this case had the landlord hired a competent contractor to promptly and properly repair the roof.

Premises cannot be used as intended

A tenant is not obligated to continue to occupy the premises and pay rent if the premises can no longer be used as intended due to the landlord's conduct.

Conversely, if the landlord's failure to repair the premises does not substantially deprive the tenant of their intended use of the premises, the tenant's right of possession and obligations under the lease agreement remain intact, including the obligation to pay future rent.

Further, the tenant may pursue the landlord in a money action for any losses experienced when:

- the landlord's failure to repair or correct conditions does not amount to a constructive eviction; or
- the landlord's failure to repair amounts to a constructive eviction, but the tenant does not vacate.

The tenant may not, however, offset rent due to the landlord by the amount of the tenant's losses. The claim for losses requires a separate civil action.

---

1 **Groh v. Kover's Bull Pen, Inc.** (1963) 221 CA2d 611

Both the landlord and the tenant are obligated to perform as agreed in the provisions contained or implied in their lease agreement. If either the landlord or tenant fails to fully perform, they breach the lease. Recall that a breach by the landlord or tenant for failure to perform as agreed is either a *minor breach* or a *material breach*.

A minor breach of a lease agreement provision by either the landlord or the tenant is not a justifiable basis for terminating the lease. Examples of minor breaches include the landlord's failure to maintain landscaping or tenant's failures which could be corrected under a three-day notice to perform or quit, or the refusal to pay late charges.

However, a material breach of the lease agreement by either the tenant or landlord justifies a termination of the tenant's right to possess the premises — their leasehold interest in the property.

If a landlord's failure to meet their obligations under the lease agreement materially breaches the lease agreement, the tenant may:

- terminate their possession of the leased premises, causing their possessory interest in the property to revert to the landlord; and
- cancel the lease agreement, including all future rent obligations.

A *constructive eviction* occurs when:

- the landlord or their agent substantially interferes with the tenant's use and enjoyment of the premises during the term of the tenancy; and
- the tenant vacates the premises due to the interference.

A constructive eviction due to the landlord's interference does not occur until the tenant vacates. An eviction cannot exist while the tenant remains in possession.

Examples of substantial interference by the landlord that justify the tenant's vacating the premises include:

- a material breach of the lease[2];
- an unauthorized and extensive alteration of the leased premises that interferes with the tenant's intended use[3];
- the sale of adjacent property owned by the landlord without reserving the tenant's parking and water rights given to the tenant as part of the lease[4]; or
- the failure to abate a sanitation, noise or safety nuisance over which the landlord, but not the tenant, has control.[5]

In a constructive eviction, neither a three-day notice nor an unlawful detainer (UD) action is used to force the tenant to vacate.[6]

Landlord's breach terminates possession

Constructive eviction on substantial interference

---

2 Groh, *supra*
3 **Reichhold** v. **Sommarstrom Inv. Co.** (1927) 83 CA 173
4 **Sierad** v. **Lilly** (1962) 204 CA2d 770
5 **Johnson** v. **Snyder** (1950) 99 CA2d 86
6 Reichhold, *supra*

Tenant's losses and remedies

Every month-to-month rental and lease agreement contains an **implied covenant**, an unexpressed lease provision, prohibiting the landlord from interfering with the tenant's agreed use and possession of the property. This implied covenant is the **covenant of quiet enjoyment**.[7]

When a landlord breaches the implied *covenant of quiet enjoyment,* or other significant provision in the lease agreement, the tenant can:

covenant of quiet enjoyment
An implied lease provision which prohibits the landlord from interfering with the tenant's agreed use and possession of a property.

- vacate the leased premises, recover their money losses incurred and cancel the lease agreement along with their obligation to pay future rents based on their constructive eviction; or
- retain possession, continue to pay rent and sue for any income lost or expenses incurred due to the landlord's interference.

The losses a tenant may recover when the tenant vacates due to a constructive eviction include:

- advance payments of rent and security deposits[8];
- the cost of removing trade fixtures[9];
- relocation expenses; and
- loss of business goodwill.[10]

The breaching landlord's remedies

A tenant who fails to pay rent and later vacates the premises due to a constructive eviction owes the landlord rent for the period of occupancy prior to vacating.

However, any unpaid back rent the landlord is entitled to collect is offset by money losses the tenant incurs due to the constructive eviction.[11]

Breach of anti-competition clause

The landlord's breach of an **anti-competition clause** in the lease agreement is a material breach. The tenant may respond by vacating the premises as a constructive eviction.

anti-competition clause
A provision in the commercial lease agreement stating the landlord will not lease space in a commercial complex to competitors of the tenant.

Consider a commercial lease containing an *anti-competition clause.* The clause states the landlord will not lease other space in the commercial complex to competitors of the tenant.

The lease agreement also contains a **remedies provision** stating the landlord may relet the premises without notifying the tenant if the tenant vacates prior to the lease expiration date.

remedies provision
A provision in a commercial lease agreement stating the nonbreaching party's available actions upon a breach of the lease agreement. [See **RPI** Form 552]

Later, the tenant holds a sale to liquidate their stock. The tenant closes down their business operations, vacates the premises and returns the keys to the landlord with instructions to find another tenant. The tenant's lease does not expire for a few years.

---

7 Calif. Civil Code §1927
8 Groh, *supra*
9 Reichhold, *supra*
10 Johnson, *supra*
11 **Petroleum Collections Incorporated v. Swords** (1975) 48 CA3d 841

The landlord does not respond by entering into an agreement to cancel (surrender) the lease, nor do they take possession of the premises. Further, the landlord does not take steps to forfeit the tenant's right of possession (by an abandonment or three-day notice).

The tenant pays no further rent and the landlord makes no demand on the tenant for delinquent rent. The landlord tries to locate a new tenant, but is unable. However, the landlord is able to lease another space in the building to a competitor of the tenant.

Several months after closing the business, the tenant re-enters the premises and prepares to reopen for business since their lease of the premises has not been terminated.

On discovering a competitor occupies the same commercial complex, the tenant vacates the premises. The tenant has elected to cancel the lease since the landlord breached the *anti-competition clause* in the lease agreement by renting another space in the building to their competitor.

The landlord makes a demand for all rents due until the expiration of the lease agreement, claiming the obligation to pay rent has not been canceled.

The tenant claims they are liable only for the rents due prior to their vacating the premises (the second time) since the landlord's breach of the anti-competition provision in the lease agreement constituted a constructive eviction.

Can the tenant cancel the lease agreement and terminate their obligation to pay rent for the remaining term of the lease?

Yes! The tenant's right of possession under the lease has been terminated. Their obligation to pay rent under the lease agreement has been canceled due to the landlord's interference with the tenant's use of the premises. The landlord's breach of the anti-competition clause is a material breach of the lease agreement. The tenant is justified in vacating the premises and canceling the lease agreement.[12]

In the prior scenario, the landlord failed to terminate the tenant's right to occupy the premises. Due to the landlord's failure to declare a forfeiture of the leasehold estate when the tenant first vacated the premises and became delinquent on rent payments, the tenant retained all their leasehold interests and lease agreement contract rights.

Failure to forfeit may lead to a breach

The landlord was able to terminate the lease when the tenant closed their business and delivered the keys to the landlord by:

- a *surrender*; or
- a three-day notice to pay rent or quit with a declaration of forfeiture of the leasehold.

---

12 **Kulawitz** v. **Pacific Woodenware & Paper Co.** (1944) 25 C2d 664

Without a termination of the tenant's leasehold rights, the tenant's right of possession granted by the lease agreement remained in effect throughout the delinquency and while out of possession.

Since the tenant's right of possession (use of the property) had not been terminated, the landlord's obligation to the tenant to abide by the anti-competition clause in the lease agreement remained in effect.

A landlord cannot reasonably expect to recover rents remaining due for the unexpired duration of a lease agreement when they are the source of the breach which resulted in the tenant's constructive eviction.

Independent obligations to perform

Now consider a tenant who leases a gas station. A modular sign on the premises advertising the gas station can be seen from a nearby freeway. However, the sign was previously installed without a permit. The city orders the removal of the sign since its proximity to the gas tanks constitutes a fire hazard.

The landlord removes the sign, replacing it with a billboard that cannot be seen from the freeway. The tenant demands the landlord provide a sign visible from the freeway, and of comparable likeness to the one removed.

When the landlord fails to provide a similar sign, the tenant stops paying rent, but remains in possession of the premises. Months later, the lease agreement is canceled by the mutual agreement of the landlord and tenant. The tenant then vacates the premises.

The landlord now makes a demand on the tenant to pay rent for the months the tenant did not pay rent prior to vacating the premises.

The tenant claims they are not liable for rent during their period of occupancy after the landlord removed the sign since the sign removal constructively evicted them from the premises. The covenant of quiet enjoyment and use of the property was breached.

Is the tenant liable for the unpaid back rent during the period they remained in occupancy?

Yes! The tenant is liable for the agreed-to rent for the period of their occupancy. A constructive eviction cannot occur until the tenant actually vacates the premises, owing no more rent.[13]

The landlord's failure to replace the sign with a similar sign significantly interfered with the tenant's use of the property as intended by the lease agreement. However, the tenant remained in possession after the breach without first negotiating a modification of the lease agreement obligating them to pay rent.

When the tenant remains in possession and fails to pay rent, the interfering landlord who also breached the lease may forfeit the tenant's right to occupy the property by use of a three-day notice to pay rent and declaration of forfeiture.

---

13 Petroleum Collections Incorporated, *supra*

A tenant leases space in a retail center under a commercial lease agreement containing a *remedies provision* stating:

- the tenant may not terminate the lease agreement on any failure of the landlord to fully perform on the lease; and

- the tenant may only recover money losses if the landlord breaches the lease.

The landlord leases the adjoining space to a dry cleaning business. The dry cleaning business emits fumes that enter the ventilation system and permeate the tenant's premises. The employees and business operations are negatively impacted. The landlord is notified of the interference but fails to remedy the ventilation problems over which they have control.

The tenant stops paying rent and vacates the premises, claiming the dry cleaning fumes were noxious and endangered their employees' health.

The landlord makes a demand on the tenant to pay rent for the remainder of the lease term. The tenant rejects the demand, and seeks to recover their lost profits. These consist of relocation expenses and employee medical expenses.

The tenant claims the landlord's failure to prevent the fumes from invading the leased premises is a breach of the implied covenant of quiet enjoyment. The breach constituted a constructive eviction, thus canceling the lease agreement when the tenant vacated.

The landlord claims the tenant is liable for the remaining rent whether or not the tenant vacated since the lease contains a **remedies provision**, waiving the tenant's right to terminate the lease based on the landlord's inaction.

Is the tenant liable for the rent due for the remaining term of the lease?

Yes! The commercial tenant is liable for the rent remaining unpaid on the lease. Here, the tenant was constructively evicted. However, they remain liable for all future unpaid rent under the lease agreement since they contracted to limit their remedies on the landlord's material breach to a demand for money. The tenant's claim for money losses is separate from the rent due under the lease.[14]

Continuing the previous example, the tenant is obligated by the remedies provision in their lease agreement to:

- remain in possession (and care) of the premises even though they have been constructively evicted;

- continue paying the agreed rent for the entire duration of the lease; and

- sue the landlord to recover any money losses caused by the landlord's breach of the lease agreement.

Commercial quiet enjoyment waiver

Tenant obligations under the remedies provision

---

14 **Lee** v. **Placer Title Company** (1994) 28 CA4th 503

Editor's note — For residential tenants, any waiver or limitation on the remedies for breach of the covenant of quiet enjoyment is void as against public policy. This is not so for commercial tenants.[15]

However, when the landlord's conduct completely prevents the tenant from operating their business on the property and forces them to vacate, then the value of the tenant's leasehold interest has been completely diminished.

While the commercial tenant waived their right to terminate the lease on the landlord's breach of the covenant of quiet enjoyment, they may vacate the property and sue for money, including:

- a 100% offset against future rents due on the lease for money losses occurring after the breach and until the landlord performs or the lease term expires; and

- lost profits, relocation expenses, rent for the replacement space and loss of goodwill.

Landlord interference with subtenants

A tenant may convey a part or all of their leasehold rights to possess the leased premises to a subtenant by entering into a *sublease*. However, most lease agreements held by single-user tenants prevent the tenant from subleasing (or assigning) without the landlord's permission.

On entering into a sublease agreement, the subtenant becomes a third-party beneficiary to the lease agreement entered into by the landlord, referred to as the *master lease*. The benefits received by the subtenant under the master lease include the implied covenant of quiet enjoyment, when:

- the master lease agreement permits subleasing; or

- the landlord consents to a sublease under a restraint on alienation provision in the master lease agreement.

The master lease agreement is attached to the sublease agreement as an exhibit. The rights of the subtenant are limited by the terms of the master lease.

*Editor's note — Both the master lease and the sublease are of the same form and contain the same provisions, except the lease agreement with the subtenant references the lease agreement held by the tenant. [See **RPI** Form 552 §2.5]*

When a landlord's conduct interferes with the subtenant's use of the premises under the sublease agreement (as limited by the referenced master lease), the subtenant may vacate and recover losses from the landlord, called a *constructive eviction.*[16]

---

15 CC §1953

16 **Marchese** v. **Standard Realty and Development Company** (1977) 74 CA3d 142

When a *subtenant* has been constructively evicted by the landlord, the master tenant may:

- vacate the entire premises, cancel the lease agreement and recover losses from the landlord for a constructive eviction of the master tenant; or
- remain in possession and recover money losses for breach of the implied covenant of quiet enjoyment.

Constructive eviction of either a residential or commercial tenant is distinct from the *implied warranty of habitability* enforceable only against residential landlords. Constructive eviction requires the tenant to vacate or pay the entire rent. The warranty of habitability requires neither.

Both residential and commercial lease agreements contain written conditions that, if breached by the landlord, result in a constructive eviction.

However, the warranty of habitability is not a written provision, it is implied. It is judicially and legislatively considered to exist in all residential rental and lease agreements.

The implied warranty of habitability requires a landlord to maintain safe and sanitary conditions in their residential units. On the landlord's failure to maintain habitable conditions, the residential tenant may remain in possession and pay a reduced rent that will be set by the court. A constructive eviction has not taken place since the residential tenant remains in possession.[17] [See Chapters 36 and 39]

However, both residential and commercial tenants can vacate the premises based on the landlord's significant interference with possessory rights and recover any losses from their landlords that flow from the constructive eviction.

Consider a commercial landlord who fails to meet their obligations under a lease agreement to maintain the property for the intended use.

The commercial tenant retaliates by refusing to pay rent. However, the tenant does not vacate the premises.

The landlord files a UD action to evict the tenant for their failure to pay rent after service of a three-day notice to pay or quit. At trial, the tenant is unable to raise the defense of a breach of the implied warranty of habitability since their lease is commercial. The commercial tenant is without a legal excuse for their failure to pay rent for the period of their actual occupancy. The commercial tenant will be evicted in spite of the landlord's material breach of lease agreement provisions.[18]

Constructive eviction vs. the warranty of habitability

---

17 **Green** v. **Superior Court of the City and County of San Francisco** (1974) 10 C3d 616; Calif. Code of Civil Procedure §1174.2
18 **Schulman** v. **Vera** (1980) 108 CA3d 552

**Chapter 33
Summary**

Both residential and commercial lease agreements contain written conditions that, if breached by the landlord, result in a constructive eviction.

Collectively, a landlord's failure to maintain the property and the tenant vacating the premises in response constitutes a constructive eviction. The tenant is not obligated to continue to occupy the premises and pay rent if the premises can no longer be used as intended due to the landlord's conduct.

Constructive eviction of either a residential or commercial tenant is distinct from the implied warranty of habitability enforceable only against residential landlords. Constructive eviction requires the tenant to vacate or pay the entire rent. The warranty of habitability requires neither.

Both residential and commercial lease agreements contain written conditions that, if breached by the landlord, result in a constructive eviction. However, the warranty of habitability is not a written provision, it is implied. It is judicially and legislatively considered to exist in all residential rental and lease agreements.

**Chapter 33
Key Terms**

anti-competition clause .... pg. 338
constructive eviction .... pg. 336
covenant of quiet enjoyment.. pg. 338
remedies provision .... pg. 338

Quiz 9 Covering Chapters 33-36 is located on page 642.

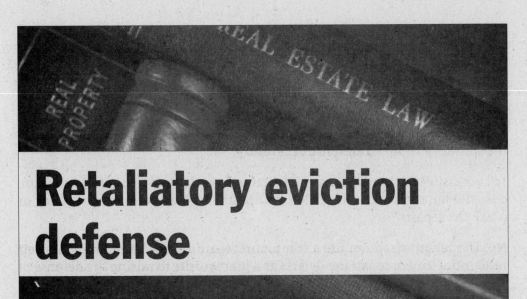

Retaliatory eviction defense

After reading this chapter, you will be able to:
- differentiate between proper and improper reasons for eviction of a tenant; and
- anticipate a tenant's allowable defenses in an unlawful detainer action.

Learning Objectives

repair and deduct remedy   retaliatory eviction

Key Terms

A tenant occupies a residential unit under a month-to-month rental agreement. [See **RPI** Form 551]

The unit has many defects which need to be repaired. The tenant requests the landlord make repairs to correct the defects. The landlord does not make the requested repairs.

The tenant complains to the landlord several more times about the need for repairs and the lack of suitable living conditions in the unit. Finally, the tenant threatens to exercise their right to perform the repairs and deduct the costs from the rent. [See Chapter 37]

Before any repairs are made, the landlord serves the tenant with a 30-day notice to vacate the premises. [See **RPI** Form 569]

The tenant remains in possession after the notice expires. Rent is tendered by the tenant, but it is refused by the landlord. The landlord files an unlawful detainer (UD) action to have the tenant evicted.

Shackling vengeful wayward landlords

retaliatory eviction
The wrongful eviction attempted by a landlord against a tenant for lawfully exercising any of their rights.

repair and deduct remedy
An option available to a residential tenant when the landlord fails to repair leased property which allows the tenant to make the repairs and deduct their cost from the next month's rent payment.

The tenant defends against the UD action, claiming the landlord seeks to evict them in retaliation for their repeated requests for repairs and complaints about the habitability of the unit.

The landlord claims the tenant may not raise the defense of **retaliatory eviction** since the tenant did not file a complaint with a government agency regarding the habitability of the unit or undertake to make the repairs under the statutory **repair and deduct remedy**.

To successfully defend against a UD action by a claim of *retaliatory eviction*, does the tenant need to first file a complaint with a government agency or make the repairs?

No! The tenant need not file a complaint regarding the habitability of their residential unit or repair the defects as a prerequisite to raising the defense of retaliatory eviction in the UD action.

Here, the residential landlord is prevented from evicting the tenant. The landlord's conduct indicates they sought to evict the tenant in retaliation for complaining about the need for repairs.[1]

The retaliatory eviction defense

A landlord's sole purpose for filing a UD action is to recover possession from a tenant.

In addition to the landlord's recovery of possession from the tenant, the UD award against the tenant may include:

- any unpaid delinquent amounts of rent accrued prior to the forfeiture of possession by a declaration in the three-day notice to quit or as granted at the UD trial;
- the reasonable rental value of the premises during the tenant's unlawful detainer which follows the date of forfeiture of the right to possession; and
- up to $600 in addition to the rent for the tenant's malicious behavior.[2]

Accordingly, UD proceedings are intended to be brief — from the use of notices to quit or vacate to the inability of the tenant to bring up frivolous defenses.

Thus, residential tenants are allowed to raise only two defenses in a UD action:

- a breach of the *warranty of habitability* [See Chapter 37];[3] and
- retaliatory eviction.

Residential tenants include mobilehome owners who rent or lease space in a mobilehome park.[4]

1   **Kemp** v. **Schultz** (1981) 121 CA3d Supp. 13
2   Calif. Code of Civil Procedure §1174(b)
3   CCP §1174.2
4   **Rich** v. **Schwab** (1998) 63 CA4th 803

For commercial tenants, the only defense allowed in a UD action is the defense of retaliatory eviction.[5]

This defense is not based on the statutory defense granted to residential tenants, but on the equivalent, long-standing common law defense of retaliatory eviction. The public policy enforced by courts entitles all tenants to exercise their rights against a landlord without retaliation. The tenant's activity outweighs the public's interest in preserving the summary nature of UD hearings provided for landlords.[6]

Further, a residential tenant may sue the landlord to recover money losses incurred due to a landlord's retaliatory acts, such as an unfair rent increase.[7]

Under a notice to vacate, a landlord may evict a tenant for any reason, or no reason at all (except rent control and Section 8 properties), but they may not evict a tenant for an improper reason.[8]

In rent control communities, ordinances require a residential landlord to state their reasons for evicting a tenant in the notice to vacate. Also, a landlord providing Section 8 housing needs to state a good reason in a notice to vacate before they may evict the tenant.[9]

Actions by a residential landlord to increase rent, decrease tenant services or evict are considered retaliatory acts if initiated by the landlord after a tenant:

- complains to the landlord or a government agency regarding the habitability of the premises;
- exercises the statutory *repair and deduct remedy*;[10]
- organizes or becomes a member of a tenants' association or tenants' rights group;[11] or
- exercises any other legal rights held by the tenant, such as notifying the police about the landlord's criminal activity.[12]

Editor's note — If a landlord fails to make repairs within 30 days after the tenant notifies them of the need for repairs, the tenant may make the repairs and deduct the cost from the rent, called the repair-and-deduct remedy.[13] [See Chapter 37]

---

5   **Custom Parking, Inc.** v. **Superior Court of the County of Marin** (1982) 138 CA3d 90
6   **Barela** v. **Superior Court of Orange County** (1981) 30 C3d 244
7   **Aweeka** v. **Bonds** (1971) 20 CA3d 278
8   **S.P. Growers Association** v. **Rodriguez** (1976) 17 C3d 719
9   **Mitchell** v. **Poole** (1988) 203 CA3d Supp. 1
10 Calif. Civil Code §1942.5(a)(1)
11 CC §1942.5(c)
12 CC §1942.5(c); Barela, *supra*
13 CC §1942

In addition, a residential landlord is prohibited from increasing the rent, decreasing tenant services or requiring the tenant to vacate within 180 days after any of the following events:

- the tenant's notice to the landlord of the need for repairs, or complaint to the landlord about the habitability of the premises;

- the tenant's filing of a written or oral complaint with a government agency regarding the habitability of the premises;

- an inspection or issuance of a citation resulting from the tenant's complaint to a government agency;

- the filing of documents to initiate an action involving the habitability of the premises; or

- the entry of a judgment or issuance of an arbitration award adverse to the landlord.[14]

Enforcing the 180-day protection rule

Consider a residential tenant holding possession under a month-to-month rental agreement who prevails in a UD action brought by a landlord. The tenant is permitted by the court to remain in possession of their unit.

Four months (120 days) after the UD judgment, the landlord serves the tenant with a notice to vacate. The notice will expire before the 180-day protective period has run.

The tenant tenders an amount of rent on the next due date representing rent due for a rental period extending beyond the expiration of the notice to vacate. The landlord refuses to accept the rent and returns it undeposited. The tenant remains on the premises after the notice to vacate expires.

The landlord next files a UD action to evict the tenant since the tenant retained occupancy after the notice to vacate expired. The UD trial is set for a date more than 180 days after the date of the prior UD trial at which the tenant prevailed.

As a defense to the current UD action, the tenant claims the landlord is barred from evicting them since a notice to vacate may not be served within 180 days after the tenant prevailed on the prior UD judgment.

The landlord claims they are not barred from evicting the tenant since the current UD trial occurs after the 180-day protective period expired.

In this example, the UD action is barred. The tenant may not be required to vacate the premises within the 180-day protection period. A UD action is based on the failure of the tenant to vacant by the expiration of the notice to vacate.

Under the notice, the tenant is required to vacate during the 180-day protection period or be guilty of unlawfully detaining the premises. Thus,

---

14 CC §1942.5(a)

*A landlord is prohibited from causing a tenant to involuntarily vacate their rental property by threatening to disclose the **immigration** or **citizenship status** of the tenant or other person associated with the tenant. [Calif. Business and Professions Code §6103.7]*

A tenant may assert the landlord's violation of this restriction as a defense in an unlawful detainer (UD) action. [Calif. Code of Civil Procedure §1161.4]

Further, a landlord and their agent are prohibited from:

- *threatening to disclose information about the immigration or citizenship status of a tenant or other person associated with the tenant to compel the tenant to vacate the property [Calif. Civil Code §1940.2];*

- *disclosing to any person or entity the immigration or citizenship status of an existing or prospective tenant with the intent of harassment, retaliation or to influence a tenant to vacate the property [CC §1942.5]; and*

- *disclosing the immigration or citizenship status of a tenant, occupant or person associated with a tenant or occupant to any immigration authority, law enforcement agency or government agency for the purpose of harassment, retaliation or to compel the tenant or occupant to vacate the property. [CC §1940.3]*

When a landlord unlawfully discloses the immigration or citizenship status of a tenant or occupant to an agency under the circumstances stated above, a court is required to:

- *order the landlord pay civil penalties to the tenant in an amount between six and 12 times the monthly rent charged for the tenant's dwelling;*

- *issue an injunctive relief to prevent the landlord from future violations;*

- *notify the district attorney of the landlord's potential violation of extortion laws; and*

- *award attorney fees and costs to the prevailing party. [CC §1940.35]*

> **Landlords prohibited from taking action against tenants based on immigration status**

the landlord may not use a UD action to evict the tenant, since the date set for the return of the premises by a notice to vacate was within the 180-day protection period.[15]

However, the landlord is not barred from serving a notice to vacate or a notice of change in rental terms within the 180-day period, as long as the notice does not expire within that period. Thus, the tenant confronted with a hostile landlord has 180 days after exercising lawful rights which antagonize the landlord to voluntarily relocate and avoid the seemingly inevitable notice to vacate or change in terms of the occupancy.

Consider a commercial tenant who occupies a property under a month-to-month tenancy. The rental agreement (or expired lease) requires the landlord to care for and maintain the exterior walls and roof of the building during the occupancy.

> **Commercial retaliatory eviction**

---

15 **Kriz** v. **Taylor** (1979) 92 CA3d 302

The roof leaks, causing damage to the tenant's personal property. On more than one occasion, the tenant notifies the landlord of the leak, and requests that the landlord repair the roof.

Several months later, the roof leaks again, and the tenant suffers more losses. The tenant repairs the roof and makes a demand on the landlord for reimbursement. The landlord rejects the demand.

The commercial tenant does not deduct the cost of the repairs from the monthly rent since the space rented is commercial. The repair and deduct remedy is only available to residential tenants and may not be used by commercial tenants. The tenant continues to pay the rent as it becomes due.

The tenant sues the landlord to recover the cost of repairing the roof. The landlord immediately serves the tenant with a 30-day notice to vacate. The tenant remains in possession after the 30-day notice expires, and the landlord files a UD action to evict the tenant.

The commercial tenant defends the UD action, claiming the landlord is attempting to evict them for an improper reason — in retaliation for the tenant's enforcement of the landlord's obligations by suing the landlord to enforce the rental agreement (or expired lease).

The landlord claims the tenant may not raise the defense of retaliatory eviction since the defense is statutory and available only to residential tenants.[16]

Here, the *common law retaliatory eviction defense*, equivalent to the statutory residential tenant defense, is available to the commercial tenant as a matter of public policy enforced by the courts. The eviction sought by the landlord is in retaliation against the tenant because the tenant exercised a legal right.

When a landlord has an improper motive to evict a tenant, the tenant, residential or commercial, may raise the common law defense of retaliatory eviction.[17]

A commercial tenant has a right to recover expenses incurred due to the landlord's breach of the lease agreement. However, when the landlord refuses to voluntarily reimburse the tenant after a demand, the tenant needs to file litigation to recover the money and enforce collection by way of a money judgment.

Losses recovered by tenant

Occasionally, a residential landlord will include a provision in the lease or rental agreement in which the residential tenant purports to waive their right to raise the defense of retaliatory eviction, or sue a landlord for retaliatory acts. However, a waiver of legal rights by a residential tenant is void.[18]

---

16 CC §1942.5
17 Custom Parking, Inc., *supra*
18 CC §1942.5(d)

If a residential landlord attempts to evict a tenant in retaliation for any lawful activity by the tenant, the tenant is entitled to recover:

- the tenant's actual money losses incurred due to the landlord's retaliatory activity;[19] and

- punitive losses of no less than $100 and no more than $2,000 for each retaliatory act where the landlord or their agent is guilty of fraud, oppression or malice with respect to the retaliation.[20]

More financially frightening for a residential landlord whose conduct subjects them to statutory punitive losses is the tenant's right to bring a class action suit. This action recovers money due to the landlord's retaliatory act of increasing the rents on all tenants who participate in a tenant association to prevent rental increases by petitioning the city for rent control.[21]

Further, the prevailing party in an action brought by a residential tenant seeking to recover losses from a landlord for retaliatory eviction is entitled to reasonable attorney fees.[22]

---

19 CC §1942.5(f)(1)
20 CC §1942.5(f)(2)
21 Rich v. Schwab, *supra*
22 CC §1942.5(g)

Chapter 34 Summary

Actions by a residential landlord to increase rent, decrease tenant services or evict are considered retaliatory acts if initiated by the landlord after a tenant:

- complains to the landlord or a government agency regarding the habitability of the premises;

- exercises the statutory repair and deduct remedy;

- organizes or becomes a member of a tenants' association or tenants' rights group; or

- exercises any other legal rights held by the tenant, such as notifying the police about the landlord's criminal activity.

Occasionally, a residential landlord will include a provision in the lease or rental agreement in which the residential tenant purports to waive their right to raise the defense of retaliatory eviction, or sue a landlord for retaliatory acts. However, a waiver of legal rights by a residential tenant is void.

Chapter 34 Key Terms

Quiz 9 Covering Chapters 33-36 is located on page 642.

Defective building components

After reading this chapter, you will be able to:

- understand the difference between a manufacturer's liability for defective building components and a landlord's liability for negligence in maintaining a building; and
- Anticipate the landlord's liability for injuries caused by defective building components.

negligence   **strict liability**

Learning Objectives

Key Terms

Liability for neglect, no strict liability

Consider a tenant of a residential rental unit who slips and falls in the bathtub, sustaining injuries. The bathtub does not have an anti-skid surface and is very slippery when wet.

The tenant claims the landlord is liable for their injuries since the bathtub without an anti-skid surface is defective.

Is the landlord liable to the tenant for the injuries caused by the defective bathtub surface?

No! Landlords are not liable for tenant injuries caused by a defective bathtub surface. To be liable for another's injuries without concern for fault, called **strict liability**, the landlord needs to be a person in the chain of distribution for the equipment or fixture that was installed and caused the injury.

It is unreasonable to extend *strict liability* to hotel operators and residential landlords for defects in products manufactured, marketed and distributed by others.[1]

strict liability
To be liable for another's injuries without concern for fault.

---

1 **Peterson** v. **Superior Court** (1995) 10 C4th 1185

Facts: A commercial landlord leases space to a tenant operating a health club. The tenant does not maintain an AED on the premises. A client of the health club suffers a fatal cardiac arrest while exercising on the premises.

Claim: The client's family seeks money losses from the landlord, claiming wrongful death of the client since the landlord failed to maintain an AED required on the premises of a health club.

Counterclaim: The landlord claims it owes no duty to ensure an AED is maintained on the premises since the definition of a health club does not include a landlord and such a requirement would impose an unreasonable duty.

*Holding: A California court of appeals holds the landlord owes no duty to ensure an AED is maintained at the site of the tenant's health club since the landlord is out of possession of the premises and such a requirement would impose an unreasonable duty on the landlord. [**Day** v. **Lupo Vine Street, L.P.** (April 11, 2018)_CA5th_]*

Strict liability

Strict liability for an injury caused by a product applies primarily to the manufacturer who places the product on the market. Manufacturers and distributors know products will not be inspected for defects before they are used. Thus, the manufacturer is liable for defects.

The primary social purpose of strict liability is to impose on the manufacturer, not the injured user, the costs of injuries caused by its products when used as intended.

Strict liability for defect-related injuries also extends to distributors and retailers who are part of the stream of commerce. Distributors and retailers are considered to be in the best position to assert influence over the manufacturer to create a product that is free of defects.

Strict liability acts as an incentive for retailers and distributors to give attention to the safety of products they purchase from manufacturers for resale to the public.

Social goal

However, the social goal of imposing strict liability on all involved in the manufacturing, distribution and resale of a product to the consumer is not to ensure the safety of the product. The goal is to distribute the risks and costs of injury due to lack of safety in the product's use among those most able to bear the burden of the costs.

The previously cited *Peterson* court held the theory of strict liability is not extended to residential landlords. Landlords are not distributors or retailers. Landlords and hotel operators, unlike distributors and retailers, cannot exert influence over the manufacturer to make a product safe. For the most part, landlords and hotel operators are not builders and do not have a business relationship with the manufacturer or the suppliers of the defective product.

Once the product is purchased and installed by the builder, the product leaves the stream of commerce — distribution and resale has come to an end. The later use of the product by occupants, be they tenants or guests, does not transform the landlord or hotel operator into a retailer of the product.

Editor's note — Peterson refused to decide whether strict liability may be imposed on a landlord or a hotel operator who participates in the construction of the building. Specifications established by planners, designers and construction contractors will play a role in deciding whether strict liability will be imposed on owner-builders of rental and hotel units.

When the landlord is **negligent** in the care and management of their property, they become liable for injury to others. A landlord is *negligent* when they are confronted with a known dangerous condition and do not act to correct the condition. Thus, a residential landlord who fails to cure known dangerous defects will be liable under general tort principles of negligence for injuries caused by the breach of their duty to correct known defects.

Tenants are able to rely on the landlord's inspection of the rented space and their correction of all visible and known defects. Residential landlords are in the business of leasing property for human occupancy.

The residential landlord will provide a clean, safe and habitable premises during the term of the lease. Further, the landlord is obligated to repair all known patent or latent defects, unless the tenant agrees to undertake repairs and maintenance.[2]

Thus, the residential landlord is personally liable to the tenant for injuries occurring on the rental property as a result of the landlord's failure to inspect, locate and repair defective and dangerous property conditions that are known or reasonably expected to be known to the landlord.[3]

The residential landlord is obligated to repair uninhabitable conditions which may affect the tenant's health and safety immediately. [See Chapter 37]

Editor's note — The tenant will be able to recover compensation from the landlord if the tenant can show the landlord may have reasonably foreseen the accident.

A landlord or hotel operator who is aware of injuries caused by latent defects in products used on the premises will be liable if other similar latent defects are not cured, since it is reasonably foreseeable injuries caused by similar defects throughout the project will occur.[4]

Duty to correct known defects

negligence
The failure to behave with the level of care that someone of ordinary prudence would have exercised under the same conditions.

---

2 Calif. Civil Code §1942
3 CC §1941
4 **Sturgeon** v. **Curnutt** (1994) 29 CA4th 301

**Chapter 35
Summary**

Strict liability for an injury caused by a product applies primarily to the manufacturer and distributors of the product which becomes a component or fixture in a building. It is the manufacturer who places the product on the market and distributors of that product who know it will not be inspected for defects before it is used. Thus, manufacturers and distributors are liable for defects in products they manufacture, market and distribute.

The residential landlord needs to provide a clean, safe and habitable premises during the term of the lease. Further, the landlord is obligated to repair all known patent or latent defects, unless the tenant agrees to undertake repairs and maintenance.

The residential landlord is obligated to repair uninhabitable conditions which may affect the tenant's health and safety.

Thus, the residential landlord is personally liable to the tenant for injuries occurring on the rental property as a result of the landlord's failure to inspect, locate and repair defective and dangerous property conditions that are known or reasonably expected to be known to the landlord.

**Chapter 35
Key Terms**

negligence ....pg. 355
strict liability ....pg. 353

Quiz 9 Covering Chapters 33-36 is located on page 642.

Chapter

36

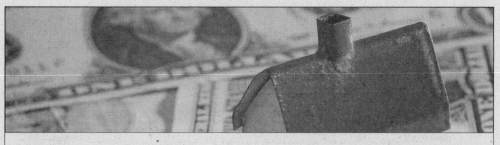

Care and maintenance of property

Learning Objectives

Key Terms

Tenant obligations and remedies

A landlord and a tenant enter into a lease agreement for a furnished unit in an apartment complex. The lease agreement contains a provision, implied if not stated, requiring the residential landlord to maintain the premises and common areas in a safe and sanitary condition, and comply with all applicable ordinances and regulations. [See **RPI** Form 550]

The lease agreement further requires the tenant to keep the unit clean and sanitary and properly operate all electrical, gas and plumbing fixtures.

Before the tenant takes possession, the resident manager and the tenant conduct a walk-through of the unit. They agree on the condition of the premises. The tenant and the resident manager complete a *condition of premises form* which is attached as an addendum to the lease agreement and signed by the tenant. [See Form 560 accompanying this chapter]

Form 560

Condition
of Premises
Addendum

Page 1 of 2

CONDITION OF PREMISES ADDENDUM

NOTE: This form is used by a property manager or landlord when conducting a pre-occupancy inspection with a residential tenant on entering into a rental or lease agreement, to document the condition of the premises and state the landlord's obligation to make any promised repairs.

DATE: _____, 20_____, at _____, California.
Items left blank or unchecked are not applicable.

FACTS:

1. This is an addendum to the following agreement:
    ☐ Lease agreement [See **RPI** Form 550]
    ☐ Rental agreement [See **RPI** Form 551]
    ☐ Occupancy agreement [See **RPI** Form 593]
    1.1   ☐ of same date, or dated _____, 20_____, at _____, California,
    1.2   entered into by _____, as the Landlord,
    1.3   and _____, as the Tenant,
    1.4   regarding real estate referred to as _____
    _____

AGREEMENT:

2. Landlord and Tenant have jointly inspected the premises and common areas and agree the premises and unchecked items such as fixtures, appliances and furnishings are in a satisfactory and sanitary condition.

3. Check only those items which are unsatisfactory and state why in "REMARKS."

4. EXTERIOR/COMMON AREAS:

☐ Garage/parking lot	☐ Garbage facilities	☐ Storage area	☐ TV antenna
☐ Pool/spa	☐ Satellite dish	☐ Patio/decks	☐ CATV hookup
☐ Stairs/railings	☐ Garage door opener(s)	☐ Hallway/lobby	☐ Laundry area
☐ Fencing	☐ Roof	☐ Exterior lighting	☐ Eaves/gutters
☐ Sprinklers/hose	☐ Mailbox	☐ Walkways	☐ _____

5. ENTRY:

☐ Door	☐ # of keys _____	☐ Doorbell/knocker	☐ Closet
☐ Intercom/security	☐ Shelves	☐ Locks	☐ _____

6. KITCHEN:

☐ Range	☐ Trash compactor	☐ Oven	☐ Water purifier
☐ Refrigerator	☐ Counters/laminate	☐ Garbage disposal	☐ Cabinets/drawers
☐ Exhaust fan(s)	☐ Pantry/shelves	☐ Dishwasher	☐ Tile/linoleum
☐ Microwave	☐ Sink/faucets		

7. BATHROOM:

☐ Sink	☐ Tile/linoleum	☐ Faucets/hardware	☐ Closets/shelves
☐ Toilet	☐ Exhaust fan(s)	☐ Shower	☐ Shower enclosure
☐ Tub	☐ Medicine cabinet		

8. ELECTRICAL:

☐ Outlets	☐ Lighting	☐ Switchplates	☐ Thermostat
☐ Fixtures	☐ Furnace	☐ Smoke detectors	☐ Ventilation
☐ Air conditioning	☐ _____		

9. PLUMBING:

☐ Water heater	☐ Washer	☐ Hot/cold water	☐ Dryer
☐ Gas hookups	☐ _____		

------ PAGE 1 OF 2 — FORM 560 ------

On the condition of premises form, the tenant notes any defects existing on the premises. For example, the tenant marks if appliances are dented, screens have holes or are missing from windows, plumbing fixtures are broken or leaking, linoleum is peeling or damaged, carpeting has stains, chipped paint, etc.

Since the unit is furnished, the tenant and the resident manager also complete a condition of furnishings addendum during the walk-through. [See Form 561 accompanying this chapter]

------------------------------------- PAGE 2 OF 2 — FORM 560 -------------------------------------

10. INTERIOR:

☐ Wall coverings	☐ Floor coverings	☐ Ceilings	☐ Walls
☐ Draperies	☐ Rods/tracks	☐ Glass doors	☐ Windows
☐ Doorknobs	☐ Fireplace	☐ Wood doors	☐ Paint
☐ Floors	☐ Baseboards/trim	☐ Hardware/fittings	☐ Shades
☐ Closets	☐ Screens	☐ Sills/jambs	☐ Kickplates/stops
☐ Chimney/flue			

11. REMARKS:

_____
_____
_____
_____
_____
_____
_____
_____
_____
_____
_____
_____
_____
_____

12. REPAIRS PROMISED:

12.1 _____
_____
_____

Completion date _____

12.2 _____
_____
_____

Completion date _____

I agree to the terms stated above.	**I accept the premises as stated above.**
☐ See attached Signature Page Addendum. [RPI Form 251]	☐ See attached Signature Page Addendum. [RPI Form 251]
Date: _____, 20_____	Date: _____, 20_____
Landlord/Manager: _____	Tenant: _____
	Signature: _____
	Tenant: _____
Signature: _____	Signature: _____
Address: _____	Address: _____
Phone: _____ Cell: _____	Phone: _____ Cell: _____
Fax: _____	Fax: _____
Email: _____	Email: _____

FORM 560	03-11	©2016 RPI — Realty Publications, Inc., P.O. BOX 5707, RIVERSIDE, CA 92517

The tenant records any defects in the furniture on the condition of furnishings form, such as tears or burns in upholstery or scratches in wood furniture. No minor or major defective conditions are observed by the tenant or the landlord during the walk-through.

Later, before the tenant vacates the unit, the tenant and the resident manager will conduct a *pre-expiration inspection*. The manager will determine if the unit and the furnishings have sustained any damage other than normal wear and tear during the tenant's occupancy. The tenant will be handed a statement of deficiencies, listing any conditions which need to be corrected to avoid a deduction of the corrective costs from the security deposit. [See Chapter 19]

Form 561

Condition of
Furnishing
Addendum

CONDITION OF FURNISHINGS ADDENDUM
and Inventory

NOTE: This form is used by a property manager or landlord when conducting a pre-occupancy inspection with a residential tenant on entering into a rental or lease agreement for a furnished unit, to document the condition of the furnishings and personal property inventory.

DATE: _____, 20_____, at _____, California.

Items left blank or unchecked are not applicable.

FACTS:

1. This is an addendum to the following
   □ Lease agreement [See **RPI** Form 550]
   □ Rental agreement [See **RPI** Form 551]
   □ Occupancy agreement [See **RPI** Form 593]
   □ _____
   1.1 □ of same date, or dated _____, 20____.
   1.2 □ entered into by
   _____, as the Landlord,
   1.3 and _____, as the Tenant,
   1.4 regarding real estate referred to as _____
   _____

AGREEMENT:

2. Landlord and Tenant have jointly inspected the furniture and furnishings and agree they are in satisfactory and sanitary condition.
3. Only those items checked are unsatisfactory and explained under "REMARKS."
4. The quantity of furnishings entered on this form are accepted by Tenant.
5. Reimbursement for any loss, damage or excess wear and tear on furnishings provided to Tenant will be deducted from Tenant's security deposit.

6. LIVING ROOM
□ Carpet □ Chairs #_____
□ Draperies □ End tables #_____
□ Window coverings □ Coffee tables #_____
□ Wall coverings □ Lamps #_____
□ Couch #____ □ Shelves
□ Pictures #____ □ _____

7. KITCHEN
□ Tile/linoleum □ Chairs #_____
□ Window coverings □ Range
□ Refrigerator □ Cabinets
□ Table #____ □ _____

8. BEDROOM:
□ Double bed #____ □ Night stands #____
□ Single bed #____ □ Lamps #____
□ Headboards #____ □ Bureau #____
□ Mattress #____ □ Pictures #____
□ Box springs #____ □ Mirror #____
□ Bed frame #____ □ _____

9. SECOND BEDROOM
□ Double bed #____ □ Night stands #____
□ Single bed #____ □ Lamps #____
□ Headboards #____ □ Bureau #____
□ Mattress #____ □ Pictures #____
□ Box springs #____ □ Mirror #____

10. BATHROOM:
□ Medicine cabinet □ Shower tub
□ Shelves/fittings □ Shower enclosure
□ Toilet □ _____

11. REMARKS:
_____
_____
_____
_____
_____
_____
_____
_____
_____
_____
_____

I agree to the terms stated above.
Date: _____, 20_____
Landlord/Agent: _____

Signature: _____
Address: _____
Phone: _____ Fax: _____
Email: _____

I agree to the terms stated above.
□ See Signature Page Addendum. [RPI Form 251]
Date: _____, 20_____
Tenant: _____

Signature: _____
Address: _____
Phone: _____ Fax: _____
Email: _____

FORM 561 11-10 ©2017 RPI — Realty Publications, Inc., P.O. BOX 5707, RIVERSIDE, CA 92517

The purpose of the condition of premises and condition of furnishings forms are to determine if any defective conditions exist in the rental unit and to repair them before the tenant takes possession. When the tenant vacates, the landlord wants to be able to recover the cost of any damage to the unit or the furnishings caused by the tenant. The completed forms document the condition of the unit and its furnishings at the time of occupancy.

On the other hand, the tenant wants to avoid liability for damage they did not cause.

A tenant is to repair all deterioration and damage to the premises caused by their failure to use ordinary care. Normal wear and tear on the unit need not be avoided or eliminated by the tenant.[1]

Further, a residential tenant has a duty of care and maintenance in the use of the leased premises which includes:

- keeping the premises clean and sanitary;
- disposing of all rubbish, garbage and waste in a sanitary manner;
- properly operating all electrical, gas and plumbing fixtures, and keeping them clean and sanitary;
- allowing no person who is on the premises with the tenant's permission to intentionally destroy, damage, waste or remove any part of the premises or the facilities, equipment or appurtenances; and
- occupying and using the premises for the purpose it is intended to be used.[2]

The landlord can agree to be responsible for the cleanliness of the common areas, and the disposal of garbage.[3]

The tenant breaches their duty to care for and maintain the premises when the tenant:

- contributes substantially to the dilapidation of the premises; or
- substantially interferes with the landlord's duty to maintain the premises.[4]

For example, a tenant does not notify their landlord of a leak in the roof that is causing damage to the ceiling of the rental unit. Eventually, the ceiling falls down, causing damage to the tenant's personal property, the walls and the floor coverings.

Here, the tenant interfered with the landlord's duty to maintain the property since the tenant failed to:

- notify the landlord of the leak in the roof; or
- repair the leak.

Also, the landlord is not liable for any damage to the tenant's personal property resulting from the falling ceiling, since the tenant neglected to report the water seepage. Conversely, the tenant is liable for the cost of the damage to the rental unit for failure to report the need for repairs on the first sign of leakage.

A landlord can recover the cost of repairs made to correct excessive wear and tear by deducting the cost of repairs from the security deposit and demanding payment for any deficiency in the deposit to cover the expenses.[5]

---

1 Calif. Civil Code §1929
2 CC §1941.2
3 CC §1941.2(b)
4 CC §1941.2(a)
5 CC §1950.5(b)

Temporary displacement for fumigation or repairs

> *When a landlord or property manager needs to temporarily displace a tenant, discretion is needed in order to not violate the tenant's right to quiet enjoyment. [Calif. Civil Code §1940.2(a)]*
>
> *Mutually agreed-to terms need to be set out in writing by the landlord and tenant when the landlord needs to repair or fumigate a property requiring temporary displacement. Unless otherwise agreed to, the landlord is responsible for the tenant's costs of temporarily relocating, including:*
>
> - *hotel costs;*
> - *pet boarding;*
> - *meals if a kitchen at the replacement accommodation is not provided; and*
> - *any other cost and expense incurred due to the displacement.*
>
> *The **Notice of Temporary Displacement** published by **RPI (Realty Publications, Inc.)** is used by a property manager or landlord when invasive repairs or fumigation work require the temporary move-out of a tenant, to notify the tenant of the conditions for the temporary displacement. [See **RPI** Form 588]*
>
> *This notice sets forth:*
>
> - *the date and time by which the occupant needs to temporarily vacate the premises [See **RPI** Form 588 §2];*
> - *the description of the work to be performed [See **RPI** Form 588 §3];*
> - *the date and time the occupant may reoccupy the premises [See **RPI** Form 588 §4]; and*
> - *the compensation offered by the landlord for the tenant's temporary displacement. [See **RPI** Form 588 §6]*

If the tenant fails to pay any charges remaining unpaid after deductions from the security deposit, the landlord can file an action against the tenant to recover amounts not covered by the security deposit.[6]

Landlord's duty to maintain

A residential landlord has a general obligation to:

- put a residential unit in a condition fit for occupancy prior to leasing; and
- repair all unsafe and unsanitary conditions that occur during occupancy that would render the unit uninhabitable.[7]

Further, all residential rental and lease agreements automatically contain an implied *warranty of habitability*. The unwritten warranty imposes a contractual duty on a landlord to keep their residential units fit for human occupancy at all times.[8] [See Chapter 37]

The landlord's statutory obligation to maintain their residential units requires the landlord to correct *major defects* interfering with the tenant's ability to live on the property, such as a lack of hot water or a leaky roof.

---

6 CC §1950.5(n)

7 CC §1941

8 **Green** v. **Superior Court of the City and County of San Francisco** (1974) 10 C3d 616

The residential landlord has an obligation to care for and maintain all major and structural components of residential rental units. They are also further obligated to repair *minor defects*. Minor defects include such conditions as:

- leaky faucets;
- faulty electrical switches; and
- failed locks or latches.

Typically, a residential landlord agrees in the rental or lease agreement to care for and maintain the property, which includes the repair of minor defects. [See **RPI** Form 550]

The landlord's failure to repair or replace minor defects constitutes a breach of provisions in the rental or lease agreement. The landlord who breaches the lease agreement by failing to make minor repairs is required to reimburse the tenant for reasonable costs incurred by the tenant to cure the defects.

When a residential landlord fails to repair minor defective conditions on the property on notice from the tenant, the tenant may exercise one of three remedies:

Tenant's option to repair

- repair the defect and deduct the costs of contracting for the repair from the rent[9];
- make the repairs, continue to pay rent and sue the landlord to recover the cost of repairs; or
- vacate the premises.[10]

However, if the premises are so unsafe and unsanitary they qualify as *uninhabitable*, the tenant can remain in occupancy and withhold payment of the rent. In an ensuing UD action, the tenant raises the defense of the landlord's breach of the implied warranty of habitability. The habitability defense forces the landlord to make the necessary repairs to eliminate the unsafe and unsanitary condition before they may collect rent. [See Chapter 37]

The court then sets the amount of rent due during the period of nonpayment of rent. The rent amount is based on the percentage of uninhabitability, usually determined in the tenant's favor.

If the leased premises is in need of repair, whether minor or major, the tenant needs to notify the landlord of the condition. The notification may be made orally, or in writing.

The repair and deduct remedy

After advising the landlord of the need for repairs, the tenant may make the repairs and deduct the cost of the repairs from the next month's rent if:

- the landlord fails to make the necessary repairs within a reasonable time after notice of the defect; and

---

9 CC §1942(a)
10 CC §1942(a)

Smoke alarm requirements for residential rental properties

A building permit issued for alterations or repairs of $1,000 or more on residential property will not be signed off until the property owner demonstrates all smoke alarms are on the current list of devices approved and listed by the State Fire Marshal. [Health and Safety Code §§13113.7, 13113.8, and 13114]

Smoke alarms will meet the following requirements to be approved and listed by the State Fire Marshal:

- *display the date of manufacture;*
- *have a hush feature;*
- *include an alarm indicating the unit needs to be replaced; and*
- *if battery operated, contain a non-replaceable battery that lasts at least ten years.*

A fire alarm system with smoke detectors may be installed in lieu of smoke alarms.

Multi-family residential properties are no longer required to have smoke detectors in common stairwells. Owners of multi-family housing properties who rent or lease their property are now responsible for testing and maintaining smoke alarms within all the units in their properties. This applies to both occupied and unoccupied units.

Residential property owners who rent out one or more units need to install any additional smoke alarms required under existing building standards. Existing alarms only need to be replaced if they are inoperable.

repair and deduct remedy
An option available to a residential tenant when the landlord fails to repair leased property which allows the tenant to make the repairs and deduct their cost from the next month's rent payment.

- the cost of repairs does not exceed the amount of one month's rent, called the **repair and deduct remedy**.

The tenant may not exercise the *repair and deduct remedy* more than twice in any 12-month period.[11]

Also, any agreement by the tenant to waive or modify their right to repair and deduct the costs from the rent is unenforceable.[12]

A reasonable time for the landlord to make necessary repairs after notice is 30 days, unless the need to repair is urgent and requires more immediate attention.[13]

The repair-and-deduct remedy is not available to the tenant when the need for repair is created by the tenant's conduct.[14]

Repairs exceeding one month's rent

If the cost of repairs exceeds one month's rent, the tenant, while continuing to occupy and pay rent, may make the necessary repairs and file an action against the landlord to recover the cost of the repairs.

However, it may be impossible for the tenant to make the necessary repairs when the tenant:

- rents a unit in a large complex; or
- is unable to cover the cost of repairs.

11 CC §1942(a)
12 CC §1942.1
13 CC §1942(b)
14 CC §1942(c)

If a commercial landlord's failure to make repairs substantially interferes with a tenant's use of the property, the tenant can vacate the premises and is relieved of any further obligation under the lease. Recall that this is called a *constructive eviction.*[15] [See Chapter 33]

Maintaining property with care

Like a residential landlord, a commercial landlord who retains responsibility for maintenance and repair under the lease agreement also has a duty to use care in doing so.

Consider a tenant, residential or commercial, who notifies their landlord a window is broken and will not stay open. The landlord begins work to repair the window, but does not complete the work. The tenant gives the landlord permission to enter the premises when the tenant is out to finish the repairs. The landlord does not enter the premises to make the repairs.

Finally, the window falls, injuring the tenant.

Here, the landlord is responsible for the injuries. Once a landlord of residential or commercial premises undertakes to make repairs on the premises to correct a dangerous condition, the landlord is to complete the repairs in a timely and proper manner.[16]

Landlords of both residential and commercial property are also responsible to tenants, guests of tenants and members of the public for injuries caused to them by the landlord's lack of ordinary care or skill in the maintenance of their property.[17]

Nondelegable duty to repair

Now consider a commercial landlord who hires a contractor to repair the roof on leased property. A tenant is injured as a result of the contractor's negligence while performing the repair.

The tenant claims the landlord is liable for their injuries since the landlord was responsible for the maintenance which created a dangerous condition.

The landlord claims they are not liable since it was the roofing contractor's negligence while on the job which caused the tenant's injury, not the landlord.

Is the landlord liable for injuries to a tenant caused by a contractor hired by the landlord to perform repairs?

Yes! A landlord's duty to exercise care (not to be negligent) in the repair and maintenance of a leased premises is a **nondelegable duty**. A *nondelegable duty* is an obligation which cannot be transferred or assumed by another person, such as a property manager or contractor.[18]

nondelegable duty
A duty which cannot be transferred or assumed by another person. In the case of a landlord, a nondelegable duty cannot be assumed by a property manager or contractor.

15 CC §1942(a)
16 **Minoletti** v. **Sabini** (1972) 27 CA3d 321
17 CC §1714
18 **Srithong** v. **Total Investment Company** (1994) 23 CA4th 721

When repairs require a contractors license

*It's common for an agent to coordinate repairs on behalf of the owner when listing property for sale or lease. Agents who order or oversee maintenance or repair projects costing $500 or more are considered **consultants**, and subject to contractor licensing requirements issued by the **California Department of Consumer Affairs Contractors State Licensing Board (CSLB)**.*

Individuals are not required to be licensed under the contractors license law if:

- *the work performed costs less than $500, including labor and materials [Business and Professions Code §7048];*
- *the work is performed by the owner of the property [Bus & P C §7044];*
- *the work is performed by a public utility [Bus & P C §7042];*
- *the work involves petroleum and gas operations [Bus & P C §7043]; or*
- *the work performed is for agricultural purposes.*

*Further, a **common interest development (CID)** manager is not required to have a contractors license when performing management services. [Bus & P C §7026.1(b)]*

When operating a residential or commercial rental property, routine maintenance is part of day-to-day property management. Routine maintenance prevents obsolescence from decreasing a property's desirability as a rental, and thus, its value and the total rents it commands.

*For repairs costing **less than $500**, the agent can contract with either:*

- *licensed contractors; or*
- *unlicensed individuals such as **handymen**.*

*However, when costs for all the proposed repairs are **$500 or more**, an agent who does not have a contractors license is limited in involvement to recommending a competent licensed contractor. All the negotiations, contracting and oversight are the responsibility of the owner directly. [Bus & P C §7048]*

The same rules apply to a property manager overseeing the ongoing repairs and maintenance of property they are managing. A broker, retained as property manager, is allowed to order out maintenance, repairs and replacements to be performed by third parties when the total cost is less than $500 per project.

*In addition, a **property management agreement** does not relieve an agent or broker from the contractors licensing requirements if they intend to solicit bids or otherwise facilitate or undertake any part of the work for repair and maintenance projects costing $500 or more.*

*Accordingly, an agent who provides property management services and is also a licensed contractor can order out work as authorized by the owner of the property regardless of the cost. [See **RPI** Form 108]*

In either situation, a professional property manager always has a predetermined limit for repairs set by the property management agreement entered into with the owner. Any repairs which exceed the limit require the owner's further authorization.

The landlord is liable for injuries caused to persons (excluding the contractor's employees) during the fulfillment of the landlord's duty to maintain the property, whether the maintenance is accomplished by the landlord or by contractors the property manager employs.

Penalty for failure to maintain

A landlord is aware that felony crimes recently occurred in the common areas of their apartment complex and parking garage.

The tenants of the complex complain to the landlord about the crimes. The tenants request the broken doors, gates and locks be repaired and adequate lighting be provided as security to prevent the crimes from reoccurring.

The landlord fails to make the repairs or provide the security measures requested. Later, while in a common area, a tenant is assaulted and suffers injuries.

The tenant seeks to recover losses from the landlord for their injuries, as well as *punitive damages*. The injured tenant claims the landlord breached their duty to protect them from known criminal activity in the complex. The landlord failed to maintain and provide adequate security measures in the common areas. Further, the tenant claims the landlord is liable for breaching the warranty of habitability.

First, can the tenant recover punitive damages from the landlord?

Yes! The landlord was aware of the dangerous condition created by the lack of maintenance. By failing to correct the deferred maintenance, the landlord acted with a conscious disregard for the rights or safety of the tenants. The landlord's deliberate failure to maintain the premises by eliminating the dangerous conditions which were known and over which they alone had the power to correct, exposes them to liability for punitive damages.[19]

Also, a landlord who fails to disclose dangerous conditions which are known to the landlord is liable for punitive damages.[20]

However, the landlord is not liable for breaching the warranty of habitability. The living quarters were habitable, and the housing complied with local codes. Thus, any tenant who fails to pay rent based on the landlord's breach of the implied warranty of habitability for lack of security in the common areas will be subject to eviction.[21]

---

19 **Penner** v. **Falk** (1984) 153 CA3d 858

20 **O'Hara** v. **Western Seven Trees Corporation Intercoast Management** (1977) 75 CA3d 798

21 Penner, *supra*

Chapter 36
Summary

A tenant needs to repair all deterioration and damage to the premises caused by their failure to use ordinary care. Normal wear and tear on the unit need not be avoided or eliminated by the tenant.

A residential landlord has an obligation to care for and maintain all major and structural components of residential rental units. They are also further obligated to repair minor defects. The landlord's failure to repair or replace defects constitutes a breach of provisions in the rental or lease agreement.

After advising the landlord of the need for repairs, the residential tenant may contract for the repairs and deduct the cost of the repairs from the next month's rent if:

- the landlord fails to make the necessary repairs within a reasonable time; and

- the cost of repairs does not exceed the amount of one month's rent.

Like a residential landlord, a commercial landlord who retains responsibility for maintenance and repair under the lease agreement also has a duty to use care in doing so. Once a landlord of residential or commercial premises undertakes to make repairs on the premises to correct a dangerous condition, the landlord is required to complete the repairs in a timely and proper manner.

Chapter 36
Key Terms

nondelegable duty .... pg. 365
repair and deduct remedy .... pg. 364

Quiz 9 Covering Chapters 33-36 is located on page 642.

Implied warranty of habitability

Learning Objectives

After reading this chapter, you will be able to:

- discuss the circumstances in which the implied warranty of habitability has been breached;
- identify the features of a dwelling which, if not properly maintained, constitute a breach of the implied warranty of habitability; and
- understand what steps residential landlords are to take when a tenant fails to notify the landlord of a condition affecting the habitability of a property.

Key Terms

habitability defense

habitable condition

implied warranty of habitability

Safe and sanitary living conditions

A landlord, aware an apartment complex they own is in a state of disrepair, does nothing to correct the defective conditions on the property. Due to the location of the property and its below market rents, the landlord is able to rent out units in the complex without repairing any of the defective conditions.

A tenant, fully aware of the *unsafe and unsanitary conditions*, enters into a lease agreement with the landlord. Soon after occupying, the tenant asks the landlord to exterminate the rodents and cockroaches in their unit. The tenant also requests that plumbing blockages, exposed electrical wiring and the collapsing bathroom ceiling in the unit be repaired.

The landlord does not correct or repair any of the defective conditions. In retaliation, the tenant stops paying rent but continues to occupy the unit.

The landlord serves a three-day notice for nonpayment of rent and declares a forfeiture of the tenant's right of possession. The notice expires without payment and the landlord files an *unlawful detainer (UD)* action to evict the tenant.

The tenant defends their right to occupy, claiming the landlord failed to maintain the premises in a habitable condition. Thus, the tenant was entitled to:

- retain possession; and
- pay a reduced rent set by the court.

Even though they failed to make repairs, the landlord claims the tenant is required to pay the amount of rent agreed-to in the lease since the tenant needs to either:

- quit the premises; or
- make the repairs themselves and deduct the cost of the repairs from their rent as authorized by law.

Can the tenant continue to occupy the premises and pay a reduced court-ordered rent to the landlord?

implied warranty of habitability
An unwritten provision, included by statute, in all residential lease agreements requiring the landlord to provide safe and sanitary conditions in the rental unit.

Yes! The landlord's failure to maintain the premises in a habitable condition constitutes a breach of the **implied warranty of habitability**. All residential rental and lease agreements are subject to the warranty of habitability regardless of the provisions in the lease agreements.

Also, the court-ordered reduced rent will remain for as long as the landlord fails to make the necessary corrections or repairs.[1]

Commercial leases are not subject to an implied warranty of habitability. [See Chapter 41]

However, if the commercial landlord fails to make the significant repairs they are obligated to make under the lease agreement, the commercial tenant has two options:

- pay for the repairs themselves, demand reimbursement from the landlord, and if unpaid, file an action against the landlord to recover the cost of the repairs; or
- vacate the premises, if justified, and file an action against the landlord for losses resulting from a *constructive eviction*. [See Chapter 33]

Implied warranty of habitability

The typical residential tenant under a lease agreement acquires a leasehold right to occupy the leased premises for a specific period of time. The tenant properly expects the premises and *appurtenances* (e.g., common areas, parking and storage) available to them to be safe, sanitary and fit for use.

---

1 **Green v. Superior Court of the City and County of San Francisco** (1974) 10 C3d 616

However, a residential tenant, especially an apartment dweller, is not just acquiring an interest in real estate; they have contracted for and are entitled to a safe and sanitary place to live, called a *habitable dwelling*. [See **RPI** Form 550]

The implied warranty requires the residential landlord to care for the premises by maintaining it in a **habitable condition**. A *habitable condition* is the minimum acceptable level of safety and sanitation permitted by a court as discussed later in this chapter.[2]

Residential property which is not in a habitable condition cannot be rented or leased "as disclosed," even though defective property conditions have been fully disclosed and the substandard conditions consented to by the tenant.

The implied warranty applies to the space rented by the tenant as housing and to all *appurtenances*.[3]

The public policy establishing the warranty of habitability was legislated due to landlord abuses during periods of scarcity in low-cost housing. This economic situation left residential tenants in lesser socioeconomic neighborhoods without the bargaining power possessed by more affluent and mobile tenants when negotiating with landlords for better property conditions.

Market forces cannot prevail over the higher public policy requiring safe and sanitary housing. The warranty of habitability serves to punish slumlords and discourage slum-like conditions in low-income housing.

A landlord who invests money in real estate needs to maintain their property. Otherwise, the value of their investment will eventually disintegrate due to competitive pressures in the rental market and court orders on tenant claims of uninhabitability.

> **habitable condition**
> The minimum acceptable level of safety, utility and sanitation permitted in a residential rental.

Landlord's breach of the warranty

The landlord breaches the implied warranty of habitability when they fail to comply with building and housing code standards that materially affect health and safety.[4]

A habitable place to live is a dwelling free of major defects, not mere inconveniences, which would interfere with the tenant's ability to use the premises as a residence.

A residential dwelling is uninhabitable if any features of the dwelling are not properly maintained or do not substantially comply with building and housing codes, including:

- effective waterproofing and weather protection of roof and exterior walls, including unbroken windows and doors;

- plumbing and gas facilities;

---

2 **Hinson** v. **Delis** (1972) 26 CA3d 62; Calif. Code of Civil Procedure §1174.2

3 Hinson, *supra*

4 CCP §1174.2(c)

- a hot and cold running water system with appropriate fixtures which are connected to a sewage disposal system;

- heating facilities;

- electrical lighting; and

- floors, stairways and railings.[5]

In applying these guidelines, a leaky faucet does not render a residential unit uninhabitable, despite the inconvenience. However, a lack of running water, or no hot water, is a significant defect that materially interferes with the tenant's ability to use the property as shelter.

At the time the rental or lease agreement is entered into, the building grounds and appurtenances, such as a pool, laundry facilities, storage areas and parking structures, need to be maintained clean, sanitary and free from all accumulations of debris, filth, rodents and vermin to meet habitability guidelines.[6]

Further, the landlord needs to provide an adequate number of garbage and rubbish receptacles in clean condition and good repair.[7]

Landlord responsibility for repairs

A residential tenant in an apartment complex is not typically expected to make repairs to major components of the complex, such as a central heating system, an electrical or plumbing system or the roof.

If a residential landlord fails to make necessary repairs, and the cost of the repair is less than one month's rent, the tenant may order out and pay for the needed repairs. The tenant may then deduct the cost from the rent, called the *repair-and-deduct remedy*.[8]

However, the repair-and-deduct remedy is not often feasible in apartment complexes since areas where repairs are made are in the possession and control of the landlord.

The residential tenant faced with inability to use self-help to cure defects may resort to other remedies, such as:

- vacating the premises, called a *constructive eviction* [See Chapter 33];

- stop paying rent and, in any ensuing UD action, prove the landlord breached the *implied warranty of habitability*; or

- raise and prove the defense of *retaliatory eviction* in any UD action.

Pre-leasing maintenance program

Before renting a residential unit in a building intended for human habitation, the landlord, in addition to continually maintaining habitability, will:

- install and maintain an operable dead bolt lock on each main entry door of a unit, unless the door is a horizontal sliding door;

---

5   Calif. Civil Code §1941.1
6   CC §1941.1(f)
7   CC §1941.1(g)
8   CC §1942

Facts: *A rental property was owned by two individuals as co-owner. One co-owner primarily managed the property while the other co-owner was passive performing only limited management duties. The co-owners held an insurance policy covering claims resulting from unknown dangerous housing conditions. The managing co-owner was aware of dangerous housing conditions on the property. A tenant of the rental property sued and was awarded money damages against both co-owners for dangerous housing conditions. The insurance company paid the damages then sought to recover the expenditures from the co-owners.*

Claim: *The insurance company claimed the damages they advanced were not covered by the insurance policy since both the co-owners were aware of the dangerous conditions due to their mutual management of the rental property.*

Counter claim: *The passive co-owner claimed their share of the damages was covered under the insurance policy since they had only limited involvement in the management of the rental property and was unaware of the dangerous housing conditions.*

Holding: *A California court of appeals held the damages awarded the tenant and advanced by the insurance company were not covered by the insurance policy and the insurance company was entitled to recover the advances from either or both co-owners since the passive co-owner's limited involvement in the management of the rental property put them on notice of the dangerous conditions.* [**Axis Surplus Insurance Company** v. **Reinoso** (2012) 208 CA4th 181]

> **Case in point**
>
> Does a co-owner's limited management of rental property expose them to liability for knowing of dangerous housing conditions on a co-owned property?

- install and maintain operable security or locking devices for windows which are designed to be opened, unless the window is a louvered window, casement window, or more than 12 feet vertically or six feet horizontally from the ground, roof or other platform; and

- install locking mechanisms on the exterior doors leading to common areas with access to dwelling units in an apartment complex.

Editor's note — Installation of a door or gate is not required if none existed on January 1, 1998.[9]

A tenant is responsible for promptly notifying the landlord of an inoperable dead bolt lock, window security or locking device in the unit. The landlord will only be liable for injuries caused by their failure to correct the defect within a reasonable period of time after being notified or becoming aware of the defect.[10]

A residential landlord failing to comply with required security measures entitles the tenant to:

- repair and deduct the cost from rent;

- vacate the premises;

- recover money losses incurred due to the condition of an uninhabitable building;

- recover losses caused by any landlord retaliation;

- file an action for breach of contract; or

---

9 CC §1941.3(a)
10 CC §1941.3(b)

- seek injunctive relief to stop the landlord from maintaining an uninhabitable building.[11]

Landlord's warranty of habitability defense

In a UD action, a tenant who successfully raises the *habitability defense* will be allowed to:

- retain possession of the premises;
- pay a reduced amount of rent based on the uninhabitable condition of the property; and
- recover attorney fees and costs of litigation.[12]

To retain possession, the tenant pays the rent awarded to the landlord, offset by the tenant's attorney fees, within:

- five days of the entry of judgment; or
- ten days, if the UD judgment is served on the tenant by mail.[13]

If the tenant fails to pay the rental amounts set by the court in a timely manner, the landlord is awarded possession of the premises.[14]

The UD judgment may or may not require the landlord to make all repairs necessary to return the premises to a safe and sanitary condition. When a landlord is ordered to correct the uninhabitable conditions by returning the premises to a safe and sanitary condition:

- the tenant remaining in possession pays the reasonable monthly rental value of the premises in its uninhabitable condition until the repairs are completed; and
- the court retains control to oversee compliance by the landlord.[15]

habitability defense
A residential tenant's pursuit of a legal remedy due to a landlord's failure to maintain habitable conditions on the rented premises.

The tenant who raises the **habitability defense** instead of paying the rent takes the risk of being evicted. The landlord's failure to make repairs may not rise to the level of a substantial breach of the warranty of habitability if the repairs are minor and are judged to create only an inconvenience or annoyance to the tenant.

If the landlord has not substantially breached the warranty of habitability:

- the landlord is awarded the right of possession; and
- the tenant is liable for rent accrued through the date of judgment.[16]

Further, the prevailing party in a UD action is entitled to their attorney fees, even if the rental or lease agreement does not contain an attorney fees provision. The prevailing party is the party awarded possession of the premises.[17]

---

11 CC §1941.3(c)
12 CCP §1174.2(a)(1)
13 CCP §1174.2(a)
14 CCP §1174.2(b)
15 CCP §1174.2(a)
16 CCP §1174.2(b)
17 CCP §1174.2(a), (b)

To calculate the reasonable rental value of the premises when a breach of the implied warranty of habitability exists, the court will:

- establish the percentage attributable to the tenant's diminished habitability or use of the premises due to the substandard living conditions; and

- use the percentage to reduce the agreed-to monthly rental payment.[18]

When determining the percentage of habitability or usability lost caused by the landlord's failure to maintain, criteria includes:

- the area of the rental unit affected;

- the duration of the tenant's exposure to the defect;

- the degree of discomfort the defect imposes on the tenant;

- whether the defect is health-threatening or just intermittently annoying; and

- the extent to which the defect caused the tenant to find the premises uninhabitable.[19]

If the agreed-to monthly rent is already below market rent due to the condition of the premises, the landlord who has breached the warranty of habitability may receive only a minimal amount of rent from the tenant. The court-ordered rent properly may be so minimal as to result in a financial penalty to the landlord.

Editor's note — While this penalizing rental amount actually may be unfair to the landlord until they repair the premises, courts are unsympathetic.[20]

The purpose of the warranty of habitability is to prevent illegal, substandard housing from having any market rental value. It also encourages landlords to maintain their premises in a condition where market rents can be charged and actually enforced in a UD action.

The mere existence of unsafe and unsanitary conditions, whether or not they are known to the tenant, establishes the landlord's breach of the implied warranty of habitability.

Consider a prospective tenant who contacts a property manager to rent a unit in an older apartment building. The tenant inspects the unit and notices wall cracks and broken windows. Considering the condition of the unit and the tenant's financial condition, the tenant offers to rent the premises in exchange for a reduced rent. The landlord agrees, and the property manager rents the unit.

The tenant takes possession. Soon afterwards, the tenant notifies the property manager of an inoperable heating system, electrical fixtures with exposed

---

18 **Cazares** v. **Ortiz** (1980) 109 CA3d Supp. 23

19 Cazares, *supra*

20 Cazares, *dicta*

wiring, no hot water and a rodent infestation. The property manager advises the landlord of the need for repairs and pest control. The landlord does not correct the defective conditions in the unit.

The tenant remains in possession but refuses to pay any rent, claiming their unit has substandard living conditions making the unit uninhabitable. The tenant is served with a three-day notice to pay or quit. The tenant still does not pay, and a UD action is filed.

The tenant claims they are not obligated to pay rent since the landlord breached the implied warranty of habitability. The landlord claims the tenant is barred from claiming a breach of the warranty since the tenant was fully aware of the extent of the defective conditions at the time they took possession.

Here, the landlord is not relieved of their duty under the implied warranty of habitability even though the tenant was fully aware of unsafe and unsanitary conditions when they took possession. It is the state of the premises, and not the disclosure of existing uninhabitable conditions that determines whether a breach of the implied warranty of habitability took place.[21]

Unlike the sale of property, when a landlord fails to care for and maintain their residential property in a habitable condition, they cannot rent the property "as-disclosed" and escape liability for having fully informed the tenant about the conditions.

Landlord has no time to respond

A landlord may not allow a tenant to take possession of a property known to be unsafe or unsanitary. Before renting out such a unit, the landlord is to ensure the premises is fully repaired.

The warranty of habitability is breached when the need for repairs is:

- known by the landlord, either through notice from the tenant or by the physical state of the property at the time it is rented; and
- the landlord fails to immediately correct the defective conditions.

Landlords have a duty to inspect and maintain their property and improve or correct known substandard conditions before renting it. Landlords are not granted a reasonable time to repair uninhabitable conditions if they are known to the landlord to exist before renting out the property to a tenant. This rule is based on the notion that landlords are to be aware of the condition of the physical components of the premises at the time the unit is rented.[22]

However, if a tenant has possession of the property, the tenant is to make the landlord aware of the unsafe or unsanitary conditions before the landlord can be held responsible for repairing them.

21 **Knight v. Hallsthammer** (1981) 29 C3d 46
22 CC §1714

Consider a tenant who rents a single-family residence that is in a safe and sanitary condition when they take possession. The condition of the premises is documented at the time possession is transferred.

During the tenant's occupancy, the toilet begins to leak and the linoleum floor does not repel the water. On noticing the leak, the tenant has a duty to notify the landlord and give them a reasonable amount of time to make the repairs before taking other action.[23]

However, the tenant fails to notify the landlord of the need for repairs. The bathroom floor rots due to the toilet leak, weakening the subfloor and eventually creating a hole. When the rent is due the tenant notifies the landlord of the unsafe and unsanitary bathroom conditions, but does not pay the rent.

Due to their refusal to pay rent, the tenant is promptly served with a three-day notice to pay rent or quit. The landlord begins repairs on the unit. The three-day notice expires and a UD action is filed and served on the tenant. The landlord completes the repairs prior to the UD hearing.

At the UD hearing, the tenant claims the landlord breached the implied warranty of habitability.

The landlord claims the warranty of habitability has not been breached since they did not have notice of the need for repairs until the tenant complained and refused to pay rent.

Has the landlord breached the implied warranty of habitability?

No! The tenant brought about the unsafe and unsanitary condition by failing to promptly notify the landlord of the need for repairs.[24]

New landlord steps into the breach

Consider a landlord of an apartment building whose tenants notify them of seriously unsafe living conditions in the units.

The landlord is financially incapable of paying for the repairs needed, and sells the complex. The new landlord inspects the building and is aware of defective and substandard conditions in the units. The new landlord proceeds to correct the conditions by renovating the building.

The new landlord notifies the tenants of the complex's change in ownership and an increase in their monthly rent to amortize their costs of renovation.

A tenants' association is organized. The tenants refuse to pay rent due to the ongoing state of disrepair in the units. The landlord serves three-day notices on the tenants who fail to pay the agreed rent. Unlawful detainer actions are filed, and the tenants raise the breach of the implied warranty of habitability as a defense to avoid eviction and reduce rents.

---

23 CC §1942
24 CC §1942

The landlord claims the landlord is not breaching the warranty of habitability since the previous landlord breached the warranty of habitability.

The tenants claim the change in ownership did not terminate their right to raise the warranty of habitability defense. The breach was a condition of the property that continued after the new landlord took possession, whether or not the landlord knew of the breach.

Can the tenants raise the warranty of habitability defense against a new landlord who did not cause the existing unsafe conditions?

Yes! The tenants have a valid implied warranty of habitability defense that justifies their failure to pay rent since:

- the premises were uninhabitable during the new landlord's ownership; and
- the new landlord is attempting to evict the tenants for rental amounts due under their ownership.[25]

Even though the landlord did not cause the premises to become uninhabitable and began rehabilitating the property when they purchased it, the tenants can still refuse to pay the agreed-to rent and avoid eviction.

Duty to avoid foreseeable injury

A tenant can recover more than a rent adjustment when the landlord breaches the implied warranty of habitability.

For example, a tenant inspects a rental unit and enters into a month-to-month rental agreement with the landlord. When the tenant takes occupancy of the unit, the tenant discovers faulty electrical wiring, a clogged kitchen sink and a leak in the roof, later damaging the tenant's personal property.

The tenant notifies the landlord (and the county health department) of the defective property conditions and asks the landlord to make the necessary repairs.

The landlord fails to make any repairs. The tenant continues to reside on the premises.

Eventually, the county health department issues a notice condemning the building as unfit for occupancy. The tenant relocates.

The tenant then makes a demand on the landlord for water damage to their personal property and the cost of relocating to a new residence since the landlord breached their duty of care to repair the defective conditions.

Here, the landlord owes a duty of care to the tenant, apart from the implied warranty of habitability, to properly maintain the premises and avoid the risk of the tenant's foreseeable financial loss.

25 Knight, *supra*

A rodent infestation is a breach of the implied warranty of habitability, inherent in all residential rental and lease agreements as though it is a written provision. [**Green** v. **Superior Court of California** (1974) 10 Cal. 3d 616]

A dwelling is considered uninhabitable if it is not "substantially free" from rodents and vermin. This, of course, raises the question of what constitutes "substantial." [Calif. Civil Code § 1941.1(a)(6)]

Under the implied warranty of habitability, an infestation is considered substantial enough to constitute a breach of the warranty if there is a "continued presence of rats, mice and cockroaches on the premises." [Green, supra]

When a residential property is thus infested, the tenant has the right to withhold rent for the duration of the infestation, until the landlord returns the property to a habitable condition. In the event the landlord proceeds with servicing notices and an unlawful detainer (UD) action for the tenant's failure to pay rent, the tenant defends their occupancy by claiming the landlord breached the implied warranty of habitability.

If the tenant successfully defends against the UD action, the tenant is still required to pay rent for the period of the landlord's breach. However, the court will reduce the rent by an amount proportional to the infestation's impact on the unit's habitability. In cases where a unit's habitability is severely affected, that amount can be reduced to almost nothing.

In multi-family properties infestations are not usually limited to one unit, frequently affecting areas beyond the control of an individual tenant. Lack of control makes it difficult or impossible for the tenant to eliminate an infestation on their own.

Bear in mind that a tenant may not withhold rent for a habitability issue they caused. Also, if the tenant never notified the landlord a condition had arisen that renders the unit uninhabitable, the landlord is not in breach of the implied warranty. Further, a tenant's request to repair the defect needs to be made in writing since proving the landlord breached the implied warranty is the tenant's responsibility.

Ultimately, rent will continue to accrue on an uninhabitable unit. However, policy mechanisms are in place to severely reduce the economic viability of an uninhabitable unit for the landlord. The goal is to prevent substandard units from entering the marketplace to begin with.

How many mice are too many?

The landlord is liable for the costs incurred by the tenant to replace damaged personal property and relocate. The costs the tenant incurred were a result of the landlord's breach of their duty of care by failing to make the necessary repairs to eliminate unsafe and uninhabitable conditions.[26]

Additionally, the tenant can recover excessive rent paid for periods of their occupancy when the unit was uninhabitable.

A tenant who fails to raise the warranty of habitability defense in a UD action and is evicted or otherwise vacates can later recover any excessive rent paid during the period the landlord failed to maintain the unit in a habitable condition.[27]

---

26 **Stoiber** v. **Honeychuck** (1980) 101 CA3d 903
27 **Landeros** v. **Pankey** (1995) 39 CA4th 1167

Bed bugs: a new kind of controlled pest

*A habitable condition is the minimum acceptable level of safety and sanitation — i.e., a property that is clean, sanitary and free of debris, garbage, rodents and vermin, such as **bed bugs**. [Calif. Civil Code §1941.1]*

Bed bugs pose a particularly challenging problem for California residential landlords. In multi-family properties, infestations frequently affect areas beyond the control of an individual tenant. Thus, properly coordinated and timely intervention is necessary to prevent a bed bug infestation from getting out of control.

*Landlords are to provide a written **bed bug notice** to prospective tenants when entering into a rental or lease agreement. [See **RPI** Form 550 and 551]*

The notice contains information about:

- *bed bug identification, behavior and biology;*
- *the importance of cooperating in bed bug prevention and treatment;*
- *the importance of prompt written reporting of bed bug infestations to the landlord; and*
- *the procedure for reporting suspected bed bug infestations to the landlord. [See **RPI** Form 563-2]*

*When a residential landlord enters into a rental or lease agreement, the notice is included an as addendum attached to the agreement. Effective 2018, the landlord is also required to hand the notice to tenants under existing rental or lease agreements which did not contain the bed bug attachment. [See **RPI** Form 563-2]*

Landlord and tenant duties

*The bed bug notice advises tenants to cooperate in the prevention and treatment of bed bugs. It also notes the tenant is to promptly hand their **written notice** of a suspected bed bug infestation to the landlord or property manager.*

*When a tenant reports a suspected infestation, the landlord or property manager will promptly contact a **structural pest control operator** requesting they investigate and correct the reported infestation.*

*Prior to the pest control operator's entry, the landlord serves the tenant a written 24-hour **Notice of Intent to Enter Dwelling**. [See **RPI** Form 567]*

When a pest control operator identifies an infestation and takes actions to cure the infected area, tenants are to cooperate with the pest control operator's treatment strategy, such as:

- *reducing or removing clutter;*
- *washing clothing, linens and furniture;*
- *clearing items from closets, shelves, drawers and other storage areas;*
- *thoroughly vacuuming and cleaning the infested and surrounding areas;*
- *allowing the operator to conduct their investigation unhindered or temporarily leaving the unit during the pest control operator's inspection or treatment; or*
- *destroying any untreatable items identified by the pest control operator.*

Bed bugs: a new kind of controlled pest

cont'd

When a landlord has no notice or suspicion of a bed bug infestation, they do not need to call for an inspection of a dwelling unit or common areas for bed bugs. However, when a bed bug infestation is visually detectable during any landlord inspection, the landlord is deemed to be on **constructive notice** *of the infestation.*

Further, a landlord may not show a prospective tenant any residential rental unit the landlord knows is infested by bed bugs.

The landlord has two business days after receiving a bed bug inspection report from a pest control operator to notify the affected tenants about the units or common areas inspected of the pest control operator's findings. [See **RPI** *Form 563-3]*

Editor's note — When a bed bug infestation exists in a **common area**, *the landlord is to provide notice of the infestation and inspection results to all tenants. [See* **RPI** *Form 563-3]*

Conditions creating a nuisance

Now consider a tenant of an apartment unit forced to relocate due to unsafe flooring and unsanitary conditions. The unsanitary conditions cause the local health department to issue an order condemning the apartment complex.

The tenant makes a demand on the landlord to pay their relocation expenses. The tenant claims the defective conditions in the rental unit constitute a nuisance since they are deprived of the safe and healthy use and enjoyment of the leased unit.

The tenant also seeks the recovery of *punitive damages* from the landlord. The tenant claims the landlord's failure to correct the defective conditions that created the nuisance was intentional and malicious.

The landlord claims the tenant cannot recover losses based on a nuisance, much less receive a punitive award for money. The landlord claims their interference with the tenant's use and enjoyment of the unit is a breach of the contractual warranty of habitability implied in the lease agreement, not the tortious creation of a health nuisance.

Here, the landlord has both breached the implied warranty of habitability and created a nuisance for the tenant. The landlord's failure to make repairs and properly maintain the rental unit substantially interfered with the tenant's continuing use and enjoyment of the unit.[28]

Recall that a *nuisance* is any condition that:

- is injurious to health;
- obstructs the free use of property; or
- interferes with the comfortable enjoyment of property.[29]

Further, the landlord's continued failure to maintain and repair the premises in a safe condition during the health department's investigation

---

28 Stoiber, *supra*
29 CC §3479

and condemnation action indicates the landlord intentionally maintained a nuisance on the premises — an ongoing disregard for the safety and health of the tenant.

Tenant recovery for landlord's failure

The tenant can recover their relocation expenses. They are also entitled to an award for punitive damages since the landlord maintained a nuisance when they failed to repair the unit. [30]

Further still, the landlord's liability to the tenant for creating a nuisance is additional to any refunds of rent and rent reduction for breaching the warranty of habitability in the rental agreement.

The tenant can also recover any medical expenses due to an intentional infliction of mental distress or personal injury if the landlord's failure to maintain the unit in a habitable condition is the result of the landlord's extreme and outrageous conduct. [31]

---

30 Stoiber, *supra*
31 Stoiber, *supra*

Chapter 37 Summary

A residential landlord's failure to maintain the premises in a habitable condition constitutes a breach of the implied warranty of habitability. A habitable condition is the minimum acceptable level of safety and sanitation permitted by public policy. All residential rental and lease agreements are subject to this implied warranty regardless of the provisions in the lease agreement. Commercial leases do not contain an implied warranty of habitability.

The implied warranty requires the residential landlord to care for the premises by maintaining it in a habitable condition. On noticing a condition that breaches the implied warranty of habitability, the tenant has a duty to notify the landlord and give them a reasonable amount of time to make the repairs before taking other action.

Chapter 37 Key Terms

Quiz 10 Covering Chapters 37-40 is located on page 643.

Fire safety programs

After reading this chapter, you will be able to:
- comply with the landlord's responsibility to provide fire safety programs; and
- identify the variety of methods which deliver fire safety information to tenants.

Learning Objectives

liability

Key Term

A residential apartment building contains state-approved smoke detectors in each individual unit and in the common areas.

A tenant informs the landlord the smoke detector in their unit does not operate, even with new batteries. The landlord and their manager do not repair or replace the broken smoke detector. Later, a fire breaks out in the tenant's unit.

The tenant is injured in the fire and their property is damaged as a result of the defective smoke detector. The tenant claims the landlord is **liable** for their losses since the landlord has a duty to repair or replace the defective smoke detector on notice from the tenant.

Is the landlord *liable* for property damage and personal injuries caused by the defective smoke detector?

Yes! On receiving notice that the smoke detector is inoperable, the landlord is required to promptly repair or replace it.[1]

Smoke detectors, security bars and safety information

liability
A financial debt or obligation owed to others.

---

1 Calif. Health and Safety Code §13113.7(d)

Further, a landlord will be subject to a $200 fine for each failure to:

- install a smoke detector in each unit and in common areas as required; and

- repair or replace a faulty smoke detector on notice from the tenant.[2]

Tenant's duty to notify

Smoke detectors are to be installed and maintained in all dwelling units intended for human occupancy, including single-family residences, duplexes, apartment complexes, hotels, motels, condominiums and time share projects.[3]

The smoke detector will be in operable condition at the time the tenant takes possession of the unit.[4]

If a smoke detector does not work when tested by the tenant, the tenant is responsible for notifying the landlord or property manager. The landlord is not obligated to investigate whether detectors are operable during the tenant's occupancy.

If the tenant does not notify the landlord about an inoperable smoke detector and the landlord is unaware of the condition, the landlord is not responsible for injuries caused by the faulty smoke detector.[5]

To repair or replace a faulty smoke detector, the landlord may enter the unit 24 hours after serving a written notice on the tenant of their intent to enter, unless the tenant gives permission for an earlier entry.[6] [See **RPI** Form 567; see Chapter 4]

Duty to install and maintain

An ordinary battery-operated smoke detector installed according to the manufacturer's instructions satisfies the requirement for both single- and multiple-unit dwellings, unless another type is required by local ordinances.[7]

For example, some local ordinances require the smoke detector to receive its power from the building's electrical system.

To determine the smoke detector requirements for a property, the landlord may contact the local fire department or the county fire planning department.

As of January 1, 2014, a building permit issued for alterations or repairs of $1,000 or more on residential property will not be signed off until the property owner demonstrates all smoke alarms are on the current list of devices approved and listed by the State Fire Marshal.

---

2 Health & S C §13113.7(e)
3 Health & S C §§13113.7(b), 13113.8
4 Health & S C §13113.7(d)
5 Health & S C §13113.7(d)
6 Health & S C §13113.7(d)
7 Health & S C §13113.7(a)

Smoke alarms are to meet the following requirements to be approved and listed by the State Fire Marshal:

- display the date of manufacture;
- have a hush feature;
- include an alarm indicating the unit needs to be replaced; and
- if battery operated, contain a non-replaceable battery that lasts at least ten years.

Housing units with a fire sprinkler system are not exempt from smoke alarm installation requirements. However, a fire alarm system with smoke detectors may be installed in lieu of smoke alarms.

Multi-family residential properties are not required to have smoke detectors in common stairwells. However, as of January 1, 2014, owners of multi-family housing properties who rent or lease their property are responsible for testing and maintaining smoke alarms within all the units in their properties. This applies to both occupied and unoccupied units.

As of January 1, 2016, residential property owners who rent out one or more units are to install any additional smoke alarms required under existing building standards. Existing alarms only need to be replaced if they are inoperable.[8]

The landlord of an apartment building is to provide emergency fire safety information to all tenants if the building consists of:

- two or more stories;
- three or more units; and
- a front door that opens into an interior hallway or lobby area.[9]

The information is to be on signs using international symbols. The signs are to be located:

- at every stairway and elevator landing;
- at the intermediate point of any hallway exceeding 100 feet in length and all hallway intersections; and
- immediately inside all public entrances.[10]

Further, the landlord is to provide fire information to all tenants through brochures, pamphlets or videotapes, if available, or conform to adopted State Fire Marshal regulations.[11]

If the rental or lease agreement the landlord negotiates is in a language other than English, the required information provided to the tenant is to be in English, international symbols and the four most common foreign languages in California.[12]

Posting fire safety information

8 Health and Safety Codes §§13113.7, 13113.8, and 13114
9 Health & S C §13220(c)
10 Health & S C §13220(c)(1)
11 Health & S C §13220(c)(2)
12 Health & S C §13220(c)(3)

A consumer-oriented brochure in English, international symbols and the four most common foreign languages is available from the State Fire Marshal.[13]

The State Fire Marshal has adopted California Code of Regulations Title 19 §3.09 concerning the dissemination of fire information to tenants in hotels, motels, office buildings and high-rises. Health and Safety Code §13220 addresses these issues for tenants in apartment complexes. However, information does not exist as to which four languages will be used to translate fire information.

Further, if the landlord has any questions about the enforcement or the requirements for posting and informing tenants of fire information, they are to contact their local fire department or the county fire planning department. The codes and regulations are enforced on a local level. Each county or city may have different requirements for complying with fire information regulations.

Emergency procedures for office buildings

Emergency procedures and information for office buildings of two or more stories are to be provided to the building's occupants.[14]

The emergency procedures information for an office building of two or more stories may be published in the form of literature (pamphlets, etc.). It is to be made available to all persons entering the building and to be located immediately inside all entrances to the building.[15]

In lieu of literature, floor plans describing emergency procedures are to be posted at every stairway landing, elevator landing, and immediately inside all public entrances.[16]

For high-rise structures, fire safety requirements include:

- posting emergency procedures on a floor plan at every stairway landing, elevator landing, and immediately inside all public entrances; and
- appointing a Fire Safety Director to coordinate fire safety activities, train employees in the building, develop an emergency plan, etc. (which is also required of operators of hotels, motels and lodging houses).[17]

A high-rise structure is a building rising more than 75 feet above the lowest floor level providing access to the building.[18]

Release mechanism in security bars

Security bars on residential property are to have release mechanisms for fire safety reasons. The release mechanisms are not required if each bedroom with security bars contains a window or door to the exterior which opens for escape purposes.[19]

---

13 Health & S C §13220(d)
14 Health & S C §13220(a)
15 19 California Code of Regulations §3.09(a)(1)(A)
16 19 CCR §3.09(a)(1)(B)
17 19 CCR §3.09(c), (d)
18 Health & S C §13210(b)
19 Health & S C §13113.9(e)

Also, the owner of an apartment complex is to install exit signs that can be felt or seen near the door of the exit.[20]

Editor's note — Any questions concerning fire safety requirements or whether an owner has properly complied with the requirements are to be directed to the local fire department or the county fire planning department. Some departments provide checklists of requirements that are to be met.

---

20 Health & S C §17920.8

Chapter 38 Summary

The landlord of an apartment building is to provide emergency fire safety information to all tenants if the building consists of:

- two or more stories;
- three or more units; and
- a front door that opens into an interior hallway or lobby area.

The information will be on signs using international symbols. The signs are to be located:

- at every stairway and elevator landing;
- at the intermediate point of any hallway exceeding 100 feet in length and all hallway intersections; and
- immediately inside all public entrances.

For high-rise structures, fire safety requirements include:

- posting emergency procedures on a floor plan at every stairway landing, elevator landing, and immediately inside all public entrances; and
- appointing a Fire Safety Director to coordinate fire safety activities, train employees in the building, develop an emergency plan, etc. (which is also required of operators of hotels, motels and lodging houses).

Chapter 38 Key Term

liability ....pg. 383

Quiz 10 Covering Chapters 37-40 is located on page 643.

Notes:

Chapter
39

Security to prevent crimes

After reading this chapter, you will be able to:
- identify the landlord's responsibilities to reduce the risk of reasonably foreseeable crime; and
- understand the landlord's responsibilities to reduce the risk of crime or warn tenants upon obtaining knowledge of criminal activity on the leased premises.

reasonably foreseeable

Learning Objectives

Key Term

Protective measures and warnings

The landlord of an apartment complex is aware of recent assaults on tenants in the common areas of the property. The landlord has also received a composite drawing of the criminal and a description of the criminal's mode of operation released by the local police.

The landlord does not undertake any of the *security steps* available to reduce the risk of a recurrence of the same or similar criminal activities.

The landlord later rents a unit to a new tenant. The landlord does not disclose the recent criminal assaults or the criminal's mode of operation. The tenant is not given a copy of the composite drawing of the perpetrator developed by the police. Further, the landlord represents the complex as safe and patrolled by security.

Later, the tenant is assaulted by the same perpetrator inside the tenant's apartment unit, not in the areas open to the public. The tenant seeks to recover their money losses caused by the assault from the landlord. The tenant claims the landlord failed to disclose the prior assaults and misrepresented the safety of the apartment complex to induce the tenant to rent and occupy the unit.

The landlord claims they are not liable for the tenant's injuries since the assault occurred within the tenant's apartment unit and not in the common areas where the prior attacks occurred.

Here, the landlord is liable for injuries suffered by the tenant inside the apartment unit. The landlord knew of criminal activity on the premises and owed a duty to care for and protect the tenant by either:

- providing security measures in the common areas; or
- warning the tenant of the prior assaults.[1]

reasonably foreseeable
The possibility a crime or danger may occur due to a previous crime on the premises. A landlord has a duty to take reasonable measures to prevent harm to persons on the property or warning tenants of the prior criminal activity.

Based on the prior criminal incidents, the likelihood of similar future assaults on tenants is **reasonably foreseeable**. When criminal activity is *reasonably foreseeable* due to known prior criminal activity, the landlord has a duty to take reasonable measures to prevent harm to persons on the property from future similar criminal activities.

The landlord's failure to warn the new tenant about known criminal activity creates a risk that a tenant may be injured. Due to the landlord's further failure to put security measures in place to prevent harm, the landlord is liable for compensating the injured person by the payment of money, called **damages**.

Alternatively, the landlord may also be liable for the tenant's losses based on their intentional misrepresentation to the tenant regarding the safety of the apartment complex.

Editor's note — Like a landlord, a homeowners' association (HOA) has exclusive control over the maintenance of the common areas. Thus, like a landlord, an HOA has the duty to maintain the common areas.

An HOA is liable for money losses due to any injury caused by a dangerous condition which it knows about or should have known about.[2]

Degree of foreseeability of harm

Consider the landlord of a shopping center who has exclusive control over the maintenance and repair of the common areas. Burglaries and purse snatchings have recently occurred on the premises. However, the landlord is unaware of this criminal activity in the shopping center.

At tenant association meetings, concerns about the lack of security in the center are addressed. The tenant association decides not to hire security guards on account of the expense. The tenants do not discuss or bring their security concerns to the attention of the landlord.

Later, a tenant's employee is physically assaulted and injured on the leased premises.

The employee claims the landlord is liable for their injuries since the landlord failed to provide security guards to protect employees of tenants from an unreasonable risk of harm.

1 **O'Hara** v. **Western Seven Trees Corporation Intercoast Management** (1977) 75 CA3d 798
2 **Frances T.** v. **Village Green Owners Association** (1986) 42 C3d 490

The landlord claims they are not liable since the assault on the tenant's employee was a type of crime that was unforeseeable by the landlord.

Here, the landlord has no duty to provide security guards in the common areas. The prior crimes (theft) were not of a similar nature that would have made a physical assault foreseeable.[3]

The landlord's duty to provide protection is determined in part by balancing the **foreseeability of harm** against the burden imposed on the landlord to remove or prevent the harm. A high degree of foreseeability is necessary to impose a duty on a landlord or HOA to hire security guards.

Unless *prior incidents* of similar crimes are brought to the landlord's attention, the high degree of foreseeability required to impose a duty on the landlord to take steps to prevent or eliminate future injury does not exist.

However, prior similar incidents are not the only factor used in determining whether a landlord has a duty to take measures to prevent future criminal activity. The foreseeability of an injury is also determined by the circumstances surrounding the injury and its occurrence, such as the nature, condition and location of the premises.[4]

Consider a landlord of an office building and parking structure located in a high-crime neighborhood. Many petty thefts and acts of vandalism have occurred on the premises, but no assaults have taken place. The security system maintained by the landlord to monitor the parking structure is in disrepair and does not function.

A visitor returning to their car enters the parking structure while an armed robbery is taking place. The visitor is shot and killed.

The visitor's spouse seeks to recover money losses from the landlord, claiming the death of the spouse was reasonably foreseeable and could have been prevented by the landlord. The spouse also claims the landlord, who was aware of criminal activity on the premises, breached their duty to take measures to prevent further criminal activity.

The landlord claims the injury was not reasonably foreseeable since the prior criminal acts were not similar to the act causing the visitor's death.

Is the landlord liable for failing to provide adequate security in the parking structure?

Yes! The landlord's failure to properly maintain existing security features in light of prior criminal activity and the nature of a public parking structure is a breach of the duty of care the landlord owes to persons who enter the structure. Although the foreseeability of the type of criminal activity causing the death is low, the landlord is liable since the burden of maintaining the existing security system is minimal.

Reasonably foreseeable criminal activity

---

3 **Ann M.** v. **Pacific Plaza Shopping Center** (1993) 6 C4th 666

4 Ann M., *supra*

Not only was the landlord aware of vandalism and thefts regularly occurring in the parking structure, the landlord knew the parking structure was located in a high-crime area. Further, parking structures by their dark and private nature tend to invite criminal activity. Death resulting from a visitor's accidental disruption of an armed robbery is reasonably foreseeable, even though no other armed assaults had previously occurred on the premises.[5]

No liability if not foreseeable

The extent of the security measures a landlord is required to provide is dictated by the degree of foreseeability of any future harm to others.[6]

When an injury is not foreseeable due to the nature, condition and location of the leased premises which do not indicate a person entering or using the property is at risk, a landlord is not liable if an injury which security measures may have prevented occurs on the premises.

Consider an apartment complex where previous criminal activity has not occurred. However, the community where the complex is located is generally known as a high-crime area.

The light bulb installed at the entrance to a tenant's apartment burns out. The tenant asks the landlord to replace the light bulb. The lighting in the common area is functional.

Before the landlord replaces the bulb, the tenant is assaulted in their unit, suffering injuries. The tenant claims the landlord is liable for their injuries since the landlord has a duty to provide adequate lighting as a security measure.

The landlord claims they are not liable since the light bulb outside the tenant's unit is for the tenant's convenience, and is not intended as a security measure to protect tenants.

Here, the landlord is not liable. Prior criminal activity had not occurred on the premises that would put the landlord on notice of foreseeable risks. The landlord has no duty to take security precautions against criminal activity. Further, lighting alone is not considered an adequate security measure for deterring crime.[7]

On-site, not off-site prevention

Tenants occupying an apartment complex have been victimized by numerous assaults and robberies in the garage area and courtyard. The landlord is aware of the criminal activity on the premises.

In response to tenants' complaints, the landlord promises to install additional lighting.

A tenant parks on the street instead of in the garage due to the inadequate lighting in the common areas. One night, while parking on the street, the

---

5 **Gomez** v. **Ticor** (1983) 145 CA3d 622

6 Ann M., *supra*

7 **7735 Hollywood Boulevard Venture** v. **Superior Court** (1981) 116 CA3d 901

tenant is attacked and injured. The tenant claims the landlord is liable for their injuries since the landlord's failure to provide adequate on-site lighting created a dangerous condition, forcing them to park on the street.

Is the landlord liable for the tenant's injuries that occurred on a public street?

No! The landlord does not have a duty to protect a tenant from criminal acts committed by others that injure the tenant when they are not on the leased premises.[8]

While the landlord's conduct may have caused the tenant to park in the street, the tenant's decision to park on the public street imposes no duty on the landlord to also eliminate dangerous off-premises conditions. A landlord's duty of care is to prevent harm to others in the maintenance and management of the leased premises, not adjoining properties.[9]

The landlord's duty of care is derived from their ability to prevent the existence of dangerous conditions from existing on the property they control, not adjacent properties or public right of ways over which they have not taken control. A landlord is liable only when a connection exists between the harm suffered by the tenant and the landlord's care and maintenance of their property and any adjacent property over which the landlord takes control.

Prevent dangers within your control

While the landlord in the prior scenario failed to exercise care in the maintenance and repair of their premises, the landlord exercised no control over the public street, nor did they create or permit the dangerous condition in the street which caused the tenant's injury.

The purpose for providing adequate lighting in the common areas of leased premises is to help protect tenants or others against the risk of criminal attacks on the leased premises, not on a public street where the responsibility for lighting and security lies with government agencies. The lack of adequate lighting in the apartment complex was not the cause of the attack suffered by the tenant on the public street; it only caused the tenant to use the street.[10]

Now consider a landlord who is aware of criminal activity occurring on public property adjacent to the leased premises. A visitor leaves the leased premises at night via a public sidewalk adjacent to the premises. Lighting is not installed on the public side of the premises to illuminate the sidewalk.

Ability to control is not control

While walking on the public sidewalk, the visitor is assaulted and injured. The visitor makes a demand on the landlord to recover money losses incurred due to their injuries. The visitor claims the landlord has a duty to protect patrons of tenants from criminal assaults on public sidewalks that provide access to the premises.

---

8 **Rosenbaum** v. **Security Bank Corporation** (1996) 43 CA4th 1084
9 Calif. Civil Code §1714
10 Rosenbaum, *supra*

The visitor contends the landlord knew criminal activity had occurred on the sidewalk and had the power to exert control over the sidewalk by installing lights on the outside of the building. The sidewalk was the means of ingress and egress to the building.

Is the landlord liable for the client's injuries due to a dangerous condition on adjacent property?

No! The landlord does not owe a duty of care to anyone to take control over an adjoining property and remove or prevent injury from dangerous conditions existing on the adjoining property. The landlord is not liable for failing to take steps to prevent possible injuries from occurring on a public sidewalk adjacent to the leased premises that are regularly used by tenants for access to their units.[11]

The landlord's failure to provide lighting for a public sidewalk that the landlord does not own or control did not create the dangerous condition that caused the assault against the tenant's client. The fact the landlord can influence or alter the condition of the public sidewalk by voluntarily adding lighting in no way indicates they have control over the sidewalk, which would impose liability for failure to provide off-site security.[12]

---

11 **Donnell** v. **California Western School of Law** (1988) 200 CA3d 715
12 Donnell, *supra*

Chapter 39 Summary

When criminal activity is reasonably foreseeable due to known prior criminal activity, the landlord has a duty to take reasonable measures to prevent harm to persons on the property from future similar criminal activities.

A landlord is to properly maintain existing security features on the leased premises. However, the landlord does not have a duty to take control over an adjoining property and remove or prevent injury from dangerous conditions existing on the adjoining property.

Chapter 39 Key Term

reasonably foreseeable .... pg. 390

Quiz 10 Covering Chapters 37-40 is located on page 643.

Chapter
40

Dangerous on-site and off-site activities

After reading this chapter, you will be able to:
- identify the duty of care a landlord has to inspect the leased premises and remove on-site dangers;
- identify conditions imposing a liability on the landlord; and
- understand how a landlord is to properly address dangerous conditions existing on the premises.

comparative negligence

Learning Objectives

Key Term

Duty to all to remove on-site dangers

A landlord, by their exercise of reasonable care in the management of their property, will take steps to prevent foreseeable injury to all who enter the leased premises.[1]

If a person is injured due to the landlord's breach of their duty of care to remove or correct a known dangerous on-site condition, the landlord is liable for the person's money losses incurred due to the injury. The person can be a tenant, guest, invitee or trespasser.[2]

The duty of care for others owed by the landlord applies to all persons on the property whether they enter the premises with or without permission, unless the person is committing a felony on the property.

Before liability can be imposed on a landlord for an injury suffered by any person on the leased premises, several factors are considered:
- the foreseeability of the type of injury suffered by the individual;

Conditions imposing responsibility

---

1   **Rowland** v. **Christian** (1968) 69 C2d 108; Calif. Civil Code §1714
2   CC §1714

- the closeness of the connection between the landlord's conduct and the injury suffered;

- the moral blame attached to the landlord's conduct;

- the public policy of preventing future harm;

- the extent of the burden on the landlord and the consequences to the community of imposing a duty to exercise care to prevent the injury suffered; and

- the availability, cost, and prevalence of insurance for the risk involved.[3]

For example, the landlord with knowledge of a dangerous situation created by the presence of a tenant's dog is liable for injuries inflicted on others by the dog based on many of these factors. The landlord's failure to cause the dangerous condition to be removed from their property is closely connected to injuries inflicted by the dog.

The landlord is sufficiently aware of the dangerous condition created by the presence of the dog to reasonably foresee the possibility of injury to others. Also, the landlord has the ability to eliminate or reduce the dangerous condition and prevent future harm by serving on the tenant a three-day notice to remove the dog or vacate.[4]

Landlord's duty to inspect

To prevent harm, the property is to be inspected by the landlord whenever entry is available to the landlord.

Each time a landlord enters into, renews or extends a rental or lease agreement, a reasonable inspection of the leased premises for dangerous conditions is completed as part of their duty of care. If the landlord fails to inspect when the opportunity exists, the landlord is still charged with knowledge of any dangerous condition discoverable by an inspection.

Consider a landlord and tenant who enter into a commercial lease agreement. [See **RPI** form 552]

The lease agreement allows the landlord to enter the premises for yearly inspections. Also, the tenant is required to obtain the landlord's approval before making any improvements.

With the landlord's consent, the tenant builds a roadside marketing structure and operates a retail produce business. The structure's concrete floor is improperly constructed and unfinished. Produce is often littered on the floor.

More than a year after construction, a customer slips and falls on produce littered on the floor, causing the customer to be injured. The customer claims the landlord is liable for their losses due to the injuries since the landlord's right to inspect the property puts them on notice of the dangerous condition.

---

3 Rowland, *supra*
4 **Uccello** v. **Laudenslayer** (1975) 44 CA3d 504

Facts: A single family residence (SFR) includes an in-ground swimming pool on the property. The pool complied with all safety codes when it was built 25 years prior and the owner has not modified conditions by installing a security fence. The owner later rents the property to a tenant. A guest of the tenant visits, bringing their 4-year-old child to the property. The only door leading from the home to the pool is left open during the visit. The door does not have a self-closing mechanism. The child falls into the swimming pool and drowns.

Claim: The guest makes a demand on the owner for money losses due to the death of the child, claiming the owner's negligence contributed to the child's death since the swimming pool was not maintained by the owner in a reasonably safe condition for tenants and guests by installing a security fence or other safety mechanism to prevent access to the pool.

Counter claim: The owner claims they are not liable for the child's death since the pool complied with safety codes when built and the owner need only to implement additional safety features if the pool is newly-constructed or being remodeled.

Holding: A California court of appeals held the owner is liable for the child's death since the owner's failure to implement safety features around the pool constituted neglect as the pool was not maintained in a reasonably safe condition for tenants and guests. [*Johnson v. Prasad* (2014) 224 CA4th 74]

Here, the injury was foreseeable and preventable by the landlord. The court further concluded the burden of installing safety features to comply with safety code was outweighed by the benefits of that burden—i.e., saved lives. Additionally, this burden is lessened with the availability of homeowners' insurance, which is typically available to cover these risks.

The landlord claims they are not liable for the customer's injuries since they had no actual notice of the dangerous condition created by the temporary deposit of produce on the floor.

However, the landlord is liable for the customer's injuries if the construction of the concrete floor:

- is a dangerous condition; or
- poses a dangerous condition when littered with produce from a permitted use.[5]

A landlord is required to conduct an inspection of the leased premises for the purpose of making the premises safe from dangerous conditions when:

- a lease is executed, extended or renewed; and
- the landlord exercises any periodic right to re-enter or any other control over the property, such as an approval of construction.[6]

Here, the landlord would have observed the condition of the floor had they conducted the yearly inspection of the premises called for in the lease agreement. The landlord is liable for slip and fall injuries when the condition of the floor is determined to be dangerous.[7]

The landlord's inspection

5　**Lopez** v. **Superior Court** (1996) 45 CA4th 705
6　**Mora** v. **Baker Commodities, Inc.** (1989) 210 CA3d 771
7　Lopez, *supra*

A reasonable inspection on any entry

A landlord has a duty to inspect the leased premises when they enter the premises for any single purpose. This includes maintenance, water damage or some other exigency causing them to make an emergency visit.

A landlord who enters the premises during a lease term is not required to make a thorough inspection of the entire leased premises. However, the landlord who enters will be charged with the knowledge of a dangerous condition if the condition would have been observed by a reasonable person.[8]

A landlord of a leased premises containing areas open to the public will be liable for injuries caused by a dangerous condition in the public area if the condition would be discovered during a landlord inspection.

However, if the landlord is not responsible under the lease agreement for repair and maintenance of nonpublic areas, the landlord will not be liable for failing to discover a dangerous condition. The landlord is not required to expend extraordinary amounts of time and money constantly conducting extensive searches for possible dangerous conditions.[9]

For example, a management-free net lease agreement transfers all or nearly all responsibility for maintaining and repairing the property to the tenant.

Under a net lease agreement, the landlord is not liable for injuries to persons caused by a dangerous condition on the leased premises if:

- the dangerous condition came about after the tenant takes possession; and
- the landlord has no actual knowledge of the dangerous condition.

Editor's note — Landlords concerned about tenant maintenance of leased premises will often reserve the right to enter the premises every six or twelve months. However, frequent inspections of a leased premises create a greater potential of liability for the landlord.

Landlords often reserve the right to conduct frequent inspections to assure that the tenant is not damaging or wasting the premises and reducing its market value. The right to enter brings with it the obligation to inspect for dangerous conditions. Also, the landlord may erroneously tend to overlook possible dangerous conditions they can control that are connected to the tenant's use, rather than maintenance of the property. [See Sidebar, "The agency duties of property managers"]

Knowledge of dangerous conditions

Consider a landlord and tenant who enter into a residential rental agreement giving the tenant permission to keep a German Shepherd dog on the premises.

After the tenant takes possession of the property, the landlord never visits the premises. Later, an employee from a utility company enters the yard and suffers injuries when they are attacked by the tenant's dog.

---

8 Mora, *supra*
9 Mora, *supra*

Often, landlords employ real estate licensees to act as their property managers.

When acting as an agent for the landlord, the property manager has a duty to notify the landlord of the property manager's activities and observations regarding the maintenance and management of the landlord's property. [Calif. Civil Code §2020]

However, the landlord is considered to have the same knowledge about the condition of the landlord's property as the property manager. [CC §2332]

Further, since the property manager is the landlord's representative, the landlord is liable for the property manager's actions performed in the scope of their representation. [CC §2330]

However, the landlord is entitled to indemnity from the property manager if the landlord is held liable for the property manager's failure to perform their duties and keep the landlord informed. The property manager who breaches their agency duty owed to the landlord is liable to the landlord for any losses the landlord suffers due to the failure, called **indemnity**. *[CC §2333]*

The utility company employee seeks to recover money from the landlord as compensation for the injuries inflicted on them by the tenant's dog. The employee claims the landlord should have known the dog was dangerous since German Shepherds are a breed with the propensity for viciousness.

Is the landlord liable for the employee's injuries?

No! The landlord did not have knowledge the tenant's dog was vicious and presented a danger to others.[10]

A landlord's obligation to prevent harm to others arises only when the landlord is aware of or should have known about the dangerous condition and failed to take preemptive action.

For example, the landlord receiving complaints from neighbors about the behavior of a tenant's dog may deduce the dog creates a dangerous condition, even if the dog has not yet injured anyone.

Editor's note — The landlord's duty to protect others from an injury inflicted by a dog does not yet include asking the tenant if their dog is dangerous. However, it is feasible the legislature could enact a law or the courts could impose a duty of inquiry on landlords when authorizing the tenant to keep a dog on the premises. Dogs genetically are European wolves hybridized to their present condition.

The pet authorization provision in the rental or lease agreement could include a declaration that the authorized pet is not dangerous. Further, the owner of a dog is neither civilly nor criminally liable for a dog bite suffered by a person who enters the dog owner's property, lawfully or otherwise, unless the person is invited onto the property by the owner of the dog, is an employee of a utility company, a police officer or a U.S. mail carrier.[11]

---

10 **Lundy** v. **California Realty** (1985) 170 CA3d 813

11 CC §3342(a)

The landlord ought to have known

Now consider a landlord who leases commercial property to a tenant who operates a retail sales business on the property. The tenant keeps a dog on the premises and posts a "Beware of Dog" sign. A newspaper article written about the dog's vicious temperament is also posted on the premises. The landlord visits the leased premises several times a year and knows the dog is kept in the public area of the premises.

After the lease is renewed, a delivery man is attacked and injured by the dog. The delivery man claims the landlord is liable for their injuries.

The landlord claims they are not liable since they were personally unaware the dog was dangerous.

Is the landlord liable for the delivery man's injuries?

Yes! The landlord owes a duty to the delivery man as a member of the public to:

- exercise reasonable care in the inspection of their property to discover dangerous conditions; and

- remove or otherwise eliminate the dangerous condition that may be created by the presence of a vicious dog.

The injured person can recover when the landlord is personally unaware of the dog's vicious propensities since a reasonable inspection of the premises on renewal of the lease would have revealed to the landlord the newspaper article and the "Beware of Dog" sign.[12]

Also, it is foreseeable that a guard dog kept on a premises during business hours might injure someone.

Further, the landlord's failure to require the tenant to remove the dog from the premises on discovery that the dog constitutes a dangerous condition is closely connected to the delivery man's injuries.

The landlord has control over the condition. They may serve a three-day notice on the tenant to require the tenant to either remove the dog from the premises during business hours or vacate the premises.

A landlord can often remove a dangerous condition by merely exercising their responsibility to make repairs that will eliminate the condition. However, a dangerous condition caused by a tenant's activity may require a three-day notice requiring the tenant to correct for the dangerous condition, or vacate the premises. [See Form 576 in Chapter 26]

On-site danger leads to off-site injury

Now consider a landlord and tenant who enter into a rental agreement for a residential dwelling. The agreement allows the tenant to keep dogs on the premises.

---

12 **Portillo** v. **Aiassa** (1994) 27 CA4th 1128

After the tenant occupies the residence, the landlord visits the premises monthly to collect the rent payments. During their visits, the landlord observes the dogs. The landlord is aware of the dogs' vicious nature.

One day, a neighbor and their dog are attacked and injured by the tenant's dogs two blocks away from the leased premises. The neighbor demands the landlord pay for losses resulting from the injuries. The neighbor claims the landlord owes them a duty of care to prevent injuries arising from dangerous animals the tenant keeps on the landlord's premises.

The landlord claims they are not liable since the injuries occurred off the leased premises.

Here, the landlord is liable for the off-site injuries since the landlord:

- was aware of the vicious propensities of dogs housed on their premises; and
- had the ability to remove the dangerous condition by serving a three-day notice on the tenant to remove the dogs or vacate the premises.[13]

The landlord's liability for injuries inflicted by a tenant's dog off the premises is the same as their liability for injuries inflicted by the dog that occur on the premises.

While the landlord did not have control over the property where the injury occurred, the landlord did have control over the tenant's right to keep and maintain a known dangerous condition.

The landlord's failure to have dangerous dogs removed from the premises caused the injuries suffered by the neighbor. The injury would not have occurred if the landlord had not allowed the dogs, which they knew to be vicious, to remain on the premises they controlled.[14]

Consider a landlord who is aware the tenant of their single family rental unit occasionally discharges a firearm in the backyard. One day, a bullet fired by the tenant enters the backyard of the neighboring residence and kills the neighbor.

Tenant's dangerous on-site activity

The neighbor's spouse makes a demand on the landlord for the financial loss resulting from the neighbor's death. The spouse claims the landlord breached their duty to individuals on the neighboring property by failing to exercise care in the management of their property.

Is the landlord liable for the neighbor's death?

Yes! Even though the injury occurred off the leased premises, the landlord is liable since the landlord:

- knew of the dangerous on-site activity carried on by the tenant who inflicted the injury; and

---

13 **Donchin** v. **Guerrero** (1995) 34 CA4th 1832
14 Donchin, *supra*

> • had the ability to eliminate the dangerous condition by serving a three-day notice on the tenant to refrain from discharging the gun or quit the premises.[15]

The landlord had a duty to prevent the tenant from continuing to fire the gun on the premises. Once again, a landlord is liable for any injury resulting from a known dangerous condition or activity occurring on their property that they have the ability to remove. This is the case even if the actual injury is suffered off the leased premises.

However, had the tenant left the landlord's premises with their gun and then shot and killed an individual, the landlord would not be liable.[16]

Failure to avoid obvious dangers

Some dangerous conditions are obvious to persons entering or using the premises. Obviously dangerous conditions impose a duty of care on each person to avoid injury to themselves.

For example, a person wearing cleats walks on a concrete path. Alongside the concrete path is a rubber walkway used to prevent slip and fall injuries. The person wearing cleated shoes walks on the concrete path and slips, becoming injured in the fall. A sign does not exist explaining the danger of the person's activity.

Here, a landlord has no duty to warn or guard others against a dangerous condition that is obvious.[17]

While a landlord is liable for injuries caused to others by their failure to use skill and ordinary care in the management of their property, the liability has its limits.

A person, who willfully or by their own lack of ordinary care injures themselves, exonerates the landlord, wholly or in part, from liability.[18]

A person has a duty of care to themselves to be sufficiently observant and keep themselves out of harm's way.

When the injured person's lack of care for themselves contributes to their injury, the money losses recoverable by the injured person will be diminished in proportion to the percent of negligence attributable to the injured person. This injured person's share of the negligence causing their injury is called **comparative negligence**.[19]

Consider a trespasser who illegally enters a property and fails to conduct themselves with care to avoid harm.

comparative negligence
An injured person's share of the negligence causing their injury when the injured person's lack of care for themselves contributes to the injury.

---

15 **Rosales** v. **Stewart** (1980) 113 CA3d 130
16 **Medina** v. **Hillshore Partners** (1995) 40 CA4th 477
17 **Beauchamp** v. **Los Gatos Golf Course** (1969) 273 CA2d 20
18 CC §1714
19 **Li** v. **Yellow Cab Company of California** (1975) 13 C3d 804

When the trespasser is negligent in exercising care to prevent harm to themselves, any losses recoverable by the injured trespasser will be reduced by the percentage amount of their negligence which caused the injury.[20]

The landlord's liability will be further limited if the trespasser was in the process of committing a felony on the property when they were injured.[21]

Now consider a person who enters leased commercial property and wants to look inside the building.

Next to the building, below a window, stands a vat of acid maintained by the business authorized to operate on the leased premises. The vat is covered with plywood for the purpose of keeping out dirt and dust.

In order to see through the window, the person climbs up and steps onto the plywood cover which collapses. The person falls into the vat, suffering injuries.

The injured person attempts to recover money from the landlord for losses resulting from their injury.

Here, the landlord is not liable for the person's injuries since the vat is not a dangerous condition that presents a risk of harm. The vat of acid is an integral part of the business run on the leased premises and is not a danger to any person who conducts themselves with care around the vat.

The injured person undertook the risk of harm to themselves by climbing on top of the vat and creating the dangerous situation leading to their injuries.[22]

Now consider a landlord of an apartment complex used by gang members as a base for planning their off-site criminal offenses. One of the gang members is a named tenant on a rental agreement.

The tenants and law enforcement officials complain to the landlord about the gang. However, the gang members do not harm or pose a threat of danger to the tenants.

Later, a pedestrian walking past the complex in the public right of way is chased by the gang members. One of the gang members, who is not the tenant, shoots and kills the pedestrian on a street adjacent to the complex.

The spouse of the pedestrian claims the landlord is liable for the death since they failed to remove the presence of gang members from their premises.

However, the landlord does not have a duty to protect members of the public using adjacent public streets from assaults by gang members who congregate on the leased premises.[23]

Not a dangerous condition

---

20 **Beard** v. **Atchison, Topeka and Santa Fe Railway Co.** (1970) 4 CA3d 129
21 CC §847
22 **Bisetti** v. **United Refrigeration Corp.** (1985) 174 CA3d 643
23 Medina, *supra*

Facts: A residential tenant rents a room on a property. The property contains a flight of steps with a functioning light located over the steps. The landlord advises the tenant to turn on the light before walking down the steps. The tenant, unable to find the light switch, uses the steps in the dark and falls, injuring themselves.

Claim: The tenant makes a demand on the landlord for these losses claiming the steps constitute a dangerous condition since the tenant did not locate the light and injured themselves falling down the steps.

Counter claim: The landlord claims the steps did not constitute a dangerous condition since a functional light was located over the steps.

*Holding: A California court of appeals held the landlord was not liable for the tenant's injuries since the steps did not constitute a dangerous condition as a functional light was located over the steps. [**Castellon** v. **US Bancorp** (2013) 220 CA4th 994]*

The congregation of gang members on the leased premises is not itself a dangerous condition. Thus, the landlord's failure to take steps to prevent the gang members from congregating on the leased premises is not the cause of the off-site shooting of a pedestrian by one of the gang members.

Again, the landlord is not liable for injuries that occur off the leased premises, since the landlord has no control over the activities of individuals or tenants while they are on public property, only when they are on their property.[24]

Dangerous off-site conditions

Now consider a landlord who leases a residence to a tenant. The residents of the neighboring property own a dog the landlord knows to be vicious. The neighbor brings their leashed dog onto the leased premises. The neighbor invites the tenant's child to pet the dog.

The dog breaks free from the leash and attacks the child, causing injuries. The tenant claims the landlord is liable for their child's injuries since the landlord failed to warn them of the dangerous condition created by the neighbor's vicious dog.

Is the landlord liable for injuries inflicted on-site by the neighbor's dog, which they knew was vicious?

No! The dangerous condition was not maintained on the leased premises. The landlord has no control or authority to remove the dangerous condition from the neighbor's property.[25]

While a landlord owes a duty to others to remove a dog from their property that they know to be dangerous, they do not have a duty to warn their tenants of the presence of vicious animals located on other properties in the neighborhood.

---

24 Medina, *supra*
25 **Wylie** v. **Gresch** (1987) 191 CA3d 412

The landlord's failure to warn the tenant about the neighbor's dog did not create a dangerous condition on the leased premises that caused the tenant to be injured. A landlord's duty to correct or prevent injury from dangerous conditions does not extend off the premises.[26]

While the landlord has a duty to make the leased premises safe, they are not required to ensure the tenant's safety from off-site hazards.[27]

The public right of way for a street fronting a leased premises includes part of the front lawn, located between the street curb and the property line. The landlord maintains the entire lawn up to the curb.

A water meter is located on the lawn in the street right of way. Several tenants inform the landlord the water meter box is broken and needs repair.

A tenant trips on the broken water meter box and suffers injuries. The tenant makes a demand on the landlord for losses caused by their injuries, claiming the landlord has a duty to eliminate dangerous conditions located in the public right of way within the lawn maintained by the landlord.

The landlord claims they are not liable since the water meter box is not located on their property and the landlord does not own or control the meter box.

However, the landlord is liable for the injuries suffered by the tenant. While the broken water meter box is located in a public right of way, the surrounding lawn is maintained by the landlord.[28]

Also, a landlord or other property owner who installs trees adjacent to or in the lawn area between the public sidewalk and the street-side curb owes a duty of care to prevent the trees from causing injury.

For example, trees planted and maintained by the property owner grow and eventually produce roots that crack and lift the sidewalk. The owner is aware of the hazard created by the tree roots but undertakes no steps to have the hazardous condition repaired or replaced.

Here, the owner has taken control over the off-site area containing the public sidewalk since the roots of the trees on their property have damaged the sidewalk. Thus, the owner will be liable to any pedestrian who is injured by the cracked sidewalk.[29]

Off-site injuries under landlord control

---

26 Wylie, *supra*

27 **7735 Hollywood Boulevard Venture** v. **Superior Court** (1981) 116 CA3d 901

28 **Alcaraz** v. **Vece** (1997) 14 C4th 1149

29 **Alpert** v. **Villa Romano Homeowners Association** (2000) 81 CA4th 1320

Chapter 40 Summary

Before liability can be imposed on a landlord for an injury suffered by any person on the leased premises, several factors are considered:

- the foreseeability of the type of injury suffered by the individual;

- the closeness of the connection between the landlord's conduct and the injury suffered;

- the moral blame attached to the landlord's conduct;

- the public policy of preventing future harm;

- the extent of the burden on the landlord and the consequences to the community of imposing a duty to exercise care to prevent the injury suffered; and

- the availability, cost, and prevalence of insurance for the risk involved.

Each time a landlord enters into, renews or extends a rental or lease agreement, a reasonable inspection of the leased premises for dangerous conditions needs to be completed as part of their duty of care. A landlord who enters the premises during a lease term is not required to make a thorough inspection of the entire leased premises. However, the landlord who enters will be charged with the knowledge of a dangerous condition if the condition would have been observed by a reasonable person.

A landlord is liable for any injury resulting from a known dangerous condition or activity occurring on their property they have the ability to remove or correct. This is the case even if the actual injury is suffered off the leased premises. However, a landlord's duty to correct or prevent injury from dangerous conditions does not extend to conditions that exist off the premises.

Chapter 40 Key Term

comparative negligence.. pg. 402

Quiz 10 Covering Chapters 37-40 is located on page 643.

Chapter
41

Commercial lease agreements

After reading this chapter, you will be able to:

- distinguish the various types of commercial lease agreements and use them to meet the objectives of the landlord and tenant;
- recognize the separate provisions of a lease agreement and understand what conduct they control;
- use an offer to lease or a letter of intent to initiate and document negotiations prior to entering into a written lease agreement; and
- determine whether the tenant or the landlord is responsible for paying property operating expenses and attending to the care and maintenance of the leased premises under lease agreement provisions.

Learning Objectives

ad valorem taxes

attorney fees provision

bona fide purchaser

choice-of-law provision

constructive notice

corporate resolution

eminent domain

entire agreement clause

full-service gross lease

gross lease

heirs, assigns and successors clause

license

net lease

reasonable certainty

reformation action

reversionary interest

Key Terms

A lease agreement is a *contract* entered into by a landlord and tenant setting forth tenant and landlord responsibilities, namely, the payment of money and the care of the real estate.

The conveyance of a leasehold

The lease agreement also acts to convey a possessory interest in real estate, called a **leasehold estate**, or simply referred to as a **lease**.[1]

By entering into a lease agreement and delivering possession of the leased property to the tenant, the landlord conveys to the tenant the exclusive right to occupy a parcel of real estate, or space in a parcel, for a fixed period of time. The continued right to occupancy of the real estate is conditioned on the tenant's performance of their obligations under two sets of provisions in the lease agreement:

- one calls for the payment of rent; and
- the others call for various levels of property maintenance and payment of operating expenses.

On expiration of the term of the lease, the right of possession to the real estate reverts to the landlord. During the term of the lease, the landlord as the fee owner holds only a **reversionary interest** in the leased parcel or space.

reversionary interest
A landlord's temporarily suspended right to occupy property leased to a tenant for the duration of the lease term.

Once the landlord and tenant have entered into a lease agreement and the tenant takes occupancy, the *right of possession* of the leased real estate is controlled by landlord/tenant law, not contract law.

On the other hand, the rent provisions in the lease agreement which evidences the debt the tenant has agreed to pay to the landlord over the term of the lease is controlled by contract law, not landlord tenant law. The landlord may prematurely repossess the real estate by declaring a forfeiture of the tenant's leasehold interest and right of possession when the tenant breaches a material provision in the lease agreement, the nexus between landlord-tenant and contract laws.

Recall from prior chapters that a forfeiture of the right of possession, the lease, does not automatically cancel the underlying lease agreement, the contract. The lease agreement requiring the tenant to pay rent and other amounts for the duration of the term of the lease remains intact and enforceable.

Conversely, the tenant's obligation to pay as agreed in the lease agreement is avoided on a cancellation of the lease agreement prior to expiration of the term of the lease. For example, a landlord's conduct due to their misunderstanding of the forfeiture provision in a notice to quit on a tenant's breach may bring about a *surrender* of the lease.[2] [See Chapter 30]

Validity of the lease agreement form

A lease agreement conveying a term of occupancy exceeding one year needs to be written to be enforceable, a *statute of frauds* requirement.[3]

Provisions in a lease agreement are separated into three categories of activities:

- *conveyance* of the leasehold interest;
- money obligations of the tenant, a debt called *rent*; and

---

1 Calif. Civil Code §761(3)
2 **Desert Plaza Partnership** v. **Waddell** (1986) 180 CA3d 805
3 CC §1624(a)(3)

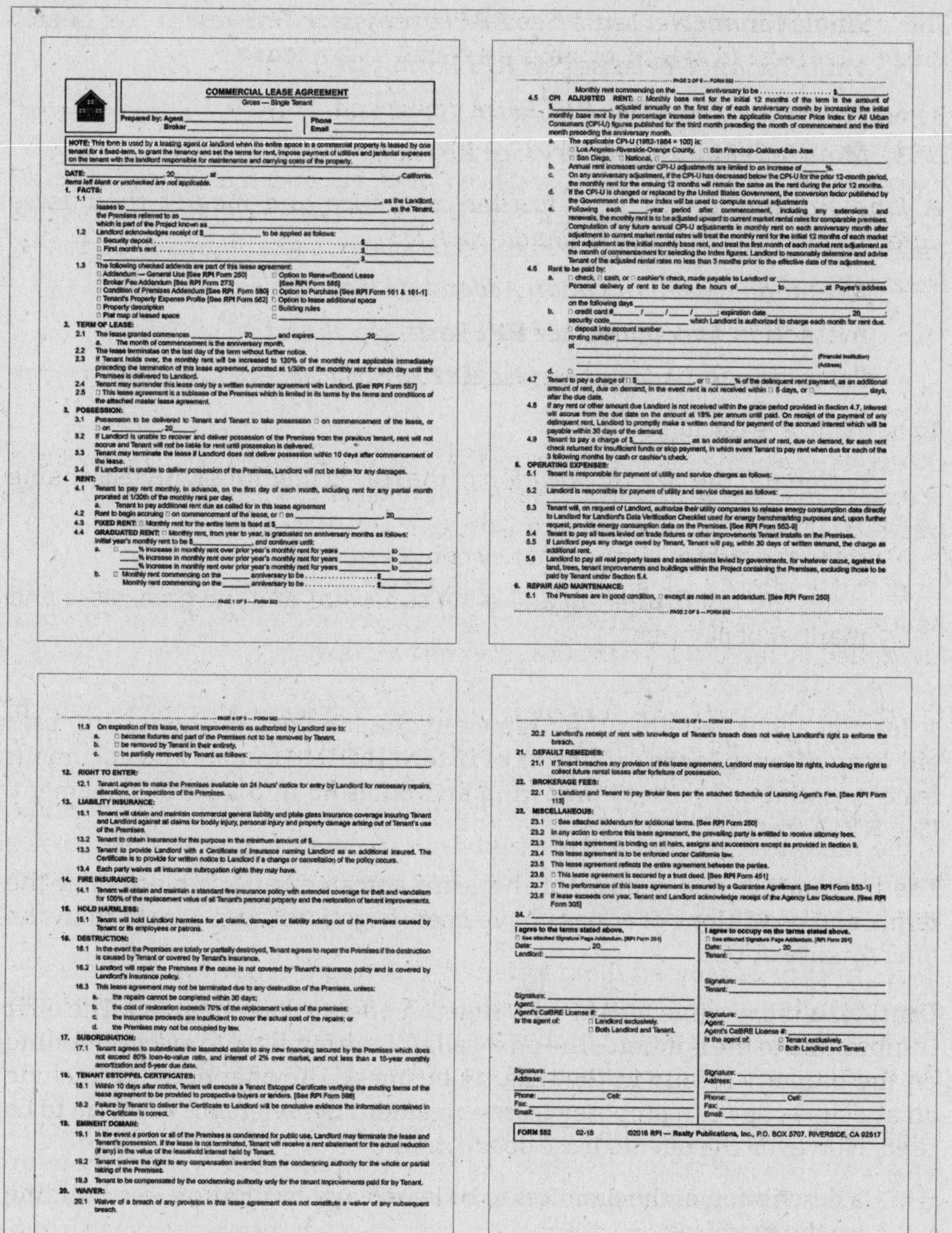

Figure 1

Form 552

Commercial Lease Agreement

Gross — Single Tenant

- responsibility of the tenant and the landlord for care and maintenance of the leased premises and other property operating expenses. [See Figure 1, Form 552]

Editor's note — Many variations of the commercial lease exist. Which of these the landlord and tenant choose depends on the specifics of the tenancy. RPI provides gross and net lease agreements tailored to common variations in commercial lease agreements, including:

- *Single Tenant Gross Lease [See RPI Form 552];*
- *Multi-Tenant Gross Lease [See RPI Form 552-1];*

- *Single Tenant Net Lease [See **RPI** Form 552-2];*
- *Multi-Tenant Net Lease [See **RPI** Form 552-3];*
- *Percentage Lease [See **RPI** Form 552-4]; and*
- *Month-to-Month Tenancy [See **RPI** Form 552-5].*

A landlord and tenant may further customize and modify their lease agreements with different addenda, such as:

- *Maintenance Modification Addendum [See **RPI** Form 552-6];*
- *Alienation Addendum [See **RPI** Form 552-7]; and*
- *Subordination Addendum [See **RPI** Form 552-8].*

To be valid, a lease agreement:

- designates the *size* and *location* of the leased premises with reasonable certainty;
- sets forth a *term* for the tenancy conveyed; and
- states the *rental amount* and other sums due, and the time, place and manner of payment.[4]

Condemnation conditions in an offer or LOI

A leasing agent, whether they represent the landlord or the tenant, uses either an **offer to lease** or a **letter of intent (LOI)** to initiate and document lease negotiations prior to preparing and entering into a lease agreement. [See **RPI** Form 556]

The preparation and signing of the lease agreement takes place after the terms and conditions of a lease have been negotiated and agreed to in the offer to lease or LOI.

Consider a prospective tenant who signs an offer to lease property. The offer is submitted to the landlord. The offer calls for the landlord to erect a building on the property for use in the tenant's business. The offer does not include an attached copy of a proposed lease agreement nor reference the form to be used. However, the offer to lease does contain:

- a description of the premises to be leased and its location — a building on the premises;
- a lease term — five years; and
- the amount of periodic rent and when it will be paid.

The landlord accepts the offer to lease, agreeing to lease the premises to the tenant. Occupancy is to be delivered on the completion of the improvements by the landlord. The offer to lease also states the tenant will lease the premises for five years, commencing on completion of the improvements. The tenant is to begin making rental payments once the improvements are completed. A formal lease agreement is not prepared or entered into by the landlord and tenant for various reasons.

---

4   **Levin** v. **Saroff** (1921) 54 CA 285

After construction of the building is complete, the tenant takes possession. Monthly rental payments are made to the landlord when due.

Both the landlord and the tenant perform according to the terms stated in the offer to lease, except for their failure to enter into the lease agreement.

Later, the property becomes the subject of an *inverse condemnation* action. Persons with an interest in the property, including the tenant, are entitled to share in the money paid by the government agency for the taking of the property.

The landlord claims the tenant is not entitled to any amount from the condemnation award since there is no lease agreement which memorializes the tenant's interest in the property.

The tenant claims they have a leasehold interest in the property under the offer to lease and delivery of possession. Further, the tenant claims they are entitled to recover the value of their lost leasehold interest in the property resulting from the condemnation of the property.

Here, the tenant will participate in the condemnation award; they hold a leasehold interest in the property that was not limited by agreement. The written agreement entered into by the landlord and the tenant — an offer to lease on the terms stated — becomes the lease agreement when the tenant takes possession of the premises without entering into a formal lease agreement.[5]

The *agreement to lease* (the offer or LOI) signed by the landlord contained all the essential terms needed to create a lease. Since all the elements necessary to create a lease are agreed to in writing, the landlord's act of delivering possession to the tenant conveys the agreed five-year leasehold interest to the tenant.

To record or not to record

A lease agreement need not be recorded. Between the landlord and the tenant, and all other parties who have actual or constructive knowledge of the lease, the agreement is enforceable whether or not it is recorded.[6]

An unrecorded lease agreement with a term exceeding one year in length is only unenforceable against a new owner if the new owner qualifies as a **bona fide purchaser**.[7]

To qualify as a *bona fide purchaser*, the buyer needs to:

- lack knowledge the lease agreement exists; and
- purchase the leased real estate for valuable consideration or accept the real estate as security for a debt (foreclosure).

Regardless of whether the lease agreement is recorded, the buyer is charged with the knowledge of the tenant's leasehold interest if the tenant occupies

bona fide purchaser
A buyer of leased real estate who lacks knowledge that a lease agreement exists and purchases the property for valuable consideration or accepts the real estate as security for a debt.

---

5 **City of Santa Cruz** v. **MacGregor** (1960) 178 CA2d 45

6 CC §1217

7 CC §1214

constructive notice
To be charged with the knowledge observable or recorded conditions exist on the property. When a tenant occupies a property under a lease agreement, a buyer is charged with constructive notice of the tenant's leasehold interest by the occupancy.

the property at the time it is purchased. The tenant's occupancy puts the purchaser on **constructive notice** a lease (or some other arrangement with the occupant) exists.[8]

However, when a lease agreement is recorded, the content of the recorded agreement may be relied on by a purchaser as a statement of all the rights of the tenant.

Editor's note — The above rules also apply to lenders when the landlord uses the property as security for a mortgage.

Also, if the lease agreement is recorded but the tenant holds an unrecorded option to buy the leased property or extend the lease, the option cannot be enforced against a buyer or lender who later acquires an interest in the property if:

- *the buyer or lender had no actual knowledge of the option at the time of acquisition; or*

- *the unrecorded options are not referenced in the recorded lease.*[9]

The contents of a lease agreement

A commercial lease agreement form has five main sections:

- identification of the parties and the premises, and the conveyance and term of the lease;

- the terms for payment of rent and other amounts owed, collectively called the **rent provisions** [See Chapter 42 and Chapter 46];

- the provisions setting forth the responsibility for care and maintenance of the leased property, collectively called **use-maintenance provisions** [See Chapter 46];

- miscellaneous provisions for circumstances unique to the transaction; and

- the signatures of the parties.

The identification section of a real estate lease agreement contains facts:

- the names of the landlord and the tenant;

- a description of the leased premises;

- words of conveyance of the leased property;

- a receipt for prepaid rents and the security deposit; and

- a list of the addenda which contain exhibits or additional terms. [See Form 552 §1.1-1.3]

The leasehold conveyance

The lease agreement includes words of transfer by which the landlord conveys — grants — a leasehold interest in the property to the tenant. [See Form 552 §1.1]

---

8 **Manig** v. **Bachman** (1954) 127 CA2d 216
9 **Gates Rubber Company** v. **Ulman** (1989) 214 CA3d 356

The conveyance of a lease is typically achieved with the words "landlord... leases to...tenant the real estate referred to as..." [See Form 552 §1.1]

Consider the landlord of a department store who enters into an agreement with a tenant to occupy space in the store for three years. The tenant will use the space to conduct their business.

The agreement states the space to be occupied by the tenant will be designated by the landlord at the time of occupancy.

The agreement also:

- outlines the formula for the monthly rent to be paid for the space;
- gives the tenant the sole and exclusive right to conduct their business in the store without competition;
- restricts transfer of the tenant's right to occupy the space without the landlord's consent; and
- requires the tenant to surrender the occupied premises on the last day of the rental term.

The tenant takes possession of the space designated by the landlord. Before the term for occupancy expires, the landlord notifies the tenant they are terminating the agreement and the tenant is to vacate the premises. The tenant does not comply with the landlord's notice to quit.

As a result, the landlord removes the tenant's fixtures, equipment and inventory, and bars the tenant from entering the premises.

The tenant claims the landlord can neither terminate the occupancy nor remove their possessions without first filing a UD action and obtaining a judgment to recover possession. The occupancy agreement constitutes a lease which conveyed a leasehold interest in the occupied space to the tenant which needs to terminate before the tenant has to vacate.

The landlord claims the occupancy agreement is a mere **license** to conduct business in the store. It is not a lease since no defined space was described in the agreement to identify the location of the leased premises.

license
The personal, unassignable right held by an individual to the non-exclusive use of property owned by another.

Here, the agreement to occupy the space conveyed a leasehold interest in the space provided for the tenant to occupy, not a *license* to use. While the agreement itself does not identify the space to be occupied by the tenant or contain words of conveyance, the agreement becomes a lease on the tenant's occupancy of the premises designated by the landlord since the agreement states:

- possession of the premises is to be delivered to the tenant for their *exclusive use* in exchange for monthly rent;
- assignment of the lease calls for the *prior consent* of the landlord; and

- the premises need not be delivered up to the landlord until expiration of the right of occupancy.[10]

The agreement entered into by the landlord does not contain the words "landlord...leases to...tenant" as words of conveyance. However, the contents of the agreement indicate the landlord's intention to convey a leasehold estate to the tenant, not create a license to use.

Sale disguised as a lease

Conversely, an occupancy agreement does not automatically convey a lease just because it uses words of leasehold conveyance. The economic function of a "lease transaction" may actually be something quite different, that of a sale which has been recharacterized by the parties under the guise of a lease.

For instance, a lease-option agreement that allocates option money or a portion of each rental payment, or both, toward the purchase price or down payment set for the purchase of the property is not a lease at all. The lease-option agreement is a disguised security device for executing an installment sale since it evidences a credit sale by a carryback seller.

Taxwise, the lease-option agreement is a sale requiring the seller (the "landlord", in this scheme) to report any profit in the down payment when the monies are received. Since this is a sale, the down payment cannot be deferred as option money under option rules.[11]

Proper identification of the parties

Each party to a lease agreement needs to be properly identified. On the lease agreement form, the identification of the tenant indicates how their ownership of the lease conveyed will be vested. Ownership of the lease can be vested as:

- community property;
- community property with right of survivorship;
- joint tenancy;
- tenancy-in-common;
- sole ownership;
- a trustee for themselves or for someone else; or
- a business entity.

When the ownership interest of the landlord is community property, both spouses need to consent to agreements leasing the community property for a fixed term exceeding one year. If not, the community is not bound by the lease agreement. Also, if challenged within one year after commencement by the nonconsenting spouse, the tenant cannot enforce the conveyance of the leasehold interest.[12]

---

10 **Beckett** v. **City of Paris Dry Goods Co.** (1939) 14 C2d 633

11 **Oesterreich** v. **Commissioner of Internal Revenue** (9th Cir. 1955) 226 F2d 798

12 Calif. Family Code §1102

In addition to individuals, **business entities** which may own or lease property include:

- corporations and out-of-state entities qualifying as a corporation such as business trusts;
- limited liability companies (LLCs);
- partnerships, general or limited;
- real estate investment trusts (REITs);
- nonprofit organizations; and
- governmental agencies.

Business entities as owner or tenant

When the landlord or tenant is a partnership or LLC, the lease agreement indicates:

- whether the partnership is a limited (LP), general (GP) or limited liability partnership (LLP);
- the partnership's or LLC's state of formation, and if out of state, whether it is qualified to do business in California; and
- the name of the partners or members authorized to bind the partnership.

With information on the partnership or LLC, the landlord and any title company insuring the leasehold can review recorded documents to confirm the authority of the general or managing partner or managing member to bind the partnership or LLC.

Whether a corporation is the landlord or tenant, the full corporate name and the state of incorporation needs to be stated. Also included is the name and title of the officer who will be signing the lease agreement as the agent committing the corporation to the lease agreement.

The corporate information will allow for confirmation of:

- the corporation's good standing to operate in the state; and
- the officers registered with the state to act on behalf of and bind the corporation under resolution by the corporation's board of directors.

Premises identified with certainty

The commercial lease agreement describes the premises to be leased sufficiently to be located with **reasonable certainty**. A description is *reasonably certain* if it furnishes a "means or key" for a surveyor to identify the parcel's location.[13]

> **reasonable certainty**
> The degree of certainty expected from a reasonable person.

If the premises is a building or a space in a building, the common street address, including the unit number, is a sufficient description to identify the premises.

If the premises is not easily identified by its common address, a plot map or floor plan needs to be included as an addendum to the lease agreement. The

---

13 **Beverage** v. **Canton Placer Mining Co.** (1955) 43 C2d 769

Case in point

A sufficient description

A tenant signs and hands a landlord an offer to lease together with the proposed lease agreement for space in a retail commercial center. Attached to the proposed lease agreement is a plot plan outlining the location of the leased premises.

The lease agreement contains a provision requiring the landlord to provide the exact legal description of the premises as an addendum to the lease agreement. The landlord is to deliver this addendum no sooner than 30 days after the leased premises is occupied by the tenant.

After submitting the offer to lease, the tenant decides to lease space at another location. The tenant mails a revocation letter to the landlord for the withdrawal of their offer.

However, the tenant receives the signed offer and lease agreement from the landlord before the landlord receives the tenant's revocation letter. The lease agreement does not include a copy of the plot plan addendum that was attached to the proposed lease.

The tenant refuses to perform under the lease agreement, claiming the lease agreement is unenforceable since the landlord failed to deliver the plot plan addendum that designated the size of the leased premises.

The landlord seeks to enforce the tenant's performance of the lease agreement.

*Here, a lease has been entered into which is enforceable. The precise size of the leased premises is not crucial to the lease transaction since the location of the premises is known due to the plot plan attached to the proposed lease agreement. Also, the lease agreement states the exact size of the premises identified on the plot plan will be determined after the tenant takes possession. [**Mabee** v. **Nurseryland Garden Centers, Inc.** (1978) 84 CA3d 968]*

space to be rented is highlighted or otherwise identified. A plot map or floor plan eliminates confusion over the location of the leased parcel or space in the building, and initially establishes the parameters of the leased space.

An attached floor or plot plan noting square footage is useful when rent is calculated based on square footage occupied by the tenant, or on the percentage of square footage within a project leased to the tenant.

However, an inaccurate or incomplete description of the leased premises will not prevent a landlord from conveying, and the tenant from accepting, a leasehold interest in a parcel of real estate. When the premises described in a lease agreement is incomplete or inaccurate, the tenant's actual possession of the premises will set the boundaries.[14]

Further, an incomplete or inaccurate description of the leased premises which the tenant has occupied does not release a tenant from liability under the lease for the space they actually occupied.[15]

Addenda to the lease agreement

Terms common to commercial lease agreements are contained in the provisions of a regular form. [See **RPI** Form 552—552-5]

14 Beckett, *supra*
15 City of Santa Cruz, *supra*

However, the terms and conditions peculiar to the leasing of a particular type of commercial tenancy, such as commercial, industrial, office, farming operation or hotel, or provisions unique to the parties and their advisors, are handled in an addendum attached to the lease agreement.

The use of an addendum to house extraordinary and atypical provisions not in common use prevents a later surprise.

Also, any handwritten or typewritten provisions added to an agreement control over conflicting pre-printed or boilerplate provisions. When inconsistencies arise between provisions in the pre-printed lease agreement form and an attached addendum, the provisions in the addendum control.[16]

The use of addenda for making changes or additions to leasing provisions allows parties to tailor the lease agreement to meet their unique needs.

Addenda occasionally attached to a commercial lease agreement include:

- terms unique to the type of property leased;
- a property description addendum, such as a plot map or site plan;
- a structural or tenant improvement agreement;
- a condition of premises addendum [See Form 560 in Chapter 36];
- a maintenance modification addendum [See **RPI** Form 552-6];
- an alienation addendum [See **RPI** Form 552-7];
- a building rules addendum;
- an option or right of first refusal to renew or extend [See **RPI** Form 566];
- a brokerage fee addendum [See **RPI** Form 273];
- a tenant leasehold subordination agreement regarding a future mortgage [See **RPI** Form 552-8];
- a non-disturbance and attornment provision [See Chapter 59];
- a signage or tenant association agreement;
- an option or right of first refusal to lease additional space [See **RPI** Form 579-1];
- authority to sublease or assign; and
- an option or right of first refusal to buy. [See **RPI** Form 161 and Form 579 in Chapter 6]

If the lease agreement is for a sublease of the premises, a copy of the master lease is referenced in and attached to a regular lease agreement thus creating a sublease. [See Form 552 §2.5]

A commercial lease agreement is an agreement to rent real estate for a **fixed term**, as opposed to a periodic rental term. Thus, the lease agreement indicates the dates the lease term commences and expires.[17] [See Form 552 §2.1]

Addenda to the lease agreement

The term of the tenancy

---

16 **Gutzi Associates** v. **Switzer** (1989) 215 CA3d 1636
17 CC §761(3)

SCHEDULE OF LEASING AGENT'S FEE

NOTE: This form is used by a leasing agent as an addendum when entering into a listing agreement or preparing a letter of intent (LOI), offer to lease or lease agreement, to set their fee due on the lease agreement and on any modification, extension or renewal of the lease agreement or purchase of the premises by the tenant.

DATE: _____, 20_____, at _____, California.
Items left blank or unchecked are not applicable.

FACTS:

1. This is an addendum to the following agreement:
   ☐ Lease Agreement [See **RPI** Form 550 and 552]   ☐ Rental Agreement [See **RPI** Form 551]
   ☐ Offer to Lease [See **RPI** Form 556]   ☐ Exclusive Authorization to Lease Property [See **RPI** Form 110]
   ☐ Exclusive Authorization to Locate Space [See **RPI** Form 111]
   1.1 dated _____, 20 _____, at _____, California,
   1.2 entered into between _____, as the Landlord, and
   1.3 _____, as the _____.
   1.4 regarding real estate referred to as _____.

2. **Fees due and payable** to Broker by Landlord under the above referenced agreement include:
   2.1 Leasing agent's fees on the initial lease of the premises in the following amounts:
      a. For leases with a term of five years or less:
         1. _____% of the total rent for the first year;
         2. _____% of the total rent for the second year;
         3. _____% of the total rent for the third year;
         4. _____% of the total rent for the fourth year; and
         5. _____% of the total rent for the fifth year.
      b. For leases with a term of more than five years:
         1. _____% of the total rent for the first five years;
         2. _____% of the total rent for the second five years; and
         3. _____% of the total rent for the remaining years.
   2.2 Leasing agent's fees on any modification, extension, renewal, new lease or other leasehold arrangement for the continuing occupancy by Tenants, or Tenant's successors or agents, of the property or any other property owned or controlled by Landlord or Landlord's successors, in the amounts calculated under the fee schedule in paragraph 2.1 above, as though the occupancy was a continuation of the original lease.
   2.3 A brokerage fee on the acquisition of ownership by Tenant, or Tenant's successors or agents, of any property which is the subject of a leasing agent's fee, in the following amounts:
      a. _____% of the first $_____ of the purchase price paid by Tenant;
      b. _____% of the next $_____ of the purchase price paid by Tenant; and
      c. _____% of the balance of the purchase price paid by Tenant.

3. **Fees due and payable** to Broker by Tenant under the above referenced agreement include:
   3.1 Fees due Broker under paragraphs 2.2 and 2.3 on Tenant's renewal or extension of their occupancy and acquisition of ownership of the property if Tenant, during Tenant's continuing occupancy of the property, renews or extends their occupancy or acquires ownership of the property from a party other than Landlord or Landlord's successors bound by paragraphs 2.2 and 2.3 above.

4. Buyer's Broker and Seller's Broker, respectively, to share the brokerage fee ☐ _____ : _____
   or ☐ _____

I agree to the terms stated above.	I agree to the terms stated above.
☐ See attached Signature Page Addendum. [RPI Form 251]	☐ See attached Signature Page Addendum. [RPI Form 251]
Date: _____, 20____	Date: _____, 20____
Landlord's Broker: _____ CalBRE #: _____	Landlord: _____
Signature: _____	Signature: _____
Tenant's Broker: _____ CalBRE #: _____	Tenant: _____
Signature: _____	Signature: _____
Phone: _____ Cell: _____	Phone: _____ Cell: _____
Email: _____	Email: _____

FORM 113   07-14   ©2016 RPI — Realty Publications, Inc., P.O. BOX 5707, RIVERSIDE, CA 92517

The date for delivery and acceptance of possession are addressed separately from the date of the lease agreement. Further, the date given at the top of a lease agreement is for the purpose of identifying the document. [See Form 552 §3.1]

On expiration of the lease term on the date stated in the lease agreement, the tenant's right of possession automatically terminates. The tenant vacates the property on the lease expiration date unless further occupancy agreements exist. No further notice is required from the landlord or tenant to terminate the tenancy or to vacate.[18]

Recall that a *holdover tenancy* is created when:

- the tenant remains in possession after the lease term expires without a right to renew or extend the tenancy; and
- the landlord refuses to accept further rent payments.

The holdover tenancy ends when the tenant vacates or is evicted.

The lease agreement contains a holdover rent provision calling for a set dollar amount of rent due for each day the tenant holds over. The holdover rent is due and payable when the tenant vacates or is evicted, not before. The daily rent rate is usually significantly higher than the fair market rate. As a result, holdover rent is considered unreasonable in a UD action. UD actions typically allow only market rent rates for the holdover period. [See Form 552 §2.3]

Holdover provision

If the amount of holdover rent is not set in the lease agreement, a fair market rate will be recoverable during the holdover (which is also the ceiling for rent awarded in a UD action to evict the holdover tenant).

The landlord may initiate UD proceedings to evict the holdover tenant immediately on expiration of the tenant's right to possession.[19]

Lease agreement provisions set the date the tenant will take possession of the leased premises. The agreement also address the consequences when a landlord fails to deliver the premises to the tenant as agreed. [See Form 552 §3.2]

Delivery and acceptance of possession

The tenant is given the opportunity to terminate the lease agreement if possession is not delivered within an agreed-to number of days after commencement of the lease. [See Form 552 §3.3]

A landlord sometimes fails to deliver possession to the tenant due to their inability to recover the premises from a previous tenant. For the tenant to cover this risk, the lease agreement states the tenant is not liable for rent payments until possession is delivered. [See Form 552 §3.2]

Conversely, the lease agreement states the landlord will not be liable for damages if they are unable to deliver possession. [See Form 552 §3.4]

A tenant may contract away their right to receive any compensation awarded to the landlord in a condemnation action by a government agency to take the real estate (fee and leasehold), also known as **eminent domain**.[20]

Eminent domain

---

18 CC §1933
19 CCP §1161(1)
20 **New Haven Unified School District** v. **Taco Bell Corporation** (1994) 24 CA4th 1473

Commercial leases typically reserve for the landlord all rights to any condemnation award. This reservation is made under the *eminent domain* provision. [See Form 552 §19]

eminent domain
The right of the government to take private property for public use on payment to the owner of the property's fair market value.

Also, the landlord may reserve their right to terminate the lease in the event of a partial condemnation. If the landlord does not choose to terminate the lease when a partial taking occurs, the tenant is entitled to rent abatement for the reduction in value of their leasehold interest. [See Form 552 §19.1]

A tenant under a lease has a right to receive compensation for their leasehold interest if their lease is terminated due to a condemnation proceeding.[21]

However, if a lease provision eliminates the tenant's rights to any compensation awarded to the landlord, the tenant looks to the condemning authority to recover other losses, such as:

- relocation costs;
- loss of goodwill;
- bonus value of the lease (due to below market rent); or
- severance damages when a partial taking occurs.

Brokerage fees

Initially, the responsibility for assuring payment of a broker fee for leasing services is controlled by employment provisions in:

- an *authorization to lease* [See Chapter 12];
- an authorization to locate space [See **RPI** Form 111]; or
- a *property management agreement*.

Secondly, the payment of fees is controlled by the placement of a brokerage fee provision within the tenant's *offer to lease* or *LOI* signed by the tenant.

Lastly, a provision for payment of the broker fees is included in the lease agreement. This redundancy allows the broker to enforce payment of the brokerage fees in case the prior documents did not include a commitment from either the tenant or the landlord to pay the brokerage fees. Also, fee arrangements are negotiable and change between the initial employment and signing of a leasing agreement. [See Form 552 §22 and Form 113 accompanying this chapter]

Miscellaneous provisions

An **attorney fee provision** is essential in a lease agreement if the landlord is to recover costs incurred to enforce payment of rent or evict the tenant. Regardless of how an *attorney fee provision* is written, the prevailing party is entitled to their fee.[22] [See Form 552 §23.2]

attorney fees provision
A provision in an agreement permitting the prevailing party to a dispute to receive attorney fees when litigation arises due to the agreement. [See **RPI** Form 552 §23.2]

The **heirs, assigns and successors clause** binds those who later take the position of the landlord or tenant to the existing lease (or rental) agreement through a(n):

---

21 CCP §1265.150
22 CC §1717(a)

- grant;
- assignment; or
- assumption.[23] [See Form 552 §23.3]

A **choice-of-law provision** in the lease agreement assures application of California law when a dispute arises between the tenant and the landlord. [See Form 552 §23.4]

Application of California law in disputes over property located in California adds stability to the legal expectations of the landlord and tenant. It also produces greater commercial certainty in real estate transactions and stabilizes property values.

Additionally, the lease agreement reflects the entire agreement between the parties and is best modified only in writing.

An **entire agreement clause** serves two key purposes. The objective is to avoid disputes over "just what are" the terms of the lease agreement resulting from negotiations to enter into or modify the agreement. An *entire agreement clause* limits the ability for the tenant or the landlord:

- to imply terms into the lease based on oral statements made before entering into the lease agreement; and
- to later orally modify terms of a lease agreement. [See Form 552 §23.5]

Performance assurance provisions address the tenant's performance of their lease obligations, including:

- security for lease agreement obligations provided by a trust deed encumbering real estate owned by the tenant (or others) [See **RPI** Form 451; see Form 552 §23.6]; and
- guarantees given by a corporate tenant's officer or another person. [See **RPI** Form 553-1; see Form 552 § 23.7]

If the tenant fails to pay rent or otherwise breaches the lease, the landlord may evict the tenant. Then, after a demand for payment, the landlord may foreclose under the performance trust deed to recover rent due, attorney fees and costs of the trustee's sale.[24]

Individuals who sign a lease agreement on behalf of the landlord or the tenant need to have the capacity and the authority to act on behalf of and bind the landlord or tenant.[25]

Unless the landlord is aware that the persons signing do not have authority to enter into a lease on behalf of the corporation, the lease entered into by a corporate tenant is valid if it is signed by:

- the chairman of the board, president or the vice president; and

---

heirs, assigns and successors clause
A clause in a lease agreement which binds those who later take the position of landlord or tenant to the existing agreement. [See **RPI** Form 552 §23.3]

choice-of-law provision
A provision specifying California law applies if a dispute arises with a tenant regarding the lease. [See **RPI** Form 552 §23.4]

entire agreement clause
A clause in a lease agreement which limits the tenant's ability to imply terms into the lease based on oral statements made before entering into the lease. [See **RPI** Form 552 §23.5]

Signatures on behalf of the parties

---

23 **Saucedo** v. **Mercury Savings and Loan Association** (1980) 111 CA3d 309
24 **Willys of Marin Company** v. **Pierce** (1956) 140 CA2d 826
25 CC §§2304; 2307

Sidebar

Americans with Disabilities Act (ADA) disclosure

*All commercial rental and lease agreements include an **Americans with Disabilities Act (ADA)** disclosure. Without it, landlords expose themselves to tenant litigation for fraud (or indemnity) when the tenant is hit with an ADA violation claim. [See Figure 1, Form 552 §7.6 and 7.9]*

*An ADA risk compliance disclosure provision is included in **RPI's** commercial lease agreements. California's Disabled Access Law makes disclosure of ADA conditions a **material fact.***

To avoid misrepresenting property conditions, a commercial lease agreement needs to declare whether the property has undergone an inspection by a Certified Access Specialist (CASp). Further, if the property has been inspected, a statement whether it does or does not meet ADA standards is included. [See Figure 1, Form 552 §7.9]

While the landlord needs to disclose ADA conditions, they need not obtain a CASp inspection. It is the failure to make ADA disclosures, as with code violations, which exposes the landlord to claims of fraud. [Calif. Civil Code §1938 and §55.53]

- the secretary, assistant secretary, chief financial officer or assistant treasurer.[26]

corporate resolution
A document from a corporation's board of directors which gives the officers of a corporation the authority to sign and bind the corporation to a lease.

However, a **corporate resolution** is the best evidence of the corporate officers' authority to act on behalf of the corporate tenant. A *corporate resolution* is a document from a corporation's board of directors which gives the officers of a corporation the authority to sign and bind the corporation to a lease.[27]

When an LLC or LLP enters into a lease agreement, the manager signing on behalf of the LLC or LLP needs to be the person named as the manager in the LLC-1 or LLP-1 certificate filed with the Secretary of State and recorded with the local county recorder.

However, an LLP or an LLC will still be bound to a lease agreement if:

- a partner or member, other than the general partner or manager, signs the lease agreement; and

- the landlord believes the partner or member is acting with the authority of the entity due to their title as chairman or president.[28]

The economics of commercial leases

Commercial lease agreements are used in transactions involving industrial, commercial, office and other types of commercial income-producing property.

A tenant who acquires a leasehold interest in commercial real estate agrees to be obligated for none, some or all of the **operating costs** of the real estate incurred directly or paid as additional rent. These obligations are in addition to payment of the base rent and periodic adjustments to the rent.

Editor's note — Residential lease agreements generally do not require the tenant to undertake the full care and maintenance of the premises. Usually, residential tenants only have the duty to prevent excessive wear and tear.

26 Corp C §313
27 Calif. Corporations Code §300
28 Corp C §17154(c)

Typically, the longer the term of the commercial lease, the more extensive the shift of ownership costs and responsibilities to the tenant, including:

- property operating expenses;
- all or future increases in real estate taxes, called **ad valorem taxes**;
- hazard insurance premiums;
- repair and maintenance of the improvements; and
- the risk of an increase in interest payments on an adjustable rate mortgage encumbering the property.

When a long-term lease obligates the tenant to pay for all expenses incurred in the ownership and operation of the property, the tenant incurs the expenses in one of two arrangements:

- directly, the tenant contracting for services and paying the costs, including payment of property taxes and insurance premiums; or
- indirectly, the landlord incurring operating expenses and in turn billing the tenant for payment, commonly called *common area maintenance charges (CAMs)*.

The responsibility for the payment of operating costs is reflected by the titles given to commercial lease agreements as either:

- a **gross lease**; or
- a **net lease**.

Lease variations

Variations and modifications exist for both types of lease agreements provided by addendums. For example, a gross lease calling for the tenant to pay some of the operating expenses is called a **modified gross lease.** When the landlord enters into a net lease agreement and retains responsibility for some of the operating expenses, the lease is called a **modified net lease**.

A commercial lease is typically called a *gross lease* if the tenant pays for their utilities and janitorial fees, but is not responsible for any other care, maintenance or carrying costs of the property.

When the landlord of an office building retains the responsibility for payment of all costs of care and maintenance, including the tenant's utilities and janitorial services, the gross lease is referred to as a **full-service gross lease**. [See **RPI** Form 552 and 552-1]

Conversely, a commercial lease that transfers to the tenant the obligation to pay some or all of the costs and responsibilities of ownership, in addition to utilities and janitorial services, is referred to as a *modified gross lease* (or a *modified net lease* if the tenant is obligated for most operating expenses). [See **RPI** Form 552-2 and 552-3]

A lease becomes more net (and less gross) as the landlord shifts ownership responsibilities and operating costs to the tenant.

ad valorem taxes
Real estate taxes imposed on property based on its assessed value. [See **RPI** Form 552-2 §5.1]

gross lease
A commercial lease specifying that the tenant pays for their utilities and janitorial fees, but unless modified is not responsible for any other care, maintenance or carrying costs of the property. [See **RPI** Form 552 and 552-1]

full-service gross lease
A commercial lease specifying that the landlord retains the responsibility for payment of all costs of care and maintenance, unless modified, including the tenant's utilities and janitorial services. [See **RPI** Form 552 and 552-1]

net lease
A commercial lease which transfers to the tenant the obligation, unless modified, to pay all of the costs of ownership in addition to utilities and janitorial services. [See **RPI** Form 552-2 and 552-3]

Sidebar

Agent Survey
Sheet for
Commercial
Property

A leasing or buyer's agent enters into an employment agreement with a user-client as the client's representative to locate and negotiate a lease or purchase commercial space to house their business operations. On determining the client's space requirements, the agent turns to the task of collecting information on available properties. From the data assembled, qualifying properties most likely to satisfy the client's needs are identified.

Here, when a leasing agent seeks out information on available properties the issue becomes: "what is the best way to quickly gather pertinent details on available properties for later analysis?"

The answer lies in the use of a **quick-fact** *checklist to itemize the types of data and information required on a property to determine its suitability for the client's need for space. One such itemized checklist is the* **Agent Survey Sheet for Commercial Property**. *[See* **RPI** *Form 320-3]*

The Agent Survey contains a series of questions to be asked of the owner's agent, or the owner if the property is not listed with a broker. Armed with detailed information on available properties, the agent and their user-client can determine which of the available properties best meets the client's needs. At this point, enough is known about a property to determine whether or not to submit a **letter of intent (LOI)** *or an offer to lease or buy, and if so, on what terms. Essentially, the survey is used as a prudent* **risk mitigation** *practice for the broker. [See* **RPI** *Form 556]*

The Agent Survey Sheet for Commercial Property contains probing questions relating to:

- *the usable square footage of the improvements and the lot and its age;*
- *facilities within the improved space including the number of bathrooms, and descriptions of the kitchen and breakroom/staff lounge;*
- *warehouse specifications, including usable square footage, ceiling clearance height, type of flooring and type of lighting;*
- *asking rent amount or base rent sought;*
- *move-in incentives offered by the owner;*
- *whether the owner or tenant pays the property taxes, insurance premiums, and like items;*
- *a description of the property's surrounding area;*
- *problems with vandalism or crime reported in the area, known earthquake faults and seismic hazards, or noise nuisances; and*
- *a description of the existing internet connections and phone lines, existing energy efficiency improvements and the ENERGY STAR® Energy Performance Score.*

The Agent Survey Sheet for Commercial Property functions as a thorough **quick-reference guide**. *By using it, the agent has compiled and considered all the advantageous and adverse information on a property in a single document. It makes for an easy, focused review by the agent and the user-client.*

Reformation of the lease agreement

During lease negotiations, a landlord orally assures a tenant they will enter into a lease for an initial term of five years with two five-year options to renew. The landlord and tenant do not memorialize the offers to lease or LOIs in writing.

However, the lease agreeent the landlord prepares and hands to the tenant sets the lease term at 15 years. Without reviewing the lease agreement, the tenant signs the lease agreement and takes possession of the premises.

The business operated by the tenant on the leased premises later fails, and the tenant defaults on the rent payments. The tenant then discovers for the first time the length of the lease term is 15 years. The landlord seeks to collect the unpaid rent for the 15-year period under the lease agreement (subject to any mitigation and present-worth discounting).

The tenant seeks to rescind the lease agreement due to the landlord's oral misrepresentation about the length of the lease term. The tenant claims the lease provisions contradict the oral agreements between the landlord and the tenant which predated the lease agreement.

Can the tenant rescind the lease agreement?

No! The landlord's oral representations regarding the lease term prior to execution of the lease agreement do not render the lease unenforceable. The terms set forth in the written lease agreement control over prior oral understandings.[29]

Rescission of lease agreements is rare since intentional misrepresentation or other fraud in the inducement is required to be shown by the tenant. As an alternative remedy, the tenant in this scenario may pursue a **reformation action** to alter the terms of the written lease agreement to conform to the terms of the oral agreement.

Another reason for reformation of lease provisions arises when a significant difference exists between the square footage contained in the leased space and the square footage given in the lease agreement for calculating rent.

---

29 **West** v. **Henderson** (1991) 227 CA3d 1578

Reformation of the lease agreement, cont'd

reformation action
A court action by a tenant seeking to reform the terms of a lease agreement to include prior agreements, oral or written, intended to be part of the lease agreement.

Chapter 41 Summary

A lease agreement is a contract entered into by a landlord and tenant addressing the tenant's primary responsibilities: the payment of money and the care of the real estate. The lease agreement also acts to convey a possessory interest in real estate to the tenant. By entering into a lease agreement and delivering possession to the tenant, the landlord conveys to the tenant the exclusive right to occupy a parcel of real estate, or space in a parcel, for a fixed period of time. On expiration of the term of the lease, the right of possession to the real estate reverts to the landlord.

The provisions contained in a written lease agreement fall into one of three categories of activities:

- conveyance of the leasehold interest;
- the money obligation of the tenant, a debt called rent; and

- responsibility of the tenant and the landlord for care and maintenance of the leased premises and other property operating expenses.

A broker, whether they represent the landlord or the tenant, uses either an offer to lease or a letter of intent (LOI) to initiate and document lease negotiations prior to entering into the lease agreement itself. The preparation and signing of the actual lease agreement remains to be done after its terms and conditions have been negotiated and agreed to in the offer to lease.

A commercial lease agreement form has five main sections:

- identification of the parties and the premises, and the conveyance and term of the lease;

- the terms for payment of rent and other amounts owed, collectively called rent provisions;

- the provisions setting forth the responsibility for care and maintenance of the leased property, collectively called the use-maintenance provisions;

- miscellaneous provisions for circumstances specific to the transaction; and

- the signatures of the parties.

A lease agreement conveying a term of occupancy exceeding one year is required to be written to be enforceable.

Chapter 41 Key Terms

Quiz 11 Covering Chapters 41-45 is located on page 644.

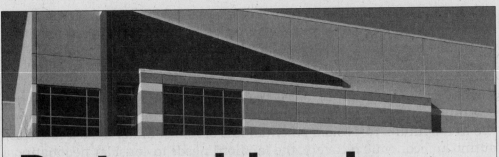

Rent provisions in commercial leases

After reading this chapter, you will be able to:

- understand the rent provisions in a regular lease agreement, such as the dollar amount of the rent, and the time, place and manner of payment;
- distinguish fixed-rent provisions from adjustable, graduated and percentage rent provisions, and describe the attributes of each;
- identify the rent provisions which periodically adjust a tenant's rent; and
- negotiate the operating costs to be paid by the tenant in addition to rent in long-term commercial leases.

Learning Objectives

base rent

percentage lease

fixed-rent lease

Key Terms

Various rent formulas exist to meet the financial needs of landlords and tenants. All commercial lease agreements set a minimum amount of monthly rent to be paid by the tenant. This minimum monthly rent is called **base rent**. [See **RPI** Form 552 §4.4]

Typically, the *base rent* is the monthly amount paid during the first year of the lease (with the exception of *percentage leases*). [See **RPI** Form 552-4]

However, in many short-term leases (e.g. leases of two to five years), the base rent is paid during the entire term of the lease, without an adjustment.

A lease agreement which sets monthly rent payments at a specific dollar amount over the entire life of the lease results in what is called a **fixed-rent lease**. [See **RPI** Form 552 §4.3]

Setting the rent

base rent
The minimum monthly rent due under a commercial lease agreement. [See **RPI** Form 552 §4.3]

fixed-rent lease
A lease agreement with monthly rent payments set at a specific dollar amount for the life of the lease. [See **RPI** Form 552]

In a rising local economy or period of general price inflation, a long-term *fixed-rent lease* will prove to be a financial disaster for the landlord. Fixed rent shifts the inflation hedge appreciation in the property's value to the tenant for so long as the fixed rent continues. [See Chapter 43]

However, a landlord may be forced to accept fixed-rent leases during economic downturns or static rental markets when interest rates are anticipated to rise in the future. To avoid a potential loss of return under a fixed-rate lease during an economic recovery, the landlord needs to consider negotiating a short-term lease or month-to-month tenancy.

When leasing space in larger, multi-tenant retail properties, landlords often negotiate a rent provision that calculates the total amount of rent the tenant will pay annually as a percentage of the tenant's gross sales. This type of lease is called a **percentage lease**. [See **RPI** Form 552-4]

Under a *percentage lease*, the tenant pays the greater of the base rent or the percentage rent. [See **RPI** Form 552-4]

percentage lease
A commercial lease agreement for a retail operation that sets the total amount of rent the tenant will pay as a percentage of the tenant's gross sales. [See **RPI** Form 552-4]

Periodic rent adjustments

Many commercial lease agreements contain provisions under which the base rent is adjusted periodically, usually on each anniversary of the lease commencement date and again every three to five years. Price adjustment provisions include:

- an *inflation-adjusted rent provision* which adjusts for annual price inflation as measured by the Consumer Price Index (CPI) [See **RPI** Form 552 §4.5];

- a *graduated rent provision* which annually adjusts rents upward in set percentage or dollar amounts; and

- an *appreciation-adjusted rent provision*, which adjusts the base rent every five years or so for property appreciation in excess of inflation due to changes in local market conditions. [See Chapter 43; see **RPI** Form 552 §4.5e]

Editor's note — These price adjustment provisions are discussed in great detail in Chapter 43.

As an alternative to the CPI, rent provisions may call for an annual percentage increase in rent over the base rent, or simply state an increased dollar amount for rent in each year of the lease term. This type of annual rent adjustment is called *graduated rent*. [See **RPI** Form 552 §4.4]

The lease agreement rent provisions need to precisely state any rent adjustment formulas to be enforced by the landlord. [See Sidebar, "Rent provisions and the NOI"]

Setting the grace period and late charge

The rent provisions in a commercial lease agreement include the:

- dollar amount of the rent;
- time for payment;

*The rent payments a landlord actually receives from all tenants constitutes the landlord's effective rental income from the property for the period analyzed. [See **RPI** Form 352 §2.2]*

The current rent and the terms for setting future rents as called for in the rent provisions of the lease agreement greatly influence the:

- *market value of the real estate;*
- *amount of long-term financing available;*
- *property's attractiveness to potential buyers; and*
- *landlord's future return on their investment.*

The calculation for setting the market value of a commercial income property is based primarily on its anticipated future net operating income (NOI). A property's NOI is composed of the property's gross operating income less operating expenses. Without a future flow of NOI, improved real estate has little value greater than the value of the land. Unless rental income exists to be capitalized, the property's value cannot be properly established.

Brokers and investors rely on the present and anticipated future NOI of a property to arrive at its current fair market value.

The NOI is initially capitalized at the current yield obtainable on comparable investments. The capitalization rate sets the property's fair market value for the price (present worth) a buyer will likely pay, and the amounts a lender will likely lend, based on the property's fundamentals.

Lenders limit mortgage amounts secured by real property based on:

- *the property's NOI; and*
- *the financial strength of the tenants to meet their lease obligations.*

Likewise, buyers determine what purchase price they will set in an offer based on (among other things):

- *the property's NOI;*
- *a review of the tenants' financial track records; and*
- *the landlord's control over operating costs.*

Thus, the leasing agent or property manager negotiating a commercial lease for a landlord ensure that lease agreements produce rents and control costs effectively to produce a maximum return, now and in the future.

- place for payment; and
- manner of payment.[1]

Additionally, if the landlord is to receive prepaid rent, the lease agreement needs to include a provision stating the tenant will pay rent in advance.[2] [See **RPI** Form 552 §4.1]

Rent payments not timely received by the landlord are considered **delinquent**. Rent is not delinquent until any **grace period** expires. In

---

1 **Levin** v. **Saroff** (1921) 54 CA 285

2 CC §1947

commercial (and residential) lease agreements, the grace period is negotiable by the landlord and the tenant. There are no legal mandates on the length of a *grace period,* or that a grace period even be granted. [See **RPI** Form 552 §4.7]

Having established a grace period by agreement or conduct, the landlord may not serve a three-day notice to pay until the grace period expires. [See Chapter 28]

The landlord may contract for a late charge as reimbursement for their delinquent rent collection efforts. The charge needs to be reasonably related to the landlord's out-of-pocket costs incurred during collection efforts or the delay in receipt of the untimely payment.

Late charges are typically assessed in leases as either a percentage of the rent due or a flat rate charge. The flat rate charge is to approximate the costs incurred to enforce collection and the loss of use of the rent money. In addition to dollar amounts equivalent to reimbursement of collection costs, the accrual of interest on any delinquent amount is often included to cover loss of the use of rent monies. [See **RPI** Form 552 §4.8]

Place and manner of payment

Rent is to be paid in U.S. dollars at a set location, such as at the landlord's or leasing agent's office. The rent may be delivered personally or by mail. [See **RPI** Form 552 §4.6a]

However, rent does not have to be paid with money. Rent may be paid by the delivery of crops, precious metals, services, assets or other currencies.[3]

The manner of rent payment is also established. Typically, landlords will accept cash, check, credit card, electronic transfer or other means of transmitting funds.

A landlord may charge a flat rate for a check returned for insufficient funds. However, the charge must be memorialized in the lease agreement in order for the landlord to shift this expense item to the tenant. [See **RPI** Form 552 §4.9]

If the tenant's check is returned for insufficient funds, the landlord may require payment of rent in cash or by money order. However, this cash requirement may not apply to rents after a three month period. After three months, the landlord is required to again accept alternate forms of payment.[4] [See **RPI** Form 552 §4.9]

When square footage sets the rent

In commercial leases for industrial, commercial, office and retail space, the base rent is generally set as a dollar amount, determined by multiplying the total number of square feet rented by a per-square-foot rate.

For example, a tenant leases 4,000 square feet at $2 per square foot. The base rent is set for the lease as $8,000, payable monthly.

---

3   **Clarke** v. **Cobb** (1898) 121 C 595
4   CC §1947.3

The per-square-foot rent formula is used to negotiate the lease, and then a specific dollar amount of rent is stated in the lease agreement. The per-square-foot formula used in negotiations usually is not mentioned in the lease agreement unless the footage is uncertain at the time the lease is entered into.

When the base rent or any additional rent, such as **common area maintenance charges (CAMs)**, is based on square footage stated in the lease, the space attributable to the leased premises is to be clearly defined and accurately measured.

To avoid disputes, the landlord and tenant agree on how the square footage will be measured:

- from the interior walls;
- from the middle of common walls;
- from the exterior of the walls; or
- to include a portion of the common hallways, lobby, restrooms or other interior areas of the structure.

The standard for determining how the square footage will be measured is negotiated through the offers and counteroffers to lease, and the competitive availability of space.

As additional rent, the commercial tenant may pay some or all of the costs of operating the property, producing various modifications of a gross or net lease agreement. Operating costs include:

- expenses incurred in the ownership and operations of the property; and
- future increases in these expenses. [See **RPI** Form 552-3]

Additional rent and other sums due

CAM provisions obligate the tenant to pay a pro rata share of the costs incurred by the landlord to maintain the common areas of the property and otherwise defray the costs of ownership, which may include:

- utilities (water, electric, etc.);
- heating, ventilation and air conditioning (HVAC);
- sewage;
- garbage;
- janitorial services;
- landscaping;
- security;
- insurance premiums;
- management fees; and
- property taxes and assessments. [See Figure 1, Form 552]

Figure 1

Excerpt from Form 552

Commercial Lease Agreement

Gross — Single Tenant

5. OPERATING EXPENSES:

5.1 Tenant is responsible for payment of utility and service charges as follows: _____

5.2 Landlord is responsible for payment of utility and service charges as follows: _____

5.3 Tenant will, on request of Landlord, authorize their utility companies to release energy consumption data directly to Landlord for Landlord's Data Verification Checklist used for energy benchmarking purposes and, upon further request, provide energy consumption data on the Premises. [See **RPI** From 552-9]

5.4 Tenant to pay all taxes levied on trade fixtures or other improvements Tenant installs on the Premises.

5.5 If Landlord pays any charge owed by Tenant, Tenant will pay, within 30 days of written demand, the charge as additional rent.

5.6 Landlord to pay all real property taxes and assessments levied by governments, for whatever cause, against the land, trees, tenant improvements and buildings within the Project containing the Premises, excluding those to be paid by Tenant under Section 5.4.

6. REPAIR AND MAINTENANCE:

6.1 The Premises are in good condition, ☐ except as noted in an addendum. [See **RPI** Form 250]

6.2 Tenant will keep the Premises and its improvements in good order, condition and repair, including all fixtures related to plumbing, HVAC components, electrical, lighting, and ☐ _____

   a. ☐ See attached maintenance modification addendum. [See **RPI** Form 552-6]

6.3 Except as stated in Section 6.2, Landlord will maintain in good order, condition and repair the structures and common area components and equipment within the Premises which exist on the commencement of this lease agreement, including but not limited to existing HVAC, plumbing and sewers, electrical systems, structural foundations, exterior walls, store front, plate glass in exterior walls, roof, government-mandated retrofitting, parking areas, lawns and shrubbery, sidewalks, driveways/right of ways, and ☐ _____

Additional rent and other sums due, cont'd

CAMs are classified as additional rent and generally arise in multi-tenant projects. Customarily, CAMs owed by a tenant are based on the ratio between the space leased by the tenant and the total rentable space in the project.

The term *"common area"* is broadly defined to include sidewalks, corridors, plazas, halls, restrooms, parking facilities, grounds, etc.

The term "maintenance" is defined to include garbage removal, janitorial services, gardening and landscaping, repairs and upkeep, utilities and other specified operating costs.

The allocation of responsibility for operating expenses depends on:

- the type of property and its use;
- the relative bargaining positions of the landlord and tenant in the current real estate market;
- the financial objectives of the landlord and tenant; and
- the length of the lease term.

The landlord and tenant may agree the property operating expenses will be paid by the tenant directly to the provider or creditor, or indirectly to the landlord as a CAMs reimbursement.

Taxes and assessments

Tenants with long-term leases often agree to pay some or all of the real estate taxes, insurance premiums and special assessments when the leased premises is an industrial or other free-standing, single-use building.

Simply put, the annual cost to a tenant is basically the same whether the landlord receives rent (a greater amount) and pays operating expenses out of the rent, or the tenant pays rent (a lesser amount) plus operating costs. Expenses are always eventually paid by the tenant, whether paid directly or indirectly through the landlord. If the tenant directly pays operating expenses or reimburses the landlord via CAMs, then the tenant, not the landlord, carries the risk they will increase.

Property is reassessed by the county assessor when the landlord sells their interest, even if the tenant remains in possession.[5]

If the landlord sells the leased property and the property is reassessed at a higher valuation, the increase is attributed to the landlord, not the tenant. [See **RPI** Form 552 §4.5]

A savvy tenant will demand a cap on any rent increases due to reassessments caused by the landlord. When a cap is agreed to in the lease, the landlord is responsible for any property tax increases exceeding the cap. However, the tenant is held responsible for the payment of assessments and taxes caused by their own improvements and trade fixtures. [See **RPI** Form 552 §4.3]

The *utilities provision* covers the cost of utilities used in the space leased by the tenant. They are separate and distinct from the utilities required to operate the common areas. [See Figure 1, Form 552 §§5.1, 5.2]

Utility charges

To protect against the increased cost of utilities consumed by the tenant, the landlord who pays for utilities may negotiate to pass the responsibility on to the tenant. The landlord may determine the tenant's pro rata share, or have each leased premises privately metered to determine the charge for the tenant's consumption.

Tenants who use a lot of energy or utilities should be required to contract with the utility companies themselves.

As a practical matter, the landlord avoids paying the utilities whenever possible, except, perhaps, for water. However, if the landlord pays the utilities and charges the tenant, the charge is additional rent to all other rent agreed to be paid.

---

5 Calif. Revenue and Taxation Code §60

Chapter 42 Summary

Various rent formulas exist to meet the demands of the marketplace and the financial needs of the landlord and tenant.

A lease agreement which sets monthly rent payments at a specific dollar amount over the entire life of the lease is called a fixed-rent lease. A lease agreement with a rent provision that calculates the total amount of rent the tenant will pay as a percentage of the tenant's gross sales is called a percentage lease.

Many commercial lease agreements contain provisions under which the base rent is adjusted periodically. Common price adjustment provisions include:

- an inflation-adjusted rent provision, which adjusts for annual price inflation as measured by the Consumer Price Index (CPI);
- a graduated rent provision which increases rent from year to year in set percentage or dollar amounts; and
- the appreciation-adjusted rent provision, which adjusts for property price appreciation every five years or so due to changes in local market conditions.

In a rising local economy or period of general price inflation, a long-term fixed-rent lease will prove to be a financial disaster for the landlord. However, a landlord may be forced to accept fixed-rent leases over a short period of time due to economic downturns or static rental markets.

When leasing space in larger, multi-tenant retail properties, landlords often negotiate a rent provision that calculates the total amount of rent the tenant will pay as a percentage of the tenant's gross sales. Tenants with long-term leases often agree to pay some or all of the property taxes, insurance premiums and special assessments when the leased premises is an industrial or single-use building.

The rent provisions in a commercial lease agreement include the:

- dollar amount of the rent;
- time for payment;
- place for payment; and
- manner of payment.

Chapter 42 Key Terms

Quiz 11 Covering Chapters 41-45 is located on page 644.

Adjustable rent provisions

After reading this chapter, you will be able to:

- structure rent and expense provisions in commercial lease agreements to protect a landlord's capital investment;
- use a graduated rent provision on a short-term commercial lease to increase the monthly rent due based on either a specific dollar amount or percentage of the base year rent;
- protect the property's income by including an inflation-adjusted rent provision in the lease agreement to keep the property's annual rental income increasing to match the annual rate of inflation; and
- use a percentage lease to have additional rent calculated as a percent of the tenant's gross sales year be paid separately from the base rent due monthly.

Learning Objectives

appreciation-adjusted rent provision	**graduated rent provision**
	inflation-adjusted rent
base rent	**provision**

Key Terms

Rent earned from leased space generates a yield on the landlord's investment in the real estate. Conceptually, rent is economically similar to a lender's receipt of interest for the use of money loaned.

At the end of their right-to-use periods, the real estate and the money are returned to the landlord and the lender, respectively.

Like interest rate provisions in a note, **rent provisions** in a commercial lease agreement are structured to anticipate future market changes that will affect the investment (value, income, expenses and debt). Even creditworthiness standards applied to both are the same, based on income.

Economic goals of commercial landlords

Figure 1

Excerpt from Form 552

Commercial Lease Agreement

Gross — Single Tenant

4.4   **GRADUATED RENT:** ☐ Monthly rent, from year to year, is graduated on anniversary months as follows:
Initial year's monthly rent to be $_____, and continues until:
a.   ☐ _____% increase in monthly rent over prior year's monthly rent for years _____ to _____,
        _____% increase in monthly rent over prior year's monthly rent for years _____ to _____,
        _____% increase in monthly rent over prior year's monthly rent for years _____ to _____,
b.   ☐ Monthly rent commencing on the _____ anniversary to be . . . .$_____,
        Monthly rent commencing on the _____ anniversary to be . . . .$_____,

As discussed in the previous chapter, *fixed-rent leases* do not anticipate future changes in the investment's fundamentals. However, variable or adjustable-rent leases do anticipate negative market changes. Properly structured, variable- or adjustable-rent leases shift increased costs and positive demographic influences to the tenant by way of an equal increase in rent.

Landlords have a financial need to protect the growth and value of their capital investment in commercial income property. The sole method a landlord has for maintaining the value of income property from year to year is through rent and expense provisions in lease agreements.

To accomplish this feat, the landlord's leasing agent anticipates the type of rent and use-maintenance provisions for a lease agreement that will deliver the maximum **net operating income** throughout the life of the lease. Applying the care and protection owed the landlord in negotiations, the agent will provide the landlord with future benefits of rents that stay in line with inflation and demographic-driven appreciation.

Since net income from operations sets value and pricing, attention to any ability to shift future cost increases to the tenant will further enhance future value. Future capitalization rates following 2014 will play a role, driving values inversely to the inevitably rise in rates.

Types of adjustable rent

graduated rent provision
A rent provision in a commercial lease agreement which increases the initial monthly rent in pre-set increments over the term of the lease. [See **RPI** Form 552 §4.4]

The three basic types of commercial *rent adjustment provisions* (also known as **rent escalation clauses**) are:

- **graduated rent provisions** [See Figure 1];
- **inflation-adjusted rent provisions** paired with **appreciation-adjusted rent provisions** [See Figure 2 and Figure 3]; and
- **percentage lease rent provisions.** [See Figure 4]

The economic goals a leasing agent reviews with their commercial landlord-client when negotiating provisions for future rents include:

- adjustments for lost purchasing power due to future consumer price inflation;
- adjustments in rent to reflect the rate of appreciation on comparable properties (beyond the rate of inflation), a demographics issue; and
- the absorption or pass-through of increased operating expenses or interest adjustments on mortgage debt.

4.5 **CPI ADJUSTED RENT:** ☐ Monthly base rent for the initial 12 months of the term is the amount of $_____, adjusted annually on the first day of each anniversary month by increasing the initial monthly base rent by the percentage increase between the applicable Consumer Price Index for All Urban Consumers (CPI-U) figures published for the third month preceding the month of commencement and the third month preceding the anniversary month.

    a.   The applicable CPI-U (1982-1984 = 100) is:
           ☐ Los Angeles-Riverside-Orange County,   ☐ San Francisco-Oakland-San Jose
           ☐ San Diego, ☐ National, ☐ _____.
    b.   Annual rent increases under CPI-U adjustments are limited to an increase of _____%.
    c.   On any anniversary adjustment, if the CPI-U has decreased below the CPI-U for the prior 12-month period, the monthly rent for the ensuing 12 months will remain the same as the rent during the prior 12 months.
    d.   If the CPI-U is changed or replaced by the United States Government, the conversion factor published by the Government on the new Index will be used to compute annual adjustments

Figure 2

Excerpt from Form 552

Commercial Lease Agreement

Gross — Single Tenant

To protect the property's income (and its value) due to inflation, rent is adjusted periodically by including an *inflation-adjusted rent provision* in the lease agreement. An inflation clause calls for annual rent increases based on figures from an inflation index, such as the **Consumer Price Index (CPI)** or the **Cost of Funds Index**. [See Figure 2]

Rent may also be adjusted to reflect an increase in the property's dollar value brought about by local appreciation. This is accomplished in long-term leases by including an *appreciation-adjusted rent provision* in the lease agreement calling for the adjustment to be made every few years, commonly five. [See Figure 3]

Also, a landlord passes on increased operating and ownership costs to the commercial tenant by shifting responsibility for payment to the tenant for:

- all or some of the operating expenses;
- future increases in operating expenses; and/or
- a pro rata share of CAMs, property taxes and hazard insurance premiums. [See Chapter 46]

Future increases in the cost of carrying debt on the property due to variable interest rate mortgage financing is passed on to the tenant as increased rent to provide the landlord with a *net lease* arrangement.

A landlord with knowledge and understanding about the economic and financial consequences of proposed lease terms makes a more informed financial decision whether to accept, counter or reject the tenant's offer to lease. The level of negotiations is no better than the level of leasing knowledge held by the landlord and their leasing agent.

The most common rent adjustment provision used in short-term commercial lease agreements is the *graduated rent provision*. [See Figure 1]

Graduated rents from year to year

base rent
The minimum
monthly rent due
under a commercial
lease agreement. [See
RPI Form 552 §4.3]

Graduated rent provisions increase the monthly rent due in the years following the first year's payment of a **base rent**. The adjustments are made annually, or sometimes semi-annually. The periodic upward adjustment is either:

- a specific dollar amount as the rent due; or
- a percentage of the base year rent or rent paid during the previous period. [See Figure 1]

When setting the rent adjustment amount, be it a dollar or percentage figure, the landlord takes into account:

- expected rate of future inflation, say 2% as now anticipated by wisdom of the long-term bond market;
- local market conditions, such as expected user demand and scarcity of like properties, demographics of increased density and incomes, traffic counts and infrastructure improvements contributing to property appreciation; and
- the tenant's evolving use and its burden on the property and improvements.

Rather than being tied to a formal index, the rent increases set by a graduated rent provision are negotiated. No paradigm exists, but increases of, say, 3% are customary in some markets, as it provides returns to the landlord exceeding inflation.

Recession and recovery

During recessionary times and recovery stages in a business cycle, graduated rent provisions are popular when the landlord seeks to incentivize tenants to lease vacant space. The landlord agrees to a low initial *teaser rent*, in addition to a few months of rent-free possession to offset the tenant's initial set up or relocation costs. The graduated rent provision then bumps up the rent so any below-market rents paid in the early years are picked up in future rents that may even exceed market rates. This is similar to the negative amortization feature in Millennium Boom *adjustable rate mortgages (ARMs)*.

Any up-front, rent-free period needs to be viewed as part of a vacancy and lost rents factor since no rent is received to contribute to gross income. The cost of any *tenant improvements (TIs)* the landlord pays is recovered by totaling:

- the monthly amount of an amortized payment of the costs of the TIs over the initial term of the lease; and
- the amount of monthly rent the property commands before TIs.

Inflation-adjusted rent provisions

Inflation-adjusted rent provisions keep the property's annual rental income increasing to match the annual rate of consumer price inflation. An inflation provision calls for annual upward rent adjustments based on figures from an inflation index, such as the *CPI* or the *Cost of Funds Index*. [See Figure 2]

The CPI is an index of fluctuations in the dollar price the local population pays for consumable goods and services. Use of the CPI to adjust rents

> *Consider a commercial lease agreement with a use provision calling for the tenant to operate a movie theater on the premises for ten years.*
>
> *The lease agreement contains a rent appreciation clause stating the landlord will adjust the base rent in five years to reflect the then-current fair market rent.*
>
> *At the time for the appreciation adjustment five years later, the landlord determines the fair market rent for the property by using rent amounts received by comparable properties put to higher and better uses than a movie theater.*
>
> *The tenant disputes the amount of the adjusted rent demanded by the landlord.*
>
> *The tenant claims the fair market rental value of the premises is based on the present use of the property as intended by the lease. The tenant argues that the lease agreement does not provide for the landlord to adjust the rent to reflect a return on the fair market value of properties that have been put to a higher and better use.*
>
> *Here, the lease agreement states the tenant will use the property to operate a movie theater for the term of the lease. The rent may only be adjusted to reflect the fair market value of the property based on its use as a movie theater. [**Wu** v. **Interstate Consolidated Industries** (1991) 226 CA3d 1511]*

recovers the dollar's annual loss of purchasing power to pay for goods and services. Occupancy of property is a service consumed by the public using dollars to pay rent.

The CPI-U is the value for urban consumers, and is the benchmark used to adjust rents for inflation. For simplicity, we'll refer to CPI-U as just the CPI. The CPI is a widely recognized index, easily understood and inexpensive to administer.

Here are some basic guidelines to follow when using the CPI method:

- set a base rent payable monthly during the first year of the lease, also called the **minimum rent** (floor);
- indicate the exact index to be used for the CPI adjustment figures (e.g., the Los Angeles-Riverside-Anaheim CPI);
- indicate an alternative index if the one selected is discarded or altered;
- note the month for the CPI figure to be used to compute annual adjustments (the third month prior to commencement); and
- state the month payments begin at the adjusted amount (e.g., anniversary month for the commencement of possession under the lease agreement).

A good practice is to use CPI figures for the third month preceding commencement of the lease to compute periodic adjustments. But why not use the CPI for the month in which rent is adjusted?

When the CPI figure hasn't been released, which will be the case when using the figure for the month of commencement, the landlord needs to

inflation-adjusted rent provision
A rent provision in a commercial lease which calls for periodic rent increases based on changes in inflation index figures during the period. [See **RPI** Form 552 §4.5]

Implementing the CPI method

e.   Following each _____-year period after commencement, including any extensions and renewals, the monthly rent is to be adjusted upward to current market rental rates for comparable premises. Computation of any future annual CPI-U adjustments in monthly rent on each anniversary month after adjustment to current market rental rates will treat the monthly rent for the initial 12 months of each market rent adjustment as the initial monthly base rent, and treat the first month of each market rent adjustment as the month of commencement for selecting the Index figures. Landlord to reasonably determine and advise Tenant of the adjusted rental rates no less than 3 months prior to the effective date of the adjustment.

estimate the rent due for the anniversary month. When the CPI figure for the anniversary month is later released and the rent adjustment is calculated, the landlord then needs to account for the rent received beginning with the anniversary month. Using a CPI figure for the third month prior to the adjustment guarantees an actual figure is available with plenty of time to calculate the rent adjustment and advise the tenant of the adjusted rent amount.

Calculating the CPI: Year-to-year CPI adjustment

Under annual rent inflation adjustment provisions, the prior year's rent and CPI are used to set the adjusted rent. [See Figure 2]

Thus, the year-to-year adjustment formula is:

$$(current\ CPI \div last\ year's\ CPI) \times current\ rent$$

Though widely used, CPI only addresses inflation resulting from the Federal Reserve's (the Fed's) **monetary policy**. CPI is limited to measuring changes in the purchasing power of the dollar as reflected in the prices of consumer goods and services, which include rents. The CPI does not reflect changes in the property's actual rental value, only in the amount of rent. Thus, to capture both inflation and long-term appreciation in rents, inflation-adjusted rent provisions are often paired with appreciation-adjusted rent provisions.

Appreciation-adjusted rent provisions: local demographics

Rents are also forged by public *appreciation* for a property's location, the result of a combination of:

- local demographics (density and income sets the level of demand for space);
- government investments and programs in the community; and
- supply of available units or space in the local market. [See Figure 3]

Long-term commercial lease agreements need rent provisions which capture the financial benefits these conditions create for property owners (and tenant businesses) over time. To garner the value of evolving local economic conditions, appreciation-adjusted rent provisions are included in the commercial lease agreement. Through the provision, rents are adjusted every three to five years to capture any increase in rents brought about by the effect of local appreciation, increasing rents beyond the inflation-adjusted increase in rent.

4.4 ADDITIONAL PERCENTAGE RENT: Additional percentage rent equal to _____% of gross sales income made from the Premises during each calendar year, less credit for base rent, real estate taxes, insurance, assessments and common area maintenance (CAM) charges paid by Tenant for the calendar year, is to be paid as described below:

    a.   The percentage rent due for each month of the lease will be paid and delivered with a signed written statement of the gross sales income and percentage computation by the tenth day of the following month.

    b.   The additional percentage rent computed for each month to be credited for base rent, taxes, insurance, assessments and CAMs paid by Tenant for the month.

    c.   Within one month after each calendar year and on expiration of the lease, Tenant to compute and deliver a written statement of the year's sales and the additional percentage rent calculated for the calendar year, less credit for base rent, taxes, insurance and CAMs paid for the calendar year, to annually determine the percentage rent remaining due from Tenant or to be refunded to Tenant by Landlord, which difference will be paid on delivery of the annual statement.

    d.   Gross sales income includes all money or equivalent received by Tenant, subtenant, licensees or concessionaires, in the ordinary course of business, whether wholesale or retail, cash or credit, less credit for goods returned by customers.

    e.   Landlord has the right, on reasonable notice, to audit Tenant's books regarding sales information.

Figure 4

Excerpt from Form 552-4

Commercial Lease Agreement — Percentage Lease

The longer the lease term, the more likely an appreciation-adjusted rent provision will be negotiated and included in the lease agreement. [See **RPI** Form 552 §4.5e]

The amount of rent increase due to appreciation is determined by a rental market analysis of comparable properties at the time of the rent adjustment. This includes situations unique to the leased property, such as:

- new developments or increased business activity at the location of the property;
- demand for like properties in the immediate area; and
- traffic counts and patterns directly affecting the property, often determined by the location of big anchor tenants.

Again, appreciation-adjusted rent provisions work in tandem with the inflation-adjusted rent provisions. The inflation adjustment is annual; the appreciation adjustment takes place every three to five years.

appreciation-adjusted rent provision
A rent provision found in a commercial lease agreement which adjusts rent every several years to reflect an increase in the rental value of a property exceeding the rate of inflation brought about by local demographics. [See **RPI** Form 552 §4.5e]

Percentage lease rent provisions for high traffic sites

The percentage lease rent provision works a little differently from other rent adjustment provisions. While using different formulas for adjusting rent, rent provisions have one common feature – the *base rent*. The base rent is the minimum rent paid by the tenant to the landlord each month.

Percentage lease rent provisions have a formula for additional rent to be paid separately from the monthly base rent due, called **percentage rent** or **overage rent.** *Percentage rent* due is typically calculated as a percent of the tenant's gross sales less the amount of base rent paid monthly during the year, a natural breakpoint arrangement. Percentage lease rent provisions are commonly negotiated with restaurants and retail tenants dependent on high vehicular or foot traffic to drive their sales. [See Figure 4]

Pairing the base rent amount with a percentage rent formula assures the landlord a full return at the appreciated rental value for the property due to its location. Thus:

- the base rent provides the landlord with a minimum return on investment for the tenant's use of the property; and

- the additional percentage rent provides the landlord with a return on their investment based on the contribution of the property's location to the tenant's operating success.

The additional rent is triggered when the tenant's gross income from sales exceed a negotiated dollar threshold, known as the **breakpoint.** The *natural breakpoint* is the point at which the calculated percentage rent amount for a period, say one year, exceeds the base rent paid during the period. However, landlords and tenants may negotiate a higher or lower breakpoint for the additional rent to kick in than the amount of base rent paid. A lower breakpoint increases the rent the landlord receives.

Formulating and negotiating additional rent under a percentage lease

To determine the formula for additional rent under a percentage lease rent provision, the landlord relies on an estimate of the tenant's gross sales for the first 12 months of operations, as well as:

- the traffic count and traffic patterns at the location of the premises;
- the dollar amount of anticipated sales and average dollar sales; and
- the price range of the goods and services to be offered.

The landlord then negotiates with the tenant to set the percentage of the tenant's annual gross sales for calculating the additional rent. With a natural breakpoint, when the percentage amount exceeds the base rent paid, the tenant pays the excess amount as additional rent.

Percentage rent is typically due within a month or two after the end of the year, when the tenant's gross income for the period is known. The frequency of the additional rent payment is negotiable, based on:

- whether the tenant's sales trends are constant or seasonal; and
- the financial strength of the tenant.

Calculating percentage rent

Consider a landlord and tenant who agree to a base rent of $5,000 per month, or $60,000 per year. The percentage rent provision calls for the payment of rent equal to 6% of the tenant's gross income, paid monthly at the base rent amount with the balance due annually. The landlord and tenant agree to a natural breakpoint.

At the end of the year, the tenant has a gross income of $1,500,000. The total percentage rent due is $90,000 ($1,500,000 x 0.06). The percentage rent exceeds the annual base rent by $30,000. Thus, the total rent owed to the landlord for the year is:

- $60,000 in base rent, paid monthly during the year; and
- $30,000 in excess percentage rent, paid within 30 to 60 days after the end of the year.

Landlords have a financial need to protect the growth and value of their capital investment in commercial income property. The sole method for maintaining the value of income property from year to year is through rent and expense provisions in lease agreements.

The three basic types of commercial rent adjustment provisions are:

- graduated rent provisions;
- inflation-adjusted rent provisions paired with appreciation-adjusted rent provisions; and
- percentage lease rent provisions.

The most common rent adjustment provision used in short-term commercial lease agreements is the graduated rent provision. Graduated rent provisions increase the monthly rent due in the years following the first year's payment of a base rent. The periodic upward adjustment is either a specific dollar amount or a percentage of the base year rent or rent paid during the previous period.

To protect the property's income due to inflation, rent is adjusted periodically by including an inflation-adjusted rent provision in the lease agreement. An inflation clause calls for annual rent increases based on figures from an inflation index, such as the Consumer Price Index (CPI) or the Cost of Funds Index.

Rent may also be adjusted to reflect an increase in the property's dollar value brought about by local appreciation. This is accomplished by including an appreciation-adjusted rent provision in the lease agreement.

Alternatively, percentage lease rent provisions have a formula for additional rent to be paid separately from the base rent due monthly, called percentage rent. Percentage rent due is typically calculated as a percent of the tenant's gross sales less the amount of base rent paid monthly during the year. Percentage lease rent provisions are commonly negotiated with restaurants and retail tenants dependent on high vehicular or foot traffic to drive their sales.

Chapter 43 Summary

Chapter 43 Key Terms

Quiz 11 Covering Chapters 41-45 is located on page 644.

Notes:

Chapter

44

Rent increases and CPI

After reading this chapter, you will be able to:

- understand the interrelationship between rents, inflation and appreciation;
- distinguish the effect of inflation from appreciation in any increase in a property's rents; and
- provide for a shift of rent inflation and appreciation to the tenant in lease agreement rent provisions.

Learning Objectives

appreciation-adjusted rent provision	Consumer Price Index (CPI) inflation

Key Terms

A long-term investment goal of an owner of rental property is to generate future **annual net operating income** sufficient to keep the property's value rising in line with consumer inflation.

Coping with inflation through rent

An income property owner's primary goal is to negotiate the best possible rental rate consistent with the highest occupancy rate attainable when entering into a lease agreement. Part of this income goal is to bargain for periodic upward rent adjustments over the life of the lease. Rent adjustments are needed to cover the loss of purchasing power in the initial rent amount brought on by annual consumer price inflation.

For example, rent adjustments may be set to match the annual price inflation experienced in the region. Thus coupled with inflation, rental income will increase from year to year to maintain the original purchasing power of the property's initial rental income over the life of the lease.

Consumer Price Index (CPI)
The CPI measures and tracks the rate of consumer inflation. This is presented as an index of fluctuations in the general price of a wide selection of consumable products – goods and services.

appreciation-adjusted rent provision
A rent provision found in a commercial lease agreement which adjusts rent every several years to reflect an increase in the rental value of a property exceeding the rate of inflation brought about by local demographics. [See **RPI** Form 552 §4.5e]

inflation
The price change in consumer goods and services, stated in the consumer price index (CPI) as a figure which is reported as a percentage change over one year ago.

For decades prior to the mid-1970s, rent adjustments in an environment of slowly rising interest rates were of little concern as inflation and appreciation rates remained low. The 1980s saw marked increases in rents and operating costs to reflect the excessive inflation of the 1970s.

By the early 1990s, rents declined and appreciation rates in California reversed, stabilizing during the late-1990s. After the turn of the century, rents again began to increase, exceeding the rate of inflation as reflected in the **Consumer Price Index (CPI)**. By 2007, rent increases began to stabilize in all areas and on all types of properties, as the real estate boom years of the mid-2000s came to a halt.

Unlike rent **appreciation** experienced by a property due to enhanced local demographics, rent **inflation** is limited by any decline in the quantity of a consumer item a dollar will buy due to a general price increase for the same item. In this case, the item is the square footage of space which can be purchased at a certain amount of rent.

Inattentive landlords and agents occasionally fail to anticipate trends in *inflation*. They saddle themselves with long-term lease agreements containing rent provisions which do not adjust rent for inflation or *appreciation*. Since future rents are formulated in lease agreement rent provisions, the worth and equity of the property can be calculated at any time during the term of the lease based on the capitalization rate then applied by investors. [See **RPI** Form 552 §4.5]

Unless rent is periodically increased over the life of a long-term lease or a lease with renewal options, lease provisions setting future rents may be economically disastrous for the landlord. The periodic upward adjustments in rent amounts to be considered include:

- the rate of consumer price inflation; and
- local demographic price appreciation.

A number of methods exist to keep pace over the term of a lease with consumer inflation, property rent appreciation and increases in the landlord's operating and ownership expenses beyond the rate of inflation.

CPI covers price inflation

The best method for coping with the uncertainty of future inflation is to tie the amount due as future rents to figures published in the federal government's *CPI*. The monetary policy for the dollar is set by the Federal Reserve (Fed) at 2% annually. However, inflation of greater amounts may be engineered by the Fed for a short period of time to offset declines in government spending. This Fed action boosts consumer spending, which in turn creates more jobs, raising employment to the level sought by the Fed.

Commercial lease agreements usually set a base monthly rent which is constant for the first year. For the following years, annual rent is adjusted by factoring in the annual change in local or regional CPI figures. [See Figure 1]

For residential rent increases, most rent control communities use a form of the CPI to allow for the amount of automatic annual rent adjustments permitted by ordinance. The rent control formulas have worked well for landlords, especially when rents slip for reason of increased supply (construction and SFR conversion to rentals) or reduced demand (job loss during a recession).

Residential leases only infrequently exceed one year. Thus, most residential lease agreements do not need to address an adjustment in monthly rents to compensate for inflation. Rent increases are negotiated at the end of the leasing period and set based on comparable market rates or, in noncompetitive environments due to restrictive zoning, as dictated by rent control.

CPI figures are published monthly, bi-monthly or semi-annually by the U.S. Bureau of Labor Statistics for numerous metropolitan areas across the states. The CPI is the most widely used indicator of inflation.

The CPI measures the overall price change from month to month, positive or negative, for a "basket" of consumer goods and services people are believed to buy or consume. The CPI-U is based on the price of food, clothing, shelter, fuel, transportation fares, routine medical charges, drugs and other goods bought for day-to-day living.

Real estate lease agreements with provisions for annual adjustments based on the **rate of inflation** most commonly use inflation figures from the regional CPI-U, the CPI for the area's urban consumers. A regional CPI-U covers the buying habits of approximately 80% of the population within the designated area. [See Figure 1]

The three CPI regions within California are:

- Los Angeles-Anaheim-Riverside (issued monthly);
- San Francisco-Oakland-San Jose (issued bi-monthly); and
- San Diego (issued semi-annually).

If property does not fall within or near one of the regions, a landlord may also use the CPI-U for a larger geographical area such as:

- the West Region CPI-U; or
- the U.S. City Average CPI-U.

CPI and its regions

The San Francisco-Oakland-San Jose CPI-U is issued bi-monthly covering consumer expenditures for two months — the month of issuance and the preceding month. The bi-monthly CPI-U for the San Francisco area is issued on even-numbered months such as February, April, June, etc.

Thus, the landlord with an adjustment index tied to the January CPI-U for the San Francisco-Oakland-San Jose area uses the CPI-U which comes out in February.

Issuance date for the CPI figure

However, the landlord located in the San Francisco-Oakland-San Jose or San Diego areas may wish to switch to a larger geographical area CPI-U index which is issued on a monthly basis. For example, the landlord may consider using the West Region CPI-U.

If the landlord seeks to switch to a different index after entering into the lease agreement, the landlord and tenant needs to agree to the use of the new index.

Inflationary cycles and the CPI

A few basic principles of real estate economics need to be considered when applying CPI figures to periodically adjust rent upward. A rent adjustment based on consumer price inflation covers the negative effect inflation has on the purchasing power of the landlord's rental income. With each inflation adjustment made in rent by the landlord, the commercial tenant in turn passes on the rent increase to consumers when pricing the goods and services they produce and sell.

Also, real estate rents on the reletting of comparable properties sometimes increase in excess of consumer inflation. Any annual increase in rents paid beyond the rate of inflation is appropriately called appreciated rents. Appreciated rents directly translate on application of a capitalization rate (to the NOI) to set the property's market value. The portion of the annual property value increase beyond the rate of inflation is the appreciated value of the property.

The appreciation of rent amounts (and thus property value) is driven by population density increase in the immediate area and increased personal income beyond the rate of inflation for local residents and companies. Thus, the location of the property is "appreciated" by more families and businesses.

How CPI works

Rent may not be increased during the term of a lease without an adjustment provision in the lease agreement. For instance, rent payments under a fixed-rent lease remain constant over the life of the lease. In contrast, rent under a month-to-month rental agreement may be increased by serving a notice of change in the terms of tenancy, limited for most residential units located in cities burdened with rent control.[1]

To increase rents annually for inflation, the lease needs to provide a formula for calculating the rent increases. [See Figure 1; see Chapter 43]

A lease provision that calls for adjustments based on the CPI-U may be worded to provide a *base-to-current year* increase or a *year-to-year* increase. The resulting rent amount is the same under either calculation. [See Figure 1]

---

1 Calif. Civil Code §827

When the landlord decides to use the CPI method to raise rents, some basic guidelines are to be followed:

- set, in advance, a base rent payable monthly during the first year of the lease which is the "minimum" rent (floor) below which the rent will never fall;

- indicate the exact index to be used (e.g., the Los Angeles-Riverside-Anaheim CPI-U);

- indicate an alternative index if the one selected is discarded or altered;

- note the CPI beginning month for computing annual adjustments (often the third month before the commencement month and anniversaries of the lease);

- state the actual date for the adjusted annual graduations (e.g., September 1); and

- include provisions to cover future changes in the property's appreciated value and operating costs (e.g., reappraisal, CAMs, etc.) whether the tenant has assigned or sublet the premises, or liened their leasehold interest. [See Figure 1]

CPI provision checklist

Choosing the beginning CPI month

Regardless of the method of adjustment, base-to-current year or year-to-year, the landlord will need to select a beginning CPI-U month.

The best month to select for the CPI-U figure used to compute periodic adjustments is the third month preceding commencement of the lease and each anniversary of the commencement. The CPI-U figure for the third month prior to the adjustment is readily available by the time the rent adjustment needs to be calculated, and the tenant is advised of the adjusted amount of rent due.

Otherwise, if the CPI-U figure chosen is for the month in which the rent will be adjusted, the landlord will need to estimate the CPI-U figure at the time of the adjustment. The actual CPI-U figure for the anniversary month will not be available for another two months. Computation of the annual adjusted rent is either by base year CPI-U to current year CPI-U, or by year-to-year CPI-U. [See Sidebar, "CPI provision checklist."]

Base-to-current year adjustment

Consider a lease rent provision which provides for a base-to-current year adjustment. [See Figure 1]

The lease commenced on January 1, 2018. The base rent is $5,000 per month for the first year. The rent is to be adjusted each January and the CPI-U index to be used is the Los Angeles-Anaheim-Riverside index.

The CPI-U figure for the October prior to January, the month of adjustment, is selected as the base month figure for rent adjustments. The CPI-U figure for the third month preceding commencement will be available to calculate the amount of the adjusted rent before the January rent is due. The CPI-U for October 2017 is 196.3, the base month figure.

In January 2019, the first rent adjustment takes place. The CPI-U for October 2014 is 206.9.

Figure 1

Excerpt from Form 552

Commercial Lease Agreement

Gross — Single Tenant

4.5   **CPI   ADJUSTED   RENT:** ☐ Monthly base rent for the initial 12 months of the term is the amount of $_____, adjusted annually on the first day of each anniversary month by increasing the initial monthly base rent by the percentage increase between the applicable Consumer Price Index for All Urban Consumers (CPI-U) figures published for the third month preceding the month of commencement and the third month preceding the anniversary month.

a.   The applicable CPI-U (1982-1984 = 100) is:
☐ Los Angeles-Riverside-Orange County,   ☐ San Francisco-Oakland-San Jose
☐ San Diego,   ☐ National, ☐ _____

b.   Annual rent increases under CPI-U adjustments are limited to an increase of _____%.

c.   On any anniversary adjustment, if the CPI-U has decreased below the CPI-U for the prior 12-month period, the monthly rent for the ensuing 12 months will remain the same as the rent during the prior 12 months.

d.   If the CPI-U is changed or replaced by the United States Government, the conversion factor published by the Government on the new Index will be used to compute annual adjustments

e.   Following each _____-year period after commencement, including any extensions and renewals, the monthly rent is to be adjusted upward to current market rental rates for comparable premises. Computation of any future annual CPI-U adjustments in monthly rent on each anniversary month after adjustment to current market rental rates will treat the monthly rent for the initial 12 months of each market rent adjustment as the initial monthly base rent, and treat the first month of each market rent adjustment as the month of commencement for selecting the Index figures. Landlord to reasonably determine and advise Tenant of the adjusted rental rates no less than 3 months prior to the effective date of the adjustment.

To calculate the base-to-current year adjustment, the current CPI-U is divided by the base CPI-U and the quotient multiplied by the base rent: (current CPI-U ÷ base CPI-U) × base rent.

For the second year (2019) of the lease, the rent is $5,270 — (206.9 ÷ 196.3) × $5,000.

For 2020, the third year of the lease, the October 2019 CPI-U is 211.4. Thus, in January 2020, the rent adjusts to $5,385 — (211.4 ÷ 196.3) × $5,000.

Year-to-year adjustment

Under year-to-year rent adjustment provisions, the prior year's rent, not the base year's rent, is used to set the adjusted rent. The base year's CPI-U is not used to make the future adjustment.

Thus, the year-to-year adjustment formula is the current CPI-U divided by last year's CPI-U, multiplied by the current rent: (current CPI-U ÷ last year's CPI-U) × current rent.

CPI advantages

Three advantages are provided by using the CPI as a basis for rent adjustments. The first and most obvious advantage is the CPI is universally known and easily understood. Little room exists for the parties to disagree over the amount of a rent increase if it is tied to a government published index.

Second, the CPI is inexpensive to administer. It only takes a few minutes and a calculator to adjust the rents each year.

Third, the CPI is a widely published index and easy to locate and conform.

CPI limitations on yield

Despite the advantages, the CPI has its limitations. The CPI bears little to no relationship to changes in the property's actual rental value. The CPI only measures changes in the purchasing power of the dollar as reflected in consumer prices, which includes residential rents (not prices). Rents are forged by a combination of local demographics (density and income), government programs and supply of available units or space. However, commercial leasing arrangements need to be worded to capture these conditions over a longer period of time. Residential leases do not have this concern as the term is generally shorter. [See **RPI** Forms 550 and 551]

Each parcel of real estate is a unique asset. The location of a property makes the primary difference since no two locations have exactly the same desirability factors affecting value.

An individual property experiences an increase or decrease in rental value for a number of reasons other than inflation, including:

- traffic counts and access to the property;
- tenant demand and changes in the size and wealth of the surrounding population;
- operating expenses;
- mortgage interest rates and investor capitalization rates; and
- construction starts.

The regional CPI as a factor for diminished purchasing power of a dollar takes none of these local economic factors into consideration (other than to the extent they are reflected in residential rents, which is just one aspect of CPI). Interest rates charged to homebuyers are indirectly included in the CPI by using implicit rent as the cost of possession. The effect of interest rates on real estate values is not included since debt is capital and real estate is a **capital asset**, the value of which is not itself consumed.

Cyclically, and in the short term, asset values run opposite to the direction interest rates move. When interest rates go down, values of real estate (and other assets) accelerate even as rents remain the same, and vice versa.

Also, the CPI does not mirror actual variations in the landlord's operating costs. An owner who does nothing to maintain their property can, in a high-demand location, enjoy rent increases due to the public's appreciation for the property's desirable location.

Astute tenants insist on an annual cap when rent increases are linked to CPI. For example, if the rise in the CPI figure is greater than 4% in any year, a 4% cap limits the increase despite a greater increase in the CPI.

The key is to analyze where inflation is headed. If inflation is expected to rise in the future, the CPI will initially benefit the landlord. Conversely, when inflation has topped off and is dropping, the CPI will appear to benefit the tenant. Also, a shock to local rental market conditions, such as overbuilding or the exodus of a rental age or business group, can completely eliminate inflationary and interest rate effects on rent.

Again, the CPI is a good method for controlling the *inflationary reduction of the purchasing power* of the U.S. dollar received in payment of rent.

Further limitations of the CPI

Alternatives to the CPI

OPERATING EXPENSES:

5.1 Tenant is responsible for payment of utilities and services supplied to the Premises.

5.2 Tenant to pay all taxes levied on trade fixtures or other improvements Tenant installs on the Premises.

5.3 As additional base rent, Tenant to pay _____% of the real property taxes and assessments levied by governments, for whatever cause, against the land, trees and buildings within the Project containing the Premises, within 30 days after written demand from Landlord.

    a. Tenant is not liable for increases in real property taxes and assessments resulting from a change in ownership.

5.4 If Landlord pays any charge owed by Tenant, Tenant will pay, within 30 days of written demand, the charge as additional rent.

5.5 As additional monthly base rent, Tenant to pay _____% of the common area maintenance (CAM) for the Project incurred each month, within 10 days of written statement and demand for payment.

    a. CAMs are the cost to landlord of maintaining and operating the "Common Areas" of the Project, including all sidewalks, corridors, plazas, hallways, restrooms, parking areas, interior and exterior walls and all other open areas not occupied by tenants.

    b. CAMs include all costs incurred by Landlord relating to the operation of the Project containing the Premises including hazard insurance premiums maintained by Landlord and charges for property management of the Common Areas.

Inflation's effect on rent amounts covered by the annual CPI adjustments is not the only concern of the property manager. Property appreciation and increased operating costs need to be managed to increase, or at worst maintain, the property's NOI, and thus the property's value.

It is advisable to add a **reappraisal** and rent adjustment provision to long-term leases rather than rely solely on the CPI. However, *reappraisal* methods are costly, time consuming and not always without argument. Managers may feel it is too involved to reappraise the property every few years to set the new rents.

Also, appraisal provisions usually call for a reappraisal and recast of the rent schedule at three- to five-year intervals or on exercise of renewal options when the rental rates are set to adjust to market rents. [See **RPI** Form 552 §4.5]

Upward shifts in rent

Some leases allow the landlord to use their judgment to set the rent for the adjustment, which needs to be exercised reasonably.

A provision for the periodic adjustment of rents to current rental rates is good insurance for a landlord. It captures any upward shifts in rents paid in the local rental market beyond those brought about by inflation.

This periodic recast of the rent payment is economically comparable to the rollover feature some lenders include in their three- or five-year adjustable rate or rollover mortgages.

In addition to base rents, CPI adjustments and rollover features, percentage rent provisions also capture the increase in rents due to appreciation based on a change in local demographics. [See Chapter 45]

If the property is in an outstanding location, or promoted by the landlord resulting in an increase in the tenant's gross income, the landlord needs to consider negotiating a percentage rent adjustment provision to better "cash in" on the draw of the property's location.

Adjustments for operating expenses

Many commercial leases include an additional rent provision to reimburse the landlord for their operating expenses. Rent may be adjusted to include the operating expenses and any taxes and assessments incurred by the property, called **common area maintenance (CAM)** expenses. [See Figure 2]

CAM provisions obligate the tenant to pay a pro rata share of the costs to maintain the common areas of the property including:

- utilities (water, gas, heat, etc.);
- air conditioning and venting;
- sewage;
- garbage;
- janitorial services;
- landscaping;
- security;
- insurance premiums;
- management fees; and
- real estate taxes.

The more operating costs passed on to the tenant, the closer the lease comes to a full net lease.

Chapter 44 Summary

To increase rents annually for inflation, the lease needs to provide a formula for calculating rent increases.

A provision for the periodic adjustment of rents to current rental rates is prudent insurance for a landlord. It captures upward shifts in rents paid in the local rental market beyond those brought about by inflation.

The best method for coping with the uncertainty of future inflation is to tie the amount due as future rents to figures published in the federal government's consumer price index (CPI).

CPI figures are published monthly, bi-monthly or semi-annually by the U.S. Bureau of Labor Statistics for numerous metropolitan areas across the states. The CPI is the most widely used indicator of inflation.

Chapter 44 Key Terms

Quiz 11 Covering Chapters 41-45 is located on page 644.

Percentage lease rent provisions

After reading this chapter, you will be able to:
- implement the use of a percentage rent provision; and
- identify retail lease situations appropriate for using a percentage rent provision to set the amount of rent due.

base rent   **percentage lease**

Learning Objectives

Key Terms

A landlord of a newly constructed commercial building negotiates a **percentage lease** with a prospective tenant. The prospective tenant intends to operate a franchised restaurant on the premises. They prepare an estimate of the gross sales amount anticipated for the first 12 months of operations, based on:

- the traffic count and traffic patterns at the location of the premises;
- the volume of anticipated sales; and
- the nature of the product and service to be offered by the restaurant.

The rent to be paid by the tenant comprises a **base rent** and additional rent.

The landlord and tenant agree the *base rent* for the first year, payable monthly, will be set at 6% of the tenant's estimated annual gross sales. The base rent is set in the lease agreement as a specific dollar amount. The monthly base rent amount is annually adjusted to increase at the rate of inflation as reflected by CPI figures.

The *percentage lease* agreement includes provisions for additional rent to be paid annually. The percentage rent provision is set to be triggered and additional rent due if 6% of the tenant's gross annual sales is greater in amount than the base rent paid during the preceding 12 months.

Rental income driven by gross sales

percentage lease
A commercial lease agreement for a retail operation that sets the total amount of rent the tenant will pay as a percentage of the tenant's gross sales. [See **RPI** Form 552-4]

base rent
The minimum monthly rent due under a commercial lease agreement. [See **RPI** Form 552 §4.3]

The percentage rates used to calculate the amount of additional rent to be paid for each consecutive 12-month period of the lease are set at:

- 6% of the first $2,000,000 in gross annual sales; and
- 7% on any greater amounts during the period.

From the total dollar amount calculated by these percentages, the *additional rent due* is the difference between the base rent paid during the 12 months and the total rent owed based on these percentages of gross annual sales. The additional rent is to be paid annually, within 45 days after the end of each 12-month period.

At the end of the first 12 months of business operation, the percentage rental rates are applied to the tenant's gross sales for the first year of occupancy. If the percentage amount is greater than the base rent paid, the tenant pays additional rent, also called percentage rent.

Base vs. percentage rent

The amount of rent paid for retail space in multiple tenant shopping complexes or other high traffic locations is based on a percentage of the tenant's gross sales. Lease agreements containing a percentage rent provision are called *percentage leases*. [See **RPI** Form 552-4]

A prudent landlord negotiating a percentage lease agreement includes as part of the rent provisions a clause calling for payment of a base rent. This base rent serves as a minimum monthly rent a tenant pays during each year of the lease. Base rent is payable monthly without regard to any amount of additional annual rent called for under the percentage rent clause. [See Figure 1]

The base rent is set by landlord/tenant negotiations, and is either:

- calculated as a percentage of the estimated gross sales the tenant will likely receive during the first year of operations; or
- based on current rents paid for comparable premises.

The monthly base rent is adjusted upward on each anniversary of the lease by either:

- pre-set increments, called graduated rent; or
- adjustments based on CPI figures, called adjustable rent. [See Chapter 44]

The total amount of rent the tenant will actually pay monthly, quarterly or annually under a percentage lease is the greater of either the base rent or the percentage rent.

Typical percentage rent rates for satellite tenants in a large shopping complex are 4% or 10% of the tenant's gross sales. However, the percentages for gradations of sales depend largely on the type of merchandise and services sold by the tenant, the pricing and volume of these sales and the traffic count at the location. Well-branded heavy advertisers, called anchor tenants, pay lesser rates than satellite tenants who surround the large anchor tenants.

Figure 1

Excerpt from Form 552-4

Commercial Lease Agreement — Percentage Lease

A tenant who retails small ticket items at high volume in a high traffic area, such as a kiosk in the center of a mall, will have a percentage rental rate, as high as 20% to 30% of sales.

Conversely, a tenant who retails big ticket items in low volume, such as an antique furniture store, will have a lower percentage rental rate.

When is percentage rent paid?

The tenant usually pays the additional percentage rent after the rental period has ended. The additional amount of the percentage rent is normally due within 10-to-45 days after the end of the period used to calculate the percentage rent.

Landlords and tenants agree to a monthly, quarterly, semi-annual or annual accounting period for payment of the percentage rent depending on:

- whether the tenant's sales tend to be constant or seasonal; and
- the financial strength of the tenant.

Further, percentage rent paid more than once a year is adjusted annually in a final accounting. This determines if any percentage rent remains due or is to be refunded to the tenant for the preceding 12 months of rental payments.

A landlord initially relies on their tenant to provide in good faith an accurate accounting of their gross sales for the period.

However, the landlord needs to reserve in the lease agreement the right to, on reasonable notice, audit the tenant's books regarding sales information and sales tax reports to the State Board of Equalization (SBOE). [See Figure 1]

Gross sales defined

The landlord and tenant also negotiate which sales will be subject to the percentage rental rate.

Gross sales is the actual price received for:

- all merchandise or services sold, leased, licensed or delivered in or from the premises by the tenant, for cash or on credit; and

- "layaway" sales at the time of the layaway transaction.

For the sale of lottery tickets, the tenant receives a 5% fee which is the amount included in the *gross sales*, not the price paid by the customer.[1]

Gross sales also include any sums received by the tenant for the licensing of vending machines, pay telephones, public toilet locks, etc., not the price paid to receive product from these machines.

For example, the tenant gives a vending machine operator the right to install vending machines on the leased premises for a one-time fee. The sums generated through the machine's sales are not included in gross sales since the tenant does not receive the sales proceeds.

Also, a periodic licensing fee received by a tenant from a vending machine operator for a license to use space is correctly considered part of the tenant's gross sales generated as a result of subleasing the premises.[2]

Further, money received by the tenant and disbursed while receiving no benefit, such as Medi-Cal funds received for direct disbursement to the staff as additional subsidized pay, is not included in the gross sales under a percentage lease. The funds did not increase the tenant's business, the tenant received no additions to sales and the funds were not for the tenant's use.[3]

The same exclusion rule applies to tips received by employees.

Excluded items

Items customarily excluded from gross sales in a percentage lease include:

- the selling price of merchandise returned for full credit;
- sums and credits received in the settlement of claims for damage to or loss of merchandise;
- sales tax;
- proceeds from the sale of fixtures, trade fixtures or other personal property used in the tenant's trade or business that are not merchandise;
- sales made to employees at a discount;
- refundable deposits; and
- uncollectible debts charged off by the tenant.

In practice, gift certificates are not considered part of the gross sales until they are redeemed and a sale is recorded.

---

1 Calif. Government Code §8880.51
2 **Herbert's Laurel-Ventura** v. **Laurel Ventura Holding Corporation** (1943) 58 CA2d 684
3 **Western Medical Enterprises, Inc.** v. **Albers** (1985) 166 CA3d 383

Finance charges or interest on accounts receivable held by the tenant may or may not be included, depending on negotiations between the landlord and tenant, and whether the receivables are administered on or off the premises.

A landlord enters into a percentage ground lease with a tenant who will build and operate a gas station on the premises. No provision requires the tenant to actually operate a gas station on the premises. The base monthly rent is set at $1,000 for the life of the lease without CPI or graduated adjustment. The percentage rent is set at 6.5% of gross sales.

A fair rent for failure to use

The tenant builds and operates the gas station on the premises. Additional rent is paid since the amount of percentage rent always exceeds the base rent.

However, before the lease expires, the tenant closes the gas station. Then, the tenant pays only the base monthly rent since no sales exist. The base rent is significantly less than the percentage rent the tenant paid during the last year of operation.

The landlord claims the tenant owes them the percentage rent as if the tenant continued to operate their business on the premises.

The tenant claims they owe no more than the monthly base rent since the lease agreement does not contain a provision requiring the tenant to operate the gas station at all times during the term of the lease.

Is the tenant liable to the landlord for the same percentage rent owed the landlord if the tenant had continued operations on the premises?

Yes! An **implied covenant** exists in a percentage lease as a promise to continue to use the premises as anticipated by the lease agreement, when:

- the base monthly rent does not represent a fair return to the landlord; and
- the tenant decides not to operate their business on the property.[4]

By entering into a percentage lease, the tenant is expected to continually operate their business during the lease term.

Continual operation

However, due to changes in market conditions, demographics, traffic patterns or other economic factors, the base monthly rent originally negotiated in a percentage lease may not always represent a fair return to the landlord — a fair rental value for the premises.

The landlord relies on the percentage rent to provide a yield on their investment that will keep pace with local rental conditions in the future.

A tenant who ceases to use the property to operate the business as anticipated by the use provision in a percentage lease agreement still owes percentage

---

4 **College Block** v. **Atlantic Richfield Company** (1988) 206 CA3d 1376

rent. The amount due is based on the gross sales the tenant expected to experience had they continued to use the property as permitted by the lease agreement.

A prudent landlord includes a use provision in a percentage lease requiring the tenant to operate the business for the entire term of the tenancy.

Chapter 45 Summary

The amount of rent paid for retail space in multiple tenant shopping complexes or other high traffic locations is set as a percentage of the tenant's gross sales. Lease agreements containing a percentage rent clause are called percentage leases.

The amount of rent the tenant will actually pay monthly, quarterly or annually for the percentage rent is the greater of either the base rent or the percentage rent.

The base rent is set by landlord/tenant negotiations and either:
- set as the dollar amount of a percentage of the estimated gross sales the tenant will likely receive during the first year of operations; or
- set as a dollar amount based on rents currently paid for comparable premises.

The monthly base rent set for the first year is adjusted upward periodically, usually on each anniversary of the lease by either:
- pre-set increments, called graduated rent; or
- adjustments based on CPI figures, called adjustable rent.

Chapter 45 Key Terms

Quiz 11 Covering Chapters 41-45 is located on page 644.

Commercial use-maintenance provisions

After reading this chapter, you will be able to:

- act on provisions in a commercial lease regarding the performance of tenant and landlord responsibilities for the use and maintenance of the leased premises; and
- explain the remedies available to the landlord if a tenant fails to fulfill their use and maintenance obligations.

Learning Objectives

appurtenance

compliance-with-laws clause

destruction provision

hold harmless provision

rent provision

right-to-enter provision

signage provision

tenant improvements and alterations clause

triple-net lease

use-maintenance provision

use-of-premises provision

waste provision

Key Terms

A commercial lease agreement contains two basic categories of provisions establishing the tenant's obligations to the landlord:

- *rent provisions* for the payment of amounts owed [See Chapter 42]; and
- *use-maintenance provisions* for the use, care and preservation of the grounds and improvements.

Rent provisions evidence the promise to pay money owed to the landlord in exchange for the tenant's exclusive possession of the leased premises. This monetary obligation is separately enforceable from the use-maintenance provisions. [See Chapter 42]

Shifting ownership obligations to tenants

> **rent provision**
> A provision contained in a lease agreement establishing the tenant's obligations to pay rents for occupancy and use of the premises leased. [See **RPI** Form 552 §4]

use-maintenance provision
A provision in a commercial lease agreement which establishes the landlord's and tenant's responsibility for the care and maintenance of the premises during the lease term.

Use-maintenance provisions in a commercial lease agreement establish whether the landlord or the tenant is responsible for the care and maintenance of the premises during the lease term. [See **RPI** Form 552]

Use-maintenance obligations are unrelated to the payment of rent. Instead, they identify who will perform or contract for the repairs and maintenance of the leased premises and who will pay for the services — the landlord or the tenant.

If the landlord retains the majority of the maintenance obligations such as under a gross lease agreement, the **base rent** the tenant will pay will likely be higher than on a net lease. If the tenant assumes the majority of the maintenance obligations such as under a net lease agreement, the base rent the tenant pays will likely be lower than on a gross lease.

Just as a tenant breaches a lease agreement by failing to pay rent, they also breach the lease agreement when they fail to perform, or violate a use-maintenance provision.

The tenant's breach of an essential use-maintenance obligation triggers enforcement action by the landlord by serving the tenant with either:

- a three-day *notice to perform or quit* stating precisely what is to be done by the tenant within three days; or
- a three-day *notice to quit* if the breach is incurable. [See Chapter 26]

Recall that when the performance called for in the notice to eliminate a curable breach is not completed prior to expiration of the notice period, the tenant loses their right of possession (provided the notice contains a declaration of forfeiture). When the notice to quit addresses an incurable breach, the tenant automatically loses any right to continue in possession at the time of the breach.[1]

Which use-maintenance provisions to include

The contents of each provision in a commercial lease agreement are fully negotiable. The results of negotiations depend on the respective bargaining power of the landlord and the tenant, as tempered by market conditions and the leasing agents involved.

As with any negotiations, lease provisions vary, depending on the:

- intended use of the property;
- delegation of operating costs and responsibility for the property's physical conditions and any TIs required; and
- length of the lease term.

Occasionally, professional landlords and franchised tenants will use a lease agreement form especially prepared by their respective attorneys for repetitive use, i.e., when the landlord has many properties to let or the tenant leases many locations.

---

1 **Kendall** v. **Ernest Pestana, Inc.** (1985) 40 C3d 488

Figure 1

Excerpt from
Form 552

Commercial
Lease
Agreement

Gross — Single
Tenant

7. USE OF THE PREMISES:

7.1   The Tenant's use of the Premises will be _____.

7.2   No other use of the Premises is permitted.

     a.   Tenant may not conduct any activity which increases Landlord's insurance premiums.

7.3   Tenant will not use the Premises for any unlawful purpose, violate any government ordinance or building and tenant association rules, or create any nuisance.

7.4   Tenant will not destroy, damage, or remove any part of the Premises or equipment, or commit waste, or permit any person to do so.

However, landlords more frequently use published lease agreements that contain provisions basic to commercial lease transactions. They then attach addenda for provisions not included in the form or contrary to provisions in the form. [See **RPI** Form 552 through 552-8]

*Editor's note — The following discussion of use-maintenance clauses refers to provisions in **RPI** Form 552 — Commercial Lease Agreement — Gross — Single Tenant.*

Use of the premises provision

On entering into a commercial lease agreement, a landlord and tenant agree the premises will be used by the tenant for a single specified purpose, such as a retail clothing store or an auto mechanics shop. This purpose is specified in the **use-of-premises provision**. [See **RPI** Form 552 §7.1; see Figure 1]

When lease provisions do not restrict or specify the tenant's use of the leased premises, the premises may be used for any lawful purpose.[2]

Conversely, a lease may prohibit any change in use, or set conditions to be met before a change from the use specified in the *use-of-premises provision* may be implemented.[3]

If the use provision requires the landlord's consent to a change in use, but gives no standard or condition to be met for the consent, the landlord needs evidence of a commercially reasonable basis for withholding their consent to the tenant's proposed new use.[4]

The standard of reasonableness applied to the landlord's consent is the same as applied to assignment and subletting restrictions — *restriction-on-transfer provisions* — calling for the landlord's consent. [See Chapter 48]

In the *use-of-premises provision*, the tenant agrees to deliver up the premises on expiration of the lease in as good condition as it was when they took possession, less reasonable wear and tear.

Even if the tenant's use of the leased premises is unrestricted, the tenant cannot impair the premises by damaging it, creating a nuisance, engaging in illegal activities or subjecting the premises to greater wear and tear than the use contemplated when the lease was entered into. [See Figure 1 §7.4]

use-of-premises provision
A provision contained in a commercial lease agreement which establishes the single specified purpose for the tenant's use of the leased premises.

---

2 Calif. Civil Code §1997.210(b)

3 CC §1997.230

4 CC §1997.250

10. SIGNS AND ADVERTISING:

10.1   Tenant will not construct any sign or other advertising on the Premises without the prior consent of Landlord.

10.2   ☐   Landlord will maintain a directory in the lobby of the Premises displaying the name and suite number of Tenant. Landlord has the right to determine the size, shape, color, style and lettering of the directory.

10.3   ☐   Landlord will provide a sign to be placed on the primary door to Tenant's suite. The fees for the cost and installation will be paid by Tenant.

In addition to the use allowed, the tenant agrees not to conduct any activities on the property which:

- increase the landlord's liability or hazard insurance premiums; or

- violate any laws, building ordinances or tenant association rules, called a *compliance-with-laws clause*. [See Figure 1]

Appurtenances to the leasehold

Property or rights belonging to but not located within the leased space are called **appurtenances**. A tenant's use of appurtenances is often necessary for the use and enjoyment of the space leased.[5]

Leasehold *appurtenances* include rights belonging to real estate owned by the landlord and located outside the leased space, such as:

appurtenance
A right belonging to real estate owned by the landlord to use property located outside the leased premises for purposes such as parking or access.

- a right of way for vehicular travel through an industrial or office complex;

- parking for employees and customers;

- storage space, lobbies and restrooms; and

- access by ingress and egress from public roads to the leased premises, such as a road or driveway.

Signs and advertising for conformity

A **signage provision** in the lease agreement gives a landlord control over the size, style, content and location of signs constructed or installed on the premises to advertise the location or existence of the tenant's business. This allows the landlord to maintain the integrity of the building's physical and aesthetic appearance. [See **RPI** Form 552 §10; see Figure 2]

The cost of sign installation can be charged to either the landlord or tenant as negotiated and stated in the terms of the lease.

Tenant improvements and alterations

A tenant's right to make alterations or further improve the premises during the tenancy is governed by the lease provision called **tenant improvements (TIs) and alterations clause**, or more simply a *TI clause*. [See **RPI** From 552 §11; see Figure 3]

To ensure the landlord retains control over the structures on the leased premises, the tenant agrees not to alter or further improve any part of the

---

5   CC §662

Figure 3

Excerpt from Form 552

Gross — Single Tenant

11. TENANT IMPROVEMENTS/ALTERATIONS:

11.1 Tenant may not alter or improve the Premises without Landlord's prior consent to include tenant improvements necessary for Tenant to occupy.

   a. Tenant will keep the Premises free of all claims for any improvements and will timely notify Landlord to permit posting of Notices of Nonresponsibility

11.2 Any increases in Landlord's property taxes caused by improvements made by Tenant will become additional rent due on demand.

11.3 On expiration of this lease, tenant improvements as authorized by Landlord are to:

   a. ☐ become fixtures and part of the Premises not to be removed by Tenant.

   b. ☐ be removed by Tenant in their entirety.

   c. ☐ be partially removed by Tenant as follows: _____

building without first obtaining the landlord's written consent. The tenant will pay all costs incurred in the construction (unless the lease agreement is altered to call for different treatment).

A lease agreement for retail space, especially in malls, includes provisions which require the tenant to renovate their storefront and interior every number of years. Renovations by tenants every four to six years will help maintain a fresh appearance which is vital to the overall success of retail shopping centers.

When the landlord later consents to alterations by the tenant, the tenant is to promptly notify the landlord of the commencement of construction so the landlord can post and record a **notice of nonresponsibility**. [See Chapter 5]

The *notice of nonresponsibility* is a form which releases the landlord from responsibility for any claims made by contractors for improvements the contractors construct on the leased premises under their contract with the tenant.[6] [See Form 597 in Chapter 5]

The notice bars *mechanic's liens* on the landlord's fee interest and denies contractors employed by the tenant the ability to pursue the landlord for unpaid amounts due.

Increases in property taxes due to alterations made by the tenant are the tenant's responsibility and are to be paid to the landlord on demand.

Unless otherwise agreed, tenant improvements become the property of the landlord at the end of the lease term and cannot be removed by the tenant, with the exception of the tenant's trade fixtures.[7] [See Chapter 5]

Further, when the tenant alters or improves the premises resulting in a new and different use of the premises, the tenant has a duty to comply with all building code requirements. This responsibility is separate from the contractual duty imposed by a **compliance-with-laws clause**. [See Figure 1 §7.3]

If the tenant's installation of improvements violates building codes and ordinances, the tenant will be liable for the costs the landlord incurs to conform the tenant-installed improvements to codes and ordinances.[8]

signage provision
A provision in a commercial lease agreement which gives the landlord control over the size, style, content and location of signs constructed or installed on the leased premises. [See **RPI** Form 552 §10]

tenant improvements and alterations clause
A clause in a commercial lease agreement which specifies the tenant's right to make alterations or further improve the premises during the tenancy. [See **RPI** Form 552 §11]

compliance-with-laws clause
A provision in a commercial lease agreement controlling the conduct of tenant activities on the property to conform with public laws, building ordinances or tenant association rules. [See **RPI** Form 552 §7.3]

---

6 CC §8444

7 **Wolfen** v. **Clinical Data, Inc.** (1993) 16 CA4th 171

8 Wolfen, *supra*

Government-ordered repairs

When determining whether the landlord of the tenant is responsible for government-ordered repairs, the terms of the lease agreement do not always control. Instead, the determination of whether the landlord or the tenant is to bear the burden of government-ordered repairs is based on the analysis of six factors:

- the ratio of the cost of repairs to the amount of rent due over the entire life of the lease;

- the length of the lease, including renewal options;

- whether the landlord or the tenant will benefit more from the repairs in terms of the useful life of the building and the remaining term of the lease;

- whether the repairs are structural or nonstructural;

- whether or not the repairs will substantially interfere with the tenant's enjoyment of the premises; and

- whether or not the government-ordered repairs were foreseeable at the time the lease agreement was entered into by the landlord and the tenant.

Each burden-of-compliance factor is weighed based on the circumstances surrounding the execution of the lease agreement, the text of the lease provisions and the economic realities of the lease transaction.

For example, a landlord and tenant enter into a 15-year commercial net lease agreement. A boilerplate use-maintenance provision transfers to the tenant all ownership duties, including structural repairs.

Less than two years into the 15-year lease, the county discovers friable asbestos on the premises and issues an abatement order to the tenant. Neither the landlord nor the tenant had previous knowledge asbestos existed on the premises as it was a pre-existing condition of the building. The tenant seals off the contaminated area and conducts business out of another section of the building.

The costs of repairing the building is a sum roughly equal to 5% of the aggregate amount of rent due over the entire 15-year life of the lease.

Here, the provisions in the lease agreement and the circumstances under which the lease was entered into imply the duty to comply with the government order was transferred to the tenant, since:

- the cost of repairs amounted to less than 5% of the aggregate amount of rent due over the life of the lease;

- the lease was for 15 years, thus the cost of repairs are easily amortized by the tenant during the remaining tenancy;

Who does the repair and maintenance?

The tenant's responsibilities for the payment of the costs to repair and maintain the premises are of equal financial importance and effect as the amount of rent to be paid under a commercial lease agreement. Ultimately, the tenant bears them, either directly by incurring the costs or indirectly through the payment of basic rent or additional rent in the form of *common area maintenance charges (CAMs)*. [See Chapter 14]

The extent of the maintenance and repair obligations assumed by the tenant depends on the type of space leased, the length of the lease term and of course market conditions of inventory and users — supply and demand issues.

- *the asbestos removal most benefits the tenant since the contamination was discovered less than two years into the lease;*

- *the repairs are structural and the lease clearly transfers structural repairs to the tenant;*

- *the tenant's use of the premises is not greatly interfered with during the abatement; and*

- *neither the tenant nor the landlord had reason to believe asbestos existed on the premises, yet the tenant was experienced in retail leasing and elected not to investigate the premises. [**Brown** v. **Green** (1994) 8 C4th 812]*

Now consider a landlord and a tenant who enter into the same commercial net lease agreement but for a term of three years. The lease also contains an option to renew the lease for five additional years. The net lease agreement contains the boilerplate compliance-with-laws and use-maintenance provisions which shift the duties of ownership to the tenant. Under these provisions, the tenant has the duty to complete structural repairs.

After the tenant exercises their option to renew the lease for the additional five years, the landlord receives a compliance order from the city requiring the leased premises to be earthquake-proofed.

The cost of earthquake-proofing the building roughly equals 50% of the aggregate amount of the rent due over the entire life of the lease, which is now in its 4th year.

Here, even though the lease agreement shifted the major burdens of ownership from the landlord to the tenant, an application of the six-factor test determines the landlord bears the burden of the earthquake-proofing costs. The analysis found that:

- *the cost of earthquake-proofing the premises was roughly equal to 50% of the aggregate rent due over the total eight-year term of the lease;*

- *the eight-year lease was short-term with little time remaining for the tenant to amortize the cost of the repairs; and*

- *the earthquake-proofing primarily benefited the landlord since only a short term remained on the tenant's lease. [**Hadian** v. **Schwartz** (1994) 8 CA4th 836]*

Thus, when entering into a commercial net lease agreement, a landlord is best served considering the inclusion of a provision calling for the tenant to assume the cost of compliance orders that do not regulate the tenant's use of the premises — government-ordered retrofitting or renovation.

Yet the landlord needs to be aware that if the economic realities of the lease agreement are not in accord with the text of the lease agreement, the landlord may still be liable for government-ordered repairs.

The longer the lease term, including renewal options, the more likely the obligations for maintenance will be shifted to the tenant. The shift will be even more likely if the premises is a single-user building, such as a warehouse or bank building as opposed to a multi-tenant project.

The commercial tenant has a duty during the leasing period to notify the landlord of those repairs which are needed and are the responsibility of the landlord.

Compliance-with-laws clause

Some net lease agreement forms contain a *compliance-with-laws clause* requiring the tenant to make any government-ordered repairs, such as asbestos removal or seismic retrofitting.

If the lease agreement containing a compliance clause is a short-term lease agreement, the landlord will be the primary beneficiary of the government-ordered repairs. In spite of the wording in the lease agreement placing the financial responsibility on the tenant, the landlord may be responsible for completing and paying for government-ordered repairs.[9] [See Sidebar, "Government-ordered repairs"]

Net lease agreements contain various provisions covering the cost of items needing repair, replacement or maintenance which exceed one month's rent. [See **RPI** Form 552-2 and 552-3]

When the cost of tenant obligations for repair and maintenance of an item exceeds the equivalent of one month's rent, the landlord performs the repairs. The cost for the repairs is initially paid by the landlord.

In turn, these provisions obligate the tenant to reimburse the landlord by payment of a monthly additional amount of rent equal to 1/144 of the cost the landlord incurred. The additional rent is paid each month for the remainder of the term of the lease agreement and any lease extensions, but not to exceed 144 months. [See **RPI** Form 552-2 §6.3]

Thus, costly repairs are allocated between the tenant and landlord over 144 months. Further, interest is paid by the tenant on the total amount remaining to be reimbursed over the 144 months at an annual rate set in the provision. To require the tenant to replace an item which is costly in the last couple of months of a lease is unenforceable since the tenant will bear all the cost and receive none of the benefits. [See **RPI** Form 552-2 §6.3]

Landlord's right to enter limited

Once a tenant acquires a leasehold interest in a commercial premises, the landlord no longer has the right to enter the premises for any reason, unless agreed to the contrary or an emergency exists. [See Chapter 4]

However, the landlord can reserve the right to enter and make any necessary repairs, alterations or inspections of the premises by including a **right-to-enter provision** in the lease agreement. [See **RPI** Form 552 §12; see Figure 4]

A landlord may need to enter the premises when:

right-to-enter provision
A provision contained in a lease agreement which reserves to the landlord the right to enter the leased premises to make necessary repairs, alterations or inspections. [See **RPI** Form 552 §12]

- the landlord makes necessary or agreed-to repairs or alterations;
- the landlord is supplying necessary services to the tenant;
- the landlord shows the premises to a prospective tenant;
- the tenant has abandoned or surrendered the premises;
- the tenant requests a pre-expiration inspection [See Chapter 19];
- a court order was issued allowing the landlord to enter; or
- an emergency exists which endangers the property. [See Chapter 4]

9 **Hadian** v. **Schwartz** (1994) 8 C4th 836

12. RIGHT TO ENTER:

12.1 Tenant agrees to make the Premises available on 24 hours' notice for entry by Landlord for necessary repairs, alterations, or inspections of the Premises.

As is expected in a lease agreement, the tenant agrees not to destroy, damage or remove any part of the premises or equipment, or permit or commit waste on the premises. This clause is called the **waste provision**. [See **RPI** Form 552 §7.4; see Figure 1]

If the tenant or a person permitted on the premises by the tenant commits waste to the property, the tenant commits an incurable breach of the lease agreement and automatically forfeits their right of possession. [See Chapter 26 and 28]

The landlord may serve the tenant who has committed or permitted waste to the property with a three-day notice to quit as required to initiate an *unlawful detainer (UD)* action to evict the tenant if they do not vacate.[10]

A landlord and tenant may agree the tenant will purchase a liability insurance policy to cover losses which might occur on the premises, including:

- property damage; and
- bodily injury. [See **RPI** Form 552 §13; see Figure 5]

The lease agreement sets the policy limits or minimum amount of liability insurance the tenant is to obtain. These limits are set as a result of the landlord's discussion and analysis with an insurance agent. [See Figure 5]

Typically, a tenant's obligation to maintain liability insurance under a lease is covered under the tenant's commercial general liability insurance policy purchased by the tenant to insure the business they operate on the premises.

To protect the landlord from any dissipation of insurance proceeds by the tenant, the landlord is to be named as an additional insured on the tenant's liability and hazard insurance policies covering the leased premises.

A landlord ensures they are named on the insurance policy by drafting the lease agreement to require the tenant to provide a certificate of insurance from the carrier naming the landlord as an additional insured. [See Figure 5 §13.3]

Waste as a permanent breach

waste provision
A provision in a lease agreement in which the tenant agrees not to destroy, damage or remove any part of the leased premises. [See **RPI** Form 552 §7.4]

Liability insurance

---

10 Calif. Code of Civil Procedure §1161(4)

Figure 5

Excerpt from Form 552

Gross — Single Tenant

---

13.   LIABILITY INSURANCE:

13.1   Tenant will obtain and maintain commercial general liability and plate glass insurance coverage insuring Tenant and Landlord against all claims for bodily injury, personal injury and property damage arising out of Tenant's use of the Premises.

13.2   Tenant to obtain insurance for this purpose in the minimum amount of $_____.

13.3   Tenant to provide Landlord with a Certificate of Insurance naming Landlord as an additional insured. The Certificate is to provide for written notice to Landlord if a change or cancellation of the policy occurs.

13.4   Each party waives all insurance subrogation rights they may have.

Under the insurance provision, both the landlord and the tenant waive any insurance subrogation rights each might have against the other. Due to the clause, an insurance carrier cannot seek to recover from the landlord or tenant who was the cause of the injury or property damage.[11]

Hazard insurance

In a multi-tenant building, a landlord obtains a hazard insurance policy and passes the cost of the premiums through to the tenant, generally by way of the monthly base rent or CAMs.

The landlord and tenant may agree the tenant will purchase a standard hazard insurance policy for fire losses. It also covers theft and vandalism of all personal property and the restoration of tenant improvements, including the destruction of plate glass windows.

Requiring the tenant to maintain a hazard insurance policy assures the landlord that the tenant will be in the financial position necessary to continue to operate their business if fire, theft or vandalism occurs during the term of the lease.

When the tenant is required to maintain an insurance policy for property damage resulting from fire, theft or vandalism, the landlord is named by the carrier as an additional insured. Thus, the landlord controls the use of any insurance proceeds.

triple-net lease
A commercial lease which passes the responsibility for all costs and maintenance of the property to the tenant. [See RPI Form 552-2 and 552-3]

In a long-term, **triple-net lease** where the tenant has assumed all obligations and duties of ownership, the lease agreement shifts to the tenant:

* the obligation to maintain hazard insurance; and
* the burden of repairing any destruction of the real estate, regardless of the cause.

Hold harmless for tenant's actions

The *hold harmless provision* covers the landlord for liability from injuries occurring on the premises which:

* arise out of the tenant's negligent use of the premises; and
* are caused by the tenant, their employees or customers due to the tenant's negligence. [See **RPI** Form 552 §15; see Figure 6]

---

11 **Gordon** v. **J.C. Penney Company** (1970) 7 CA3d 280

Figure 6

Excerpt from
Form 552

Gross — Single
Tenant

15. HOLD HARMLESS:

15.1 Tenant will hold Landlord harmless for all claims, damages or liability arising out of the Premises caused by Tenant or its employees or patrons.

When a **hold harmless provision** is included in a lease agreement, the tenant needs to purchase liability insurance coverage for the risk of loss they have agreed is theirs — their contractual liability under the lease agreement. [See Figure 6]

Contractual liability insurance is separate from general liability insurance covering bodily injury and property damage.

Regardless of the type of hold harmless provision used, the landlord cannot shift responsibility to the tenant for any liability arising from their landlord's intentional misconduct or violation of law.[12]

For example, a landlord cannot escape liability to others for injuries occurring on the leased premises due to the landlord's failure to maintain the premises. [See Chapters 36 and 37]

hold harmless provision
A provision in a lease agreement that shifts liability from the landlord to the tenant for injuries occurring on the premises caused by the tenant's negligence. [See **RPI** Form 552 §15]

Initially, the responsibility for the costs of making repairs to commercial property lies with the landlord.

However, some or all of the responsibilities may be shifted to the tenant through negotiations. They are also allocated between the landlord and the tenant by a *destruction provision* in the lease agreement.

In the destruction provision, the tenant agrees to repair and pay for any destruction to the premises:

- caused by the tenant;
- covered by insurance policies held by the tenant; or
- required by other lease provisions.

When the tenant is obligated to carry insurance covering the cost of repairs, the landlord named as an additional insured controls the disbursement of any insurance proceeds available to pay for the repairs. [See **RPI** Form 552 §16; see Figure 7]

On the other hand, the landlord agrees to repair and pay for any damage to the premises which:

- is not caused by the tenant or covered by the tenant's insurance policies;
- is insured only by the landlord's policy; or
- is not insured by any policy. [See Figure 7 §16.2]

Destruction and who must repair

destruction provision
A provision in a lease agreement in which a tenant agrees to pay for any destruction to the premises caused by the tenant, covered by the tenant's insurance or required by other lease provisions. [See **RPI** Form 552 §16]

12 CC §1668

Figure 7

Excerpt from Form 552

Gross — Single Tenant

16. DESTRUCTION:

16.1 In the event the Premises are totally or partially destroyed, Tenant agrees to repair the Premises if the destruction is caused by Tenant or covered by Tenant's insurance.

16.2 Landlord will repair the Premises if the cause is not covered by Tenant's insurance policy and is covered by Landlord's insurance policy.

16.3 This lease agreement may not be terminated due to any destruction of the Premises, unless:

    a. the repairs cannot be completed within 30 days;

    b. the cost of restoration exceeds 70% of the replacement value of the premises;

    c. the insurance proceeds are insufficient to cover the actual cost of the repairs; or

    d. the Premises may not be occupied by law.

A **destruction provision** typically states the lease will not terminate due to any destruction of the premises, unless the landlord chooses to terminate it under specified conditions, such as:

- the repairs cannot be completed within 30 days;
- the cost of restoration exceeds 70% of the replacement value of the premises;
- the insurance proceeds are insufficient to cover the actual cost of the repairs; or
- the premises may not be occupied by law. [See Figure 7]

Thus, the landlord may opt to terminate the lease if the casualty is underinsured.

However, if the landlord fails to begin repairs which are their responsibility or, alternatively, terminates the lease within a reasonable time, the tenant may:

- abandon the premises due to a *constructive eviction* and be excused from further performance under the lease[13] [See Chapter 33]; or
- pay rent and recover from the landlord any losses suffered due to the landlord's failure to repair.[14]

---

13 CC §1942

14 **Ng** v. **Warren** (1947) 79 CA2d 54

A commercial lease agreement contains two basic categories of provisions establishing the tenant's obligations to the landlord:

- rent provisions for the payment of amounts owed; and
- use-maintenance provisions for the use, care and preservation of the grounds and improvements.

Use-maintenance obligations are unrelated to the payment of rent. Use-maintenance provisions in a commercial lease agreement establish whether the tenant or the landlord is responsible for the care and maintenance of the premises during the lease term.

Just as a tenant breaches a lease agreement by failing to pay rent, they also breach the lease agreement when they fail to perform, or violate a use-maintenance provision.

The tenant's breach of an essential use-maintenance obligation triggers enforcement action by the landlord by serving the tenant with either:

- a three-day notice to perform or quit stating what needs to be done by the tenant within three days; or
- a three-day notice to quit if the breach is incurable.

Chapter 46 Summary

Chapter 46 Key Terms

Quiz 12 Covering Chapters 46-49 is located on page 645.

Notes:

Lease renewal and extension options

After reading this chapter, you will be able to:
- distinguish between a renewal and extension of a lease; and
- take the proper steps to exercise an option to renew or extend a lease

option to extend   **option to renew**

Learning Objectives

Key Terms

Don't forget to exercise

A broker arranges for a tenant to lease improved commercial real estate. The lease is for a three-year term and contains options to renew the lease for additional three-year periods to avoid violation of the **due-on clause** in a trust deed encumbrance. [see **RPI** Form 552]

The lease renewal options require the tenant to exercise each renewal option in writing at least three months before the lease term expires. Otherwise, the renewal options expire three months before the lease itself expires. [See Form 566 accompanying this chapter]

During occupancy, the tenant's business improves. As a result, they make substantial improvements to the building with the owner's consent.

Business demands require the tenant to also lease an adjacent building. The two buildings are operated as one complex by the tenant. The cul-de-sac street fronting the building is even renamed after their business.

As the expiration date of the renewal option approaches, the tenant installs new air conditioning units, again with the owner's consent.

However, the tenant fails to give the owner the written notice required to exercise their option to renew the lease before the renewal option expires.

After the option expires, but before the lease expires, the tenant attempts to exercise the renewal option.

The owner refuses to waive or extend the expiration date of the option to renew. The tenant is told they need to vacate on expiration of the current three-year term since the renewal option expired unexercised.

The tenant claims their tenant improvement activity was sufficient to place the owner on notice of their intent to exercise the renewal option since their improvements were inconsistent with vacating the premises on expiration of the lease.

When the option to renew expires unexercised as agreed, does the lease automatically expire at the end of its term?

Yes! The tenant's further improvements of the premises prior to expiration of the renewal option are not proper notice to the owner of the tenant's intent to renew. An option is an irrevocable offer, separate and independent of the lease agreement, whether it is a provision in the lease agreement or an addendum to it. [See Form 565 accompanying this chapter]

An option expires by its own terms, as does any offer. If acceptance is not given by exercise as specified in the option agreement, the option expires.[1]

The lease term

Absent an agreement to the contrary, a lease terminates automatically, without further notice, on expiration of the lease term stated in the lease agreement.[2]

A tenant who remains in possession after the lease term expires is commonly referred to as a **holdover tenant**, legally called a **tenant at sufferance**.

A landlord subjected to a holdover may initiate an unlawful detainer proceeding to evict the holdover tenant immediately after expiration of the lease — no notice to quit is necessary.[3]

Alternatively, when a renewal option does not exist and the tenant continues in occupancy and tenders rent which the landlord accepts, a month-to-month tenancy is created. Consequently, the landlord needs to serve the tenant with the appropriate notice to vacate to terminate the periodic tenancy.[4]

Options to renew/extend

Frequently, lease agreements contain provisions or addendums which allow the tenant to continue in lawful possession after the initial lease term expires. A prior agreement allowing continued occupancy is called an **Option to Renew/Extend the Lease**. [See Form 565]

For a tenant, a lease renewal/extension option can be financially advantageous. The tenant has time during the option period to examine

---

1   **Bekins Moving & Storage Co. v. Prudential Insurance Company of America** (1985) 176 CA3d 245
2   Calif. Civil Code §1933(1)
3   Calif. Code of Civil Procedure §1161(1)
4 . CC §§1945, 1946

OPTION TO RENEW/EXTEND LEASE

Prepared by: Agent _____ Phone _____
Broker _____ Email _____

NOTE: This form is used by a leasing agent or landlord when negotiating a residential or commercial lease agreement, to provide in an addendum the landlord's grant to the tenant the option to extend possession under the original lease agreement or renew under a new lease agreement on the same conditions as the expiring lease.

DATE: _____, 20_____, at _____, California.
Items left blank or unchecked are not applicable.

FACTS:

1. This option to renew or extend is an addendum to the lease agreement

　1.1　dated _____, 20_____, at _____, California,

　1.2　entered into by _____, as the Tenant,

　1.3　and _____, as the Landlord,

　1.4　recorded _____, 20_____, as Instrument No. _____,

　1.5　in _____ County, California, regarding real estate referred to as
　　　_____

AGREEMENT:

2. Landlord hereby grants to Tenant the following option(s) to ☐ renew, or ☐ extend, the term of the lease agreement referenced above.

　2.1　The first option is for a term beginning on expiration of the original term of the lease and ending _____ year(s) thereafter.
　　　The rental payment schedule during the term of this renewal/extension to be _____
　　　_____
　　　_____

　2.2　The second option is for a term beginning on expiration of the immediately preceding term and ending _____ year(s) thereafter.
　　　The rental payment schedule during the term of this renewal/extension to be _____
　　　_____
　　　_____

　2.3　The third option is for a term beginning on expiration of the immediately preceding term and ending _____ year(s) thereafter.
　　　The rental payment schedule during the term of this renewal/extension to be _____
　　　_____
　　　_____

　2.4　Other _____
　　　_____

3. Each option to renew/extend the lease expires _____ months prior to the expiration of the lease term which immediately precedes the renewal/extension period provided by the option.

4. A written notice of Exercise of Option to Renew/Extend Lease needs to be delivered prior to expiration of the option exercised and no sooner than _____ months before expiration of the option exercised. [See **RPI** Form 566]

　4.1　Exercise of each option to be delivered to Landlord by certified mail or personal delivery, or by personal delivery to Broker/Property Manager who is _____.
　　　Address _____

　4.2　Tenant's failure to timely exercise any option will cause the lease to expire unrenewed and unextended.

---

whether the economic and financial conditions of their trade or business at this location favor an exercise of the option and continued possession. If not, the tenant is under no obligation to exercise the option. If they do not exercise the option, they need to vacate the premises on expiration of the lease.

Thus, the well-informed tenant will consider negotiating one or more renewal/extension options when entering into a lease agreement for a short term.

On the other hand, the landlord may not share the tenant's enthusiasm for a renewal/extension option since the decision seems to only benefit the tenant. A renewal/extension option leaves the landlord in a somewhat uncertain

-- PAGE 2 OF 2 — FORM 565 --

5. This addendum's provisions supersede any inconsistent provisions contained in the lease agreement.

6. Other _____

_____

_____

_____

_____

_____

_____

_____

_____

I agree to the terms stated above.

Date: _____, 20_____
Landlord: _____
Agent: _____

Signature: _____
CalBRE #: _____
Address: _____

Phone: _____
Cell: _____
Email: _____

I agree to the terms stated above.
☐ See attached Signature Page Addendum. [RPI Form 251]
Date: _____, 20_____
Tenant: _____

Signature: _____
Tenant: _____

Signature: _____
Phone: _____
Cell: _____
Email: _____

FORM 565   03-11   ©2016 RPI — Realty Publications, Inc., P.O. BOX 5707, RIVERSIDE, CA 92517

position as they do not know who will occupy the premises in the future. Meanwhile, the tenant is left to decide whether to exercise the option and extend the occupancy or vacate on expiration of the lease.

Future uncertainty

One solution to the landlord's anxiety about locating a new tenant is to set the expiration of the renewal/extension option several months before the lease expires. Thus, the expiration of the option unexercised gives the landlord sufficient time in which to locate a replacement tenant. [See Form 565 §3]

A renewal option encourages a tenant to enter into the lease in the first place since the tenant has the right to continue in possession if the property proves beneficial to their business. Additionally, the renewal/extension option encourages the tenant to improve and promote the location in anticipation of remaining in possession. Also, three-year terms do not violate the due-on clause in any trust deed encumbering the property.

Consider a lease agreement which grants a tenant an option to renew the lease every three years at the same rental rate. It does not state a date for expiration of the continuing option renewal periods. When the tenant attempts to exercise the renewal option, the landlord claims the lease is unenforceable since the lease agreement and the option grant the tenant the right to renew the lease forever — a violation of the rule against perpetuities.

However, the lease is valid. Commercial lease transactions are no longer controlled by laws governing perpetuities. The total term of the commercial lease, including extensions or renewals, is limited to 99 years by statute if not limited by its terms.[5]

A technical but obvious processing distinction exists between a **renewal** and an **extension** of a lease.

An *extension* is a modification of the original lease term by extending its expiration date for an additional period. On the other hand, a *renewal* requires the execution of a new lease on identical conditions to the original lease agreement, not a continuation of the old lease.[6]

A renewal involves the preparation and signing of a new lease which creates an entirely new tenancy. The new tenancy is subject to any change in law affecting the rights and obligations of the landlord or the tenant. It is also subordinate to any encumbrances which occurred during the term of the prior lease.

Alternatively, an extension merely modifies the original lease by extending its expiration date. Thus, the modified lease is not subject to changes in the law or encumbrances occurring after the term of the original lease.

However, the terms are often used interchangeably, neglecting to maintain clarity of purpose, legal rights and the paperwork involved.

For instance, a lease agreement granting the tenant an "option to renew" which does not specify the manner or method for exercise of the option nor call for the signing of a new lease is considered an extension. As a result, the provisions of the original lease apply on exercise of the option, but with a new expiration date by modification.[7]

To exercise a lease renewal/extension option, the tenant needs to notify the landlord of their unqualified intention to renew or extend the lease on the terms in the option. The notice of exercise needs to be timely delivered to the landlord, unequivocal and precise in its terms for the specific period offered in the option. If not, the notice of exercise is ineffective and may be ignored by the landlord.

Consider a tenant who enters into a lease agreement which includes a provision or an attachment granting the tenant an option to renew the lease for an additional two-year period.

During the period for exercise of the renewal option, the tenant notifies the landlord of their intention to renew the lease, but notes they will only occupy for one year.

Renew vs. extend

option to renew
An agreement granting a tenant the right to continue in possession upon expiration of the existing lease under a new lease agreement on the same conditions as the expiring lease agreement on terms for payment of rent set out in the option to renew. [See **RPI** Form 565]

option to extend
An agreement granting a tenant the right to extend possession under the original lease agreement on terms set out in the option to extend. [See **RPI** Form 565]

Exercise of the option

---

5   **Shaver** v. **Clanton** (1994) 26 CA4th 568
6   In **re Marriage of Joaquin** (1987) 193 CA3d 1529
7   In re Marriage of Joaquin, *supra*

In this example, the tenant's notice to renew is an ineffectual attempt to exercise the option to renew the lease. The tenant's notice is a proposal to renew for a different period than the period stated in the option — an irrevocable offer to renew the lease.

Thus, the notice is not an acceptance of the offer to renew housed in the option granted, but an attempt to alter the original terms of the option. Here, the communication constitutes a rejection of the offer in the original option. It is a counteroffer calling for an alternative performance by the tenant, not an unequivocal acceptance.[8]

Strict compliance

Also, when the renewal/extension option agreement specifies the steps to be taken and the time period in which they are to occur, the tenant needs to strictly comply if they intend to exercise the option.[9]

Usually, the tenant is required to give written notice of their exercise of the option several months before the current term of the lease expires (often a period of three to six months before the lease itself expires).

Advance notice requirements give the landlord ample time to locate a new tenant when the present tenant elects not to renew/extend the lease.

The option needs to state the method for delivery of the tenant's notice of their intent to exercise the option to renew/extend. Notice of exercise needs to be required in writing and personally handed or sent by certified mail to the landlord within a specific period of time, such as a three-month window six months prior to the lease's expiration.

If notice is to be delivered by certified mail, the risk of the notice being lost in the mail is on the landlord. When a receipt for certified mail is issued by the post office, the tenant is no longer responsible for its physical delivery to the landlord. It is unnecessary to request a return receipt.[10]

Failure to comply

Failure to timely comply with delivery of a written notice of exercise within the period for exercise of the option causes the lease to automatically expire at the end of its original term. To prevent an unintended expiration of a lease, the tenant's broker might prepare and hand the tenant an exercise of option to renew/extend lease form or make one available to the tenant during the period for exercise of the option. [See Form 566]

An exercise of option to renew/extend lease form provides the tenant with the paperwork needed to properly exercise the option. The notice of exercise states the tenant's intent to exercise the renewal/extension option on its terms and conditions, without qualification or equivocation.

Usually, the broker's fee arrangement on the original lease calls for a fee on any extension or renewal. Not only is the exercise by the tenant a benefit for the tenant, the leasing agent benefits by earning a fee. [See **RPI** Form 113]

---

8 **Hayward Lumber & Investment Co.** v. **Construction Products Corp.** (1953) 117 CA2d 221
9 Bekins Moving & Storage Co., *supra*
10 **Jenkins** v. **Tuneup** Masters (1987) 190 CA3d 1

Form 566

Exercise of Option to Renew/Extend Lease

EXERCISE OF OPTION TO RENEW/EXTEND LEASE

Prepared by: Agent _____   Phone _____
Broker _____   Email _____

NOTE: This form is used by a tenant or their agent when they have been given the option to renew or extend their lease on the expiration of its term, to inform the landlord of the tenant's intent to exercise the renewal/extension option on its terms and conditions, without qualification or equivocation.

DATE: _____, 20_____, at _____, California.
Items left blank or unchecked are not applicable.

FACTS:

1. A lease agreement dated _____, 20_____, at _____, California,

    1.1 entered into by _____, as the Landlord,

    1.2 and _____, as the Tenant,

    1.3 recorded _____, as Instrument No. _____, in _____ County, California,

    1.4 regarding real estate referred to as _____
    _____
    _____

    1.5 provides for the renewal or extension of its term, or is subject to an option to renew or extend this lease granted by Landlord and dated _____, 20_____.

NOTICE TO LANDLORD:

2. Tenant hereby elects to exercise the option to renew or extend the term of this lease following expiration of the current lease term for the additional period and on the conditions stated in the option.

3. Landlord is hereby requested to respond in writing to Tenant regarding any further actions necessary on the part of Tenant to exercise this renewal/extension option, or implement this election to exercise the option, and result in a binding agreement for the additional term.

4. _____
    _____
    _____
    _____
    _____
    _____
    _____

☐ See attached Signature Page Addendum. [RPI Form 251]

Date: _____, 20_____
Tenant: _____

Signature: _____
Title: _____
Address: _____

Phone: _____
Cell: _____
Email: _____

FORM 566   03-11   ©2016 RPI — Realty Publications, Inc., P.O. BOX 5707, RIVERSIDE, CA 92517

A renewal option need not set forth the time period and manner for its exercise. However, clarified steps ands dates make the process simple.

Consider a renewal option which is silent as to the time and manner for exercise, simply stating the tenant has the right to renew for three years. The tenant constructs substantial improvements on the property and remains in possession throughout the entire lease term.

Continued possession as exercise

The lease term expires without the tenant giving any notice to the landlord of their intent to renew the lease, yet the tenant remains in possession. The tenant then tenders the correct amount of rent as though they had already exercised their renewal option. The landlord refuses the tender of rent.

The landlord serves a notice to quit on the tenant claiming the tenant did not take steps to exercise the option to renew prior to the expiration of the lease and is unlawfully detaining the premises.

Does the tenant's continued possession of the property after the lease expires constitute exercise of the renewal option when delivery of a notice of intent to exercise is not called for in the option?

Yes! When the tenant has a renewal option and the time and manner for exercise is not specified, the tenant's continued possession and timely tender of rent indicates their election to renew.[11]

Waiver of notice to exercise

A tenant is bound by the terms for exercise of the renewal/extension option unless the landlord has, by their conduct, waived the requirements for exercise.[12]

A **waiver** is the relinquishment by the landlord's conduct of a known right, claim or privilege, such as the tenant's delivery of a notice to exercise the option to extend, since they benefit from the right they granted.

For example, a tenant fails to exercise their option to renew the lease as called for in the renewal option since they do not notify the landlord in writing of their intent to renew prior to expiration of the option.

On expiration of the lease, the tenant remains in possession and tenders rent to the landlord at the new rate called for in the option to renew. The landlord accepts the rent.

Later, the landlord serves a 30-day notice to vacate on the tenant. The tenant claims the renewal option has been exercised and the renewed lease bars the landlord's use of the 30-day notice to vacate to terminate possession since the landlord accepted rent called for in the renewal option.

Is the landlord's acceptance of rent when the tenant continued in possession a waiver of the written notice to exercise?

Yes! The landlord's acceptance of rent at the renewal rate after expiration of the lease waived their right to object to the tenant's prior failure to exercise the renewal option as agreed.[13]

Prior acceptance of rent

Now consider a tenant whose long-term lease contains options to extend the lease. The options will expire unless exercised in writing during a two-month period expiring 60 days prior to the expiration of the lease.

11 **ADV Corp.** v. **Wikman** (1986) 178 CA3d 61
12 **Simons** v. **Young** (1979) 93 CA3d 170
13 **Leonhardi-Smith, Inc.** v. **Cameron** (1980) 108 CA3d 42

The lease agreement is entered into and dated two years prior to the transfer of possession to the tenant (due to construction). The lease term is set to expire on the fifth anniversary of the date of the lease agreement.

Five years pass after the date of the lease agreement. The tenant remains in possession, paying the rent due during the original term of the lease. The tenant then gives the landlord written notice to extend the lease 60 days prior to expiration of five years after the date of possession, not the date of the lease agreement as called for.

The tenant then remains in possession and pays rent at the increased amount called for in the option to extend. The landlord does not object to the notice of intent to exercise the option to extend and continues to accept rent payments.

Later, a new owner becomes the landlord.

The new landlord serves the tenant with a 30-day notice to vacate. The landlord claims the tenant's occupancy under the lease is a periodic month-to-month tenancy which can be terminated at the will of the landlord since the original lease expired without being extended due to the untimely notice to exercise the renewal option.

The tenant claims the prior landlord's acceptance of the tardy notice to exercise the renewal option and the rent called for in the option waived the landlord's right to enforce the conditions for exercise of the option.

Did the tenant exercise their option to extend due to a waiver of the notice requirement by the prior landlord when the landlord accepted rent after the lease expired and failed to object to delivery of the notice of exercise?

Yes! The landlord's prior acceptance of the rent without objection and receipt of the untimely exercise waived the notice requirement for the exercise of the extension option. Thus, the lease and all its terms remained in effect for the period of extension, barring any attempts by the landlord to terminate the tenant's occupancy as a month-to-month tenancy.[14]

For the landlord to avoid waiving the requirement of a timely and unconditional written notice from the tenant to exercise an option to extend, the property manager and landlord cannot accept rent from the holdover tenant. Unless the rent is paid under a newly negotiated lease agreement unrelated to the expired lease, the landlord effectively extends the expiration date of a lease when they accept rent and allow the tenant to remain in possession.

When the holdover tenant refuses to vacate or refuses to accept an offer from the landlord for a new and different tenancy, the landlord may, without further notice, begin an unlawful detainer action to remove the holdover tenant.

Prior acceptance of rent, cont'd

No acceptance of rent

14 **Oxford Properties & Finance LTD** v. **Engle** (9th Cir. 1991) 943 F2d 1150

When the tenant neglects to properly exercise the renewal option, the lease term will itself expire without renewal or extension. The property manager may evict the holdover tenant and relet the premises. Here, the lease has expired and no new arrangement for continued occupancy has been agreed to, either in writing or by the landlord's conduct.[15]

Finally, to exercise the lease renewal option, the tenant needs to be in full compliance with all conditions of the lease. Thus, the tenant may not be in default on rent payments or allow any other material breach of the lease to exist at the time they exercise the option.

The payment of rent is an implied condition which needs to be satisfied, in addition to any other material conditions in the lease agreement, before the renewal option may be properly exercised. When the tenant is in default, their right to exercise their option is suspended.[16]

Notice of option's expiration

A leasing agent negotiating a renewal option on behalf of a tenant needs to consider arranging for the inclusion of a notice provision. The provision requires the landlord to give the tenant notice of the option's expiration 60 to 180 days prior to the expiration of the option.

This notice from the landlord to the tenant of the option's expiration eliminates the element of surprise for both landlord and tenant.

The tenant's inadvertent failure to exercise the lease renewal option can prove disastrous for the tenant who plans to continue in occupancy.

If the landlord will re-rent to the existing tenant despite the tenant's failure to exercise a renewal/extension option, the tenant will be forced to negotiate the terms of a new lease under the existing market conditions. Thus, the landlord may be in a position, if availability of space is extremely scarce, to take unconscionable advantage of the tenant, a situation the landlord needs to be careful to avoid. [See Chapter 48]

Renegotiation of rent and lease terms on expiration of a lease can result in increased rental rates, higher common area maintenance fees and other landlord charges. When the landlord chooses to negotiate a lease with the holdover tenant, it may change the tenant's responsibilities.[17]

Thus, a tenant's broker needs to inform the client as to when and how the renewal option has to be exercised, and then provide the tenant with the necessary forms.

The leasing fee due on renewal is sufficient incentive for the broker to take action and assist the buyer to exercise the option.

---

15 Simons, *supra*

16 **Nork** v. **Pacific Coast Medical Enterprises, Inc.** (1977) 73 CA3d 410

17 Bekins Moving & Storage Co., *supra*

Frequently, lease agreements contain provisions or addendums which allow a tenant to continue in lawful possession after the initial lease term expires. A prior agreement allowing continued occupancy is called an Option to Renew/Extend the Lease.

An extension is a modification of the original lease term by extending its expiration date for an additional period. On the other hand, a renewal requires the execution of a new lease on identical conditions to the original lease agreement, not a continuation of the old lease.

A renewal involves the preparation and signing of a new lease which creates an entirely new tenancy. The new tenancy is subject to any change in law affecting the rights and obligations of the landlord or the tenant. It is also subordinate to any encumbrances which occurred during the term of the prior lease.

**Chapter 47
Summary**

**Chapter 47
Key Terms**

Quiz 12 Covering Chapters 46-49 is located on page 645.

Notes:

Chapter
48

Lease assignments and subleases

After reading this chapter, you will be able to:
- apply the standards for a landlord's review of a tenant's request for the landlord's consent to the tenant's transfer of their leasehold interest; and
- identify permissible landlord exactions for their consent to tenant assignments and subletting, the subject of restriction-on-transfer provisions in lease agreements.

Learning Objectives

assumption	**successor tenant**
novation	**tenant-mitigation provision**
overriding rent	**transfer**
restriction-on-transfer provision	

Key Terms

A commercial lease agreement entered into by a tenant contains an assignment and subletting provision, called a **restriction-on-transfer provision** or a *restraint-on-alienation provision*.

The *restriction-on-transfer provision* either prohibits transfer of the tenant's interests or requires the landlord's consent prior to assigning, subletting or further encumbering the tenant's leasehold interest. If the provision permits an assignment or subletting, it states the landlord's consent will not be unreasonably withheld. [See **RPI** Form 552; see Figure 1]

Further, the lease agreement signed by the tenant contains a *cancellation provision*. The cancellation provision allows the landlord to cancel the lease agreement and terminate the tenant's occupancy on the landlord's receipt of the tenant's written request to sublet the premises.

Consent conditioned on exactions

> **restriction-on-transfer provision**
> A provision in a lease agreement calling for either the landlord's consent to any transfer of the tenant's leasehold interest or the prohibition of any transfer of that interest. [See **RPI** Form 552 §9.2]

Figure 1

Excerpt from Form 552

Gross — Single Tenant

> 9. **ASSIGNMENT, SUBLETTING AND ENCUMBRANCE:** [Check only one]
>   9.1   ☐ Tenant may not assign this lease or sublet any part of the Premises, or further encumber the leasehold.
>   9.2   ☐ Tenant may not transfer any interest in the Premises without the prior consent of Landlord.
>   a. ☐ Consent may not be unreasonably withheld.
>   b. ☐ Consent is subject to the attached alienation provisions. [See **RPI** Form 552-7]

After taking occupancy, the tenant vacates the premises and relocates their operations to another property. The tenant has no intention of returning to the leased premises.

The tenant finds a new tenant who will pay rent at current market rates for the space. The current market rates exceed the rent owed under the lease agreement. The amount by which the current market rates exceed the rents under the lease is called **overriding rent**.

overriding rent
The amount the current market rent rates exceed the rents set in the lease agreement, attainable by the tenant on a sublease to a successor tenant.

The tenant requests the landlord's consent to sublease to the new tenant. The landlord responds by cancelling the lease agreement and terminating the tenant's leasehold interest under the cancellation provision.

The landlord, having terminated the tenant's leasehold by cancellation of the lease agreement, negotiates directly with the new tenant. The landlord enters into a lease of the premises with the new tenant at current rental rates.

The previous tenant makes a demand on the landlord for the overriding rent they lost due to the landlord's refusal to consent to the sublease, claiming the landlord's consent was unreasonably withheld since no conditions for the consent were agreed to that entitled the landlord to the *overriding rent*.

The landlord claims their cancellation of the lease is valid, even though cancellation is an absolute restraint on the proposed *transfer* of the tenant's leasehold interest. The tenant and landlord bargained for the cancellation provision that was triggered by the tenant's request for the landlord's consent to a sublease.

transfer
Any assignment, sublease or further encumbrance of the leasehold by the tenant. [See **RPI** Form 552 §9]

May the landlord cancel the lease agreement on receipt of the tenant's request for consent to an assignment even though they agreed not to unreasonably withhold their consent?

Yes! The two provisions in the lease, the *consent-to-assignment provision* and the *cancellation provision*, are mutually exclusive alternative remedies. They give the landlord a choice between two different and separate courses of action when confronted with a request for consent to a sublease.

Cancellation nullifies the need to consider request for consent

In the previous example, the landlord exercised the cancellation provision on receipt of the tenant's request for consent. Thus, the tenant is relieved of any further obligation under the lease agreement. Cancellation also terminated the tenant's right of possession and any potential profit between the lease agreement rent rate and the property's appreciated rental value.

Thus, the issue as to whether the landlord refused their consent never arises. The landlord cancelled the lease as agreed, nullifying any need to consider the request for consent.

If the landlord chooses not to cancel the lease agreement and terminate the tenancy on the tenant's request for consent to an assignment, the landlord is then obligated to analyze whether or not to consent. In an analysis, they are required to be reasonable about any objection they may have to the assignment since no other standard was set in the lease.

The cancellation provision in the lease agreement is bargained for and not the unconscionable result of an interference with an assignment of the lease.

Here, the tenant contracted away their leasehold right to retain the benefit of increased rental value of the property by assignment or subleasing when they included the cancellation provision in the lease agreement. The leasehold was eliminated by the cancellation of the lease agreement. With the lease agreement cancelled and the leasehold terminated, the right to assign or sublet did not become an issue. Thus, the landlord did not interfere with the tenant's right to assign or sublet since the leasehold no longer existed to be assigned or sublet.[1]

A *restriction-on-transfer provision* in a lease agreement typically calls for the tenant to acquire consent from the landlord before the tenant may transfer their leasehold interest.[2] [See Form 552-7 accompanying this chapter; see Figure 1 §9.2]

A **transfer** by the tenant includes an assignment, sublease or further encumbrance of the leasehold.[3] [See Figure 1]

An *assignment* of the lease agreement transfers the original tenant's entire interest in the property to a **successor tenant**, leaving no interest held by the original tenant. However, the original tenant named on the lease agreement remains liable for the *successor tenant's* performance on the lease, even though the landlord consents to the assignment and the successor tenant becomes primarily responsible for the lease obligations. The act of taking over a previous tenant's lease agreement and right of possession is called an **assumption**.

For the original tenant to be released of their liability under the lease agreement on an assignment, a **novation** (also known as a substitution of liability) is negotiated and entered into by the landlord and both tenants.[4] [See Form 552-7]

On the other hand, when entering into a *sublease* with a *subtenant*, the original tenant (or *master tenant*) transfers to the subtenant less than all of the master tenant's interest in the property. Also, possession reverts back to the master tenant on expiration of the sublease.

Transfer of any interest

assumption
The promise by a successor tenant to fully perform all obligations under the lease agreement they are taking over by assignment from the previous tenant.

novation
An agreement entered into by a landlord and tenant shifting responsibility for obligations owed the landlord under a lease agreement to another the tenant, releasing the original tenant of liability.

---

1 **Carma Developers, Inc.** v. **Marathon Development California, Inc.** (1992) 2 C4th 342
2 Calif. Civil Code §1995.250
3 CC §1995.020(e)
4 **Samuels** v. **Ottinger** (1915) 169 C 209

The master tenant granting the sublease remains obligated to perform on the *master lease agreement*. The subtenant does not assume liability of the master lease. However, the subtenant may not act in any way that constitutes a breach of the master lease agreement. A copy of the master lease agreement is provided to the subtenant as an attachment to the sublease. [See **RPI** Form 552 §2.5]

The *further encumbrance* of a tenant's leasehold interest is a transfer and occurs when the tenant places a lien on their leasehold to secure a mortgage, such as a trust deed or a collateral assignment.

Editor's note — For simplicity's sake, the following discussion will only refer to an assignment of a lease. However, the discussion fully applies to transfers by any sublease or further encumbrance transaction.

Various alienation provisions

Leases include various types of *restriction-on-transfer provisions*, which may:

- entirely prohibit any assignment of the tenant's leasehold interest[5];
- require the landlord's consent prior to an assignment without referencing *approval standards* or placing any *monetary conditions* on the tenant for obtaining the landlord's consent, called **exactions**[6];
- require the landlord's consent prior to an assignment, stating consent will not be unreasonably withheld[7];
- require the landlord's consent, subject to conditions first being met by the tenant[8]; or
- contain conditions for a valid assignment without requiring any consent from the landlord.[9] [See Figure 1]

Approval standards lay out the analytical process to be applied by the landlord when judging whether or not to withhold consent.

Monetary conditions are sums of money or modified leasing terms to be met by the tenant as a pre-requisite to the landlord's consent.

No standards for withholding consent

Consider a lease agreement with a *restriction-on-transfer provision* calling for the landlord's consent prior to the tenant's assignment. However, the lease does not contain any standard or condition for the landlord's consent.

Here, for lack of agreement to the contrary, the standards and conditions for the landlord's consent are set by law.

---

5   CC §1995.230
6   CC §1995.260
7   CC 1995.250(a)
8   CC §1995.250(b)
9   CC §1995.240

Any lease agreement entered into without stating a standard for the landlord's consent to an assignment, requires the landlord to have a commercially reasonable basis for any denial of consent. The landlord cannot arbitrarily deny consent.

Also, the landlord may not impose conditions on the consent, such as a higher rent rate, unless the condition was included in the lease agreement.[10]

Commercial reasonability standards relate to the landlord's ability to:

- protect their ownership interest from property waste and financial deterioration caused by the conduct of the *successor tenant*; and
- ensure the future performance of the lease by an assignment to a creditworthy tenant.

Commercially reasonable objections for withholding consent to an assignment include:

- the successor tenant's financial responsibility, net worth, prior operating history and creditworthiness;
- the successor tenant's intended use, care and maintenance of the property;
- the suitability of the successor tenant's use, product marketing and management style for the property; and
- the need for tenant alterations to the premises.[11]

For example, the *use provision* in a lease agreement gives the tenant the right to operate their service business in a landlord's shopping center. The landlord also runs a retail business outlet in the same shopping center. The lease agreement restricts the tenant's use to an "office use related to the business" of the tenant.

The restriction-on-transfer provision in the lease agreement requires the tenant to obtain the landlord's prior consent to an assignment of the lease agreement. The provision sets no standard for withholding consent and provides for no conditions to be met (paid/lease modification) by the tenant for the consent.

Later, the tenant seeks to transfer the lease to a successor who will operate a retail business from the premises. The successor tenant's retail business will be in direct competition with the landlord's retail outlet. Since the successor tenant's use will be a change in the use of the premises, the landlord refuses to consent to the assignment.

The tenant claims the landlord's refusal is commercially unreasonable since it amounts to economic protectionism unrelated to the landlord's ownership and operation of the rental property.

Commercial reasonability standards

successor tenant
On a transfer, the new tenant who acquires by assignment the original tenant's entire leasehold interest in the property. [See **RPI** Form 552 §9]

10 **Kendall** v. **Ernest Pestana, Inc.** (1985) 40 C3d 488
11 Kendall, *supra*

Here, the landlord's refusal is a commercially reasonable application of the use restriction in the lease agreement. The landlord sought only to retain the use originally intended by the lease. The refusal is not due to improper economic protectionism in the management and operation of the real estate since the landlord did not demand an *exaction* through an increase in rent or other economic benefits to enhance themselves as a condition for their consent to the assignment of the lease.[12]

Also, the landlord may reasonably refuse their consent to a trust deed lien the tenant seeks to place on the leasehold interest when the proceeds of the mortgage are not used to enhance or improve the property.[13]

Reasonable increases in rent

Consider a commercial tenant who agrees to a *percentage lease*. [See **RPI** Form 552-4]

The restriction-on-transfer provision in the lease agreement requires the tenant to obtain the landlord's consent before assigning the lease. The provision does not include standards or conditions for the landlord's consent to an assignment.

The tenant enters into an agreement to sell their business and assign the lease to a new operator. The operator buying the tenant's leasehold interest (and the business) is to pay the tenant the *overriding rent* over the remaining life of the lease.

The tenant requests consent for the assignment of the lease agreement from the landlord. On investigation, the landlord determines the operator will manage the business in a manner that will not generate gross sales at the same level as the current tenant. Thus, under the percentage lease, the new operator will not become obligated to pay the amount of rent currently being paid by the tenant seeking consent.

However, the landlord agrees to consent to the assignment conditioned on the landlord receiving the overriding rent premium the tenant is to be paid for the assignment.

The tenant claims the landlord cannot condition consent on exacting the rent premium since no standards or conditions for consent exist in the lease and thus cannot now be imposed.

Here, the landlord's conditional consent to the assignment is commercially reasonable. When granting consent, the landlord is entitled to preserve the rental income they currently receive from the existing tenant. The landlord does not need to accept the certain risk of a lower monthly percentage rent from the assignee while the original tenant receives a monthly premium.[14]

12 **Pay 'N Pak Stores, Inc.** v. **Superior Court of Santa Clara County** (1989) 210 CA3d 1404

13 **Airport Plaza, Inc.** v. **Blanchard** (1987) 188 CA3d 1594

14 **John Hogan Enterprises, Inc.** v. **Kellogg** (1986) 187 CA3d 589

Now consider a commercial lease agreement that contains a restriction-on-transfer provision authorizing the landlord to demand all the consideration the tenant will receive for an assignment of the lease as a condition for their consent to the assignment.

The landlord does not bargain for any other exaction, such as key money, lease assignment-assumption fee or a portion of the purchase price the tenant will receive on a sale of the business that the tenant operates from the premises.

Later, the tenant agrees to assign the lease to a new operator as part of the sale of their business. The operator will pay the tenant a lump sum for the lease as part of the purchase price since rent due under the lease agreement is below market rates.

The landlord demands the tenant pass on to the landlord the price received for assignment of the lease as a condition for their consent to the assignment. The tenant rejects this demand.

The tenant claims the landlord's demand in exchange for consent is commercially unreasonable, and thus unenforceable, since the landlord has no lawful justification for the premium or additional rent.

Here, the landlord may condition consent on their receipt of the payment made for the assignment of the lease. Commercial lease agreements granting the landlord the right to receive any consideration the tenant is to receive related (and limited) to the value of the lease to be assigned are enforceable.[15]

Absent unconscionable or discriminatory provisions, commercial landlords and tenants are free to place commercially reasonable restrictions — limited to the value of the leasehold, not any part of the price the tenant received on the sale of the business — on any assignment of the lease.[16]

Again, it is commercially reasonable for a commercial lease agreement to provide for the landlord to receive all consideration the tenant receives for the assignment of the lease in exchange for the landlord's consent.[17]

However, the consideration the landlord may receive for their consent to an assignment is limited to financial benefits related to the value of the lease assigned.

For example, a tenant occupies commercial property under a lease agreement.

The lease agreement includes a *profit-shifting clause* calling for the tenant to pay the landlord 25% of the consideration the tenant receives for *business goodwill* on the sale of the tenant's business, in exchange for the landlord's consent to an assignment.

Proceeds from assignment demanded

More than rental value demanded

---

15 CC §1995.240
16 Carma Developers, Inc., *supra*
17 CC §1995.240

Both agree it is the location of the leased property which will give the tenant's business its goodwill value.

The tenant's business is a success and the tenant locates a buyer for the business and the remaining term on the lease. The tenant seeks the landlord's consent for an assignment of the lease.

As agreed, the landlord demands 25% of the consideration the tenant will receive for their business goodwill. The tenant refuses to meet the demand and the landlord refuses to consent to the assignment.

As a result, the sales transaction does not close. The tenant makes a demand on the landlord for 100% of their lost profits on the sale.

The tenant claims the landlord's demand for a share of the profits on the sale of the business as agreed to in the lease agreement was a commercially unreasonable and unenforceable condition for granting consent to the assignment.

The landlord claims the profit-shifting provision is enforceable since all consideration received by the tenant on a transfer of the lease, even in excess of the value of the lease, may be agreed to and taken in exchange for consent.

Here, the landlord's right to receive consideration in exchange for their consent to an assignment is limited to the consideration the tenant receives for the value of the lease.[18]

Unconscionable advantage situations

Now consider a subtenant who needs to negotiate a new lease with the landlord or be evicted. The master tenant's lease agreement has been terminated by the landlord due to no fault of the subtenant.

The landlord submits a proposed lease agreement to the subtenant which differs significantly in its terms and conditions from the wiped out sublease agreement the subtenant held with the master tenant. When the subtenant attempts to negotiate a reasonable rent and eliminate unacceptable provisions, the landlord tells the subtenant to "take it or leave it." The subtenant is told they will be evicted if the proposed lease agreement is not signed.

The proposed lease agreement includes a restriction-on-transfer provision calling for a 200% increase in rent as a condition to be met before the landlord will consent to an assignment of the lease.

The subtenant signs the lease. Later, the subtenant seeks the landlord's consent to an assignment of the lease on sale of their business. The landlord demands a modification of the rent provision to reflect the 200% increase in monthly rent as agreed, which the subtenant's buyer refuses to sign.

The tenant claims the provision was the result of an **unconscionable advantage** held as a negotiating advantage by the landlord. When the lease

18 **Ilkhchooyi** v. **Best** (1995) 37 CA4th 395

was negotiated, the tenant could not refuse to rent due to the goodwill they had built up for their business through a heavy investment in advertising at the location.

The landlord claims the restriction-on-transfer provision is enforceable since the clause was freely bargained for.

Can the tenant avoid enforcement of the restriction-on-transfer provision?

Yes! The restriction-on-transfer provision agreed to was the result of the landlord taking *unconscionable advantage* of the subtenant's adverse situation. The subtenant was in possession under a wiped out sublease without any power to freely bargain. The subtenant was already in possession and operating a business that had developed goodwill that will be lost if they vacate.

Collection of future rents so hugely excessive as to effectively shift profits from the sale of the business to the landlord for their consent to an assignment of a lease was overreaching on the landlord's part. Thus, the restriction-on-transfer provision was unenforceable as the product of the unconscionable advantage taken by the landlord.[19]

Also, any consideration the landlord seeks which is beyond the value of the leasehold interest or the landlord's interest in the real estate is not reasonable, whenever or however bargained for. The right to freely bargain is not intended to give the landlord the right to freely fleece a tenant of the tenant's assets beyond the lease in the name of freedom of contract.[20]

Unconscionable and unenforceable

When a commercial lease agreement contains a **tenant-mitigation provision** and the tenant breaches the lease, the landlord may leave the lease in place and recover rent for the life of the lease. [See **RPI** Form 552 §21.1; see Figure 2]

Under a *tenant-mitigation provision*, the breaching tenant who has vacated the property has the duty to:

- find a replacement tenant;
- pay for any tenant improvements (TIs); and
- collect rent.[21]

In other words, the tenant-mitigation provisions shifts to the tenant the responsibility of mitigating the landlord's losses for the tenant's breach.

However, if the lease agreement also provides for the landlord's prior consent to an assignment of the tenant's leasehold interest, the tenant-mitigation provision is enforceable only if the landlord's consent to an assignment is not unreasonably withheld.[22]

Tenant-mitigation provisions

tenant-mitigation provision
A provision in a commercial lease agreement allowing the landlord to leave the tenant's leasehold and the lease agreement intact on the tenant's breach, and then recover rent from the tenant for the life of the lease without the landlord first taking steps to mitigate losses. [See **RPI** Form 552 §21.1]

---

19 Ilkhchooyi, *supra*
20 Ilkhchooyi, *supra*
21 CC §1951.4
22 CC §1951.4(b)(3)

21.   DEFAULT REMEDIES:

21.1   If Tenant breaches any provision of this lease agreement, Landlord may exercise its rights, including the right to collect future rental losses after forfeiture of possession.

A landlord who prohibits assignments or unreasonably withholds consent retains the duty to mitigate their loss of rents on the tenant's breach.

Broker's role in assigning or subletting

Restriction-on-transfer provisions become a concern of the business-opportunity (bus-op) or industrial leasing agent when:

- negotiating the assignment of a lease in a bus-op sale (or negotiating a sublease or a further encumbrance);
- relocating a tenant whose current lease has not yet expired; or
- negotiating the origination of any lease.

A broker handling a bus-op sale or relocation of a business or industrial tenant needs to determine the tenant's ability to assign the existing lease to a potential buyer or other successor tenant.

The broker starts the analysis by ascertaining the type of restriction-on-transfer provision the lease agreement contains. The broker can then determine the tenant's assignment rights.

Now consider a leasing agent who is negotiating a lease on behalf of a prospective tenant. The tenant's agent limits the wording of a restriction-on-transfer provision to include:

- the landlord's consent "will not be unreasonably withheld"; and
- any exaction to be paid for the consent is limited to the consideration the tenant receives for the rental value of the premises.

Here, a prohibition against assignment is eliminated by including the "with consent" provision.

Compensation for consent

Conversely, the landlord's leasing agent reviews the restriction-on-transfer provision and suggests the tenant pay compensation to the landlord in exchange for any consent to a transfer. For example, in exchange for consent, the landlord may:

- adjust rents to current market rates;
- receive fees and costs incurred to investigate the successor tenant's credit;
- receive any *overriding rent* or lump sum payment the tenant receives that is attributable to the value of the lease;

Form 552-7

Commercial
Lease
Agreement
Addendum
— Alienation of
Leasehold

COMMERCIAL LEASE AGREEMENT ADDENDUM

Alienation of Leasehold

NOTE: This form is used by a leasing agent or landlord as an addendum when the landlord negotiating a commercial lease is concerned about the tenant selling their business or their leasehold to another operator, to include provisions in an addendum to a lease agreement requiring the landlord's consent for the tenant to assign, sublet or further encumber their leasehold interest in the property.

DATE: _____, 20_____, at _____, California.
Items left blank or unchecked are not applicable.

FACTS:

1. This is an addendum to a commercial lease agreement
    1.1   dated _____, 20_____, at _____, California,
    1.2   entered into by _____, as the Landlord,
    1.3   and _____, as the Tenant,
          regarding real estate referred to as _____
          _____

ALIENATION OF LEASEHOLD:

2. Any transfer by Tenant of any leasehold interest held by Tenant, voluntarily or involuntary, is a breach of this lease unless Tenant has requested and received Landlord's prior written consent, which will not be unreasonably withheld.

3. The transfer of 50% or more, cumulative, of the ownership of Tenant constitutes a transfer requiring Landlord's prior consent.

4. Upon Tenant's request for Landlord's consent to an assignment or subletting, Tenant needs to notify Landlord in writing and provide Landlord with:
    a.   the name and address of the proposed assignee or subtenant;
    b.   the nature and character of the business of the proposed assignee or subtenant;
    c.   current financial statements for the proposed assignee or subtenant prepared in accordance with generally accepted accounting principles; and
    d.   the proposed sublet or assignment agreement.

5. Tenant's transfer by assignment to include a written assumption in favor of Landlord by the assignee of Tenant's obligations under the lease.

6. Tenant may assign or sublet the premises to any entity controlling Tenant, controlled by Tenant or under common control with Tenant or affiliated with Tenant, without the prior written consent of Landlord.

7. Tenant licensing of a minimal portion of the premises (i.e., 20 square feet or less) to be used by a third-party vendor in connection with the installation of a vending machine, payphone or like equipment does not constitute the transfer of an interest held by Tenant.

8. On an unconsented transfer of any interest held by Tenant under this lease, Landlord may terminate the leasehold interest held by Tenant on a 30-day notice.

9. If Landlord approves an assignment or subletting, Tenant to pay Landlord, as additional rent, fifty percent (50%) of the difference, if any, between:
    a.   the rent due landlord under this lease agreement; and
    b.   the rent received by Tenant under the assignment or sublease consented to by Landlord, after deducting costs of customary real estate fees, tenant improvement cost or allowance and reasonable attorney's fees, if any, incurred by Tenant in connection with the assignment or sublease.

10. Tenant is to pay Landlord an administration fee of Five Hundred Dollars ($500.00) per transaction, for Landlord's review and processing of documents regarding any proposed assignment, sublease, or further encumbrance.

I agree to the terms stated above.	I agree to the terms stated above.
☐ See attached Signature Page Addendum. [RPI Form 251]	☐ See attached Signature Page Addendum. [RPI Form 251]
Date: _____, 20_____	Date: _____, 20_____
Landlord: _____	Tenant: _____
	Signature: _____
Signature: _____	Tenant: _____

FORM 552-7   12-14   ©2016 **RPI — Realty Publications, Inc.**, P.O. BOX 5707, RIVERSIDE, CA 92517

- require the successor tenant to pay operating expenses as additional rent such as maintenance, utilities, insurance and taxes; or

- alter the terms of the lease agreement and any options to extend/renew the lease or buy the property.

To be enforceable, any exactions the landlord may expect or later seek for their consent will be:

- agreed to and set forth in the lease agreement; and

- related solely to the value of the lease.

Brokerage fee addendum

A broker employed by a landlord under an *exclusive authorization to lease property* is due a fee if the premises is rented to a tenant located by anyone during the listing period. [See Form 110 in Chapter 12]

Likewise, a broker employed by a tenant under an *exclusive authorization to locate space* is entitled to a fee when the tenant rents space sought by the employment during the listing period. If the tenant rents and does not provide for the landlord to pay the fee, the tenant will owe the broker the fee. [See Form 111 in Chapter 13]

However, brokers too often fail to insist on a written fee agreement from either the landlord or the tenant before rendering services. To be assured a fee when a prior written fee agreement does not exist, the broker includes a fee provision as part of an *offer to lease* or *letter of intent*. The fee is also included as an addendum to the proposed rental or lease agreement. [See **RPI** Form 273]

Chapter 48 Summary

A transfer by the tenant of their leasehold interest in property includes an assignment, sublease or further encumbrance.

The restriction-on-transfer provision may either prohibit transfer of the tenant's interests or it may require the tenant to obtain landlord consent prior to assigning, subletting or further encumbering the tenant's leasehold interest.

The cancellation provision allows the landlord to cancel the lease agreement and terminate the tenant's occupancy on specified events, such as the receipt of the tenant's written request to assign the lease or sublet the premises.

The consent-to-assignment provision and the cancellation provision are mutually exclusive alternatives available to the landlord. They give the landlord a choice between two different and separate courses of action when confronted with a request for consent to an assignment or sublease.

Chapter 48 Key Terms

Quiz 12 Covering Chapters 46-49 is located on page 645.

Commercial rent control prohibited

After reading this chapter, you will be able to:
- work within the limitations of local rent control; and
- explain the differences between permitted residential rent control and the policy against commercial rent control.

impasse notice

Residential landlords and apartment builders in California have battled **local rent control ordinances** since the mid-1970s.

Some judicial support for de-control is taking root since the societal objectives underlying the enactment of rent control ordinances are not being met.[1]

Further, the California legislature enacted a scheme which will gradually lead to a phaseout of all *residential rent control*. The economics of rent control in the long term are not kind to tenants or the surrounding neighborhoods, while investment capital is unharmed since it simply locates elsewhere.[2] [See Chapter 57]

Most major metropolitan areas in California, including Los Angeles, San Francisco, Oakland and San Jose, have some form of residential rent control. San Diego County and Orange County do not.

However, the city of Berkeley went beyond attempts to control only residential income properties. The city passed rent control ordinances placing restrictions on the amount of rent landlords of commercial properties are able to change.

---

1   **152 Valparaiso Associates** v. **City of Cotati** (1997) 56 CA4th 378
2   Calif. Civil Code §1954.52;

The stated objective supporting the Berkeley commercial rent ordinances was to preserve the city's older business neighborhoods without change or evolvement. Inefficient owners with improperly located shops in high traffic locations saw their rents rise dramatically as their space was sought by better capitalized and more effective businessmen, a process loosely called **Economic Darwinism** or **creative destruction**. Simply put, the landlords were willing to rent to more efficient and productive businesses which pay higher rent.

Local historical preservation advocates asserted rent control was the only way to protect "mom-and-pop" shops, which otherwise are no longer financially viable operations. Conversely, landlords felt they needed to be allowed to rent the space to any tenant whose business operation conforms to existing zoning ordinances.

Local community leadership is caught politically between making a policy commitment to protect inefficient, small shop owners in historic business districts or fostering an environment that encourages the growth of existing businesses or their replacement by fresh, energetic businesses in the same or newly constructed structures.

No commercial rent control ordinances

However, no California city, county or other public agency may pass and enforce *commercial rent control ordinances*.[3]

The California legislature felt commercial rent control was economically improper since it:

- discouraged commercial development and open market competition;
- benefitted one business enterprise over another; and
- hampered business expansion.[4]

Rental limit ban

The ban on commercial rent control also covers actions by all public entities who act as landlords, as well as private landlords.[5]

A public entity includes the state and all:

- cities and counties;
- public authorities and agencies; and
- political subdivisions and public corporations.[6]

Thus, no public entity may control or limit commercial rental rates, directly as owners or indirectly by ordinances. Using the power of **eminent domain** to control rents is improper.

Commercial real estate includes all real estate except:

- dwelling units;

---

3   CC §1954.25
4   CC §1954.25
5   CC §1954.27(a)
6   Calif. Government Code §811.2

- residential hotels; and
- mobilehome parks.[7]

Thus, the marketplace of available space for rent is left to sort out who will occupy the space in our growth economy without unnecessary government interference.[8]

To meet these ends, public agencies are prohibited from designating a specific tenant with whom a landlord needs to negotiate to create, extend or renew a commercial lease. Any tenant may rent any commercial space based on negotiations unfettered by governmental imposition of rent conditions.[9]

The prohibition against commercial rent control covers all actions by local governments, whether by charter, ordinance, resolution, administrative regulations or policy statements.[10]

Local rent control ordinances cannot establish or dictate any of the terms which might be negotiated in a commercial lease agreement or in the renewal or extension of the lease.

However, not all local government powers have been curbed. What has ended is government interference with commercial lease negotiations between landlords and tenants.

Local governments may still regulate all facets of business location and development such as:

- exercising eminent domain powers;[11]
- abating nuisances;[12]
- establishing zoning (use) and business licenses (policing);[13] and
- protecting historical resources.[14]

Also, the ban on commercial rent control does not apply to redevelopment contracts entered into by a developer and a public agency.

Under redevelopment agreements, the developer rents to local businesses at a set or reduced rate in exchange for participation with the public agency.[15]

Public agencies may establish a notice procedure for an existing commercial tenant to make or solicit an offer to the landlord negotiating for a renewal or extension of the lease.

Remaining local powers

Negotiations by notice to landlords

---

7   CC §1954.26(d)
8   CC §1954.27(a)
9   CC §1954.27(a)
10 CC §1954.27(a)
11 CC §1954.28(a)
12 CC §1954.28(b)
13 CC §1954.29(a)
14 CC §1954.28(e)
15 CC §1954.28(d)

However, the agency's action may not interfere with rights held under an existing lease agreement. Thus, they cannot alter the lease expiration date or the attendant obligation of the tenant to vacate on expiration or be evicted.[16]

For example, a lease agreement exists which does not grant an option to the tenant to renew or extend the term of the lease, called a *term-only lease*.

However, the local governing agency may by ordinance create a procedure allowing the tenant to deliver a **negotiation notice** to the landlord. In the negotiation notice, the tenant makes or solicits an offer to negotiate an extension of the term of the lease.[17]

A tenant who has materially breached a significant provision in the lease agreement is not eligible to use the negotiation notice scheme.[18]

The negotiation notice acts as the tenant's offer to acquire an extension or renewal of the lease, an activity a tenant can carry out without the existence of an enabling ordinance. Of course, the tenant does not need to use a negotiation notice to contact their landlord.[19]

On the landlord's receipt of the negotiation notice, the landlord is required to respond if the notice is sent within 270 days before the expiration of the lease.[20]

However, whether or not the landlord receives a negotiation notice from the tenant, the landlord and the property manager have no duty to notify the tenant the lease is expiring at the end of the term stated in the lease agreement.

Impasse notice to tenant

impasse notice
A notice advising the tenant the lease will expire and no modification of the lease will be entered into.

If the tenant delivers the negotiation notice within 270 days before the lease expires, the landlord either:

- enters into negotiations to renew or extend the lease with the tenant; or
- delivers an **impasse notice** to the tenant no more than 180 days before the lease expires, within a time period after receipt of the negotiation notice as set by the local agency.[21]

An *impasse notice* advises the tenant the lease will expire as called for in the lease agreement and no modification of the lease will occur.[22]

For example, a city passes an ordinance requiring a landlord to respond with an impasse notice within 30 days of receiving a negotiation notice, but not prior to 180 days before the lease expires.

16 CC §1954.31
17 CC §1954.31(a)(1)
18 §1954.31(b)(1)
19 CC §1954.26(j)(2)
20 CC §1954.31(a)(2)(A)
21 CC §1954.31(a)(2)(B)
22 CC §1954.26(i)

However, if the negotiation notice is received 150 days prior to expiration of the lease, the landlord needs to respond within 30 days or they will be acting in bad faith.

The landlord is also required to send an impasse notice when they (or their agent) have received a negotiation notice and entered into renewal or extension negotiations with the tenant which are later broken off. The impasse notice indicates the lease will not be renewed or extended.

Also, negotiation and impasse notice ordinances cannot force the landlord to deal with a tenant or to make a counteroffer to the tenant. A landlord is not required to negotiate an additional or new term with the existing tenant and may reject the tenant's offer by use of the impasse notice.

One purpose served by the tenant's notice to the landlord is to allow the tenant time to negotiate a new or extended lease or find alternative space before the lease term expires. In practice, tenants have always knowingly borne these burdens as their possessory interest draws to an end.

Time to negotiate

Without conjecture as to unintended consequences, these ordinances appear to add nothing to the leasing environment except for the landlord's written impasse notice in response to a prior written offer from the tenant to negotiate.

However, the notice rules do not provide guidance for landlords who commence negotiations which become prolonged and continue beyond the response period set by ordinances for delivery of an impasse notice. If the landlord breaks off negotiations after the response period for delivery of the impasse notice has passed, it is too late to deliver an impasse notice unless the ordinance extended the time in which to respond.

The safest conduct for the landlord who receives a tenant's negotiation notice is to deliver an impasse notice within the response period set by the local ordinance, and then enter into negotiations. If negotiations result in an extension or renewal, the notice becomes irrelevant. If negotiations fail, the landlord complied with the negotiation/impasse ordinance.

A landlord or property manager who fails to deliver an impasse notice and does not enter into negotiations after the timely receipt of the tenant's negotiation notice may have acted in **bad faith**. A non-response subjects the landlord or property manager to liability for the tenant's actual money losses incurred due to the bad faith failure to deliver the impasse notice.[23]

Failure to deliver notices

When confronted with a *bad faith* claim, the landlord needs to immediately deliver an impasse notice and extend the expiration of the lease to a date after delivery of the impasse notice. This conduct provides the tenant with the period of time the tenant was to have prior to expiration of the lease had an impasse notice been timely delivered. The extension avoids loss of the tenant's reasonable expectations, induced by the notice ordinance, of up to a 180-day period to relocate after receipt of an impasse notice.

---

23 CC §1954.31(a)(3)

**Chapter 49
Summary**

No California city, county or other public agency may pass and enforce commercial rent control ordinances.

Public agencies are prohibited from designating a specific tenant with whom a landlord needs to negotiate to create, extend or renew a commercial lease. Any tenant may rent any commercial space based on negotiations unfettered by local rent control ordinances.

Public agencies may establish a notice procedure for an existing commercial tenant to make or solicit an offer to the landlord negotiating for a renewal or extension of the lease.

However, the agency's action may not interfere with rights held under an existing lease agreement. Thus, they cannot alter the lease expiration date or the attendant obligation of the tenant to vacate on expiration or be evicted.

**Chapter 49
Key Term**

Quiz 12 Covering Chapters 46-49 is located on page 645.

Chapter
50

Residential rental and lease agreements

After reading this chapter, you will be able to:

- distinguish the different terms for occupancy under residential rental and lease agreements;
- understand the operation of provisions of residential rental agreements and lease agreements;
- use addenda to incorporate additional terms into residential rental and lease agreements; and
- identify the statutory rights and duties of landlords and tenants as restatements in residential rental or lease agreements.

Learning Objectives

addendum	**rental market**
credit application	**waterbed addendum**

Key Terms

Typically, residential landlords and tenants enter into either a *periodic rental agreement* or a *fixed-term lease agreement*. Residential periodic tenancies typically take the form of month-to-month rental agreements. [See Chapter 3; see **RPI** Form 551]

Residential rental and lease agreements each grant and impose on the landlords and tenants the same rights and obligations. Their differences lie in the expectation of continued occupancy and the obligation to pay future rent.

Recall that a *month-to-month rental agreement* runs for an indefinite period of time. It automatically renews monthly, and on the same terms, until modified or terminated by notice. [See **RPI** Form 551 §3]

A review of periodic vs. fixed-term tenancies

Periodic tenancies may be terminated by either the landlord or tenant on 30 days' written notice. However, a residential landlord is to give the tenant at least 60 days' written notice if the tenant's occupancy has exceeded one year.[1] [See Chapter 26]

On the other hand, a *lease agreement* creates a tenancy that continues for a fixed period. At the end of the fixed-period, the tenant's right of possession expires. The terms in the lease agreement set the expiration date, and no further notice is required by either the landlord or tenant to terminate the tenancy. [See Figure 1, Form 550 §3]

Unlike a periodic tenancy, the lease agreement does not automatically renew, unless an option to renew or extend has been written into the lease agreement and exercised.

Rental market influences

The **rental market** is the market environment in which landlords seek tenants (and vice versa). The condition of the *rental market* is determined by:

- the population of tenants;
- the number of properties competing for these tenants; and
- the comparative position of the property and its amenities in relation to competing properties.

rental market
The market environment in which landlords seek tenants and tenants seek landlords for the occupancy of property. The rental market sets the amount of rent a property will command on any given day.

The *rental market* sets the amount of rent a landlord is able to charge on any given day to solicit and induce prospective tenants to enter into rental or lease agreements.

Generally, tenants on month-to-month rental agreements pay higher amounts of monthly rent for a unit than do tenants with lease agreements. Month-to-month tenants pay a premium for the privilege of being able to vacate the premises on 30 days' notice, without liability exposure for future rents. This privilege held by the tenant contributes to the landlord's uncertainty about their income and costs of tenant turnover, hence the rent premium to cover the risks.

Tenants typically pay lower rents when they enter into a lease agreement. In stable rental markets, the longer the lease period the lower the rent. [See Chapter 20]

Rent may, however, be subject to adjustments for future price inflation, local appreciation and management decisions. During weak market periods of generally high vacancy rates, price-competitive landlords may favor using month-to-month rental agreements rather than lease agreements. When rents begin to rise, landlords adjust rents to market by serving notice of a change in rent rates. [See Chapter 22]

Lease negotiations on expiration

Conversely, a landlord may not alter the terms of a lease agreement during the life of the lease without consideration and the tenant's consent.

---

1   Calif. Civil Code §1946

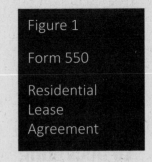

Figure 1

Form 550

Residential Lease Agreement

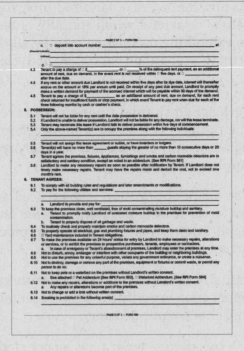

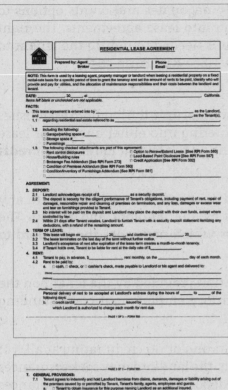

For a full-size, fillable copy of this or any other form in this book that may be legally used in your professional practice, go to realtypublications.com/forms

To extend a soon-to-expire lease agreement, the landlord may contact the tenant and offer to:

- enter into another lease agreement; or
- a month-to-month rental agreement.

If the tenant desires to remain in possession when their lease expires, the amount of rent a landlord may demand is limited only by negotiations and economic forces in the rental market, with the exception of rent control vicinities.

As an alternative, a landlord proactively negotiates and grants options to renew or extend when initially entering into lease agreements. The right to extend the occupancy may be all that is needed to induce the tenant to remain a tenant on expiration of the lease. [See **RPI** Form 565]

Requisites to accepting tenants

credit application
A document prepared by a prospective tenant which includes a provision authorizing the landlord to investigate and receive information on the tenant's creditworthiness. [See **RPI** Form 302]

On locating a prospective tenant for a residential unit, the landlord establishes the prospect's creditworthiness before entering into either a rental or lease agreement. This is accomplished by requiring the tenant to fill out a **credit application**. [See **RPI** Form 302]

The *credit application* is referenced and attached as an addendum to any rental or lease agreement entered into by the landlord and tenant. The application is part of the leasing process which persuades the landlord to accept the applicant as a tenant.

Initially, the landlord uses the authorization provided by the tenant on the application to verify the tenant's rental history, employment, credit standing and check-writing history.

If a prospective tenant has a poor credit rating or no credit rating at all, yet meets the landlord's income requirements, the landlord may seek assurances in addition to the maximum security deposit allowed. These assurances include:

- a co-signer on the lease; or
- a guarantee agreement signed by a creditworthy person. [See **RPI** Form 553-1]

With third-party assurances, the landlord will receive full performance on the lease agreement from others if the tenant defaults on their rent or otherwise causes the landlord to incur a loss exceeding the security deposit. On a default by the tenant, the landlord may hold the co-signer liable, or collect their losses from the guarantor. [See Sidebar, "Disclosing a notice of default"]

Landlord's right to avoid lawsuits

Every landlord has a duty to ensure the residential housing they rent is **safe and sanitary** throughout the tenant's occupancy. Additionally, a landlord has a duty to protect their tenants from *foreseeable* dangers.

Since environmental tobacco smoke (ETS) poses a legislatively recognized danger to tenants, a wise landlord takes steps to avoid claims.[2]

A landlord may do any of the following risk avoidance activities to alleviate the burden of future ETS disputes:

- relocate smokers so they will not affect non-smokers;
- relocate non-smokers so they are not affected by the ETS of smoking tenants; or

---

2   **Stoiber** v. **Honeychuck** (1980) 101 CA3d 903; Calif. Code of Civil Procedure §1174.2

Owners of one-to-four unit residential rental property subject to a recorded notice of default (NOD) are required to disclose the NOD in writing to any prospective tenants before entering into a lease agreement.

If a landlord does not disclose the existence of a recorded NOD, the tenant may:

- *terminate the lease after a trustee's sale and recover all prepaid rent, plus the greater of one month's rent or twice the amount of money lost from the landlord; or*
- *if the foreclosure sale has not occurred, remain bound by the lease and deduct the amount of one month's future rent.*

The disclosure notice is required to be provided in English, and include Spanish, Chinese, Tagalog, Vietnamese and Korean translations.

It is the landlord's responsibility to ensure this notice is provided in the event an NOD has been recorded against the property. A property manager is not liable for failure to provide this notice, unless they neglect to provide the notice after being instructed by the landlord to do so. [Calif. Civil Code §2924.85]

- refuse to rent to persons who will not agree to the non-smoking provisions made a part of the rental or lease agreement.

Alternatively, the landlord may:

- designate all of the property as **smoke-free**, with the exception of any clearly defined areas where smoking will not affect others, by amending existing rental agreements or expired lease agreements; [See **RPI** Form 563-1] and
- enforce no smoking as part of the rules and policies of occupancy of the property through a *"property policies"* provision in the rental or lease agreement, then serve tenants who breach the no-smoking rule with a three-day notice perform (do not smoke) or quit (vacate). [See Figure 1, Form 550 §6.12; see **RPI** Form 576]

The above policies may be **agreed upon** by the landlord and tenant by the use of a **Non-Smoking Addendum** when entering into a rental or lease agreement. The *Non-Smoking Addendum* either prohibits smoking on the entire premises, or notes the specific location on the property where smoking is permitted. [See **RPI** Form 563-1 §3]

Nonsmoking addendum

A non-smoking policy may not be imposed on tenants under an existing fixed-term lease until renewal of the lease is negotiated, at which point the addendum may be attached. However, the use of a **property policies** provision in a lease agreement is a method for changing the rules on tenants during the term of a fixed-term lease.

However, tenants occupying under a month-to-month (periodic) rental agreement or an expired lease agreement may be given a 30-day Notice of Change in Rental Terms containing the non-smoking provision as the change. [See **RPI** Form 570 §7]

The tenant receiving a 30-day Notice of Change in Rental Terms does not need to sign a non-smoking addendum. The tenant, by remaining in possession and not giving notice to vacate, has by remaining silent agreed to the non-smoking provision. The non-smoking condition is enforceable on the running of 30 days from delivery of the notice.

Condition of premises addendum

A residential landlord has the statutory duty to maintain the rented premises in a habitable condition at all times. Similarly, a tenant has the statutory duty to refrain from damaging the premises and advising the landlord of adverse conditions which come about during the tenancy.[3]

To avoid disputes over who is responsible for any damage to the premises, the residential landlord and tenant complete and sign a **condition of premises addendum** before the tenant is given possession. [See Form 560 in Chapter 36; see Chapter 37]

Before a tenant takes possession, the landlord or their manager needs to inspect the unit with the tenant. Recall this is called a *walk-through*. Together, the landlord (or resident manager) and the tenant will use a condition of premises addendum to note:

- the premises is in satisfactory condition;
- any existing damage to the premises; and
- any repairs the landlord is to make to the premises.

If the unit is furnished, the landlord and tenant complete and sign an additional form on their walk-through called a *condition of furnishings addendum*. The condition of furnishings addendum notes:

- the inventory of furnishings located in the unit;
- the current condition of the furnishings; and
- the tenant's acceptance of the furnishings. [See Form 561 in Chapter 36]

Within thirty days before the end of a residential tenancy, the condition of premises addendum is reviewed during the *pre-expiration inspection* to help establish tenant responsibility for excess wear and tear to the unit rented. [See Chapter 19]

Pet addendum

Any provisions agreed to but not included in the boilerplate provisions of pre-printed lease or rental agreements are included in an **addendum** to the rental or lease agreement. The additional or conflicting provisions are entered on the *addendum*. The addendum is then referenced in the body of the rental or lease agreement as attached.

One such addendum is the *pet addendum*. If a landlord allows pets, they often:

- impose restrictions on the type or size of the pet; and

addendum
An attachment to a rental or lease agreement for incorporating any provision agreed to but not included in the boilerplate provisions of the agreement. [See **RPI** Form 250]

3   CC §§1941; 1941.2

- require the landlord's written consent to keep the pet on the premises. [See **RPI** Form 551 §6.9 and Form 550 §6.9]

The landlord and tenant may sign and attach a pet addendum that states:

- the type of pet and its name;
- the security deposit to be charged for the pet (but limited as part of the maximum security deposit allowed); and
- the tenant's agreement to hold the landlord harmless for any damage caused by the pet. [See **RPI** Form 563]

A landlord may not prohibit a disabled person from keeping a specially trained guide dog on the premises.[4]

Additionally, a landlord who allows pets may not:

- favor declawed or devocalized animals in any advertisement;
- refuse to rent or negotiate for rent to a tenant because their pet has not been declawed or devocalized; or
- require tenants' pets to be declawed or devocalized as a condition of renting the property.[5]

Editor's note — Although landlords may not favor declawed or devocalized pets, they may still protect against property damage or noise by including a lease provision barring specific pet behavior or prohibiting pets altogether.

Additional rules regarding pets

Lease agreements and month-to-month rental agreements also prohibit a tenant from keeping a waterbed or other liquid-filled furnishings on the premises without the landlord's written consent. [See **RPI** Form 551 §6.9 and Form 550 §6.9]

When a tenant has a waterbed, the landlord may require the tenant to sign a **waterbed addendum**. [See **RPI** Form 564]

The *waterbed addendum* indicates:

- the additional security deposit the tenant will be required to provide for keeping a waterbed on the premises (in addition to the maximum security deposit allowed); and
- the tenant's agreement to maintain an insurance policy to cover potential property damage when the waterbed leaks or bursts.

Waterbed addendum

waterbed addendum
An addendum to a rental or lease agreement setting the additional security deposit and insurance coverage the tenant will provide the landlord to keep a waterbed on the premises. [See **RPI** Form 564]

Other addenda which may be incorporated into a residential rental or lease agreement include:

- house or building rules; and
- any *rent control* disclosures required by local rent control ordinances. [See Chapter 57]

Other addenda

---

4 CC §54.1(b)(5)
5 CC §1942.7

A residential landlord seeking to sell a property may also grant the tenant an option to purchase the property. [See Form 161 in Chapter 6]

However, no portion of any option money or the rent may be applied to the purchase price. When the terms of the lease agreement or option agreement provide for any credit to be applied toward the purchase price, or to a down payment on the purchase price, the tenant has acquired an *equitable ownership* interest in the property and cannot be evicted.

This is called a **lease-option sale,** and is a masked sale of the property typically entered into in violation of all the single family residence (SFR) disclosures to the buyer/tenant, mortgage lender and county assessor. The *lease-option sale* also lacks the protective formalities and fees involved in an escrowed grant deed transfer of ownership.

Terms of residential occupancy

Residential tenants typically provide a *security deposit* to the landlord to cover the cost to clean the unit or remedy any damage caused to the unit beyond reasonable wear and tear. [See **RPI** Form 551 §2 and Form 550 §2; see Chapter 19]

In return for the use and possession of the premises, the tenant pays the landlord rent until expiration of the lease, or periodic tenancy. The tenant agrees to pay a late charge if rent is not paid on the due date, or within the established *grace period*. [See **RPI** Form 551 §4 and Form 550 §4; see Chapter 25]

Also, the number of guests the tenant may have in their unit and the period of time over which their guests may visit is limited. [See **RPI** Form 551 §5.6 and Figure 1, Form 550 §5.6]

The tenant agrees to comply with all building or project rules and regulations established by any existing *covenants, conditions and restrictions (CC&Rs)* or the landlord. [See **RPI** Form 551 §6.1 and Form 550 §6.1]

The landlord and tenant agree who will pay or how they will share the financial responsibility for the unit's utilities. Landlords of apartment buildings or complexes often retain the responsibility of providing water to the units. [See **RPI** Form 551 §6.2 and Form 550 §6.2]

In both rental and lease agreements, the tenant agrees to hold the landlord harmless from all liability for damages caused by the tenant or their guests. [See **RPI** Form 551 §7.1 and Form 550 §7.1]

Statutory rights and duties

Residential rental and lease agreements often contain provisions that restate the landlord's and tenant's statutory rights and duties.

For example, the rental agreement reiterates the landlord's statutory obligation to furnish a tenant with:

- a security deposit refund;

- a notice of the tenant's right to a joint pre-expiration inspection of the unit and delivery of an itemized statement of repairs/cleaning [See Chapter 19][6]; and

- a statement of security deposit accounting and an itemization of any deductions.[7] [See **RPI** Form 551 §2.4 and Form 550 §2.4; see Chapter 19]

Also, rental and lease agreements often advise tenants of their limited statutory right to make necessary repairs to the premises and deduct the cost from the rent when the landlord fails to make the repairs the tenant has brought to the landlord's attention.[8] [See **RPI** Form 551 §6.2 and Figure 1, Form 550 d§6.2]

A rental or lease agreement prohibits a tenant from:

- using the premises for an unlawful purpose;

- creating a *nuisance*; and

- committing *waste*. [See **RPI** Form 551 §6.7, §6.8 and Form 550 §6.7, §6.8; See Chapter 26]

Even if the lease or rental agreement does not restate these statutory prohibitions, a tenant who carries on any of these prohibited activities may be evicted with a three-day written notice to quit, no alternative performance being available to the tenant.[9] [See Chapter 26]

---

6 CC 1950.5(f)
7 CC 1950.5(g)(1)
8 CC 1942
9 CCP 1161(4)

The rental market is the market environment in which landlords seek tenants (and vice versa). The condition of the rental market is determined by:

- the population of tenants;

- the number of properties competing for these tenants; and

- the comparative position of the property and its amenities in relation to competing properties.

The rental market sets the amount of rent a residential landlord is able to charge on any given day.

A month-to-month rental agreement runs for an indefinite period of time. It automatically renews monthly, and on the same terms, until modified or terminated by notice. Tenants typically pay lower rents when they enter into a fixed-term lease. In stable rental markets, the longer the lease, the lower the rent.

Chapter 50 Summary

On locating a prospective tenant for a residential unit, the landlord establishes the prospect's creditworthiness by requiring the tenant to fill out a credit application.

Every landlord has a duty to ensure the housing they rent remains safe and sanitary. Additionally, a landlord has a duty to protect their tenants from foreseeable dangers.

Any provisions agreed to but not included in the boilerplate provisions of pre-printed lease or rental agreements maybe included in an addendum to the rental or lease agreement, such as a:

- pet addendum;
- non-smoking addendum; and
- waterbed addendum.

Chapter 50
Key Terms

Quiz 13 Covering Chapters 50-53 is located on page 646.

Chapter

51

Foreign-language residential leases

After reading this chapter, you will be able to:
- identify requirements for real estate transactions conducted in foreign languages; and
- understand how to apply these requirements to lease negotiations.

right of rescission

Learning Objectives

Key Term

A written translation addendum

A bilingual real estate broker negotiates a residential lease agreement with a tenant who is only able to speak Spanish. The lease has an initial term which exceeds one month. Thus, it is not a month-to-month rental agreement. [See **RPI** Form 550]

While negotiations between the broker and the prospective tenant are in Spanish, the lease agreement is on a form written in English.

The tenant signs the English-language lease and takes occupancy. The tenant does not receive a written Spanish translation of significant provisions in the lease.

Later, the tenant decides to relocate to another landlord's property. However, the lease entered into with the broker obligates the tenant to occupy and pay rent for its remaining term.

The tenant hands the broker a **notice of rescission** of the lease agreement and vacates the unit. The tenant claims the lease is void since the tenant did not receive a written Spanish-language translation when they entered into the English-language lease.

> **right of rescission**
> The right to cancel a completed transaction such as sale or letting of property, including restoration, after the transaction has been closed.

Can the tenant *rescind* the lease and avoid future rent obligations since the broker failed to provide a written Spanish-language translation with the written English-language lease?

Yes! A written translation is required to be delivered to the tenant in the language used to negotiate a residential real estate lease. The translation is to be handed to the tenant at the time and place the tenant signs the lease agreement when it:

- is a residential lease agreement for an initial term which exceeds one month [See **RPI** Form 550]; and

- is negotiated primarily in Spanish, Chinese, Tagalog, Vietnamese or Korean by a broker, landlord, resident manager, their employee or a person (interpreter) provided by them.

Lease agreements only

The written translation requirement to deliver a non-English language translation applies only to lease agreements, not month-to-month or shorter periodic rental agreements, on a residential dwelling, apartment, mobilehome or other residential unit.[1] [See **RPI** Form 551]

The only remedy available to a tenant who does not receive the required written Spanish, Chinese, Tagalog, Vietnamese or Korean language translation is to rescind the lease agreement and vacate by returning possession to the landlord. No money losses are recoverable by the landlord based on the lack of the additional written translation. Simply put, the tenant is not bound by the lease agreement.[2]

Transactions exempt from written translations

A written translation of a lease is not required if the tenant's interpreter assists in negotiating the lease.

However, the tenant's interpreter needs to:

- be 18 years of age or older;

- be fluent in both English and the language in which the lease is negotiated; and

- not be employed or located by the broker or landlord (or their employees) involved in the negotiations.[3]

Also, other real estate transactions exempt from the written translation requirement include:

- real estate purchase agreements [See **RPI** Form 150];

- real estate mortgages, except for small private lender mortgages brokered under California Business and Professions Code §10245 which have their own translation requirements;

- month-to-month rental agreements [See **RPI** Form 551]; and

- home improvement agreements.[4]

---

1   Calif. Civil Code §1632(b)(3)
2   CC §1632(k)
3   CC §1632(h)
4   CC §1632

Also, addenda ordinarily attached to leases do not need to be translated when referenced in the lease. Ordinary addenda include documents for the rules and regulations for the occupancy, inventories for furnishings, brokerage fees, the condition of the premises and furnishings, and waterbed and pet addenda.

The terms of a lease agreement written in English set and control the rights and obligations of a landlord and tenant. This version of the lease agreement controls over a Spanish, Chinese, Tagalog, Vietnamese or Korean translation of its significant provisions.

The written translation of the lease provided to the non-English speaking tenant may only be used to void the English lease agreement if substantial differences exist between the two documents regarding significant terms and conditions of the English-language lease.[5]

When the lease is rescinded by the tenant, the tenant needs to return the premises to the landlord. The landlord needs to then refund any unearned rent and security deposit to the tenant. Thus, on rescission the landlord loses a tenant but incurs no liabilities beyond the refund.

When a lease controlled by the translation rule is negotiated, documents later delivered to the tenant which alter the rights and obligations of the tenant, such as three-day and 30-day notices, need to be accompanied by a written translation in the language the lease was negotiated, whether Spanish, Chinese, Tagalog, Vietnamese or Korean.[6]

However, documents authorized by the original agreement which will be later delivered and do not alter the rights and obligations of the parties do not need to be translated. These include receipts, changes in rules and regulations of occupancy and notices to enter for repairs.[7]

Reliance on the English agreement

Subsequent notices to the tenant

---

5   CC §1632(j)
6   CC §1632(g)
7   CC §1632(g)

Chapter 51 Summary

The written translation requirement to deliver a non-English language translation applies only to leases, not month-to-month or shorter periodic rental agreements, on a residential dwelling, apartment, mobilehome or other residential unit.

When a lease agreement controlled by the translation rule is negotiated, documents later delivered to the tenant which alter the rights and obligations of the tenant, such as three-day and 30-day notices, need to be accompanied by a written translation in the language the lease was negotiated, whether Spanish, Chinese, Tagalog, Vietnamese or Korean.

However, documents authorized by the original agreement which will be later delivered and do not alter the rights and obligations of the parties do not need to be translated. These include receipts, changes in rules and regulations of occupancy and notices to enter for repairs.

Chapter 51 Key Term

right of rescission ....pg. 515

Quiz 13 Covering Chapters 50-53 is located on page 646.

Chapter
52

Lead-based paint disclosures

After reading this chapter, you will be able to:

- use the federal lead-based paint (LBP) disclosure to timely disclose the existence of a lead-based paint hazard on residential properties built prior to 1978;
- determine when to deliver the LBP disclosure to a buyer; and
- advise owners and buyers on the conditions of the LBP disclosure.

lead-based paint   **lead-based paint hazard**

Learning Objectives

Key Terms

Crystal clear transparency

An agent, prior to meeting with the owner to list an older SFR property for sale, gathers facts about the property, its ownership and its likely market value.

As the first step, the agent pulls a *property profile* on the SFR from a title company website. On receipt of the profile, the agent confirms their suspicion that the structure was built **prior to 1978**. The agent is now aware the property is the target of separate state and federal environmental protection disclosure programs designed to prevent the poisoning of children by the presence of **lead-based paint**.

The agent meets with the owner to review the requisite **listing and marketing** requirements laid down by the agent's broker. To prepare for the meeting, the agent fills out the listing agreement and attaches all the information disclosure forms needed to properly market the property and locate a buyer, called a **listing package**.

lead-based paint
Any surface coating containing at least 1.0 milligram per square centimeter of lead, or 0.5% lead by weight. [See **RPI** Form 313]

Disclosure of lead-based paint conditions

Among other informational forms for this pre-1978 SFR property, the agent includes two forms which address **lead-based paint conditions** on the property:

- the **Federal Lead-based Paint (LBP) disclosure** [See **RPI** Form 313]; and

- the California **Transfer Disclosure Statement (TDS)**. [See **RPI** Form 304]

On review of the listing agreement with the owner, the agent explains the **owner's legal obligation**, owed to prospective buyers and buyer's agents, to provide them with all the information:

- known to the owner or readily available to the owner's agent on observation or inquiry; and

- which might adversely affect the value of the property.

By making the **full-transparency** presentation about a property to prospective buyers before the owner enters into a purchase agreement, later renegotiations due to delayed disclosures are avoided, including demands for a price reduction, renovation or cancellation.[1]

Duties of the seller's agent

A full disclosure to the prospective buyer about adverse conditions on the property does not entail a review or explanation by the seller's agent about their effect on the buyer or the property once the facts are disclosed. Application of the facts disclosed and the potential consequences flowing from the facts which may affect the prospective buyer's use, possession or ownership of the property are not among the seller's agent's duties of affirmative disclosure.

However, federal LBP rules do require the seller's agent to advise the owner about the requirements for disclosures to be made to prospective buyer before they enter into a purchase agreement. It is the seller's agent who **insures compliance** by the owner before entering into a purchase agreement.

*Editor's note — Regarding the LBP disclosures, the owner has no obligation to have the property inspected or a report prepared on the presence of lead-based paint or any lead-based paint hazards. Also, the owner need not perform any **corrective work** to clean up or even eliminate the lead-based paint conditions, unless agreed to with the buyer.[2]*

Thus, the owner cooperates in the LBP disclosure and their agent's other marketing efforts by:

- filling out and signing the federal LBP disclosure form required on all pre-1978 residential construction [See **RPI** Form 313];

- filling out and signing the TDS containing the lead-based paint, environmental and other property conditions [See **RPI** Form 304];

---

1   **Jue** v. **Smiser** (1994) 23 CA4th 312
2   24 Code of Federal Regulations §35.88(a); 40 CFR §745.107(a)

- making a physical home inspection report available to prospective buyers as an attachment to the TDS form; and
- providing the seller's agent with copies of any reports or documents containing information about lead-based paint or lead-based paint hazards on the property.

Lead-based paint and hazards

Lead-based paint, defined as any surface coating containing at least 1.0 milligram per square centimeter of lead, or 0.5% lead by weight, was *banned* by the Federal Consumer Product Safety Commission in 1978.[3]

A **lead-based paint hazard** is any condition that causes exposure to lead from lead-contaminated dust, soil or paint which has deteriorated to the point of causing adverse human health effects.[4]

> **lead-based paint hazard**
> Any condition that causes exposure to lead from lead-contaminated dust, soil or paint which has deteriorated to the point of causing adverse human health effects. [See **RPI** Form 313]

Editor's note — A list of statewide laboratories certified for analyzing lead in hazardous material, including paint, is available from the National Lead Information Center at (800) 424-LEAD. Lists are also available on the web at http://www.leadlisting.com/lead.html and http://www.dhs.ca.gov/childlead.

LBP disclosure content

The **LBP disclosure** form includes the following:

- the *Lead Warning Statement* as written in federal regulations [See **RPI** Form 313 §1];
- the owner's statement *disclosing the presence* of known *lead-based paint hazards* or the owner's lack of any knowledge of existing lead-based paint [See **RPI** Form 313 §2];
- a *list of records or reports* available to the owner which indicates a presence or lack of lead-based paint, which have been handed to the seller's agent [See **RPI** Form 313 §2.2];
- the buyer's statement *acknowledging receipt* of the LBP disclosure, any other information available to the owner and the lead hazard information pamphlet entitled **Protect Your Family From Lead in Your Home** [See Form **RPI** 313 §3.1; see **RPI** Form 316-1];
- the buyer's statement acknowledging the buyer has received a 10-day *opportunity to inspect* the property or has agreed to reduce or waive the inspection period [See Form **RPI** 313 §3.2];
- the seller's agent's statement noting the owner has been informed of the owner's disclosure requirements and that the agent is aware of their *duty to ensure* the owner complies with the requirements [See Form **RPI** 313 §4]; and
- the *signatures* of the owner, buyer and seller's agent.[5]

---

3 24 CFR §35.86; 40 CFR §745.103
4 24 CFR §35.86; 40 CFR §745.103
5 24 CFR §35.92(a)(7); 40 CFR §745.113(a)(7)

The owner and the seller's broker each keep a copy of the disclosure statement for at least three years from the close of escrow on the sales transaction.[6]

Further, the disclosure form is to be written in the language of the purchase agreement. For example, if the purchase agreement is in Spanish, then the LBP disclosure will also be in Spanish.[7]

Opportunity to evaluate risk

A prospective buyer of a residence built prior to 1978 is put on notice of LBP conditions by handing them the disclosure forms before they make an offer.

The disclosures advise them they have a *10-day period* after their offer is accepted to evaluate the lead-based paint risks involved. The buyer may agree to a *lesser period of time* or simply waive all their rights to the federally permitted risk evaluation period.

However, disclosures about the SFR property cannot be waived by the use of an "as-is" sale provision or otherwise.[8] [See **RPI** Form 313]

Pre-contract disclosure avoids cancellation

Consider a prospective buyer who indicates they want to make an offer to buy pre-1978 residential property. The seller's agent hands the prospective buyer a lead-based paint disclosure signed by the owner of the property which discloses that lead-based paint is known to exist on the property.

The prospective buyer is also handed independent reports and documents related to the existence of the lead-based paint on the property.

The prospective buyer enters into a purchase agreement offer, but does not waive the 10-day lead-based paint risk evaluation period, wishing instead to *inspect and confirm* the accuracy of the owner's disclosure since the owner's disclosure of the property condition is not a warranty guaranteeing the actual condition of the property.

After the owner's acceptance of the offer, the buyer has the property inspected. The inspector's report states lead-based paint exists as stated in the owner's disclosure documents. The buyer now seeks to cancel the purchase agreement due to the presence of lead-based paint.

May the buyer refuse to complete the purchase of the property due to the existence of the lead-based paint as previously disclosed by the owner?

No! The buyer had full knowledge of the presence of lead-based paint and any lead-based paint hazards *prior to the owner's acceptance* of the purchase agreement offer. Thus, the buyer purchased the property *as disclosed*. Also, the purchase agreement did not contain conditions calling for removal or abatement of the lead-based paint. The risk evaluation period only enabled the buyer to cancel had the owner not disclosed the presence of any lead-based paint or lead-based paint hazards prior to acceptance.

---

6   24 CFR §35.92(c); 40 CFR §745.113(c)
7   24 CFR §35.92(a); 40 CFR §745.113(a)
8   40 CFR §745.110(a)

Thus, prior to the buyer entering into the purchase agreement, the buyer was *put on notice* – transparency – about the presence of lead-based paint on the SFR property. When timely disclosed, the buyer may not later, when under contract, use the existence of lead-based paint as justification for cancellation.

Exempt from the Federal LBP disclosures are **foreclosure sales** of residential property.[9]

Yet, a foreclosing lender still has a **common law duty** to disclose property defects known to them at the time of the foreclosure sale. A foreclosing lender is not protected from liability for intentional misrepresentation (negative fraud by omission – deceit) when the property is sold "as-is" at a foreclosure sale and the foreclosing lender previously fails to disclose a known defect to the bidders.[10]

However, the LBP foreclosure exemption *does not apply* to the resale of housing previously acquired by the lender at a foreclosure sale, commonly called **real estate owned (REO)** property, or to the resale by a third party bidder who acquired the property at a foreclosure sale.

Thus, if a lender or other bidder who acquired property at a foreclosure sale is reselling it, the resale needs to comply with the lead-based paint disclosure requirements.[11]

9   24 CFR §35.82(a)

10 **Karoutas** v. **HomeFed Bank** (1991) 232 CA3d 767

11 61 Federal Register 9063

Disclosure exemption

Lead-based paint, defined as any surface coating containing at least 1.0 milligram per square centimeter of lead, or 0.5% lead by weight, was banned by the Federal Consumer Product Safety Commission in 1978. A lead-based paint hazard is any condition that causes exposure to lead from lead-contaminated dust, soil or paint which has deteriorated to the point of causing adverse human health effects.

An owner of residential property built prior to 1978 cooperates in the lead-based paint (LBP) disclosure and their agent's other marketing efforts by:
- filling out and signing the federal LBP disclosure form required on all pre-1978 residential construction;
- filling out and signing the TDS containing the lead-based paint, environmental and other property conditions;
- making a physical home inspection report available to prospective buyers as an attachment to the TDS form; and

Chapter 52 Summary

- providing the seller's agent with copies of any reports or documents containing information about lead-based paint or lead-based paint hazards on the property.

A prospective buyer of a residence built prior to 1978 is put on notice of LBP conditions by handing them the disclosure forms before they make an offer. The disclosures advise them they have a 10-day period after their offer is accepted to evaluate the lead-based paint risks involved.

Exempt from the Federal LBP disclosures are foreclosure sales of residential property. Yet, a foreclosing lender still has a common law duty to disclose property defects known to them at the time of the foreclosure sale.

Chapter 52 Key Terms

Quiz 13 Covering Chapters 50-53 is located on page 646.

Chapter
53

Permitting pets and waterbeds

After reading this chapter, you will be able to:
- identify limitations to a tenant's right to keep a pet; and
- implement rules regulating a tenant's use of a waterbed.

security deposit **waterbed addendum**

Landlords and their property managers are frequently confronted with acceptable, prospective tenants who own pets or liquid-filled furniture which might not be so acceptable.

However, landlords may not automatically refuse to rent to a prospective tenant whose furnishings include liquid-filled furniture. Further, they may not deny an existing tenant the use of liquid-filled furniture, such as a waterbed, on the premises.

On the other hand, landlords may, as a matter of general policy, refuse to accept any prospective tenant who wants to occupy a unit with their pet, unless the tenant is disabled and uses:

- a guide dog, which is a seeing-eye dog trained by a licensed person to aid a blind person;
- a signal dog, trained to alert a deaf or hearing-impaired person to intruders or sounds; or
- a service dog, trained to aid a physically disabled person by protection work, pulling a wheelchair or fetching dropped items.[1]

---

1 Calif. Civil Code §54.1(b)(6)

Disabled persons accompanied by a specially trained dog are to keep the dog leashed and licensed by an identification tag issued by the county clerk, animal control department or some other authorized agency.

The disabled tenant accompanied by a tagged guide, signal or service dog may not be required by the landlord to pay any extra rent, charge or **security deposit** for the right to keep the dog on the premises.

However, the owner of a guide, signal or service dog is liable for the cost to repair any damages brought about by the dog's activities.[2]

Any public agency owning and operating rental accommodations is to permit any person over 60 years of age to keep two pets or fewer (i.e., dog, cat, bird or fish). The elderly pet owner is responsible for any damages caused by the pets.[3]

security deposit
A source of funds to pay tenant obligations owed the landlord on the tenant's default in the rental or lease agreement.[See **RPI** Form 550 §2.1 and 552 §1.2]

Pet addendum

A property manager allowing a tenant to occupy a unit with a pet needs to enter into and attach a pet addendum to the rental or lease agreement. [See Form 563 accompanying this chapter]

The pet addendum establishes the responsibilities of the pet owner and the acceptable behavior standards for the pet. To avoid misunderstandings as to size, type and number of pets allowed on the premises, a careful description of the pet needs to be entered on the form.

The property manager may charge an additional *security deposit* for the pet to offset any expenses or losses caused by the pet, unless:

- the rules for disabled persons and their trained dog apply; or
- the security deposit ceiling is exceeded.

A standard deposit for a pet is one-third of the first month's rent, with an extra $100 to $200 for each additional pet, limited to the ceiling amount for residential security deposits. [See Chapter 19]

Thus, the total security deposit for an unfurnished residential unit, including the pet deposit, may not exceed an amount equal to two months' rent (in addition to the first month's rent).

For a furnished unit, the security deposit, including the pet deposit, may not exceed three months' rent (in addition to the first month's rent).[4]

Also, if a pet's behavior does not conform to the terms of the pet addendum, the rental or lease agreement is breached by the tenant. The property manager may serve a three-day notice to the tenant to correct the activity or vacate the premises, called a three-day notice to perform or quit.[5] [See Chapter 26]

---

2 CC §54.2(a)
3 Calif. Health and Safety Code §19901
4 CC §1950.5(c)
5 Calif. Code of Civil Procedure §1161(3)

Case in point

Landlord liability for pets

A landlord permits a residential tenant to keep a dog on the premises. The landlord is not aware the dog is vicious. No "Beware of Dog" notice is posted by the tenant.

A utility serviceman properly enters the backyard to check the meter. The dog attacks and injures the serviceman. The serviceman attempts to recover their losses due to the injury from the landlord.

Will the serviceman recover their losses from the landlord since the landlord allowed the tenant to keep a pet that was actually dangerous?

*No! The landlord is not responsible for injury caused by dangerous domestic pets when the landlord has no actual knowledge of their ferocity. Also, the landlord has no duty to investigate or inspect the rental unit to determine if the pet is dangerous. [**Lundy** v. **California Realty** (1985) 170 CA3d 813; see Chapters 37 and 40]*

*However, if the landlord has actual knowledge of the dangerousness of a tenant's pet and fails to serve the tenant with a three-day notice to remove the pet or to vacate the unit, then the landlord is liable for injuries inflicted by the dangerous pet. [**Uccello** v. **Laudenslayer** (1975) 44 CA3d 504]*

*Also, a landlord has no responsibility to warn a prospective tenant of a dangerous pet located on a neighboring property, even when the landlord has knowledge of the ferocity of the neighbor's pet. [**Wylie** v. **Gresch** (1987) 191 CA3d 412]*

Qualifying to maintain a waterbed

The use of waterbeds or other liquid-filled bedding in a rental unit is not grounds for refusal to rent to a prospective tenant.[6]

If the prospective tenant is otherwise qualified to rent, the landlord has to rent to the tenant if the waterbed is qualified to be placed in the unit. For a waterbed to qualify, the landlord may establish conditions for the use of the waterbed on the premises, as long as the conditions meet the standards set by California waterbed state law.

These requirements are itemized in the **waterbed addendum** that is attached to the rental or lease agreement. [See Form 564 accompanying this chapter]

waterbed addendum
An addendum to a rental or lease agreement setting the additional security deposit and insurance coverage the tenant will provide the landlord to keep a waterbed on the premises. [See **RPI** Form 564]

The waterbed conditions a landlord may impose on the tenant to qualify their waterbed include:

- an insurance policy against property damage;

- a special waterbed frame;

- specific methods of installation and maintenance;

- a written receipt of installation by the manufacturer, retailer or movers;

- an increase in the maximum security deposit permitted; and

- a requirement the tenant comply with specific methods of installation or remove the bed on three-day written notice to perform or quit.[7]

---

6   CC §1940.5
7   CC §1940.5

PET ADDENDUM

NOTE: This form is used by a leasing agent or landlord as an addendum when negotiating a residential lease agreement which prohibits the possession of pets, to modify the terms of the lease agreement and provide the terms under which a specific pet may be kept on the premises in exchange for a pet security deposit.

DATE: _____, 20_____, at _____, California.

Items left blank or unchecked are not applicable.

FACTS:

1. This is an addendum to the following:

    ☐ Residential lease agreement [See **RPI** Form 550]

    ☐ Residential rental agreement [See **RPI** Form 551]

    ☐ _____

    1.1   ☐ of the same date, or dated _____, 20_____,

    1.2   entered into by _____, as the Landlord,
    and _____, as the Tenant,

    1.3   regarding real estate referred to as _____

2. The above referenced agreement allows smoking on the premises without Landlord's prior written consent.

AGREEMENT:

3. Landlord agrees Tenant may keep the following pet:

    _____

    _____

4. Landlord hereby acknowledges receipt of $_____ as a security deposit, from which Landlord may offset any expenses or losses caused by the pet. On termination of the above referenced agreement, the security deposit will be refunded to Tenant with an itemization fo its disposition.

5. Tenant agrees:

    5.1   Pet will not damage premises or annoy, endanger or inconvenience other tenants.

    5.2   Tenant will hold Landlord harmless for any damages caused by the pet.

    5.3   To comply with all laws pertaining to the keeping and leashing of the pet.

    5.4   pet is not known to be dangerous or to have injured individuals.

    5.5   _____

    _____

    _____

    _____

    _____

I agree to the terms stated above.	I agree to the terms stated above.
Date: _____, 20_____	Date: _____, 20_____
Landlord/Agent: _____	Tenant: _____
	Signature: _____
	Tenant: _____
Signature: _____	
	Signature: _____

FORM 563   03-11   ©2016 RPI — Realty Publications, Inc., P.O. BOX 5707, RIVERSIDE, CA 92517

The floor of any residence has a limited capacity for weight centralized in one area.

Since a waterbed is considerably heavier than a regular bed, the weight of the waterbed is not to exceed the weight limitation of the floor, especially if it is on an upper level.

Also, to ensure proper distribution of the weight, the tenant is required to provide an adequate bed frame specially designed to support and distribute the weight of a waterbed.[8]

---

8   CC §1940.5(b)

When a tenant qualifies to maintain a waterbed on the premises, the landlord may increase the tenant's security deposit up to an additional one-half month's rent. The waterbed deposit is in addition to the maximum security deposit otherwise allowed. [See Chapter 19]

The landlord may also charge a reasonable administrative fee to cover the time, effort and money expenditures necessary to process the waterbed paperwork, such as $50 to $100.[9]

The amounts of both the additional security deposit and administrative charges are set forth in the *waterbed addendum*. [See Form 564 §§2; 3]

The tenant may be required to provide the landlord with a waterbed insurance policy or certificate of insurance for property damage caused by the waterbed. The policy needs to name the landlord as an additional insured to eliminate any question over the disbursement of funds from a claim.

The waterbed insurance policy is to be accepted by the landlord when specific conditions are met, including:

- the policy is issued by a company licensed in California;
- the company possesses a Best Insurance Report rating of B or better; and
- the policy offers coverage of no less than $100,000.[10]

The tenant is to ensure the policy remains valid and enforceable throughout the period the waterbed is located on the premises. The landlord has the right to demand proof of insurance from the tenant at any time. If the tenant fails to provide proof of insurance when requested, a three-day notice to perform or quit may be served on the tenant to deliver the policy, remove the furniture or vacate.

Waterbed addendum

Consider the insurance policy a tenant holds on their waterbed expiring two months before they vacate. The tenant does not renew the policy since they will soon be moving. The landlord fails to purchase coverage and charge the tenant for the premium or serve the tenant with a three-day notice to get insurance, remove the bed or vacate.

No insurance policy

Sometime after the policy expires, a liner patch from a prior leak ruptures, releasing its water. The whole apartment is flooded, causing hundreds of dollars in losses as well as damage to the units and personal property on lower floors.

The landlord repairs the damage and demands payment from the tenant for all of their losses caused by the waterbed. The tenant claims the landlord had the responsibility to obtain coverage if the tenant did not.

May the landlord collect the losses from the tenant?

---

9 CC §1940.5(g)
10 CC §1940.5(a)

WATERBED ADDENDUM

NOTE: This form is used by a leasing agent or landlord as an addendum when negotiating a residential lease agreement, to establish the conditions for the use of the waterbed on the premises.

DATE: _____, 20_____, at _____, California.
Items left blank or unchecked are not applicable.

FACTS:

1. This is an addendum to the following:
    ☐ Residential lease agreement [See **RPI** Form 550]
    ☐ Residential rental agreement [See **RPI** Form 551]
    1.1   ☐ of the same date, or dated _____, 20_____, at _____, California,
    1.2   regarding a residential unit referred to as _____
    _____
    1.3   containing a provision prohibiting waterbeds and other liquid-filled furniture without the written consent of Landlord.

AGREEMENT:

2. Tenant may keep and use on the premises the following liquid-filled furniture.
    ☐ Waterbed described as _____
    _____
    ☐ _____

3. Landlord acknowledges receipt of $_____ as an additional security deposit, to be used to offset any expenses or losses incurred by Landlord due to the liquid-filled furniture.
    3.1   Within 21 days after removal of the liquid-filled furniture, the security deposit will be refunded to Tenant with an itemization of its disposition.

4. Landlord acknowledges receipt of $_____ as an additional fee to cover administrative costs incurred due to this agreement.

5. Tenant agrees:
    5.1   To maintain an insurance policy on the liquid-filled furniture for no less than $100,000 to cover property damage, naming landlord as an additional insured.
          a.   To cause Landlord to receive at least 10 days prior written notice of cancellation or non-renewal of the insurance policy.
          b.   To accept responsibility for property damage caused by the liquid-filled furniture if the policy expires unrenewed.
    5.2   To install the liquid-filled furniture according to manufacturer specifications, to operate properly all heaters and safety items, and to dispose of the liquid in a safe and sanitary manner.
          a.   To give Landlord 24 hours notice of intent to install, move or remove the liquid-filled furniture.
          b.   To provide Landlord with a written installation receipt stating the installer's name, address and place of business when the liquid-filled furniture is installed, moved or removed by anyone other than Tenant.
    5.3   To strictly abide by the maintenance and safety precautions specified in the owner's manual supplied by the manufacturer of the liquid-filled furniture.
    5.4   Landlord may enter Tenant's residence on 24 hours notice to inspect the liquid-filled furniture to ensure it is being properly maintained.
          a.   On lack of Tenant's reasonable care and maintenance of the liquid-filled furniture, Landlord may serve Tenant with a Three-day Notice to Perform or Quit regarding correction of the deficient care and maintenance or the removal of the furniture. [See **RPI** Form 576]

6. Landlord's failure to enforce these conditions does not waive their right to an insurance claim.

I agree to the terms stated above.	I agree to the terms stated above.
Date: _____, 20_____	Date: _____, 20_____
Landlord: _____	Tenant: _____
Signature: _____	Signature: _____
Signature: _____	Signature: _____

FORM 564   03-11   ©2016 **RPI — Realty Publications, Inc.**, P.O. BOX 5707, RIVERSIDE, CA 92517

Yes! Any damage resulting from the waterbed not covered by an insurance policy is the responsibility of the tenant. The landlord has no obligation to procure coverage even though they have authority to do so on the tenant's failure to provide coverage.

Further, if for some reason the tenant's waterbed liability policy is canceled, expires or is not renewed, the tenant is obligated to give the landlord a ten-day notice of cancellation or nonrenewal of the insurance policy.[11]

The notice is automatically given to the landlord by the insurer when the landlord is an additional insured on the waterbed policy.

---

11 CC §1940.5(a)

It is the tenant's responsibility to ensure the waterbed is properly installed and maintained.

The tenant is to give the property manager 24 hours' notice if they intend to move, install or remove a waterbed.

If anyone other than the tenant installs the waterbed, specifically the manufacturer, a retailer or a moving company, the tenant is to provide the landlord with a written receipt that contains the installer's name, address and place of business.[12]

To ensure safety at all times, the tenant is to comply with the manufacturer's specifications for proper use of the bed.[13]

When a landlord suspects the tenant is not meeting the provisions in the waterbed addendum, they have the right to enter the residence to inspect the waterbed and ensure it is being maintained properly. However, they need to give the tenant a 24-hour notice of entry before the inspection.[14] [See **RPI** Form 567; see Chapter 4]

The landlord may give the tenant a three-day notice to either comply with installation and maintenance standards or remove the bed from the premises (or vacate) if:

- the landlord finds the waterbed is not being properly maintained; or
- the waterbed has not been properly installed.[15]

The landlord may serve a three-day notice to perform or quit on the tenant, as long as the tenant is given the option of either curing the installation defects or removing the bed as performance in lieu of vacating. If the tenant fails to perform either alternative within three days, they are to vacate the premises. [See Chapter 26]

In lieu of the notice to perform or quit, the landlord may serve an "advisory" letter giving notice to perform.

However, the landlord will have to later serve a three-day notice to perform or quit if the tenant fails to either repair or remove the bed.

Finally, the landlord does not lose their right to make an insurance claim if they fail to exercise any of their rights to police the tenant's care and maintenance of the waterbed.[16]

Installation and care of the waterbed

12 CC §1940.5(c)
13 CC §1940.5(e)
14 CC §§1940.5(f); 1954
15 CC §1940.5(f)
16 CC §1940.5(h)

Chapter 53 Summary

A property manager allowing a tenant to occupy a unit with a pet needs to enter into and attach a pet addendum to the rental or lease agreement.

The property manager may charge an additional security deposit for the pet to offset any expenses or losses caused by the pet, unless:

- the rules for disabled persons and their trained dog apply; or
- the security deposit ceiling is exceeded.

A standard deposit for a pet is one-third of the first month's rent, with an extra $100 to $200 for each additional pet, limited to the ceiling amount for residential security deposits.

The use of waterbeds or other liquid-filled bedding in a rental unit is not grounds for refusal to rent to a prospective tenant.

If the prospective tenant is otherwise qualified to rent, the landlord has to rent to the tenant if the waterbed is qualified to be placed in the unit. For a waterbed to qualify, the landlord may establish conditions for the use of the waterbed on the premises, as long as the conditions meet the standards set by California waterbed state law.

Chapter 53 Key Terms

Quiz 13 Covering Chapters 50-53 is located on page 646.

Civil rights and fair housing laws

After reading this chapter, you will be able to:

- recognize discriminatory practices prohibited under the Federal Fair Housing Act (FFHA);
- ensure equal access is provided to residential rental units for disabled tenants;
- determine when to disclose a prior death on a property; and
- understand how federal and California anti-discrimination laws affect the management of residential and commercial rental property.

Learning Objectives

blockbusting	**familial status**
Civil Rights Act	**Federal Fair Housing Act**
disabled individual	**Steering**
Dwelling	**Unruh Civil Rights Act**

Key Terms

Regardless of race, all citizens of the United States have the right to rent real estate under the federal **Civil Rights Act**.[1]

Further, all individuals within the United States, regardless of race or legal status, are given the same rights to make and enforce contracts (rental and lease agreements), sue, be sued, enjoy the full benefits of law and be subject to the same punishments, penalties, taxes and licenses.[2]

The federal *Civil Rights Act* applies to race discrimination on the rental of all types of real estate, both residential and commercial. Racially motivated activities in any real estate leasing transaction are prohibited.

Property rights and an individual's status

Civil Rights Act
A federal law which provides broad protections to all persons in the United States against discriminatory activities.

---

1   42 United States Code §1982
2   42 USC §1981

Federal protection against racial discrimination given under the Civil Rights Act is a broad protection which applies to types of discrimination prohibited in all activities between individuals present in the country.

Anti-discrimination in residential property

While the federal Civil Rights Act provides general protection against all prohibited discriminatory activity, the **Federal Fair Housing Act (FFHA)** protections specifically limited to dwellings, including rental housing.[3]

A **dwelling** includes any building or structure that is occupied, or designed to be occupied, as a residence by one or more families. A *dwelling* also includes vacant land offered for lease for residential dwelling purposes, such as a lot or space made available to hold a mobilehome unit.[4]

The FFHA bars the use of any discriminatory actions a landlord or property manager might take against a prospective tenant when handling a residential rental based on an individual's:

Federal Fair Housing Act
A collection of policies designed to prevent the arbitrary restriction of access to housing based on an occupant's inclusion in a protected class.

- race or color;
- national origin;
- religion;
- sex;
- familial status; or
- handicap.[5]

dwelling
A building occupied or designed to be occupied as a residence by one or more families.

Familial status refers to whether a household includes individuals under the age of 18 in the legal custody of a parent or legally designated guardian.[6]

Handicapped persons are individuals who have:

familial status
A status which indicates a household includes individuals under the age of 18.

- a physical or mental impairment which substantially limits the individual's life activities; or
- a record of, or are regarded as having, a physical or mental impairment.[7]

The term "handicap" excludes individuals who illegally use a controlled substance. However, alcoholics and individuals who are considered "recovering or recovered addicts" are protected as handicapped individuals.[8]

Qualifying and processing tenants

The FFHA prohibits a landlord or property manager from unlawfully discriminating against individuals during solicitations and negotiations for the rental of a dwelling.[9]

Thus, a landlord or property manager may not:

- refuse to rent a dwelling or to negotiate the rental of a dwelling for prohibited discriminatory reasons;

---

3 42 USC §§3601 et seq.
4 42 USC §3602(b)
5 42 USC §3602
6 42 USC §3602(k)
7 42 USC §3602(h)
8 **United States** v. **Southern Management Corporation** (4th Cir. 1992) 955 F2d 914
9 42 USC §3604(a)

- impose different rental charges on a dwelling for prohibited discriminatory reasons;

- use discriminatory qualification criteria or different procedures for processing applications in the rental of a dwelling; or

- evict tenants or tenants' guests for prohibited discriminatory reasons.[10]

For example, a broker is hired by a residential apartment landlord to perform property management activities. One of the broker's duties as a property manager is to locate tenants to fill vacancies.

A tenant from a religious minority group contacts the broker about the availability of an apartment.

The broker (or their agent) informs the prospective tenant of the monthly rent. However, the rate the broker communicates to the prospective tenant is higher than the rent nonminority tenants are asked to pay for similar apartments.

When the prospective minority tenant asks the broker for an application, the broker informs the tenant a nonrefundable screening fee is charged to process the application. The creditworthy minority tenant fills out the application, pays the fee and is told the processing will take several days.

In the meantime, a nonminority tenant inquires about the rental of the same or similar apartment. The monthly rent rate the broker quotes the nonminority is lower than the rent rate the minority tenant was quoted, even though the nonminority tenant is not as creditworthy as the minority tenant. Further, the nonminority tenant is not charged a screening fee with their application. The apartment is immediately rented to the nonminority tenant.

Here, the broker's actions were racially or religiously motivated, a violation of the FFHA. The broker misrepresented the availability of the apartment based on the tenant's ethnicity or religion by using different procedures and qualification standards in accepting and processing the tenant's application.[11]

Religiously motivated actions

A landlord or property manager may not discriminate against an individual by setting different terms, conditions or privileges for their rental of a dwelling, or by providing substandard services and facilities for the dwellings than are made available to other individuals.[12]

For example, consider a prospective tenant who is a member of a **protected class**, one who is guarded from unequal or unfair treatment based on certain characteristics, such as race or ethnicity. The prospective tenant responds to an advertisement soliciting tenants for the rental of a unit in a housing project.

Different terms, different privileges

---

10 24 Code of Federal Regulations §100.60(b)

11 **United States** v. **Balistrieri** (7th Cir. 1992) 981 F2d 916

12 42 USC §3604(b)

Federal protections against a blanket ban on tenants with a criminal history

> *The Department of Housing and Urban Development (HUD) released **new guidance** for the **Fair Housing Act (FFHA)** in 2016 prohibiting landlords from enforcing a **blanket ban** against renting to all prospective tenants with any criminal record.*
>
> *Landlords are to consider a tenant's criminal history on a case-by-case basis and may exclude tenants with specific convictions. Landlords are required to be able to prove their screening policy justifiably serves a **substantial nondiscriminatory interest**, e.g., when a prospective tenant's criminal conviction poses a demonstrable threat to fellow tenants. [24 Code of Federal Regulations §100.500]*
>
> *When reviewing a tenant's criminal conviction, landlords need to consider:*
>
> - *the nature and severity of a conviction; and*
> - *the amount of time that has passed since the crime occurred. [**Green** v. **Missouri Pacific R.R.** (1975) 523 F.2d 1290]*
>
> *HUD recommends landlords also consider additional information about a tenant beyond the contents of a criminal record, such as:*
>
> - *facts and circumstances surrounding the criminal conduct;*
> - *the age of the tenant at the time of the crime;*
> - *the tenant's rental history before and after the conviction; and*
> - *evidence of rehabilitation.*
>
> *To ensure a screening policy does not run contrary to the new guidance under the FFHA, landlords need to universally apply their screening methodology to all prospective tenants equally. A landlord who uses criminal history as an alleged reason for denying housing to a member of a protected group, but fails to apply the same standard to members of other groups, is involved in perpetuating a discriminatory practice, a violation of Fair Housing laws.*
>
> *The only exception to these guidelines occurs when a tenant has a conviction for the manufacturing or distribution of **controlled substances**. [42 USC §3607(b)(4)]*

The prospective tenant informs the broker they are interested in renting the property.

The prospective tenant is informed they cannot rent this particular unit. Due to the prospect's minority status, the property manager and the landlord believe it will become more difficult to rent other units in the project with a tenant from a minority group occupying a unit.

The property manager offers to show the tenant a unit in another area of the housing project.

Here, the property manager has unlawfully discriminated against the prospective tenant. The property manager improperly refused to rent the unit to the tenant based on the **tenant's status** as a member of a protected class of people.[13]

---

13 **United States** v. **Pelzer Realty Company, Inc.** (5th Cir. 1973) 484 F2d 438

Selective reduction of tenant privileges, conditions, services and facilities offered to protected individuals is also prohibited. **Selective reduction** takes the form of:

- providing for different terms for leasing, such as the rent rate charged, security deposit amount and the term of the lease, than offered by other individuals;
- delaying or failing to perform maintenance;
- limiting use of privileges, services or facilities to different classes of individuals; or
- refusing or failing to provide services or facilities due to an individual's refusal to provide sexual favors.[14]

Further, the landlord or property manager may not discriminate based on an individual's status by representing that a dwelling is not available for rent in order to direct the individual to a particular Section 8 project or neighborhood, when the dwelling is available. This practice is called **steering**.

Steering involves the redirecting of an individual seeking to rent a dwelling in a community, neighborhood or development to another property when the guidance perpetuates segregated housing patterns.[15]

A broker or their agent releasing and publishing information when handling the rental of a dwelling unit is barred from using any wording that indicates a discriminatory preference or limitation against individuals of protected classes of people.[16]

The prohibition against prohibited discriminatory advertisements applies to all oral and written statements.

Releases and publications include any applications, flyers, brochures, deeds, signs, banners, posters and billboards used to advertise the availability of a dwelling for rent.

A residential landlord or property manager may not induce others to offer or refuse to offer a dwelling to specific classes of people to prevent their entry into the neighborhood. This prohibited practice is known as **blockbusting**.[17]

Further, a landlord's or agent's actual financial gain is not necessary to establish *blockbusting* conduct. The mere profit motivation is sufficient to establish blockbusting activity.[18]

Selective reductions and steering

steering
The discriminatory practice of restricting the rental or ownership of a property to a specific class of people to perpetuate segregated housing.

Discrimination in advertisement

Blockbusting for exploitation

blockbusting
The prohibited practice of a residential landlord inducing or attempting to induce a person to offer, or abstain from offering a dwelling to prevent the entry of a class of people into a neighborhood.

14 24 CFR §100.65(b)
15 42 USC §3604(d); 24 CFR §100.70
16 42 USC §3604(c)
17 42 USC §3604(e)
18 24 CFR §100.85(b)

Examples of blockbusting activities by a landlord or property manager include:

- encouraging an owner-occupant to offer their home for rent by insinuating that a neighborhood is undergoing or is about to undergo a change in the race, color, religion, sex, handicap, familial status or national origin of its residents; or

- discouraging an owner-occupant from offering their home for rent by claiming the entry of individuals of a particular race, color, religion, sex, familial status, handicap or national origin will result in undesirable consequences for the neighborhood or community, such as an increase in criminal activity or a decline in schools and other facilities.[19]

Aiding in discriminatory activities

Landlords and their property managers may not use any tactics to interfere with the occupancy or enjoyment of a dwelling by any person from a protected class of people.[20]

Consider a mobilehome park which effectively operates as a senior citizen housing development under local rent control ordinances. The park owner never officially declares the park a senior citizen housing development exempt from the FFHA.

Later, local rent control ordinances are amended, allowing the park management to rent vacated spaces to new residents without rent control restrictions. The park owner then decides to open the park to families with children.

Senior tenants currently renting mobilehome spaces in the park file an application with the city seeking a rent reduction, claiming families with children cause a reduction in their use of available services. The city awards the tenants the reduction in rent they sought due to the familial status of other tenants.

The park owner claims the city violated the FFHA since the rent reduction for existing tenants was a prohibited discriminatory interference. The city's action financially inhibits the owner's decision to rent to families with children.

The city claims it did not violate the FFHA since the park met the requirements of a senior citizen housing development, and was therefore exempt from the FFHA.

The court found the city did violate the FFHA by interfering with the owner's rental of the mobilehomes to families with children. The older tenants were not entitled to a reduction in rent based on the occupancy of spaces by families.

---

19 24 CFR §100.85(c)
20 42 USC §3617

The owner's rental of mobilehome spaces to families with children cannot be the basis for reducing rent paid by tenants who do not have children. Further, only an owner, not a governmental agency, can claim a housing development is exempt from the FFHA under the senior housing exemption.[21]

There are exemptions to the FFHA discrimination prohibitions. A landlord who rents out a single family residence is exempt from FFHA discrimination prohibitions if they:

- own three or fewer single-family residences;
- do not use a real estate licensee to negotiate or handle the tenancy; and
- do not use a publication, posting or mailing for any discriminatory advertisement.[22]

Thus, the FFHA prohibitions only apply to the promotion of rentals by anyone in the business of renting dwellings.[23]

A person is in the business of renting dwellings if the person:

- has participated within the past 12 months as a *principal* in three or more transactions involving the rental of any dwelling or interest in a dwelling;
- has participated within the past 12 months as an *agent*, negotiating two or more transactions involving the rental of any dwelling or interest in a dwelling, excluding the agent's personal residence; or
- is *the owner* of a dwelling structure intended to be occupied by five or more families.[24]

When a broker is the agent for either the landlord or the tenant in a residential rental transaction, the FFHA anti-discrimination rules apply without concern for any FFHA exemption available to the landlord.

Consider a landlord who is also licensed by the Department of Real Estate (DRE) as a real estate broker or sales agent. When the licensee acting as a landlord distributes their real estate office phone numbers, cards or rental signs linking the soliciting of tenants for their SFR rentals in any way with their real estate office or licensee status implies to prospective tenants that the landlord owes the tenant licensee duties. It is this implication that dissolves the exemption for active licensees since soliciting business with a public image is a vital component of earning a living acting as a real estate licensee.

However, attorneys, escrow agents, title companies and professionals other than brokers who are employed by a landlord to complete a transaction do not bring the transaction under the FFHA, unless they participate in negotiations with the tenant.[25]

Exemptions from prohibited discrimination

FFHA anti-discrimination rules

Exemptions limited and defined

21 **United States** v. **City of Hayward** (9th Cir. 1994) 36 F3d 832
22 42 USC §3603(b)(1)
23 42 USC §3603
24 42 USC §3603(c)
25 42 USC §3603(b)(1)(B)

Also, the landlord of a one-to-four unit residential rental property is exempt from discrimination prohibition rules if the landlord occupies one of the units.[26]

Religious organizations who limit the rental or occupancy of dwellings to individuals of the same religion are also exempt, provided the dwelling is owned for noncommercial reasons. No religious exemption exists if the religion is restricted to individuals of a particular race, color or national origin.[27]

Private clubs which provide their members with residential dwelling space for noncommercial purposes may limit rental or occupancy of the dwellings to members.

Finally, housing qualified for older citizens which excludes children is not considered a prohibited discrimination against tenants with children based on *familial status*. However, for housing to exclude children it needs to first qualify as housing for the elderly.[28]

Failure to comply with the FFHA

Any individual who claims they have been injured by a prohibited discriminatory housing practice under the FFHA or believes they will be injured by such a practice is considered an *aggrieved individual*.[29]

An aggrieved individual may file a complaint with the Secretary of Housing and Urban Development (HUD), within one year of the alleged discriminatory housing practice.[30]

HUD then attempts to resolve the dispute by having the parties enter into informal negotiations, called **mediation**.[31]

If mediation is not successful, a judicial action may be initiated by HUD as a complaint to resolve the issue of discrimination. The dispute will then be resolved by an administrative law judge.

Any party to the complaint may elect to have the claims decided in a civil action before a court of law in lieu of using an administrative law judge.[32]

When a real estate broker subjected to a judicial action is found guilty of discriminatory housing practices, HUD is to notify the DRE and recommend disciplinary action.[33]

When a court determines discriminatory housing practices have taken place, actual and punitive amounts of money awards may be granted. Also, an order may be issued preventing the landlord or broker from engaging in any future discriminatory housing practice.[34]

26 42 USC §3603(b)(2)
27 42 USC §3607(a)
28 42 USC §3607(b)
29 42 USC §3602(i)
30 42 USC §3610(a)
31 42 USC §3610(b)
32 42 USC §3612(a)
33 42 USC §3612(g)(5)
34 42 USC §3613(c)(1)

Further, if California's Attorney General commences a civil action against an individual for prohibited discriminatory housing practices, the court may award:

- relief preventing further discriminatory housing practices such as an injunction or restraining order;
- money losses; and
- civil penalties of no more than $50,000 for the first violation and no more than $100,000 for any subsequent violation.[35]

California's **Unruh Civil Rights Act**, another anti-discrimination law, prohibits discrimination by a business establishment based on numerous status classifications, including: an individual's sex, race, color, religion, ancestry, national origin, disability or medical condition.[36]

However, age restriction is a legitimate discrimination as long as the restriction is in a project that qualifies as a senior citizen housing development.

The *Unruh Civil Rights Act* applies to anyone in the business of providing housing. Brokers, developers, apartment owners, condominium owners and single-family residential owners renting or selling are considered to be in the business of providing housing.

As business establishments, landlords may not boycott, blacklist, refuse to lease or rent because of the race, creed, religion, color, national origin, sex, disability or medical condition of an individual's, or that individual's business partners, members, stockholders, directors, officers, managers, agents, employees, business associates or customers.[37]

A blind prospective tenant has a guide dog and seeks to rent an available unit in a multi-unit residential dwelling structure.

The landlord refuses to rent a unit to the blind tenant, claiming the guide dog violates the building's pet restriction in the *covenants, conditions and restrictions (CC&Rs)*.

The blind tenant claims the landlord is discriminating against them due to their disability since the landlord denied them housing on account of the guide dog.

Here, a landlord may not refuse to rent residential property to a blind tenant because of inclusion of the tenant's guide dog. Landlords are also prohibited from discriminating against tenants with dogs specially trained to assist deaf and other disabled individuals.[38]

California's business related Unruh Civil Rights Act

> **Unruh Civil Rights Act**
> A California law which prohibits discrimination by a business establishment based on sex, race, color, religion, ancestry, national origin, disability or medical condition.

Full and equal access guaranteed

---

35 42 USC §3614(d)
36 Calif. Civil Code §§51; 51.2; 51.3
37 CC §51.5
38 CC §54.1(b)(6)

Housing opportunities for disabled individuals

Disabled individuals are protected from discrimination when renting or leasing California residential real estate. A *disabled individual* is anyone who:

- has a physical or mental impairment which significantly limits major life activities;
- has a record of a disability; or
- is regarded as being disabled.[39]

disabled person
Anyone who has a physical or mental impairment which significantly limits major life activities, has a record of disability, or is regarded as being disabled.

People with disabilities are entitled to full and equal access to housing accommodations offered for rent.[40]

The only exception is the rental of no more than one room in a single-family residence.[41]

The examples of the blind tenant and their seeing-eye dog illustrate how a landlord might attempt to avoid anti-discrimination laws. While the landlord claims to justify their behavior based on their equal application of a single pet restriction rule to pet owners (an unprotected class of people), the refusal to rent to a disabled tenant for reason they rely on a trained dog is a prohibited discrimination.

Accommodating the disabled

A landlord is not required to structurally modify existing residential rental property to meet the special needs of disabled tenants.[42]

Although not required to modify the structure for a disabled tenant, the landlord is to allow the tenant to make reasonable modifications themselves or pay the landlord to do so. The landlord may require the disabled tenant who modifies the structure to restore the property to its original condition when the tenancy is terminated.[43]

Anti-discrimination laws require new residential properties consisting of four or more units per building to be built to allow access by disabled individuals. Required improvements include kitchens and bathrooms designed to allow access to disabled tenants in addition to wheelchair ramps.

Failure to provide the disabled with access to a newly constructed residential property with four or more units is prohibited discrimination.[44]

Remedies to stop discrimination

An individual's primary remedy for discrimination based on their physical disability is to seek an injunction to stop the discriminatory activity. The injunction may be sought by the disabled individual being discriminated against, or by the city attorney, district attorney or Attorney General.[45]

---

39 CC §54(b)
40 CC §54.1(b)(1)
41 CC §54.1(b)(2)
42 CC §54.1(b)(4)
43 Calif. Government Code §12927
44 Gov C §12955.1
45 CC §§55; 55.1

> *An ethnic or religious minority tenant seeks to rent an apartment. The landlord informs the prospective tenant they cannot rent the apartment until they complete a credit check. The landlord also declines to accept a deposit from the tenant.*
>
> *Later the same day, a nonminority tenant seeks to rent the same apartment. The landlord agrees to rent the apartment to the nonminority tenant without first requiring a credit check, and immediately accepts the tenant's check for a deposit on the apartment. The minority tenant is informed the apartment has been rented to another individual.*
>
> *The minority tenant files a complaint against the landlord, claiming the landlord discriminated against them based on their ethnicity or religion by refusing to rent them an apartment. The landlord claims no discrimination occurred since they were entitled to require a credit check of prospective tenants.*
>
> *However, requiring a credit check of minority tenants, but not nonminority tenants, is a prohibited discriminatory practice which allows the minority tenant to recover their money losses. [**Stearns v. Fair Employment Practice Commission** (1971) 6 C3d 205]*

Case in point

Unlawful discrimination

Property owners who discriminate against disabled individuals are further liable for the disabled individual's money losses. In addition to actual money losses, treble that dollar amount may be awarded as punitive damages, along with attorney fees. The minimum award of money damages for discrimination against a disabled individual is $1,000.[46]

California prohibits discrimination in the sale or rental of housing accommodations based on an individual's: race, color, religion, sex, sexual orientation, marital status, national origin, ancestry, familial status, source of income or disability. This list of protected individuals is more extensive than all others.[47]

Discriminatory activities and conduct include:

- making a written or oral inquiry into the race, sex, disability, etc. of any individual seeking to rent housing;

- ads or notices for rental of housing which state or infer preferences or limitations based on any of the prohibited discrimination factors;

- a broker refusing to represent an individual in a real estate transaction based on any prohibited factor; and

- any other practice that denies housing to a member of a protected class.[48]

The denial of housing based on the landlord or broker's perception that a prospective tenant, or any associates of the prospective tenant, has any of the protected characteristics is absolutely prohibited. An individual who has been the victim of discriminatory housing practices may recover their money losses.[49] [See Case in point, "Unlawful discrimination"]

California prohibitions against housing discrimination

---

46 CC §54.3
47 Gov C §12955
48 Gov C §12955
49 Gov C §12955(m)

Income standards for tenants

Standards of conduct applied equally by a broker to all individuals are not classified as prohibited discrimination against a protected group of individuals as they are considered reasonable and thus permitted.

For example, to qualify a tenant for occupancy based on their creditworthiness (which is not a prohibited discrimination), a landlord or property manager may establish income ratios or standards to determine a tenant's ability to pay the rent. The higher the ratio of income to rent established by a landlord, the less the risk of loss of rent borne by the landlord. The lower the income ratio established by the landlord, the greater the risk of their loss of rent. However, once set, the ratio is applied to all prospective tenants equally.

However, two or more individuals who desire to live in the same unit might apply to rent a unit. Whether related or unrelated, married or not, the income of all tenants is to be treated as the total income used by the landlord to determine their collective eligibility to qualify to pay the rent amount sought for the unit.

Separately, each prospective tenant may be unable to qualify by meeting the income standard for the total rent sought by the landlord. However, if aggregating the income of all who intend to occupy the unit and enter into the rental or lease agreement results in total income sufficient under the ratio applied to qualify a tenant or tenants for occupancy, the tenants collectively qualify.[50]

Also, under rent subsidy programs, such as *Section 8* housing arrangements, the landlord or property manager evaluate the tenant's income when determining their qualifications based on the portion of the rent that is not subsidized.[51]

The source of income for each prospective tenant includes any income lawfully received by the tenant and verifiable, whether it is directly received by the tenant or received by a representative of the tenant.[52]

Dependency on spouse's income

Consider a disabled tenant dependent on their spouse for financial support. The disabled tenant and their spouse seek to rent an apartment. Both will sign the application and lease agreement. The spouse's income meets the landlord's minimum requirement to qualify to pay the rent.

However, the landlord refuses to rent an apartment to the couple, claiming the disabled tenant does not also meet minimum income requirements.

Here, the landlord may not deny housing to the disabled tenant based on the tenant being financially dependent on their spouse. The combined incomes of the tenant and their spouse meet the landlord's minimum income requirements for the payment of the rent amount.

---

50 Gov C §12955(n)
51 Gov C §12955(o)
52 Gov C §12955(p)

The landlord's refusal to rent an apartment to the disabled tenant based on the tenant's dependency on their spouse's income is unlawful discrimination. If one tenant qualifies to rent a unit, both tenants are qualified.[53]

Recall that *familial status* in anti-discrimination law refers to whether children under the age of 18 will be living with a parent or guardian on the premises.[54]

Rental policies excluding children under the age of 18 are classified as prohibited discrimination under state, as well as federal laws, unless the property qualifies as senior citizen housing.[55]

Familial status

Consider a landlord who refuses to rent an apartment to an unmarried couple based on the landlord's religious beliefs developed about such conduct.

The couple files a complaint with California's Fair Employment and Housing commission, claiming the landlord violated fair housing laws that prohibit discrimination based on marital status.

The landlord claims they are exempt since renting to an unmarried couple violates the landlord's religious beliefs regarding the cohabitation of unmarried couples.

However, the landlord's refusal to rent to unmarried couples violates the fair housing laws. The key to the ruling is that the landlord's religious beliefs do not also require them to participate in the business of renting dwelling units.

Thus, fair housing laws prohibiting discrimination based on marital beliefs do not interfere with the practice of the landlord's religion. The landlord faithful to religious dictates is free to go into a business that does not violate their religious convictions.[56]

Marital status of co-applicants for housing

DRE regulations prohibit discriminatory practices by real estate brokers acting on behalf of a client. A broker or their agent engaging in discriminatory business practices which generate a complaint may be disciplined by the DRE.[57]

Prohibited practices include any situation in which a broker, while acting as an agent, discriminates against anyone based on race, color, sex, religion, ancestry, disability, marital status or national origin.

Examples of discriminatory practices include:

- refusing to negotiate for the rental of real estate;

Conduct guidelines for the broker

53 CC §54.1(b)(7)
54 Gov C §12955.2
55 Gov C §12955.9
56 **Smith** v. **Fair Employment and Housing Commission** (1996) 12 C4th 1143
57 Department of Real Estate Regulations §2780

- refusing to show property or provide information, or steering clients away from specific properties;
- refusing to accept a rental listing;
- publishing or distributing advertisements that indicate a discriminatory preference;
- any discrimination in the course of providing property management services;
- agreeing with a client to discriminate when leasing the client's property, such as agreeing not to show the property to members of particular minority groups;
- attempting to discourage the rental of real estate based on representations of the race, sex, disability, etc. of other inhabitants in an area; and
- encouraging or permitting employees to engage in discriminatory practices.

For example, a broker is aware a licensed care facility for disabled people is located in a single family residence near a residence the prospective tenant is interested in renting.

The presence of the facility might influence the tenant's decision to rent the property. However, for the broker or their agents to inform the tenant of the facility would be unlawful discrimination. The broker may not attempt to influence the tenant's decision based on representations of the disability of other inhabitants in the area.[58]

However, on a direct inquiry from a tenant, the broker or agent are required to respond based on their knowledge of the existence of a care facility.

The broker's duty to manage employees

A broker has a duty to advise their employees of anti-discrimination rules, including DRE regulations, the Unruh Civil Rights Act, the California Fair Employment and Housing Act, and the FFHA.[59]

The broker, in addition to being responsible for their personal conduct, owes the public a duty to ensure their employees follow anti-discrimination regulations when acting as agents on the broker's behalf.

Disclosure of HIV/AIDS

A property manager negotiates the rental of a residential unit to a prospective tenant. The previous occupant of the property was afflicted with AIDS. Neither the property manager nor the landlord disclose the prior occupant's AIDS affliction, whether or not asked by the prospective tenant.

The tenant rents the property and later discovers the previous occupant was afflicted with AIDS while residing on the property. The tenant claims the property manager had a duty to disclose the previous occupant had AIDS.

---

58 73 Ops. Cal. Atty. Gen. 58 (1990)
59 DRE Reg. §2725(f)

However, the tenant has no basis for a claim against the property manager for the property manager's failure to disclose any prior occupant was infected with the HIV virus or afflicted with AIDS. No duty exists to disclose the prior tenant's affliction.[60]

Further, California public policy prohibits a broker from responding to a tenant's inquiry for disclosure of a prior occupant's affliction with AIDS.[61]

Individuals afflicted with the HIV virus are considered handicapped and are protected by the FFHA.[62]

A landlord or property manager occasionally has reason to believe a death on the premises offered for rent might affect a prospective tenant's decision to lease. Here, they will voluntarily disclose to the prospective tenant when negotiating the lease of a dwelling the death of a prior occupant on the premises which occurred more than three years earlier.

Further, the landlord or property manager will disclose their knowledge of any deaths which took place on the property in response to a direct inquiry by a prospective tenant.

Consider a tenant who asks the property manager if any AIDS-related deaths occurred on the property.[63]

If the property manager is aware an AIDS-related death occurred on the property, they have a duty on direct inquiry from the tenant to disclose:

- the prior occupant's death; and
- the death was AIDS-related.

If the property manager has no knowledge of any AIDS-related deaths occurring on the property, they will disclose:

- their lack of knowledge; and
- whether or not they intend to undertake an investigation to determine if an AIDS-related death occurred on the property.

However, consider a property manager who is aware a death, from any cause, occurred on the property within three years of the commencement of a tenant's lease agreement. The tenant has not inquired if any deaths have occurred on the property.

Here, the property manager will need to determine if the death on the property is a *material fact* which might affect the tenant's decision to lease and occupy the property.

The property manager as good practice discloses *any death* occurring on the property within three years when they have reason to believe the fact might

Disclosing a death

60 CC §1710.2(a)
61 CC §1710.2(d)
62 24 CFR §100.201
63 CC §1710.2(d)

affect the tenant's decision to lease. However, on inquiry from the tenant, the property manager discloses their knowledge of any death, including AIDS-related deaths, which occurred on the property within the last three years.

Chapter 54 Summary

A broker has a duty to inform their agents and employees of anti-discrimination rules, including Department of Real Estate (DRE) regulations, the Unruh Civil Rights Act, the California Fair Employment and Housing Act, and the Federal Fair Housing Act.

California law prohibits discrimination in the sale or rental of housing accommodations based on race, color, religion, sex, sexual orientation, marital status, national origin, ancestry, familial status, source of income or disability.

The federal Civil Rights Act applies to race discrimination on the rental of all types of real estate, both residential and commercial. Racially motivated activities in any real estate leasing transaction are prohibited.

The Federal Fair Housing Act prohibits any discriminatory actions a landlord or property manager may take in the handling of a residential rental based on an individual's race or color, national origin, religion, sex, familial status or handicap.

Disabled individuals are protected from discrimination when renting or leasing California residential real estate. However, a landlord is not required to structurally modify existing residential rental property to meet the special needs of disabled tenants.

Rental policies excluding children under the age of 18 are classified as prohibited discrimination, unless the property qualifies as senior citizen housing.

Chapter 54 Key Terms

Quiz 14 Covering Chapters 54-57 is located on page 647.

Adults-only policies prohibited in housing

After reading this chapter, you will be able to:
  • identify various fair housing laws; and
  • understand the protections and limitations of fair housing laws as they relate to a tenant's familial status.

Learning Objectives

California Fair Employment and Housing Act (FEHA)

familial status

Federal Fair Housing Act (FFHA)

senior citizen housing

Unruh Civil Rights Act

Key Terms

The landlord of a residential property may not adopt an "adults-only" or "no children" policy, regardless of the number of units on the property, unless the housing development qualifies as **senior citizen housing**.

A development qualifies as *senior citizen housing* when:

  • the housing units are occupied solely by persons 62 years of age or older; or

  • the housing units are intended and operated for occupancy by persons 55 years of age or older, and at least 80% of the occupied units have one or more residents at least 55 years old.[1] [See Chapter 56]

State and federal anti-discrimination laws prohibit a landlord's screening policies from discrimination based on a tenant's **familial status.** Specifically, landlords may not prevent children from living in non-exempt residential property.

Familial status is protected social activity

senior citizen housing
Housing intended for persons 55 or 62 years of age or older.

familial status
A status which indicates a household includes individuals under the age of 18.

[1]   42 United States Code §3607(b)(2)

Federal Fair Housing Act (FFHA)
A collection of policies designed to prevent discrmination in the access to housing based on an occupant's inclusion in a protected class.

California Fair Employment and Housing Act (FEHA)
Legislation which prohibits landlords from using discriminatory rental policies to avoid renting to a tenant based on familial status.

Unruh Civil Rights Act
A California law which prohibits discrimination by a business establishment based on sex, race, color, religion, ancestry, national origin, disability or medical condition. A real estate practice is a business establishment.

Conversely, senior citizen housing is exempt from unlawful discrimination based on familial status provided it meets the senior housing criteria.[2] [See Chapter 54]

Rental policies or conduct excluding pregnant women or families that contain one or more children under the age of 18 discriminate against a tenant based on *familial status*. Thus, residential policies resulting in "adults-only" tenants are unlawful.

An individual submitting an application to rent may not be discriminated against if the individual is the parent, legal custodian or a person authorized by written permission to take care of a child who will reside with the individual on the premises.[3] [See **RPI** Form 302]

The Federal Fair Housing Act (FFHA) also prohibits a landlord from using rental screening policies that discriminate against a tenant based on familial status.[4]

Further, the **California Fair Employment and Housing Act (FEHA)** prohibits landlords from using discriminatory rental policies to avoid renting to a tenant based on familial status.[5]

Additional California tenant protection under the **Unruh Civil Rights Act** prohibits a business establishment (landlord) from discriminating against a tenant based on their age, unless the property is qualified as senior housing.[6]

Each of these acts provides a variety of remedies and recoveries for a tenant who, since they reside with a child, has been discriminated against by a landlord. With the exception of senior housing, discrimination in the rental of housing based on familial status violates all three acts. For a landlord, property manager or resident manager, these violations may result in civil liability, civil penalties and suspension of a real estate license.

Discrimination prohibited

Consider the landlord of a two-bedroom residential unit. The unit is vacant and is advertised for rent.

A prospective tenant contacts the landlord regarding the rental unit. Before agreeing to show the tenant the property, the landlord asks the tenant how many family members will occupy the unit.

The prospective tenant informs the landlord they, their spouse and a child will occupy the unit. The landlord informs the tenant they do not qualify to rent the unit since families with children increase maintenance costs by causing excessive wear and tear to the property. The tenant is forced to look elsewhere for housing.

---

2 Calif. Civil Code §51.2(a)

3 Calif. Government Code §12955.2; 42 United States Code §3602(k)

4 42 USC §3602

5 Gov C §12955(k)

6 Calif. Civil Code §51.2(a)

Has the landlord unlawfully discriminated against the tenant by refusing to rent the unit to the tenant based on their familial status?

Yes! A residential landlord unlawfully discriminates against a potential tenant when they refuse to rent a residential unit to a tenant based solely on the fact a child will occupy the unit — a violation of *FEHA*.[7]

Also, FEHA prohibits a residential landlord from inquiring, as part of the screening process, into whether a prospective tenant has children when the purpose of the inquiry is to exclude families.[8]

However, a landlord who targets families with children as prospective tenants is not necessarily acting in a prohibited discriminatory manner when they inquire about children. They may be intending to push advantages their property offers to tenants who have children, such as playground facilities or day care.

Whether or not an inquiry into familial status was made with discriminatory intent is shown by the landlord's subsequent behavior, i.e., refusal to rent, a higher security deposit, an increase in rent to anyone with children or the "steering" of families to other units or facilities.

No targeting of families in the selection process

The California Unruh Act prohibits a business establishment from discriminating in the rental of housing based on an occupant's age.[9]

Owners of apartment complexes and condominium associations fall under the definition of a business establishment for purposes of unlawful discrimination.[10]

Editor's note — Landlords of one-to-four units fall under California's FEHA, as well as the state's Unruh Act. The term "business establishment" under the Unruh Act applies in the broadest reasonable manner, which includes landlords.[11]

While it does cover condominium projects (CIDs), California's Unruh Act does not control mobilehome park owners.[12]

However, a mobilehome park owner discriminating against tenants based on familial status violates federal law and California's FEHA, unless the mobilehome park is operated as qualified senior citizen housing.[13]

Discrimination based on familial status is permitted under all these laws when the housing qualifies as senior citizen housing.[14]

The Unruh Act and the FFHA

7 Gov C §§12955(a), 12955(k)
8 Gov C §12955(b)
9 CC §51.2(a)
10 CC §51.2(b)
11 **O'Connor** v. **Village Green Owners Association** (1983) 33 C3d 790
12 **Schmidt** v. **Superior Court** (1989) 48 C3d 370
13 CC §798.76; Gov C §12955.9; 42 USC §3607(b)
14 CC §§51.2, 51.10; Gov C §12955.9; 42 USC §3607(b)(1)

Rental discrimination under the FFHA

Landlords, property managers and resident managers regularly engage in proper discrimination when the purposes are legitimate, such as in screening potential tenants for their rental units.

For example, a potential tenant's income, credit rating, rental and employment history are properly considered by the landlord as a basis for creditworthiness. The landlord's tenant analysis is intended to reduce the risk of lost rent when renting a unit to a tenant.

Landlords become less (or more) discriminatory when analyzing creditworthiness and risk based on economic conditions. In economic downturns, landlords tend to be more lenient in their rental practices, lowering rental deposits and rates, and relaxing credit requirements. They tend to accept less-qualified tenants than they might otherwise accept in better economic times.

Conversely, when activity in the real estate rental market turns up and multiple-family starts do not keep up with demand, landlords become more selective in the screening process to reduce the risk they take with a tenant. Landlords raise rental rates and tighten credit standards during a strong demand for units.

However, as credit standards are raised, they are to be equally applied to all prospects. Some landlords in strong rental markets overstep by cultivating an exclusive living atmosphere desired by older, wealthier tenants. This conduct is similar in result to application of criteria used in the screening process that tends to prevent families with children from renting.

Prohibited rental practices

Prohibited discriminatory rental practices toward families include the direct refusal to rent. Also prohibited is the use of different rental or credit analyses or qualification criteria between competing tenants, such as:

- using different income standards for competing tenants;
- applying a different credit analysis to competing tenants;
- using different tenant screening and approval procedures to file a vacancy; or
- imposing different rental charges on tenants competing for the same vacant units.[15]

Thus, a landlord may not require tenants with children to have a higher family income or a better credit rating than tenants without children.

Also, a landlord who rents to a tenant with children may not include different terms in the lease or rental agreements, such as higher security deposits or rental rates.[16]

---

15 24 Code of Federal Regulations §100.60
16 24 CFR §100.65(b)

Case in point

Discriminatory intent not required

Consider a landlord of an apartment complex who has a policy limiting occupancy of units to two persons. Each unit has two bedrooms and two baths. A prospective tenant contacts the property manager of the apartment complex. The tenant intends to rent a unit for them, their spouse and two children.

The property manager advises the prospective tenant an application will not be processed even though units are available, since the complex has a policy limiting occupancy of each unit to two persons. The prospective tenant is not shown any of the units in the complex.

The tenant files an action against the landlord to recover money losses incurred in their extended search for housing, claiming the landlord violated the Fair Housing Act based on their refusal to rent a two-bedroom apartment to a family of four.

The landlord claims their two-or-less occupancy restriction is not discriminatory since the restriction is even-handedly applied to all rental applicants with the intent of preventing excessive wear to the units, reducing maintenance costs and increasing the property's value.

Is the landlord liable for the costs incurred by the tenant to find new housing since the landlord's refusal to rent is based on a two-tenant occupancy restriction?

*Yes! The landlord's occupancy restriction limiting use of a two-bedroom residential unit to two persons automatically results in discrimination against families with children. Economically, this conduct leads also to an improper allocation of national wealth to oversized units. [**Fair Housing Council of Orange County, Inc.** v. **Ayres** (1994) 855 F.Supp. 315]*

Nationally, a landlord may not refuse to rent to families with children or adopt rental policies that result in discrimination against families with children. Households with children have to be free to move about the country. [24 CFR §100.60(b)]

Any rental practice or policy that has the effect of discouraging or preventing families with children from renting a dwelling violates federal and state discrimination laws.[17]

A landlord's intent to discriminate against children is not necessary for them to violate the Fair Housing Act. An occupancy restriction needs only to result in discrimination against families with children, regardless of intent.[18]

An occupancy restriction limiting the number of persons allowed to reside in the unit is enforceable if reasonable and applied equally to all tenants. However, the restriction becomes an unlawful discriminatory housing practice when it has a negative effect on the availability of suitable rental units for families with children.

For example, a parent and their child locate a one bedroom unit they want to rent in an apartment complex. The apartment complex has a longstanding practice of only renting one bedroom units to a single occupant out of concern for the lack of parking in the complex. Thus, the property manager refuses to show the prospective tenant the available unit. The local zoning ordinances require a minimum of 250 square feet for two persons in a unit, and the one bedroom unit has 650 square feet.

Occupancy restrictions allowed if uniformly applied to all tenants

17 **Marina Point, Ltd.** v. **Wolfson** (1982) 30 C3d 721
18 **Fair Housing Council of Orange County, Inc.** v. **Ayres** (1994) 855 F.Supp. 315

Here, the occupancy standard of the owner, which applies to all prospective tenants equally, violates the Fair Housing Act. The occupancy by one is unreasonable since it results in an adverse impact on a protected class of people: family groups. Thus, the restrictions denied the family housing for impermissible reasons — parking availability for the second occupant, who is a child.[19]

Number-of-occupants restriction

Now consider an owner of several single-family residences (SFRs) which they operate as rentals. The owner imposes a five-person occupancy restriction on some of their rentals.

One rental unit has a four-person restriction. It has a small yard and 1,200 square feet of living space, which includes two modestly-sized bedrooms, a den opening onto the living room, a large kitchen and one large bathroom.

The unit becomes vacant and is advertised for rent by the owner's property manager. A prospective tenant is shown the rental. The prospective tenant completes a rental application, makes a deposit and passes the credit screening.

The property manager informs the owner they have located a family of five as tenants for the unit. The landlord advises the property manager they will only rent this unit to a family of four and rejects the application, claiming the family is too large to occupy the property. The tenant files a complaint with the Secretary of Housing and Urban Development (HUD), claiming the landlord discriminated against them since they had children.

The landlord claims the occupancy restriction is not intended to and does not discriminate against families with children, but is the result of a business decision necessary to prevent excessive wear and tear to property which is not designed to accommodate a family larger than three or four members.

Is the landlord liable for the tenant's losses and the civil penalty because of their occupancy restriction?

No! Here, the landlord is able to demonstrate that their occupancy restriction does not unreasonably limit or exclude families with children. The landlord's occupancy restriction is based on the size of the residence. Therefore, it is a reasonable means of preventing dilapidation of the property without barring families.[20]

The purpose of limiting the number of occupants is to preserve the economic value of a property designed to house fewer occupants. Families with children are not prohibited. Therefore, the landlord may properly impose a reasonable numerical occupancy restriction.

19 **United States** v. **Badgett** (8th Cir. 1992) 976 F2d 1176

20 **Pfaff** v. **U.S. Department of Housing and Urban Development** (1996) 88 F3d 739

State and federal anti-discrimination laws prohibit a landlord's screening policies from discrimination against a tenant based on familial status. This includes preventing children from living in the rented property. Conversely, senior citizen housing is exempt from unlawful discrimination based on familial status provided it meets the senior housing criteria.

A residential landlord unlawfully discriminates against a potential tenant when they refuse to rent a residential unit to a tenant based solely on the fact a child will occupy the unit — a violation of FEHA.

A landlord may only impose an occupancy restriction as a reasonable means of preventing dilapidation of the property without barring families.

California Fair Employment and Housing Act (FEHA) ..pg. 550
familial status ....pg. 549
Federal Fair Housing Act (FFHA) ....pg. 550
senior citizen housing ....pg. 549
Unruh Civil Rights Act ....pg. 550

**Chapter 55
Summary**

**Chapter 55
Key Terms**

Quiz 14 Covering Chapters 54-57 is located on page 647.

Notes:

Chapter
56

Seniors-only housing

After reading this chapter, you will be able to:
- identify a qualified senior citizen housing project; and
- apply the limitations on age discrimination to senior citizen housing projects.

senior citizen housing   **Unruh Civil Rights Act**

Learning Objectives

Key Terms

California's fair housing laws

A landlord of an apartment complex with an "adults-only" rental policy enters into a lease agreement with a pregnant tenant. The lease contains an exclusion provision prohibiting individuals under 18 years of age from residing in the leased unit.

The tenant gives birth to a child prior to the expiration of the lease.

The landlord immediately serves the tenant with a three-day notice to remove the child from the premises or vacate. The tenant does neither. [See **RPI** Form 576]

The landlord files an unlawful detainer action to evict the tenant since the tenant remains in possession and has failed to perform under the notice.

The tenant claims they may not be evicted since the "adults-only" policy is an unlawful discriminatory practice and violates the child's civil rights.

May the tenant avoid the landlord's "adults-only" policy agreed to in the lease agreement and remain in the unit with the child?

Unruh Civil Rights Act
A California law which prohibits discrimination by a business establishment based on sex, race, color, religion, ancestry, national origin, disability or medical condition. A real estate practice is a business establishment.

Yes! The landlord may not refuse to rent to an individual based on age unless the individual may be excluded under **senior citizen housing** laws. The landlord's "adults-only" policy violates California's **Unruh Civil Rights Act** since it does not qualify as *senior citizen housing*.[1]

When locating, negotiating with or handling tenants for the occupancy of real estate, civil rights and fair housing laws prohibit landlords, property managers and leasing agents from discriminating against protected individuals. These class discrimination rules apply to both residential and commercial real estate. [See Chapter 54]

However, discrimination is allowable so long as it is not based on a tenant's protected status.

Discriminatory standards not based on a protected status include ensuring the tenant:

- is financially able to pay the rent based on equally-applied creditworthiness standards;
- will not damage the property, based on prior conduct as a tenant or owner of property; or
- will properly conduct themselves in the use and enjoyment of the leased premises.

Senior citizen housing

senior citizen housing
Housing intended for persons 55 or 62 years of age or older.

A lease or rental agreement provision is void if it prohibits the use or occupancy of real estate based on an individual's actual or perceived:

- age;
- sex;
- race;
- color;
- religion;
- ancestry;
- national origin;
- disability;
- medical condition;
- genetic information;
- citizenship;
- primary language;
- immigration status;
- marital status; or
- sexual orientation.[2]

---

1 **Marina Point, Ltd.** v. **Wolfson** (1982) 30 C3d 721
2 Calif. Civil Code §§51, 53

However, if the lease provision relates to the age of occupants in qualified *senior citizen* housing, age discrimination is allowed within specific parameters.

Senior citizen housing is housing intended for occupancy:

- only by individuals 62 years of age or older; or
- by at least one person 55 years of age or older.[3]

Landlords and owners of qualified retirement communities or senior citizen apartment complexes may exclude children to meet the particular needs of older individuals.

To qualify as senior citizen housing, the development or renovation project needs to have at least 35 dwelling units and obtain a public report issued by the California Bureau of Real Estate (CalBRE).[4]

For a housing development to qualify as senior citizen housing with the CalBRE, the project needs to provide:

- access throughout for individuals using a wheelchair;
- railings or grab-bars in common areas;
- bright common area lighting for individuals with difficulty seeing;
- access throughout without the need to use stairs;
- a common room and open space for social contact; and
- compliance with the Federal Fair Housing Act (FFHA) and Americans with Disabilities Act (ADA).[5]

Qualified senior housing may limit occupancy to individuals who are 62 years of age or older under an exemption from federal anti-discrimination law.

A housing project qualifies as senior housing by limiting the occupancy exclusively to individuals 62 or older.[6]

Qualified senior housing projects may allow management employees and their families under 62 years of age to live on the premises. The employees need to perform substantial duties directly related to the management or maintenance of the housing.[7]

The age restriction may exclude all individuals under the age of 62, even if one spouse is 62 or older and the other is not.[8]

If a project owner elects not to qualify or cannot qualify for the 62-or-older exemption, the project may still qualify under the broader 55-or-older exemption.

Qualified retirement communities

Qualified senior citizen housing

3 CC §51.3(b)(1); 42 United States Code §3607(b)
4 CC §51.3(b)(4)
5 CC §51.2(d)
6 24 Code of Federal Regulations §100.303(a)(1), (2)
7 24 CFR §100.303(a)(3)
8 24 CFR §100.303(b)

The 55-or-older 80% rule

To qualify for the federal 55-or-older exemption, the housing project needs to have 80% of the units occupied by at least one individual 55 years of age or older.[9]

For newly constructed projects, the 80% occupancy requirement does not apply until the real estate is 25% occupied.[10]

If a residential complex is renovated for senior citizen housing, it needs to be used for that purpose immediately following the renovation in order to qualify for senior citizen housing.[11]

Underage occupants

An underage individual may occupy a residential unit in a seniors-only project, other than a mobilehome park, if the individual:

- resides with a senior citizen prior to the senior's death, prolonged absence or their divorce; and
- is at least 45 years of age, a cohabitant, or an individual providing primary economic or physical support for the senior citizen.[12]

A family member or employee may reside with the senior citizen if they act as caregiver to the senior.[13]

Also, a disabled child or grandchild may live with the senior citizen if their disabilities require it.[14]

Also, a mobilehome park may not discriminate against a 55-or-older tenant who is married to a younger occupant. Federal law does not allow any discrimination when one occupant is at least 55 years of age.[15]

Penalties for discrimination

A leasing agent found guilty of discrimination may be liable for damages of no less than $4,000 and no more than three times the amount of the actual damages and any attorney fees.[16]

9 24 CFR §100.305(a)
10 24 CFR §100.305(d)
11 CC §51.3(f)
12 CC §51.3(b)(2)
13 CC §51.3(b)(7)
14 CC §51.3(b)(3)
15 CC §798.76
16 CC §52(a)

When locating, negotiating with or handling tenants for the occupancy of real estate, civil rights and fair housing laws prohibit landlords, property managers and leasing agents from discriminating against protected individuals. These class discrimination rules apply to both residential and commercial real estate.

However, if leasing conditions relate to the age of occupants in qualified senior citizen housing, age discrimination is allowed within specific parameters.

Senior citizen housing is housing intended for occupancy:

- only by individuals 62 years of age or older; or
- by at least one person 55 years of age or older.

An underage individual may occupy a residential unit in a seniors-only project, other than a mobilehome park, when the individual:

- resides with a senior citizen prior to the senior's death, prolonged absence or their divorce; and
- is at least 45 years of age, a cohabitant, or an individual providing primary economic or physical support for the senior citizen.

**Chapter 56
Summary**

**Chapter 56
Key Terms**

Quiz 14 Covering Chapters 54-57 is located on page 647.

Notes:

Residential rent control

After reading this chapter, you will be able to:

- understand the purpose and function of local rent control ordinances;
- apply rent adjustments to properties subject to rent control; and
- establish a landlord's good cause for evicting a tenant in a rental control community.

general adjustment

individual adjustment

police power

rent control

strict rent control

vacancy decontrol

Learning Objectives

Key Terms

Police power and rent control

A city's or county's ability to establish *rent control* by passing ordinances comes from the authority of its **police power**.

Police power is the basis for enacting local ordinances such as zoning, traffic, health and safety regulations, and rent control, as long as the ordinances enacted are for the public's benefit.[1]

To be valid, rent control ordinances need to be reasonably related to the prevention of excessive rents and maintaining the availability of existing housing. No case has yet found an ordinance lacking in this purpose, regardless of its inability to attain, much less come close to, its stated purposes.[2]

police power
The basis for enacting local ordinances such as zoning, traffic, health and safety regulations and rent control.

---

1 Calif. Constitution Article XI §7
2 **Santa Monica Beach, Ltd.** v. **Superior Court** (1999) 19 C4th 952

Application for rent increases

Before increasing rent on residential rentals located within rent control communities, a prudent property manager determines:

- Is this rental unit subject to any rent control ordinances?
- Does the unit fall within an exemption?
- What type of rent adjustment does the ordinance allow?

Units covered by controls

rent control
Local ordinances that are reasonably related to the prevention of excessive rents and maintaining the availability of existing housing. [See **RPI** Form 550 §1.3]

Frequently, **rent control** ordinances do not cover all the rental units in a city. Examples of the types of property that may be exempt from a rent control ordinance in a city include:

- owner-occupied buildings;
- single family residences (SFRs) and duplexes;
- luxury apartments;
- condominiums; or
- substantially rehabilitated buildings.

Rent control ordinances may also exempt newly constructed units from regulations to stimulate construction of additional housing. Zoning ordinances permitting sufficient new construction to keep up with demand for all price and rent tiers of housing eliminates the need for rent control ordinances.

Types of rent control

strict rent control
A type of rent control ordinance that limits rent increases on all rental units.

vacancy decontrol
A type of rent control ordinance that applies rent ceilings only to existing tenants.

Despite the complexity and variety of rent control ordinances, two primary types exist:

- *strict rent control*; and
- *vacancy decontrol*.

Under **strict rent control**, rent increases are limited on all residential dwellings. The restrictions on rent amounts apply to landlords renting to either new or existing tenants. Even when a tenant vacates and a new one moves in, the rent restrictions continue to apply to the unit.

The more common type of rent regulation is **vacancy decontrol**. Under vacancy decontrol, the rent ceilings apply only to existing tenants as long as they choose to remain in occupancy of the unit. When the tenant vacates, the landlord may raise the rent and charge the new tenant market level rents.

Rent adjustment standards

Once the property manager determines a unit is governed by a rent control ordinance, the manager then determines the type of rent adjustments allowed.

Under a **general adjustment**, rents in all rental units in the city are adjusted using:

- an amount tied to an economic index, such as the *Consumer Price Index (CPI)*;

Facts: An owner purchases a mobile home park in a location governed by a rent control ordinance. The ordinance limits the increase in monthly rent charged to new buyers to 75% of the change in the consumer price index (CPI).

Claim: The owner sought money damages, claiming the rent control ordinance was an unconstitutional taking of profit from the owner since the ordinance limited the ability of the owner to charge fair market rent for their mobile home lots.

Counter claim: The city sought to enforce the rent control ordinance, claiming the owner purchased the property when the rent control ordinance was already in effect, and thus, no taking occurred as the owner did not experience an unforeseeable economic **disadvantage.**

Holding: A California court of appeals held the rent control ordinance was not an unconstitutional taking since the owner purchased the property when the rent control ordinance was already in effect and the owner did not experience unforeseeable economic disadvantage. *[MHC Financing Limited Partnership v. City of San Rafael (9th Cir. 2013) 714 F3d 1118]*

Case in point

Is a rent control ordinance limiting the increase in rent an unconstitutional taking?

- a maximum annual percentage rate increase; or
- an amount determined at the discretion of the rent control board.

However, in most rent control cities, a landlord or property manager may also seek an **individual adjustment** from the rent control board (RCB). The individual adjustment is usually determined at a hearing before a rent control board.

Individual adjustments are sought when the *general adjustment* fails to provide a fair return on the residential property.

Rent increases may be based on:

- cash flow requirements to cover mortgage payments and operating expenses;
- a percentage of the *net operating income (NOI)*; or
- a set return on value.

Also, almost all rent control cities allow individual adjustments for capital improvements made to upgrade the units.

individual adjustment
A type of rent adjustment sought by a landlord when the general adjustment established by local rent control ordinances fails to provide a fair return on their residential property.

general adjustment
A type of rent adjustment under rent control which uniformly adjusts rents for all rental units. [See **RPI** Form 552 §4.4 and 4.5]

When a rent control ordinance bases rent increases for existing tenants on NOI, the landlord's operating expenses include fees and costs incurred by the landlord for professional services used to seek the rent increases. Thus, the cost of the procedure for getting the increase in rent is paid for by the tenant through higher rents.[3]

Reasonable fees incurred by the landlord in successfully obtaining a judicial reversal of an adverse administrative rent control decision on a petition for upward adjustment in rents will be paid by the public agency that issued the adverse decision, not by the tenant. Unrecovered fees cannot be used to calculate the net operating income on the property.[4]

Reasonable expenses recovered as rent

3 Calif. Civil Code §1947.15(b)
4 CC §1947.15(c)

Case in point

Rent control and reduction of tenant services

Facts: *A landlord of a residential unit governed by rent control laws decreases tenant services by lowering the temperature of a common area hot tub and shortening its heating cycle. Upon the tenant's petition, the city rent control board (RCB) orders the landlord to decrease the rent, reducing their resulting profit to comply with rent control limits.*

Claim: *The landlord sought to avoid the RCB's order, claiming they were wrongly required to decrease the tenants' rent since no evidence was presented to prove the landlord profited from the decreased tenant services.*

Counter claim: *The RCB claimed the landlord must lower the rent since a landlord's profits can reasonably be presumed to increase beyond rent control thresholds as a result of decreased operating expenses related to tenant services.*

Holding: *A California appeals court held the landlord was not required to decrease rents since no evidence was presented to prove the decreased services increased their profit.* [**Santa Monica Properties** v. **Santa Monica Rent Control Board** (2012) 203 CA4th 739]

Editor's note — The reduction of tenant services in this case was so minor that an increase in the landlord's profit could not be presumed. A RCB bases any reduction of rent on the dollar amount of the increase in the landlord's profit due to a reduction in services.

When the landlord's appeal of an adverse administrative decision is frivolous, the public agency will be awarded its reasonable expenses incurred to defend against the landlord's action. These expenses include attorney fees.[5]

When a landlord's petition for a rent increase is without merit and the landlord is assisted by attorneys or consultants, the tenant will be awarded a reduction in the rent to compensate for the costs incurred to defend against the landlord's petition.[6]

Evicticting Section 8 tenants

In addition to restricting rent increases, rent control ordinances restrict the landlord's ability to evict existing tenants.

In communities free of rent control, the landlord does not need to give a reason for serving a 30-day notice to vacate on a month-to-month tenant.[7] [See Chapter 29]

A residential landlord is required to provide **good cause** for terminating the tenancy of a tenant whose rent is subsidized by HUD's Section 8 housing voucher program. The *good cause* is to be set forth as the reason for the termination of tenancy, either in a notice to vacate or a notice to quit.

Good cause for termination includes:

- the tenant's violations of the terms and conditions of the lease (i.e. failure to pay rent);
- the tenant's violations of federal, state or local law in connection with the occupancy or use of the premises;

---

5   CC §1947.15(h)(2)

6   CC §1947.15(h)(1)

7   CC §827

- criminal activity; and
- other good cause.[8]

Criminal activity may also be grounds for termination, including:

- criminal drug activity on or near the premises by the tenant, household member, guest of the tenant or any person under the tenant's control;
- patterns of illegal drug use that interfere with the health, safety or right to peaceful enjoyment of the premises by other residents;
- any other criminal activity that threatens the health, safety or right to peaceful enjoyment of the residence by other occupants of the premises (including property management staff) or residents in the immediate vicinity;
- the tenant's avoidance of prosecution, custody or confinement for a crime, after a conviction or an attempt to commit a crime, which is considered a felony under local laws from which the tenant is fleeing; and
- the tenant's violation of the conditions of probation or parole imposed by federal or state law.[9]

However, a landlord may only terminate a tenancy due to criminal activity if the lease provides that the criminal activity in question is grounds for termination.[10]

*Editor's note — **RPI's** rental and lease agreement forms require the tenant to agree not to use the premises for unlawful purposes, violate any government ordinance or create a nuisance.*

State and local ordinance ultimately control what is considered "other good cause." However, during the initial lease term (established by Section 8 as at least one year, unless shortened for good reason by the local *public housing agency (PHA)*) "other good cause" may only be based on the tenant's behavior, such as:

- disturbing the neighbors; or
- destruction or damage of the premises.[11]

After the initial lease term ends, "other good cause" includes:

- the tenant's failure to accept the offer of a new lease or revision;
- the owner's intent to use the residence for personal or family use; and
- business or economic reasons, such as sale of the property, renovations or the landlord's desire to lease the unit at a higher rental rate.[12]

---

8 24 Code of Fed. Regs. §982.310(a)
9 24 CFR §982.310(c)
10 24 CFR §982.310(c)
11 24 CFR §982.310(d)(2)
12 24 CFR §982.310(d)

<table>
<tr><td>

Case in point

Terminating a rent-controlled tenancy under a buyout agreement

</td><td>

Facts: A landlord of a rent-controlled property intends to move into a currently occupied unit. The landlord and the tenant enter into a buyout agreement in which the tenant agrees to vacate in exchange for an agreed-upon sum of money to avoid an owner move-in eviction under the rent control ordinance. The tenant vacates and the landlord moves in. A year after taking occupancy, the landlord vacates, then rents the unit to a new tenant at a higher price.

Claim: The former tenant seeks to rescind the buyout agreement, claiming the landlord misrepresented their intention to occupy the unit in accordance with the rent control ordinance since the landlord later rented the unit to a new tenant at a higher price in violation of the ordinance.

Counter claim: The landlord claims they did not misrepresent their intent to occupy and the buyout cannot be rescinded since the landlord occupied the unit, and the ordinance only applies in the event of an owner move-in eviction.

Holding: A California court of appeals holds the buyout agreement cannot be rescinded since the landlord did not mislead the tenant about their intent to occupy the unit, and the rent ordinance does not apply as the buyout agreement avoided the move-in eviction procedures under the ordinance. [**Geraghty v. Shalizi** (January 24, 2017) _CA4th_]

</td></tr>
</table>

Written notice

Prior to termination for any reason, the landlord is required to first provide the tenant with a written notice of good cause informing the tenant their specific conduct constitutes a basis for termination of tenancy. This notice may be served with the notice to vacate.[13]

The landlord is required to also provide the local PHA with a copy of the notice to vacate.[14]

Phase-out of rent control

When a city's rent control laws conflict with state law, state law controls.

The Legislature enacted rent control *phase-out measures* to provide a more economically efficient statewide housing policy than allowed by local rent control.

The economics of local rent control and zoning ordinances have generally debilitated investment in new and existing apartments. Rent control limits market rental rate returns on investments. Further, archaic zoning restrictions deprive local markets of sufficient housing needed to meet demand. Thus, rents go up, driven by excessive unfulfilled demand for housing.

However, any state law to the contrary overrides local rent control ordinances. One such state law allows landlords of residential rental property to establish rent for each unit, provided the unit:

- was newly constructed and exempt from rent control on or before February 1, 1995;
- was issued a certificate of occupancy after February 1, 1995; or

---

13 24 CFR §982.310(e)
14 24 CFR §982.310(e)(2)(ii)

- is a separately described parcel of real estate (single-family residence or condominium unit) or a unit in a community apartment project, stock operative or limited-equity housing cooperative.[15]

Also, the landlord of a *single family residence (SFR)* or condominium unit may set rental rates for all new tenancies when the prior tenant's occupancy was entered into on or before December 31, 1995.[16]

However, the landlord of an SFR or condo unit may not set the rental rates even though the previous tenant occupied before 1996, when:

- that previous tenancy was terminated by a 30-day notice to vacate or a 30-day notice of change of rental terms; or

- it is a condominium unit still owned by the subdivider.[17]

Further, when any residential tenant vacates (other than on a 30-day notice to vacate from the landlord), abandons the property or is evicted, the landlord may establish the rent rate without concern for rent control.

A landlord who maintains a unit that has been previously cited for violations of health, fire or building codes may not increase the rent charged to new tenants when the violation is not corrected at least six months before the unit is vacated.[18]

Further, the landlord may not set new rental rates when the landlord has contracted with a local agency to establish low-income housing.[19]

Rental units located in rent control communities and sublet under an agreement entered into before January 1, 1996 do not fall under State law allowing landlords to set rental rates.[20]

Demolition of residential rentals

A landlord who wants to demolish a rental building, whether or not it is under rent control, is required to apply to a local governmental agency for a demolition permit.

A landlord is entitled to demolish a unit since they may not be compelled to continue to provide residential rentals when the landlord chooses to withdraw their property from the market.[21]

Before applying for a demolition permit, the residential landlord needs to first give a written notice of their intent to apply for a permit to all tenants in the structure which will be demolished.[22]

---

15 CC §1954.52(a)
16 CC §1954.52(a)(3)(C)(ii)
17 CC §1954.52(a)(3)(B)
18 CC §§1954.52(d); 1954.53(f)
19 CC §1954.52(b)
20 CC §1954.53(d)
21 Calif. Government Code §7060(a)
22 CC §1940.6(a)(2)

A residential landlord who has applied for a demolition permit gives written notice to prospective tenants about the application before accepting the tenant's application to rent, a screening or other fee, or entering into a rental or lease agreement.[23]

This notice includes the earliest possible approximation of the date the demolition is to occur and the approximate date the tenants' occupancy will be terminated by the landlord.[24]

---

23 CC §1940.6(a)(1)
24 CC §1940.6(b)

Chapter 57 Summary

Despite the complexity and variety of rent control ordinances, two primary types exist:

- strict rent control; and
- vacancy decontrol.

Once the property manager determines a unit is governed by a rent control ordinance, the manager then determine the type of rent adjustments allowed.

Under a general adjustment, rents in all rental units in the city are adjusted using:

- an amount tied to an economic index, such as the Consumer Price Index (CPI);
- a maximum annual percentage rate increase; or
- an amount determined at the discretion of the rent control board.

However, in most rent control cities, a landlord or property manager may also seek an individual adjustment from the rent control board.

Further, in rent control communities, the landlord may only evict a tenant for good cause.

Chapter 57 Key Terms

Quiz 14 Covering Chapters 54-57 is located on page 647.

Chapter
58

Leaseholds as security for mortgages

After reading this chapter, you will be able to:
- identify different reasons for a tenant to encumber their leasehold; and
- understand how to encumber a leasehold as security for a mortgage.

Learning Objectives

leasehold estate	trust deed
note	

Key Terms

A commercial tenant holding a long-term lease on real estate needs financing to fund the construction of tenant improvements and the purchase of equipment to accommodate their expanding business.

As a condition for originating the mortgage, a commercial lender wants security in the form of:

- the new equipment;
- the tenant's inventory, tools and trade fixtures;
- existing equipment, furniture and accounts receivable; and
- a lien on the real estate.

The tenant's real estate broker advises the tenant to offer the lender a trust deed lien on their **leasehold** interest since it will have far greater value on completion of the improvements. The tenant thought only fee ownership interests in real estate, such as the landlord's interest, may be encumbered by a trust deed as security for a mortgage.

Financing business expansions

leasehold estate
The right to possess a parcel of real estate, conveyed by a fee owner (landlord) to a tenant.

The broker explains any **marketable interest** in real estate can be given as security for a mortgage, including a tenant's *leasehold* interest in the premises they occupy, such as a ground lease.

Can a mortgage be secured by a trust deed lien on a commercial tenant's leasehold interest in the premises where they conduct their business?

Yes! A fee estate is not the only real estate interest which can be encumbered by a trust deed. Any *marketable interest* in real estate which is transferable can be used to secure a mortgage.[1]

The two operative and coupled documents used in real estate mortgage financing are the **note** and **trust deed**.

The *note* is evidence of an obligation to pay money to a creditor — usually a lender or carryback seller. The *trust deed* secures the money obligation by encumbering some marketable interest in real estate, be it the fee, a leasehold or a life estate, with a lien in favor of the lender.

The lender needs to determine whether the market value of the tenant's remaining term under the lease, on completion of improvements, has sufficient value to satisfy the lender's mortgage condition of a trust deed lien on the tenant's interest in the real estate.

> **note**
> A document, often secured by a trust deed on real estate, evidencing an obligation to pay money to a creditor, usually a lender or carryback seller. [See **RPI** Form 421 and 424]

> **trust deed**
> A security device which attaches a money obligation as an encumbrance on a marketable interest in real estate. [See **RPI** Form 450]

Estates as a transferable interest

The phrase "transferable interest in real estate" is applied broadly. An interest in real estate which is transferable includes the right to exclusive possession and is legally called an **estate**.

Each *estate* in property is fully capable of being encumbered with a lien by the owner of the estate.[2]

In California, four recognized estates exist in real estate:

- **fee simple** (simply called a **fee**);
- **life estates**;
- **leaseholds**; and
- **estates at will**.[3]

Each estate can be vested as one's sole property, or in a co-ownership such as:

- a *tenancy-in-common*;
- *joint tenancy*;
- *community property*, with or without the right of survivorship; or
- *limited liability company (LLC), corporation, real estate investment trust (REIT) or partnership entity vestings*.[4]

The fact the ownership of the estate has been fractionalized between several concurrent co-owners does not automatically destroy each co-owner's

---

1 Calif. Civil Code §2947
2 CC §2947
3 CC §761
4 CC §682

ability to encumber their interest in the real estate. The separately vested interests may be individually encumbered. However, community property or property used in a partnership for the mutual benefit of all the co-owners may not be individually encumbered.

Tenants in common are often partners who hold title for the benefit of the group venture. No co-owner may individually encumber partnership assets they hold in their name.

Also, a spouse with a vested interest in title cannot encumber that interest if it is community property unless the other spouse consents.[5]

Even contract rights to buy an ownership interest in real estate, such as an option to buy, may be encumbered by placing a lien on the option.[6]

A trust deed lien on real estate encumbers only the interest in the real estate held by the person executing the trust deed.

A trust deed describing a parcel of real estate signed by the tenant occupying the property under a lease creates a lien only on the tenant's leasehold interest. The trust deed cannot attach as a lien to the landlord's fee interest in the described real estate — unless the landlord also signs the trust deed and the description does not exclude their fee.

When the tenant defaults on a mortgage secured by their leasehold, the lender forecloses on the tenant's leasehold estate. A trustee's sale or judicial foreclosure sale is used to repossess the right to possession owned by the tenant under the lease. The foreclosing lender, as the **successful bidder** at the foreclosure sale, becomes the tenant entitled to occupy the property as the new owner of the leasehold interest, which was security for their trust deed lien.

The lender, as the new tenant, is required to make the lease payments and otherwise fully perform under the lease to avoid a forfeiture of the leasehold interest by the landlord on a default. The lender who is now the tenant may retain the leasehold interest.

Alternatively, they may sell the lease to a user of the property, or sublet the property. They now own the leasehold interest, subject to the provisions in the lease agreement limiting alienation.

Encumbering real estate interests

Occasionally, a tenant holds an *option to buy* the leased real estate. If a tenant with a trust deed lien on their leasehold later acquires fee title to the real estate, the fee acquired automatically becomes security for the mortgage. The two possessory interests in the real estate, the leasehold and the fee, owned by the same individual merge into the greater interest — the fee. Thus, the leasehold is extinguished and the lender automatically becomes secured by the fee.[7]

Option to buy leased property

---

5 Calif. Family Code §1102
6 **Chapman** v. **Great Western Gypsum Co.** (1932) 216 C 420
7 Chapman, *supra*

On the merger, the lender's security interest attaches to the fee. The fee is the only interest remaining in the property held by the trustor who signed the trust deed describing the real estate.[8]

Leases as security for financing

Commercial tenants encumber their leasehold interest with a trust deed when borrowing funds to:

- acquire an existing business opportunity together with the lease to the premises occupied by the business;
- construct improvements on vacant ground or in airspace controlled by the tenant under a long-term lease;
- expand the tenant's existing business and facilities on the leased premises; or
- acquire a home or investment property under an existing ground lease.

For example, an investor wants to acquire the current master tenant's leasehold position in the ownership of a shopping center.

To finance the acquisition, the investor arranges a purchase-assist mortgage as if they were buying the shopping center under a grant deed conveyance.

At the close of the purchase escrow, the tenant under the master lease they are selling assigns their leasehold ownership interest in the center to the investor.

The investor delivers mortgage documents to the lender which includes a trust deed to encumber the leasehold interest the investor will acquire by assignment. The lender funds the purchase-assist mortgage.

The tenant and lender obtain separate **American Land Title Association (ALTA)** title insurance policies on their respective interests in the recorded leasehold estate.

The tenant defaults on the mortgage and the lender forecloses. The successful bidder at the trustee's sale becomes the new master tenant, since they purchased ownership of the leasehold estate at the trustee's sale.

The foreclosure does not wipe out the fee ownership interest which remains unaffected. The fee was not security for the mortgage.

However, the successful bidder at the lender's foreclosure sale of the leasehold steps into the shoes of the leasehold tenant (as of the date the trust deed was recorded). The tenant's interest in the real estate, the right to possess or sublet to users of the premises, was sold to the highest bidder as authorized by the tenant under the trust deed's power of sale provision.

---

8 CC §2930

A landlord may restrict a tenant's right to encumber the lease with a trust deed lien or collaterally assign the lease as security for a mortgage. If encumbrance restrictions are not written into the lease, the tenant may assign or encumber their leasehold as they choose.[9]

A landlord includes a provision in the lease which defines the conditions under which the tenant may encumber the lease. These conditions are defined in the lease's alienation provision. [See Chapter 48; see Figure 1; see **RPI** Form 552-7]

In the alienation provision in the lease, the landlord may:

- prohibit the tenant from encumbering the leasehold[10] [See Figure 1];
- allow the tenant to encumber the leasehold subject to previously agreed conditions, such as the payment of a fee or higher rent[11] [See Figure 1]; or
- require the landlord's consent before the tenant may encumber the leasehold.[12] [See Figure 1]

If the lease requires the landlord's consent to encumber the leasehold, conditions for the payment of money contained in the alienation provision need to be met before the landlord grants consent. If no conditions for the landlord's consent are stated in the lease, consent needs to be granted unless a commercially reasonable basis exists for the denial of consent.[13] [See Figure 1; see **RPI** Form 552-7]

Conversely, a tenant may require the landlord's consent to be subject to the standard of reasonableness by writing a provision into the lease.[14]

It is commercially reasonable for the landlord to withhold consent when the encumbrance interferes with their interest, such as the tenant's:

- poor business track record;
- lack of creditworthiness;
- damage to property; or
- inadequate management skills.

Consider a commercial tenant who borrows money to expand their business. The security devices available to secure the mortgage include:

- a trust deed;
- a collateral assignment of the lease; or
- a lease hypothecation, such as a UCC-1 financing statement. [See **RPI** Form 436-1]

Restricting the right to encumber

Financing a business expansion

---

9 CC §1995.210
10 CC §1995.230;
11 CC §1995.240
12 CC §1995.250
13 CC §1995.260
14 CC §1995.250(a)

Figure 1

Excerpt from
Form 552

Gross — Single
Tenant

9.   ASSIGNMENT, SUBLETTING AND ENCUMBRANCE: [Check only one]
9.1   ☐ Tenant may not assign this lease or sublet any part of the Premises, or further encumber the leasehold.
9.2   ☐ Tenant may not transfer any interest in the Premises without the prior consent of Landlord.
    a.   ☐ Consent may not be unreasonably withheld.
    b.   ☐ Consent is subject to the attached alienation provisions. [See **RPI** Form 552-7]

When a lender agrees to accept a lease as security, the trust deed is the preferred security device used to document the lender's lien on the real estate. The secured lender or carryback seller of a leasehold interest who uses a trust deed as the security device may foreclose on the leasehold estate by a trustee's sale.

Use of any type of security device not containing a power of sale provision will require judicial foreclosure if the tenant defaults.[15]

Financing a business opportunity purchase

Consider a buyer of a business opportunity who makes a down payment on the purchase price. The seller carries back the balance of the price on a note secured by the business equipment and furniture, the trade fixtures, and the lease on the premises.

The buyer signs a UCC-1 financing statement to impose a lien on the personal property (equipment, furniture, trade fixtures and accounts receivable) and a collateral assignment of the lease on the premises (or a trust deed). The documents are delivered to the seller as security for the carryback note. [See **RPI** Form 436-1]

Later, the buyer defaults on the note. The lease and the business have no remaining value. The seller sues directly on the promissory note to enforce collection without concern for the lien of the leasehold.

Can the seller waive the leasehold as security and sue directly on the note?

No! The seller cannot first sue on the note since the debt is secured by an interest in real estate (the leasehold). The seller needs to first foreclose on the lease (unless it has been exhausted by termination of the leasehold estate on a forfeiture declared by the landlord). The lease of the premises, as an interest in real estate, requires the lender holding the lease as security to foreclose judicially to enforce collection of the mortgage before a money judgment can be awarded, called the one-action rule.[16]

---

15 CC §2924
16 Calif. Code of Civil Procedure §726

Chapter 58 Summary

Any marketable interest in real estate which is transferable can be used to secure a mortgage.

If ownership of an estate has been fractionalized between several concurrent co-owners, this does not automatically destroy each co-owner's ability to encumber their interest in the real estate. The separately vested interests may be individually encumbered. However, community property or property used in a partnership for the mutual benefit of all the co-owners may not be individually encumbered.

To restrict or control a tenant's ability to encumber their leasehold interest, a landlord includes a provision in the lease which defines the conditions under which the tenant may encumber the lease. These conditions are defined in the lease's alienation provision.

A trust deed lien on real estate encumbers only the interest in the real estate held by the person executing the trust deed.

Chapter 58 Key Terms

Quiz 15 Covering Chapters 58-62 is located on page 648.

Notes:

Chapter
59

Attornment clauses in commercial leases

After reading this chapter, you will be able to:
- identify the mortgage lender's use of attornment, lender subordination, future subordination and nondisturbance clauses in commercial lease agreements; and
- properly apply the use of provisions as a landlord or lender to alter the priorities of leaseholds and trust deed liens.

Learning Objectives

attornment clause	nondisturbance clause
future subordination clause	nondisturbance agreement
lender subordination clause	

Key Terms

Altering priorities for lenders

Consider a mortgage lender who holds a recorded trust deed lien on the fee interest in a parcel of commercial income-producing real estate. The trust deed contains a *due-on clause* that states the landlord may not sell, lease or encumber the secured property without the prior written consent of the lender. [See Chapter 61]

The lender has advised the landlord it will consent to new leases under the due-on clause, provided the lease agreements contain an **attornment clause** and a **lender subordination clause**. [See **RPI** Form 552-8]

A tenant later enters into a lease agreement with the landlord that contains an *attornment clause*. The lease agreement is approved by the lender.

The attornment clause in application

The *attornment clause* states the tenant will:

- recognize the buyer who purchases the property at a foreclosure sale on a trust deed of record as the new landlord under the tenant's lease agreement entered into with the current landlord; IF
- the buyer exercises their right to restore the leasehold interest and enforce the lease agreement as the substitute landlord. [See Figure 1; see **RPI** Form 552-8 §3]

Later, the landlord defaults on the lender's trust deed. The lender notices a foreclosure sale and acquires the property.

On taking title to the property, the lender mails a written notice to the tenant stating:

- the lender is the new landlord under the lease agreement; and
- the tenant is to pay rent to the lender.

The tenant does not pay rent and vacates the premises.

The lender claims the tenant is required to accept the lender as the new landlord under the attornment clause in the tenant's lease agreement with the prior landlord.

The tenant claims the attornment clause is unenforceable since the lease agreement that contained the clause was junior to the lender's trust deed and was eliminated by the lender's foreclosure sale.

Is the tenant required to accept the lender as the new landlord and perform under the lease?

Yes! The lease agreement is a contract and remains enforceable after the foreclosure sale. Further, the real property leasehold interest held by the tenant was eliminated from title by the foreclosure sale. However, on notice from the lender that the lender is enforcing the lease agreement under its attornment clause, the tenant is bound to recognize the lender as the substitute landlord.

Since the lender purchased the property at the foreclosure sale and declared itself to be the landlord under the lease agreement, the tenant now pays rent to the substitute landlord and abides by the lease agreement.

Restored and reattached

By the lender's (or other purchaser's) notice to be the substitute landlord by their exercise of the attornment clause, the leasehold interest under the lease agreement is restored and reattached to title.[1]

The attornment clause contracts around the permanent elimination of a tenant's junior leasehold interest on completion of a foreclosure sale by a senior trust deed lender. The clause allows the purchaser at the lender's foreclosure sale to restore the extinguished leasehold as though it was unaffected by the foreclosure sale.

---

1   **Miscione** v. **Barton Development Company** (1997) 52 CA4th 1320

Figure 1

Excerpt from Form 552-8

Lender Subordination and Attornment Provisions

> **3. Attornment clause:** In the event Tenant's estate is exhausted by an elimination of Landlord's estate, Tenant will recognize the new owner who acquires Landlord's estate as Landlord under this Lease should the new owner, within 30 days of acquisition, notify Tenant in writing of the new owner's election to be substituted as Landlord under this Lease.

Priority on foreclosure

A tenant's leasehold interest, whether or not the lease agreement granting the property interest is recorded, has priority on title over an interest in the property held by another person when:

- the lease agreement is recorded before the other interest is recorded or, if unrecorded, is actually known to the person holding the other interest[2]; or

- the tenant takes possession before the other interest is recorded or the tenant's right of possession is actually known to the person holding the other interest.[3]

For example, a trust deed is recorded junior in time to a tenant's occupancy of the secured real estate. The trust deed is foreclosed. The tenant's lease, being prior in time, is undisturbed by the foreclosure — the tenancy established by the lease agreement remains in full effect.

Thus, the buyer at the foreclosure sale of a junior trust deed acquires title "subject to" the lease. Since the leasehold right of possession held by the tenant has priority, the buyer will perform the landlord's obligations under the lease agreement.

Tenant's leasehold interest is junior in time

Now consider a leasehold interest acquired by a tenant under a lease agreement entered into after a trust deed or judgment lien is recorded on the property. Later, the trust deed or judgment lien is foreclosed.

Here, the tenant's leasehold is wiped out by the foreclosure of the trust deed lien or judgment lien. The tenant's leasehold interest in title is junior in time and subordinate to the lien. Again, the lease agreement remains intact as a contract.

On elimination of a junior leasehold by a foreclosure sale of the premises under a lien with priority, the tenant loses their leasehold interest, the right to possession of the premises.[4]

After foreclosure by the senior lienholder, the tenant's continued use and possession of the property is an *unlawful detainer (UD)* and the tenant can be evicted. A three-day notice to quit due to foreclosure is served. On expiration of the notice, a UD action may be filed and the occupant evicted. [See **RPI** Form 578]

2 Calif. Civil Code §1214
3 **Gates Rubber Company** v. **Ulman** (1989) 214 CA3d 356
4 **Hohn** v. **Riverside County Flood Control and Water Conservation District** (1964) 228 CA2d 605

Editor's note — Different rules apply to a residential rental property sold in foreclosure. The new landlord serves the tenant with a 90-day notice to vacate to terminate a prior month-to-month tenancy, but not a prior lease agreement with more than 90 days remaining. When the buyer intends to occupy the residential property as their primary residence, the 90-day notice terminates the tenant's right to occupancy after foreclosure.

Altering the priorities

Consider a commercial tenant who enters into a lease agreement with a provision permitting the mortgage lender to unilaterally alter the priority of the tenant's leasehold and the lender's trust deed liens on the property.[5]

Commercial lease agreements often contain boilerplate provisions relating to the priority of the leasehold against trust deeds, present and future. These provisions include:

- *attornment clauses* [See Figure 1; see **RPI** Form 552-8 §3];
- *lender subordination clauses* [See Figure 2; see **RPI** Form 552-8 §2];
- *future subordination clauses* [See Figure 3; see **RPI** Form 552 §17]; and
- *nondisturbance clauses*.

The attornment clause allows an owner-by-foreclosure who acquires title at a foreclosure sale on a trust deed senior to the tenant's leasehold interest to unilaterally avoid the automatic elimination and unenforceability of a junior leasehold interest by the foreclosure sale.

The *lender subordination clause* gives a senior trust deed lender the right to unilaterally subordinate the lender's trust deed to a previously junior leasehold interest by written notice to the tenant prior to the foreclosure sale. Thus, the leasehold interest in title is not wiped out by a foreclosure of the lender's trust deed; the trust deed has been subordinated and the leasehold has priority.

Under a *future subordination clause*, the tenant agrees to subordinate their leasehold interest in the property to a trust deed to be recorded in the future. Here, the tenant remains involved since they need to sign a specific subordination agreement to give the later recorded trust deed priority to their leasehold interest in the property.

The *nondisturbance clause* when included in a lease agreement is coupled with a future subordination clause. These two clauses, paired together, allow the tenant's leasehold interest in the property to remain unaffected for its full term even though the tenant subordinates their leasehold to the lender's trust deed.

A knowledgeable lender will require the landlord's lease agreements to include both a lender subordination clause and an attornment clause as a condition for the lender's consent to the landlord's leasing of space or units in the mortgaged property. The future subordination clause is included in a lease agreement for the benefit of the landlord only.

---

5 **Dover Mobile Estates** v. **Fiber Form Products, Inc.** (1990) 220 CA3d 1494

To enforce a lease agreement which includes an **attornment clause** and reinstate the leasehold wiped-out by the foreclosure sale, the owner-by-foreclosure notifies the tenant they have elected to be the substitute landlord under the tenant's lease agreement. Thus, the tenant's leasehold interest is restored. However, the owner-by-foreclosure need not exercise their right to enforce the lease agreement, leaving the wiped-out tenant with no interest in the property.

A commercial landlord has financial justification to include an attornment clause in a lease agreement. When a senior trust deed lender forecloses, it is essential for the landlord losing ownership by foreclosure to maintain the property's value. In the event the lender judicially forecloses, the future rents collectible under an advantageous lease agreement reduces the potential of a deficiency judgment for lost property value. [See Figure 1; see **RPI** Form 552-8 §3]

A financially advantageous lease agreement, enforceable by new owners after a foreclosure, will help maintain the value of the property. On the other hand, when a financially advantageous lease agreement does not contain an attornment clause, the property's market value will be lower than had the owner-by-foreclosure been able to enforce the lease agreement and restore the tenant's leasehold interest.

When an owner-by-foreclosure elects to enforce a financially advantageous lease agreement under its attornment clause, the lease agreement remains effective to enforce collection of rent for the remainder of its term as scheduled in the lease agreement.

Thus, the owner-by-foreclosure who makes the attornment election becomes the substitute landlord. As the new landlord, they will perform the obligations of the landlord under the lease agreement.[6]

Before the foreclosing lender or other purchaser at a foreclosure sale chooses to become the successor landlord, they will consider whether the lease agreement provides for rents at or above market rates. To help make the attornment decision, the owner-by-foreclosure:

- obtains the equivalent of a *tenant estoppel certificate (TEC)* from each tenant to discover if the prior landlord has breached their lease agreement [See **RPI** Form 598]; and
- inspects the property to be assured its physical condition is acceptable to the owner-by-foreclosure.

The attornment clause and foreclosure

attornment clause
A lease agreement provision which allows an owner-by-foreclosure to unilaterally avoid the automatic elimination of a junior leasehold interest by a foreclosure sale and become a substitute landlord under the tenant's lease agreement. [See **RPI** Form 552-8 §3]

Subleases and attornment

Lease agreements allowing a tenant to sublet the use and occupancy of all or portions of the property to others, known as *subtenants*, contain *restriction-on-transfer provisions*. These are also known as *restraint-on-alienation provisions*, *transfer restrictions* or *assignment and subletting provisions*. [See Chapter 48; see **RPI** Form 552-7]

---

6 Miscione, *supra*

Under a prohibition of subletting, the tenant is to first obtain the landlord's consent to sublet. When setting up the guidelines for consenting to a sublease agreement, the landlord requires an *attornment provision* to be included in the lease agreement with the subtenant.

If the landlord ever terminates the master tenant's right of possession under a three-day notice and forfeiture, the landlord may enforce the sublease agreement by exercising their right to be the substitute landlord provided by the attornment clause.

The landlord electing to enforce the sublease agreement under the attornment election is substituted as the landlord (sublessor) under the lease agreement. Due to the election, the subtenant will continue paying rent as agreed, but to the new landlord.

No assurance of continued occupancy

Conversely, an attornment clause does not give the tenant the reciprocal right to enforce the lease agreement against the buyer at the foreclosure sale. The attornment agreed to by the tenant to recognize the buyer as their landlord is not triggered until the owner-by-foreclosure elects to enforce the provision.

Thus, a tenant who enters into a lease agreement with an attornment clause, whose leasehold is junior to a lender's trust deed, has no assurance the leasehold will be restored on the lender's foreclosure.

Yet tenants, when agreeing to an attornment clause, believe the clause states the obvious — the tenant will perform on the lease agreement for anyone who becomes the new owner of the property. The tenant views it as a *nondisturbance agreement* with the lender, but it is not. The lender is not a party to a subordinate lease agreement and has agreed to nothing contained in it.

However, when a junior leasehold is eliminated at a foreclosure sale, the owner-by-foreclosure is unlikely to elect to enforce the lease agreement if:

- the owner-by-foreclosure acquired the property to occupy it as a user; or
- the rents due under the exhausted lease agreement are significantly less than the rents available in the market.

The tenant protects their interest

Further, a tenant will regret the inclusion of an attornment clause when:

- rents called for in the lease agreement exceed market rates at the time of foreclosure, as in a time of recession; or
- the location or premises are no longer desirable for the tenant when a foreclosure sale occurs, such as economic obsolescence.

All these foreclosure related events typically converge during economically depressed times for all involved, not when the lease agreement is entered into.

For a tenant to avoid the unilateral adverse economic impact of an attornment clause upon entering into a long-term lease, the tenant is best served by a leasing agent who:

- obtains an abstract of title or lessee's policy of title insurance to ascertain the trust deeds and other liens of record and the risk of loss they present to the tenant, after initially pulling a title profile from a title insurance company;

- obtain beneficiary statements or other assurance of mortgage balances and defaults on the mortgages/liens of record;

- records a request for notice of default (NOD) [See **RPI** Form 412 and 412-1]; and

- records a request for notice of delinquency (NODq) on the lender. [See **RPI** Form 412 and 412-2]

With the information from these documents, the tenant is positioned to take timely steps to protect their interest when the landlord defaults on senior liens or the underlying ground lease, long before any foreclosure sale occurs to terminate the tenant's lease.

An owner-by-foreclosure elects to enforce the tenant's lease agreement under an attornment clause. The owner-by-foreclosure gives the tenant a written notice:

- stating the owner-by-foreclosure is exercising their right to enforce the lease agreement under the attornment clause; and

- instructing the tenant to make all future rent payments due under the lease agreement to the owner-by-foreclosure.[7]

The attornment clause indicates a specific time period within which the owner-by-foreclosure is to notify the tenant it they elect to enforce the lease. [See Figure 1]

The owner-by-foreclosure loses the right to enforce the attornment clause when:

- the attornment clause does not contain a specific time period for enforcing recognition of the owner-by-foreclosure as landlord; and

- the owner-by-foreclosure does not elect to enforce the lease agreement within a *reasonable period of time*.

Instead of exercising the right to retain a lease, the owner-by-foreclosure of a commercial property may choose to serve the tenant with a three-day notice to quit due to foreclosure. This notice gives the landlord the right to evict the tenant by unlawful detainer (UD) when the tenant remains in possession past the three-day notice period.[8] [See **RPI** Form 578]

Avoidance of the adverse impact of an attornment

Notifying the tenant

---

7 Miscione, *supra*
8 Calif. Code of Civil Procedure §1161a(b)

No right to continued occupancy

The three-day notice is served as soon as possible to avoid conduct by the landlord or property manager that could be construed as an enforcement of the lease.

For example, an owner-by-foreclosure under a senior trust deed who elects not to enforce the lease agreement may not accept rent from the tenant. Accepting rent in the amount called for in the lease agreement may indicate the owner-by-foreclosure intends to accept the lease under its attornment clause, regardless of the owner-by-foreclosure's actual intent.[9]

When the owner-by-foreclosure accepts rent payments from a tenant following the sale of the property under a senior trust deed and an attornment clause does not exist in the extinguished lease, a *periodic tenancy* is created. Here, neither the tenant nor the owner-by-foreclosure can enforce the lease agreement since the tenant's leasehold interest has been eliminated.[10]

Lender subordination clauses

A commercial lender requiring an attornment clause in a lease agreement will also require the landlord to include a **lender subordination clause** in the lease agreement. The lender subordination clause allows the lender to elect to subordinate its trust deed lien to leases the landlord enters into after the trust deed is recorded. [See Figure 2; see **RPI** Form 552-8 §2]

A lease agreement containing both a lender subordination clause and an attornment clause gives the lender flexibility to:

- subordinate its trust deed to the leasehold before the foreclosure sale under the lender subordination clause and then enforce the lease agreement after foreclosure;

- complete a foreclosure sale and exercise the attornment clause to enforce the lease agreement by acting within the attornment election period; or

- do neither and treat the tenant as a holdover in unlawful possession.

Some attornment clauses are worded to state the lender acquires the premises "subject to" the leasehold at the time of the foreclosure sale.

No automatic subordination

Occasionally, an attornment clause in a lease agreement literally states the lender is to acquire the property "subject to" the lease. However, the attornment clause does not automatically subordinate the trust deed to the leasehold when a foreclosure sale occurs since the lender is not a party to the lease agreement. The lender did not agree to the terms of the lease agreement, even when the lender previously reviewed it and waived due-on clause enforcement by consenting to the lease.

When the lender notifies the tenant prior to the foreclosure sale of its election to subordinate its trust deed lien to the tenant's lease, the election need not be recorded to give public notice. The change in priority only

9 **Rubin** v. **Los Angeles Federal Savings and Loan Association** (1984) 159 CA3d 292
10 **Colyear** v. **Tobriner** (1936) 7 C2d 735

> **2. Lender subordination clause:** Any master lessor or holder of a lien on the leased premises may elect to subordinate its interest in the premises to this lease by service of written notice on Tenant of the election, and thereafter Lease will have priority regardless of the priorities set by law.

affects the parties to the agreements, namely the lender, the tenant and their successors who are charged with knowledge of the provision's existence in the lease agreement.[11]

A trust deed that becomes junior to a tenant's leasehold interest in the property by the lender's election to subordinate prior to foreclosure gives the leasehold priority over the trust deed. Thus, the tenant's leasehold interest is not eliminated from title by the foreclosure sale under the now-junior trust deed.

When the leasehold is not wiped out at the foreclosure sale because of the lender's prior election to subordinate, a later election under the attornment clause after foreclosure becomes unnecessary.

When a lender elects to subordinate its trust deed to the lease, the high bidder at the foreclosure sale acquires the property *"subject to"* the tenant's leasehold interest since the leasehold has priority over the trust deed.

After the foreclosure sale, by either a prior election by the lender to subordinate or a later election to have the tenant attorn to the owner-by-foreclosure, the lease agreement becomes enforceable by both the tenant and the new landlord.[12]

Electing to subordinate

Now consider a lender holding a first trust deed on commercial real estate. After the trust deed is recorded, the landlord enters into a lease agreement granting a tenant a leasehold interest in the property.

The lease agreement contains a lender subordination clause, included to satisfy the lender's conditions for waiver of the due-on clause in their trust deed as consent to the landlord entering into a lease agreement with a term greater than three years.

During the term of the lease, the landlord defaults on the lender's trust deed. The lender records an NOD, initiating a trustee's foreclosure. The lender has the property appraised and discovers the rent due over the remaining term of the tenant's lease exceeds current prevailing rental rates.

For the same economic reasons that cause the lender to decide to preserve the lease agreement, the tenant wants out of the lease agreement.

---

11 CC §1217
12 Miscione, *supra*

Before holding the trustee's sale, the lender becomes aware of negotiations between the landlord and the tenant to modify the lease agreement. The lender does not want the landlord to alter the agreement prior to foreclosure and an attornment. The lender serves written notice on the tenant of its exercise of the election to subordinate the trust deed to the tenant's lease. This notice alters priorities, subordinating the lender's trust deed to a position junior to the tenant's leasehold interest and the terms of the lease agreement.

After receipt of the notice of subordination, the tenant and the landlord modify the lease agreement, granting the tenant the right to terminate the leasehold and cancel the lease agreement at any time on 30 days' written notice, in exchange for the tenant paying the landlord a modification fee.

The trustee's sale is held and the lender acquires the property. The lender notifies the tenant that the lender is the owner-by-foreclosure of the property and all rent payments under the lease agreement are to be made to the lender. The tenant serves the lender with a written 30 days' notice exercising the tenant's election to terminate the leasehold and cancel the lease agreement under the lease modification agreement.

The lender claims the tenant cannot terminate the leasehold or cancel the lease agreement since the modification agreement, but not the original lease agreement, was rendered ineffective as against the lender by the foreclosure sale.

Lender subordination prior to modification

Can the tenant in the previous example terminate the leasehold by canceling the lease agreement under the conditions stated in the lease modification entered into prior to the landlord's loss of the property to foreclosure?

No! The original terms of the lease agreement and the right of occupancy held by the tenant remain unaffected by the foreclosure sale. The lender had elected to subordinate their trust deed to the leasehold and lease agreement prior to the tenant entering into the modification of the lease agreement. Thus, the agreement modifying the lease agreement for termination of the leasehold is unenforceable against the subordinate lender.

The modification agreement was junior in time to the subordination of the trust deed. On subordination, the leasehold became a senior (unrecorded) encumbrance on title to the property with priority to the lender's trust deed, a condition unalterable without the lender's consent.[13]

By the lender subordinating its trust deed to the tenant's leasehold, the lender acted to maintain the property's value based on future rents scheduled in the lease agreement at the time of the subordination. Subordination allows the lender to avoid the effect of any later modification of the lease agreement prior to foreclosing and acquiring ownership at the trustee's sale.

---

13 **In re 240 North Brand Partners, Ltd.** (9th Cir. BAP 1996) 200 BR 653

Figure 3

Excerpt from Form 552

Gross — Single Tenant

17. SUBORDINATION:

17.1 Tenant agrees to subordinate the leasehold estate to any new financing secured by the Premises which does not exceed 80% loan-to-value ratio, and interest of 2% over market, and not less than a 15-year monthly amortization and 5-year due date.

In the event the lender proceeds with a judicial foreclosure, the landlord would normally prefer for the property to remain encumbered by a financially advantageous lease agreement to avoid a deficiency in the property's value as insufficient to satisfy the mortgage at the time of a judicial foreclosure sale.

Thus, the risk of loss due to a deficiency in the value of the property at the time of the remaining judicial foreclosure sale is reduced for both the lender and the landlord. The tenant, however, is required to pay future rent as scheduled in the leasing agreement.

A landlord's ability to further encumber or refinance their property during the term of a lease is greatly diminished unless the lease agreement contains a **future subordination clause**. [See Figure 3]

Like the attornment clause and lender subordination clause, a future subordination clause is an agreement to alter priorities on title. Under a future subordination clause, the tenant agrees to subordinate their leasehold (right of possession) to a trust deed to be recorded by the landlord sometime in the future.

Thus, the tenant agrees to place their leasehold in a financially junior position on title, whether or not the lease agreement is recorded, than they enjoyed at the time they entered into the lease agreement and took possession. The tenant's leasehold will be subordinated to a new trust deed based on the terms agreed to in the future subordination clause.

For a future subordination clause to be enforceable at the time the landlord arranges a new trust deed lien, the clause needs to specify:

- the use of the mortgage proceeds, such as refinancing existing encumbrances or improving the property;
- the dollar amount of the mortgage or the loan-to-value ratio of the financing;
- the payment schedule;
- the interest rate; and
- the due date.[14]

Future subordination clauses

future subordination clause
A lease agreement provision in which the tenant agrees to subordinate their leasehold interest in property to a trust deed to be recorded in the future. [See **RPI** Form 552 §17]

---

14 **Handy** v. **Gordon** (1967) 65 C2d 578

The clause also contains any other terms that might be unique to the future financing that would, if agreed to by the tenant, further impair the tenant's lease.

When the landlord later arranges financing for the property on terms within the parameters agreed to in the subordination clause, the tenant is obligated to sign a specific subordination agreement. The agreement to subordinate needs to set out the specifics of the mortgage to which the tenant's leasehold will be subordinate. A title company will not insure the priority of the new trust deed over the tenant's recorded or unrecorded leasehold interest without a tenant-executed *subordination agreement.* Automatic subordination agreements are not enforceable.

Tenant refusal to sign

However, the tenant may properly refuse to sign a subordination agreement when the financing terms are not substantially similar or within the parameters of the subordination clause in the lease agreement. The tenant has not agreed to subject their lease to the uncertainties of a greater risk of loss than the risks established by the terms of the lease agreement's future subordination clause.

Editor's note — When the landlord wants to record a new trust deed to secure a mortgage and the tenant refuses to sign a specific subordination agreement, the landlord's primary recourse is to serve a three-day notice to perform or quit. When performance is not forthcoming, the landlord may file a UD action to evict the tenant or file an action against the tenant for declaratory relief and specific performance of the future subordination clause in the tenant's lease agreement.

Nondisturbance and subordination clauses

A **nondisturbance clause** gives the tenant the right to require a new trust deed lender to enter into a written agreement with the tenant, called a **nondisturbance agreement**. The *nondisturbance agreement* states the tenant's leasehold interest will remain in effect for its full term under the lease agreement after the leasehold is subordinated to a new mortgage.

A nondisturbance clause is included in a lease agreement only when the lease agreement also contains a *future subordination clause*. The tenant is the primary beneficiary of the *nondisturbance clause*.

nondisturbance clause
A lease agreement provision which is coupled with the future subordination clause to allow a tenant's junior leasehold interest to remain unaffected by a lender's foreclosure under a senior trust deed. [See **RPI** Form 552-8]

A nondisturbance clause is typically used by the landlord and leasing agents to avoid negotiating the terms of a subordination clause with the tenant when initially hammering out the terms of the lease agreement.

When the nondisturbance clause and an enforceable future subordination clause are included in a lease agreement, the tenant may refuse to sign a subordination agreement unless the lender provides the tenant with a nondisturbance agreement. Any standoff between the tenant and the lender poses a serious problem to a landlord attempting to record financing.

Informed lenders on originating a mortgage secured by a first trust deed are not likely to provide a tenant with a nondisturbance agreement when a tenant has agreed to subordinate their leasehold to the lender's trust deed lien. Without the subordination of the leasehold to the new trust deed, no reason exists for the tenant to have a nondisturbance agreement.

A nondisturbance agreement negates the effect of the subordination agreement by reversing the very priorities agreed to by subordinating the leasehold to the trust deed, a sort of *self-destruct provision*. The lease, in effect, will not be subordinate to the lender's trust deed if the lender agrees to recognize the continued existence of the leasehold after a foreclosure of the trust deed.

> **nondisturbance agreement**
> An agreement with mortgage lender providing for the tenant's lease agreement to remain in effect for its full term after the leasehold is subordinated to a new mortgage.

A knowledgeable landlord, contrary to the needs of a tenant, does not want a nondisturbance clause in the lease agreement. Landlords are better served by an enforceable *future subordination clause*.

Unlike the purpose of an attornment clause, a leasehold that is subject to a nondisturbance agreement will not be eliminated by foreclosure nor need to be later restored by election of the owner-by-foreclosure. The nondisturbance agreement states the leasehold will remain in effect for its full term without regard to foreclosure.

Since the leasehold subject to a nondisturbance agreement with the lender is not extinguished by foreclosure, it cannot also be junior to the trust deed.

Thus, a subordination of the leasehold to the trust deed does not occur when the lender concurrently enters into a nondisturbance agreement.

Also, when a new lender executes a nondisturbance agreement, an attornment clause serves no purpose for the lender's trust deed rights. Like many clauses in some lease agreements, it makes other provisions superfluous.

The tenant's possession and lease agreement when subject to a nondisturbance agreement remains undisturbed and continuously enforceable by both the tenant and the owner-by-foreclosure after the foreclosure sale.

By entering into a nondisturbance agreement, the lender (or other high-bidder at the foreclosure sale) is forced to become the landlord under the lease agreement if the lender forecloses.

A landlord eliminates the issue of a nondisturbance clause in a lease agreement by their leasing agent negotiating an enforceable future subordination clause outlining the mortgage parameters acceptable to both the landlord and the tenant when entering into the lease. By doing so, the landlord placates both the tenant and any future lenders that might otherwise balk at a lease agreement requiring the landlord to deliver a nondisturbance agreement from a new lender.

Future subordination clause benefits the landlord

Chapter 59 Summary

Commercial lease agreements often contain boilerplate provisions relating to the priority of the leasehold against trust deeds, present and future. These provisions include:

- attornment clauses;
- lender subordination clauses;
- future subordination clauses; and
- nondisturbance clauses.

An attornment clause allows an owner-by-foreclosure who acquires title at a foreclosure sale on a senior trust deed to unilaterally avoid the automatic elimination and unenforceability of a junior leasehold by the foreclosure sale.

A lender subordination clause gives a senior trust deed lender the right to unilaterally subordinate the lender's trust deed to a previously junior leasehold interest by written notice to the tenant.

Under a future subordination clause, the tenant agrees to subordinate their leasehold interest in the property to a trust deed to be recorded in the future.

A nondisturbance clause, when coupled with a detail-deficient future subordination provision, allows a tenant's junior leasehold interest to remain unaffected by a foreclosure under a new trust deed which is given priority to the lease.

Chapter 59 Key Terms

Quiz 15 Covering Chapters 58-62 is located on page 648.

Chapter

60

Tenant estoppel certificate

**Learning
Objectives**

After reading this chapter, you will be able to:

- understand the obligations imposed by a Tenant Estoppel Certificate (TEC); and
- use a TEC on the sale or financing of tenant-occupied property.

Key Terms

annual property operating data sheet (APOD)	**Tenant Estoppel Certificate (TEC)**

Protection for buyers and lenders

A real estate broker representing an owner who wants to sell or refinance their tenant-occupied property customarily prepares an **annual property operating data sheet (APOD)** form to be included in the marketing package. The completed *APOD* is handed to prospective buyers and lenders to induce them to enter into a transaction with the owner. [See **RPI** Form 352]

An APOD prepared on a due diligence review of the property provides buyers and lenders with an accurate summary of financial information on the operating income and expenses generated by the property.

Buyers and lenders who rely on APOD figures need to corroborate the income and expense numbers and other leasing arrangements prior to closing. A strategic method is to condition the closing on their receipt and further approval of **Tenant Estoppel Certificates (TEC)**, one signed and returned by each tenant occupying the property. [See Form 598 accompanying this chapter]

The *TEC* summarizes the financial and possessory terms of the tenant's lease agreement, and whether the landlord and tenant have fully performed their obligations.

> **annual property operating data sheet (APOD)**
> A worksheet used when gathering income and expenses on the operation of an income producing property, to analyze its suitability for investment. [See **RPI** Form 352]

Tenant Estoppel Certificate (TEC)
A statement which summarizes the monetary and possessory terms of a lease agreement, and whether the landlord and tenant have fully performed their obligations. [See **RPI** Form 598]

The objective of the TEC is to confirm the current status of:

- rent schedules;
- security deposits;
- possessory and acquisition rights; and
- the responsibility for maintenance and other operating or carrying costs.

Thus, the TEC will reveal any option or first refusal rights held by the tenant to:

- extend or renew the lease;
- buy the property;
- lease other or additional space; or
- cancel the lease on payment of a fee.

However, the lease agreement needs to contain a TEC provision before the owner may require a tenant to sign and return a TEC to confirm the leasing arrangements. [See Figure 1; see **RPI** Form 552 §18]

The TEC provision calls for the tenant to:

- sign and return a TEC, which has been filled out and sent to them, within a specific period of time after its receipt; or
- waive their right to contest its contents if the tenant fails to sign and return the TEC submitted for their signature.

Tenant response on receipt of a TEC

In addition, a TEC includes a statement indicating a buyer or lender will rely on the information provided by the TEC when making a decision to lend or purchase. [See **RPI** Form 598 §10]

In the TEC, the tenant acknowledges the accuracy of its contents by either:

- signing and returning it; or
- failing to respond, which waives the right to contest the accuracy of its contents.

Either way, a buyer or lender may rely on the TEC's content as complete and correct statements on the terms and condition of the lease.[1]

The properly submitted TEC prevents any later claims made by the tenant in a dispute with the buyer or lender that its terms are in conflict with the contents of the lease agreement.

A buyer or lender asserts their right to rely on and enforce the terms stated in the TEC by presenting the tenant's TEC as a defense to bar contrary claims made by the tenant, called **estoppel**. Thus, the tenant is *estopped* from denying the truth of the information in the TEC or later claiming conflicting rights.

---

1 Calif. Evidence Code §623

Figure 1

Excerpt from Form 552

Gross — Single Tenant

> **18. TENANT ESTOPPEL CERTIFICATES:**
>
> 18.1 Within 10 days after notice, Tenant will execute a Tenant Estoppel Certificate verifying the existing terms of the lease agreement to be provided to prospective buyers or lenders. [See **RPI** Form 598]
>
> 18.2 Failure by Tenant to deliver the Certificate to Landlord will be conclusive evidence the information contained in the Certificate is correct.

Security deposits confirmed

Lease agreements entered into by tenants and the seller of income property are assigned to a buyer by the seller on the close of a sale. As part of the adjustments and prorates at closing, the buyer requires the seller, through escrow, to account for any security deposits collected from the tenants. The amount of the remaining security deposits goes to the buyer as part of the escrow process, called **adjustments**.

With a TEC, the tenant confirms the accounting and dollar amount of security remaining on deposit with the seller. Thus, the TEC avoids the transfer of insufficient amounts of security deposits on closing and establishes the extent of the buyer's liability for refunds due the tenant.

The buyer needs to condition their purchase on receipt of TECs to confirm the current accounting of the security deposits. Otherwise, the buyer may be required to pay tenants more than the security deposit amounts they received from the seller on closing.[2]

Any deficiency in the amount of credit the buyer receives on closing for security deposits the buyer is later required to pay to the tenants is recovered by pursuing the seller.

TEC substantiates prior representations

A completed APOD form received by a buyer presents an accounting summary of a property's income and expenses. It represents the present income flow and operating expenses a prospective buyer can expect the property to generate in the immediate future.

Prior to closing, the buyer needs to:

- review and analyze all the lease agreements the owner has entered into with the tenants;

- compare the results of an analysis of rent and maintenance provisions in the lease agreements to the figures in the APOD received before the offer was submitted; and

- confirm the rent schedules, possessory rights, maintenance obligations and expiration of the leases by serving conforming TECs on the tenants and reviewing their responses before closing.

---

2 Calif. Civil Code §1950.5(i)

Form 598

Tenant Estoppel
Certificate

TENANT ESTOPPEL CERTIFICATE

NOTE: This form is used by an escrow officer or owner's broker when handling the sale or refinance of a tenant-occupied property which is contingent on confirmation of rents, deposits and other leasing arrangements between the tenant and owner, to provide the buyer or lender a summary of the financial and possessory terms of the tenant's lease agreement and whether the owner and tenant have fully performed their obligations.

DATE: _____, 20 _____, at _____, California.
Items left blank or unchecked are not applicable.

FACTS:

1. This certificate pertains to terms and conditions under the following agreement:
    □ Lease agreement   □ Month-to-month rental agreement   □_____
    1.1 dated _____, 20_____, at _____, California.
    1.2 entered into by _____, as the Landlord,
    1.3 and _____, as the Tenant,
    1.4 regarding real estate referred to as _____
    _____

STATEMENT:
Tenant certifies as follows:

2. The rental or lease agreement is:
    □ Unmodified and in effect.
    □ Modified and in effect under a modification agreement dated _____, 20 _____.
3. Tenant is in possession of the premises, and has not assigned or sublet any portion of the premises, except _____.
4. If the agreement is a lease, the current term is for _____ years, ending _____, 20_____.
    4.1 Lease term under all renewal/extension options will run until _____, 20 _____.
    4.2 Tenant holds no privilege to terminate the lease prior to its expiration.
5. The amount of monthly rent is $_____.
    5.1 No incentives, bonuses, free rent, discounts or refunds on the rental amount were given Tenant, except _____.
    5.2 Rent is paid through the period ending _____, 20 _____.
    5.3 Tenant has not prepaid future rent, except the amount of $_____ for the rental period of _____.
    5.4 No Tenant liens, claims, offsets or charges exist against Landlord, except _____.
6. A security deposit of $_____ is held by Landlord to cover any expenses or losses caused by Tenant's breach of the agreement.
7. Personal property in Tenant's possession and owned by Landlord includes _____.
8. Any improvements required to have been made by Landlord or Tenant have been satisfactorily completed.
9. No breach of the agreement by Landlord or Tenant presently exists, except _____.
10. Tenant holds no contract, option or right of first refusal or other right to buy any interest in the real estate.
    10.1 Tenant holds no right to lease additional or substitute space in the real estate.
11. Tenant has caused no lien or encumbrance to attach to the leasehold interest in the property.
12. Tenant understands this certificate will be relied on by a buyer of the property or a lender secured by the real estate.
13. _____
    _____

I certify the above is true and correct.
Date: _____, 20_____
Tenant's Name: _____

Signature: _____
Phone: _____ Fax: _____

FORM 598   03-11   ©2016 RPI — Realty Publications, Inc., P.O. BOX 5707, RIVERSIDE, CA 92517

Close on receipt of TECs

When signed and delivered to the buyer, the TEC statement reflects the financial and possessory arrangements existing at the time the tenant signs and returns the TEC.

Consider a tenant who signs and returns a TEC that is reviewed and approved by the buyer. However, before escrow closes, the seller breaches, modifies or enters into other leasing arrangements with the tenant.

The seller's post-TEC activities are not noted on the TEC, and will be unknown to the buyer when escrow closes unless brought to the buyer's attention. Thus, on receiving the TECs, a buyer or lender needs to review them and close the transaction as soon as possible to avoid a change in conditions in the interim.

The Tenant Estoppel Certificate (TEC) verifies the following:

- *whether possession is held under a lease or rental agreement;*
- *the current monthly amount of rent and the basis for rent increases;*
- *the date rent is paid each month;*
- *the date to which rent has been paid;*
- *any incentives given to obtain the tenant;*
- *whether the tenant has prepaid any rents;*
- *the term of the lease and whether an early cancellation privilege exists;*
- *whether and in what manner the lease/rental agreement has been modified;*
- *whether the tenant holds any options to renew or extend, acquire additional or substitute space, or a right of first refusal to rent vacated space;*
- *whether the tenant holds any options to buy the real estate;*
- *the amount and status of any security deposit;*
- *any improvements the tenant needs to or can remove on vacating the premises;*
- *any landlord commitments to further improve the premises;*
- *whether the landlord or tenant is in breach of the lease or the rental agreement; and*
- *whether the tenant has assigned or sublet the premises, or liened their leasehold interest.*

Figure 2

Status of the lease

Consequence of no TEC

A buyer or lender may be confronted at the time of closing with a tenant who has not signed and returned a TEC. Before closing, it is good practice for the buyer and their agent to investigate whether differences actually exist between the owner's representations on the TEC and the tenant's expectations under the lease agreement.

The buyer or lender may legally rely on the contents of an unreturned TEC when the tenant's lease agreement contains a TEC clause. However, an inquiry by the buyer or their agent into the tenant's failure to return the TEC is a prudent measure to prevent future surprises.

Consider an owner of income-producing real estate who needs to generate cash. They will do so by borrowing money using the equity in their property as security for repayment of the mortgage.

Tenants occupy the property under lease agreements that include options to renew at fixed rental rates. The lender does not condition the origination of the mortgage on the lender's receipt and approval of TECs from each tenant. The lender, unfamiliar with real estate ownership interests, makes the mortgage based on the value of comparable properties without regard for a schedule of the tenants' rent. [See **RPI** Form 380]

The owner defaults. The lender forecloses and acquires the property at the trustee's sale. As the new owner, the lender reviews the rent being paid by the tenants.

Consider a tenant who signs and returns unaltered a Tenant Estoppel Certificate (TEC) on the landlord's sale of commercial property. The TEC is erroneously prepared, stating an expiration date earlier than the date for termination provided in the lease agreement.

The buyer relies on the TEC and purchases the property. The tenant remains in possession of the premises after the expiration date stated in the TEC. The buyer seeks to enforce the expiration date in the TEC by filing an unlawful detainer (UD) action to evict the tenant.

The tenant claims the buyer cannot enforce the expiration date in the TEC by a UD action since the TEC was not a written agreement modifying the lease, binding them to a different expiration date than actually stated in the lease agreement. The buyer claims the tenant is barred from contradicting the expiration date stated in the TEC.

*Here, the new landlord may enforce the expiration date in the TEC and evict the tenant by a UD action. The TEC is a statement signed by the tenant certifying facts with respect to the lease which were relied on by the buyer. Thus, the tenant is barred from later using the contrary provision in the lease agreement to contradict the TEC. [**Plaza Freeway Limited Partnership v. First Mountain Bank** (2000) 81 CA4th 616]*

Consequence of no TEC, cont'd

The new owner decides to increase the rents to current market rates in order to bring the property's market value up to prices recently received on the sale of comparable properties. However, the tenants who occupied the premises before the lender's trust deed was recorded claim their lease agreements, which provide options to extend at old rental rates, are enforceable against the lender as the new owner.

The lender claims their foreclosure sale wiped out all the owner's rights in the property and established the lender as the new title holder with priority over the leases. Further, the lease agreements were not recorded.

May the tenants who occupied the property prior to the recording of the lender's trust deed enforce their renewal options even though their pre-existing lease agreements were not recorded?

Yes! The lender originating a trust deed mortgage on income-producing property they now own by foreclosure recorded the trust deed after the tenants were in possession of the property. Thus:

- the tenants' rights and obligations under lease agreements, recorded or not, retain priority over the lender's trust deed lien recorded after the tenants were in possession; and
- the lender is bound by the rent schedules in the pre-existing lease agreements and renewal/extension options because of the seniority of the leases.[3]

The tenants' occupancy of the premises prior to originating the mortgage puts the lender on constructive notice, or knowledge, of the lease agreements, renewal options and rent schedules.[4]

---

3   CC §1214
4   **Evans** v. **Faught** (1965) 231 CA2d 698

The condition for funding a motgage requiring lender approval of a TEC from each tenant informs the lender of the tenants' rights and obligations to occupy and pay rent and other amounts under their lease agreements.

The owner's scheduled future income needs to represent amounts the tenants expect to pay. Every buyer or lender acquiring an interest in income-producing real estate needs to require tenant approval of TECs based on lease arrangements the owner/seller purports to hold with each tenant.

Now consider a purchase agreement for commercial rental property that requires the seller to provide the buyer with TECs for the buyer's further approval or cancellation of the purchase agreement.

One tenant's lease agreement does not state the rent amounts but contains a formula for calculating rent. The seller instructs the buyer on how to calculate the rent due from the tenant based on the provisions in the tenant's lease agreement.

The seller enters the rent amounts on the TEC based on the same calculations given the buyer and sends it to the tenant to be signed and returned to the buyer.

The tenant refuses to sign the TEC since the tenant is not obligated under their lease agreement to provide a TEC. The seller hands the buyer a copy of the tenant's unsigned TEC to satisfy the purchase agreement condition. The buyer accepts it without further investigation and confirmation.

After escrow closes, the buyer discovers the tenant's actual rent is significantly lower than the seller's estimate. The buyer makes a demand on the seller for the difference between the actual rent paid by the tenant under the lease and the rent amounts calculated by the seller to be paid by the tenant.

Is the seller liable for the difference in the rent?

Yes! The buyer recovers lost rent from the seller in the amount of the difference between the seller's calculated estimate of rent and the actual amount owed by the tenant. The seller is obligated under the purchase agreement to provide the buyer with an accurate TEC. The buyer based their decision to purchase the property on representations made by the seller, not on the rent provisions in the lease agreement.[5]

The erroneous, unsigned TEC

A seller avoids liability for errors in the TEC prepared and sent to tenants by including a TEC clause in the tenant's lease agreement, calling for the tenant to sign and return a TEC on request. The failure of the tenant to provide the TEC as called for in the lease agreement is conclusive evidence any contrary information contained in the TEC is correct. [See Figure 1]

Thus, a tenant's refusal to sign a TEC when a TEC clause exists in the lease agreement results in the tenant, not the seller, being liable for the erroneous rent amount stated in the TEC prepared by the seller.

Sellers avoid liability

---

5 **Linden Partners** v. **Wilshire Linden Associates** (1998) 62 CA4th 508

Chapter 60 Summary

The Tenant Estoppel Certificate (TEC) summarizes the monetary and possessory terms of the lease agreement, and whether the landlord and tenant have fully performed their obligations.

The objective of the TEC is to confirm the current status of:
- rent schedules;
- security deposits;
- possessory and acquisition rights; and
- the responsibility for maintenance and other operating or carrying costs.

Thus, the TEC will reveal any option or first refusal rights held by the tenant to:
- extend or renew the lease;
- buy the property;
- lease other or additional space; or
- cancel the lease on payment of a fee.

Chapter 60 Key Terms

Quiz 15 Covering Chapters 58-62 is located on page 648.

Chapter 61

Due-on-leasing regulations

After reading this chapter, you will be able to:

- explain a lender's right to call or modify a mortgage under a due-on clause in a trust deed when the landlord leases the property for a period of more than three years or enters into a lease for any period when the lease is coupled with an option to buy;
- understand a lender's impetus to enforce the due-on clause in order to increase the interest yield on their portfolio in times of consistently rising interest rates;
- negotiate a waiver of the lender's due-on rights when entering into a lease, or limitation on the lender's due-on rights on origination of the mortgage; and
- discuss the liability imposed on a leasing agent who assists the landlord or tenant to hide the lease and purchase option from the lender in an effort to avoid due-on enforcement.

Learning Objectives

call	**recast**
due-on clause	**retroactive interest differential**

Key Terms

A property encumbered by a first trust deed containing a **due-on clause** is offered for sale or lease. The owner locates a tenant for the property. The tenant enters into a two-year lease agreement with an option to purchase the property.

Does the lease agreement and option to buy trigger the *due-on clause* in the trust deed and allow the lender to call the mortgage secured by the trust deed lien on the property?

Rising interest rates bring lender interference

Yes! A trust deed's due-on clause is triggered by a lease agreement for any period of time when coupled with an option to buy the property. Thus, the trust deed lender may call the mortgage on discovery of the lease-with-option transaction, and foreclose if not paid in full.[1]

Interference under federal mortgage law

When real estate is encumbered by a trust deed containing a due-on clause, the transfer of any interest in the real estate allows the lender to enforce the clause under federal mortgage law. Thus, by preemption, Californians are deprived of their state law right to lease, sell or further encumber real estate free of unreasonable lender interference.[2]

For the landlord of property encumbered by a trust deed, due-on enforcement is triggered by:

- leasing the property for a period of more than three years; or
- entering into a lease agreement for any period of time when coupled with an option to buy.

On the trust deed lender's discovery of these leasing arrangements, the lender may either:

- **call** the mortgage, also known as *accelerating the mortgage*, by demanding the remaining balance be paid in full; or
- **recast** the mortgage, requiring the mortgage terms be modified and additional fees be paid as a condition for the lender's consent to the triggering event, called a *formal assumption*.

call
A lender's demand for the balance of the mortgage to be immediately paid in full. [See **RPI** From 418-3]

recast
A mortgage holder's demand to modify the note terms and receive payment of additional fees in exchange for waiving the due-on clause in their mortgage.

Economics of the due-on clause

In times of consistently rising interest rates (as expected over the next two or three decades), lenders will seize on any opportunity to enforce the due-on clause as a method of increasing the interest yield on their portfolios. This enforcement shifts the lender's risk of loss due to rising interest rates to the property owner by increasing their payments. Federal policy favors this interference on the sale, lease or further encumbrance of any type of mortgaged real estate as a means of maintaining mortgage lender solvency.

due-on clause
A trust deed provision used by lenders to call the mortgage due and immediately payable, a right triggered by the owner's transfer of any interest in the real estate.

A real estate interest, be it an owner's fee simple or a tenant's leasehold estate, when encumbered by a due-on trust deed becomes increasingly difficult to transfer to new owners and tenants as interest rates rise. Lender interference is then virtually guaranteed in a relentless cyclical pursuit for ever higher portfolio yields.

The increasing inability of owners to lease their properties and retain existing financing has an adverse economic effect on real estate sales, equity financing and long-term leasing. Ultimately, as mortgage rates rise bringing on lender interference, many buyers, equity lenders and long-term tenants will be driven out of the market. The result is an increase in depressed property values due to the reduced ability to sell, lease, assign a lease or encumber an equity in real estate.

---

1   12 Code of Federal Regulations §591.2(b)
2   12 United States Code §1701j-3; Calif. Civil Code §711

Unless the existing lender's consent is obtained, the possibility of due-on enforcement and a call creates uncertainty for the landlord when leasing property with an initial or extension period longer than three years. The risk a lender will call rise as interest rates increase.

To best represent landlords and tenants, leasing agents need to understand which events trigger the lender's due-on clause, which do not, and how to avoid or handle the lender's consent.

Consider a landlord with a short-term interim construction mortgage on commercial rental property who obtains a conditional mortgage commitment from a lender for long-term, take-out financing.

Editor's note — Take-out financing is a commitment to provide permanent financing after a construction project has been completed and the requisite occupancy has been attained.

Funding of the take-out mortgage is conditioned on the property being 80% occupied by tenants with initial lease terms of at least five years.

The landlord locates tenants for 80% of the newly constructed property, all with lease terms of five years or more. The condition is met and the lender funds the mortgage. The trust deed securing the mortgage contains a due-on clause.

The five-year leases already entered into to qualify for the refinancing precede the recording of the refinancing. Thus, the leases do not trigger the due-on clause in the new lender's trust deed.

However, after recording the trust deed, the landlord continues to lease space on their property for five-year terms. None of the new leases are submitted to the lender for approval. Thus, no waiver of the due-on clause is obtained before entering into these leases.

In a few months, mortgage interest rates rise. Then, an officer of the lender visits the property or requests a rent roll and discovers new tenants. The officer learns the new tenants have five-year leases.

The lender sends a letter informing the landlord that the lender is calling the mortgage since "It has recently come to our attention..." that the landlord has entered into lease agreements with terms longer than three years without first obtaining the lender's consent. This is an incurable violation of the due-on clause in the trust deed.

The landlord claims the lender cannot call the mortgage since the lender required medium-term leases as a condition for funding the mortgage. Thus, the lender is *estopped* from invoking the due-on clause.

Can the lender call the mortgage due or demand a recast of its terms?

Due-on-leasing clauses

Yes! Requiring leases with terms exceeding three years as a condition for funding the mortgage did not waive the lender's right to later call or recast the mortgage when the landlord entered five-year leases after the trust deed was recorded.

It has recently come to our attention...

When a trust deed lien encumbers income property, the landlord prior to entering into a lease agreement is to:

- obtain consent from the lender before leasing;
- lease the property for an initial three-year period with options to extend for three-year periods; or
- negotiate the elimination of the due-on clause from the trust deed.

Assignment or modification of the lease

The tenant's assignment of their leasehold interest in property does not trigger the due-on clause in a trust deed encumbering the landlord's fee interest. However, a modification of an existing lease agreement triggers the due-on clause if:

- the modification extends the term beyond three years from the date of modification;
- the modification adds a purchase option.

For example, consider a landlord who enters into a long-term lease agreement with a tenant. Later, the landlord takes out a mortgage secured by a trust deed containing a due-on clause.

After the trust deed is recorded, the tenant assigns their leasehold interest in the property which has more than three years remaining to another person who will take occupancy, all with the landlord's approval, as agreed to in the lease agreement.

Here, the lender's due-on clause is not triggered by the lease assignment. The lender's trust deed only encumbers the landlord's fee interest, subject to the outstanding leasehold. The trust deed does not encumber the leasehold interest owned by the tenant (which if it did would produce a different result). Thus, the tenant's assignment of their unencumbered leasehold does not trigger the lender's due-on clause in the trust deed lien on the fee ownership. The leasehold assignment was not a transfer of the fee interest which is the lender's security.

However, consider a landlord who enters into a release of liability with the original tenant, releasing the tenant from all liability under the lease agreement as part of an assumption of the lease by a new tenant. A trust deed with a due-on clause encumbers the landlord's fee interest, whether the trust deed is junior or senior to the lease.

Here, the release of the original tenant from the lease agreement coupled with an assumption of the lease agreement by the new tenant creates a

novation. The *novation* legally cancels the original lease agreement and establishes a new lease agreement with the landlord conveying an interest in the secured property to the new tenant on the same terms.[3]

Thus, the lender's due-on clause has been triggered if the lease "assumed" by the tenant on the novation has a remaining term of over three years or includes an option to purchase.

With the federal due-on regulation, lenders have the power to dictate the fate of most long-term real estate leasing transactions since most real estate is encumbered by trust deeds.

However, a landlord intending to lease their real estate and avoid lender interference needs to consider:

- eliminating or placing some limitation on a lender's due-on-clause use when negotiating the origination of the trust deed mortgage; or

- negotiating a waiver of the lender's due-on rights when entering into a lease. [See Chapters 41 and 50]

Waiver agreements are basically trade-offs. The lender will demand some consideration in return for waiving or agreeing to an elimination or limitation of its future due-on rights. This consideration can take the form of increased points on origination, additional security, increased interest, a shorter due date and an assumption fee for each consent. [See **RPI** Form 410]

The lender's waiver of its due-on rights applies only to the current lease transaction under review for consent. Unless additionally agreed, any later leasing of the property will again trigger the due-on clause, allowing the lender to call or recast the mortgage again, due in part to the *nonwaiver provision* in the trust deed.

Besides obtaining a written waiver agreement, waiver of the lender's due-on rights may occur by conduct. When a lender fails to promptly enforce its due-on rights upon gaining knowledge of a lease transaction, the lender loses its right to later enforce the clause based on that lease.

For example, a landlord enters into a lease agreement for a term exceeding three years. The leased property is encumbered by a mortgage secured by a trust deed containing a due-on clause. The lender is informed of the leasing arrangements by letter or during an annual audit.

The lender then calls the mortgage under its due-on clause based on the lease transaction disclosed or delivered. However, the lender continues to accept payments from the landlord for 12 months after the call, stating it is unilaterally reserving its due-on rights. The lender has no further contact regarding the call.

Here, the lender by its conduct waived the right to enforce the due-on clause. The lender accepted payments from the landlord for an extended period of time after calling the mortgage.[4]

Negotiations and conduct as waiver

---

3   **Wells Fargo Bank, N.A.** v. **Bank of America NT & SA** (1995) 32 CA4th 424

4   **Rubin** v. **Los Angeles Federal Savings and Mortgage Association** (1984) 159 CA3d 292

Broker liability for due-on avoidance

Again, a lender can call the mortgage only when it discovers a lease agreement with a term longer than three years, or a lease with an option to buy.

If the tenant's option to purchase is not recorded and the lease agreement is for a term under three years, the lender might not discover the transfer which triggered its due-on clause.

However, if the lender later discovers the lease with its option to purchase, the lender's only remedy against the landlord or the tenant is to call the mortgage due, or agree to recast the mortgage as a condition for retroactively waiving its right to call.

The lender cannot recover any **retroactive interest differential** from the landlord or tenant for a higher rate they would have charged at the time the clause was actually triggered. Also, if the lender calls the mortgage, it cannot add the *retroactive interest differential* to the mortgage payoff amount.[5]

However, an advisor, such as a leasing agent or attorney, assisting the landlord or tenant to hide the lease and option to purchase from the lender to avoid due-on enforcement may be found to have wrongfully interfered with the lender's legal right to call or recast the mortgage.

Thus, the advisor may be held liable for the lender's losses, called **tortious interference** *with prospective economic advantage*.

The advisor's liability is dependent upon:

- the extent the actions were intended to conceal the lease agreement and prevent a call by the lender; and
- the foresight that the advisor had regarding the lender's likely losses due to the concealment.[6]

The lender's losses caused by the advisor's wrongful interference are calculated based on the interest differential between the note rate and the market rate at the time the lease commenced, retroactive to the date of the commencement. Hence, the title of *retroactive interest differential*.

retroactive interest differential
The mortgage holder's losses, calculated based on the interest differential between the note rate and the market rate on the date of a third party's unlawful interference with the mortgage holder's right to call a mortgage.

---

5   **Hummell v. Republic Fed. Savings and Mortgage Assn.** (1982) 133 CA3d 49
6   **J'Aire Corporation v. Gregory** (1979) 24 C3d 799

In times of consistently rising interest rates, lenders seize on any opportunity to enforce the due-on clause in order to increase the interest yield on their portfolios.

For the landlord of property encumbered by a trust deed, due-on enforcement is triggered by:

- leasing the property for a period of more than three years; or
- entering into a lease agreement for any period of time when the lease agreement is coupled with an option to buy.

When the trust deed lender discovers these leasing arrangements, the lender may either call or recast the mortgage.

A landlord intending to lease their real estate and avoid lender interference needs to consider:

- eliminating or placing some limitation on a lender's due-on-clause use when negotiating the origination of the mortgage; or
- negotiating a waiver of the lender's due-on rights when entering into a lease.

Chapter 61 Summary

due-on clause .... pg. 602
call .... pg. 602
recast .... pg. 602
retroactive interest differential .... pg. 606

Chapter 61 Key Terms

Quiz 15 Covering Chapters 58-62 is located on page 648.

Notes:

Gaining possession after foreclosure

Chapter

62

After reading this chapter, you will be able to:
- understand how to evict tenants using proper notices; and
- identify special protections granted to tenants of a foreclosed property.

owner-by-foreclosure   **unlawful detainer**

Learning Objectives

Key Terms

A residential income property is encumbered by a recorded trust deed. Tenants occupy the property under *month-to-month rental agreements* entered into after the trust deed was recorded. [See **RPI** Form 551]

Payments on the trust deed note are delinquent, causing the lender to initiate a trustee's **foreclosure**.

Prior to the foreclosure sale, the lender employs a broker to inspect the physical condition of the improvements and determine the property's fair market value for immediate resale.

Based on the broker's inspection and market review, they advise the lender to:

- complete the foreclosure proceedings;
- evict all tenants;
- renovate the property;
- relet the property to creditworthy tenants at market rates; and
- sell the property.

The lender acquires the property at the trustee's sale.

Notice required to remove occupants

To meet the resale objectives recommended by the broker, the lender wants the tenants to immediately vacate the property. The property now owned by the lender is referred to as **real estate owned (REO)** property.

The broker has each tenant served with a 90-day notice to quit due to foreclosure. [See Form 573 accompanying this chapter]

Have the tenants been properly notified and thus required to vacate the premises?

Yes! The residential tenants whose unexpired month-to-month rental agreements were junior (in time) to the recording of the trust deed, and thus eliminated by the foreclosure sale, are entitled to 90 days written notice to vacate.[1]

owner-by-foreclosure
The winning bidder at a trustee's sale who takes title to the property sold on a trustee's deed.

After the expiration of the 90-day notice to vacate, a residential tenant under a month-to-month rental agreement who does not vacate the foreclosed property, may be evicted by the **owner-by-foreclosure** in an **unlawful detainer (UD)** action. This general rule does not apply to rent controlled or Section 8 properties.

unlawful detainer
The unlawful possession of a property. [See **RPI** Form 575 -578]

Evicting occupants after foreclosure

A rental or lease agreement entered into after a trust deed is recorded is wiped out on completion of a foreclosure sale on the trust deed.

If a prior owner or occupant under a junior rental or lease agreement remains in possession after a foreclosure sale, the new *owner-by-foreclosure* may serve the appropriate notice to quit due to foreclosure. They may remove the occupants, residential or commercial, in a *UD* eviction action.

An owner-by-foreclosure is defined as a buyer of real estate which is sold at:

- a sheriff's sale on a judgment lien;
- a judicial foreclosure sale; or
- a trustee's foreclosure sale.[2]

An owner-by-foreclosure follows different rules to evict occupants remaining in possession of the foreclosed property under a wiped-out lease or month-to-month rental agreement.

Evicting residential tenants

A tenant who occupies a residential property under a periodic tenancy at the time the property is sold in foreclosure needs to receive at least 90 days' written notice to quit.

Residential tenants with a fixed-term lease entered into prior to the foreclosure sale have the right to possess the rented property until the end of their lease, unless:

- the new owner will use the property as their primary residence;

---

1   Calif. Code of Civil Procedure §1161b
2   CCP §1161a(b)

- the tenant is the owner of the property who defaulted on the mortgage;
- the tenant is the child, spouse or parent of the owner who defaulted;
- the lease was not the result of an arm's length transaction; or
- the rent was substantially less than fair market rent without subsidization or reduction per court order.

A fixed-term tenancy can be terminated for any of the above reasons by serving the tenant with a 90-day notice to quit. [See **RPI** Form 573]

The new owner bears the burden of proof in establishing the tenant is not eligible to possess the property through the end of the lease term.

This law will sunset on December 31, 2019.[3]

Additionally, tenants living in Section 8 housing or rent control communities are protected from unqualified termination of their occupancy after a foreclosure sale.

The appropriate period of notice to vacate due to foreclosure depends on whether:

- the property is residential or commercial; and
- the occupants are former tenants or former owners.

Unlike a residential tenant, a commercial tenant whose junior lease is wiped out by a foreclosure is only entitled to a three-day notice to quit, regardless of whether the tenant paid rent monthly, quarterly or annually.[4]

A former owner who remains as an occupant is only entitled to a three-day notice to quit, whether the property is residential or commercial.[5]

Thus, to remove a commercial tenant or the former owner of a property, the owner-by-foreclosure serves them with a three-day notice to quit due to foreclosure. On expiration of the three days after service of the notice and the failure of the prior owner or the tenant to vacate, a UD is established. Thus, the tenant may be evicted by court order. [See **RPI** Form 578]

A notice to quit due to foreclosure is served in the same manner as a three-day notice to pay rent or quit.[6] [See Chapter 25]

An attempt at personal service on the occupant is first made at both the occupant's residence and place of business, if known.[7]

Evicting commercial tenants

Service of notice

---

3 CCP §1161b(f)
4 CCP §1161a(b)
5 CCP §1161a(b)
6 CCP §1161a(b)
7 CCP §1162

90-DAY NOTICE TO QUIT DUE TO FORECLOSURE
To Holdover Residential Tenant

NOTE: This form is used by an owner-by-foreclosure, a successor owner or their agent when they have acquired ownership of residential property at or following a foreclosure sale and seek removal of a tenant who occupied the property at the time of the foreclosure sale, to notify the tenant to vacate within 90 days.

DATE: _____, 20_____, at _____, California.
TO FORMER RESIDENTIAL TENANT: _____
Items left blank or unchecked are not applicable.

The attached notice means that your home was recently sold in foreclosure and the new owner plans to evict you.

You should talk to a lawyer NOW to see what your rights are. You may receive court papers in a few days. If your name is on the papers it may hurt your credit if you do not respond or simply move out.
Also, if you do not respond within five days of receiving the papers, even if you are not named in the papers, you will likely lose any rights you may have. In some cases, you can respond without hurting your credit. You should ask a lawyer about it.

You may have the right to stay in your home for longer than 90 days. If you have a lease that ends more than 90 days from now, the new owner must honor the lease under many circumstances. Also, in some cases and in some cities with a "just cause for eviction law," you may not have to move at all. But you must take the proper legal steps in order to protect your rights.

How to Get Legal Help
If you cannot afford an attorney, you may be eligible for free legal services from a nonprofit legal services program. You can locate these nonprofit groups at the California Legal Services Internet Web site (*www.lawhelpca.org*), the California Courts Online Self-Help Center (*www.courtinfo.ca.gov/selfhelp*), or by contacting your local court or county bar association.

FACTS:

1. You were a residential Tenant under a rental or lease agreement
   1.1 dated _____, 20_____, at _____, California,
   1.2 entered into by _____, as the Tenant,
   1.3 and _____, as the Landlord,
   1.4 regarding real estate referred to as _____
   _____

NOTICE:

2. On _____, 20_____, the real estate you occupy was sold at a foreclosure sale which extinguished your interest in the property.

3. Within ninety (90) days after service of this notice, you are required to vacate and deliver possession of the premises to the new owner-by-foreclosure, or _____
   _____

4. If you fail to vacate and deliver possession within ninety (90) days, legal proceedings will be initiated to regain possession of the premises and to recover money damages for wrongful possession and costs.

Owner-by-foreclosure:
☐ See attached Signature Page Addendum. [RPI Form 251]
Date: _____, 20_____
Name: _____

Signature: _____
Address: _____

Phone: _____ Cell: _____
Email: _____

FORM 573   10-12   ©2016 RPI — Realty Publications, Inc., P.O. BOX 5707, RIVERSIDE, CA 92517

If the occupant cannot be located for personal service, the server may leave the notice with a person of suitable age and discretion at the occupant's residence or business address, and mail the notice to the occupant's residence, called substituted service.[8]

Finally, if no person of suitable age or discretion is available at either the occupant's residence or place of business, the server may post the notice on the leased premises and mail a copy to the premises, called service by **"nail and mail."**[9]

8 CCP §1162(a)(2), §1162(b)(2)
9 CCP §1162(a)(3), §1162(b)(3)

The day after the notice is served is day one of the period during which the occupant needs to vacate.[10]

In a UD action, an owner-by-foreclosure is entitled to recover rent from the occupant. The amount recoverable is the reasonable rental value of the property for the period the occupant resides on the property after the foreclosure sale, not the penalty holdover rate.[11]

UD award of rental value

The secured lender who acquires the premises at the foreclosure sale cannot collect unpaid pre-foreclosure rents in a UD action.

However, any rents which were due and unpaid by a tenant before the foreclosure sale belong to the lender under an assignment of rents provision in the lender's trust deed. These unpaid rents are collectable in a separate action unrelated to the UD action, called **specific performance** of the assignment of rents provision.

When residential income property subject to local rent control ordinances or a Section 8 contract is acquired by an owner-by-foreclosure, the owner-by-foreclosure needs to comply with the ordinances and Section 8 rules.

UD action as a remedy, not a right

Consider a trust deed lender who forecloses on residential rental units by a trustee's sale and acquires the property at the foreclosure sale. The lender wants to remove the former tenants under wiped-out rental or lease agreements. The lender intends to renovate the property and resell it.

The lender, now the owner-by-foreclosure, serves each tenant with a statutory 90-day notice to quit due to foreclosure. However, the property is located in a rent control community.

The occupants claim they cannot be evicted by the lender since the rent control ordinance does not permit eviction on a change of ownership. The rent control ordinances limit the circumstances which are cause for a tenant to be evicted. Change of ownership for any reason is not a permitted basis for eviction of a tenant protected by rent control.

The lender claims the tenants can be evicted due to foreclosure since the local ordinance is preempted by state law allowing a tenant to be evicted after a foreclosure sale.

Can the tenants be evicted by the lender since the lender is an owner-by-foreclosure?

No! Residential tenants protected under rent control ordinances cannot be evicted after a foreclosure, except as permitted by local ordinances. The 90-day notice requirement for evicting a residential tenant after a foreclosure sale in a UD action does not preempt the local rent control ordinance. [See Form 573]

---

10 Calif. Civil Code §10
11 CCP §1174(b)

No tenancy for wiped-out occupants

An occupant of property whose leasehold or ownership interest has been eliminated by foreclosure has no right to possession and is not a tenant. Any landlord/tenant relationship under the rental agreement or lease which was junior to the foreclosing lienholder is wiped out at the foreclosure sale.

No tenancy in real estate is recognized for occupants who lost their possessory interest due to a foreclosure. The wiped-out occupant, whether they are a prior owner or held a tenancy interest in the property, is not a holdover tenant, and thus is not a tenant-at-sufferance.

Also, the occupant is not a tenant-at-will since they did not occupy the property with the owner-by-foreclosure's consent.

Even though no landlord/tenant relationship exists, an owner-by-foreclosure is permitted to remove occupants from the foreclosed property by evicting them in an unlawful detainer (UD) action. [CCP §1161a(b)]

However, a buyer at a foreclosure sale does not qualify as an owner-by-foreclosure for a UD eviction of a prior occupant when the property is purchased at:

- *a federal or state tax lien sale;*
- *a property tax lien sale; or*
- *a Mello-Roos sale, or sale under other improvement bonds or government agency assessments.*

Purchasers of property at tax sales or improvement bond sales which are occupied:

- *are not permitted to remove occupants by filing a UD action; and*
- *are limited to filing an **ejectment action** against the occupant to recover possession of the premises*

While an ejectment action and a UD action are alternative remedies for recovering possession from occupants, the UD action is faster and less expensive, and thus more desirable for the owner-by-foreclosure.

The UD notice and eviction process merely provides a legal remedy for a lender who has grounds to recover possession from the tenants, in lieu of using self-help to remove tenants. Under rent control, it is the ordinance which establishes the grounds for the eviction of a tenant.[12]

---

12 **Gross** v. **Superior Court** (1985) 171 CA3d 265

Chapter 62 Summary

A rental or lease agreement entered into after a trust deed is recorded is wiped out on completion of a foreclosure sale on the trust deed.

If a prior owner or occupant under a junior rental or lease agreement remains in possession after a foreclosure sale, the new owner-by-foreclosure can serve the appropriate notice to quit due to foreclosure. They may remove the occupants, residential or commercial, in a UD eviction action.

A tenant who occupies a residential property under a periodic tenancy at the time the property is sold in foreclosure needs to receive at least 90 days' written notice to quit.

Unlike a residential tenant, a commercial tenant whose junior lease is wiped out by a foreclosure is only entitled to a three-day written notice to quit, regardless of whether the tenant paid rent monthly, quarterly or annually.

Chapter 62 Key Terms

owner-by-foreclosure ....pg. 610
unlawful detainer ....pg. 610

Quiz 15 Covering Chapters 58-62 is located on page 648.

Notes:

Glossary

A

abandonment **313**
A unilateral termination of a tenancy by forfeiture, delivered by the landlord based on notices from the landlord. [See **RPI** Form 581]

accommodation party **226**
An individual who signs a note to include liability for a debt evidenced by the note and receives no direct benefit from the debt.

ad valorem taxes **423**
Real estate taxes imposed on property based on its assessed value. [See **RPI** Form 552-2 §5.1]

addendum **510**
An attachment to a contract, rental or lease agreement for incorporating any provision agreed to but not included in the boilerplate provisions of the agreement. [See **RPI** Form 250]

agency duty **138**
The fiduciary duty a broker owes a client to use diligence in attaining the client's real estate goals. [See **RPI** Form 305]

agent-for-service clause **118**
A section in the property management agreement which appoints the owner's agent-for-service. [See **RPI** Form 590 §11.3]

agent-for-service process **117**
An individual who acts on behalf of the owner, accepting service of legal documents and notices initiated by tenants.

annual property operating data sheet (APOD) **593**
A worksheet used when gathering income and expenses on the operation of an income producing property to analyze its suitability for investment. [See **RPI** Form 352]

anti-competition clause **338**
A provision in the commercial lease agreement stating the landlord will not lease space in a commercial complex to competitors of the tenant.

applicant screening fee **175**
A nonrefundable fee charged to the tenant to reimburse the landlord for the cost to obtain the tenant's credit report.

appreciation-adjusted rent provision **441, 446**
A provision found in a commercial lease agreement which adjusts rent every several years to reflect an increase in the rental value of a property exceeding the rate of inflation brought about by local demographics. [See **RPI** Form 552 §4.5(e)]

appurtenance **464**
A right belonging to real estate owned by the landlord to use property located outside the leased premises for purposes such as parking or access.

assignment **261**
A tenant's sublease of a portion of the leased premises.

assumption **489**
The promise by a successor tenant to fully perform all obligations under the lease agreement they are taking over by assignment from the previous tenant.

attorney fees provision **420**
A provision in an agreement permitting the prevailing party in a dispute to receive attorney fees when litigation arises due to the agreement. [See **RPI** Form 552 §23.2]

attornment clause **583**
A lease agreement provision which allows an owner-by- foreclosure to unilaterally avoid the automatic elimination of a junior leasehold interest by a foreclosure sale and become a substitute landlord under the tenant's lease agreement. [See **RPI** Form 552-8 §3]

B

balance sheet **178**
An itemized, dollar-value presentation for setting an individual's net worth by subtracting debt obligations (liabilities) from asset values. [See **RPI** Form 209-3]

base rent **427, 438, 455**
The minimum monthly rent stated in a commercial lease agreement. [See **RPI** Form 552 §4.3]

blockbusting **537**
The prohibited practice of a residential landlord inducing or attempting to induce a person to offer, or abstain from offering a dwelling to prevent the entry of certain classes of people into a neighborhood.

bona fide lease agreement **298**
A lease agreement with a fair market rent held by a residential tenant when ownership of a property is transferred by a foreclosure sale. [See **RPI** Form 550]

bona fide purchaser **411**
A buyer of leased real estate who lacks knowledge that a lease agreement exists and purchases the property for valuable consideration or accepts the real estate as security for a debt.

business goodwill **45**
The earning power of a business.

C

call **602**
A lender's demand for the balance of the loan to be immediately paid in full. [See **RPI** Form 418-3]

call option **63**
An agreement giving a buyer the right to buy property within a specified time or upon an event at a specified price with terms for payment. [See **RPI** Form 161]

California Fair Employment and Housing Act (FEHA) **550**
Legislation which prohibits landlords from using discriminatory rental policies to avoid renting to a tenant based on familial status.

cancellation provision **290**
A lease agreement provision permitting the tenant to terminate their occupancy and rent obligation by paying a set sum of money.

certified CID manager **75**
A non-required professional designation certifying an individual has met legislated educational requirements specific to managing common interest developments.

choice-of-law provision **421**
A clause which sets the state law applicable in the event of a dispute. [See **RPI** Form 552 §23.4]

Civil Rights Act **533**
A federal law which provides broad protections to all persons in the United States against discriminatory activities.

commingling **101**
The mixing of personal funds with client or third-party funds held in trust.

common area maintenance charge **149**
Property operating expenses incurred by a commercial landlord and paid by the tenant as rent additional to the base rent, adjustments and percentages. [See **RPI** Form 552 §6]

common interest developments **85**
Condominium projects, cooperatives or single family residences in a planned unit development. [See **RPI** Form 135]

comparative cost analysis **146**
A comparison of the costs a tenant will incur to occupy and operate in a particular space against the costs to operate in other available space. [See **RPI** Form 562]

comparative negligence **402**
An injured person's share of the negligence causing their injury when the injured person's lack of care for themselves contributes to the injury.

compliance-with-laws clause **465**
A provision in a commercial lease agreement controlling the conduct of tenant activities on the property to conform with public laws, building ordinances or tenant association rules. [See **RPI** Form 552 §7.3]

compounded base rent **409**
Rent that adjusts yearly by a certain percentage of the prior year's rent.

constructive eviction **336**
A termination of the tenant's right of possession and cancellation of the lease agreement on vacating due to the landlord's failure to maintain the premise as stated in the lease. [See **RPI** Form 552 §6]

constructive notice **412**
To be charged with the knowledge observable or recorded conditions exist on the property. When a tenant occupies a property under a lease agreement, a buyer is charged with constructive notice of the tenant's leasehold interest by the occupancy.

consultation fee **138**
A fee the broker charges for the time spent locating rental property if the tenant decides not to lease space during the exclusive authorization period. [See **RPI** Form 111 §4.2]

Consumer Price Index (CPI) **446**
The CPI measures and tracks the rate of consumer inflation. This is presented as an index of fluctuations in the general price of a wide selection of consumable products – goods and services.

contingency fee **75**
An incentive bonus paid upon successfully completing or hitting certain benchmarks, or received as compensation on the occurrence of an event.

contingency fee clause **130**
A provision in an offer-to-lease which states the broker's fee is payable on the transfer of possession to the tenant. [See **RPI** Form 556 §15]

corporate resolution **422**
A document from a corporation's board of directors which gives the officers of a corporation the authority to sign and bind the corporation to a lease.

covenant of quiet enjoyment **338**
An implied lease provision which prohibits the landlord from interfering with the tenant's agreed use and possession of a property.

credit application **508**
A document prepared by a prospective tenant which includes a provision authorizing the investigation and receipt of information on the applicant's creditworthiness. [See **RPI** Form 302]

credit reporting agency **170**
A private agency which collects and reports information regarding an individual's credit history.

curable breach **254**
A breach of the lease agreement which can be remedied by action from the tenant.

D

A lease or rental agreement provision declaring a tenant's failure to cure a breach of the agreement constitutes a forfeiture of the tenant's right of possession. [See **RPI** Form 575 §5]

A lease agreement provision authorizing the landlord on termination of the tenant's lease due to the tenant's default to collect rents for the remaining unexpired lease term. [See **RPI** Form 550 §3.1 and 552 §2.1]

A tenant's or borrower's failure to pay the agreed amounts on or before the due date or expiration of any grace period.

A provision in a lease agreement in which a tenant agrees to pay for any destruction to the premises caused by the tenant, covered by the tenant's insurance or required by other lease provisions. [See **RPI** Form 552 §16]

Anyone who has a physical or mental impairment which significantly limits major life activities, has a record of disability, or is regarded as being disabled.

The property benefitting from an easement on a servient tenement.

The agency relationship that results when a broker represents both the buyer and the seller in a real estate transaction. [See **RPI** Form 117]

The date provided in the rental or lease agreement on which rental payments are due. [See **RPI** Form 550 §4.1 and 552 §4.1]

A trust deed provision used by lenders to call the mortgage immediately due and payable, a right triggered by the owner's transfer of any interest in the real estate, with exceptions for intra-family transfers of their home.

A building occupied or designed to be occupied as a residence by one or more families.

E

A provision which assures payment of the broker's fee if the owner withdraws the property from the market during the listing period. [See **RPI** Form 110 §3.1(c)]

A fee paid to the landlord by the tenant to cancel the lease agreement in exchange for returning possession. [See **RPI** Form 587 §2.2]

The right of the government to take private property for public use on payment to the owner of the property's fair market value.

A clause in a lease agreement which limits the tenant's ability to imply terms into the lease based on oral statements made before entering into the lease.

The ownership interest a person may hold in real estate.

An unlawful detainer action filed to physically remove a tenant from actual possession.

exclusive authorization to lease **124**
A written agreement between a broker and client employing the broker to render services in exchange for a fee on the leasing of the property to a tenant located by anyone. Also known as a listing. [See **RPI** Form 110]

exclusive authorization to locate space **136, 153**
An employment agreement by a broker and a prospective tenant which authorizes the broker to act as the tenant's leasing agent to locate suitable space and negotiate a lease agreement. [See **RPI** Form 111]

exclusive right-to-collect clause **128**
A provision which assures payment of the broker's fee if anyone procures a tenant on the terms in the listing, or on terms the landlord accepts. [See **RPI** Form 110 §3.1(a)]

F

familial status **534, 549**
A status which indicates a household includes individuals under the age of 18.

Federal Fair Housing Act (FFHA) **534, 550**
A collection of policies designed to prevent discrimination in the access to housing based on an occupant's inclusion in a protected class.

fee estate **2**
An indefinite, exclusive and absolute legal ownership interest in a parcel of real estate.

final inspection **193**
An inspection of the premises conducted by the landlord within 21 days after a residential tenant vacates the property. [See **RPI** Form 585]

fixed-rent lease **427**
A lease agreement with monthly rent payments set at a specific dollar amount for the life of the lease. [See **RPI** Form 550 and 552]

fixed-term tenancy **5**
A leasehold interest which lasts for the specific lease period set forth in a lease agreement. A fixed-term tenancy automatically terminates at the end of the lease period. [See **RPI** Form 550 and 552]

floor rent **410**
A minimum rent rate the landlord receives throughout the lease term.

forcible entry **41**
The unlawful entry of any party into a rented property without permission, prior notice or justification.

forfeiture of possession **231**
A termination of the tenant's right of possession triggered by a declaration of forfeiture in a notice to quit. [See **RPI** Form 575 §5]

full listing offer **127**
A buyer's or tenant's offer to buy or lease on terms substantially identical to the employment terms in the owner's listing agreement with the broker. [See **RPI** Form 556]

full-service gross lease **423**
A commercial lease specifying that the landlord retains the responsibility for payment of all costs of care and maintenance, unless modified, including the tenant's utilities and janitorial services. [See **RPI** Form 552 and 552-1]

further-approval contingency **149**
A provision in an offer to rent property which allows the tenant time to investigate and confirm the property information disclosed by the landlord.

futher-improvements provision **48**
A commercial lease provision which allows a landlord to retain tenant improvements or require the restoration of the property to its original condition upon expiration of the lease. [See **RPI** Form 552 §11.3]

future subordination clause **589**
A lease agreement provision in which the tenant agrees to subordinate their leasehold interest in property to a trust deed to be recorded in the future. [See **RPI** Form 552 §17]

G

general adjustment **565**
A type of rent control rent adjustment which uniformly adjusts rents for all rental units. [See **RPI** Form 552 §4.4 and §4.5]

general duty **138**
The duty a licensee owes to non-client individuals to act honestly and in good faith with up-front disclosures of known conditions which adversely affect a property's value. [See **RPI** Form 305]

grace period **246**
The time period following the due date for a payment during which payment received by a lender or landlord is not delinquent and a late charge is not due. [See **RPI** Form 550 §4.3 and 552 §4.7]

graduated rent provision **436**
A rent provision in a commercial lease agreement which periodically increases the initial monthly rent in pre-set increments over the term of the lease. [See **RPI** Form 552 §4.4]

gross lease **423**
A commercial lease specifying that the tenant pays for their utilities and janitorial fees, but unless modified is not responsible for any other care, maintenance or carrying costs of the property. [See **RPI** Form 552 and 552-1]

ground lease **6**
A leasehold interest for which rent is based on the rental value of the land, whether the parcel is improved or unimproved.

H

habitability defense **374**
A tenant's pursuit of a legal remedy due to a landlord's failure to maintain habitable conditions on the rented premises.

habitable condition **371**
The minimum acceptable level of safety, utility and sanitation permitted in a residential rental.

heirs, assigns and successors clause **421**
A clause in a lease agreement which binds those who later take the position of landlord or tenant to the existing agreement. [See **RPI** Form 552 §23.3]

hold harmless provision **471**
A provision in a lease agreement that shifts responsibility from the landlord to the tenant for injuries occurring on the premises caused by the tenant's negligence. [See **RPI** Form 552 §15]

holdover rent **24**
Rent owed by a holdover tenant for the tenant's unlawful detainer of the rented premises as a tenant-at-sufferance. [See **RPI** Form 550 §3.3]

holdover rent provision **230**
A rental or lease agreement provision which sets the rent rate during a tenant holdover period. [See **RPI** Form 550 §3.3 and 552 §2.3]

holdover tenant **24**
A tenant who retains possession of the rented premises after their right of possession has been terminated, called a tenant-at-sufferance.

I

impairment **4**
The act of injuring or diminishing the value of a fee interest.

impasse notice **502**
A notice advising the tenant the lease will expire and no modification of the lease will be entered into.

implied warranty of habitability **370**
An unwritten provision, included by statute, in all residential lease agreements requiring the landlord to provide safe and sanitary conditions in the rental unit.

incurable breach **244**
Nonmonetary defaults in leases or mortgages that cannot be cured or undone. [See **RPI** Form 577]

individual adjustment **565**
A type of rent adjustment sought by a landlord when the general adjustment established by local rent control ordinances fails to provide a fair return on their residential property.

inflation **446**
The price changes over time in consumer goods and services, stated in the consumer price index (CPI) as a figure which is reported as a percentage change over one year ago.

inflation-adjusted rent provision **439**
A rent provision in a commercial lease which calls for periodic rent increases based on changes in inflation index figures during the period. [See **RPI** Form 552 §4.5]

irrevocable license **16**
The right to enter and use property when the specific activity granted by the license is maintained by the licensee's ongoing expenditure of money or equivalent labor, and remains feasible.

itemized statement of deductions **195**
A document accounting for the tenant's security deposit, delivered by the landlord to a residential tenant after the tenant vacates. [See **RPI** Form 585 §4.3]

J

joint pre-expiration inspection **189**
An inspection conducted by a residential landlord or the property manager to advise a tenant of the repairs the tenant needs to perform to avoid deductions from their security deposit. [See **RPI** Form 567-1]

L

landlord-initiated disposition procedure **325**
The process of a landlord mailing a notice of the right to reclaim personal property to a tenant who vacated and left personal property on the premises. [See **RPI** Form 581 and 584]

late charge notice **285**
A landlord's written notice demanding payment of a late charge on a delinquent rent payment. [See **RPI** Form 586]

late charge provision **247**
A provision in the lease agreement which imposes an additional administrative charge if rent payments are not received when due or within a grace period for payment.

late payment clause **279**
A provision in a rental or lease agreement establishing the landlord's right to demand and receive a late charge when a rent payment becomes delinquent. [See **RPI** Form 550 §4.3 and 552 §4.7]

material breach **243**
Failure to pay rent or perform other significant obligations called for in the rental or lease agreement.

mechanic's lien **56**
A lien entitling a contractor or subcontractor to foreclose on a job site property to recover the amount due and unpaid for labor and materials they used.

minor breach **230**
Failure to pay late charges, interest penalties, bad check charges or security deposits.

monetary breach **254**
A tenant's failure to timely pay rent or other money obligation due.

money action **234**
Litigation which seeks to recover future rents and any previously unpaid rent earned but not included in an unlawful detainer judgment.

N

negligence **355**
The failure to behave with the level of care that someone of ordinary prudence would have exercised under the same conditions.

net lease **423**
A commercial lease which transfers to the tenant the obligation, unless modified, to pay some or all of the costs of ownership in addition to utilities and janitorial services. [See **RPI** Form 552-2 and 552-3]

net operating income **198**
The net revenue generated by an income producing property as the return on capital, calculated as the sum of a property's gross operating income less the property's operating expenses. [See **RPI** Form 352 §4]

nondelegable duty **365**
A duty which cannot be transferred or assumed by another person. In the case of a landlord, a nondelegable duty cannot be assumed by a property manager or contractor.

nondisturbance agreement **591**
An agreement with the mortgage lender for providing for the tenant's lease agreement to remain in effect for its full term after the leasehold is subordinated to a new mortgage.

nondisturbance clause **590**
A lease agreement provision which is coupled with the future subordination clause to allow a tenant's junior leasehold interest to remain unaffected by a lender's foreclosure under a senior trust deed. [See **RPI** Form 552-8]

nonmonetary breach **254**
A tenant's breach of any obligation other than an obligation to pay money.

nonrecurring deposits or charges **145**
One-time costs for which the tenant is responsible. [See **RPI** Form 550 §2]

nonwaiver of rights provision **209**
A commercial lease or rental agreement provision containing the landlord's reservation of rights. [See **RPI** Form 552 §20]

nonwaiver provision **263**
A provision in the lease agreement that states a landlord's waiver of a tenant's breach of the lease is not a waiver of similar or future breaches. [See **RPI** Form 550 §7.4 and 552 §20.1]

note **572**
A document, often secured by a trust deed on real estate, evidencing an obligation to pay money to a creditor — usually a lender or carryback seller. [See **RPI** Form 421 and 424]

option period **63**
The time period during which an optionee/buyer may exercise their right to buy under an option agreement. [See **RPI** Form 161 §4]

option to buy **62**
An agreement granting an irrevocable right to buy property within a specific time period. [See **RPI** Form 161]

option to extend **62, 479**
An agreement granting a tenant the right to extend possession under the original lease agreement on terms set out in the option to extend. [See **RPI** Form 565]

option to renew **64, 479**
An agreement granting a tenant the right to continue in possession upon expiration of the existing lease under a new lease agreement on the same conditions as the expiring lease agreement on terms for payment of rent set out in the option to renew. [See **RPI** Form 565]

overriding rent **488**
The amount the current market rent rates exceed the rents under the lease agreement, attainable by the tenant on a sublease to a successor tenant.

owner-by-foreclosure **297, 610**
The winning bidder at a trustee's sale who takes title to the property sold by a trustee's deed.

P

parcel **2**
A three-dimensional portion of real estate identified by a legal description.

partial payment agreement **205**
An agreement for receipt of partial rent, specifying the amount of deferred rent remaining unpaid and the date for its payment. [See **RPI** Form 558 and 559]

percentage lease **428, 455**
A commercial lease agreement for a retail operation that sets the total amount of rent the tenant will pay as a percentage of the tenant's gross sales. [See **RPI** Form 552-4]

periodic tenancy **22**
A leasehold interest which lasts for automatic successive rental periods of the same length of time, terminating upon notice from either party. [See **RPI** Form 551 and 552-5]

permissive improvement **52**
A nonmandatory improvement the tenant is authorized to complete without further landlord consent.

police power **563**
The basis for enacting local ordinances such as zoning, traffic, health and safety regulations and rent control.

power of attorney **73**
A temporary authority granted to an individual to perform activities during a period of the owner's incapacity or travel. [See **RPI** Form 447]

present value **237**
Unearned rent that is discounted at the time of the court's money award at the annual rate of 1% over the Federal Reserve Bank of San Francisco's discount rate.

pro rata rent **218**
Rental payment amount due for the portion of the rental period remaining after a change in the rent amount due. [See **RPI** Form 552 §4.1]

profit a prendre **3**
The right to remove minerals from another's real estate.

R

right of first refusal **62**
A pre-emptive right to buy a property if the owner decides to sell. [See **RPI** Form 579]

right of rescission **515**
The right to cancel a completed transaction such as sale or letting of property, including restoration, after the transaction has been closed.

right-to-enter provision **468**
A provision contained in a lease agreement which reserves to the landlord the right to enter the leased premises to make necessary repairs, alterations or inspections. [See **RPI** Form 552 §12]

S

safety clause **129**
A provision in an exclusive listing agreement earning the broker a fee during an agreed safety period after expiration of the employment for marketing efforts with identified buyers, tenants or properties, if the client sells the listed property to an identified buyer or purchases or leases an identified property during the safety period. [See **RPI** Form 102 §3.1(d), 103 §4.1(c) and 110 §3.1(d)]

Section 8 housing **296**
A government housing program for low income households which provides qualifying tenants with rent subsidies and minimum habitability standards.

security deposit **183, 526**
A source of funds to pay tenant obligations owed the landlord on the tenant's default in the rental or lease agreement. [See **RPI** Form 550 §2.1 and 552 §1.2]

self-help **38**
A landlord's own method of recovering possession from a tenant outside the legal eviction process.

senior citizen housing **549, 558**
Housing intended for persons 55 or 62 years of age or older.

servient tenement **9**
A property burdened by a license or easement.

signage provision **465**
A provision in a commercial lease agreement which gives the landlord control over the size, style, content and location of signs constructed or installed on the leased premises. [See **RPI** Form 552 §10]

start-up fee **98**
A flat, one-time fee charged by a property manager for the time and effort taken to become sufficiently familiar with the operations of the property to commence management.

statement of deficiencies **193**
A document a residential landlord presents to a vacating tenant specifying any repairs or cleaning to be completed by the tenant to avoid deductions from their security deposit. [See **RPI** Form 567-3]

statutory breach **258**
A breach of the lease agreement which automatically forfeits the tenant's right of possession.

"stay-or-pay" clause **198**
An unenforceable provision calling for the residential tenant to forego a return of their security deposit if they move before a set date.

steering **536**
The discriminatory practice of restricting the rental or ownership of a property to a specific class of people to perpetuate segregated housing.

strict liability **353**
To be liable for another's injuries without concern for fault.

strict rent control **564**
A type of rent control ordinance that limits rent increases on all rental units.

sublease **7**
A leasehold interest subject to the terms of a master lease.

substituted service **272**
In place of personally serving the tenant, a notice is personally delivered to a person of suitable age at the tenant's residence or place of business and is mailed to the leased premises, or posted on and mailed to the premises.

successor tenant **491**
On a transfer, the new tenant who acquires the original tenant's leasehold interest in the property. [See **RPI** Form 552 §9]

surrender **304, 313**
A mutual cancellation of a lease agreement by the landlord and tenant, written or by their conduct, when the tenant vacates the leased premises. [See **RPI** Form 587]

T

tenancy-at-sufferance **5**
A leasehold interest created when a tenant retains possession of the rented premises after the tenancy has terminated. [See **RPI** Form 550 § 3.3]

tenancy-at-will **5**
A leasehold interest granted to a tenant, with no fixed duration or rent owed. A tenancy-at-will can be terminated at any time by an advance notice from either party.

Tenant Estoppel Certificate (TEC) **594**
A statement which summarizes the monetary and possessory terms of a lease agreement, and whether the landlord and tenant have fully performed their obligations. [See **RPI** Form 598]

tenant improvements **47**
Improvements made to a leased property to meet the needs of the occupying tenant. [See **RPI** Form 552 §11]

tenant improvements and alterations cause **465**
A clause in a commercial lease agreement which specifies the tenant's right to make alterations or further improve the premises during the tenancy. [See **RPI** Form 552 §11]

tenant lease worksheet **155**
A document the leasing agent uses to analyze the tenant's current financial condition and needs for leased space. [See **RPI** Form 555]

tenant-initiated recovery procedure **326**
The recovery process initiated by a tenant to retrieve personal property from a landlord within 18 days after vacating rental property. [See **RPI** Form 582]

tenant-mitigation provision **318, 495**
A provision in a commercial lease agreement allowing the landlord to leave the tenant's leasehold and the lease agreement intact on the tenant's breach, then recover rent from the tenant for the life of the lease without the landlord first taking steps to mitigate losses. [See **RPI** Form 552 §21.1]

termination-of-agency clause **127**
A provision in an exclusive listing agreement which calls for a broker fee to be earned and payable when the client cancels the employment without cause. [See **RPI** Form 102 §3.1(c), Form 103 §4.1(b) and Form 110 §3.1(c)]

trade fixture **54**
A fixture used to render services or make products in the trade or business of a tenant.

transfer **488**
Any assignment, sublease or further encumbrance of the leasehold by the tenant. [See **RPI** Form 552 §9]

Property Management, Sixth Edition Quizzes

Instructions: Quizzes are open book. All answers are Multiple Choice.
Answer key is located on Page 650.

Quiz 1 — Chapters 1-4, Pages 1-46

_____ 1. Four types of estates exist in real estate, including:

   a. family estates.
   c. personal estates.
   b. leasehold estates.
   d. None of the above.

_____ 2. A _____ lasts for a specific period of time agreed to in a lease agreement between a landlord and tenant.

   a. periodic tenancy
   c. fixed-term tenancy
   b. tenancy-at-sufferance
   d. tenancy-at-will

_____ 3. A lease conveys a(n) _____ in real estate to a tenant.

   a. exclusive possessory interest
   b. personal privilege
   c. nonexclusive possessory interest
   d. irrevocable privilege

_____ 4. When a broker offers space in their office under a written agreement providing for lockable office space and a specific period for occupancy, the agreement is a:

   a. lease.
   c. Both a. and b.
   b. license.
   d. None of the above.

_____ 5. The characteristic(s) of a tenancy-at-will include:

   a. no provision for the payment of rent.
   b. possession for an indefinite and unspecified period.
   c. possession delivered to the tenant with the landlord's knowledge and consent.
   d. All of the above.

_____ 6. A tenant-at-sufferance is also known as a(n):

   a. nuisance.
   c. landlord.
   b. tenant-at-will.
   d. holdover tenant.

_____ 7. When a landlord accepts rent from a holdover tenant after a fixed-term tenancy expires, the expired lease agreement is _____ on the same terms except for the period of occupancy.

   a. cancelled
   c. Both a. and b.
   b. renewed
   d. Neither a. nor b.

_____ 8. A landlord may not permit the police to enter and search a tenant's unit without a:

   a. previous request from the police.
   b. warrant.
   c. written notice delivered in advance to the tenant.
   d. None of the above.

_____ 9. A 24-hour notice of entry to a tenant's unit or space may reasonably be served by:

    a. handing a written notice to the tenant personally.

    b. posting the notice on the entry door.

    c. Neither a. nor b.

    d. Both a. and b.

_____ 10. A landlord is prohibited from entering a unit unless:

    a. the tenant's right of possession has been terminated.

    b. the tenant has vacated the unit.

    c. Both a. and b.

    d. Neither a. nor b.

Quiz 2 — Chapters 5-8, Pages 47-86

_____ 1. If a tenant fails to make mandated improvements that are to remain with the property on expiration of the lease, the tenant is liable to the landlord for _____ incurred by the landlord to make the improvements.

    a. none of the cost   c. the full cost

    b. half the cost   d. None of the above.

_____ 2. Tenant improvements become part of the leased property and remain with the property on expiration of the lease unless:

    a. the landlord and tenant previously agreed otherwise.

    b. the tenant paid for the improvements.

    c. the landlord does not intend to use the improvements.

    d. All of the above.

_____ 3. _____ revert(s) to the landlord on expiration of the lease.

    a. The tenant's furniture   c. The security deposit

    b. Real estate fixtures attached to the property   d. None of the above.

_____ 4. A(n)_____ is a preemptive right to purchase property if the owner later decides to sell the property.

    a. surrender   c. offer to purchase

    b. notice of abandonment   d. right of first refusal

_____ 5. When options to renew or extend a lease are included in the lease terms, the expiration of the option to buy is tied to:

    a. the expiration of the initial lease term.   c. Either a. or b.

    b. the expiration of any renewal or extension.   d. Neither a. nor b.

_____ 6. The tenant's right of first refusal is _____ when the landlord agrees to sell the property on terms different from those terms offered to the tenant.

    a. renewed   c. reinstated

    b. extended   d. cancelled

_____ 7. A temporary manager of real estate who has _____ is not required to hold a real estate broker's license.

    a. past experience in property management

    b. a personal relationship with the landlord

    c. a leasehold interest in the property

    d. power of attorney

____ 8. Anyone who receives a percentage or contingency fee for continuously locating tenants or managing income properties for another:

    a. needs to hold a DRE license.

    b. needs to hold a DRE license only if the fee is greater than $1,500.

    c. needs to hold a DRE license only if the fee is greater than $2,500.

    d. does not need a DRE license.

____ 9. The property management agreement authorizes the property manager to:

    a. locate tenants.   c. collect rents.

    b. enter into rental and lease agreements.   d. All of the above.

____ 10. A landlord is entitled to a statement of accounting:

    a. at least once every quarter.   c. Both a. and b.

    b. when the property management agreement   d. Neither a. nor b.
        is terminated.

Quiz 3 — Chapters 9-13, Pages 87-142

____ 1. A property manager's obligations to a landlord include:

    a. serving notices on tenants and filing unlawful detainer (UD) actions as needed.

    b. advertising for prospective tenants.

    c. negotiating and executing rental and lease agreements.

    d. All of the above.

____ 2. A property manager is required to deposit all funds collected on behalf of a landlord into a(n)_____ within three business days of receipt.

    a. trust account   c. general savings account

    b. impound account   d. checking account

____ 3. A resident manager who continues to occupy a unit after their employment is terminated becomes a(n):

    a. tenant-at-will.   c. occupant-in-capacity.

    b. holdover tenant.   d. equity purchase (EP) investor.

____ 4. Apartment buildings with _____ or more units need to have a landlord, resident manager or responsible caretaker living on the premises to manage the property.

    a. 12   c. 16

    b. 14   d. 18

____ 5. Tax-wise, the rental value of an apartment unit is not reportable income for the resident manager when the unit they occupy is:

    a. for the property manager's or landlord's convenience.

    b. located on the premises managed.

    c. occupied by the manager as a condition of their employment.

    d. All of the above.

____ 6. Addresses given to residential tenants for the landlord, property manager and resident manager need to be:

    a. street addresses.   c. identified on a plot map.

    b. email addresses.   d. clarified using a metes and bounds description.

_____ 7. Without the _____ promising to pay, the broker cannot enforce collection of an orally promised fee.

    a. broker's signature

    b. client's signature

    c. broker's documentation of the oral agreement

    d. client's cooperative conduct

_____ 8. The _____ grants a broker the right to a fee if, within a fixed period after the exclusive authorization period expires, the property is leased to a tenant the broker dealt with during the listing period.

    a. right of first refusal

    b. safety clause

    c. Both a. and b.

    d. Neither a. nor b.

_____ 9. Under a(n) _____, a broker has earned a fee if the tenant enters into a lease agreement.

    a. option listing

    b. net listing

    c. exclusive authorization to locate space

    d. None of the above.

_____ 10. A broker acting as an agent on behalf of both the landlord and tenant is a:

    a. single agent.

    b. dual agent.

    c. double agent.

    d. None of the above.

Quiz 4 — Chapters 14-18, Pages 143-182

_____ 1. The amount of the common area maintenance (CAM) cost of a property is a(n) _____ a broker needs to disclose to a prospective tenant who agrees to pay these costs.

    a. assessment

    b. CC&R

    c. material fact

    d. immaterial fact

_____ 2. A leasing agent best determines the tenant's intentions for leasing property by preparing a(n):

    a. tenant lease worksheet.

    b. offer to lease.

    c. property management agreement.

    d. disclosure form.

_____ 3. An offer to lease contains four sections, including:

    a. identification of the parties and premises.

    b. rental payment schedules and period of occupancy.

    c. property maintenance and terms of possession (use).

    d. All of the above.

_____ 4. A(n) _____ is a non-binding proposal signed and submitted to a property owner to start negotiations to rent or buy a property.

    a. lease agreement

    b. offer to lease

    c. letter of intent (LOI)

    d. Both a. and b.

_____ 5. In order to form a binding agreement, an offer or counteroffer:

    a. needs to be accepted in its entirety and without conditions.

    b. may be accepted with minor changes in conditions.

    c. may be accepted with minor changes in conditions if both parties agree to address the conditions within 15 business days.

    d. None of the above.

_____ 6. Property managers advising landlords on tenants' creditworthiness need to subscribe to the services available from a:

    a. prior landlord.

    b. credit reporting agency (CRA).

    c. personal reference.

    d. employer.

_____ 7. Credit checks on prospective tenants can only be used to establish eligibility for:

    a. employment purposes.

    b. personal, family or household purposes.

    c. the rental of a dwelling unit.

    d. All of the above.

_____ 8. A tenant is entitled to request a clarification by a credit reporting agency of the results of a(n) _____ against the tenant if the report is true but misleading.

    a. unlawful detainer (UD) action

    b. criminal conviction

    c. traffic violation

    d. None of the above.

_____ 9. A residential landlord may charge a fee to cover the costs of obtaining a prospective tenant's:

    a. employment history.

    b. former street address.

    c. financial statements.

    d. credit report.

_____ 10. A property manager needs to consider a prospective tenant's _____ before agreeing to lease commercial property.

    a. race and sexual orientation

    b. business acumen and style of marketing

    c. religion and net worth

    d. business plan and gender

Quiz 5 — Chapters 19-21, Pages 183-212

_____ 1. A residential landlord who sets the security deposit amount based on creditworthiness needs to apply these credit standards equally to:

    a. all prospective tenants.

    b. all senior citizen housing tenants.

    c. all prospective tenants without children.

    d. None of the above.

_____ 2. A landlord _____ security deposits with other funds in a general account.

    a. is prohibited from commingling

    b. may commingle

    c. may spend

    d. Either a. or b.

_____ 3. The notice advising the tenant of their right to a joint pre-expiration inspection is best given to the tenant at least __ days prior to the end of the lease term.

    a. 10

    b. 15

    c. 30

    d. 45

_____ 4. On completion of the joint pre-expiration inspection, the landlord gives the tenant an itemized:

    a. statement of deficiencies.

    b. trust account ledger.

    c. notice of delinquency.

    d. statement of inventory.

_____ 5. Within _____ after a residential tenant vacates, the landlord needs to provide the tenant with an itemized statement of all deductions from the security deposit.

    a. two weeks

    b. 20 days

    c. 21 days

    d. 24 hours

_____ 6. A residential landlord who fails to refund a tenant's security deposit in bad faith may be subject to a penalty of up to _____ the amount of the security deposit.

    a. twice

    b. three times

    c. four times

    d. five times

_____ 7. A stay-or-pay clause which calls for a tenant to forfeit their security deposit is:

    a. illegal.

    b. unenforceable.

    c. enforceable if the tenant stays less than 180 days.

    d. Both a. and b.

_____ 8. The landlord's best method for recovering turnover costs is to:

    a. require a security deposit equal to eight months' rent.

    b. include a "stay-or-pay" clause in the lease agreement.

    c. rent only to month-to-month tenants.

    d. rent to creditworthy tenants on a lease agreement with a one-year term or longer.

_____ 9. A commercial landlord can accept a partial payment of rent after serving a three-day notice and before eviction under a(n):

    a. subordination agreement.

    b. windfall provision.

    c. reservation of rights clause.

    d. attorney fees provision.

_____ 10. A residential unlawful detainer (UD) action based on a three-day notice which overstates the amount of the delinquent rent due is:

    a. valid.

    b. invalid.

    c. valid if two or more tenants occupy the property.

    d. invalid unless the landlord holds a broker license.

Quiz 6 — Chapters 22-24, Pages 213-240

_____ 1. _____ in a residential or commercial month-to-month rental agreement may be changed on 30 days' written notice by the landlord.

    a. Addendums

    b. Provisions and conditions

    c. Clauses and terms

    d. All of the above.

_____ 2. Upon receipt of a 30-day notice of change in terms on a periodic rental agreement, the new terms take effect _____ after the expiration of the notice.

    a. immediately

    b. 15 days

    c. 15 business days

    d. 30 days

_____ 3. A residential landlord subject to rent control can make adjustments to rents based on:

    a. the maximum percentage of the consumer price index (CPI) as set by ordinance.

    b. the maximum percentage set by ordinance.

    c. the maximum amount previously set by the rent control board.

    d. All of the above.

_____ 4. In a small claims action for recovery against a guarantor, the amount of recovery is limited to _____ or less.

    a. $1,500   c. $3,500

    b. $2,500   d. $4,500

_____ 5. In a municipal court action, the landlord seeking to recover unpaid rents may:

    a. represent themselves.   c. perjure themselves.

    b. be represented by an attorney licensed in California.   d. Both a. and b.

_____ 6. An unlawful detainer occurs when a tenant refuses to pay rent and _____ the property after the expiration of a three-day notice to pay rent or quit.

    a. remains in possession of   c. terminates possession of

    b. vacates   d. None of the above.

_____ 7. When a tenant remains in possession of a property without a valid right of possession, this is referred to as:

    a. waste.   c. Both a. and b.

    b. a holdover tenancy.   d. Neither a. nor b.

_____ 8. After mitigating their losses by reletting the premises, a landlord has a right to recover future rents without a default remedies provision in the lease agreement under the theory of:

    a. loss mitigation.   c. statutory recovery.

    b. unlawful detainer (UD).   d. attorney fees provision.

_____ 9. The landlord who recovers future rent under an unexpired lease agreement is only awarded _____ of the unearned future rents.

    a. the present value   c. a partial value

    b. the future accumulated value   d. None of the above.

_____ 10. A landlord is entitled to recover _____ after the tenant fails to perform on the lease.

    a. costs to clean up the property

    b. legal fees to find a new tenant

    c. permit fees to construct necessary renovations

    d. All of the above.

Quiz 7 — Chapters 25-28, Pages 241-288

_____ 1. A tenant's failure to pay late charges, interest penalties, bad check charges or security deposits is known as a(n):

    a. material breach.   c. minor breach.

    b. incurable breach.   d. None of the above.

_____ 2. After a landlord serves a tenant with a three-day notice to pay rent or quit containing a declaration of forfeiture provision, the tenant needs to cure the breach in _____ to avoid forfeiture.

a. three business days   c. one week

b. three calendar days   d. one month

_____ 3. Rent does not become delinquent until:

a. the business day following the due date, unless a grace period exists.

b. the business day following the last calendar day of the grace period.

c. 15 days after mailing if posted within the grace period.

d. Either a. or b.

_____ 4. A landlord needs to allow a tenant to cure a material breach of the lease when the tenant is capable of curing the breached provision within:

a. three days.   c. one month.

b. 15 days.   d. two months.

_____ 5. A tenant may be evicted for maintaining a(n) _____ the property.

a. unlawful use of

b. nuisance on

c. unorthodox or unprofessional business style on

d. Both a. and b.

_____ 6. In order to evict a tenant for laying waste to the premises, the landlord needs to prove the waste _____ the market value of the premises.

a. substantially improved   c. had no influence on

b. substantially diminished   d. None of the above.

_____ 7. A three-day notice cannot be upheld when:

a. the notice is incorrectly prepared.

b. a proof of service form is not completed.

c   the notice is not properly served to the tenant.

d. All of the above.

_____ 8. Personal service is accomplished when _____ signs the postal receipt acknowledging receipt of the three-day notice in the mail.

a. the landlord   c. Either a. or b.

b. the tenant   d. Neither a. nor b.

_____ 9. A three-day notice to pay or quit may include:

a. delinquent rent.   c. Both a. and b.

b. unpaid amounts due under the lease which are not labeled rent.   d. Neither a. nor b.

_____ 10. A late charge is only permissible when the amount is _____ cost of collecting the delinquent rent and the loss due to the delay in its receipt.

a. greater than the   c. reasonably related to the

b. less than the   d. None of the above.

Quiz 8 — Chapters 29-32, Pages 289-334

_____ 1. Once the 30-day notice to vacate expires and the month-to-month tenant does not vacate, the landlord may file a(n) _____ to evict the tenant without further notice.

   a. unlawful detainer (UD) action
   c. offer to surrender
   b. three-day notice to vacate
   d. notice of termination

_____ 2. To evict a tenant under HUD's Section 8 program, the landlord needs to state a valid reason for the eviction in:

   a. the notice to vacate.
   b. the lease agreement.
   c. the three-day notice to perform or quit.
   d. None of the above.

_____ 3. A(n)_____ reconveys the real estate to the landlord in exchange for cancellation of the lease agreement.

   a. notice of termination
   c. impasse notice
   b. notice to vacate
   d. surrender

_____ 4. A surrender may only occur by the:

   a. mutual consent of the landlord and tenant.
   c. conduct of the tenant.
   b. operation of law.
   d. Both a. and b.

_____ 5. General abandonment and surrender rules apply to:

   a. residential property.
   b. commercial property.
   c. Both a. and b.
   d. Neither a. nor b.

_____ 6. A Notice of Abandonment expires __ days after the date the notice is sent by first-class mail.

   a. 5
   c. 18
   b. 10
   d. 30

_____ 7. A tenant, after being served a Notice of Belief of Abandonment, may stop the abandonment procedure by:

   a. reoccupying the property.
   b. handing a written statement of no intent to abandon the property to the landlord.
   c. accepting the Notice of Belief of Abandonment.
   d. None of the above.

_____ 8. After a tenant pays storage costs to the landlord, the tenant needs to pick up their personal property within __ hours.

   a. 72
   c. 12
   b. 24
   d. 2

_____ 9. Abandoned personal items worth _____ or more may be sold at a public sale by the landlord if they are not reclaimed.

   a. $1,000
   c. $700
   b. $500
   d. $1,700

____ 10. Personal property subject to a public sale needs to be surrendered to the tenant:

   a. at no time.
   c. 15 days after the public sale.
   b. two business days after receiving request for the return of the property from the tenant.
   d. any time prior to the sale.

Quiz 9 — Chapters 33-36, Pages 335-368

_____ 1. A constructive eviction occurs when the tenant vacates the premises due to:

    a. waste committed on the property by the tenant.

    b. the landlord's substantial interference with the tenant's use and enjoyment of their property during the term of the rental or lease agreement.

    c. the neighbor's substantial interference with the tenant's use and enjoyment of their property

    d. eminent domain.

_____ 2. When a tenant vacates due to a constructive eviction, they may recover:

    a. relocation expenses.

    b. unaccrued prepaid rent and security deposits held by the landlord.

    c. loss of business goodwill.

    d. All of the above.

_____ 3. Any waiver or limitation on the remedies for breach of the covenant of quiet enjoyment for _____ is void as against public policy.

    a. residential properties

    b. commercial properties

    c. Both a. and b.

    d. Neither a. nor b.

_____ 4. In an unlawful detainer (UD) action, residential tenants are allowed to raise two defenses, retaliatory eviction and:

    a. breach of the warranty of habitability.

    b. eminent domain.

    c. refusal to reimburse tenant for cost of repairs.

    d. None of the above.

_____ 5. Actions by a residential landlord are considered retaliatory acts if initiated by the landlord after the tenant:

    a. organizes or becomes a member of a tenants' association or tenants' rights group.

    b. exercises the statutory repair and deduct remedy.

    c. commits waste.

    d. Both a. and b.

_____ 6. After prevailing in an unlawful detainer (UD) action, a residential tenant is entitled to_____ of protection against eviction without cause.

    a. 90 days

    b. 30 days

    c. 180 days

    d. 60 days

_____ 7. In addition to a tenant's actual money losses incurred due to the landlord's retaliatory act, the tenant is also entitled to recover ___ for each retaliatory act where the landlord acts maliciously with respect to the retaliation.

    a. punitive losses between $100 and $500

    b. punitive losses between $50 and $1,000

    c. punitive losses between $1,200 and $1,500

    d. punitive losses between $100 and $2,000

_____ 8. A landlord who is confronted with a known dangerous condition and does not act to correct the condition is:

    a. negligent.

    b. retaliatory.

    c. wasteful.

    d. malicious.

_____ 9. A residential tenant has a duty of care and maintenance in the use of leased property, which includes:

    a. disposing of all waste in a sanitary manner.

    b. properly operating all electrical, gas and plumbing fixtures.

    c. using the property for the purpose it is intended to be used.

    d. All of the above.

_____ 10. A residential tenant may make necessary repairs that the landlord fails to make and deduct _____ from the rent.

    a. the full costs of the repairs

    b. a partial cost of the repairs

    c. the cost of the repairs limited to one month's rent

    d. no amount of the cost of repairs

Quiz 10 — Chapters 37-40, Pages 369-406

_____ 1. Part of a residential tenant's entitlement to a safe and sanitary dwelling includes:

    a. marble flooring.

    c. a hot and cold running water system.

    b. an external air-conditioning unit.

    d. new carpeting.

_____ 2. A tenant who successfully raises a warranty of habitability defense in an unlawful detainer (UD) action may:

    a. retain possession of the premises.

    c. recover attorney fees and the costs of litigation.

    b. pay a reduced amount of rent.

    d. All of the above.

_____ 3. _____ are to be installed and maintained in all dwelling units intended for human occupancy.

    a. A washer and dryer

    c. Smoke detectors

    b. Dead bolt locks

    d. None of the above.

_____ 4. Security bars on residential bedroom windows do not need to have release mechanisms if the bedroom has:

    a. a window leading out of the premises.

    c. Either a. or b.

    b. a door leading out of the premises.

    d. Neither a. nor b.

_____ 5. Landlords owe a duty to care for and protect the tenant by:

    a. providing security measures in the common areas.

    b. providing the tenant with a firearm.

    c. offering on-site self-defense classes.

    d. hiring a private investigator.

_____ 6. When criminal activity is _____, the landlord has a duty to take reasonable measures to prevent harm to persons on the property from future similar criminal activities.

    a. decreasing in the area

    c. remotely possible

    b. reasonably foreseeable

    d. reasonably unforeseeable

_____ 7. The landlord's duty of care to protect a tenant from injury is derived from their ability to prevent the existence of dangerous conditions from existing on:

    a. the property they control.

    b. adjacent properties.

    c. public right of ways over which they have not taken control.

    d. All of the above.

_____ 8. Liability is imposed on a landlord for an injury suffered by any person on the property if:

    a. the type of injury suffered by the individual is foreseeable.

    b. the injury suffered is closely connected to the landlord's conduct.

    c. Both a. and b.

    d. Neither a. nor b.

_____ 9. A landlord has a duty to _____ a leased premises when they enter the premises for any single purpose.

    a. repair all minor defects in   c. reasonably inspect

    b. thoroughly inspect   d. fumigate

_____ 10. When an injured tenant's lack of care for themselves contributes to their injury, recovery for their losses is limited to the percentage of the negligence attributed to them, called:

    a. comparative negligence.   c. nondelegable negligence.

    b. constructive negligence.   d. reasonable negligence.

Quiz 11 — Chapters 41-45, Pages 407-460

_____ 1. To be valid, a lease agreement needs to:

    a. designate the size and location of the leased premises.   c. state the rental amount.

    b. set forth a term for the tenancy conveyed.   d. All of the above.

_____ 2. On expiration of a lease, a holdover tenancy is created when the tenant remains in possession of the property and:

    a. enters into a new lease agreement with the landlord.

    b. is subject to an eminent domain action.

    c. the landlord refuses to accept further rent payments.

    d. All of the above.

_____ 3. The right to receive a condemnation award on the leased property can be contracted away by a:

    a. landlord.   c. government agency.

    b. tenant.   d. None of the above.

_____ 4. If a tenant has a history of writing bad rent checks due to insufficient funds, the landlord may serve a 30-day notice on the tenant requiring them to:

    a. vacate the property on expiration of the notice.

    b. forfeit their security deposit.

    c. tender payment of future rents in cash or by money order.

    d. All of the above.

_____ 5. _____ are typically based on the ratio between space leased by the tenant and the total rentable space in a project.

    a. Common area maintenance (CAM) charges   c. Fair market rent

    b. Operating expenses   d. None of the above.

_____ 6. Types of rent adjustment provisions found in commercial leases include:

    a. graduated rent provisions.   c. appreciation-adjusted rent provisions.

    b. inflation-adjusted rent provisions.   d. All of the above.

_____ 7. Graduated rents are _____ on a periodic basis.

    a. adjusted to accommodate for an increase in local appreciation

    b. decreased in pre-set increments

    c. increased in pre-set increments based on a specific dollar amount or a percentage of the base year rent

    d. None of the above.

_____ 8. Inflation adjustments are usually made:

    a. annually   c. daily

    b. monthly   d. None of the above.

_____ 9. Under _____ rent adjustment provisions, the prior year's rent, not the base year's rent, is used to set the adjusted rent.

    a. base-to-current year   c. base-to-future

    b. year-to-year   d. Both a. and b.

_____ 10. _____ is the actual price received for all merchandise or services sold, licensed, leased or delivered for purposes of percentage rent calculations.

    a. Gross sales   c. Median sales

    b. Net sales   d. Total receipts

Quiz 12 — Chapters 46-49, Pages 461-504

_____ 1. Leasehold appurtenances include rights in real estate owned by the landlord located outside the leased space, such as:

    a. a right of way for vehicular travel through an industrial or office complex.

    b. parking for employees and customers

    c. storage space, lobbies and restrooms.

    d. All of the above.

_____ 2. A _____ relieves a landlord's property from becoming security for any claims made by contractors for improvements they construct on the leased premises.

    a. notice of forfeiture   c. notice of default

    b. notice of abandonment   d. notice of nonresponsibility

_____ 3. If not limited by its terms, the total term of a commercial lease, including extensions or renewals, is limited to ____ years by statute.

    a. 99   c. 101

    b. 100   d. 130

_____ 4. When the terms of a lease are _____, a new lease is created.

   a. extended

   b. renewed

   c. cancelled

   d. negotiated

_____ 5. For a tenant to be released from liability on the assignment of their lease agreement, a(n) _____ needs to be negotiated and entered into by the landlord and both tenants.

   a. novation

   b. substitution of liability

   c. subrogation agreement

   d. Either a. or b.

_____ 6. Unless unconscionable or discriminatory, commercial landlords and tenants are free to place _____ restrictions, limited to the value of the leasehold, on the tenant's assignment of the lease.

   a. commercially unreasonable

   b. commercially reasonable

   c. economically damaging

   d. economically unreasonable

_____ 7. No _____ may pass and enforce commercial rent control ordinances.

   a. city

   b. county

   c. public agency

   d. All of the above.

_____ 8. Commercial real estate includes all real estate except:

   a. industrial property.

   b. commercial property.

   c. dwelling units.

   d. warehouse space.

_____ 9. Local governments can regulate all facets of business location and development, such as:

   a. abating nuisances.

   b. exercising eminent domain powers

   c. protecting historical resources.

   d. All of the above.

_____ 10. After receiving a commercial tenant's _____ under a local ordinance, the landlord needs to enter into negotiations to renew or extend the lease with the tenant.

   a. negotiation notice

   b. letter of intent (LOI)

   c. offer to lease

   d. impasse notice

Quiz 13 — Chapters 50-53, Pages 505-532

_____ 1. Some landlords allow pets but frequently:

   a. impose restrictions on the type or size of the pet.

   b. require the landlord's written consent to keep the pet on the premises.

   c. Both a. and b.

   d. Neither a. nor b.

_____ 2. A lease or rental agreement may prohibit a tenant from:

   a. creating a nuisance.

   b. using the premises for an unlawful purpose.

   c. committing waste.

   d. All of the above.

_____ 3. A written translation of a residential lease agreement is required to be delivered to the tenant if its term exceeds _____ and is negotiated primarily in Spanish, Chinese, Vietnamese, Korean or _____.

   a. one year; Japanese

   b. one month; Tagalog

   c. one year; Russian

   d. one month; German

___ 4. Real estate transactions exempt from the written translation requirement include:

    a. purchase agreements.

    b. month-to-month rental agreements.

    c. home improvement agreements.

    d. All of the above.

___ 5. The mandated lead-based paint disclosure laws do not obligate a landlord to:

    a. abate or remove any lead-based paint.

    b. conduct an inspection to determine whether any lead-based paint exists.

    c. Both a. and b.

    d. Neither a. nor b.

___ 6. A lead-based paint disclosure is required for all _____ residential units which have not been certified as lead-based paint free.

    a. post-1970

    b. pre-1978

    c. pre-1975

    d. post-1982

___ 7. A _____ is any condition that causes exposure to lead from lead-contaminated dust, soil or paint which has deteriorated to the point of causing adverse human health effects.

    a. lead-based paint hazard

    b. lead-based paint disclosure

    c. seismic activity hazard

    d. dangerous off-site condition

___ 8. Landlords can refuse to accept tenants who want to occupy a unit with their pet unless the tenant is disabled and the pet is a:

    a. signal dog.

    b. service dog.

    c. guide dog.

    d. All of the above.

___ 9. For a furnished unit, the security deposit, including the pet deposit, may not exceed:

    a. one month's rent.

    b. two month's rent (in addition to first month's rent).

    c. three month's rent (in addition to first month's rent).

    d. three month's rent.

___ 10. A tenant needs to give the property manager ___ if they intend to move, install or remove a waterbed.

    a. 24 hours' notice

    b. 3 weeks' notice

    c. reasonable notice

    d. None of the above.

Quiz 14 — Chapters 54-57, Pages 533-570

___ 1. Handicapped persons refer to individuals who have:

    a. a physical or mental impairment which substantially limits the person's life activities.

    b. a record of having a physical or mental impairment.

    c. relatives who have a record of having a physical or mental impairment.

    d. Both a. and b.

___ 2. A person who believes they have been discriminated against needs to file a complaint with the Secretary of Housing and Urban Development (HUD) within _____ of the alleged discriminatory practice.

    a. 24 hours

    b. 12 days

    c. one month

    d. one year

_____ 3. A broker found guilty of discrimination by the Secretary of Housing and Urban Development (HUD) may face disciplinary action from the:

a. Department of Real Estate (DRE).

b. local police department.

c. Department of Motor Vehicles (DMV).

d. All of the above.

_____ 4. A landlord of newly constructed _____ unit residential property needs to provide disabled access.

a. four or more

b. four or less

c. eight or more

d. 12 or more

_____ 5. Rental policies excluding children under the age of 18 are considered _____ unless the property qualifies as senior citizen housing.

a. reasonable

b. unlawful discrimination

c. lawful discrimination

d. None of the above.

_____ 6. Requiring families with children to _____ than other prospective tenants when screening rental applications is prohibited.

a. have a higher family income

b. pay a higher security deposit

c. have a better credit rating

d. All of the above.

_____ 7. Senior citizen housing is property:

a. intended for occupancy only by individuals 62 years of age or older.

b. intended for occupancy by at least one person of 55 years of age or older.

c. Both a. and b.

d. Neither a. nor b.

_____ 8. A senior citizen and their disabled _____ may live in senior citizen housing.

a. child

b. grandchild

c. Both a. and b.

d. Neither a. nor b.

_____ 9. Two primary types of rent control ordinances exist, called:

a. strict rent control and variable rent control.

b. market rent control and vacancy decontrol.

c. vacancy decontrol and strict rent control.

d. variable rent control and market rent control.

_____ 10. In addition to restricting rent increases, rent control ordinances restrict the landlord's:

a. ability to enter a tenant's unit.

b. ability to evict existing tenants.

c. Both a. and b.

d. Neither a. nor b.

Quiz 15 — Chapters 58-62, Pages 571-615

_____ 1. In addition to fee estates, there are three other estates which exist in California, including:

a. life estates

b. leaseholds

c. estates at will.

d. All of the above.

_____ 2. In the alienation provision in a lease, the landlord may:

    a. prohibit the tenant from encumbering the leasehold.

    b. allow the tenant to encumber the leasehold subject to previously agreed conditions.

    c. require the landlord's consent before the tenant may encumber the leasehold.

    d. All of the above.

_____ 3. Examples of boilerplate provisions in commercial lease agreements which relate to the priority of the lease against trust deeds are:

    a. future subordination clauses.   c. nondisturbance clauses.

    b. attornment clauses.   d. All of the above.

_____ 4. A _____ gives a tenant the right to require a new trust deed lender to enter into a written agreement which states the tenant's lease agreement will remain in effect for its full term after the lease is subordinated to a new mortgage.

    a. nondisturbance clause   c. future subordination clause

    b. self-destruct provision   d. power of sale provision

_____ 5. A _____ confirms the correct amount of security deposit held by the seller.

    a. UCC-1 Financing Statement   c. notice of default (NOD)

    b. Tenant Estoppel Certificate (TEC)   d. None of the above.

_____ 6. On the discovery of a long-term leasing arrangement which triggers due-on enforcement under the lender's trust deed, the lender may:

    a. call the mortgage.   c. Either a. or b.

    b. recast the mortgage.   d. Neither a. nor b.

_____ 7. The due-on clause is triggered when an owner of property secured by a due-on trust deed enters into a lease:

    a. with a term over two years or an option to purchase.

    b. with a term under three years without an option to purchase.

    c. with a term over three years or an option to purchase.

    d. with a term under two years without an option to purchase.

_____ 8. A broker who advises a buyer not to disclose a sale to a lender secured by a trust deed on the property may be held liable by the _____ for their right to additional interest.

    a. buyer   c. seller

    b. lender   d. All of the above.

_____ 9. Residential tenants whose month-to-month rental agreements were junior to the recording of the trust deed, and thus eliminated by the foreclosure sale, are entitled to a _____ written notice to vacate.

    a. three-day   c. 90-day

    b. 25-day   d. one-year

_____ 10. Tenants living in _____ are protected from unqualified termination of their occupancy after a foreclosure sale.

    a. Section 8 housing   c. Both a. and b.

    b. rent control communities   d. Neither a. nor b.

Answer References

The following are the answers to the quizzes for *Property Management, Sixth Edition* and the page numbers where they are located.

Quiz 1			**Quiz 2**			**Quiz 3**			**Quiz 4**			**Quiz 5**		
1.	b	2	1.	c	49	1.	d	89	1.	c	148	1.	a	185
2.	c	5	2.	a	53	2.	a	98	2.	a	155	2.	b	187
3.	a	12	3.	b	54	3.	b	106	3.	d	162	3.	c	191
4.	a	15	4.	d	62	4.	c	107	4.	c	165	4.	a	192
5.	d	23	5.	c	63	5.	d	110	5.	a	167	5.	c	193
6.	d	24	6.	c	68	6.	a	118	6.	b	170	6.	a	195
7.	b	26	7.	d	73	7.	b	125	7.	d	174	7.	d	198
8.	b	32	8.	a	75	8.	b	127	8.	a	173	8.	d	202
9.	d	34	9.	d	80	9.	c	136	9.	d	175	9.	c	206
10.	c	38	10.	c	82	10.	b	140	10.	b	178	10.	b	208

Quiz 6			**Quiz 7**			**Quiz 8**			**Quiz 9**			**Quiz 10**		
1.	d	214	1.	c	244	1.	a	292	1.	b	337	1.	c	372
2.	a	217	2.	b	244	2.	a	296	2.	d	338	2.	d	374
3.	d	218	3.	d	246	3.	d	305	3.	a	342	3.	c	384
4.	b	223	4.	a	256	4.	d	305	4.	a	346	4.	c	386
5.	d	224	5.	d	258	5.	c	314	5.	d	347	5.	a	390
6.	a	230	6.	b	261	6.	c	315	6.	c	348	6.	b	390
7.	b	231	7.	d	264	7.	b	316	7.	d	350	7.	a	393
8.	c	236	8.	b	277	8.	a	328	8.	a	354	8.	c	395
9.	a	237	9.	c	280	9.	c	333	9.	d	361	9.	c	398
10.	d	238	10.	c	282	10.	d	332	10.	c	363	10.	a	402

Quiz 11			**Quiz 12**			**Quiz 13**			**Quiz 14**			**Quiz 15**		
1.	d	410	1.	d	464	1.	c	510	1.	d	534	1.	d	572
2.	c	419	2.	d	465	2.	d	513	2.	d	540	2.	d	575
3.	b	419	3.	a	479	3.	b	516	3.	a	540	3.	d	582
4.	c	430	4.	b	479	4.	d	516	4.	a	542	4.	a	590
5.	a	432	5.	d	489	5.	c	520	5.	b	545	5.	b	595
6.	d	436	6.	b	491	6.	b	520	6.	d	552	6.	c	602
7.	c	438	7.	d	500	7.	a	521	7.	c	559	7.	c	606
8.	a	438	8.	c	500	8.	d	525	8.	c	560	8.	b	606
9.	b	450	9.	d	501	9.	c	526	9.	c	564	9.	c	610
10.	a	458	10.	a	502	10.	a	531	10.	b	566	10.	c	611